Human Resources
and Higher Education

Human Resources and Higher Education

Staff Report of the Commission on
Human Resources and Advanced Education

JOHN K. FOLGER
HELEN S. ASTIN
ALAN E. BAYER

RUSSELL SAGE FOUNDATION
NEW YORK, 1970

© 1970
RUSSELL SAGE FOUNDATION

Printed in the United States of America
Library of Congress Catalog Card Number: 68-58129

MEMBERS OF THE COMMISSION ON HUMAN RESOURCES AND ADVANCED EDUCATION

Contents

Preface by Dael Wolfle   xi

INTRODUCTION: AN INTERVIEW BY MEMBERS OF
THE COMMISSION   xv

1. Summary of Manpower Problems and Issues Facing the Nation   1
    The Current Status of Research on Specialized Manpower, 4
    The Changing Pattern of Supply and Demand for Educated Persons, 6
    Feedback into Education—Changes in the Demands for Teachers, 9
    Supply-Demand Balance in Other Selected Professions, 10
    Planning Career Shifts, 12
    The Flow of Students Through College, 13
    The Mobility of Professional Manpower, 15
    Criteria of Effective Professional Performance in the Sciences, 16
    The Development of Talent Among Special Groups, 18
    Professional Careers for Women, 18
    Socioeconomic Background and College Completion, 19
    Foreign Contributions to High-Level Manpower, 20
    Conclusion, 20

SECTION I   23

2. The Market for College Graduates   25
    Problems in Manpower Forecasting, 26
    Estimating the Supply of College-Educated Manpower, 26
    Estimating the Demand for College-Educated Manpower, 29
    The Overall Picture to 1980, 34
    The Bureau of Labor Statistics Model, 35
    The Need for College Graduates to Achieve National Goals, 37
    Educational Improvement of the Occupational Structure, 38
    Summary and Discussion, 41

3. The Supply and Demand for Graduates in the Arts and Sciences   44
    The Growth in the Supply of Arts and Science Graduates, 46
    Stipend Support and the Growth of Graduate Enrollments, 54
    Other Limits on Graduate Enrollment, 59
    The Demand for College Teachers, 61
    The Humanities, 64
    The Social Sciences and Psychology, 65
    Mathematics and the Physical Sciences, 67
    Biological Sciences, 68
    Summary and Discussion, 68
    The Demand in Research and Development Activities, 69
    Summary, 74

4. Manpower Supply and Demand in Selected Professions   75
  Law, 76
    Student Demand for Legal Education and Institutional Capacity, 78
    Means of Accommodating Student Demand, 82
    Characteristics of Future Supply, 83
    Summary, 84
  Medicine, 84
    Output of Medical Schools, 85
    The Availability of Medical Services, 90
    Components of Demand for Medical Services, 91
    Increasing the Physician's Productivity, 92
    Summary, 93
  Engineering, 94
    The Shortage of Engineering Graduates, 94
    Estimates of the Demand for Engineers, 97
    Mechanisms for Redressing the Balance, 101
    Summary, 103
  Elementary and Secondary School Teaching, 103
    The Supply of Potential Entrants, 105
    The Slackening of Demand for Teachers, 108
    Characteristics of Persons Entering Teaching, 111
    Summary, 114
  The Social Welfare Occupations, 114
    Trends in Social Welfare Employment, 115
    The Competitive Position of Social Workers, 116
    Characteristics of Persons Entering Social Welfare Occupations, 119
    Training in Social Work, 120
    Summary, 122
  Nursing, 122
    Recent Trends in Supply and Demand, 125
    The Competitive Position of Nursing, 130
    Summary, 132
  The Performing Arts, 132
    The Status of Professionals in the Arts, 133
    Projections of Future Demand, 137
    Summary, 140
  Summary, 142

SECTION II   144

5. The Flow of Students Through the Educational System   147
  Entry into College, 148
    Estimating Talent Loss, 149
    Factors That Determine College Entry, 153
    The Ability Level of Entering College Students, 158
  Patterns of College Attendance, 161
    Institutional Growth Rates and Selectivity, 161
    Factors That Determine the Kind of College Attended, 164
    Student Progress in Different Kinds of Colleges, 165
  Graduate School Attendance, 182
    Factors Affecting Graduate School Entry, 185

The Ability of Entering Graduate Students, 188
Trends in the Length of Doctoral Training, 191
Summary, 194

6. Career Plans of High School and College Students 197
Stability and Change in Career Choice, 198
Trends in Career Plans, 206
Personal and Environmental Determinants of Career Outcomes, 207
Summary and Conclusions, 216

7. The Mobility of High-Level Manpower 217
Geographic Mobility and Regional Gain and Loss of Educated
Persons, 219
What Is Regional "Gain" or "Loss"?, 220
A Migration Paradigm, 222
Migration Patterns and Educational Quality of Doctoral Training, 223
Regional Gain and Loss Through Migration, 226
Changes in Career Field After the Baccalaureate Degree, 232
The Occupational Mobility of College Graduates, 235
Changes in Job Setting, 241
The Employment of Postdoctoral Fellowship Recipients, 245
Summary and Conclusions, 249

8. Determinants of Professional Achievement and Rewards
Among Scientists 253
Criterion Measures of Scientific Productivity, 256
Background Factors Affecting Citation Frequency, 258
Occupational Factors Affecting Citation Frequency, 260
Summary of Determinants of Scientific Productivity, 265
Determinants of Professional Income, 268
Summary of Determinants of Professional Income, 275

SECTION III 277

9. The Educational and Vocational Development of Women 280
Factors Affecting the Education of Women, 281
The Career Plans of Women, 287
Labor Force Participation of Women Doctorate Recipients, 288
Employment Conditions of Women Doctorate Recipients, 294
The Scientific and Scholarly Productivity of Women Doctorate
Recipients, 298
Barriers to the Career Development of Women Doctorate Recipients, 300
Women Doctorate Recipients as Compared with Other Groups of
Women, 301
Summary and Conclusions, 302

10. Talent Development Among Low Socioeconomic Groups 305
Socioeconomic Status and Measured Ability, 307
Socioeconomic Status and College Attendance, 309
Socioeconomic Status and Educational Progress, 316
Socioeconomic Status and Career Aspirations, 321
Summary and Conclusions, 321

11. The Effect of International Interchange of High-Level Manpower on
   the United States   325
 Immigration of High-Level Manpower, 327
 Foreign Student Inflow, 329
 U.S. Students Abroad, 335
 U.S. High-Level Manpower Abroad, 336
 The U.S. "Brain Gain," 336
 Estimated Costs and Benefits of International Student Exchange, 338
 Manpower Gains Through the Second Generation, 339
 Summary and Discussion, 340

SECTION IV   345

12. Manpower Planning and Manpower Market Operations   347
 Manpower Adjustment Mechanisms, 348
 Adjustments in the Educational System, 348
 The Labor Reserve, 352
 Changing the Age of Retirement, 353
 Entry Standards and Quality Substitution, 354
 Using Subprofessional Personnel to Expand Professional Services, 355
 Geographic and Occupational Mobility, 356
 The Effectiveness of Manpower Planning, 358

13. Research Needed on Talented Manpower   360
 Research on the Quality of Human Resources, 364
 Research on the Development of New Specialties and
  Subprofessional Roles, 365
 Research on the Processes of Occupational Choice and
  Educational Effects, 367
 Research on the Development of Human Resources Investment
  Models, 369
 Summary and Conclusions, 370

APPENDICES   373

 Appendix A: Projections of Enrollments and Degrees, 375
 Appendix B: Studies Utilizing the Project TALENT Data Files, 407
 Appendix C: Career Plan Studies, 422
 Appendix D: The National Register—Doctoral Files Collated Data Tape
      and Estimated Coverage of the National Register, 433
 Appendix E: Sample and Procedures of Analysis in the Survey of Women
      Doctorate Recipients, 449
Publications That Resulted from the Commission Staff Efforts   453

TABLES AND FIGURES   455

INDEX   465

Preface

INTEREST IS widespread in understanding more clearly how the nation identifies, educates, and utilizes men and women of high ability. The Commission on Human Resources and Advanced Education has shared this interest with the Bureau of Labor Statistics, the National Science Foundation, the Office of Education, and other government agencies, and also with the American Council on Education, the Educational Testing Service, Project TALENT, the National Academy of Sciences, and a variety of other nongovernmental groups. Studies and analyses carried out by these agencies and institutions have provided much valuable information for educational planning, government policy formation, and individual guidance in making educational and career decisions.

Most of the studies have been planned in terms of the purposes of their sponsoring agencies, or have concentrated on a particular group—such as scientists—of special national interest. The Commission's responsibility has been broader: to look at the whole matter of how the United States educates and utilizes young men and women in the upper ranks of the distribution of intellectual ability.

The decision that such a broad study would be timely and desirable was made by the American Council of Learned Societies, the American Council on Education, the National Academy of Sciences–National Research Council, and the Social Science Research Council. The Conference Board of Associated Research Councils—which represents the four councils on matters with which they are jointly concerned—appointed the 12 Commission members whose names appear on page v. The Commission thereafter functioned as an autonomous body. We are grateful to the four councils for their sponsorship and encouragement, but we must also free them of any responsibility for how we have carried out our work or for any conclusions or recommendations based upon the work.

We are also grateful to Carnegie Corporation of New York and Russell Sage Foundation, the two foundations that shared equally in providing the necessary financial support. They, too, are free from responsibility for how the work has been done and reported.

The National Academy of Sciences administered the grants from the two foundations and provided the Commission staff with office space and with administrative and fiscal services.

The Commission was responsible for outlining in general terms the area of inquiry to be undertaken, for selecting the director, for periodic discussions with the staff, and for reviewing and criticizing earlier drafts of this report. The members of the Commission also felt a responsibility to state their collective judgment on three questions: *Why are such studies as those reported here essential and what was the setting in which this effort was undertaken? What were the highlights or major results? What policy issues demand attention as the work of the Commission draws to a close?* The Commission's answers to these questions are given in the Introduction which precedes the 13 chapters written by Doctors Folger, Astin, and Bayer. The manuscript was completed in April of 1968.

Anyone who is familiar with the ways in which similar commissions and committees work understands that the most important decision made by the Commission was the selection of a director, and understands also that all compliments merited by the final product should be addressed to the director and staff, not to the Commission.

We were fortunate in persuading John K. Folger, Dean of the Graduate School of Florida State University (and now Executive Director of the Tennessee Higher Education Commission) to take two years away from his academic responsibilities to direct the studies. And he, in turn, was fortunate to get the competent and stimulating help, throughout the whole period of the Commission's studies, of Helen S. Astin (now with the Bureau of Social Science Research) and Alan E. Bayer (now with the American Council on Education). This team of three planned the studies in detail, saw them through to completion, and wrote the report.

They had substantial help from several persons who served as consultants or who for a period were part-time members of the staff. Donald S. Bridgman, formerly of the American Telephone and Telegraph Company, prepared the projections of enrollments and degrees which are used in many parts of the report and which are presented in abridged form in Appendix A. W. Lee Hansen of the University of Wisconsin made a number of contributions to the thinking of the staff and provided much of the basic analyses for the section on supply and demand for engineers in Chapter 4. A. G. Holtmann (now of Florida State University) provided analyses of the economics of teacher supply and demand, which are included in Chapter 4, and also analyzed the factors affecting salaries of scientists, which are presented in Chapter 8. Simon Marcson of Rutgers University made some special studies of manpower utilization and prepared a review of the literature on productivity.

The Commission staff were fortunate to have Dee Burton, Jill Smith, and Dave Yochim as capable research assistants for various periods of time. All three worked on several parts of the report. Miss Burton made a major contribution to the material on supply and demand for lawyers. Olive Bennett and Milda Vivada were valuable secretaries who typed and retyped the manuscript many times. Mary Pat Peacock and Linda Pate also assisted in preparing the manuscript. Carol Ames designed and prepared the graphic art work.

Numerous suggestions and criticisms on the project and valuable advice on various parts of it were provided by Alexander W. Astin of the American Council on Education, Henry David of the National Science Foundation and later of the National Research Council, R. Thayne Robson of the National Commission on Technology, Automation, and Economic Progress, and Lindsey R. Harmon of the National Academy of Sciences' Office of Scientific Personnel.

The Office of Scientific Personnel of the National Academy of Sciences furnished a large number of tabulations from their files on doctoral graduates. Herbert Soldz of that Office assisted the Commission staff with a number of special analyses.

The staff of Project TALENT, particularly William W. Cooley (now with the University of Pittsburgh) and Lyle F. Schoenfeldt (now with the University of Georgia) were especially helpful in providing several analyses of data and in consulting on various aspects of the Project TALENT tabulations.

The staff members of the Office of Research of the American Council on Education cooperated extensively, provided unpublished data, and gave access to some of their reports in advance of publication.

The Educational Testing Service, particularly J. A. Davis, was helpful in providing information and reports about the numerous research activities of ETS.

Leonard A. Lecht of the National Planning Association, Joseph L. Spaeth of the National Opinion Research Center, Laure M. Sharp of the Bureau of Social Science Research, and Milton Levine of the National Register of Scientific and Technical Personnel of the National Science Foundation all cooperated by providing special tabulations and analyses of data for the commission studies.

A draft of the entire manuscript was read by Leonard A. Lecht of the National Planning Association and Henry W. Riecken of the Social Science Research Council. Both made numerous helpful suggestions and criticisms. The entire report was edited by Laura M. Kent, who contributed a great deal to its clarity and readability.

We are grateful to all of these persons for their generous and valuable assistance. They all helped to produce this volume, as did others who are not named here but whose works are cited at appropriate places throughout. All helped, yet it was the three authors who selected, analyzed, organized, and presented the material to be found in the following chapters. Because their work was a group effort, and because each rewrote sections that were initially prepared by one of the others, separate authorship simply could not be indicated for the individual chapters. All three contributed ideas, suggestions, and criticisms to all parts of the report. Dr. Folger was the director, and his name appears first on the title page. The contributions of Dr. Astin and Dr. Bayer were equivalent and therefore their names appear alphabetically.

All three acknowledge with gratitude the help they have received and have asked me to say, on their behalf, that they assume responsibility for any errors and unclear passages that remain. They feel obligated to make this disclaimer, but I, on behalf of the Commission, can add that the credit is also theirs, credit for what we hope is an illuminating analysis and a useful reference source to persons interested in the richer and fuller development of our human resources.

Dael Wolfle
Chairman, Commission on Human
Resources and Advanced Education

June, 1968

Introduction:

An Overview by

Members of the Commission*

How THE nation develops and utilizes its human resources is determined by millions of individual decisions, each made for quite personal reasons. Involved are the high school student's decision to take another year of mathematics, the college student's decision to major in fine arts, the engineer's decision to leave one job and accept another, the nurse's decision to return to professional work when her youngest child starts to school, the older worker's decision to retire. These and countless other decisions, each made individually and each made in terms of the individual's own interests, opportunities, aspirations, and capabilities, collectively determine the nation's development and utilization of human resources.

The decisions individuals make are influenced and sometimes circumscribed by another set of decisions that are often also made in relative independence of each other: the decision to establish a junior college in a growing community; the decision to raise admission requirements to a particular college; the decision to institute a program of graduate fellowships in a particular field; the decision to increase or decrease the size of the military forces or to change the procedures by which young men are selected for induction; the decision to change tax policies or salaries or other factors that make one or another kind of work more or less attractive.

* The names of the Commission members appear on page v.

In the open, democratic society that has been the pride of the United States, it has been national policy to encourage great individual freedom in the making of decisions. Private enterprise and local responsibility have been hallmarks of the American system, and we have treated education and training as a personal right and privilege more than as a calculated means of achieving nationally determined objectives.

To the individual, this system represents freedom of opportunity to fulfill his own potential as fully as he wishes. From the standpoint of most individuals, the system has worked reasonably well, though some groups have not had full opportunity to benefit.

And from the standpoint of the nation, it has also worked well. The net result of all of the millions of individual decisions has been to give the nation a very large number of educated and competent teachers, doctors, lawyers, engineers, scientists, scholars, diplomats, legislators, poets, philosophers, and leaders in other human endeavors.

Indeed, some would argue that the system works so well in bringing forth the numbers and kinds of specialists needed to keep the whole complex machinery of a large industrial nation running effectively that we should simply let it alone.

But there are many who note imperfections that require attention. The system is sometimes criticized for not producing enough engineers, or physicians, or specialists in other fields. It is charged with not really being equally open to all young people, but as discriminating unfairly against those from the lower socioeconomic groups. It is said to be so costly that only a very wealthy nation, one willing to be careless and even wasteful in spending its money, could permit such uncontrolled individual freedom.

The critics are not challenging the fundamental characteristics of the system. They have no wish to abandon the principle of free choice. But they believe the system could be helped to work more efficiently if we knew in greater detail just how it does work.

To help to understand better how it is working was the task of the Commission on Human Resources and Advanced Education. The Commission's approach has been to examine the system from the outside, from the point of view of society rather than that of the individual, from the point of view represented by such terms as *manpower, supply and demand, shortage, surplus, utilization of supply,* or *adjustment of supply and demand,* rather than from the viewpoint of an individual making his own individual decisions. Some people object to such terms as *manpower* or *the output of an educational institution* as demeaning to the individual human beings involved. The humane concerns represented by these objections must be respected, but in dealing with professional and specialized persons en masse, such terms are descriptive and convenient. They will be used without apology, for they imply no disregard for the rights and sensibilities of individuals.

THE STAFF STUDIES

If the Commission staff had been able to do all they would have liked to do, they would have analyzed individually and in their interrelations half a dozen different aspects of the system and its operation:

• The educational processes employed to prepare young men and women for work in each of the professional and specialized fields that call for advanced education;

• The qualitative and quantitative characteristics of the output of the educational system;

• The effectiveness with which men and women with specialized abilities and education are utilized in the economic, educational, artistic, religious, and other spheres of national life;

• Present or prospective mismatches between the numbers and characteristics of persons prepared to do each major kind of work and the requirements or needs for such persons;

• Wastes, inequities, and other faults in the system;

• The variety of governmental and other policy-making arrangements that influence the education and utilization of specialized and professional manpower.

It was not possible to accomplish so much. Not all of these half-dozen areas of inquiry, nor all aspects of any one of them, could be analyzed. Thus, the first thing to say about the studies reported in the following chapters is that they are a series of related contributions to the better understanding of the processes involved in developing and utilizing professional and specialized personnel, but they do not pretend to be a comprehensive analysis.

A small staff working together for two or three years simply could not cover all aspects of so vast a subject. Moreover, the kind of information available was not of uniform value. For some matters, excellent data were at hand. For others, partial information could be brought together from several sources. Still others simply had to be laid aside for lack of data to build on. The studies carried out by the staff were therefore necessarily selective, with the selection being partly determined by the time available, partly by the nature of the available information, and partly by the interests of the staff members. If some spottiness seems to result, it is an inevitable spottiness. The high spots are significant contributions to our understanding of how a complex and multifaceted system of adjustment mechanisms operates. The low spots and the blanks show the need for further work by other people.

Predicting the Future

Section I of the report analyzes supply-and-demand trends in the arts and sciences and in several professions.

The words *supply and demand*—the words we usually use when we talk about manpower trends in the United States—are too simple; they mask the variety of forces that determine how educated men and women are allocated among the various competitors for their services. In the years since World War II, many countries have tried to look into the future to see what their manpower needs would be and then have attempted to plan and control their educational systems to produce the needed numbers and kinds of specialists. In the United States we often talk as if we were engaged in a similar effort. We speak of the demand for engineers or the supply of teachers. We project college graduation trends and economic trends. We talk of a shortage of physicians or a surplus of some other kind of specialist.

But in reality there are not large numbers of vacant positions in a "shortage" field. Nor are there large numbers of unemployed persons in a "surplus" field. We employ educated and able people in a wonderfully flexible fashion and use a great variety of means to maintain effective adjustment between the work that requires trained intelligence and the people qualified to perform such work.

The analyses of trends presented in Section I therefore involve three elements:

1. Projections of the new supply available to enter each field in the next ten or twenty years;

2. Estimates of the demand or need for a like time into the future;

3. Analysis of the adjustments that are likely to be made to rectify imbalances between supply and demand.

With considerable confidence one can project for several years the numbers of students who will complete their education at different degree levels in different fields of specialization. These graduates will constitute the new supply. Those who remain identified with the fields for which they have been trained will be employed in three ways: some will replace older workers who retire or die; some will fill new positions; and some will change the educational level of the field by displacing a less well-qualified worker or by substituting for a better-educated one.

It is also possible to forecast demand in some fields with fair confidence. For example, it is not hard to project the number of children who will be in elementary schools in 1975, and with that figure in hand it is easy to project the number of elementary school teachers needed in 1975. For many other fields, however, demand projections are less certain, for they will depend upon the state of the economy, military requirements, unforeseen changes in social conditions, the possible development of new materials or processes, and other factors that are much harder to foresee than is the progression of students through the educational system. Moreover, major national decisions may suddenly change manpower requirements. The number of engineering jobs was rapidly expanded as a result of the decision to expand the nation's space effort and send a man to the Moon. The demand for workers in the health fields was sharply increased by congressional adoption of the Medicare bill and other recent health and medical legislation.

Despite these uncertainties, projections of demand can be made, although they should usually be treated as less precise than the projections of supply.

Supply and demand influence each other and tend to move together. In the long run, the number of students who are educated for and who enter a particular field tends to change to fit changing demands. The timelag is substantial, however, and the expected condition of the market four to eight years later is only one of the many factors that influence students' college plans and career choices.

More rapid adjustments are achieved by the migration of already trained persons from one kind of work to another, by lowering or raising the entrance standards, by increasing or reducing the attractiveness of employment to women in the labor reserve, by the greater or lesser use of subprofessional personnel to carry part of the workload, and by other adjustment mechanisms.

The detailed projections of Section I show a continuing increase for the decades immediately ahead in the numbers of persons earning degrees. During the same period, the need for teachers, lawyers, engineers, scientists, economists, and a wide variety of other kinds of specialists will continue to increase. To some extent the greater demand merely reflects the population increase. More people need more teachers, more doctors, and more engineers, just as they need more grocers, more policemen, and more undertakers. But in many fields the demand goes up more rapidly than the population. An expanding economy calls for more engineers, scientists, accountants, and lawyers. New specialties develop as invention provides opportunities for new goods and services. The deprivations of the city ghetto call for more social workers and for the start of school opportunities at earlier ages. We are sending more expert consultants and aides to other countries to assist with the agricultural, industrial, educational, and governmental planning and development that are essential for the economic growth their peoples want.

The comparisons of projected future demand and projected future supply show different relationships in different fields. In engineering, law, medicine, nursing, and social welfare work the number of openings is expected to exceed the number of new graduates for the next decade or two.

In the creative arts, the future looks like the past, with more people seeking openings than can find employment.

In teaching, at all levels from kindergarten to graduate school, we appear to be heading toward significant transition points in the relationships between the number of positions and the numbers of prospective new entrants. Ever since the baby boom that followed World War II we have been warned of the tidal wave of students that would move relentlessly through elementary, secondary, and collegiate classrooms. The annual birth cohorts are a little smaller now. The birth rate was lower in 1967 than in any other year in American history. The total number of children born was 3.53 million, down from 3.61 million in 1966 and down farther from the high plateau of over 4 million a year from

1954 through 1964. Changes in the birth rate, plus changes in the educational attainment of successive age groups, are expected to have the following results:

• The annual number of bachelor's degrees will continue to increase, from about 650,000 in 1967–1968 to about 925,000 in 1975, an increase of more than 40 per cent.

• The annual number of doctor's degrees is expected to increase from approximately 22,000 in 1967–1968 to approximately 43,000 in 1975, an increase of nearly 100 per cent.

• Depending on how birth rates change in the next few years, elementary school enrollment may range from a slight decline in the next 20 years to an increase of as much as 30 to 35 per cent.

• High school enrollment is expected to increase by approximately 15 per cent between 1967–1968 and 1977–1978, and remain at approximately that level for a few years.

• College enrollment is expected to increase by 40 to 50 per cent between now and 1975, to continue to increase until about 1982, and then to remain about level or perhaps to show a slight decline for a few years.

Putting these projections together leads to the following implications:

The number of college graduates preparing for teaching positions in elementary and secondary schools will probably be more than adequate in the next decade. (Compare the 40 per cent increase in college graduates with the smaller percentage increases in elementary and secondary school enrollment.)

For each person who graduated from college with a major in education in 1960, about one and a half new teaching positions were open. The "extra" positions were filled by new college graduates in other fields, by the employment of women who had been out of the labor force for a few years, and by the employment of a variety of other persons. The ratio of new education graduates to employment opportunities is changing as a result of the trends just described. In 1969 the ratio will be about one to one. If graduation trends continue as projected, by 1977 there are expected to be only about two-thirds of a teaching job for each new education graduate. As the facts become more widely known, a number of students may decide to change to other fields. Perhaps significant numbers of women who might otherwise have planned to teach will switch to such fields as nursing and social welfare work that have also traditionally been primarily women's fields of professional work.

The relationship between the number of new recipients of advanced degrees and the number of openings on college and university faculties will also change. The rate of increase of federal research funds for colleges and universities has already slowed down markedly from the average increase of 26 per cent a year that prevailed from 1955 through 1964; indeed, the colleges and universities must plan on reductions in 1969. The rate of increase of college population will also slow down. In fact, the expansion will probably be less in the period from 1971 to 1975 than in the 1966 to 1970 period. The number of doctor's and master's degrees conferred will, however, continue to increase for years after the undergraduate population boom has ended. All of this means that the colleges and universities will not need to employ as large a fraction of the recipients of graduate degrees in the future as in the past. Faculty appointments can therefore become more selective. The proportion of newly appointed faculty members holding the doctor's degree is likely to increase, and the number holding only the master's degree to drop. We will approach this condition gradually, of course, and the situation will vary somewhat from one field of study to another, but there will be opportunities to engage more persons with Ph.D. degrees in other kinds of employment; for example, in junior college teaching and in industry, government, and nonprofit organizations. It may be possible to pay more attention to improving the quality of graduate education when the pressure for numbers become less acute.

Career Choices

Section II of the report concerns some of the factors that help determine how many graduates there are in each field and some of the principal means of keeping supply and demand in adjustment.

There is a substantial body of information about the differences among students who attend different kinds of institutions of higher education, such as the highly selective and prestigious college or university, the large state university, and the community or junior college that is open to almost anyone who wants to enter. But too little is understood of how these different kinds of institutions affect their different groups of students.

College provides students with an opportunity to consider various occupational alternatives and to compare their interests and abilities with the requirements of alternative fields of work. As students gain additional insight and experience, there are many shifts in career plans. Graduating seniors who plan to enter a particular field tend to be more like each other than were the freshmen four years earlier who expected to enter that field.

The sorting process continues after leaving the university. With the exception of some professional men and women whose work requires geographic stability—the physician and the dentist are probably the best examples—the nation rather than the city or the region constitutes the employment market for specialized and professional personnel. Geographic mobility is fostered by the uneven distribution of opportunities for graduate and professional education, and continues as the graduates take advantage of occupational opportunities.

In the geographic shuffling of talent there are some interesting discrepancies between quantitative and qualitative aspects. Some regions of the country have been complaining that they feed, clothe, and educate the students who then go elsewhere to work. (Not all of the brain drain crosses national boundaries!) But for some areas a quantitative loss may be a qualitative gain, when the young men and women from elsewhere are superior to the students who emigrate.

For other areas the opposite effect occurs. These findings add a new dimension to discussions of the geographic mobility of educated manpower.

There is also mobility from one kind of work to another: from teaching to research, from industry to education, from a lower to a higher level of responsibility, from the profession or specialty in a narrow sense to the wider responsibilities of administration. And there is more migration from one field to another than is usually recognized. Many college graduates do not enter work in the fields in which they majored, and within a few years after receipt of a bachelor's degree many others are employed in specialties different from those of their college majors. Migration across fields is less likely at the doctoral level, but even so, in approximately five years a quarter of the recipients have moved into different fields from those in which their degrees were granted. By 25 years after the doctorate, 40 per cent use different labels to identify their fields of specialization from those they used at the time of receiving the doctorate. Some of these changes probably represent changing terminology and confusion of labels, but much represents real intellectual migration made possible and attractive by the development of new opportunities in electronics, computers, space research, international aid, and so forth. The substantial amount of transfer from the field in which a person's highest degree was earned to the field in which he is employed some years later represents one of the most rapidly effective means of keeping the supply of educated persons adjusted to the constantly changing needs for their services. Industry, education, government, and society would be much more sluggish if a chemist could never change his label and become a physicist, or a physicist become a space scientist, or a historian become an administrator, or a lawyer turn into a philosopher.

Special Groups

Most of the statistics and most of our assumptions and attitudes concerning the education and utilization of professional and specialized personnel disregard or conceal the special problems of three groups that are discussed in Section III: women, persons from the lower socioeconomic levels, and immigrants.

Women earn about 40 per cent of the bachelor's degrees conferred in the United States, about a third of the master's degrees, and about a tenth of the doctor's degrees. Statistically, therefore, women are clearly underutilized in the fields that require graduate and specialized training.

As pointed out earlier, two fields in which women outnumber men, nursing and social welfare work, and two in which men outnumber women, law and engineering, are likely to show demand in excess of supply for some time to come. How many additional women will enter these fields appears likely to be primarily determined by their own interests and attitudes, for jobs will be available.

To a substantial fraction of young people, access to higher education and to the professional and specialized fields becomes gradually but firmly closed by a complex set of barriers associated with low socioeconomic status. The earliest barriers are in the home: poverty, ignorance, apathy, lack of intellectual stimulation, and absence of motivation. These barriers, which start in the cradle and continue through early childhood, lead to indifference and poor performance in often inadequate schools, neglect of visual and other handicaps, delinquency, and dropping out of the educational system. Failure to make normal progress through elementary and secondary school closes the gate to higher education and the professional and specialized fields based on higher education.

Part of the differences in achievement of children from low and high socioeconomic levels is associated with differences in ability, but substantial differences remain even when ability is equated. One of the analyses shows that of 100 male high school graduates who stood high in scholastic ability and who came from homes of high socioeconomic level, 66 graduated from college and 36 continued immediately in graduate or professional schools. In contrast, of 100 male high school graduates of comparable scholastic ability, but from homes of low socioeconomic status, only 37 graduated from college and only 15 continued immediately in graduate or professional schools.

Low socioeconomic status is an educational handicap, but socioeconomic status is not as highly correlated with college attendance, college graduation, or entrance into graduate or professional school as are the scores students make on tests of intellectual ability or the grades they make in school and college. It is not possible to separate socioeconomic status completely from these measures of ability, for ability is influenced by environment and the ability measures are correlated with family background factors. Nevertheless, if all students of comparable measured academic aptitude equaled the college entry rates and the college completion rates of the top fifth in socioeconomic standing, and if they chose selective colleges in the same proportions, the number of college graduates in 1965 would have almost been doubled. The larger number of graduates would in itself be important to the nation, but less beneficial than would be the elimination of educational discrimination on socioeconomic grounds.

The United States benefits greatly from the immigration of educated persons from other lands. Although total immigration is much smaller than it was half a century ago, the proportion of all immigrants who are classified in the professional, technical, and kindred category of occupations has been increasing. In 1910, only about one per cent of immigrants were so classified; in 1965, 10 per cent were in the professional, technical, and kindred occupations. In some fields, the contributions of immigrants are much more significant than in others. Scientists and engineers coming to the United States from other countries are now equal in number to about five or six per cent of the students earning bachelor's or higher degrees in science and engineering. Between a quarter and a third of all physicians serving in internships and residencies in the United States are graduates of foreign medical schools. Some return to their homelands, but many stay on, and in doing so contribute substantially both to American health care and to international clamor over the brain drain.

POLICY ISSUES

Socioeconomic Differences in Access to Higher Education

In 1954 the first Commission on Human Resources wrote: "A society which permits a significant portion of its members to work at levels below their capabilities is failing to achieve its full potential strength. . . . Judged by this standard the United States has failed to reach the strength which it might attain, for it wastes the abilities of many of its most capable sons and daughters and thereby loses the contributions they might have made."[1]

Since 1954 there has been a gratifying decrease in the percentage of able young people who fail to enter college. The 1954 report estimated that 47 per cent of the top fifth of all high school graduates in the country (measured in terms of rank in high school graduating classes) did not go on to college. Data in Chapter 10 of this report show that only 15 per cent of the boys and 24 per cent of the girls graduating from high school in the top fifth in terms of academic ability do not go to college immediately. Both figures will drop a few percentage points when account is taken of those who entered college after a delay of a year or two.

If one goes down to the next level, the second fifth of all high school graduates, the comparable decrease was from 56 per cent reported as not entering college in the 1954 report to 27 per cent of the boys and 51 per cent of the girls in the mid 1960's.

Many fewer bright students are stopping their educational careers at the end of high school than were stopping at that point 14 years ago. The relationship between academic ability and the probability that a high school graduate will enter college is greater now than it was at the time of the earlier report.

It is gratifying to be able to report these changes, but there are still serious inequalities associated with socioeconomic level. Among boys in the top fifth of all high school graduates, 91 per cent of those who are also in the top fifth in socioeconomic status enter college immediately, while only 69 per cent of the boys of similar ability who come from the bottom fifth of homes in terms of socioeconomic status do so. For girls, the comparable figures are 90 per cent and 52 per cent.

So far, the data have been in terms of high school graduates. A considerable number of young people drop out of school before reaching that stage, and here, too, there is socioeconomic selection. The child of the ghetto is much more likely than the child of suburbia to drop out of school before getting his high

---

[1] Wolfle, Dael, *America's Resources of Specialized Talent*. Harper and Bros., New York, 1954, p. 137.

school diploma. So is the child brought up in one of the rural pockets of poverty that are scattered across the land.

The low socioeconomic group includes both white and black youth. The political and operational problems of securing better educational opportunities differ somewhat according to color. But from the standpoint of the goals sought, the color of the skin is irrelevant. Intellectual starvation in childhood, poor schools, apathy, and absence of motivation operate in much the same way regardless of skin color; and each failure to let a bright child acquire whatever education and experience are required to develop his full potential is a loss to the individual and a loss to the nation, whether the child's skin is black or white.

Several implications of the data presented in this report are relevant to the various programs intended to overcome socioeconomic discrimination:

1. If students from all socioeconomic levels could be brought up to the college attendance and completion rates of students from the top fifth of homes in terms of socioeconomic status, the annual number of college graduates in the United States would be almost doubled.

2. It is not money alone that spells the difference between the educational achievement of students of different socioeconomic levels. Attitudes deeply rooted in the cultural characteristics of the home shape the child's development and determine what his educational interests and aspirations will be.

3. Efforts to overcome the cultural and educational disadvantages of early home environment must start earlier than the usual school-entering age. By the time children enter first grade, those from culturally poor homes have already fallen well behind their more favored schoolmates who have had the kind of stimulation and encouragement that is normal in a middle-class or upper-class home.

4. It will take at least a generation, and probably longer, to minimize the educational differences attributable to socioeconomic differences. As an analogue, consider the immigrant from a foreign country. The differences between the culture into which he was born and the one into which he has migrated are clearly evident. Although his children are aware of their parents' first-generation status and can see many differences between their parents and the neighboring families who have been here longer, they are, nevertheless, educated and adjusted to American customs and values. And their children are full-fledged Americans. The problems of assimilation are somewhat comparable for the children of the bottom socioeconomic level; culturally, Scarsdale, New York, is as far from Harlem as it is from many foreign countries. The fact that it will take a generation or more to overcome the educational handicaps of low socioeconomic status should not be permitted to serve as an excuse for delay in pushing ahead on the necessary social, educational, and economic actions. Rather it is reason for getting started as quickly as possible to learn what corrective actions will work most effectively.

Mounting concern over the plight of the Negro calls for work on many aspects of the American scene, but one of the fundamental requirements is improved education. At the preschool and elementary levels we need special efforts to compensate for the impoverishment of spirit, the lack of intellectual stimulation, and the cultural drag of the homes into which so many are born. And at all levels we need to provide as good education as we know how to give. It will be some years before the percentage of Negro students qualified and wishing to enter the professions and other specialized fields catches up with the percentage of white students. As it does, we must expect a further expansion of the higher educational system and can look forward to an expansion of the numbers of persons educated to take their places in the professional and specialized occupations.

Fostering Occupational Mobility

In the next couple of decades there are likely to be as many opportunities and needs for occupational change and mobility as there have been in recent ones. The fact that knowledge gained in college or in graduate or professional school will no longer last a man through his professional career has often been stated, as has the corollary that we must develop improved means of continuing or adult education to enable men and women in mid-career to refresh their knowledge or to equip themselves for an occupational change.

A related matter for schools and colleges to worry about is the need for education that will equip graduates for mobility. It has always been true that a college graduate has taken to his first job not only a body of knowledge but also some habits of study, some attitudes toward work and thought, and, of course, the abilities that enabled him to earn a college degree. The problem of how to foster those habits and attitudes and methods of work that will be helpful in a man's first professional job and that will continue to be helpful as he moves into new jobs with different obligations and requirements is by no means a new puzzle for educational philosophers and curriculum planners. But the puzzle has not been solved. The importance of finding a solution becomes more evident when we recall that job mobility serves as a major means of adapting an ever-changing supply of educated manpower to an ever-changing set of social and economic demands.

Selection for What

The fear has often been expressed that quality standards must go down as the number of college students continues to increase. There are two things to say in reply to this fear. One is that it has not happened yet and may never happen, and the other is that it will not hurt much if it does happen.

It has not happened yet. The comparison a few pages back of the percentage of high school graduates entering college now with the percentage entering some years ago showed that the greatest increase was among students at the upper end of the ability scale. All along the ability scale—except, of course, at its lower reaches—more students are completing high school than did formerly, and more are going to college. But the increases have been numerically larger toward the upper end of the scale than lower down, and consequently the increase in college attendance has not meant a dilution of quality as measured by any of the available means of assessing intelligence or academic ability.

How long this trend will continue is a matter of conjecture. If one assumes a constant distribution of ability in the population, a decrease in the average ability of college students must be predicted. At the high end of the scale the number going to college is approaching the ceiling of 100 per cent. Within a decade or two, if enrollment trends continue as projected, the average ability will have to decrease.

But a constant distribution of ability may be the wrong assumption over the long term. The tests used to assess ability depend very much on earlier learning, and ability—in a more abstract and general sense—is thought to be influenced by early childhood nutrition. Better child care, more extensive preschool education, and better elementary schools may raise the average level of ability significantly.

And even if one expects the measured average ability of college entrants to decline, it is important to remember that the average being considered is the average of all college students in the nation, and that there is great diversity among colleges. Some will continue to be highly selective in choosing their students. A slight drop in average ability level of the student body as a whole would go unnoticed on most campuses and would have very little influence on what graduates do, or how well they do it, after leaving college.

Much effort has been devoted to predicting who will succeed. The selective colleges examine grade records, scores on entrance examinations, and other credentials in selecting their freshman classes. National panels are convened to select the winners of graduate fellowships. Employers screen diligently through the records and credentials of applicants. We usually assume all this work to be justified and that the methods employed provide better selection than would less careful methods.

There is much empirical evidence that the selection methods do predict which applicants will succeed in earning a degree. The predictions are significantly better than chance, but whether they are good enough or whether alternative methods might serve better is frequently argued.

When we go beyond the degree to ask if the selection methods predict which graduates will succeed best in their careers, there is another story to tell. It is extremely difficult to get reliable and satisfactory measures of success in most professions. Who is a successful teacher? How should we compare the effectiveness or success of a pediatrician with that of a surgeon? Is the community pastor or his foreign missionary brother more successful? Such measures of professional effectiveness or success as we have—unsatisfactory and incomplete as they are—are only partially predicted by measures of student selection or by the grades they earn in college, or in professional or graduate school.

One reason is that the information available at the time of selection, even if perfectly reliable—which it is not—and significantly related to later measures of success, constitutes only a portion of the whole set of variables that later on in time will determine relative merit or success. It is also true that no one yet knows how to measure satisfactorily at the time of selection some of the characteristics or elements that contribute to success. And it is also true that the fact of being selected (for admission to a highly selective university, for a graduate fellowship, or for a coveted job) is a very different fact from that of being rejected, and may have a very different impact on one's career. For all these reasons, our ability to predict relative degrees of success in a professional or specialized field is not very good. One practical outcome is that an applicant usually has a second, and often a third chance. If he is not admitted to one college, another will take him; if one employment interview ends in rejection, another is likely to end more favorably. And another practical consequence, as pointed out in the report, is that if in the years ahead there is a slight downward shift in the average intelligence score of students entering a particular field, or if there is a change in the socioeconomic level from which the recruits to a particular profession usually come, or if there is some similar change in the population of entrants to a field, it will probably be impossible to find, later on, any cause-and-effect relationship with changes in the quality or nature of the work being done in that field.

The Role of the Federal Government

Federal funds now provide a quarter of the money annually spent by American colleges and universities. The percentage will probably go higher.

Increasing federal support has provided higher education with buildings, equipment, research facilities, financial aid for students, and means of increasing faculty salaries. College and university officers know that their institutions have been greatly aided by generous federal government support. They also know, however, that higher education has come to be more influenced by decisions made in Washington. How much individual colleges and universities have lost in freedom of action and local autonomy is subject to debate. But that the federal government has come to play a larger role in shaping university affairs and in influencing the education of students preparing for careers in the professions and specialized fields is beyond argument. Increasingly these decisions help to determine the supply of such persons and the demand for their services. Increasingly, therefore, governmental actions help to keep supply and demand in balance, or help to disturb an imbalance.

From the viewpoint of an economist, the adjustment mechanisms of students, educational institutions, and employers constitute the means by which the manpower market is kept in balance. It is useful to think of manpower supply-and-demand questions in market terms, but it is necessary also to understand that this market differs greatly from the simple, free market of classical economic theory. There are many constraints on its operation. The costs of education are partly consumption costs and partly investments. Long timelags are involved. Many kinds of substitutions are possible. It is not one market but many.

Nevertheless, it is useful to think of the matter in market terms and to ask— as some economists do—if public action is necessary to keep supply and demand in better balance. In this simple form, the question is unrealistic, for public actions are continuously affecting the market. The scholarship and fellowship programs that have assisted students to earn degrees, the draft policies that take some men into military service, the government subsidization of medical expenses, the decision to build a great network of national highways, the tax and economic policies that help determine the rate of economic growth, and a whole host of other governmental actions affect supply, affect demand, and affect the means by which supply and demand can be adjusted to each other.

There is no point in asking whether public action is needed. Public action is constantly being taken.

The question to ask is whether the adjustment mechanisms work well enough to make it undesirable for the federal government to take action specifically intended to improve the adjustment processes. Several kinds of action are possible. On a few occasions in the nation's history it appeared necessary to freeze workers into their jobs, to establish wage controls, or in other ways to restrict individual freedom to decide whether and when and where to work. There is general agreement that such controls should be imposed only under the most exceptional conditions.

Without attempting to limit individual freedom through the imposition of manpower controls, it is possible to influence supply and demand by various governmental actions, and especially if the actions and policies of different government agencies are coordinated so that they will reinforce each other. Often there appears to be conflict rather than coordination. Tax policies of the Internal Revenue Service discourage mothers of school-age children from working outside the home, while other agencies of government try to encourage their employment. At a time when many federal agencies have sought to increase the number of graduate students, Selective Service policy has gone in the opposite direction.

It is sometimes argued that the best role of government is to allow each agency to go its own way in establishing policies to achieve its own purposes, that the influences of different government agencies should be handled no differently from the various other influences that act upon the adjustment mechanisms. But not everyone agrees with this position. From time to time there have been proposals that the nation needs a council on manpower policy comparable to the President's Council of Economic Advisers, a council that would keep manpower problems under constant review and that would help to develop a coordinated, government-wide policy for manpower development and utilization. This proposal has never been adopted, but recommendations for greater coordination continue to be made.

On another point there is greater certainty. Federal funds now provide so large a fraction of the costs of higher education and of the costs of scientific activities that sudden fluctuations and withdrawals can be disastrous. Too rapid expansion can be wasteful and inefficient. Too rapid contraction can be even more disturbing, and can waste funds already spent on partially completed activities. Yet on several occasions agencies of the federal government have called upon the universities to expand rapidly and have then reduced financial support so rapidly as to cause a good part of what they had helped to build up to collapse. If federal funds constituted only a small fraction of university budgets, there would be maneuvering room in which to adapt to sudden governmental changes. But with the federal portion as large as it is—and in some of the best universities it is much larger than 25 per cent—it has become imperative to build greater continuity into the government-support programs to protect universities against the inefficiencies and disruption of too rapid fluctuations.

Finally, there is need for a continuing series of inquiries into the whole system of educating and utilizing highly trained men and women so that we might better understand how the various facets are interrelated, how the supply-and-demand adjustment mechanisms work, and how to help the whole system to work more effectively.

The federal government already strongly influences both the supply and the demand for educated men and women, and its influence can be expected to increase. Inevitably, federal executive agencies must conduct studies of manpower problems and formulate manpower policies. But at the same time, educators, scholars, scientists, and professional men and women can and ought to claim the right to make their own assessments of the nation's needs and their own judgments as to how its human resources can best be nurtured and given optimal opportunities for development. The present Commission therefore believes that it should be succeeded by a permanent body that will continue to review and appraise the findings and policies of official agencies and of unofficial special-interest groups, and where necessary will undertake its own inquiries, untrammeled by considerations of political expediency, or of the self-interests of particular professions. Private financial support without strings attached is indispensable to the effective performance of such a role.

The Objectives of Manpower Policy

Several criteria may be used to judge the soundness of manpower policies. One that has been used widely is the criterion of production. We have tried to determine whether or not there are enough engineers by asking whether or not industry would employ more engineers if they were available. Similarly, questions concerning adequacy of the numbers of physicians, or school teachers, or other kinds of specialists have often been answered in terms of the numbers of jobs filled or empty, or in terms of production records, using the term *production* broadly.

A second criterion is that of self-fulfillment. An American dream has been to provide every child with the education that best helps him fulfill his own potentialities for development. That the dream is not always attained is painfully evident, but the degree to which we achieve it is one criterion of the effectiveness of our manpower policies.

A third criterion, which is of a different order from the first two, is cost. We devote a substantial fraction of our national resources to education. Economic analyses have shown the money so spent to have paid good dividends both socially and individually. At some level, however, such analyses may later show that some of the money spent on education might better be spent on improved health, on remedying urban blight, or on other means of social betterment.

Perhaps even so we will want to increase educational expenditures, for economic return is not the only valid measure of value. Nevertheless, comparisons between costs and returns constitute a legitimate criterion for judging manpower policies and actions.

The final criterion, which is of a still different order, is the attainment of national goals. The goals of earlier generations were sometimes clearly formulated and supported by governmental action; an educated citizenry and the opening of the West are examples. But in recent years, with a central government of greatly increased power and with much of the labor force engaged in service instead of in production activities, there has been greater effort to plan and give explicit statement to national goals. President Eisenhower asked a blue-ribbon commission to formulate national goals. Presidential declarations, acts of Congress, and papers prepared by influential private groups have stated the goals of the nation with respect to civil rights, health, the exploration of space, the rate of economic growth, and other objectives.

Many national goals have manpower implications, and may imply future needs substantially greater than the projections of present trends. The overall projections of demand for college graduates between 1966 and 1975 and the projections of the supply of new college graduates in that period (as given in Table 2.5) show a reasonably good balance between the totals, although, of course, there are expected to be discrepancies between supply and demand in some fields. In contrast, Table 2.6 indicates that the total supply of new college graduates will fall well short of the number needed to meet all of the national goals analyzed by the National Planning Association's National Goals Project. Of course, it takes more than a given number of men and women to achieve national goals. Money and productive capacity and perhaps new knowledge are also required. But people are always involved, and the ways in which manpower decisions contribute to or interfere with the attainment of national goals provide one criterion for judging those decisions.

The objective of manpower policy is to help us get where we want to go. In this sense, manpower policy is analogous to economic policy. There are other similarities. Neither is a single policy but rather a complex of many policies dealing with various parts of an interrelated system of variables. Neither should have as its objective the establishment of rigid controls over all of the individual decisions involved, but rather the acquisition of enough knowledge of how a complex system operates to enable us to take the actions necessary to keep it in a healthy state.

We have not yet reached this level of understanding. There does not yet exist an adequate theoretical apparatus for predicting the results of actions in the manpower field. But there is beginning to be enough understanding of educational trends, market adjustment mechanisms, and the dynamics of human behavior to give hope that we can progress beyond pure empiricism. The development of a more adequate theoretical basis for policy will require the collaborative efforts of economists, psychologists, sociologists, and workers from still other disciplines.

As we have previously observed, manpower matters are not determined in a completely decentralized fashion, and it is not safe to act as if they were. There is already enough concentration of influence in the federal government to make it urgent to try to understand the whole system better. We should be pushing forward toward the development of a more detailed understanding and a theoretical formulation of the set of interrelated forces that determine the education and utilization of our major national asset, able and educated men and women. This task we commend to interested scholars and to the next Commission on Human Resources.

1 Summary of Manpower Problems and Issues Facing the Nation

THE UNITED STATES provides more opportunities for collegiate, advanced professional, and graduate education than any other nation in the world's history. Nearly half of the young Americans reaching adulthood in 1970 will attend college for some period of time, and between a fifth and a fourth of each age group will graduate from college. Approximately 10 per cent of these age cohorts will attend graduate or professional school and more than half-of them will receive an advanced degree. By comparison with other nations, or with our own figures for earlier decades, these statistics on educational attainment are very impressive. But if we compare them with the demands of our society and economy for educated specialists, our pride of accomplishment must be tempered with concern for occupations and professions where the supply of entrants still fails to meet the demands for graduates. If we compare our educational accomplishments with our ideals of equal educational opportunity for all citizens, we also find our system short of the goal.

The quarter of a century since the end of World War II has seen our economy and society become larger, more complex, more urbanized, more technologically oriented, and more concerned about equality of opportunity. The educational aspirations of the American people, which have always been substantial, have increased even more in the past twenty years. Young people are seeking more education; their parents want them to have more, and the nation's leaders see education as a necessity for dealing with the problems of growth and change in our economy and society.

1

Has the expansion and change of our educational system at the collegiate, graduate, and professional levels kept pace with the changes in our society, and with the requirements of our economy for specialized graduates? This question is extremely complex, and the remainder of this book will examine the answers that can be given to the many facets of this question.

Americans have been concerned with the development of talent, and with the identification and measurement of talent, for a long time, but the systematic study of manpower problems and the collection of information about manpower resources have largely developed in the post-World War II period. The national interest in specialized and professional manpower problems increased greatly during and in the period immediately after World War II. The requirements for specialists for the war effort, the problems of peacetime readjustment, and the sharp wartime drop in the inflow of graduates created a number of manpower problems that provided an impetus for better and more comprehensive information about our human resources.

One of the important results of this heightened interest in specialized manpower problems was the report of the first Commission on Human Resources, *America's Resources of Specialized Talent*,[1] which provided one of the first comprehensive assessments of the numbers and kinds of specialized personnel needed in our society. This report underlined the need for more systematic and comprehensive information about our human resources, and a number of government agencies either began or expanded their efforts to provide information about a wide variety of specialized and professional personnel. In addition, nongovernmental organizations like the National Manpower Council and the Office of Scientific Personnel of the National Academy of Sciences have carried on active programs of study and data collection during and since the 1950's.

By the early part of the 1960's a large amount of manpower information was being collected on a recurring basis by a number of different government and nongovernmental agencies, and a number of special studies had been completed or were under way. The person with an interest in manpower problems was confronted, not with an absence of information, but with a problem of assembling information from diverse sources, resolving inconsistencies in the data, and relating this information to policy problems or theoretical issues.

Despite the increase in manpower studies and information available, manpower shortages and underdeveloped human potentials continued to exist in our society. Our specialized manpower problems were not simply the result of temporary wartime disruptions, but were of long-run derivation because they arose from rapid technological change, urbanization, discrimination, and a variety of other social forces. The studies and statistical information that were gathered helped policy-makers understand the complexities of the issues involved, but they left more policy questions unanswered than were resolved.

[1] Wolfle, Dael, *America's Resources of Specialized Talent*. Harper and Bros., New York, 1954. See the Preface in that volume for a statement about the origins of the report.

Why, after more than a decade of fact-gathering and studies, were people still complaining about a shortage of engineers? Not only were the shortages still being identified, but people were not clear on exactly what steps would be most effective in alleviating the shortages, or how big the shortage was. Similar uncertainties about the best way to alleviate manpower problems can be found, for example, in the problems of unemployment and underutilization of human resources, or the problems of providing adequate medical care.

The need for reassessment of the results of more than a decade of information gathering, research, and special studies was highlighted by these policy dilemmas. In the governmental sector, it led to a provision of the Manpower Development and Training Act of 1962 which specified that: "The Secretary of Labor shall report to the President on the Nation's manpower requirements, resources, use, and training, and the President shall transmit a Manpower Report to the Congress."[2] This annual report attempted to consolidate manpower information from a variety of sources and discuss the principal issues facing governmental manpower policy planners.

In the nongovernmental sector, these same interests led to the second Commission on Human Resources, which was concerned with manpower problems in the specialized occupations and professions, and with the development of human resources among persons with outstanding potential. To some extent the interests of the Commission were complementary to those of the governmental manpower planners. Government agencies represent a concern with the entire spectrum of manpower problems, but the greatest political and governmental attention has been devoted to the problems of unemployment, undereducation, and the ineffective use of manpower in our society. The Commission, by contrast, limited its concern to persons who have above average potential; while a few of them do not have much formal education, on the average they are very well educated, and they have a much lower than average unemployment rate. Some of them may not perform up to the level of their capacity, but by most of the societal standards, they are successful, and they provide most of the leadership in the various segments of our society.

In its studies the Commission drew very heavily on governmental statistics and the results of government-sponsored studies of specialized manpower. Indeed, without the efforts of the federal government, there would be practically no manpower information available today. But in its synthesis and interpretations of these and other studies the Commission, hopefully, will provide its major contribution to a current appraisal of specialized manpower.

The problem of defining the scope of the second Commission's concern was no easier than it was for the first Commission. Who is included in "specialized manpower"? We can offer no better definition than Wolfle did in the report of the first Commission:

[2] *Manpower Report of the President, 1963*. Government Printing Office, Washington, 1963, p. xxvii.

[The study is concerned with] . . . those persons who are educated, intelligent, able to work with ideas, and qualified to plan and understand and direct the nation's complex web of industrial, technological, social, scientific, and governmental institutions and problems. This limited portion of the population is easier to illustrate than to define. It includes the engineers and doctors, the philosophers and historians, the scientists and teachers, the business executives. . . . No term in common usage covers all these groups.[3]

A decade and a half later there is still no general term for all these groups— and there are more specialties and quasi-specialties today then there were in the early 1950's. We will refer to them as specialized manpower, as educated manpower, as professionals, although the population we are interested in is both more and less than any one of these terms. In some chapters of this book (see Chapter 8) the analysis and discussion is limited by the availability of data to a much smaller group, for example, scientists with Ph.D. degrees, but to the extent feasible and possible we have tried to include as much of the "specialized," "educated," and "talented" population in our study as the limitations of space and relevant information would permit.

The Current Status of Research on Specialized Manpower

It is always difficult to characterize the development of any research field in simple terms, but the postwar period up to about 1960 to 1965 was the time in which manpower research emerged as an identifiable specialty. It was a period when great emphasis was placed on data collection and empirical analysis. More than a dozen major sample surveys, longitudinal studies of cohorts, and professional registration projects were either launched or greatly expanded during the 1950's and early 1960's.

Development of new manpower theories and concepts made less progress during the period; researchers were generally content to use ideas and methods of demography, labor economics, and vocational psychology as the basis for their investigations. Much of the data collection and analysis was focused on practical policy questions that determined the scope and content of the surveys; methodological and conceptual issues were of secondary importance in determining the scope of the studies.

Studies conducted in the past two decades have focused on quantitative problems—how many people will want to become teachers, engineers, doctors, or other types of specialists? How many will be needed? What factors affect the choice of a specialty? Much less attention has been given to the problems of quality of our human resources. Stated in layman's language, the quality question is: Will the teachers (or doctors, or other specialists) be good enough? If we paid them more, would they be better? If we gave them a different education, would they be better? The qualitative dimension of manpower problems is very complex, and research has made little headway in measuring the basic dimen-

---

[3] Wolfle, Dael, *op. cit.*, p. 5.

sions of effective performance in any of the professions, or in linking the measures we do have to antecedent factors in the educational, familial, or personal background of professionals or other specialists.

We have already pushed the quantitative "numbers approach" to the study of manpower problems about as far as it can go in providing useful policy information. We need information linking the numbers to the quality of people entering and remaining in the specialized occupations, and hopefully research and data collection in the next decade will devote a great deal more attention to the qualitative criteria that are needed in manpower research. Progress in development of measures of quality and effectiveness seems likely to be slow; the problems involved are very complex, and although a number of researchers have been exploring the dimensions of creativity and of effective professional performance,[4] the validation of measures that can be used in manpower studies in large samples is still in the beginning stages. Research on these questions is likely to be slowed in the future by the concern of public officials about the invasion of personal privacy in social research, as well as by the resistance of professional organizations generally to research about professional competence that is not carefully controlled by the profession itself. For these reasons, while we can be hopeful about research on the quality dimension, we cannot be optimistic about the rate of progress in this important area of manpower research.

It has been clear for some time that manpower problems, like nearly every other research problem, were complex and that many variables were involved in the understanding of any particular problem or outcome. In recognition of these complexities, manpower researchers have used increasingly complex multivariate methods of analysis; often examining the simultaneous effects of 40 to 60 variables on some particular result or outcome. As a result, there is a better understanding of the relative effects of any one variable such as high school grades, or mathematical aptitude, on an outcome such as entering college, or becoming an engineer, for example. Our knowledge of the range of situations in which these variables are important has also been broadened by the number of national and other large samples that have used the same variables. Some of these conclusions and generalizations are discussed later in this chapter, and in subsequent parts of the book. It seems safe to predict that multivariate analysis will dominate future manpower research, and that systems analysis, as a specialized methodology for examining the effects of complex systems of variables on complex outcomes, will be increasingly applied to manpower problems.

The present may be an especially appropriate time to take a new look at our

[4] See, for example, the work of Calvin W. Taylor and Frank Barron, editors, *Scientific Creativity: Its Recognition and Development,* John Wiley and Sons, New York, 1963; and the work of Donald McKinnon and associates at the Institute for Personality Assessment of the University of California on the personality characteristics of professionals who were considered leaders by their peers. McKinnon, "The Nature and Nurture of Creative Talent," *American Psychologist,* vol. 17, July, 1962, pp. 484–495.

knowledge about talented manpower, because we are moving from an emphasis on the problems of data collection, and the analysis of the quantitative aspects of manpower problems, to a future in which systems analysis and other complex methods will be applied to both quantitative and qualitative facets of manpower questions. The following chapters of this book reflect the transition in methods. Some of the analyses reported utilize multivariate techniques, while others involve simpler studies of relationships between only two or three variables. The last two chapters contain a more detailed discussion of the present status and future prospects of manpower planning, manpower research, and manpower theory.

These brief comments about the status of manpower research are necessarily an oversimplification; they do not indicate what the results of the studies and surveys have been, but they may give some perspective to the remainder of this summary.

The Changing Pattern of Supply and Demand for Educated Persons

The rapid and sustained growth of higher education in America is well known. Degree output rose an average of about 4 per cent a year in both the forties and the fifties; in the sixties it is expected to rise about 6 per cent a year, and is projected to rise another 4 to 5 per cent a year during the 1970's. These growth rates, which have consistently been greater than the peacetime average economic growth rate or the rate of growth in the civilian labor force in the United States, have meant an enormous increase in the inflow of graduates to our labor force. In 1940 there were fewer than 200,000 college graduates; during 1968 there will be about 650,000, and by 1980 there will be between 1,000,000 and 1,100,000 graduates each year—between five and six times the number produced in 1940. In the same forty-year period (1940 to 1980) the total labor force will increase by about 80 per cent, so that college graduate entrants have made up and will continue to make up relatively a much larger share of the total entrants to the working population. These gross statistics indicate that our educational system has been growing more rapidly in the past than our economy or labor force, and that these differences seem likely to continue in the next ten to fifteen years.

Will the recent more rapid expansion of our educational system, referred to at the beginning of this chapter, produce more graduates in the future than our economy and society will demand? In general, the answer to this question seems to be "No"; for the foreseeable future college graduates will have a preferred place in the job market. Like other answers about the future, this one is subject to reservations and qualifications.

The *demand*[5] for educated persons in the economy can be separated into three

[5] *Demand* is used in the economic sense, and refers to the existence of positions and funds to employ persons. *Need* is used in the social sense of the number of people that would be required to meet some social goal. Need may be larger than demand, or smaller.

components: (1) replacement of persons dying, retiring, or otherwise leaving the labor force; (2) occupational growth requirements; and (3) requirements for raising the educational level of occupations. The first two components of demand can be measured fairly well from available data but the third component cannot. We know that some occupations have become more complex and require more education, and many occupations will employ better-educated people, if they can get them. We can estimate the amount of educational upgrading that has occurred in the past, but this does not give us any indication of how much of this upgrading was required, and how much was merely desirable. Nor can we measure effectively how much of the educational upgrading of occupations was economically beneficial, in the sense of adding to the average productivity in the occupation. (See Chapter 2 for a detailed discussion of this topic.)

It may be surprising to some people, but our educational system has been producing more graduates than are required for replacement and occupational growth in the period from 1950 to 1965, and it seems likely to continue to produce more graduates in the next fifteen years than are needed to fill the first two components of demand. In the 1950 to 1959 period about one-fourth of the college graduates entering the labor force were available to raise the educational level of occupations in the labor force. In the 1960 to 1969 period the more rapid growth of the labor force slowed the educational upgrading of occupations, but in the 1970 to 1979 period it seems likely that between 25 and 30 per cent of the college graduate entrants to the labor force will again be available to raise the educational level of occupations. While the preceding holds true for the aggregate of all college graduates, in a number of occupations the educational level has changed very little.

These projections assume about a 4 per cent annual rate of economic growth, which was larger than the growth rate achieved in the 1950 to 1959 period; if we fail to achieve our future economic and labor force growth targets, the educational upgrading of occupations will occur at an even more rapid rate than we have projected.

A large part of the educational upgrading (at the college graduate level) has occurred in the managerial, sales, and in those professional occupations where college graduation has not been in the past a requirement for obtaining a job. The occupations that have traditionally required college degrees, such as law, medicine, and college teaching, will provide employment for a much smaller fraction of our future college graduate output.

Even though our output of college graduates is growing at a slightly more rapid rate than is needed for occupational growth and replacement, some occupations have continued to experience shortages. The health professions, especially medicine and dentistry, have grown very slowly in relation to the demand for their services, and shortages of engineers are widely reported. In the 1950's, for example, college graduates entered managerial occupations at a rate that almost doubled the percentage of college graduates in these occupations in a decade, while the proportion of college graduates in engineering did not rise during the decade. Even though a bachelor's degree is the expected standard for occupational entry into engineering, the occupation was expanding so rapidly during the 1950's that a substantial number of nongraduates had to be recruited to the occupation. These examples illustrate the problems of distribution of graduates to the occupations where demand is greatest. These problems of distribution of graduates are likely to continue into the future even if the total supply of graduates is adequate to meet occupational requirements. New occupations will arise in which college graduation is expected or required, and the reorientation of students toward the new (and often rapidly growing) occupations through our democratic processes of counseling and persuasion will mean that we will continue to have problems of distribution of our total supply of college graduates to the right specialties.

We cannot determine just how much educational upgrading of the occupational structure is optimum from the point of view of economic growth. Other nations with much smaller proportions of persons in the labor force with postsecondary school training than the U.S. has, have had economic growth rates considerably higher than those the U.S. has maintained in the postwar period, but since economic growth occurs as a result of a large number of influences, only one of which is the educational level of the labor force, these comparative studies of different countries raise more questions than they answer.

We should not conclude from these examples that the proportion of college graduates in the labor force of a modern industrialized society has no effect on economic growth rates; we just have not been able to measure the relationship with sufficient precision to be able to identify optimum levels or proportions of college graduates who are needed in the labor force. It does appear that the output of college graduates will be sufficient to continue the educational upgrading of occupations at the rate that was achieved in the 1950's, even with a more rapid rate of economic growth, and larger increases in the labor force projected for the 1970's than occurred in the 1950's.

In Chapter 2 there is a discussion of college-educated manpower needed to achieve national goals that were defined by a Presidential commission in 1960; these educated manpower needs would be substantially greater than the number of college graduates who would be produced by 1975. National goals achievement by 1975 also implies a higher rate of economic growth than seems likely to be achieved, so that even if the number of college graduates was expected to be sufficient, the resources to employ them probably would not be available.

Tested against projected economic growth (demand), we cannot be certain whether or not we are expanding our educational system at an optimum rate; tested against the criteria of achievement of national goals (need), we will not produce enough graduates in the next decade. Problems of distribution of the total supply of graduates among the specialized occupations are likely to persist in the future, with some occupations experiencing a shortage while others may have a relatively adequate supply.

Feedback into Education—Changes in the Demands for Teachers

A large part of the demand for bachelor's and advanced degree graduates comes from the educational system itself. The rapid growth of elementary and secondary education in the postwar years (especially in the 1953 to 1965 period) led to a continuing heavy demand for teachers; in addition, educational standards for entry into the profession have been rising. In the late 1950's and early 1960's nearly a third of all college graduates entered teaching. Over half of all women college graduates who entered the labor force during this period became teachers. While many of these teachers married, had children, and dropped out of teaching after only a few years, teaching was the dominant occupational destination for college graduate women.

In the late 1960's and the 1970's elementary and secondary enrollments will grow more slowly than they did from 1950 to 1965; this smaller demand for teachers can be filled from college graduating classes that continue to expand rapidly. By 1970 only about 22 per cent of college graduates will be required in teaching, and by 1980 only 12 to 14 per cent will be needed, assuming that the staffing pattern and teacher-pupil ratios continue at 1966 levels. Even if additional teachers for kindergartens, compensatory education, and other new programs were added in the next decade, as suggested in the report of the National Goals Commission of 1960, the proportion of graduates required for teaching by 1980 would be less than 20 per cent. A substantial redirection of career goals of future college graduates is implied in these figures.

More than 60 per cent of all doctoral graduates enter academic employment; even when persons employed full time in research, administration, and service are excluded, about 45 to 50 per cent of all Ph.D.'s enter regular college teaching positions.[6]

In 1967–1968 about half of the 22,000 doctorate recipients would have to enter college teaching in order to maintain the present level of Ph.D.'s on college faculties; by 1975 fewer than one-fourth of the 40,000 to 42,000 doctoral graduates of that year would be required to maintain the present level of doctorates on faculties. The present level of doctorates on college faculties does not represent a desired level, and college employment of Ph.D.'s is likely to continue at the present level (45 to 50 per cent of all graduates entering teaching) until some of the backlog of unmet demand for college teachers is satisfied. Sometime between 1975 and 1985 the demand for additional doctorates to upgrade college faculties will be satisfied in most fields, and at that point, the

---

[6] Cartter, Allan M., "Future Faculty: Needs and Resources," *Improving College Teaching.* Background Papers at the 49th Annual Meeting of the American Council on Education, Washington, 1966, p. 108.

proportion of doctorates required for college teaching positions will decline sharply. The timing of the decline in the proportion of graduates entering academic employment will vary in different fields, but will probably occur first in the sciences, and last in the humanities.

These large shifts in the proportion of graduates required for teaching at both elementary and secondary levels and college levels will mean reorientation of career plans for many people now enrolled as undergraduates in college, or alternatively, the development of new programs that provide more teachers in relation to students, and/or programs to teach persons who are not now served by formal educational programs. Although our assumptions about enrollment growth lead to higher projections of both enrollments and degrees than those provided by the Office of Education and the Census Bureau, the share of all graduates who will be employed in education will decline unless new programs to employ additional teachers are developed, and even these seem likely to be insufficient to continue the ratios at their present levels. Since teaching employs so large a fraction of all Ph.D.'s and college graduates, these prospective shifts will have a substantial effect on career plans, and on the availability of personnel to enter a number of related occupations, such as the social welfare occupations, managerial and governmental jobs, and other related occupations. The increases in the supply of doctoral graduates will have the effect of reducing demand for master's graduates, but the greater supply of master's graduates will, in turn, reduce the demand for bachelor's graduates. Educational standards for jobs are likely to change with changing supplies of graduates prepared for teaching.

Supply-Demand Balance in Other Selected Professions

While the magnitude of shifts anticipated in the requirements for teachers are numerically greater than the shifts expected in other occupations, none of the fields of specialization presents a static picture of future demand. Several of these occupations are examined in detail in Chapter 4, to see how each occupation has supplied the personnel to meet the demand for them. Several different ways of responding to changing demand are utilized in different occupations.

Changes in the inflow of graduates to the occupation is usually the first approach considered to meet a change in demand, but it is only one way of adjusting supply to demand, and it is often a slow and relatively ineffective approach. The inflow of persons to each occupation is based on the choices of a large number of individuals acting independently. These patterns of choice are slow to change, and are further channeled by institutional arrangements that are also slow to change. For example, the flow of M.D. graduates has been quite steady and quite predictable; changing the institutional arrangements (that is, expanding medical school student capacity) has proved to be difficult and slow, despite the addition of large sums of money.

Other approaches to meeting the demand have been more effective in the short run. In professions like teaching and nursing, which employ a large proportion of women, there is a reserve of trained housewives and mothers who can be and have been drawn back into the labor force in periods of high demand. The combination of family and career has become the norm among well-educated women in the postwar period. They work until the first child is born, drop out of the labor force to rear a family, and then reenter the profession when their children are in school. Since the timing of reentry into the labor force can be varied in response to market demand, the women provide a reservoir of professional skills that will be available to meet demand. Teaching and nursing are examples of occupations where the reentry of women to the occupation has been of great importance in meeting the demand for graduates.

Another means of meeting demand has been through the employment of more subprofessional workers, and through improved technology, both of which can add to the effectiveness of the professional. Both medicine and dentistry have met the rising demand for health services by employment of assistants, and by the use of new drugs and equipment that have increased the average amount of service provided by each professional.

Still another means of meeting demand is through the use of flexible standards for the profession, and the employment of persons with less than desired professional qualifications. Engineering has employed a large number of persons with less than a bachelor's degree because the demand could not be filled with college graduates. Similarly, college teaching positions have been filled by many persons who do not have a doctor's degree, simply because persons with the prerequisite qualifications were not available.

In licensed professions with rigidly defined entry standards, the pattern has been to use subprofessional assistants; in professions with more flexible entry requirements, the pattern has been to incorporate them into the profession itself. A large part of the answer to the question, "Why don't we have more subprofessional engineering technicians and engineering aides?" is that they can call themselves engineers and be counted as professionals.

In some of the professions we have examined in detail, it is very difficult to predict future demand. This is true of the law, of social work, and of the performing arts. In law and social work, whatever supply of graduates is produced seems likely to have no difficulty in finding employment within their respective professions. The use of lawyers and of social service personnel in our society is widespread, and covers a very wide variety of activities. The social forces that generate employment opportunities for these occupations seem likely to generate even more opportunities in the future.

But because the criteria of demand in these professions are difficult to reduce to quantitative terms, it is difficult to make comparisons between the relative magnitude of demand in one occupation as compared with another. In both engineering and social work, future demand will be very high, and will be greater than increases in demand for teachers, or for lawyers, or professionals in the arts. But these generalizations are not very precise, and give us inadequate guidance in planning expansion of educational facilities, or in advising students who have choices to make about which field to enter.

Planning Career Shifts

These changing career opportunities pose a real challenge to our ability to redirect the career aspirations of students. In the past, as materials in Chapters 6 and 9 will indicate, we have had limited success in redirecting the career plans of students at either the graduate or undergraduate level. There is a great deal of shifting of career plans during the college years, and some shifting between the baccalaureate and graduate school entry, but these shifts seem to be less determined by market forces and the demand for graduates than they are by the efforts of students to select careers that are congruent with their interests and aptitudes, and by the effects of academic pressures that move students from the more demanding toward the less demanding occupations.

The smaller proportions of graduates who are required for elementary and secondary teaching will probably have little or no effect in raising the proportion of graduates who are engineers. Very few students who initially aspire to be teachers shift into engineering, and the difference in academic aptitudes between the two groups is substantial. In addition, the two occupations attract persons with very different patterns of interests and values. On the other hand, there are many similarities between the interests and academic aptitudes of elementary and secondary teachers and social workers, and the gains to social work from a relative decline in demand for teachers would probably be substantial. A change from teaching to social work may be the kind of career shift that will occur fairly frequently without the need for extensive efforts to redirect career plans, or change institutional arrangements. A shift from elementary teaching to nursing, on the other hand, may require considerably more intervention in current institutional arrangements. A decision to enter nursing is usually required at the time of high school graduation, because the majority of nurses are trained in hospital schools of nursing which are programs that are difficult to transfer into or out of. The opportunities for a transfer from teaching to nursing are made much more difficult by these institutional arrangements, and this constitutes a barrier to career mobility in the direction of future market needs. The patterns of interests and aptitudes of teachers and nurses are different, but not to an extent that would prevent many of them from shifting their career objectives. The further expansion of collegiate nursing programs, and the delay of the differentiation between nursing and other majors in the four-year collegiate programs to the end of the sophomore year, would be institutional arrangements that would facilitate career shifts in the direction of market needs.

The flow of entrants into teaching can be regulated by raising the degree requirements for entry to the master's level, by being more selective in admission to teacher certification programs, or by both. The trend to require more education is already evident, and is likely to accelerate in the future. Some potential entrants to teaching will be discouraged by the longer period of preparation required, and may consider alternatives such as business (for men), or social work and nursing (for women).

There are no general solutions to the problem of redirection of career plans and interests that will work for all occupations. Instead, each occupation attracts a particular type of student, has a set of relationships with other occupations, and a set of institutional arrangements for facilitating the flow of personnel into the occupation. The steps that will increase the flow into nursing are different from the steps that will increase the flow into engineering. A good deal of evidence is already available to indicate which procedures are likely to be successful, and which procedures will not work. In spite of this information, the problem of redirecting the voluntary choices of today's youth is formidable, and a great deal more research is needed if we are to be able to give the kind of career guidance, and make the institutional changes, required by rapidly shifting occupational options in tomorrow's world.

The Flow of Students Through College

Colleges and universities are the primary institutions in our society that affect and direct the flow of students into the professional occupations. From the viewpoint of the manpower planner, the colleges not only provide an education for the professions and specialized occupations, they also serve a critical function in channeling students into occupations and careers, and in eliminating students who seem to lack the prerequisites for entry to a professional occupation. We have already indicated that the evidence is inconclusive about the effect of expansion in the total size of the collegiate enterprise on economic growth. We have also indicated that the number of entrants into some occupations will not expand rapidly enough to meet demand, even if the total system of higher education is growing sufficiently. From this point of view the problem is to expand the enrollments and graduates of those college major fields where demand will be greatest. In some cases, as in the health professions, like medicine and dentistry, institutional bottlenecks are clearly evident. If we had more medical schools or larger medical schools, we would eventually have more doctors. In other shortage fields the evidence of institutional barriers is less clearcut. Additional students could be accepted in many engineering schools, for example. Engineering has a high dropout rate, and this is partly an institutional problem, but unless dropouts can be reduced without reducing the quality of the education provided, the results of changing institutional practices may be less beneficial rather than more beneficial.

Apart from the question of institutional arrangements to facilitate entry into shortage occupations, there is the more general question of how our colleges and universities select and retain students, and what the consequences are for the development of the abilities of our population. To what extent do socioeconomic barriers thwart the development of talent? Does our diverse system of higher education contain deadends, or rigidities that in unintended ways hamper the process by which people select a major and a career and make progress toward a degree?

The size and diversity of our system of higher education is one of its most striking features. A few students from the bottom 10 per cent of high school graduates go to college, and some of these manage to attain a bachelor's degree. The poorest students at our most selective colleges have more academic potential than the best students at our least selective institutions. While there is very little overlap in student aptitude between our best and our poorest colleges, there is a wide overlap for most institutions. Our large public universities, which attract a wide spectrum of students, actually educate more of the top ability students than our highly selective liberal arts colleges, which admit only about 4 per cent of the students entering college. The overlap in student populations served by different institutions, and the similarities of their curricula, facilitate student transfers, and about one student out of every three attends more than one institution during his college career. Progress in college is slowed down slightly for the student who transfers, but the percentage of transfers who completed a bachelor's degree was almost as high as the percentage among the total group of entrants. These figures exclude the transfers from junior college, who are somewhat less likely to complete college.

The most striking loss of talent occurs among high ability students who enter junior colleges. Among the top fifth of high school graduates who go to college, those who enter the junior colleges are less than half as likely to complete a college degree within five years as are students of equivalent aptitude who initially entered a four-year institution. The more selective the institution, the greater the probability of graduating and going on to graduate school. The initial choice of college turns out to have a substantial influence on the chances of college completion, even among students of equivalent ability. Part of the difference is undoubtedly self-selection—those students who have uncertain plans or less motivation may enroll in the local junior college, while those who enter a selective college must plan well in advance, and probably are much more motivated toward academic pursuits. The extent to which the difference in rate of completion is the result of initial self-selection or the result of institutional influences that could be modified is not clear, and deserves further study. A major influence on talent development is involved when it is remembered that nearly a third of all college entrants begin their careers in junior college, and that this reduces the chance of completing college by half for persons of equivalent academic aptitude.

The highly selective colleges, which have very low dropout rates and send a very high percentage of their graduates on to graduate and professional schools, select students largely on the basis of academic aptitude, and they also tend to get students from high socioeconomic backgrounds, even though socioeconomic background is usually not a selection criterion. A boy from the top fifth in academic aptitude and the top fifth in socioeconomic status (SES) is almost ten times as likely to enter a selective college as a boy of equivalent academic aptitude who is from the bottom fifth in socioeconomic status. The chances of attending college at all are about 30 per cent greater for the boy from the top fifth in SES than from the lower fifth in SES, a much smaller differential than in selective colleges.

About four out of five boys from the top fifth of their high school graduating classes now go to college, a substantial improvement over the figures reported in the first Commission study. For girls the proportions are a little lower, and for both sexes the nonattenders are concentrated among the lower SES groups.

It is also encouraging to note that the rapid expansion of higher education seems to have occurred without a decline in the average academic aptitude of entering students. Although the evidence is based on samples that are not entirely representative, average academic aptitude of entering freshmen seems to have risen slightly since the early 1950's; if true, it indicates that the additional high school graduates who have entered college have included increases among high ability students as well as average or below average students. Nearly all the high ability students now enter college (over 90 per cent of those in the top 10 per cent in high school go on to college) and further expansion of college enrollment will be drawn more heavily from average and below average students. It would be theoretically possible for college enrollments to increase until about 1975 without any decline in the average ability of entering students if we are successful in attracting those high ability high school graduates (mostly of lower socioeconomic background) who do not go to college now; achievement of the projected increases in college enrollment after 1975 would necessarily lead to a slight decline in the ability levels of entering college students. A more detailed discussion of these trends can be found in Chapter 5.

The Mobility of Professional Manpower

It should be evident from this summary that a great deal of uncertainty exists about the future level of demand in many occupations, and about the kinds of work that will be demanded, as well as uncertainty about the way in which the educational and career plans of youth can be encouraged or changed. This uncertainty about the future is one of the important realities affecting manpower and educational planning. Since the rate of change in occupations is increasing, the uncertainty about the future may increase too, despite our research efforts.

In this context of uncertainty, mobility, both occupational and geographic, is necessary to a functioning economy and to individual career development as well. Since we cannot plan careers completely, we must have effective ways of adapting careers to changing circumstances. The high level of specialization required for the professions inhibits occupational mobility. The more specialized the level of education required, the more difficult occupational mobility becomes.

The reverse is true for geographic mobility. For most professions, a national labor market (as contrasted with a regional or local labor market) exists, and this leads to a high degree of geographic mobility and more long distance movement.

There has been a great deal of interest in the effects of geographic mobility on the redistribution of talent among the various regions of the country. Young people migrate for college and graduate education, and the best schools draw their students from all parts of the country. The best students are the ones who are most mobile; they attend the high prestige "national" graduate schools and enter a national labor market that leads to higher posteducational mobility.

Although there are substantial state and regional differentials in the availability of high quality educational opportunities, especially at the graduate level, the effects of migration for education and posteducational migration tend to equalize the distribution of talent among the regions. While our sample studies were confined to the study of quantitative and qualitative effects at the graduate level, other studies of the migration of persons with a bachelor's degree suggest that the same influences are operative at other levels of education. For the entire population of adults, the net effects of migration exert a relatively small influence in changing the educational level of the adult population of states or regions,[7] although for highly specialized groups like Ph.D. scientists, the effects can be quite substantial in redistributing talent.

Since support for higher education, and in particular for graduate education, is unequal in different states and regions of the United States, and since the quality of education is related to these different levels of support, migration has the effect of counterbalancing some of the geographic inequities in educational opportunity. Current federal support efforts are putting more emphasis on distribution of funds geographically and the development of additional centers of excellence in graduate work. This diffusion of support has a great deal of backing, but its value ought to be weighed against the alternative of promoting the mobility of good students to existing institutions with good programs, especially in those specialized fields where the number of qualified and interested students is smaller than the number of institutional places that are available for graduate students. To some degree, we have had both policy emphases in educational support programs. While the growth of many fields requires the addition of more educational programs, in other fields it probably will be cheaper and quicker to take the good students to the good programs than to develop additional quality programs in new geographic locations.

Criteria of Effective Professional Performance in the Sciences

Implied in some of the preceding comments about the supply and demand for specialized personnel was the idea that quality of future personnel was a

---

[7] Folger, John K., and Charles B. Nam, *Education of the American Population*. Government Printing Office, Washington, 1967, pp. 184–186.

more important consideration than quantity. In teaching, in the law, and in the performing arts, for example, the number of people available to enter these occupations will probably be adequate, but the shortage of well-qualified entrants may be substantial. In nearly every profession, and in most other occupations as well, the concern is for more highly qualified and more effective entrants. Good people are always in short supply. To the extent that this is simply the expression of a relative judgment, little can be done about it, because only 25 per cent of the people can be in the top quarter. But to the extent that it represents inadequate selection or education of the entrants to an occupation, there is possibility of improvement. How good are the entrants to various occupations? Do they perform effectively? What is effective performance? What relation is there between the quality of education received and the quality of subsequent performance? These are important questions, but they are very complex. Effective professional performance is difficult to reduce to measurable terms, although everyone has opinions about it. Indices of professional performance such as income or publications (for scientists and scholars) have been used in a number of studies. These studies have demonstrated more about the difficulties of measuring professional performance and its determinants than they have provided answers that would be useful in determining either selection or education procedures. While academic performance (grades) and quality of school attended at one level (for example, high school) are quite predictive of success at the next level (for example, college), grades have only a little predictive power for future income, research productivity, or other measures of career success. Chapter 8 reviews some of these studies and reports on some additional studies that attempt to relate the quality of graduate school attended and personal characteristics to later career development among scientists. Even though the measures of scientific accomplishment used were more carefully developed and the studies were more comprehensive in design, the results were not greatly different from earlier studies. The quality of graduate school attended has some relation to scientific productivity, but the relationships are not large. The type of employer and the amount of emphasis given to research on the job have more relation to research productivity, but it would be surprising if these did not prove to be important influences.

These studies make it very clear that there is no single group of institutions, and no single pattern of education or career development that is "the" way to scientific accomplishment. While the persons who pursue an uninterrupted graduate program at a high quality university follow it with a postdoctoral fellowship and then go to another high quality university where they spend the greater part of their time in research are most likely to have works published and have a high citation count, there are a large number of other patterns that produce people with substantial research accomplishment and many citations. Until we have much more definitive research linking personal characteristics and educational experiences with accomplishment, our ideas for educational program improvement will not be capable of being validated. Research has shown that no particular program or kind of institution has a monopoly on the development of talent. Leaders of our professions come from a wide variety of backgrounds and from all sorts of educational institutions. In view of the low correlations between institutional effects and later career success, the diversity of our educational system is probably a strength.

The Development of Talent Among Special Groups

The problems of talent development in our society center around the problems of special groups of the population: women, Negroes and other ethnic minorities, and disadvantaged youth. The academically able, white middle-class male finds an educational system that has been developed to serve his interests and to facilitate his entry into the professional world. Our nation is highly successful in providing a college education and entry to a specialized occupation to nearly all the members of this favored group; those few who do not enter a profession, or become a business manager, enter other occupations by choice and not by necessity. In the future the question of talent development and of adequate supplies of entrants for the professions will be largely determined by the remaining population groups: women, persons from disadvantaged socioeconomic backgrounds (regardless of race and ethnic origin), and persons who do not perform well on standard measures of academic ability but who nevertheless have creative potential. In the third section of this book we examine women and persons from low socioeconomic background in more detail (Chapters 9 and 10) to see what barriers limit their achievement, as well as identifying their patterns of career development. Foreign manpower contributions to the supply of entrants to the specialized occupations are also examined (Chapter 11) since they have been an important part of the nation's manpower supply for a long time.

Professional Careers for Women

Women constitute the largest potential for further expansion of the professions and specialized occupations. While the percentage of women who develop their potential through higher education has been increasing, they still lag behind the men in achievement of bachelor's degrees, and at the advanced degree level the sex differences favoring the men are even greater. As we have indicated earlier, most college-educated women plan both a family and a career, and they usually interrupt their career to rear children to the point (which usually occurs between the ages of 35 and 45) where they can resume their careers, at least on a part-time basis.

Professions like law, medicine, and university teaching, which require extended training beyond the bachelor's degree, and where a high level of career commitment is expected on the part of their entrants, attract relatively few women, and the proportion of women entering these occupations has remained relatively stable. Engineering, another high demand occupation with uncertain prospects for an adequate supply of entrants, has also failed to attract more women, and only about one per cent of the employed engineers are women.

The problem of getting more women to enter the high demand occupations is partly one of changing the image of these occupations so that more women will be attracted to them. While some employer discrimination against women undoubtedly exists, the main reason there are so few women engineers or physical scientists is that women do not choose these occupations. Their parents, counselors, teachers, and friends do not encourage them to enter these occupations, and so a process of self-selection keeps them out.

Another important barrier to entry of more women to some of the predominantly male occupations is the limited reentry to a career (which may involve refresher educational programs for any of the professions with technical content) or for part-time work while family responsibilities are high. As long as the occupation or profession requires (or expects) continuous full-time commitment of all entrants, few women will be attracted, for few are willing to give up the opportunity for marriage and a family.

The changes in women's aspirations about entry to some professions and in the work expectations of some professions will be slow to come, but if demand in the occupation is sufficiently high, more women entrants are likely to be recruited. In any event, the future will see more women seeking both a career and marriage, and more married women and mothers entering or reentering the labor force. The extent to which these long-term trends for women's work help to resolve some of the more chronic manpower shortage problems will depend on some of the changes described above, which are described more fully in Chapter 9.

Socioeconomic Background and College Completion

The lower rates of college entry and completion of persons from lower socioeconomic backgrounds have been documented in a number of recent studies, which are described in both Chapter 5 and Chapter 10.[8] While the undereducated segment of the lower socioeconomic groups has been getting proportionately smaller, it is still substantial in size. Compared with the number of able women who fail to obtain a college education, the able low SES group represents a much smaller potential, but one that is of greater concern because it is a much clearer failure to realize our ideals of equal educational opportunity.

Elimination of SES differentials in college attendance and completion rates is not simply a matter of providing more scholarships or low-cost college opportunities, even though these would help. It also involves changing aspirations and

[8] Inasmuch as Negro Americans and some other ethnic minorities are disproportionately concentrated among low socioeconomic groups, these chapters implicitly deal with their talent development problems. We have not, however, attempted a comprehensive review of talent development problems among minority groups.

motivations for college and professional careers, a complex process that should begin at an early age and extend throughout the school years. High ability girls from low SES backgrounds are least likely to attend college; for them marriage and family represents a familiar and acceptable alternative to college. Until these traditional sex-role values are changed, higher education, even if it were free, would draw only a portion of the bright low SES girls. While we do not have reliable longitudinal data on college attendance rates by SES with ability, controlled, indirect evidence indicates that attitudes about college-going have been shifting rapidly among low SES groups; if these attitudes are reinforced by the extension of low-cost college opportunities, SES related differentials in college attendance among high ability youth, which are still substantial in magnitude, may become smaller in the next decade.

Foreign Contributions to High-Level Manpower

The interest in the "brain-gain" and the "brain-drain" has risen in recent years, but contributions of foreign-born persons to our professions and specialized occupations have been substantial for a long time. The inflow of both foreign students (who may later be recruited as permanent residents of this country) and of immigrants with professional and specialized backgrounds has been rising in recent years. While the annual contribution of immigrants to the professional occupations in this country is only about 5 per cent of the total, it is heavily concentrated in fields like medicine and science and engineering, and for some of the sending countries represents a major loss of their most capable people.

The concern of some of the sending countries over their losses indicates that they will take remedial action of some kind. Whether such action will be in the form of restrictive immigration quotas (which is likely to be an ineffective way of dealing with the problem in the long run) or whether these countries will raise salaries, modernize their educational systems, utilize merit criteria for promotions, and take other steps to improve their competitive position in international manpower exchange will undoubtedly vary from country to country. The major initiative for these reforms lies with the countries that are losing manpower; the United States cannot "solve" the problem by excluding foreign-trained persons, or adopting more rigid quota systems.

Conclusion

This brief nonstatistical summary of the manpower problems and issues facing the United States is developed in more detail in the subsequent chapters of this book, which concludes with two chapters that discuss the need for manpower planning and the need for further research.

There is much to be pleased with in America's record of manpower and educational development in the postwar period. We have expanded our educational system rapidly, have greatly reduced the proportion of bright students who do not go to college, and have provided specialists and professionals to meet the manpower demands of most (but not all) of the important occupations.

We can speak with less assurance about the changes in the quality of education provided, and about the adequacy with which America's specialists and future leaders are being prepared for the complex world of tomorrow. The quality dimension is the most important aspect of most manpower problems today and it is the part of the problem that we know the least about. We know, for example, that there are enough teachers in the sense that there are few if any classes that have no teachers. We also know that the percentage of teachers without a college degree has declined rapidly in the past fifteen years. But we cannot say how much the average effectiveness of teachers has changed in the past decade, either for better or worse, or whether today's school systems come closer to or farther from the goals of an adequately educated population. We could say the same things about engineering, about social work, and most other occupations. In many of these occupations our expectations for the quality of service have risen; the educational system, the medical system, and the engineering service that we had in 1920 or even 1950 would be considered inadequate by today's standards. But we cannot measure very well whether our educational preparation has kept pace with our rising goals for service. We have plenty of opinions about the inadequacies of schools, hospitals, and other services, but we do not have the information needed for planning effective qualitative improvements in manpower and educational programs.

Even though we are beginning to learn something about the various flows of personnel into, between, and out of professional occupations, the remainder of this book will demonstrate that our knowledge is often superficial and quite limited. While we can conclude that in most professions the flow seems to be adequate in size (if not in quality) and that the various processes by which the flow is adjusted to meet changing demands seem to work reasonably well in most cases, there is no basis for complacency on our part. We have shown little ability to modify any of these manpower flows by planned action if they did not seem to be meeting the demands.

In the future the rate of social change will increase our aspirations and goals for professional service, and the subsequent demands for better service. If a cure for cancer is discovered, there will be the expectation that it should be almost immediately available to everyone. Progress in obtaining a cleaner environment, safer cities, and other complex goals will also generate demands for many new professions in a hurry. If an answer is in sight, Congress will appropriate the funds, and the expectation is that somehow the professionals to carry out the programs will be found.

Today's professional manpower recruitment based on voluntary choices of individuals, and adjustment processes (occupational and geographic mobility, increased productivity per professional, for example) that operate on the same basis of individual choice may be severely strained by the quickening pace of change in society. If we are to avoid compulsory or quasi-compulsory manpower allocation, and at the same time make adequate use of manpower to achieve national objectives, we must greatly expand the information base we have about talented manpower, and our ability to use that information wisely in the interests of both the individuals concerned and the society that uses their services.

Section I

2 The Market for
College Graduates

IF MANPOWER planning is to be effective, it is essential that we have some overall perspective on the relation of supply to demand for a fairly long time into the future. We need knowledge of past and current trends that may continue to develop, of sudden changes in the rate or direction of these trends and the effects that such changes will have on the supply of college graduates and on the demands of the economy as a whole and of specialized fields within the economy, and of the areas of uncertainty that make more precise projections impossible. In the last connection, a full assessment of what we do not know—and there is admittedly a great deal—will not only temper our projections with the proper spirit of humility but, more important, will help to direct the attention of educators, government officials, and others concerned with manpower planning to those questions most in need of consideration and research.

This chapter attempts to provide a general framework for the examination of supply and demand in specific occupations which follows in Chapters 3 and 4. In the first part of this chapter, the method usually used in manpower forecasting is described and some of the difficulties that arise in estimating supply (particularly the colleges' output of graduates) and demand are discussed. In the second part, the Bureau of Labor Statistics input-output model for the total economy, industry by industry, is made the basis for projections to 1975 of the number of college-educated people required to satisfy three components of demand and the number needed to achieve national goals. Some of the variables that may affect these projections are also examined.

Problems in Manpower Forecasting

The most widely used method for approaching manpower problems is to make projections, based on past trends and on assumptions about continuities or changes in these trends in the future, of the demand that will exist for people with certain qualifications and of the supply of such people who will be available to fill these demands.[1]

By identifying jobs that require college graduates and then making projections of the number of people that will be required to fill these jobs, we will arrive at an estimate of the demand for college graduates. If, according to these estimates, the number of such jobs will be greater than the number of college graduates available to fill them, then a "shortage" is said to exist; if the number of college graduates exceeds the number of jobs available, a "surplus" will be identified.

Most manpower projections of this nature have dealt with single occupations, such as medicine, or with groups of related occupations, such as the health professions. Some efforts have also been made to examine the relation of supply and demand for college-educated manpower generally.[2]

In general, the most useful supply-demand projections are those that look at least ten years into the future. Short-range projections have less value for the planner and administrator simply because they do not allow enough time to plan for expansion of the educational system, to inform entering students about the major fields that offer the greatest career opportunities, or to make other necessary adjustments.

Estimating the Supply of College-Educated Manpower

To make projections of the supply of trained manpower that will be available in the next ten or fifteen years, we must estimate first the number of college graduates who will be entering the labor force in that period. Although we have reliable figures, by degree level and field of specialization, that extend back for several decades, past projections have usually proved to be underestimates of actual college enrollment and degree output. Indeed, as Rivlin points out, most of the projections made in the 1950's for the 1970's had already fallen below the actual figures by 1961. She concludes from this: "It does not seem likely that anything useful can be accomplished by fitting more trend curves to the same basic data on enrollment trends. . . . It is time to begin looking at college

---

[1] In this volume we have primarily concerned ourselves with high-level occupations that employ persons with advanced training—bachelor's degree holders or better. Of course, one could also make projections of future supply and demand for unskilled laborers, office workers, sales clerks, and other persons in jobs where college training is not necessary.

[2] See, for example, Harris, Seymour, *The Market for College Graduates*, Harvard University Press, Cambridge, Mass., 1949; Havighurst, Robert, *American Higher Education in the 1960's*, Ohio State University Press, Columbus, 1960; and Mushkin, Selma, editor, *Economics of Higher Education, Part 1*, OE-50027, Government Printing Office, Washington, 1962.

enrollment as a dependent variable."[3] In other words, if we are to avoid the errors of past enrollment projections, we must consider what factors have influenced the unforeseen large increases in college enrollment and what impact they (or other new factors) are likely to have in the future.

With the wisdom afforded by hindsight, it can be said that these errors arose from a failure to recognize the rising expectation of young people for a college education. Larger percentages of youth have been graduating from high school, and more high school graduates going on to college, than foreseen in the 1950's. The question is: Will student demand for college education continue to increase in the next decade or two at the same rate, at a lower rate, or at a still higher rate?

To answer, we can offer only negative evidence. At present there is nothing to indicate that more young people will not seek a college education. A number of studies have shown that more students hope or expect to go to college than actually get there and that parents are even more optimistic than their offspring in their expectations, particularly when their children are young. Though at present slightly less than half of those in their late teens or early twenties actually get any college experience, it seems reasonable to assume that the aspirations of students and their parents will more and more be realized.

It is sometimes argued that, instead of expanding to accommodate these aspirants, our colleges will simply become more selective in their admissions policies, thus screening out students of low ability, which would have the effect of keeping enrollment figures relatively stable. That likelihood seems remote. The rapid growth of the junior college system (which enrolled 21 per cent of all entering freshmen in 1955, 28 per cent by the fall of 1965, and which may enroll as many as one-third of all entering freshmen by 1975) shows no signs of slackening. Moreover, even at present, our system of higher education is not so strained as it appears to be when one looks only at the more selective and more prestigious instiutions. While they turn away large numbers of applicants, evidence suggests that those who apply to less selective institutions are admitted. There is a college for everyone who is persistent enough. For instance, Klock and Hills found that nearly every student who had been rejected by one public institution in Georgia was accepted at some other college if he made a second application.[4]

Granting that these trends toward greater college attendance will continue to develop in the future, our long-range projections are still subject to rather wide margins of error because of our relative ignorance about specific determinants of college attendance. We know enough about the general determinants—aca-

[3] Rivlin, Alice, "The Demand for Higher Education," in Orcutt, Guy H., and others, *Microanalysis of Socioeconomic Systems.* Harper and Row, New York, 1961, Table 47 and pp. 258–262.

[4] Klock, Joseph, and John Hills, "Rejected Students in the University System of Georgia, 1961–63," Board of Regents of the University System of Georgia, Research Bulletin, 65–2, January 30, 1965. Mimeographed.

demic ability, socioeconomic status, and so forth (see Chapter 5)—to say that there is one group of high school graduates who will almost certainly go to college under any conditions, and another (smaller) group who will almost certainly not go, however favorable the circumstances. But among each year's high school graduates, there is a relatively large group—15 to 20 per cent—who must be classified as "undecided" and whose plans may be influenced by the availability of jobs, their selective service status, their friends' plans, their immediate likelihood of marriage, the proximity of a college, and other immediate factors. If more were known of how the college attendance of this undecided group is affected by scholarship and loan programs, tax incentives, guidance and counseling in high school, and so forth, our projections would be a good deal more adequate (and, of course, our policies better based). Moreover, because of the large proportion of students who delay entry to college for a year or more, 27 per cent of each year's male high school graduates, according to a National Science Foundation report,[5] enrollment projections for particular years may be substantially affected by the timing of college entry among those who do not go directly from high school to college.

Table 2.1 shows degree output by level in the period from 1956 to 1965 and

TABLE 2.1. *Total Number of Degrees Granted, by Level: 1956–1965, with Projections for 1966–1975 (figures in 000's)*

	Total Number for Decade 1956–1965	Projected Decade Total 1966–1975		Percentage Increase 1966–1975 over
	Actual	Low	High	1956–1965
Bachelor's Degrees	3,795	6,970–7,710		84–103
Master's Degrees	797	1,620–1,790		103–125
Advanced Professional Degrees	365	583– 643		60– 76
M.D. Degrees	76	89– 92		17– 21
Doctoral Degrees	111	231– 290		108–161

SOURCE: Projections by Donald S. Bridgman for the Commission on Human Resources. See Appendix A for details. Bachelor's degree figures exclude advanced professional degrees (L.L.B., D.D.S., and so forth) that usually follow receipt of a bachelor's degree. Advanced professional degrees include degrees in medicine, law, theology, library science, social work, business, and a few smaller fields. Doctoral degrees include all earned doctorates—Ph.D., Ed.D., Sc.D., and so forth.

projections of degree output in the 1966 to 1975 decade. The last column indicates the percentage increase of the second decade over the first in number of degrees awarded. Figures for M.D. degrees are included to show that not all fields are expanding as rapidly as overall trends would indicate.

These degree projections, which are limited to a decade in the future, are more

[5] National Science Foundation, *The Duration of Formal Education for High Ability Youth*, NSF 61–36, Table 8. Even higher estimates of delayed entry were found in a Census sample survey ERS (P-27), No. 3, *Educational Status College Plans and Occupational Status of Farm and Non-farm Youth: October, 1959*, U.S. Bureau of the Census, *Current Population Reports,* August, 1961.

likely to be accurate than are longer-range projections simply because about 40 per cent of the graduates of the next decade are already in college; even if the figure for the last year of the decade were off by 10 per cent, our figures for the total number of degrees to be awarded during the 1966 to 1975 period would change only about 1 to 1.5 per cent. College enrollments are subject to influences that cause them to fluctuate from year to year, but the overall trends for the past decade have been remarkably consistent. Barring a major war or some other cataclysmic event, total degree output for the next decade should come to within 5 per cent of the projected figures.

In addition to failure to take into account the student's rising educational aspirations and the consequent expansion of the educational system, another factor that has made previous projections inaccurate is the tendency to overlook sources of supply other than recent college graduates. For instance, married women may return to the labor force after their children are in school (see Chapter 9), or foreign nationals may migrate to the United States for employment (see Chapter 11). Moreover, people may change from one occupation to another—for instance, they may leave jobs in business and industry to take up jobs in teaching—and this occupational mobility (see Chapter 7) will affect the supply in particular occupations (though it will not affect the total number in the labor force).

Estimating the Demand for College-Educated Manpower

The concept of demand has proved even more troublesome than the concept of supply. Too often, projections have tended to confuse *demand* (the number of jobs that can be financed with current or future funds in a given occupation) with *need* (the number of persons in a field who will be required to provide a given level or amount of service judged to be desirable). The distinction is between social ideals (what people feel ought to be done) and economic realities (what people are able to pay for).[6]

In practice, demand and need may be identical. More often, estimates of need are higher than estimates of demand. For instance, it is generally acknowledged that in such occupations as social work, psychiatry, and teaching, the need (expressed in terms of the number of professional workers per unit of population required to meet standards set for services) is greater than the demand (the money available to pay these professional workers). Sometimes, however, demand may exceed need, although conclusions in this regard will be highly subjective and will vary according to the individual's value system. For instance, many people may feel that the demand for researchers in chemical warfare is greater than our society's need for such researchers.

A few manpower forecasters have painted a gloomy picture of the future for college graduates seeking jobs, implying that the supply will far outstrip the

[6] This distinction is discussed in more detail in Chapter 4. See also Fein, Rashi, *The Doctor Shortage: An Economic Diagnosis,* The Brookings Institution, Washington, 1967.

demand. This pessimism is unwarranted in that it fails to distinguish among occupations for which a degree is required and occupations for which a degree is expected or preferred. Many occupations—particularly those in which work activities are diverse, such as teaching and engineering—are highly flexible in their educational requirements for entry, and indeed this flexibility is one of the most important mechanisms for adjusting supply to demand (see Chapter 12).

Table 2.2 shows the distributions of all college graduates among occupations, categorized on the basis of their educational requirements, in 1950 and in 1960. Only about 20 per cent of college graduates were employed in occupations where a degree was a requirement, and the proportion declined slightly between 1950 and 1960. In 1960 about 24 per cent of all men graduates and 45 per cent of all women graduates were employed in fields where a college degree was expected but not required, and 55 per cent of the men and 39 per cent of the women were in occupations—professional and nonprofessional—where the col-

TABLE 2.2. *Distribution of All College Graduates in Occupations for Which College Graduation Is Required, Expected, or Not Expected, by Sex: 1950 and 1960 (figures in 000's)*

Sex and Occupational Group	1950		1960	
	Number	Per Cent	Number	Per Cent
Men				
Total College Graduates	2,658	100.0	4,445	100.0
Professional Occupation, College Required	627	23.6	927	20.9
Professional Occupation, College Expected	623	23.4	1,079	24.3
Professional Occupation, College Not Expected	222	8.4	526	11.8
Nonprofessional Occupation, College Not Expected	1,186	44.6	1,913	43.0
Women				
Total College Graduates	1,054	100.0	1,768	100.0
Professional Occupation, College Required	221	21.0	281	15.9
Professional Occupation, College Expected	401	38.0	792	44.8
Professional Occupation, College Not Expected	123	11.7	251	14.2
Nonprofessional Occupation, College Not Expected	309	29.3	444	25.1

SOURCE: U.S. Bureau of the Census, *Census of Population: 1960*, PC(2)7A, Table 9.
U.S. Bureau of the Census, *Census of Population: 1950*, Vol. IV, Part B, Table 8.
Occupations where 90 per cent or more of the people employed were college graduates are classified in the "college required" group; occupations where 50 to 90 per cent of the people employed are college graduates were classified in the "college expected" group; occupations where less than 50 per cent of the people employed were college graduates are classified in the "college not expected" group. For consistency, secondary teachers in 1950 were classified in the "college required" group; although in that year less than 90 per cent of all secondary teachers were college graduates, the percentage was over 90 in 1960. The professional occupations for which college was expected but not required include engineering, elementary teaching, the ministry, pharmacy, and so forth. The nonprofessional occupations include white-collar occupations such as manager, proprietor, and official.

lege degree was not yet the norm. For both men and women, the total proportion of the college graduates employed in occupations requiring a college degree
declined slightly in the ten years between 1950 and 1960.

Partly as a result of the increased supply of college graduates, certain occupations are in the process of being upgraded educationally—that is, of moving
from the "college not expected" to the "college expected" group or from the
"college expected" to the "college required" group. (We measure this educa-
cational upgrading of an occupation by an increase in the proportion of people
in a given field who have college degrees.) Thus, the desirability of having a
college degree increases for young people entering certain fields, even though
a substantial proportion of older people still employed in the field may not be
college graduates. For instance, in elementary education, where the number of
jobs increased 40 per cent between 1950 and 1960, the percentage of college
graduates among the total employed in the field increased from about 55 per
cent to almost 70 per cent in the ten-year period, and nearly all new entrants
to the field were college graduates. In another rapidly expanding occupation,
engineering, the educational upgrading was not as marked: the percentage of
college graduates in the field increased only slightly between 1950 and 1960,
and about one-third of the entrants did not have a college degree. The sharp
increase (about 65 per cent between 1950 and 1960) in number of engineering
jobs available probably accounts for the differences between this field and education (where the growth was about 40 per cent) in the extent of educational
upgrading. When demands are very high and college graduates are simply not
available to fill jobs, employers will accept persons with less educational attainment.[7]

In the 1950 to 1959 period about one-third of all the male college graduates,
and about 10 per cent of the women college graduates were available to raise
the educational level of the occupational structure. During the 1960's more
rapid expansion of the occupational structure is occurring and the process of
educational upgrading of occupations has slowed down for men, and probably
has halted entirely for women (see Tables 2.3 and 2.4). In the 1970's we expect
the educational upgrading to proceed at about the same rate for men as in the
1950's, and for women the educational upgrading should actually be greater
in the 1975 to 1980 period than it was in the 1950's. Since these estimates of
the overall rate of educational upgrading of occupations are residual figures after
estimated replacement and occupational growth requirements have been subtracted from the total of college graduates, any errors in estimating occupational growth rates or numbers of college graduates (to mention the two most
likely sources of error) will affect this residual figure.

If the projected figures are accurate, enough college graduates will be available to raise educational levels so that some new occupations in the managerial

---

[7] See Chapter 4 for a fuller discussion of the educational level of entrants to engineering
occupations.

TABLE 2.3. *Average Annual Supply of Male College Graduates, Compared with Demands for Occupational Growth and Replacement, Indicating the Estimated Number Available to Raise the Educational Level of Occupations: 1950–1980 (figures in 000's)*

Period	(1) Average Annual Supply of Male Graduates	(2) Replacement Requirements	(3) Occupational Growth Requirements	(4) Available to Raise the Educational Level of Occupations	(5) Column 4 as Percentage of Column 1 (Percentages)
1950–1959	209	63	78	68	32
1960–1964	243	91	109	43	18
1965–1969	332	105	197	30	9
1970–1974	456	128	187	142	31
1975–1979	552	159	205	188	34

SOURCE: Number of college graduates, 1950–1964, from U.S. Office of Education, *Projections of Educational Statistics to 1973–74*, and *Historical Statistics of the U.S. Colonial Times to 1951*, Series H327-38. Projections made by Commission on Human Resources (see Appendix A), with estimated duplicate first professional degrees subtracted. Replacement requirements are estimated from age-specific death rates and retirement rates based on Census survival rates by occupation. Requirements for occupational growth are based on changes in the size of each occupation projected by the Bureau of Labor Statistics with Commission on Human Resources extensions to 1980. The column, Available to Raise the Educational Level of Occupations, is a residual based on subtraction of the other two columns from the total supply.

and sales class, as well as some additional professional occupations, will move into the college expected category between 1970 and 1980. As the supply of college graduates becomes proportionately large in professional occupations, possession of a college degree becomes a requirement for entry. The process is

TABLE 2.4. *Average Annual Supply of Female College Graduates, Compared with Demands for Occupational Growth and Replacement, Indicating the Estimated Number Available to Raise the Educational Level of Occupations When Only 80 Per Cent of the Women Enter the Labor Force: 1950–1980 (figures in 000's)*

Period	(1) Average Annual Women College Graduates	(2) Estimated Number Entering the Labor Force	(3) Replacement Requirements	(4) Occupational Growth Requirements	(5) Available to Raise the Educational Level of Occupation	(6) Column 5 as Percentage of Column 1 (Percentages)
1950–1959	108	87	47	27	12	11
1960–1964	161	129	69	93	−34	—
1965–1969	257	205	91	130	−16	—
1970–1974	353	283	122	91	70	11
1975–1979	443	354	145	93	116	26

SOURCE: See Table 2.3. Eighty per cent of the women are assumed to enter the labor force. In the 1960–1969 period when this assumption produces too few women college graduates to meet occupational growth and replacement needs, more than 80 per cent might enter the labor force, and/or more housewives might reenter the labor force. Replacement requirements for women assume an annual average of 4 per cent replacement, consistent with an average career of 25 years for working women.

complete when professional standards or licensing requirements (or both) turn a flexible educational standard for entry into a rigid one.

In short, college graduates need not fear that they will be unemployed in the future; the jobs open to them will probably expand to accommodate the available supply. Of course, the most prestigious positions may not be open to them, and consequently they may have to "spill over" into nonprofessional white-collar occupations. That such a process has been occurring is indicated by the rising proportion of younger men (25 to 34 years old) with college degrees employed as managers, proprietors, officials, and salesmen. Of the total number who held such positions, the proportion of college graduates increased from 15 per cent in 1950 to 25 per cent in 1960. In the same time period the proportion of professionals who were college graduates increased from 58 to 62 per cent, although the more rapid growth of the professional occupations means that college graduates were as heavily concentrated in these occupations in 1960 as in 1950.

The aggregate of occupations where a degree is now expected or required is projected to grow more slowly than the group of occupations where a degree is not the norm. However, the concept of an oversupply of college graduates lacks meaning, since as the supply of graduates grows the standards for occupations also shift, so that some growth in demand for college-educated persons will occur.

The problem of assessing either demand or need is further complicated by the difficulty of making accurate assessments of the quantity and quality of the services a given person provides. In the last analysis, it is services, not bodies, that are demanded: the number of persons employed in a field is merely a proxy variable for these services. Thus, when we speak of there being a shortage of 10,000 teachers or 2,000 engineers, what we really mean is that the demanded quantity of teaching or engineering services is not being provided.

In our projections we usually assume that the average amount of service provided by each professional will remain the same over time. In fact, however, changes in the professional's productivity may be occurring fairly rapidly in some fields. Thus, what appears to be a decline, judged on the basis of number of entrants into the field, may actually represent an improvement, judged on the basis of services provided.

Several factors operate to increase the productivity of the professional. For instance, subprofessionals may be introduced into a field to take over some of the "junior" services formerly performed by the professional, thus freeing him for more demanding tasks. The increasing use of teacher aides offers one example of how this works: the aide takes over the routine "bookkeeping" duties that used to be the responsibility of the teacher, thus enabling him to devote more attention to instruction. Medicine and dentistry, too, are making increasing use of subprofessional assistants. (See Chapter 12 for a more detailed discussion of this adjustment mechanism.)

Technological improvements are another factor that may increase the quantity and quality of the services performed by the professional. A good deal of attention has been devoted recently to the probable impact of technology on the labor force,[8] but there is little agreement among economists, businessmen, and labor leaders about how large that impact will be or how it should be planned for. Studies have not looked very closely at how technological innovation will affect productivity in high-level occupations, and a good deal more research is needed in this area.

Finally, the educational system may improve its selection procedures and training methods enough to increase considerably the professional's productivity.[9] For example, although the demands for medical services and the number of applicants to medical schools have increased greatly in the past decade, medical schools have been expanding at a very slow rate. But it does not necessarily follow that the quantity and quality of medical services have declined. Rather, medical schools are becoming more and more selective in accepting applicants. Not only may this greater selectivity lead to less attrition among medical students, but also it may increase the ability level of graduates, which, in turn, may increase their average productivity and their subsequent total contribution as physicians. To take another example, because the number of persons certified to teach will rise rapidly in the next decade, at the same time that the growth of schools is leveling off, schools can be more selective in hiring teachers. This greater selectivity may result in improved teaching and greater student learning.

In assessing the adequacy of supply to fill demand, we must recognize, then, that changes in the average professional's productivity may be as important or more important in meeting manpower needs than is the number of professionals added to the field. Because of the potential importance of changes in productivity of professionals in the overall assessment of demand, it is unfortunate that we have so little information on the changes in the quality and quantity of service delivered per professional. In the examples cited above, there is no conclusive evidence that brighter doctors deliver more service[10] or that schools will select the teachers who will have a maximum impact on student learning.

The Overall Picture to 1980

The problems involved in assessing the number of graduates who will enter various fields, in differentiating demand and need, in determining how quality

---

[8] See, for instance, Bureau of Labor Statistics, National Commission on Technology, Automation, and Economic Progress, *Technology and the American Economy*, Government Printing Office, Washington, 1965; and *The Outlook for Technological Change and Employment*, Appendix to Vol. I, Government Printing Office, Washington, 1966.

[9] For a discussion of the relative contributions of ability and of training to productivity, see Becker, Gary, *Human Capital*, National Bureau of Economic Research, New York, 1964, chap. 4.

[10] Probably, brighter doctors are more likely to enter medical research or teaching careers, so that in the short run their delivery of services may be lower than that of average doctors; the long-run benefits of the research and teaching may, of course, outweigh the short-run decline in services; see Fein, Rashi, *op. cit.*, p. 72.

substitutions and changing entry standards will help to adjust supply and demand, and in predicting what improvements in the professional's productivity may occur are factors that contribute to the difficulty of making adequate supply-demand projections. Compounding the difficulty, the supply in one field is affected by trends in adjacent fields, which may draw recruits from an occupation or, conversely, provide additional recruits to an occupation. Within the framework of the limitations that have been stated, the following assessment is presented.

The Bureau of Labor Statistics Model

The Bureau of Labor Statistics has developed an input-output model—industry by industry, for the total economic system—that gives a comprehensive view of future employment prospects in broad occupational categories.[11] These projections have two distinct advantages over independent projections for single occupations or groups of related occupations. First, because they are tied to explicit economic and employment targets, they make it easier to appraise how changes in the targets will affect employment in specific occupations. Second, the projections are internally consistent in the sense that the sum of individual occupational projections adds up to the total growth in the labor force. If one occupation is projected for above-average growth, others will be projected for lower-than-average growth. Independent projections for a single occupation, on the other hand, may give a distorted picture because they make implicit assumptions about total employment growth that are unrealistic.

Table 2.5 shows a projection of the demand for college graduates to 1975

TABLE 2.5. *Projected Demand and Supply of College Graduates: 1966–1975 (figures in 000's)*

Demand for Graduates		Men	Women	Total
White-Collar Occupations				
Professional		2,370	1,900	4,270
Managers and Officials		1,130	110	1,240
Clerical		210	330	540
Sales		300	40	340
Blue-Collar Occupations		100	30	130
Total Demand		4,110	2,410	6,520
Supply of				
College Graduates, 1966–1975	Low	3,937	2,439[a]	6,373[a]
	High	4,354	2,698[a]	7,052[a]

[a] Based on the assumption that only 80 per cent of the 3,049,000 to 3,372,000 women college graduates will enter the labor force. This makes the totals lower than those shown in Table 2.1.

SOURCE: Table 2.1 and based on Bureau of Labor Statistics projection of a total employment of 88.7 million in 1975, as shown in Table E-8 of the 1967 *Manpower Report of the President.* The projections assume continuation of the 1950–1960 trend in the educational level of broad occupational groups, and indicate numbers needed for both replacement and occupational growth.

[11] Bureau of Labor Statistics, *The Outlook for Technological Change and Employment.*

consistent with the Bureau of Labor Statistics model. These projections assume an economic growth rate of 4.3 per cent a year, a total labor force of 88.7 million by 1975, and a 3 to 4 per cent annual unemployment rate. If we compare this projected demand with the projected number of college graduates (see Table 2.5), excluding those graduates—mostly women—who are not expected to enter or remain in the labor force, we find that there will be an overall supply of 6.4 to 7.1 million graduates entering the labor force to meet a projected total demand for 6.5 million college graduates. If the low projection of college graduates is achieved, the educational upgrading of the occupational structure in the next decade will continue at about the 1950–1960 rate, even though the labor force will be expanding more rapidly in the 1965 to 1975 period (19.5 per cent) than was the case in the period from 1950 to 1960 (12.9 per cent). If the high projection of college graduates is achieved, the educational upgrading of occupations will be slightly accelerated during the next decade.

Although it provides the best available basis for studying the future occupational structure, the Bureau of Labor Statistics projection has certain shortcomings. For one thing, it does not explore alternative assumptions about economic growth rates and unemployment rates. Thus, if its economic targets are not realized, its projections will be inaccurate. If, for example, we achieve only a 2 to 3 per cent annual growth rate and have a 6 to 8 per cent unemployment rate in 1975, the occupational distribution of those employed will obviously be affected. Also, even if the assumptions are accurate, we may achieve the growth rate and unemployment targets through a different combination of industry-by-industry or occupation-by-occupation growth rates which could affect the demand for college graduates.

Moreover, when we use this set of occupational projections as a basis for projecting the demand for college graduates in different fields and at different degree levels, additional sources of variation are introduced. For all the reasons given earlier, educational requirements for entry into an occupation may be highly flexible. An occupational projection indicates a range of employment possibilities for college graduates. If occupational growth exceeds the growth in the number of college graduates, such comparisons may show the limits imposed on achievement of occupational and economic goals because of a shortage of educated manpower. But even these limits may not be rigid. In the face of a high demand, productivity can be increased by encouraging people to work longer hours, by inducing part-time workers to become full-time, and so forth.

The comparisons between the number of college graduates and the growth of the occupational structure during the next decade indicate that the overall supply of college graduates will be at least as adequate, and possibly more adequate, to the demands of the economy than it has been in the recent past. Since a number of occupations have had fewer qualified entrants than were demanded, the indication that things are not getting worse may be small comfort to those who have been dissatisfied with the number and quality of entrants to their profession in the past.

To some extent, the shortages of educated manpower we have experienced in the past are problems of distribution; that is, we have enough people finishing college in some fields, but in other fields, like medicine and engineering, the numbers are inadequate. In Chapters 3 and 4 we examine the adequacy of supply and demand in a number of specific fields, and in Chapters 5 and 6 we discuss the influences that affect educational and occupational choice, which will give an indication of what may be done to improve the distribution of manpower.

To a considerable extent, our concern with the adequacy of manpower supplies arises from the gap between our ideals for service and the number and quality of people who are available to provide that service. This view of our manpower problem compares the supply with the need for personnel, rather than with the demand estimated from past trends in the economy. A projection of needs, compared with available supplies, is provided below, and indicates a big gap between the estimated number of college-educated people our society could use, and the number of college graduates we have projected to be available in the next decade.

The Need for College Graduates to Achieve National Goals

The need for college graduates—"need" here being understood, as already indicated, to apply to numbers required to fulfill socially desirable goals—was estimated from projections developed by Leonard A. Lecht for the National Goals Project.[12] The projections in Table 2.6 indicate the number of college graduates required if the United States is to achieve specified goals in health, education, transportation, housing, and other areas. The demand may, of course, fall considerably short of these projections, because the growth in national income will probably not be sufficient to pay for the services needed. The highest projection indicates, in a general way, the potential needs of our society for college-educated manpower.

The number of male college graduates necessary to fill the projected need by 1975 is 1.5 to 2 million more than the number of male college graduates who will graduate by that time. To achieve the national goals projections for women by 1975, 500,000 to 800,000 more women college graduates would have to enter the labor force in appropriate occupations than are expected to be available by that date. There are probably enough educated women now in the labor reserve to provide the 800,000 needed, but they may not be in the right occupational field nor can we determine very accurately the number of them who

---

[12] The goals were defined by the National Goals Commission in 1960. See also Lecht, Leonard A., *Goals, Priorities and Dollars*, The Free Press, New York, 1966. This book contains dollar-cost estimates of each goal; manpower requirements are described in Lecht, Leonard A., *Manpower Needs and National Goals for the 1970's*, Frederick A. Praeger, Inc., New York, 1969.

TABLE 2.6. *Projected Needs for Additional College Graduates to Meet National Goals, and Projected Supply of College Graduates: 1965–1975 (figures in 000's)*

Total Needs		Men	Women	Total
White-Collar Occupations				
Professional		3,730	2,590	6,320
Managers and Officials		1,430	140	1,570
Clerical		250	420	670
Sales		370	40	410
Blue-Collar Occupations		140	40	180
Total Needs		5,920	3,230	9,150
Supply of				
College Graduates, 1965–1975	Low	3,937	2,439[a]	6,373[a]
	High	4,354	2,698[a]	7,052[a]

[a] Based on the assumption that only 80 per cent of the 3,049,000 to 3,372,000 women college graduates will enter the labor force. This makes the totals lower than those shown in Table 2.1.

SOURCE: Occupational distribution from unpublished estimates made by Leonard A. Lecht for the National Planning Association's National Goals Project, with educational levels projected by the Commission on Human Resources to continue rising at the 1950–1960 rate. Figures above include estimated replacements for death and retirement, as well as projected growth in the size of each occupation.

might be induced to return to the labor force. If marriage patterns and the timing of the arrival of the first child were to change so that more women were to enter the labor force immediately upon graduation from college, an additional 600,000 educated women workers would potentially be available between 1965 and 1975, but changes of this magnitude would be difficult to produce except under emergency conditions.

Educational Improvement of the Occupational Structure

A more detailed examination of demand can be made by separating the total demand for college graduates into the three components shown in Table 2.3 for men and Table 2.4 for women. These components are: (1) the graduates needed to replace persons who die or retire from the labor force, (2) the graduates needed for the growth in the size of occupations, and (3) the graduates available for raising the educational level of occupations. This last component of "demand," as we indicated earlier, is a "residual" estimated by subtracting the first two components from the total number of graduates. We cannot determine just how much of the educational upgrading of each occupation is required by the increasing complexity of jobs and how much is simply the effort of each employer to fill vacancies with the best available persons. A college education may not actually be necessary for many of the jobs where graduates are employed, but to the extent that graduation measures motivation, proper attitudes, and general ability, it may be among the best criteria for an employer to use in selecting new employees. Since we cannot separate the "selection" demand for more college graduates from the "higher educational requirements" demand, we can only indicate the relative changes in this component of demand. In periods of rapid labor force expansion, as typified by the 1960's, the proportion of college graduates available for upgrading the educational level of the labor force is small (see Tables 2.3 and 2.4). If we had a static labor force with only replacement demand and demand generated by changes in the occupational structure, between 45 and 50 per cent of our college graduates in the 1950 to 1960 period would have been available to raise the educational level. In the 1960 to 1970 period, between 40 and 45 per cent of the graduates would have been available to raise the educational level under similar conditions, while in the 1970 to 1980 period the rapid expansion of the colleges would make 50 to 55 per cent available for this purpose.

These calculations for a static labor force size indicate that our colleges are producing graduates at a rate that is considerably above the rate of change in the occupational structure. When labor force expansion is added to the rate of change in the occupational structure, then the rate of educational upgrading (expressed as a percentage of the total number of college entrants and shown in the last column of Table 2.3 and 2.4) is much lower in the 1960 to 1970 period, but it was substantial for the 1950 to 1960 period, and is expected to rise again to the 1950–1960 rate in the 1970 to 1980 period.

In the 1952 to 1965 period, increases in the proportion of the labor force who were college graduates were greater for men (the total was 8 per cent in 1952 and slightly over 12 per cent in 1965) than for women (where the total was 8 per cent in 1952 and 10 per cent in 1965). In the 1962 to 1965 period, the extremely rapid growth of the economy—with the concomitant growth in the total labor force—slowed the rate of increase in the proportion of college graduates in the labor force. The rapid growth in the output of college graduates in the 1970's will mean that, despite a continued rapid increase in the size of the labor force, the proportion of college graduates in the total labor force will rise an additional 5 to 7 percentage points for men, and 4 to 6 percentage points for women between 1965 and 1980. This would mean that by 1980, 17 to 19 per cent of the men and 14 to 16 per cent of the women in the labor force would be college graduates.

Between 1950 and 1965, colleges produced almost 900,000 more male graduates than were required for replacement and occupational growth purposes; and from 1965 to 1980, they may be expected to produce almost 1,800,000 more than are necessary. Insofar as educational upgrading for men is concerned, the number of graduates available for upgrading did not increase as rapidly during the 1960 to 1970 period as in the preceding decade, primarily because of the rapid growth of the occupational structure as a whole and of the occupations that attract college graduates in particular. In the 1970 to 1980 period, the rate of overall occupational expansion is projected to be higher than in the 1950's, but the colleges will expand their output enough so that the rate of educational improvement in the 1970's will approximate or slightly exceed the rate that occurred in the 1950's. It is interesting to note that the changes in the occupational structure have been so rapid that twice as large a numerical increase in college graduates is required in the 1970's as in the 1950's to slightly exceed, in the 1970's, the rate of educational improvement observed in the 1950's.

Projections of supply and demand for women are more subject to error than are projections for men, primarily because it is difficult to estimate how many women graduates will never enter the labor force, how many will enter it for a short period of time only and then withdraw when their children are born, and how many who do withdraw will reenter the labor force at a later date. (See Chapters 9 and 12 for a fuller discussion of the career patterns of women.)

The projections in Table 2.4 are based on the assumption that only 80 per cent of women college graduates will ever enter the labor force, a figure consistent with results found for sample surveys of college graduates in 1958 and 1961.[13] This proportion is extremely sensitive to short-run economic fluctuations and to long-run trends in age of marriage and average time lapse between marriage and the birth of the first child.

The projected replacement requirements are further based on the assumption that about one-fourth of the college-educated women in the labor force will not have responsibilities that will cause them to drop out of the labor force and that the remaining three-fourths will shorten their working careers by about 15 years as a result of their family responsibilities. These assumptions are consistent with the notion that having a career outside the home is becoming more and more the norm among college-educated women.

The rate of educational upgrading of the occupational structure in the 1950's for women was only about one-third the rate for men (see Tables 2.3 and 2.4, last column). This difference is explained in part by the fact that there was a 25 per cent increase in the number of women in the labor force during the decade, and only a 7.5 per cent increase in the number of men. The greater increase in labor force participation of women than men meant that most of the women college graduates were needed for the rapidly expanding occupations, and few were available to raise the educational level of women in these occupations.

As Table 2.4 indicates, after 1970 much larger supplies of women college graduates will be available than were available during the 1960's. One reason for this is that the labor force participation of women has been increasing rapidly in the past decade, but this increase is projected to slow down by about one-third during the next 15 years.[14] Were the economy to expand at more than the assumed 4 per cent annual rate, the percentage of working women required might continue to rise rapidly, with the consequence that the supply of college women would not be as adequate to the demand as our projection indicates.

[13] See National Science Foundation, *Two Years After the College Degree*, NSF 63–26, Government Printing Office, Washington; and Bureau of Social Science Research, "Five Years After the College Degree," mimeographed research report to NSF.
[14] *Manpower Report of the President, 1966*, Government Printing Office, Washington, 1966, Tables A-4 and E-2.

The figures in Table 2.4 indicate that a quarter of a million fewer women graduates will enter the labor force in the 1960's than are required for replacement and occupational growth. This shortage of women college graduates may not actually be developing because: first, there may be higher employment of men in occupations where the two sexes compete (this has been occurring in both secondary teaching and social work); second, as women remain in the labor force even during the period of their maximum family responsibility, the replacement requirements may be lower than we have assumed; third, the educational level of women entering some occupations may decline; and finally, the proportion of women college graduates entering the labor force today may be above the assumed 80 per cent level.

In the 1970's about 900,000 more women college graduates will enter the labor force than will be required for replacement and occupational growth, which should make possible a slightly greater rate of educational improvement of occupations employing women than occurred in the 1950's.

Summary and Discussion

America has developed an educational system that produces more college graduates than are required to replace graduates leaving the labor force and more than are required to provide for the growth of the occupational structure. The additional college graduates over and above those needed for replacement and occupational growth are available to raise the educational level of occupations. A large part of this educational upgrading, as has been indicated, is occurring in managerial, sales, and professional occupations where college graduation has not been in the past a requirement for obtaining a job.

Educational upgrading of the occupational structure occurs more rapidly in periods of slow expansion and change in the occupational structure. Conversely, in periods of very rapid economic expansion, where manpower demands are high, all of the graduates may be needed to staff the expanding occupations, and few if any will be available to provide educational improvements.

Since high level manpower is specialized and has only limited flexibility in moving from one occupation to another (see Chapter 7), there may be situations where some occupations are being upgraded educationally, while in others there are not enough entrants to staff the expansion of the occupation. This occurred in the 1950's when college graduates entered managerial occupations at a rate which almost doubled the percentage of college graduates in the occupation in a decade, while engineering was expanding so rapidly that the proportion of college graduates in the occupation did not rise during the decade. Furthermore, engineering is an occupation where a bachelor's degree is the expected standard for occupational entry, but a substantial number of nongraduates entered the occupation because it was expanding more rapidly than the college graduate output could staff the new jobs.

These are illustrations of problems of *distribution* of graduates to the occupations where they are needed. Such problems are likely to continue in the future and to become more complicated as the number of occupations employing college graduates expands. Chapters 5 through 7 deal with these problems of occupational choice and distribution in more detail.

In terms of total degree output, our higher educational system has been expanded to serve the requirements of a rapidly expanding economy. In each five-year period since 1955, the bachelor's degree output of our higher educational institutions grew at a more rapid rate than the growth of professional occupations, which are the employment destination for nearly two-thirds of all graduates. We expect the growth rate of college degrees to exceed that of the professional occupations until 1980, and possibly beyond that date.

If the growth of the professional and other white-collar occupations slows down, either as a result of lower economic growth rates or slower change in the occupational structure, our educational system would provide many more graduates to upgrade the educational level of occupations. Even in periods of continued economic growth such as are forecast for the next decade, over a fourth of the graduates would be available to upgrade the educational level of occupations.

There is an optimum relationship (from the standpoint of economic growth) between the size of our higher educational system and the size of the labor force occupations that employ college graduates. Beyond a certain point, the expansion of the number of college graduates will probably not contribute to economic growth, but in a dynamic economy the optimum size of the educational system cannot be specified very precisely; in addition, as indicated above, we don't know enough about the economic benefits associated with the educational upgrading of an occupation to be able to say just when educational upgrading of an occupation ceases to add to economic productivity. Also, as our economy changes, the optimum size and composition of the educational system will change.[15]

The cost to the economy of an inadequate supply of educated persons is probably greater than the expenditure of resources involved in creation of an excess of graduates beyond the needs of the economy, and in this sense an over-expanded educational system is less costly than an underdeveloped one. Since we are not able to specify the exact size of the educational system that is optimum for our present economy, nor to specify in detail what it should be like in the future, we cannot say in terms of economic criteria whether the rates of growth of higher education in America should be accelerated or slowed down. The analysis in this chapter does indicate that the output of our colleges will fall considerably short of providing the graduates needed to achieve national

[15] For a more complete discussion of the relation between the economy and the educational system, see Anderson, C. A., and M. J. Bowman, "Theoretical Considerations in Educational Planning" in *Educational Planning,* The World Yearbook of Education, 1967, Harcourt Brace and Co., 1967, pp. 11–37.

goals by 1975; but our economy probably will not grow fast enough to achieve these goals even if the educated manpower were available. Tested against economic growth targets, we cannot be certain whether we have expanded our higher educational system at an optimum rate; tested against the criteria of social needs, we will not produce enough graduates in the next decade to meet the goals that have been outlined.

At the present time the resolution of problems of distribution of manpower is a priority issue. Our data do not indicate that the total number of graduates is inadequate, but we do know that the number of graduates entering some fields has been short of the demand. Research and planning attention should continue to be concentrated on ways to attract more people to the shortage occupations. As subsequent chapters will reveal, enrollments and degrees in higher education will continue to expand because student demand for more education will provide a steady pressure for growth in enrollment. The most pressing problem appears to be that of getting young people to choose the career areas where future demand is likely to be highest.

3 The Supply and Demand for Graduates in the Arts and Sciences

IN THIS CHAPTER, we will focus on the supply of and demand for graduates at the bachelor's, master's, and doctoral degree levels in the arts and sciences, divided into four broad areas: the humanities, the social sciences and psychology, the physical sciences and mathematics, and the biological sciences. The arts and sciences have long constituted the central core of the higher educational enterprise; each year approximately half of the first-level degrees, one-third of the master's degrees, and two-thirds of the Ph.D.'s are awarded in one of these fields.

One of the characteristics of the arts and sciences is that the bachelor's degree represents a general, liberal education which enables the recipient to work in occupations that do not demand a high degree of specialized training. Consequently, the B.A. graduate often does not work in his major field. For instance, in 1962, less than 5 per cent of the bachelor's graduates in the social sciences, about 10 per cent of those in the humanities, a fourth of those in the biological sciences, and about a third of those in the physical sciences were working in the field in which they had been trained.[1] The occupations that employed arts and sciences bachelor's graduates were nonprofessional white

[1] Schwartz, Mildred A., *The United States College-Educated Population: 1960*, National Opinion Research Center, University of Chicago, Report No. 102, October, 1965, based on a 1960 Census follow-up sample of scientists, engineers, and a smaller sample of other college graduates (total cases approximately 51,000). Data in text are from Table 3.23.

collar jobs in management, sales, clerical, or secretarial work (about a third of the graduates), teaching (7 to 10 per cent), and other professional jobs such as engineering and the health professions (one-fourth of the graduates). This situation is by no means unfortunate; the broad training of the bachelor's graduate in the arts and sciences gives him occupational mobility, which constitutes one important adjustment mechanism in overall supply and demand. (See Chapter 12.) The low percentage of bachelor's graduates working in the same field as their degree also illustrates another important point about the arts and sciences; advanced degrees are needed to provide a reasonable assurance of employment in the same field where the degree is earned.

At the master's level, a higher proportion of graduates (approximately half of the physical scientists and humanists and a third of the biological and social scientists) find employment in the field for which they were trained. At the doctoral level, the proportions increase: 80 to 90 per cent of the graduates are working in occupations directly related to their major field.[2]

Because advanced degrees are the primary route of occupational entry in fields of arts and sciences, this chapter will deal mostly with people who have advanced degrees, especially the doctorate. The two main sources of employment demand for these people are college teaching and research and development. In 1965, for instance, out of the total number of Ph.D.'s in the labor force, almost 60 per cent were employed—as teachers, research workers, or both—in colleges and universities, about 30 per cent worked in nonacademic research jobs, and about 10 per cent were in other occupations (Table 3.1).

The first section of this chapter discusses degree output (both past and projected) in the arts and sciences and examines the effects of such programs as stipend support on the production of graduates. The next two sections deal with the demand for college teachers and for research workers, respectively. No doubt some error has been introduced into this analysis because of the difficulty of dividing academic employment into its teaching and research components,[3] but such a division has been attempted. It should be remembered, too, that frequently the Ph.D. graduate engages in administrative or managerial activities

[2] *Ibid.,* Table 3.23. The size of the percentages quoted is partly a function of the Census classification of occupations: for instance, a psychologist working in a mental hospital might be classified as a medical scientist rather than a psychologist. There is substantial response error in describing specific occupations.

[3] Unfortunately, university methods for reporting division between teaching and research are not uniform. If college teachers are asked, "What is your major assignment?" 90 per cent of physical scientists and over 80 per cent of biological scientists report "teaching" (unpublished tabulations from the Office of Education survey of college teachers, 1962–1963). If, on the other hand, they are asked, "How do you spend your time?" physical scientists indicate that one-half time is spent in teaching, one-quarter to one-third spent in research, and the remainder in administration (Allan M. Cartter's *Assessment of Quality in Graduate Education,* American Council on Education, Washington, 1966, data for 1964). Cartter's figures are similar to data collected from colleges by the National Science Foundation for 1964–1965; about one-half of all scientists' and engineers' time was spent in teaching, and 25 to 30 per cent in research (*Reviews of Data on Science Resources,* August, 1966, Table 6).

TABLE 3.1. *Estimated Total Employed Ph.D.'s in Arts and Sciences Fields: 1965 (figures in 000's)*

Field	Total Employed	Type of Employer and Type of Work					
		Colleges and Universities			Nonacademic Employer[a]		
		Total	Teaching	Re-search	Total	Research and Res. Mgt.	Other
Physical Sciences and Mathematics	49 to 51	20 to 21	13 to 14	7	29 to 30	23 to 24	6
Social Sciences and Psychology	36 to 38	22 to 23	16 to 17	6	14 to 15	7 to 8	7
Biological Sciences	29 to 31	16 to 17	10 to 11	6	13 to 14	11 to 12	2
Arts and Humanities	24 to 26	22 to 24	17 to 19	5	2	———	2
Total Arts and Sciences	138 to 146	80 to 85	56 to 61	24	58 to 61	41 to 44	17

[a] Federal contract research centers operated by universities and medical schools are shown under "Nonaca-demic Employer" rather than under "Colleges and Universities."

SOURCE: Total estimated from Dael Wolfle's *America's Resources of Specialized Talent*, Appendix Table C.2, which gives an estimate of the number of living Ph.D.'s in 1953. This number was reduced by esti-mated deaths and retirements between 1953 and 1965 and increased by Ph.D. output since 1953, minus foreign Ph.D.'s who have returned home. Distribution by field and function from Lindsay R. Harmon's *Profiles of Ph.D.'s in the Sciences*, National Academy of Sciences-National Research Council, Publication No. 1293, Washington, 1965, which is consistent with distributions from the Ph.D.'s in the National Register of Scientific and Technical Personnel (physical and biological scientists).

in the academic setting or in nonacademic research and development occu-pations.

THE GROWTH IN THE SUPPLY OF ARTS AND SCIENCES GRADUATES

In the 1955 to 1965 decade the output of bachelor's and master's graduates increased more rapidly in the arts and sciences than in all fields, but output at the doctoral level grew a little more slowly than in all fields. Compare figures in Table 3.2 with the projected degree level output, at each level and in each of the four major areas of the arts and sciences, as shown in Figures 3.1 through 3.3. Table 3.3 compares past and projected growth in arts and sciences fields with that in all fields.

The increasing popularity of arts and sciences was most evident in the period from 1960 to 1965, when they grew about a third more than other fields at the bachelor's level. As a result, by 1965, 50 per cent of all bachelor's degrees were in the arts and sciences fields, and by 1975, the figure is projected to rise to 57 per cent.

In view of the heavy emphasis on science in our society recently, we might expect that, at the bachelor's level, the science fields would grow much more rapidly than the humanities or social sciences, but such has not been the case. It is true that in the period from 1955 to 1959 mathematics and the physical

TABLE 3.2. *Projections of Bachelor's, Master's, and Doctor's Degrees, by Sex: 1956–1975 (figures in 000's)*

Academic Year	Bachelor's			Master's			Doctor's		
	Total	Men	Women	Total	Men	Women	Total	Men	Women
1955–1956	287	178	109	59.3	39.4	19.9	8.9	8.0	.9
1956–1957	315	200	115	62.2	41.5	20.7	8.8	7.8	1.0
1957–1958	339	219	120	65.5	44.1	21.4	8.9	8.0	.9
1958–1959	357	230	127	69.9	47.6	22.3	9.4	8.4	1.0
1959–1960	366	230	136	74.3	50.8	23.5	9.8	8.8	1.0
1960–1961	373	230	143	78.1	54.0	24.1	10.6	9.5	1.1
1961–1962	391	236	155	85.0	58.7	26.3	11.6	10.4	1.2
1962–1963	419	247	172	91.4	62.9	28.5	12.8	11.4	1.4
1963–1964	470	272	198	101.2	69.1	32.1	14.5	13.0	1.5
1964–1965	505	290	215	112.1	76.0	36.1	16.5	14.7	1.8
				Projected					
1965–1966	522	295	227	122.4	82.1	40.3	18.2	16.2	2.0
1966–1967	550	314	236	133.4	88.3	45.1	20.1	17.9	2.2
1967–1968	651	361	290	143.6	94.0	49.6	22.3	19.8	2.5
1968–1969	713	398	315	157.0	101.9	55.1	24.6	21.8	2.8
1969–1970	744	418	326	171.7	111.4	60.3	26.9	23.7	3.2
1970–1971	753	422	331	189.4	122.2	67.2	29.1	25.6	3.5
1971–1972	816	464	352	204.0	130.8	73.2	32.1	28.1	4.0
1972–1973	844	476	368	220.7	141.0	79.7	35.5	31.0	4.5
1973–1974	888	499	389	236.0	150.8	85.2	39.2	34.1	5.1
1974–1975	927	518	409	252.6	161.4	91.2	42.9	37.2	5.7

SOURCE: Projections made for the Commission on Human Resources. See Appendix A for description of assumptions and methods.

sciences had the highest rate of growth, but the biological sciences had the lowest. Moreover, in the 1960 to 1965 period the physical sciences (including mathematics) grew about 35 per cent, the biological sciences (excluding health professions) grew about 45 per cent, and both the social sciences and the humanities grew about 70 per cent, or nearly twice as fast as the first two areas.

TABLE 3.3. *Past and Projected Growth in Degree Output in Arts and Sciences Fields and All Fields Combined, by Level: 1956–1975*

	Percentage Increase During Five-Year Intervals			
	1955–1960	1960–1965	1965–1970	1970–1975
Bachelor's				
Total	38	38	47	25
Arts and Sciences	44	61	60	29
Master's				
Total	27	51	53	47
Arts and Sciences	43	74	80	54
Doctor's				
Total	11	68	63	60
Arts and Sciences	15	56	61	66

SOURCE: Table 3.2 and Figures 3.1 through 3.3.

FIGURE 3.1 *Actual and Projected Number of First-Level Degrees in Arts and Sciences Fields: 1956–1976 (figures in 000's)*

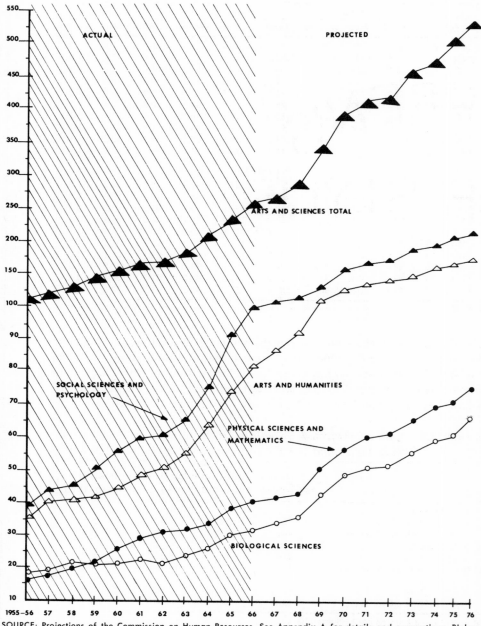

SOURCE: Projections of the Commission on Human Resources. See Appendix A for details and assumptions. Biological Sciences exclude health professions, and Arts and Humanities exclude Religion and Theology.

FIGURE 3.2 *Actual and Projected Number of Master's Degrees in Arts and Sciences Fields: 1956–1976 (figures in 000's)*

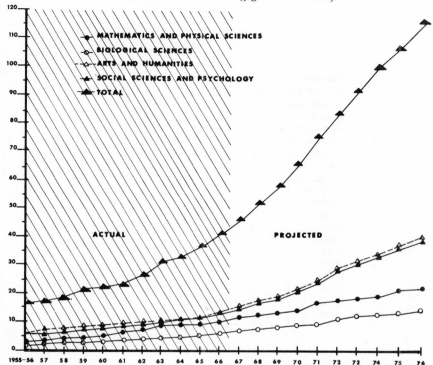

SOURCE: Projections of the Commission on Human Resources. See Appendix A for details and assumptions.

And if we exclude mathematics (which, along with psychology, has been the most rapidly growing arts and sciences field at the bachelor's level during the 1955 to 1965 decade), we find that the physical sciences actually have the lowest growth rate for the decade.

These differences in growth rate can be attributed in part to the rising proportion of women among bachelor's recipients: in 1956 and in 1960, they constituted about 37 per cent, and by 1965, 43 per cent. In particular, more women have been choosing the humanities, while the percentage of all male graduates in this area has remained fairly stable since 1955. Conversely, few women major in scientific fields; the proportion of women majoring in the physical sciences at the baccalaureate level declined slightly in the past decade, and although the proportion majoring in the biological sciences (3.5 per cent) and in mathematics (3 per cent) rose sharply, it was still small.

Although reasons for the increased popularity of the arts and sciences at the

FIGURE 3.3 *Actual and Projected Number of Doctoral Degrees in Arts and Sciences Fields: 1956–1975*

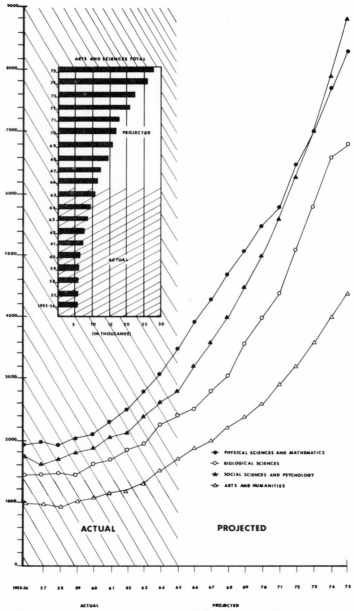

SOURCE: Projections of the Commission on Human Resources. See Appendix A for details and assumptions.

FIGURE 3.4 *Proportion of All Bachelor's, Master's, and Doctoral Degrees in Arts and Sciences Fields: 1956–1975*

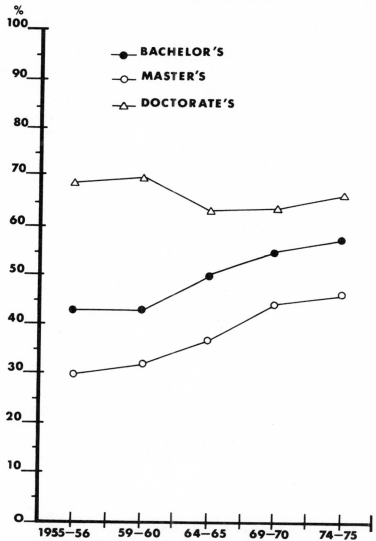

SOURCES: Table 3.2; Figures 3.1, 3.2, and 3.3.

bachelor's level may be difficult to define precisely, its consequences for graduate enrollment in these fields are obvious. The increase in the base of bachelor's degree recipients produces a larger pool of potential graduate students, which is one component of the subsequent growth in the number of advanced degrees awarded. The second part is the growing tendency of college students to undertake graduate training,[4] a tendency that may operate particularly among arts and sciences students because of their recognition that, in order to get jobs in their field, they must have advanced degrees. For all fields combined, about 40 per cent of the increase in master's degrees (between 1958 and 1965) is attributable to the first component and about 60 per cent to the second. For arts and sciences fields, however, the increased base is the more important factor.

At the master's degree level, some of the same trends observed at the bachelor's degree level are apparent. In both the 1955 to 1960 period and the 1960 to 1965 period, output in arts and sciences fields grew approximately one and one-half times as rapidly as output of master's degrees in all fields (see Table 3.3). The growth rate of the biological sciences was conspicuously lower than that of the other three arts and sciences areas, partly because of the very small increases in graduate degrees in agriculture and forestry (if we omit these two fields, we find that the growth of the biological sciences approximated that of the social sciences and physical sciences/mathematics) and partly because of the relatively small increase in the number of bachelor's degrees. (The proportion of bachelor's degree recipients going on into graduate work actually increased more in the biological sciences than in any of the other arts and sciences areas, but the bachelor's degree base from which they were drawn expanded more slowly.)

At the doctoral level 20 per cent of the increase in degree output (between 1958 and 1965) can be attributed to growth of the base[5] and about 80 per cent to the increasing popularity of graduate study. Increasing popularity of graduate study accounted for 10 per cent of the growth in doctoral-level output in the social sciences, 20 to 25 per cent in mathematics and the humanities, 50 to 60 per cent in psychology and the physical sciences, and nearly all the biological sciences.

Expressed in another way, much but not all of the increases in graduate degree output in recent years in arts and sciences fields can be traced to their having attracted more students to undergraduate majors, whereas professional fields—though less successful in recruiting students in the early college years—have compensated somewhat by increasing the proportions of their students who go on to advanced study.[6]

---

[4] Alexander W. Astin, in a survey of freshmen classes in a national sample of colleges, found that about 65 per cent of the college freshmen of 1965 planned to earn a graduate degree, as compared with only about 45 per cent of 1961 college freshmen. (*Proceedings of the Association for Institutional Research*, 1966.)

[5] The base is determined separately for each field and consists of the approximate percentage of different bachelor's cohorts which make up the bulk (80 to 90 per cent) of the graduate degree recipients of the given year. The bulk of the Ph.D. graduates of 1958 through 1965 are drawn from the bachelor's graduates of 1947–1960, for the master's graduates of 1958–1965, the bachelor's graduates of 1952–1962 made the greatest contribution. The growth of the base was much smaller for doctoral cohorts than for master's graduates.

[6] It should be noted that because the arts and sciences have always had higher rates of recruitment to graduate study than have most professional fields, they have less opportunity to register further increases. In the arts and sciences, between one-half and two-thirds of

The physical sciences appear to face the greatest problems in expanding graduate degree output, because a large proportion of their bachelor's degree recipients already go on to graduate study (for example, 75 per cent in physics) and because their extensive prerequisites make it difficult for them to recruit students from other fields for graduate study. Moreover, although they are successful in attracting students at the freshman level, they are not able to retain students throughout the four years of undergraduate study, with the consequence that, of all arts and sciences fields, the physical sciences (excluding mathematics) have had the smallest increases in bachelor's degree output.[7] This problem is particularly acute in physics: between 1962 and 1966 the number of seniors majoring in the field did not increase at all, and bachelor's degree output rose only 2 per cent between 1962 and 1965. To the extent that freshmen planning to major in physics make only minor changes in their major fields (out of physics and into mathematics, for instance), the total growth of the sciences will not be affected. But the National Opinion Research Center's studies of career shifts, as well as longitudinal studies of a large sample of freshmen who entered college in 1961, indicate that many students shift out of the sciences entirely.

Part of the undergraduate attrition in the sciences may be the result of a rigorous curriculum that weeds out the less able and less well-prepared students. But studies of National Merit Scholarship winners indicate that a large proportion of these students also shift out of science, and they, of course, are all exceptionally able students.[8] It would seem, then, that the problem of the shift out of science reflects not only the rigor of the courses, but also the kind and amount of attention that faculty members give to undergraduate instruction and to encouraging students to take up a career in the field. Recent comprehensive studies of attrition among medical students (who are even more select academically than are undergraduate science students) highlight some of the factors in faculty-student relationships that may influence the student's remaining in a program.[9] In medical schools where attrition was high, faculty contacts were impersonal and faculty spent little time on curriculum improvements or in personal counseling of students. In medical schools where attrition was low, the

---

the male graduates of 1961 went directly to graduate school, whereas in engineering, education, business, and other professions, only between one-fifth and one-third went directly to graduate school. If increases in the percentage of bachelor's degree recipients going on to graduate school were expressed as a proportion of the increase possible, the arts and sciences would register gains in attractiveness similar to those of other fields. See Spaeth, Joseph, "Undergraduate Origins and Success in Graduate School," unpublished National Opinion Research Center study, August, 1966, Table 2.

[7] See Davis, James, *Undergraduate Career Decisions,* Aldine Publishing Co., Chicago, 1965, for a description of the gains and losses of different career fields during the undergraduate years.

[8] Nichols, Robert C., "Career Decisions of Very Able Students," *Science,* vol. 144, June 12, 1964, pp. 1315–1319. See also the discussion in Chapter 6.

[9] Johnson, Davis F., and Edwin B. Hutchins, "Doctor or Dropout," *Journal of Medical Education,* vol. 41, December, 1966, p. 12.

reverse was true. These findings suggest that, important as it is to devote attention to improving undergraduate science education,[10] it is equally important to study more precisely the effects of the undergraduate environment and faculty-student interaction patterns.

Stipend Support and the Growth of Graduate Enrollments

One of the major differences between the arts and sciences fields and the professions like medicine and law is that a large proportion of the students in the former area are supported by stipends—research assistantships, teaching assistantships, or fellowships. The availability of funds to support graduate students has increased greatly in the past decade, and it is important to try to determine the extent to which it has been effective in (a) attracting students to arts and sciences fields as contrasted with professional fields, and (b) affecting the distribution of students among the arts and sciences fields. Can we attribute the higher growth of degree output in arts and sciences fields as compared with other fields to the greater availability of support in arts and sciences? Can we say that the more rapid increase of degree output in the social sciences than in the physical sciences is the result of greater stipend support in the former than the latter? Large sums of money are involved in current fellowship programs; the federal support of fellowships and traineeships alone in 1965–1966 was over 150 million dollars; a conservative estimate of the total support from all sources for all graduate student stipends (including teaching and research assistants) in 1965–1966 would be half a billion dollars.

In spite of the magnitude of these programs, it is very difficult to get comparable figures on the number and size of stipends in different fields. There have been a number of surveys of graduate student finances that have used different definitions of students (some covered all students, some covered only full-time students, some were limited to science students, and so forth) and have asked questions about stipend holding in various ways. (Stipends generally include fellowships, scholarships, and teaching and research assistantships.) Some surveys have excluded some kinds of support (such as veterans' benefits, or students attending school who are supported by their employer) so that it is very hard to get a clear picture of trends in support that can be compared with trends in graduate enrollment and degrees.

Lindsey Harmon[11] collected data about support during graduate school for six cohorts of doctoral graduates from 1935 through 1960. For arts and sciences graduates he found that in the earliest group of graduates (1935–1940) between 37 per cent (in the social sciences) and 56 per cent (in the biological sciences) of the total support for the students' costs of graduate education (not the per-

---

[10] For an example of efforts at such improvements, see the report of the committee of the American Society for Engineering Education, *Factors Affecting Engineering Enrollments and Degrees,* Engineers' Joint Council, New York, 1965.

[11] Harmon, Lindsey R., *Profiles of Ph.D.'s in the Sciences.* National Academy of Sciences-National Research Council, Publication No. 1293, Washington, 1965, Table 13.

centage of students) came from university, government, or private foundation sources combined. For the most recent graduates (1955–1960) these percentages had risen to between 51 and 68 per cent. The increased importance of stipend support (including veterans' benefits) in the total of all types of support for students averaged about 12 per cent for all fields, and arts and sciences field differences in the amount of increase are not large. The increase was 15 per cent in the physical sciences, 14 per cent in the social sciences, 12 per cent in psychology, and 10 per cent in both mathematics and biological sciences.

In view of these modest field differences in amount of change in stipend support, it is not surprising that there is no correlation between rates of growth in degree output between 1935–1940 and 1955–1960, and changes in percentage of stipend support from different sources.

Comparison of the number of full-time science and nonscience graduate students who were receiving stipends (from any source) in 1953–1954 and 1964–1965 is possible, although the figures have to be treated as approximations since the definitions are not entirely comparable. These figures differ from those quoted previously because they referred to the percentage of all funds for graduate students' expenses that came from stipends, while these figures refer to the percentage of all students who had at least one stipend. Most of the *full*-time graduate students in the natural sciences held stipends in both 1953–1954 (82 per cent) and 1964–1965 (79 per cent). There was a very large increase in science graduate enrollment (225 per cent) during the decade, but an even larger increase in nonscience graduate enrollment (270 per cent) and in the nonscience fields, the percentage with stipends rose from 32 to 44 in the same period that the proportion with stipends remained stationary for the sciences. The greater increase in stipends in the nonscience areas is associated with a greater increase in enrollment in those areas, but this is not proof of a causal relationship.

It does indicate that stipend support is probably an important factor in the overall rate of growth of a field, and is also important in determining the rate at which students are able to complete their graduate programs. In the period from 1955 to 1965, the number of teaching assistant positions more than doubled, while the number of research assistants increased by 125 to 150 per cent in the same period. Federal predoctoral fellowships increased from 7,800 in 1960 to over 30,000 in fiscal year 1966 (see Table 3.4). In 1965 about 40 per cent of graduate student stipends were in the form of fellowships and scholarships, about a third were in the form of teaching assistantships, and about a fourth were research assistantships (Table 3.5).

What is likely to be the future level of stipend support for graduate study, and how will the number of stipends affect future enrollment trends? More specifically, does the level of stipend support seem likely to exert either an inhibiting or accelerating effect on the enrollment and degree trends that have been projected? While a precise answer to these questions is not possible, we

TABLE 3.4. *Number of Fellowships Supported by Federal Predoctoral Fellowship Programs: 1960–1966*

	1960	1961	1962	1963	1964	1965	1966
Science:							
National Science Foundation	2,155	2,373	2,720	2,904	4,249	6,430	8,040
National Aeronautics and							
Space Administration	—	—	100	886	1,957	3,132	3,646
Public Health Service;							
National Institutes of							
Health	1,600	2,000	2,700	3,000	3,800	3,900	4,000
Other	672	642	777	1,366	1,776	2,022	2,360
Atomic Energy Commission	146	197	174	197	235	323	372
National Defense Education Act	910	1,526	1,679	1,775	1,813	2,647	4,617
Total, Science	5,843	6,738	8,150	10,128	13,830	18,454	23,035
Other Fields:							
National Defense Education Act							
Humans., Soc. Sci., Education	1,510	2,389	2,434	2,250	2,307	3,236	5,877
National Defense Education Act							
Foreign Language	474	769	1,000	1,000	1,100	1,400	1,500
Total, Other Fields	1,984	3,158	3,434	3,250	3,407	4,636	7,377
Total Fellowships in All Fields	7,827	9,896	11,584	13,378	17,237	23,090	30,412

NOTES

1. Numbers indicate predoctoral fellowships and traineeships only and exclude support of postdoctorals and professionals (e.g., master's degrees for teachers of the handicapped).
2. Estimates are based on agency information, but in some cases are adjusted. Note the following:
   (a) NSF estimate includes 500 in 1965 and 750 in 1966 for student support under the science development program.
   (b) NASA makes grants to institutions for 3 full years of support for each fellow, in contrast to the annual funding practice of other agencies. The estimates have been adjusted so as to reflect the number of students supported in a given year consistent with other agencies.
   (c) NIH estimates exclude trainees under general research support grants, mental health service fellowships, and non-Ph.D. candidates.
   (d) NDEA distribution between "Science" and "Other Fields" is based on percentage relationships which have prevailed from year to year between these academic areas in award of new fellowships.

SOURCE: National Science Foundation, *First Fifteen Years,* Report of Library of Congress to Sub-Committee on Science, Research and Development, Committee on Science and Astronautics, 1965, p. 160. Information furnished by the Bureau of the Budget, March 18, 1965.

can examine the probable future level of stipends and discuss their possible impact on enrollments.

The major obstacle in expanding support for graduate students in the next decade will probably be encountered with teaching assistantships. Office of Education projections[12] indicate that lower division enrollments (where teaching assistants are usually employed) in degree-granting colleges will rise only about one-third in the next ten years. These Office of Education projections assume that a larger proportion of all entering students will be taught in junior colleges. Moreover, many universities express concern about the large amount of lower division instruction that is done by teaching assistants (although we have no reliable national figures), and thus, they may be hesitant to have a

[12] U.S. Office of Education, *Projections of Educational Statistics to 1974–75,* OE 10030–65. Government Printing Office, Washington, 1965, Table 6. Lower division enrollments were estimated from first time in college enrollment.

TABLE 3.5. *Current and Projected Patterns of Student Support for Full-Time Graduate Students (figures in 000's)*

Year and Type of Support	Total		Natural Sciences		All Other Fields	
	Total	Federally Supported	Total	Federally Supported	Total	Federally Supported
1965						
Total Full-Time Students	254		91		163	
Total Stipends	144	— 50	72	— 36	72	— 14
Fellowships and Scholarships	60	— 23	29	— 19	31	— 4
Research Assistants	35	— 27	22	— 17	13	— 10
Teaching Assistants	49		21		28	— 0
Other or None	110		19		91	
Percentage Supported	57		79		44	
1975						
Total Full-Time Students	500		179		321	
Total Stipends	238	— 104	126	— 75	112	— 29
Fellowships and Scholarships	103	— 50	54	— 41	49	— 9
Research Assistants	70	— 54	44	— 34	26	— 20
Teaching Assistants	65		28		37	
Other or None	262		53		209	
Percentage Supported	48		70		35	

SOURCE: Commission on Human Resources projections of Total Graduate Students and Support. Distribution of Total from data in Seymour Warkov's *Graduate Student Finances: 1963*, National Opinion Research Center Report 103, Table 2.3, and from estimates by the Bureau of the Budget. "All Other Fields" include professional fields (education, engineering, business, and so forth) as well as arts and humanities and social sciences. Projections of T.A. support assume a 33 per cent increase, equal to Office of Education projections of growth in lower division enrollment.

Projections of R.A. support assume a 100 per cent increase in number, based on projected increase in university research funds of 150 to 200 per cent and a continued rise in the cost of research of 4 per cent a year.

Fellowships are assumed to double in the next decade.

larger proportion of the teaching done by graduate students. Therefore, teaching assistant employment will probably not increase any more rapidly than lower division enrollment in the next decade.

Because they receive less research assistantship support than students in other fields, students in the humanities are more dependent on teaching assistantships, but according to the 1963 study by Warkov,[13] only 20 per cent of all full-time humanities students had teaching assistantships, while another 30 per cent had fellowships, scholarships, or research assistantships. A one-third growth in humanities teaching assistantships during the next decade and a doubling of other forms of support would reduce the total percentage of students with support

[13] Warkov, Seymour, *Graduate Student Finances: 1963.* National Opinion Research Center Report, No. 103, Table 2.4.

from 50 to 55 to from 43 to 48, if the total number of graduate students increases as projected. A change of this magnitude probably would have little effect on the Ph.D. proportion prior to 1975. A slowdown in the expansion of teaching assistant positions will not occur before 1968 or 1969, and by that point nearly all persons who are going to get Ph.D. degrees by 1975 are already enrolled in graduate school.

Colleges and universities generally give preference for support to students who are already enrolled, and in most situations to Ph.D. students as contrasted with terminal M.A. students. Limitations on stipend support might reduce the projected M.A. output in the humanities and other arts and sciences fields in the 1971 to 1975 period but there would probably not be more than a 5 per cent decline in any field.

The federal government currently provides support for more than two-thirds of all the science fellowships, and nearly one-third of all fellowships and scholarships. The future level of federal fellowship support is very hard to predict; the very rapid growth of support that occurred in the 1960 to 1966 period has leveled off, and will actually decline in 1968. However, a future reduction in military expenditures might lead to another period of rapid expansion in fellowship support. Private fellowship programs have not grown in a way that would counterbalance the federal declines. The largest of these programs, the Woodrow Wilson program, has been reduced even more than federal programs. In Table 3.5 federal fellowships are assumed to double between 1965 and 1975, while nonfederal fellowships are assumed to increase about 50 per cent. These assumptions are little more than educated guesses. Fellowship funds represent short-term commitments in the federal budget, and are vulnerable when budget cuts are necessary. In addition, the expansion of fellowships is likely to be affected by the views of federal and foundation administrators about the shortages of doctoral level manpower. If specialized manpower is hard to recruit, there will be pressure for more fellowships; if the manpower situation seems likely to improve, these pressures will ease. In view of these uncertainties, the projections of fellowship support shown in Table 3.5 can be regarded only as an illustration of one possible pattern of support.

Research assistantships, the third major type of student support, are projected to double between 1965 and 1975. This projection is based on the projections of growth in total university research expenditures shown in Table 3.9, which indicates a total increase of 90 to 145 per cent in the next decade. Since the costs of research per principal investigator have been rising fairly rapidly, because of rising salaries, more complex equipment, and so forth, these changes in costs will affect the number of research assistants that can be supported per million dollars of university research funds. An increase of 90 to 145 per cent in funds might mean an increase of only 75 to 120 per cent in the number of research assistants that could be supported.

If enrollment increases as projected, and if support increases according to the projections outlined above, the percentage of all full-time graduate students supported would decline from about 57 per cent in 1965 to about 48 per cent by 1975; the percentage of science students supported would decline from 79 to 70 per cent, and the percentage of nonscience students supported would decline from 44 to 35 per cent. If the projected pattern of support did materialize, it might lead to a reduction of full-time enrollment, rather than a decline in the percentage of supported students. Our graduate enrollment projections are based on a continuing rise in the proportion of baccalaureates who continue their education. The number of college graduates who can support themselves in graduate school on a full-time basis may reduce total enrollment in graduate school, and increase the fraction of all graduate students who would work and attend school on a part-time basis. While these support trends might eventually reduce the number of advanced degree graduates, we have projected that the influence prior to 1975 would be slight, especially at the doctoral level.

In the nonscience fields a lower rate of increase in stipend support may mean a higher percentage of part-time enrollment and more stretchout of graduate programs, but little reduction in total graduate enrollment. In the science fields, where full-time enrollment is more the pattern, the effect of a smaller increase in stipend support probably would be to decrease the projected growth in total enrollment. The sciences have supported about 80 per cent of their full-time students in most of the past decade; the projected fellowship support in Table 3.5 would support about 10 to 12 per cent less full-time science students than we have projected for the next decade if the 80 per cent level of support was maintained. Most of the effects of these limits on growth would appear in the degrees awarded after 1975.

We have devoted considerable attention to the effects of graduate student stipend support on enrollment levels, because we have assumed that this was one of the major influences on the level of enrollment in graduate schools. While the evidence available does not enable us to prove this assumption, there is considerable support for it. The evidence about the effects of fellowships on the distribution of graduates among the various fields is much less clearcut; science fields have had a higher proportion of supported students than the humanities or most of the professional fields for a long time, but the percentage of students entering graduate work in the sciences has not increased as rapidly as the percentage in nonsciences. Stipend support may have affected the distribution of students to different specialties within fields; but it seems to have had very little effect on the distribution of graduate students among broad fields.

Other Limits on Graduate Enrollment

The graduate education enterprise in America has been able to expand very rapidly because large increases in resources have flowed into the universities from the traditional sources of state appropriations, private gifts, and student fees, as well as from the federal government. The federal government has provided the biggest increase in funds of any of the sources, and if the contributions to the support of research are included, probably supplies more than half the support for post-baccalaureate education. The precise level of support that is provided to graduate education, and the sources of that support, cannot be identified very accurately, because colleges and universities have not segregated their costs into undergraduate and graduate portions, nor are there accepted ways to separate university research expenditures into a portion that reflects the advancement of knowledge and a portion that represents graduate training.

The enrollment projections assume implicitly that the rapid increase in support for graduate education will continue in the future, and any major cutback in support would affect enrollment, although the exact magnitude of the effect of, for example, a 10 per cent slowdown (or increase) in the growth of support, cannot be determined very precisely.

Changes in draft deferment procedures for graduate students could have a major short-run effect on graduate enrollment. In the long run, changing the pattern of military service will not appreciably affect the supply of talent (we eventually overcame the effects of the major disruption in education caused by World War II), but in the short run, changed deferment status for graduate students could have a major impact. We have not tried to calculate the effects of these changes because they are dependent on political considerations that will shift in unpredictable ways.

Whatever influence limitations of graduate student support and of the expansion of undergraduate degrees may have on graduate enrollments and degrees, especially in the sciences, they do not seem likely to influence degree output greatly prior to 1975, nor do other possible limitations on growth—through shortages of faculty, facilities, or funds—seem likely to exert major influences in the next decade. Most of the persons who will earn doctoral degrees between 1968 and 1975 are already enrolled in graduate schools. If these assumptions are true, then doctoral production in 1975 will come closer to the 40 to 42 thousand a year of the projections shown in Table 3.2 than to the 35 to 36 thousand a year projected by the Office of Education. Master's degree output is also projected to grow about 30,000 more (to about 250,000 a year by 1975) than is indicated in the Office of Education projection.

Before we can compare the projected supply of graduates with the projected demand for advanced degree graduates in the arts and sciences, we must first adjust the total number of degree graduates at the M.A. level to eliminate those individuals who continue their graduate work to the Ph.D. level, and those women who do not enter the labor force at all. At the doctoral level the number of foreign students who receive a Ph.D. degree and leave the United States must also be subtracted. The resulting "available supply" is shown in Table 3.6. The dramatic increase in the available supply at both the M.A. and Ph.D. levels projected for the next decade can be seen in these figures. The high projection indicates that master's degree entrants to the labor force will triple in the 1971

TABLE 3.6. *Estimated Advanced Degree Graduates Available to Enter United States Employment in Arts and Sciences Fields, by Period and Degree (figures in 000's)*

Field	Degree Level	Period 1956–1960	1961–1965	1966–1970	1971–1975
All Arts and Sciences	M.A.	63.6	111.8	183–202	299–331
	Ph.D.	31.4	41.8	61–68	103–114
Physical Sciences and	M.A.	10.0	22.4	34–38	48–55
Mathematics	Ph.D.	10.0	14.5	20–22	30–33
Biological Sciences	M.A.	7.0	14.5	15–18	25–30
	Ph.D.	7.5	9.0	13–15	24–27
Social Sciences	M.A.	20.2	33.8	59–65	100–110
	Ph.D.	9.0	11.6	18–20	32–35
Arts and Humanities	M.A.	26.4	41.1	75–81	126–136
	Ph.D.	4.9	6.7	10–11	17–19

SOURCE: Figures 3.1 and 3.2. The number of master's degrees in each five-year period is reduced by the estimated number who go on to obtain a Ph.D., so that double counting of entrants to the labor force is reduced. M.A. degrees awarded to women are also reduced by the percentage of women (9 to 12 per cent) who do not enter the labor force at all. Ph.D. degrees reduced 10 per cent in the sciences, 5 per cent in the social sciences and 3 per cent in the arts and humanities to make up for estimated foreign Ph.D.'s who do not continue in or return to employment in this country.

to 1975 period as compared with the 1961 to 1965 period, while Ph.D. entrants will increase about 175 per cent in the same period.

The efforts to increase the size of our graduate schools, the increase in the size of the age group, and the increased number of students with advanced degree plans and aspirations are bearing fruit in a very rapid and large expansion of graduate schools after a period of relatively slow growth in the 1950's. How will these larger numbers of well-educated graduates fare in tomorrow's labor markets? Will there be good jobs for all of them? The next section examines these supply and demand relations.

THE DEMAND FOR COLLEGE TEACHERS

As was remarked previously, academic employment has been the primary occupation for three out of every five Ph.D.'s in the arts and sciences fields (Table 3.1). In this section we have attempted to project the probable demand for college teachers in each of the four major areas of the arts and sciences, basing our estimates of need for faculty on projected trends in college enrollment. Overall, the demand for college teachers will continue to be high in all fields until 1969, will slow down somewhat until 1980, and will slow down even further in the period from 1980 to 1985 as the number of entering students declines slightly. Of the arts and sciences fields (which will experience slightly more growth than all fields combined), the physical sciences/mathematics will have the lowest average growth rate and the social sciences/psychology the highest (Table 3.7 and Figure 3.5).

The definition of "teaching demand" employed in these analyses is a narrow

FIGURE 3.5 *Actual and Projected Full-Time Equivalent Teaching Faculty in Arts and Sciences Fields: 1955–1985 (figures in 000's)*

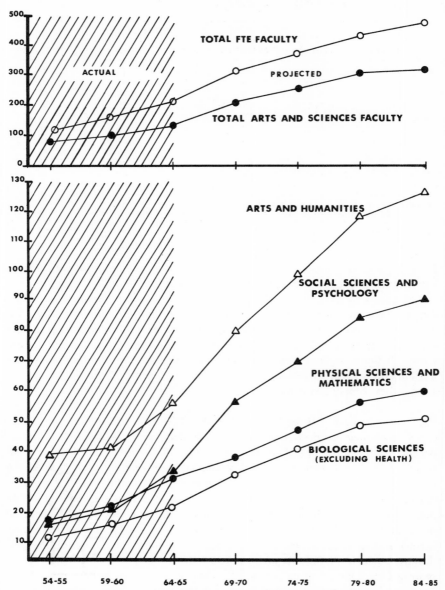

SOURCE: Commission on Human Resources projections, based on projected increases in college enrollment and assuming constant faculty-student ratio. Figures exclude: (1) junior college faculty, (2) junior staff (teaching assistants) in four year colleges, (3) estimated staff for research, (4) extension and noncollegiate staff, and (5) administration.

TABLE 3.7. *Faculty Required for Enrollment Growth and Replacement (figures in 000's)*

		1956–1960	1961–1965	1966–1970	1971–1975
All Instructional	Growth	32	57	87	72
(Full-Time-Equivalent)	Replacement	14.5	19	26	33
Faculty	Total	46.5	76	113	105
All Arts and Sciences	Growth	22.3	40.5	67.3	47.7
Faculty	Replacement	9.0	12.1	17.5	22.8
	Total	31.3	52.6	84.8	70.5
Humanities Faculty	Growth	8.2	14.7	24.7	19.0
	Replacement	3.7	4.8	6.8	8.7
	Total	11.9	19.5	31.5	27.7
Physical Sciences and	Growth	4.5	8.1	8.6	7.4
Mathematics Faculty	Replacement	2.0	2.7	3.4	4.2
	Total	6.5	10.8	12.0	11.6
Social Sciences and	Growth	5.8	10.8	23.8	13.5
Psychology Faculty	Replacement	1.9	2.7	4.5	6.3
	Total	7.7	13.5	28.3	19.8
Biological Sciences	Growth	3.8	6.9	10.2	7.8
Faculty	Replacement	1.4	1.9	2.8	3.6
	Total	5.2	8.8	13.0	11.4

SOURCE: See source for Figure 3.5. Replacement requirements are projected at 2 per cent a year for death and retirement; net loss to nonteaching occupations is estimated to be zero.

one, including only those regular full-time faculty members in four-year colleges who are employed primarily as teachers. Excluded, then, are junior college faculty—on the grounds that only 2 to 3 per cent of the annual doctoral output enter jobs in junior colleges, junior faculty in senior colleges (teaching assistants, chiefly graduate students), full-time research faculty, extension faculty, full-time administrators, and faculty for noncollegiate instruction.

In estimating supply, we have excluded foreign students who return home after receiving their doctoral degrees. In estimating demand, we have assumed that the 1964–1965 faculty/student ratio of 1 to 18 will continue—a possibly unrealistic assumption in view of the fact that one of the mechanisms operating to stretch the supply of teachers to fill the demands imposed by student enrollment has been a change in this ratio. In the tight market of the past decade, for instance, the number of students per faculty member has increased about 15 per cent, from 15 to about 18. In the future, with larger numbers of teachers available, it may be possible to reduce this figure to its 1955 level of about 1 to 15. In each section, therefore, we have made an alternative projection of need for faculty, based on the assumption of reduction in the faculty/student ratio to 1 to 15.

Because of shortages of Ph.D. graduates during the past decade, colleges and universities have often had to fill available positions with persons who hold less than the doctoral degree. In our discussion we give some consideration to probable changes in the proportions of faculty holding Ph.D. degrees, of the continued demand for those with M.A.'s, and of other occupational opportunities for M.A.'s as college teaching positions become less available to them.

The Humanities

Practically all employed Ph.D. graduates in the humanities are in colleges and universities, and over 90 per cent of them are teachers. We might expect that they would have the highest percentage of faculty with Ph.D.'s in any field; however, only about 40 per cent of humanities faculty members have Ph.D. degrees, the lowest proportion of any of the arts and sciences areas. Teachers in the fine arts and music, where the master's degree has long been the standard for entry, account for the major part of this low figure: only 25 per cent of the group have doctorates. English, languages, and philosophy are similar to other fields in that proportions with doctorates range from 50 to 75 per cent.

In the period from 1955 to 1960, only about 37 per cent of the entrants to teaching in the humanities had the Ph.D. degree (including those who earned their doctorates after entering employment); this figure was slightly below the percentage of doctorates already in the field. In the 1960 to 1965 period, when enrollments grew more rapidly, entrants with the doctorate made up only 31 per cent of the total faculty additions, and this lower proportion is expected to continue to 1970. After 1970 the ratio will improve sharply: doctorates available to enter teaching will constitute about 60 per cent of total teaching requirements.

Therefore, the proportion of faculty members who hold the Ph.D. degree can be expected to decline from 41 to 37 per cent between 1960 and 1970, but to begin to rise again after 1970, reaching 44 per cent by 1975. The best available projections suggest this rise will continue, reaching 50 to 52 per cent by 1980 and 58 to 62 per cent by 1985. These estimates hold, of course, only if the faculty/student ratio remains constant and humanists continue to be employed primarily in teaching, rather than in nonteaching jobs. It seems likely that, even with the large projected expansion of humanities doctorates, the colleges and universities will absorb all of the output for the next 20 years.

To fill their requirements, colleges will need to hire about 20,000 to 22,000 graduates with less than a Ph.D. degree in the 1965 to 1970 period (25 to 30 per cent of the total M.A. output) and another 10,000 to 12,000 in the 1970 to 1975 period (8 to 10 per cent of the total M.A. output). If the number of students per faculty member were reduced 15 per cent, or 15 per cent more time were provided for scholarly activities, then an additional 15,000 M.A. graduates would be needed by 1975. Even with this increase, colleges would provide employment for only about one-fourth of all the humanities M.A. graduates entering the labor force during the 1970 to 1975 period.[14] Little information is

---

[14] This is not inconsistent with past patterns of employment for humanities M.A. graduates, insofar as they can be estimated from data provided in the postcensal survey of college graduates. (See Schwartz, Mildred A., *op. cit.,* Table 3.18.) About 10 per cent

available now about what nonacademic occupations M.A. graduates enter. It seems probable that junior college and secondary teaching, library work, editorial and publishing work—all expanding fields—may be able to absorb a large proportion of the master's graduates. Between half and three-fourths of the humanities M.A. graduates reported that they were in occupations where they utilized their advanced degree training,[15] which suggests that demand for master's graduates in fields relevant to their training already may be less than the supply.

In summary, in the next two decades the demand for Ph.D.'s in the humanities as college teachers will be sufficient to absorb the total supply. At the M.A. level, the demand is already smaller than the supply and will probably decline in the next decade. Since humanities graduates can find employment in related fields, the real problem is not unemployment, but graduate programs that will better prepare students to utilize their talents in a wider spectrum of occupations.

The Social Sciences and Psychology

The social sciences and psychology are the most rapidly expanding area of the arts and sciences, except for mathematics. In 1953 faculty in these fields was about 13 per cent of the total faculty in all fields,[16] in 1965 it was about 15 per cent, and by 1975 it is projected to be about 18 to 19 per cent.

About 70 per cent of recent Ph.D.'s in the social sciences have been employed by colleges and universities, and the remainder have found employment in government, industry, or nonprofit organizations. Psychologists are the only arts and sciences group that have substantial employment opportunities outside teaching or research; over one-fourth of recent psychology doctoral graduates are engaged in providing personal services (largely as clinicians).

About 80 per cent of the social scientists employed in academic institutions are primarily engaged in teaching, and the remainder are mostly in research. Comparing projected requirements with projected degree output (Tables 3.10 and 3.11), we find the same pattern that emerges for other arts and sciences areas.

The proportion of entrants to teaching in the 1955 to 1960 period who held the Ph.D. degree was slightly lower than that of the existing faculty in 1963 and the percentage of entrants with Ph.D. degrees dropped further in the 1960 to 1965 period as enrollments grew rapidly. The percentage of entrants with Ph.D.

---

reported their occupation as college teaching, but others who reported themselves as music teachers, art teachers, or artists, and so forth should also be included. The M.A. graduates who enter college teaching could easily be 20 to 25 per cent of the total.

[15] See National Science Foundation, *Two Years After the College Degree*, NSF 63–26, Tables 58 and 59; also Schwartz, Mildred A., *op. cit.*, Table 3.23.

[16] Wolfle, Dael, *America's Resources of Specialized Talent*. Harper and Bros., New York, 1954, Table V.16.

degrees is expected to remain low in the period from 1965 to 1970 and then rise sharply after 1970. The projected supply of doctoral graduates available for teaching is about equal to the estimated demand in the 1970 to 1975 period (see Table 3.8).

TABLE 3.8. *Estimates of Proportions of Ph.D.'s Among Teaching Faculty and Ratio of Ph.D.'s Available to New Entrants Required: 1955–1975*

	New Entrants 1955–1960	Total Faculty 1962–1963	1960–1965	New Entrants 1965–1970	1970–1975
Total Arts and Sciences	.60	.58	.47	.48	.96
Biological Sciences	.75	.75	.53	.61	1.24
Social Sciences	.65	.69	.48	.40	.99
Arts and Humanities	.37	.42	.31	.31	.61
Physical Sciences and Mathematics	.69	.64	.60	.82	1.28

SOURCE: Tables 3.6 and 3.7 and U.S. Office of Education, *Survey of Teaching Faculty in 1962–63.*

In 1962–1963 about 70 per cent of teaching faculty members in the social sciences had Ph.D. degrees. If our projections are accurate, the figure will fall to 60 to 61 per cent by 1970, rise sharply to from 72 to 75 per cent by 1975, and to about 90 per cent by 1980. Depending on academic hiring practices, it could be close to 100 per cent before 1985. Even if faculty/student ratios were improved by 15 per cent and if only doctorates were hired for this purpose, it is still possible for 90 to 95 per cent of all members of social sciences faculties of four-year colleges and universities to have Ph.D. degrees by 1985. In short, if the expected numbers of social science Ph.D.'s are to be absorbed, new sources of demand—in research, service, or elsewhere—will need to be opened up after 1975.

The need for master's degree graduates in the social sciences as senior college teachers will approximate 50 per cent of the output in the 1960 to 1970 period, but after 1970 it will drop to almost nothing. Other sources of employment—in junior colleges, secondary schools, and research organizations—will have to be developed if these graduates are to be employed in professionally relevant work. As was true in the humanities, more M.A. graduates may thus go back to graduate school to seek a Ph.D. degree.

In summary, although the very rapid growth of social sciences enrollments in the social sciences and faculty requirements in the 1960 to 1970 period have created a tight labor market for social sciences doctorates, the rapid expansion of doctoral degree output and the anticipated slowdown of growth after 1970 will make it possible to saturate the demand for Ph.D.'s in teaching sometime between 1980 and 1985, even if there is a 15 per cent improvement in faculty/student ratios.

Mathematics and the Physical Sciences

Mathematics has been the most rapidly growing area of the arts and sciences, and the physical sciences the slowest growing. "Slow" is, of course, a relative term, since faculty in the physical sciences have increased about 60 per cent in the past decade and will increase another 50 to 55 per cent in the next decade.

The pattern of growth in physical sciences and mathematics differs slightly from that of other fields: a decline in the supply of Ph.D.'s relative to demand in the early 1960's as enrollment growth accelerated, some improvement in the 1965 to 1970 period (in contrast to the humanities and social sciences, where no improvement is projected before 1970), and a considerable increase in supply projected after 1970. In 1962–1963 about 64 per cent of physical sciences and mathematics faculty had a doctoral degree; this figure is expected to rise to nearly 75 per cent by 1970 and to more than 90 per cent by 1975.

If we take into consideration the demand for Ph.D.'s in the physical sciences to teach in engineering schools—where undergraduate curricula have become increasingly similar to undergraduate curricula in the physical sciences and which have a low proportion of Ph.D.'s on their faculties (about 40 per cent in 1962–1963)—our projections of the demand for physical sciences graduates would be even higher. If the faculty-student ratio were improved 15 per cent, from 80 to 85 per cent of the physical sciences/mathematics faculty in 1975 would have doctorates.

These projections indicate that the supply of physical scientists and mathematicians will be more than adequate to fill all teaching vacancies with Ph.D.'s after 1975; unless the number of students per faculty member declines sharply, increases in research and other kinds of demand must be greater than they have been in the past to provide employment for the supply.[17]

Requirements in the period from 1955 to 1965 for mathematics and physical sciences teachers who had less than a Ph.D. degree were 20 to 25 per cent of the master's degree output; they will fall much lower in the next decade: only 5 to 10 per cent will be needed for college and university teaching, leaving virtually all of these master's graduates available for junior college, secondary school, research and development, and other employment.

In summary, the supply of physical sciences doctorate recipients in relation to the demand for college teachers appears more adequate than is true of any of the other arts and sciences fields. By 1975 all demand for teachers can be

[17] These projections do not agree with recent unpublished projections of the National Science Foundation, which base faculty requirements on physical science bachelor's degree projections. Their projections indicate a 146 per cent growth in the next decade, as compared with the 86 per cent bachelor's degree increase projected by the Commission on Human Resources. The CHR faculty projection is based on overall changes in enrollment, not degrees, and assumes only a 50 per cent growth of faculty required. From their data, the NSF concludes: "The requirements for science doctorates will greatly exceed the probable supply available to the colleges and universities throughout most of the period. By the end of the decade the growing numbers of doctorates will begin to approximate the academic requirements, and after 1975 the situation should be greatly improved." The analysis above differs principally in the timing of improvements expected.

met by the doctoral supply, and new sources of demand will be needed in the 1975 to 1985 decade if appropriate employment is to be provided.

Biological Sciences

The biological sciences (including agricultural fields, but excluding the health professions) follow essentially the same pattern as other arts and sciences fields. The past and projected supply and demand are similar particularly to those in the social sciences: the percentage of doctorates on the faculty will fall from 75 in 1962–1963 to about 68 to 70 in 1970 and will rise to about 90 by 1975. In the period from 1975 to 1985 biological scientists will be faced with the problem of finding other sources of demand, because college teaching will not be able to absorb as great a proportion of all degree graduates. By 1975 the supply will be sufficient so that over 90 per cent of the faculty could have Ph.D. degrees.

One important source of employment not included in these figures is teaching jobs in the health professions, which constitute about 15 to 25 per cent of the total college teaching opportunities open to biological scientists. If they are included as part of the market for Ph.D.'s in these fields, the projected demand rises considerably, and the point at which an adequate supply of graduates is available to meet teaching demands moves from 1975 to the period from 1980 to 1985.

Summary and Discussion of Demand for College Teachers

The projections indicate that only in the humanities will virtually all the available Ph.D. output be required to fill the demand for college teaching positions for the next two decades. In the social sciences and the biological sciences, this demand could be completely met (meaning that 90 per cent or more of faculty in the field would have the doctoral degree) sometime between 1980 and 1985. In the physical sciences/mathematics, demand could be met sometime between 1975 and 1980. These projections assume that no change in the proportion of all doctoral degree output going into teaching would occur. In all fields, demand for college teachers with less than a Ph.D. degree will decline sharply after 1970; only a very small proportion of the M.A. output will be able to find college teaching jobs. Unless new sources of demand develop, graduate students will be under heavy pressure to stay in school and complete the Ph.D., since without it, they may have great difficulty in finding work commensurate with their training.

As supplies of Ph.D. graduates become more plentiful, various reorganizations and adjustments in the teaching function could occur. For instance, less instruction might be done by the junior staff (mostly predoctoral teaching assistants), the number of students per faculty member might be reduced, or more Ph.D.'s might go into education-related services, such as counseling and extension work. These adjustments, however, would add substantially to educational costs per student. Rising educational costs are already bringing increasing pressures for economy and educational efficiency, and only if faculty salaries rise at a lower rate in the future (as seems likely) would some of these expensive changes be likely. We could improve predictions about the way in which the supply of graduates will be absorbed by means of cost analyses that would identify the budgeting limits and alternatives for adding personnel to college and university staffs. Though complicated, such analysis should make for more efficient projections.

Allan M. Cartter, in a similar assessment of supply and demand for teachers in specific fields,[18] also emphasizes the likelihood of a rapid shift in the supply and demand balance. If nonacademic jobs increase in attractiveness, he points out, more older college teachers may transfer to nonacademic fields, with the result that new Ph.D. graduates would have greater opportunity to enter college teaching; this change might mean some financial saving to the colleges. He also predicts that earlier retirement would become the rule. Cartter closes with a valuable observation about the limitations of quantitative analysis and about the consideration that should be foremost in manpower planning:

> If this (essay) accomplishes anything, I hope it will lay to rest our recent overriding concern with quantity, and permit us to turn our attention to the really important problems of quality in higher education.[19]

> No head count of teachers can tell us how high the standard of teaching is; the possession of an advanced degree will not convert a poor teacher into an exciting and dedicated one. Just as many of the colleges and universities should be more concerned than they have been with the quality of education provided by their institutions, so should the graduate schools become more concerned with the preparation of their students for careers in college teaching.

THE DEMAND IN RESEARCH AND DEVELOPMENT ACTIVITIES

The rapid growth of research and development activities in the recent past is a familiar story, one that is pertinent here because such jobs constitute a sizable part of the employment demand for arts and sciences graduates with advanced degrees. With the federal government as the chief provider of funds, total expenditures for research and development have increased fourfold over the past decade. Moreover, basic research has received greater emphasis, and a greater proportion of the total research effort has been carried on by universities. The chief impetus to this expansion has been the increased, and often pressing, interest in such fields as space exploration, medicine, agricultural development, aviation, weaponry, and so forth. All sectors of the economy

[18] Cartter, Allan M., "A New Look at the Supply of College Teachers," *Educational Record,* vol. 46, Summer, 1965, pp. 267–277; and "Future Faculty Needs and Resources" in Lee, Calvin B. T., editor, *Improving College Teaching,* American Council on Education, Washington, 1967, pp. 113–135. Cartter's projections differ somewhat from those presented here, but his conclusions are essentially the same.

[19] Cartter, Allan M., *op. cit.,* p. 277.

are involved in research activity; government, universities, private industry, and foundations.

The number of persons who are employed in research activity is difficult to determine accurately because most Ph.D.'s perform more than one function: they teach and do research if they work for a university; they may manage research activity and do research if they work for industry. In theory, we can determine the percentage of time spent in each activity, and develop full-time equivalent numbers of persons engaged in research, administration, and teaching. But in practice, this is difficult to do; estimates of the amount of time spent in research will vary, depending on the way the questions are asked. For example, a certain part of research activity, such as the supervision of graduate students, can be classified either as teaching or research.

Table 3.1 gives an estimate of research employment in colleges and universities and in all other organizations combined, based on reports of employment patterns by samples of employed doctorate recipients.[20] In 1963 about 65,000 to 68,000 arts and sciences Ph.D. graduates were working primarily in research and development. These figures approximate a full-time equivalent number of individuals in research activity; or expressed another way, the proportion of the total employment of Ph.D.'s that is devoted to the research function.

Evidence from Lindsey R. Harmon's study of successive cohorts of Ph.D. graduates indicates a gradual rise in the percentage of total time of a Ph.D. devoted to research from about 33 per cent in the 1930's to about 43 per cent in the late 1950's and early 1960's. A counter-trend seems to be revealed in the reports of first jobs in the National Academy of Sciences doctoral graduate study. The Ph.D.'s of 1962–1963 had a higher percentage with research as their primary job than the Ph.D.'s of 1964–1966.

In the remainder of this section, we will discuss the relative employment in research and development by field, increases in expenditures during the past decade, projections to 1970 and 1975 based on alternative assumptions about proportionate growth in future research expenditures and increases in costs per man, the resultant relation of supply to demand and the adjustment mechanisms that may function to restore the balance.

As Table 3.1 shows, roughly half of the Ph.D. scientists employed in research

[20] A sample of doctorates, as reported by Lindsey R. Harmon in *Profiles of Ph.D.'s in the Sciences,* Table 8, indicated that the doctorate recipients of 1960 spent 46 per cent of their time in research in 1962. The National Register report, *American Science Manpower,* 1964 (NSF No. 66–29, Table A-4) indicates that 40 per cent of the employed doctorate scientists had research as their primary activity and another 13 per cent had the administration of research as their primary activity. In the reports of new Ph.D.'s in arts and sciences in *Doctorate Recipients from United States Universities, 1958–66* (National Academy of Sciences, Publication No. 1489, Washington) Table 19 indicates that in their postdoctoral job 48 per cent of recent (1964–1966) Ph.D.'s in the physical sciences had research as their primary activity; comparable figures for the biological sciences were 39 per cent, for the social sciences 22 per cent, and for arts and humanities only 3 per cent. These survey results are not necessarily inconsistent with each other, but the differences in question wording and differences in the population included in the survey make precise comparisons impossible.

and development in 1965 were in the physical sciences, 28 per cent in the biological sciences, and 22 per cent in the social sciences. The humanists have been excluded from the discussion of research and development employment because so few of them have jobs that are totally research. During the decade from 1954 to 1964 college and university expenditures for research expanded at an annual rate of about 16 per cent, and total research expenditures in all sectors expanded at almost as high a rate. This increase has two components: demand for more research personnel and rises in cost per professional worker. The second component accounts for about 6 to 8 per cent—a little less than half—of the total.[21] An annual increase of as much as 9 to 10 per cent in demand for research personnel must be considered unusually large, especially when it comes at a time when teaching demand is also very high. In 1964 and 1965 the increases in expenditures were smaller, only about 10 per cent. While a part of the slowdown can be attributed to the conflict in Vietnam, some of it must be regarded as the inevitable decline in the rate of increase that occurs after a period of extremely rapid growth.

Table 3.9 presents two alternative projections of research and development expenditures, based on alternative assumptions about two main components: the proportion of the gross national product that research expenditures will constitute in the future and increases in costs per professional research worker. To take the first component, the lower projection assumes that research expenditures will continue to constitute 3 per cent of the GNP, the figure reached in fiscal 1965; the higher projection assumes they will continue to accelerate as they have over the past decade until they constitute 4 per cent of the GNP

TABLE 3.9. *Research and Development Expenditures, 1954–1965, with Projections for 1970 and 1975*

Fiscal Year	Total Research and Development Expenditures	Research and Development as Percentage of GNP	Basic Research Expenditures	Basic Research as Percentage of Total R & D	College and University Research & Development Expenditures
	(in millions)	Per cent	(in millions)	Per cent	(in millions)
1954	$ 5,730	1.6	$ 455	8.0	$ 380
1961	14,500	2.8	1,324	9.2	970
1965	20,470	3.0	2,375	11.6	1,870
1970a	24,700	3.0	3,285	13.3	2,464
1970b	28,600	3.5	3,800	13.3	2,850
1975a	30,800	3.0	4,620	15.0	3,465
1975b	40,800	4.0	6,120	15.0	4,590

SOURCE: Projections of total R & D are based on assumed GNP growth of approximately 4 per cent a year. In 1965 prices, 1970 GNP is 818 billion, 1975 is 1,020 billion. Past trend in basic research as percentage of total is assumed to continue to 1975. R & D projection b and GNP projections are consistent with Leonard A. Lecht's, *Goals, Priorities and Dollars,* The Free Press, New York, 1966, Table 11.4. R & D projection "a" assumes 3 per cent of GNP for R & D; projection "b" assumes rise to 4 per cent of GNP for R & D by 1975.

[21] For a discussion of rising research costs per man, see Milton, Helen, *Cost of Research Index, 1920–65,* Research Analysis Corporation, Technical Paper, RAC-TP-209, March, 1966.

by 1975. Basic research and university research are projected to increase their share of total research and development expenditures to about 15 and 12 per cent, respectively, by 1975.

Even the higher of these projections assumes a slowdown in the rate of increase in annual research expenditures from the 16 per cent a year during the early 1960's to about 9 to 10 per cent a year. If this assumption is valid, the question of increases in cost per professional worker becomes critical. If these increases average 6 to 8 per cent a year during the next decade, the expansion of manpower in research will be small and replacement will constitute the largest component of demand. On the other hand, if the rise in costs in the past decade is attributable chiefly to rising salaries, as some data indicate,[22] a larger supply of qualified persons should result in a slowdown in salary increases and a consequent drop in the rise of research costs per man. These two possibilities provided the basis for alternative assumptions about future research costs per man: the first, that costs will increase 5 per cent a year from 1965 to 1970 and 3 per cent a year thereafter; the second, that costs will increase 4 per cent a year to 1970 and will remain stable thereafter. Table 3.10 translates research costs into demand for Ph.D. level manpower in the arts and sciences on each of the combinations of alternative assumptions. In this projection the proportion of all research and development professionals who hold the Ph.D. degree is regarded as remaining constant—an unlikely possibility.

Table 3.11, which is based on the same combinations of assumptions, compares demand with the supply that will be available if there is no change in the

TABLE 3.10. *The Number of Additional Arts and Sciences Ph.D. Research Personnel Who Could Be Supported from Projected Growth in Basic Research Funds (figures in 000's)*

	High Projection of Basic Research Expenditures		Low Projection of Basic Research Expenditures	
	High Increase in Research Cost[a] per Man	Low Increase in Research Cost[a] per Man	High Increase in Research Cost[a] per Man	Low Increase in Research Cost[a] per Man
1965–1970 Growth	14.9	18.0	5.1	7.8
1965–1970 Replacement	6.2	6.2	6.2	6.2
1965–1970 Total	21.1	24.2	11.3	14.0
1970–1975 Growth	27.7	45.6	13.2	26.1
1970–1975 Replacement	7.7	8.1	6.7	7.0
1970–1975 Total	35.4	53.7	19.9	33.1

[a] Research cost per professional worker; see text for discussion of assumptions.
SOURCE: Projections of basic research expenditures from Table 3.9. Projections of manpower demand assume: (a) constant proportion of R & D funds for personnel in Arts and Sciences R & D, (b) 2 per cent annual replacement rate for death and retirement, and (c) high increase in cost of research assumes 5 per cent annual rise to 1970, 3 per cent thereafter; low projection assumes 4 per cent annual rise to 1970, and no rise thereafter.

[22] *Ibid.* See also Searle, Allan D., "Measuring Price Change in Research and Development Purchases," in Business and Economic Statistics Section: *Proceedings, 1966,* American Statistical Association, Washington, pp. 19–28.

TABLE 3.11. *Research and Development Ph.D. Employment Demand Compared with Supply (figures in 000's)*

	1966–1970	1971–1975
Range of Demand (from Table 3.10)	11.3 to 24.2	19.9 to 53.7
Supply of Doctorates for Research and Development (Total Arts and Sciences)	39.5 to 44.2	68.1 to 75.9
Physical Sciences and Mathematics		
Nonacademic Research and Development	20.1 to 22.4	34 to 38
Academic Research and Development	9.1 to 10.2	15.4 to 17.1
Total	29.2 to 32.6	49.4 to 55.1
Biological Sciences		
Nonacademic Research and Development	3.0 to 3.4	5.5 to 6.2
Academic Research and Development	3.0 to 3.4	5.5 to 6.2
Total	6.0 to 6.8	11.0 to 12.4
Psychology and Social Sciences		
Nonacademic Research and Development	1.8 to 2.0	3.2 to 3.5
Academic Research and Development	2.5 to 2.8	4.5 to 4.9
Total	4.3 to 4.8	7.7 to 8.4

proportion of Ph.D.'s entering research as compared with teaching or other activities. The allocation of supply between teaching and research is consistent with the analysis of supply for teaching; that is, those persons not allocated to teaching earlier are here apportioned among research and other activities.[23]

Given any of the assumptions about future research support, the projections indicate that the supply will be much larger than the demand. This generalization may not apply to each scientific subfield, nor are detailed comparisons of subfields (such as meteorology or social psychology) possible. Except through special studies such as those being made by the National Academy's Committee on Science and Public Policy,[24] the data are simply not available.

This increased supply available for research positions makes it likely that several adjustments will take place. First, some of the additional Ph.D.'s can be absorbed into research positions by displacing persons who have less than Ph.D. training. At present, only about 17 per cent of research and development professionals hold the Ph.D. degree, and although the proportion is much higher in colleges and universities (an estimated 50 per cent) and in the arts and sciences fields, there is substantial room for additional employment of Ph.D.'s. Second, salaries will increase at a slower rate in the future, especially if the rate of growth in research expenditures is slow. These two adjustment processes should be more than adequate to absorb all the doctoral graduates produced

[23] Apportionment between research and other activities (primarily nonresearch and development administration and service) was made on the basis of data from the National Register of Scientific and Technical Personnel, and of data on the expected employment of recent (1962–1964) cohorts of Ph.D.'s in the National Academy of Sciences' Doctoral Files.

[24] See, for example, National Research Council, Physics Survey Committee, *Physics Survey and Outlook*, NAS–NRC Publication No. 1295, Washington, 1966. Commonly known as the "Pake Report."

between now and 1975. Projections for the 1975 to 1985 period cannot be made with much accuracy because we don't know how research costs per man will change, nor can we make long-range projections of federal research and development expenditures with any confidence.

SUMMARY

We have expanded the graduate degree-producing institutions of the United States to the level where they can supply an economy that has a very high demand for both teaching and research. If this demand grows at a slower rate than has been the case in the past, which seems almost certain, the graduate output will permit rapid proportional and quantitative increases in Ph.D. employment in research and teaching. Consequently, persons with less than a Ph.D. degree will have more difficulty obtaining jobs in these fields.

Because the structure of demand in both teaching and research is highly flexible, we will probably not need to develop new sources of employment for Ph.D.'s before 1985. By that date, however, each arts and sciences area, except the humanities, may be approaching the saturation point for doctoral level employment. As Allan Cartter has suggested, these trends may finally reduce our national preoccupation with quantity and allow us to give more emphasis to problems of quality in selecting and preparing graduate students in the arts and sciences.

4 Manpower Supply and Demand in Selected Professions*

IN THIS CHAPTER the projected supplies of graduates in seven professions are compared with the anticipated demands for high-level manpower in those professions in the next 10 to 15 years. All seven professions are large: together they employ about half of all professional workers. Although a number of other professional groups might have been included, these seven—law, medicine, engineering, elementary and secondary school teaching, social work, nursing, and the performing arts—were selected because they seem representative of the varieties and range of manpower problems that confront all professions.

The seven differ from one another in their patterns of growth, labor markets, and requirements for entry. Engineering and social work are expanding very rapidly; in the next decade they will probably grow one and one-half times as fast as all other professions. The other five groups are likely to grow at a lower-than-average rate. Most of these professions are dominated by one sex, although secondary teaching, the performing arts, and social work attract both men and women. Engineering and law are virtually all-male professions (over 97 per cent of the practitioners are men), and medicine is only slightly less so. Nursing and elementary school teaching are chiefly women's occupations. A college degree is necessary for entry into all except nursing and the performing arts. Physicians and lawyers are predominantly fee professionals, engineers are primarily salaried employees in the private sector, and teachers are salaried employees in the public sector.

* An earlier version of a portion of this chapter appeared in *The Modern Hospital*, vol. 109, 1967, pp. 75–79, under the title "Nurse Supply: It's Better Than We Thought," by Alan E. Bayer. (Copyright 1967 by McGraw-Hill, Inc.)

Because of their structural differences, the seven professional groups face different manpower problems. For each, the general outlook—with respect to the anticipated demand, the quantity and quality of the supply, and the adjustment mechanisms that may operate to bring the two into balance—is discussed, with special emphasis given in each section to the particular problems faced by the profession under consideration.

LAW

Law is one of the broadest of all professions, and the skills and knowledge of the lawyer are applied in nearly every area of modern life. Legal analysis is an important part of the operation of nearly every large organization, and the lawyer as a manager and a decision-maker is found at every level of government and in all types of business and industry.

A lawyer may work as an independent fee professional or as the salaried employee of an organization, and the past 15 years have seen a rapid shift in the employment settings of lawyers. The percentage in individual private practice declined from about 60 in 1951 to about 40 in 1963, the percentage in group practice rose slightly from 28 to 33, while the percentage working for business and industry almost doubled (from 6 to 11 per cent). The percentages in private group practice and in federal and state government employment increased slightly (see Table 4.1). Projections of trends of the past decade indicate that the proportion in private practice will decline from about 75 per cent in 1963 to about 60 per cent in 1980, and two-thirds of these will be in group practice. The percentage working for business or industry will double (to 22 per cent), and there should be a modest increase from 14 to 18 per cent in government legal employment.

The central questions confronting the legal profession with respect to manpower are: How rapidly will the supply of graduates expand? Will the demand be sufficient to provide employment for all the lawyers produced by the edu-

TABLE 4.1. *Percentage of Lawyers in Different Employment Settings: 1948–1963*

Year	Private Practice			Business and Industry	Government			
					Judicial	Executive and Legislative		
	Total	Indi-vidual	Group			Federal	State	Local
1948	89.2	61.2	28.0	3.2	4.2	—	—	4.7
1951	86.8	59.0	27.8	6.3	3.6	4.1	1.8	3.9
1954	85.5	57.5	28.0	7.5	3.6	4.5	1.6	3.9
1957	80.1	51.9	28.2	8.9	3.3	5.3	1.7	3.3
1960	76.2	46.3	29.9	9.9	3.2	5.2	1.7	3.3
1963	74.7	42.1	32.6	11.0	3.3	5.6	2.4	2.9

SOURCE: *The 1964 Lawyer Statistical Report,* American Bar Foundation, Chicago, 1965, Tables 6 and 7. Percentages add to more than 100 because a lawyer may have had more than one job (for example, a private group practice and a local government job) and would thus be counted in both categories.

cational system? To take the second question first, the pervasive involvement of lawyers in so many aspects of the public and private sector makes it very difficult to determine precisely the future demand, but current trends in corporate size, government regulation of business, emphasis on adequate legal representation for the poor, and the overall rise in the importance of law in regulating society's affairs indicate that the demand will increase to absorb the supply—indeed, that the supply will, in a sense, create its own demand.

One index of changes in the overall demand for lawyers is provided by changes in population size. With some fluctuations the number of lawyers per million population remained relatively stable from 1900 to 1963 (see Table 4.2). This

TABLE 4.2. *Ratio of Lawyers to Total U.S. Population: 1900–1980*

Year	Population (000's)	Number of Lawyers	Lawyers per Million Population			
1900	76,094	107,592	141			
1910	92,407	114,704	124			
1920	106,461	122,519	115			
1930	123,077	160,605	130			
1940	132,122	180,483	137			
1950	152,271	205,539	135			
1960	180,684	250,132	138			
1963	189,417	265,823	140			
		Institutional Capacity Projection	Low Student Demand Projection	Institutional Capacity Projection	Low Student Demand Projection
		(Number of Lawyers)		(Lawyers per Million Pop.)	
1970	206,039	317,000	320,000	154	155
1975	219,366	375,000	395,000	171	180
1980	235,212	457,000	493,000	194	210

SOURCES: (1) Total U.S. population projection was obtained from *Current Population Reports: Population Estimates,* Bureau of the Census Series, P-25 No. 359, February 20, 1967, Series C. (2) Number of lawyers for 1900–1940 was obtained from Dael Wolfle's, *America's Resources of Specialized Talent,* Harper and Bros., New York, 1954, p. 127. Number of lawyers in 1960 as given in *U.S. Census of Population: 1960, Occupational Characteristics.* The figures for 1970, 1975, and 1980 represent projections of the Commission on Human Resources and Advanced Education. See text for definitions of ''Institutional Capacity'' and ''Student Demand Projection.''

national ratio should not, however, obscure the very large differences among states with respect to the availability of legal services. If we exclude the District of Columbia (where there were over 16,000 lawyers per million population), the number of lawyers per million population ranged from 73 in Arkansas to 236 in New York. The wealthy, urbanized states like Massachusetts and Illinois had ratios of lawyers to population that were twice as high as those of poorer more rural states like Alabama, Mississippi, and North Carolina.

Another index of demand is the number of lawyers per billion dollars of the gross national product (GNP). In 1950, the ratio was 551 lawyers per billion dollars of GNP, and by 1963, this figure had decreased to 457. If volume of business (as measured by GNP) is a good indicator of demand for legal services, then during the 1950's demand was rising faster than the supply of lawyers.

Tables 4.2 and 4.3 illustrate the projected relationships between the number

TABLE 4.3. *Ratio of Lawyers to Gross National Product: 1950–1980*

Year	GNP IN Billions	Lawyers per Billion Dollars of GNP		
		Institutional Capacity Projection		Low Student Demand Projection
1950	$ 372		551	
1960	515		485	
1963	581		457	
1970	793	400		403
1975	981	382		402
1980	1,199	381		411

SOURCE: GNP projections are in 1962 constant dollars, and assume 4 per cent annual growth rate. 1970 figures have been adjusted to be consistent with projections for 1970, Bureau of Labor Statistics Bulletin No. 1536, Government Printing Office, Washington, 1967, Table 11-1.

of lawyers, population, and GNP. The independent factor in these projections is not the demand for lawyers, but the supply. That is, the projection of supply of lawyers is made independently and then compared with the projection of population and GNP. Neither the Lawyers to Population Index nor the Lawyers to Total Economic Activity Index provides a satisfactory basis for projecting demand for legal services. We cannot conclude that a stable lawyer-to-population ratio indicates that the demand is being adequately met, nor can we conclude that a smaller number of lawyers per billion dollars of GNP indicates a shrinking demand for lawyers. The relative income position of lawyers in comparison with other workers improved between 1951 and 1963 (see note 4 on page 83), which suggests an increasing, rather than decreasing demand. The decline in the ratio of lawyers to GNP indicates a slower growth in the supply of lawyers than the growth of the economy; the rising income of lawyers indicates that if the supply had been larger there would not have been any problem of finding employment for the additional graduates.

This may be an involved way of expressing the common sense idea that bright, well-educated youth will find jobs in a growing economy, but it is the basis for the subsequent concentration on the supply of lawyers as the key variable in determining the future size of the legal profession.

Student Demand for Legal Education and Institutional Capacity

The primary determinant of the supply is, of course, the legal profession's capacity for attracting and retaining student recruits to legal education. In the long run recruitment to the legal profession is influenced in a major way by job opportunities and earnings. If jobs become scarce, or if average earnings drop rapidly relative to those in other professions, the long-run recruitment of students is likely to be adversely affected; conversely, the higher-than-average earnings and plentiful job opportunities that have characterized the postwar period will encourage a larger proportion of college youth to choose law.

Table 4.4 shows law school enrollment and degree output during recent years and projections of these figures to 1980.[1] In the past decade entering law school students have ranged between 7.2 and 9.4 per cent of male bachelor's degree graduates, with the proportion rising steadily between 1959 and 1964. In the longer period from 1900 to 1953, the proportion of all degrees in law decreased; the recent trend has thus run counter to a longer-term decline in the popularity of law as a field of study.[2] Retention rates in law school fluctuated between 54 and 61 per cent in the 1953 to 1962 period. These figures represent the proportion of entering students who graduated three years later. While some students take more than three years to complete law school, if the proportion of delayed graduates is constant, the overall completion rate will not be affected.

Two projections of supply were made. The first, or low projection, assumes that law schools will attract a constant 9 per cent of college graduates and will graduate a constant 59 per cent of the entrants. The high projection assumes that law schools will attract a steadily increasing proportion of college graduates (the projected increase being .2 per cent a year) and will also steadily reduce attrition until by 1980 about two-thirds of the entrants will be graduating three years later.

According to the low projection, the annual output of law schools will almost triple in a 15-year period, from 11,792 in 1965 to 29,700 by 1980. In the high projection, the annual output of graduates is quadrupled, reaching 43,100 by 1980. Given the current rates of attrition from law school (and even with the increased retention rates assumed in the high projection, about one out of every three entrants will not complete a legal education), the degree output indicated in the low projection would require, by 1977, an annual enrollment of 125,000 to 135,000 law students, and that of the high projection would require an annual enrollment of 155,000 to 175,000.

Thus, we come to a second major determinant of future supply, the capacity of law schools to expand in order to meet student demand. In the final analysis, this factor determines the number of qualified lawyers who will be available. Another projection was made on the basis of past trends in the expansion of law school facilities. Such expansion has three components: increases in the enrollment of existing institutions, the upgrading of unapproved institutions to approved status, and the establishment of new law schools. Analysis of the

[1] Since men constitute 97 per cent of law school graduates, projections are based on figures for male graduates rather than on the total number of graduates.
[2] Wolfle, Dael, *America's Resources of Specialized Talent.* Harper and Bros., New York, 1954, Table B.1.

TABLE 4.4. *High and Low Projections of Law School Graduates Based on Student Demand*

| (A) | (B) | Low Projection | | | | | | High Projection | |
| | | (C₁) | (D₁) | (E₁) | (F₁) | (C₂) | (D₂) | (E₂) | (F₂) |
Year Y	No. of Male Bachelor's Degree Recipients	No. of First-Year Law Students Year Y	$C_1/B \times 100$ Per Cent of Male Bach. Entry Law School Year Y	Projection B No. of Law Schl. Grads. Year Y+3	Per Cent of First-Year Law Students Grad. in Year Y+3	No. of First-Year Law Students Year Y	$C_2/B \times 100$ Per Cent of Male Bach. Entr. Law School Year Y	Projection C No. of Law School Grads. Year Y+3	Per Cent of First-Year Law Students Grad. in Year Y+3
1956	178,000	16,697	9.4%	9,429	56.5%	16,697	9.4%	9,429	56.5%
1957	200,000	16,083	8.0	8,653	53.8	16,083	8.0	8,653	53.8
1958	219,000	16,651	7.6	9,261	55.6	16,651	7.6	9,261	55.6
1959	230,000	16,667	7.2	9,434	56.6	16,667	7.2	9,434	56.6
1960	230,000	17,030	7.4	9,948	58.4	17,030	7.4	9,948	58.4
1961	230,000	17,886	7.8	10,828	60.5	17,886	7.8	10,828	60.5
1962	236,000	20,012	8.5	11,792a	58.9	20,012	8.5	11,792	58.9
1963	247,000	22,933	9.3	13,600	59.5	22,933	9.3	13,600	59.5
1964	272,000	25,267	9.3	15,000	59.3	25,267	9.3	15,200	60.1
1965	290,000	26,100	9.0	15,500	59.3	26,100	9.0	15,800	60.7
1966	295,000	26,550	9.0	15,700	59.3	27,140	9.2	16,600	61.3
1967	314,000	28,260	9.0	16,800	59.3	29,516	9.4	18,300	61.9
1968	361,000	32,490	9.0	19,300	59.3	34,650	9.6	21,700	62.5
1969	398,000	35,820	9.0	21,200	59.3	39,004	9.8	24,600	63.1
1970	418,000	37,620	9.0	22,300	59.3	41,800	10.0	26,600	63.7
1971	422,000	37,980	9.0	22,500	59.3	43,044	10.2	27,700	64.3
1972	464,000	41,760	9.0	24,800	59.3	48,256	10.4	31,300	64.9
1973	476,000	42,840	9.0	25,400	59.3	50,456	10.6	33,000	65.5
1974	499,000	44,910	9.0	26,600	59.3	53,892	10.8	35,600	66.1
1975	518,000	46,620	9.0	27,600	59.3	56,980	11.0	38,000	66.7
1976	537,000	48,330	9.0	28,700	59.3	60,144	11.2	40,500	67.3
1977	557,000	50,130	9.0	29,700	59.3	63,498	11.4	43,100	67.9

ᵃ All underscores indicate end of actual numbers and beginning of projections.
See following page for "Sources by Column."

SOURCES BY COLUMN:

(B) Number of male bachelor's degree recipients excludes first professional degrees in law, medicine, and so forth which require a bachelor's degree. For further explanation of fields included, see Appendix A. Projections of bachelor's degrees are extended in the present table to 1977.

$(C_{1, 2})$ Number of first-year law students through 1963 was obtained from *The 1964 Lawyer Statistical Report*, American Bar Foundation, Table 9, p. 43. The 1964 figure was obtained from *Review of Legal Education*, American Bar Foundation, Fall, 1964, p. 19. Projected numbers are computed on the basis of percentages given in columns $D_{1, 2}$.

(D_1) The projected constant of 9.0 per cent of male bachelor's degree recipients entering law school represents an average of the percentages given for 1962, 1963, and 1964, based on the assumption that a leveling-off in percentage of males with bachelor's degrees entering law school has occurred and will last through the next decade.

(D_2) The projections given here for percentage of male bachelor's degree recipients entering law school are based on past trends and take into account the rapid increase in this percentage from 1959 to 1963. It seems likely that the decreasing percentages from 1956 to 1959 are partially representative of a return to normality after an increase following the end of the Korean War. While the average annual percentage increase in the four-year period between 1959 and 1963 is 0.5 per cent, the observation for 1964 indicates this rate of increase will not continue. The 0.2 per cent annual increase projected in this column to 1977 represents an average of the yearly rates of increase from 1957 to 1964.

$(E_{1, 2})$ Number of law school graduates for 1962 through 1965 was obtained from Appendix A. Figures for 1959–1961 are derived from third-year law school enrollment figures given in *The 1964 Lawyer Statistical Report*, Table 9, p. 43. The 1962–1964 actual yearly figures for law school graduates represent 93 per cent of the third-year enrollment for each prior year. Thus for each year from 1959–1961, 93 per cent of the third-year law school enrollment of the previous year was taken as the number of law school graduates. Projected numbers are computed on the basis of percentages given in columns $F_{1, 2}$.

(F_1) The projected constant of 59.3 per cent of first-year law students graduating from law school three years later represents an average of the percentages given for 1963, 1964, and 1965, based on the assumption that a leveling-off in the percentage of first-year law students who actually graduate has occurred and will last through 1980.

(F_2) The projections given here for percentage of first-year law students graduating from law school three years later consider the ten-year trend line from 1953 to 1963. The percentage for 1953 is 52.9 and thus, there is a total increase of 6.0 per cent between 1953 and 1963, or an average annual increase of 0.6 per cent. This rate of increase is continued to 1980.

increases in law school enrollment during the past decade shows that the average annual growth rate ranged from 1.3 per cent in large private schools to 10 per cent in small public schools. (Enrollment in unapproved schools, which were kept in a separate category, increased about 11 per cent, but these schools are relatively small, so the expansion does not affect overall figures much.) An average of one new law school has been opened in each of the past ten years.

Extending these trends into the future, and assuming that one-third of the unapproved schools will become approved, we find that law school facilities will accommodate 119,000 students in 1980—10,000 fewer than called for by the low projection of student demand, and 40,000 to 45,000 fewer than called for by the high projection—a level of enrollment that would, with a continuation of the present rates of expansion (and attrition) of law schools, produce about 25,000 to 26,000 graduates a year from a total enrollment of 119,000.

Means of Accommodating Student Demand

How can these differences between potential student demand and expected institutional growth be resolved? One means would be simply to raise standards for admission, thus diverting the students into other fields. Men entering law school are already substantially more select than the average male graduate student, though law schools vary greatly in their selectivity, and some accept students who have very low academic attainment. In an analysis of the 1961 National Opinion Research Center survey of college seniors, Seymour Warkov found that students entering the least selective law schools were below the all male graduate average in academic performance, although they had higher grades than men entering education or social work.[3] More rigorous entrance standards will undoubtedly be established by some schools, but the prospects for an overall rise in the average academic aptitude of law school students will depend more on what weaker schools are doing than on what the average and good schools do because the weak students are concentrated in the weaker schools. Moreover, raising admissions standards is a device that "solves" the student demand problem by refusing to accept it rather than by trying to accommodate it.

Another possible way of meeting the anticipated student demand is to expand existing schools at an even more rapid rate in the future than in the recent past. This growth would produce some very large law schools. The largest 35 would probably have more than 1,000 students each, and the largest 100 would each have 500 or more students. In the past the growth of large schools has been

---

[3] Warkov, Seymour, *Lawyers in the Making*, NORC Report No. 96, December, 1963. Law schools were divided into three strata on the basis of their selectivity as indicated by mean scores on LSAT. Then an Academic Performance Index (API) was computed for each stratum. The students in top-stratum schools scored 2.61; in middle-stratum schools, 1.98; and in bottom-stratum schools, 1.61. Although the top two strata contained only 24 schools (out of a national total of 135 approved schools), they enrolled more than half of the sample students. Data are taken from Table 4.2.

lower than that of small and medium-sized schools. Moreover, there are usually forces operating to slow the growth of any educational program when it gets very large. The likelihood that existing law schools will continue to increase in size for another 15 years at the rate they have increased in the recent past may be less than our projections have assumed and instead of accelerated growth, a decline may be a more reasonable expectation.

A third possibility for expanding enrollment would be to establish more new schools. Instead of launching the 18 new schools over the next 15 years as assumed in our projections, 35 to 45 might be launched to accommodate the potential student demand for enrollment. In the absence of more national concern over the supply of lawyers, however, it is extremely improbable that so many new schools will be added.

In short, none of these approaches seems likely to accommodate those students who aspire to careers in law. Limited institutional capacity means that actual figures on enrollment and degree output will probably be even lower than those indicated by the low projection of student demand.

Characteristics of Future Supply

If either the institutional capacity projection or the low student demand projection is achieved, however, the total number of lawyers will grow rapidly (see Table 4.2). Assuming that the present age-specific mortality and attrition rates remain constant, the number of lawyers will increase from about 266,000 in 1963 to from 457,000 to 493,000 by 1980. As a consequence, the number of lawyers per million population will increase from the current level of 140 to from 194 to 210 by 1980, and the number of lawyers per billion dollars of GNP (in constant dollars) will continue to decline from 460 to about 380 according to the institutional capacity projection and will decline to, then stabilize around, 400,000 to 410,000 according to the low student demand projection.

Analysis indicates that the real income of persons in the legal services industry (which includes lawyers in private practice and their secretaries and clerical help) will rise about 53 per cent in the 17-year period from 1963 to 1980 if the low student demand projection is realized, a figure almost identical with the projected rise in real income per worker (55 per cent) for the total labor force.[4] These projections demonstrate that a substantial future growth in the number of

[4] The legal services industry accounted for 0.42 per cent of the gross national product in 1951; this figure rose to 0.54 per cent by 1960, and to 0.55 per cent by 1963. (*The 1964 Lawyer Statistical Report*, American Bar Association, Chicago, 1965, p. 23.) There was about 16 thousand dollars of income per lawyer in the private sector in 1963; this figure includes secretarial and clerical income as well as that of the lawyers themselves. If the legal services profession's share of the GNP continues to increase at the same rate as between 1960 and 1963 (.003 per cent per year), and if the GNP projections of Table 4.3 are achieved, then the legal services industry would have $4.5 billion income in 1970, $5.8 billion in 1975, and $7.3 billion in 1980. If this total income is divided by the projected numbers of lawyers in private practice in each of these future years, income per lawyer (in 1962 constant dollars) would increase from $16,100 in 1963 to from $20,100 to $20,300 in 1970, to from $22,600 to $23,800 in 1975 and to from $24,700 to $26,600 in 1980.

lawyers could take place without any decrease in their relative income position. The actual level of income for lawyers might be higher than these projections if society's demand for their services grows more rapidly than the growth in the size of the profession. Since the factors discussed at the beginning of this section indicate that demand for legal service is likely to increase rapidly in the next 10 to 15 years, the relative income of lawyers (already above the average for all professional workers) is likely to improve even more between now and 1980.

So far we have dealt with the quantity of supply. Unless the legal education provided is of good quality, however, increases in mere numbers will be of little value. In 1964 there were still some 27 unapproved schools in the United States, enrolling 12 per cent of all law students and graduating 7 per cent of all lawyers. The legal education profession has been trying to get these schools either upgraded or eliminated. Their elimination would reduce the projected total size of the profession by 1980 by only 5,000 to 10,000, even if we assume that none of the students who attend unaccredited schools will enroll elsewhere.

Summary

In summary, the demand for persons with legal training is likely to be sufficient to absorb all the graduates that law schools can produce. Student demand for legal education will be at least as great and perhaps considerably greater than the capacity of law schools to accommodate the applicants. In the past law students have been a heterogeneous group, and law schools have admitted students representing a wide spectrum of abilities; it seems likely that these variable admission standards will continue. Some of the schools may become more selective, but there will still be relatively unselective schools, and they will probably experience the most rapid growth rates. The task of the legal profession is twofold; first, to improve the quality of the poorer schools that still remain, and second, to expand the number of opportunities for legal education at a faster rate in the next decade. Unless both quantity and quality of legal education can be increased, there will be unmet student demand for legal education, and unmet societal demands for legal services.

MEDICINE

One of the striking characteristics of the manpower situation in the medical profession is that the future supply of doctors is relatively easy to predict, but the demand for medical services is almost incalculable. As was the case with law, the demand seems capable of expanding indefinitely. Medicine has been the subject of public and congressional scrutiny for a number of years, but it remains a perennial "shortage" field. Stated simply, the situation is this: In the past, people wanted more medical service than was available; at present, they want more medical service than is available; and, undoubtedly, in the future, they will want more medical service than will be available. It seems to be a case of rising expectations that can never be completely fulfilled.

In part, this perpetual dissatisfaction speaks well for the value we place on health and the importance we attach to the doctor's part in maintaining it. In a sense, we can never have too much health or too many doctors.

But the statement of this ideal furnishes only the sketchiest framework for an analysis of manpower problems in medicine. In approaching these problems we must distinguish, first, between health goals and medical service goals and, second, between the number of physicians and the adequacy of medical services.[5] Health goals can be defined in terms of a goal of average length of life (such as an average life expectancy of 75 years), or in terms of the reduction in a particular cause of death (such as cancer). These goals can be achieved partly by better medical service, but safer highways, better diet, more medical research, and many other influences are involved. Medical service goals can be stated in terms of levels of diagnostic and treatment care; one dimension in assessing the adequacy of medical service is the accessibility or contact with a doctor, dentist, or other health service professional. Just as medical service is only part of the achievement of health goals, so access to or contact with a doctor is only part of the achievement of medical service goals. Further, access to a doctor is only partly determined by the doctor/population ratio. We use the doctor/population ratio as a measure when other measures are lacking, but its limitations should be kept in mind.

Nor is it easy to specify what our medical service goals should be. There is no generally accepted definition of "optimum," or even "adequate," service, and any definition will change as medical capabilities change. The level of service enjoyed by the more affluent in our population is often used as a pragmatic alternative; but it may not be very close to "optimum" in some more ideal sense.

We encounter further difficulties in attempting to translate medical service goals into manpower requirements. To do so, it is necessary to relate the goals to the average service provided by each doctor or to the services provided by specified subgroups of doctors—a complicated process in that the amount of service provided varies widely from doctor to doctor and the increasing specialization of the medical profession makes overall statistics, such as the physician/population ratio, somewhat irrelevant. In addition, the amount of service provided by the average doctor is changing now and will probably continue to change in the future. For all these reasons, it is not possible to determine precisely how much medical services will improve or decline in the next decade, but we can look at the trends and form some general impressions.

Output of Medical Schools

The output of medical schools can be projected with considerable accuracy to 1975. The number of new schools that will open in the next decade, their size, and the year that their first class will graduate are fairly well settled now

[5] For an extended discussion of these points, see Fein, Rashi, *The Doctor Shortage: An Economic Diagnosis,* The Brookings Institution, Washington, 1967, chap. 1.

(1968), since from the beginning of planning for the medical school to first graduating class, a minimum of 8 to 10 years is required and all the new schools that will produce any graduates by 1975 are already being planned now.

From 1950 to 1965 the number of graduates of American medical schools and schools of osteopathy increased about 32 per cent. Most of that growth occurred between 1950 and 1955; it slowed down considerably (to only 5 per cent) in the 1955 to 1965 period.[6] According to projections, the number will grow from 7,700 in 1965 to somewhere between 10,200 and 11,100 in 1975,[7] a 30 to 42 per cent increase of graduates in a decade (see Figure 4.1). These projected increases would produce about 88,000 to 92,000 additional M.D.'s and D.O.'s between 1966 and 1975; allowing for replacement requirements (approximately 44,000[8]), then the number of physicians would increase from the 1966 figure of about 305,000 to from 349,000 to 353,000 by 1975, a number sufficient to maintain the physician/population ratio at about 156 per 100,000 population.[9] Thus, it appears that the expanded graduate output of American medical schools will keep pace with population growth. If the physician/population ratio is to be improved, however, we must rely on the continued influx of foreign-trained doctors who become licensed and remain in the United States. If past trends continue into the future, this source of supply will increase the number of doctors for each 100,000 population to 164. Foreign-trained doctors have been a very significant source of supply in recent years. Since 1960 about a fourth of both internships and residencies in this country have been filled by foreign medical school graduates, who even in training make a significant contribution to the hospital staff's provision of medical services. Approximately 1,500 to 1,600 of these trainees each year in recent years are licensed to practice in the United States; about 200 of them are graduates of Canadian medical schools.[10] If we assume that the number of foreign doctors remaining in the United States for practice each year remains constant, then the total number of physicians would increase to from 366,000 to 370,000 and the physician/population ratio would increase about 8 points to 164. In other words, nearly all of the improvement in the ratio would be the result of the continuing inflow of foreign trained medical personnel.

Student applications for admission to medical school have been rising rapidly (see Table 4.5) since 1962, after a decade of relative stability. Since the number

---

[6] National Center for Health Statistics, U.S. Public Health Service, *Health Resources Statistics, 1965.* Government Printing Office, Washington, Table 76.

[7] The low projection is from the *Health Manpower Source Book,* Section 18, "Manpower in the 1960's," Government Printing Office, Washington, 1964, p. 38; the high one is from C. H. William Ruhe's "Present Projections of Physician Production," *Journal of the American Medical Association,* vol. 198, 1966, pp. 1094–1100.

[8] *Health Manpower Source Book,* Section 18, "Manpower in the 1960's," p. 40.

[9] This projection is consistent with Rashi Fein's analysis (in *The Doctor Shortage,* Table 3.9), although his figures include estimated graduates from foreign schools.

[10] Fein, Rashi, *The Doctor Shortage,* p. 87.

FIGURE 4.1 *Number of Graduates from Medical and Osteopathic Schools: 1950–1965, with Projections to 1975*

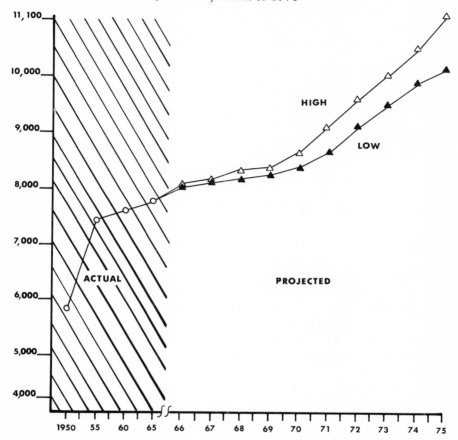

SOURCES: Actual figures from U.S. Public Health Service, *Health Manpower Source Book,* Section 18, "Manpower in the 1960's," Government Printing Office, Washington, 1964, Table 20; projections from C. H. William Ruhe's "Present Projections of Physician Production," *Journal of the American Medical Association,* vol. 198, 1966, pp. 1094–1100.

of college graduates is increasing rapidly, too, the potential number of medical school applicants will be even greater in the future. In 1960, medical school applicants constituted about 5.8 per cent of all male baccalaureate graduates; by 1965, the figure had increased to 6.1 per cent. If 6 per cent of the male baccalaureates of 1969 apply for admission, there will be over 28,000 applicants in that year. Even with the planned expansions in medical school facilities, spaces for medical school students are limited, and only about 10,000 freshmen could be enrolled in 1969; thus, the proportion of applicants accepted, which was three out of every five in 1962 and one out of every two in 1965, will

TABLE 4.5. *Applications and Acceptances to Medical Schools: 1952–1953 to 1964–1965*

First-Year Class	Total Applicants	Applications per Applicant	Accepted Applicants	Per Cent Accepted	Applicants per Place
1952–1953	16,763	3.4	7,778	46.4	2.16
1953–1954	14,678	3.3	7,756	52.8	1.89
1954–1955	14,538	3.3	7,878	54.2	1.84
1955–1956	14,937	3.6	7,969	53.4	1.87
1956–1957	15,917	3.8	8,263	51.9	1.93
1957–1958	15,791	3.9	8,302	52.6	1.90
1958–1959	15,170	3.9	8,366	55.1	1.81
1959–1960	14,952	3.9	8,512	56.9	1.76
1960–1961	14,397	3.8	8,560	59.5	1.68
1961–1962	14,381	3.7	8,682	60.4	1.66
1962–1963	15,847	3.7	8,959	56.5	1.77
1963–1964	17,668	4.0	9,063	51.3	1.95
1964–1965	19,168	4.4	9,043	47.2	2.12

SOURCE: Adapted from A.A.M.C., Division of Education, "Application Activity and MCAT Data of Applicants to the Class of 1964–65," *Datagrams*, vol. 7, October, 1965.

decline to one out of every three, unless the proportion of college graduates who apply to medical school drops.

With respect to the career choices of college students, medicine has increased slightly in popularity among freshman students recently; according to one study, in 1961, 8 per cent of the freshman men planned to be physicians, and in 1965, 9 per cent had similar plans.[11] But students tend to drop these plans during the four college years. Nearly half the 1961 sample who as freshmen had planned to be doctors named other career choices by 1965. The potential pool of applicants in 1969 is even more likely to have their plans frustrated, because there will be more of them, relative to the number of spaces in medical schools in 1969.

The rising number of applicants relative to the number of spaces available has led to a slight increase in the average ability of entering medical school students, with respect both to grades and to medical college admissions tests (see Figure 4.2). Ruhe has also shown that there is an inverse correlation between dropouts and the acceptances/applications ratio. When a large proportion of applicants are rejected, those who are accepted are more likely to finish.[12] Since more applicants are likely to be rejected in the future, the higher projections of graduate output in Figure 4.1 are based on the assumption that dropout rates are likely to fall.

The average undergraduate grades of medical students are substantially higher than those for all undergraduates who go on to graduate work, regardless of the quality of the graduate school they attend, with one exception: students who

---

[11] See Chapter 6 for a description of sample and detailed discussion of the career choice process.

[12] Ruhe, C. H. William, "Present Projections of Physician Production," Figure 2.

FIGURE 4.2 *Mean Medical College Admissions Test Scores (MCAT) of Accepted, Rejected, and Total Medical School Applicants, for Selected Years: 1952–1965*

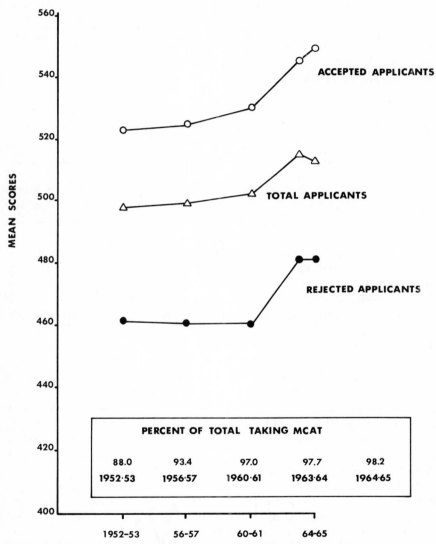

SOURCE: Adapted from American Association of Medical Colleges, Division of Education, "Application Activity and MCAT Data of Applicants to the Class of 1964–65," *Datagrams*, vol. 7, October, 1965.

TABLE 4.6. *Average Undergraduate Academic Performance Index Scores of Medical vs. All Other Graduate Students, by Overall Quality Rating of Graduate Institutions*

Quality of University	All Graduate Students		Medical Students	
	Number	Mean API	Number	Mean API
Top Quality Ph.D.	1,512	2.49	129	2.68
High-Medium Quality Ph.D.	895	2.29	72	2.75
Low-Medium Quality Ph.D.	1,492	2.09	184	2.58
Low Quality Ph.D.	2,442	1.84	346	2.09
Non-Ph.D.	1,805	1.57	21	—
Total	8,146	2.00	752	2.37

SOURCE: Special tabulations by National Research Center for the Commission on Human Resources. The composite quality ratings of universities are based on weighted Cartter quality ratings. Mean not shown where there are fewer than 25 cases. For description of the API (*Academic Performance Index*), see Davis, James, *Great Aspirations,* Aldine Publishing Co., Chicago, 1964, Appendix 3. Data are for college graduates of 1961.

take up graduate work in physical sciences or social sciences at the best Ph.D.-granting institutions[13] have better undergraduate records than the medical students who enter those same universities. But in all other comparisons with other fields in other universities in other categories of quality, the medical students are as good as, or better than, entering graduate students in other fields (see Table 4.6). Given these figures, it seems probable that the number of freshman medical student spaces, which are projected to increase about 40 per cent between 1964 and 1975, could be increased 80 to 100 per cent without any marked lowering in the academic ability of entering medical school students.

The Availability of Medical Services

As indicated earlier, the number of doctors relative to the total population is too gross a measure of the availability of medical services. Some doctors are in training (residents), others are retired, still others are engaged in research. To get a more accurate picture of the availability of medical services, we must look at the two groups who are most directly engaged in providing health services to patients: physicians in private practice and physicians in direct family service (general practice; physicians combining general and specialty practice, called limited specialty practice; pediatrics; and internal medicine).

As Table 4.7 indicates, these two groups have been decreasing in absolute numbers, thus becoming much less available, and the ratio of both specialists and generalists to population has also gone down slightly. If demand for medical services and the doctor's productivity remained constant for the next decade, the quantity of medical services would deteriorate slightly as a result of the declining ratio of physicians in private practice and physicians in direct family service. Neither demand nor physician productivity is likely to remain constant,

[13] See Fein, Rashi, *The Doctor Shortage,* chap. 2. This discussion relies heavily on his extended analysis.

TABLE 4.7. *Total Physicians, Physicians in Private Practice, and Physicians in Direct Family Service: 1955, 1965, and 1975*

	1955	1965	1975
Total Physicians	255,211	305,115	366,000
Physician-Population Ratio[a]	153	156	164
Physicians in Private Practice	169,871	190,748	214,000
Private Physician-Population Ratio[a]	102	98	96
Percentage in Private Practice	66.6	62.5	58.5
Family Physician Direct Service	114,550	106,837	100,000
Family Physician-Population Ratio[a]	69	55	45
Percentage in Family Practice	44.9	35.0	27.3

[a] Physicians per million population.

SOURCE: *Health Resources Statistics, 1965,* Tables 74 and 75. Physicians in direct family service include pediatricians, internists, general practitioners, limited specialists, and osteopaths. Figures for 1955 adapted from Rashi Fein's *The Doctor Shortage: An Economic Diagnosis,* Brookings Institution, Washington, 1967, Table III-4. Projections assume a constant rate of decrease in the percentage in private practice and direct family service.

however, and because these are the major determinants of the adequacy of medical services, each must be examined more closely.

Components of Demand for Medical Services

The demand for medical services is affected by a number of factors; some of these can be measured, and others cannot. Growth in population, which can be estimated fairly accurately, exerts a substantial influence on demand, and this part of demand is measured by the physician/population ratio. In the 1965 to 1975 period population growth alone will account for an increase of about 14 to 15 per cent in demand, and by 1980 it will lead to a 23 to 25 per cent increase. Rashi Fein identifies and discusses a number of other less easily quantifiable factors that influence demand. He uses patient visits to doctors as a measure of demand.[14] For instance, demographic and socioeconomic factors affect demand. Changes in the age-sex-color composition of the population, and in its rural, urban, and regional distribution, may lead to greater or lesser pressures for medical services. Older people and babies demand more medical care; nonwhites and rural residents demand less, even allowing for income differences. The effects of these demographic changes over a decade are relatively slight, however, because the composition of the population changes slowly, and because those groups that differ most widely from the norm in the extent to which they utilize doctors' services are the smallest. Demographic changes in the next decade will increase demand by only about one per cent, a very negligible impact.

Increases in the educational level of the population may increase demand another 1.5 to 2 per cent (more highly educated persons see the doctor more often), rising incomes might add 6 to 7 per cent, and Medicare legislation

[14] *Ibid.,* p. 87.

another one per cent. Taken together, these socioeconomic and demographic changes (apart from population growth itself) may boost demand 8 to 10 per cent by 1975.

Even more difficult to quantify is what Fein calls "potential demand," the demand that would exist if doctors were available to provide the service, and any attempt to estimate its magnitude ten years hence, under different conditions of practice and with higher levels of medical effectiveness, can be only the airiest speculation. Fein's illustrations of "shortage" problems suggest that potential demand could easily equal the additional demand associated with demographic and socioeconomic changes (that is, 10 per cent), and it might even be larger.

To meet, say, a 2 per cent increase in demand, about 45,000 more doctors than are projected for 1975 would be required, and that assumes that all of them would go into private practice. This figure is equivalent to the output of all of our medical colleges for five years. Moreover, these estimates are probably conservative. Projections of needs for doctors (that is, the number required to provide health care at some particular level or standard) and other assumptions about demand might produce even larger estimates of the number of additional doctors needed.

The important point here is that even though the estimates may be crude, the smallest of them is so large that we cannot expect to expand medical school output rapidly enough to make any dent in meeting this demand during the next two decades. Expanding medical education beyond the present planned growth is an expensive and essentially long-range solution; it will make no contribution toward alleviating demand by 1975, and very little by 1980.

The importation of foreign-trained physicians has been one way to increase the supply of doctors in the short run, and has supplied 15 to 20 per cent of the new licentiates in the past few years. But this method of meeting the demand for physicians has come under more and more criticism lately. The foreign doctor is usually needed even more in his own country than here, and if we encourage further increases in immigration by foreign doctors, we are likely to pay a high price in international ill will. The number of foreigners entering American internships and residencies seems to be leveling off, in any event, and the contributions made to this country by foreign-trained physicians may be balanced by the expenditures involved in our training foreign students in our intern and residency programs.

Increasing the Physician's Productivity

Our principal hope for improving medical services in the next decade is the possibility of further increasing physician productivity. Existing information is inadequate to give a picture of past changes in productivity, and provides an even shakier base for projection. Weiss, on the basis of constant dollar changes in health expenditures and shifts in occupational employment patterns, estimates that there was an increase of 50 per cent in the output of health services between

1950 and 1960. If this increase in output had not occurred, 21 per cent more doctors would have been required in 1960 to deliver the same amount of medical service.[15]

A number of factors contribute to increasing the productivity of doctors. One is more extensive use of auxiliary personnel—nurses, technicians, and assistants —to relieve the physician of routine tasks. Another is the group medical practice, which allows the doctor to concentrate on his specialty and use his time more efficiently. A third consists of such innovations as new drugs, technological advances in equipment, and other products of research that may speed up the doctor's services as well as improve their quality. Rashi Fein, reviewing a number of these possibilities, concludes that many of them have promise for increasing physician productivity, but that we do not know enough about their potential to measure precisely the effect of any particular change on future productivity, nor do we know enough to choose the combination of changes that will lead to the greatest increase in productivity.[16]

Moreover, there are forces that may work against increases in productivity. Many doctors work very long hours, and were they able to provide the same amount of service through one of the means just described, they might cut down on their working hours, thus canceling any gains in productivity. Changes in work patterns, such as those involved in group practice or increased use of auxiliary personnel, may be difficult to introduce among established practitioners who have limited incentives to adopt new methods.

If the estimate of an approximately 3 per cent annual increment in physician productivity during the 1950's is reasonably near the true increase and if these annual gains can be maintained through the 1965 to 1975 period, the effect on the availability in 1975 of medical services would be equivalent to the addition of 40,000 to 45,000 doctors working at today's average productivity levels. The potential importance of improved productivity is so great, and the alternatives for increasing the supply so impractical or expensive, that a great deal of attention should be given to these possibilities.

Summary

Medical services have been in a state of perpetual crisis over the past few decades. Medical schools are unable to expand rapidly enough either to grant admission to all qualified applicants or, more important, to produce doctors in sufficient numbers. Whatever the forces operating to increase demand—population growth, demographic and socioeconomic changes, or the less tangible forces of rising expectations and higher standards—and however clumsy our efforts to estimate that demand, one thing is clear: the demand will increase, and we cannot expect to meet that demand just by adding more doctors who provide

[15] Weiss, Jeffrey, "The Changing Job Structure of Health Manpower," Ph.D. Dissertation, Harvard University, 1966, pp. 112–119.
[16] Fein, Rashi, *The Doctor Shortage,* chap. 4.

the same amount of service that the average practitioner provides today. It is imperative, then, that we turn our attention to making the average doctor more productive. Widescale investigation of methods for doing so is certainly called for. As compared with the cost of establishing one new medical school, the total costs of such a program of research and experimentation would seem to be a small investment.

ENGINEERING

Like law and medicine, engineering is virtually an all-male occupation. Indeed, it is the largest professional occupation for men, employing more than a million persons. As is true of many large occupations, it is very heterogeneous in composition: engineers range all the way from doctoral degree holders in research and development to persons with a high school diploma only. Although the term "professional engineer" is usually taken to mean the graduate of an engineering school, only about 56 per cent of the "engineers" in the 1960 Census had college degrees.[17] Almost a fourth of all "engineers" reported in the Census in 1960 had not attended college at all, a fact that underlines the continuing importance of practical experience as a route into engineering and at the same time indicates some of the problems involved in defining who is an engineer.

Engineering is also a rapidly growing occupation; the number of engineers by Census definition grew more than 80 per cent between 1950 and 1964, a figure just slightly lower than the 90 per cent growth in the same period for all professional workers. Because of this rapid growth of demand for engineers in the 1950's and early 1960's, and because there was neither a reserve of professionally trained women engineers who could be drawn back into employment nor an adequate supply of engineering bachelor's degree graduates, the demand had to be met by employing less well-educated men, many of whom had obtained their experience on the job. The short supply of bachelor's degree engineering graduates has been a matter of concern for a long time, but in spite of efforts to relieve the shortage, the number of engineering graduates grew only about two-thirds as much as the number of bachelor's degree graduates in other fields in the 1955 to 1965 period. Although starting salaries for engineering graduates are substantially higher than the average starting salaries for all male college graduates, persistent shortages of qualified engineers continue to exist.

The Shortage of Engineering Graduates

An examination of the major field and career choice patterns of students during the undergraduate years throws some light on the problem. At the ninth-grade level, nearly one-third of the male students say they plan to be scientists or engineers. But many change their minds during the high school years. In 1965 only 14 per cent of the male college freshmen entered engineering programs. Moreover, the attrition among engineering students is slightly higher

---

[17] Hansen, W. Lee, "Another Look at the Engineer Projections," 1966, p. 8. Mimeographed.

than the average for all college students; only about 12 per cent of the male college graduates of 1965 were engineers. In the process of educational sorting that takes place during high school and college, many more young men change their career choice away from engineering than change their choice to the field. (See Chapter 6.)

With respect to this situation, a committee of the American Society for Engineering Education stated: "Both the secondary school student and the general public believe that the profession of engineering demands top talent and great effort while it returns only medium income and status."[18] The committee added that entrance standards had risen and that the undergraduate curriculum had become more rigorous, and presented statistics showing that the percentage of entering engineering students who got a degree in engineering declined from about 63 in 1950 to 49 by 1959; the figure rose slightly to 53 per cent in 1965. Not all this attrition involves students who drop out of college permanently; a fair number transfer from engineering into other programs. The percentage of beginning engineers who graduated *in some other field* rose from 15 per cent in 1950 to 23 per cent by 1959.

The problem is not so much one of initially attracting more students to a career in engineering; at the beginning of high school, there are more than enough potential aspirants to fill all the demands projected a decade hence. Nor is the problem simply one of attracting better students; the students who enter engineering are drawn largely from the more academically able high school graduates. Therefore, it would seem that although attrition weeds out the unfit and the ill-equipped, many talented students are being lost, too. Rather, the problem is one of retaining a larger portion of the highly qualified students who enter the program. Whatever the causes of attrition—an overly rigorous curriculum, ineffective teaching practices, failure to hold the student's interest in an engineering career—engineering schools would do well to follow the example of medical schools, which have recently made intensive studies of factors affecting retention of students in their programs.

Since the evidence indicates that the number of students dropping out of engineering has grown in recent years, it is likely that the basic pressures which have limited the growth of engineering in the past will continue to operate in the future. There is some disagreement, however, on just how slowly the supply will grow. Figure 4.3 compares three different degree projections for selected years between 1966 and 1976. All three projections indicate that, while the absolute numbers of graduates will, of course, increase, engineering output will decrease relative to other fields; that is, the proportion of engineering graduates among all college graduates will decline. The U.S. Office of Education (OE) and the Engineering Manpower Commission (EMC) projections assume a sharper decline at the bachelor's level than does the Commission on Human

[18] Committee for the Analysis of Engineering Enrollment, *Factors Influencing Engineering Enrollment*. American Society for Engineering Education, Washington, 1965, p. 4.

96

FIGURE 4.3 *Actual and Projected Number of Bachelor's, Master's, and Doctoral Degrees in Engineering: 1955–1976 (figures in 000's)*

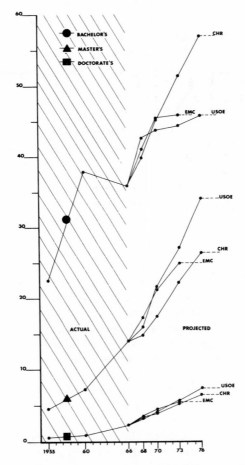

SOURCES: (a) U.S. Office of Education, *Projections of Educational Statistics, 1975–76*, Government Printing Office, Washington, 1966, pp. 31–35. (*USOE*). (b) Engineering Manpower Commission, *The Placement of Engineer Graduates, 1966*, Engineers Joint Council, New York, October, 1965, p. 18. (*EMC*). (c) Projections made by the Commission on Human Resources assume that bachelor's graduates in engineering will continue to decline as a percentage of all male degree recipients from 14.7 per cent in 1955 to 12.4 per cent in 1966, and 10.8 per cent in 1976. Master's degrees, which have increased from 19 per cent of the B.A. base in 1956 to 34 per cent in 1965, are projected to increase to 55 per cent in 1975; for doctorates, the comparable percentages of the base are 2.0 in 1958, 6.4 in 1965, 10.9 in 1970, and 14.8 in 1975. (*CHR*).

Resources (CHR) projection, which assumes that the declining trend will continue at the same rate as in the past ten years. The OE projection indicates that in the 1967 to 1976 decade there will be a total of 437,000 bachelor's engineering graduates, about 83,000 more than in the past decade, but 40,000 less than projected for the same period by the Commission on Human Resources.

Though growth at the bachelor's level may be relatively slow, the projections indicate a continued rapid expansion in graduate enrollments and degrees. According to the OE projection, the output of master's degrees will be three times as high in the 1967 to 1976 decade as it was in the preceding ten years (the OE projection is larger by about 43,000 master's graduates than the CHR projection), and the output of doctorates in engineering will be four times as high. Even the lower projection of the Commission on Human Resources indicates that about 60 per cent of the engineering graduates of 1975 will eventually earn an advanced degree. By the end of the next decade, graduate work may be as important in engineering as it is in a science like physics today.

Nevertheless, the prospects for meeting the demand for engineers at the bachelor's level are very poor. Even the most optimistic projections of engineering graduates fall short of the projected demand by a large margin; the additional engineering jobs will be filled, if at all, by persons without a college degree or a degree in some other field. The number of engineering jobs filled by people without an engineering degree will be determined by the extent to which the supply of engineering graduates will fall short of the demand, since there is no other source of supply. The National Science Foundation has estimated that about 61 per cent of the entrants to the field of engineering in the 1960's would be made up of engineering graduates, and about 39 per cent would be drawn from other sources (23 per cent would be people with no college degree, and 16 per cent would be graduates in other fields).[19] In a reanalysis of these data, Hansen has shown that if engineering employment in 1970 actually reaches the 1.37 million projected in the NSF study, then an additional 266,000 new engineers would be required during the decade over and above the projected output of engineering degree graduates.[20] In this eventuality, engineering schools would supply less than half of the new entrants during the decade 1960 to 1970. He points out that most of the engineers who did not having engineering degrees in the 1950 to 1960 period were drawn from among those who had no college degrees and that they would probably continue to be the main source of additional supply.

Estimates of the Demand for Engineers

A great deal of effort has been expended in the postwar years on trying to develop estimates of the future demand for engineers. Some people are highly

[19] National Science Foundation, *Scientists, Engineers, and Technicians in the 1960's: Requirements and Supply,* NSF 63–34.
[20] Hansen, W. Lee, "Another Look at the Engineer Projections."

skeptical of the effectiveness of these efforts; for example, a committee that studied engineering enrollment trends concluded: "Methods do not exist for making reliable and meaningful forecasts of demand for engineering graduates, whether long-term or short-term forecasts. If it is possible to develop such methods it will be at great cost. Both short-term and long-term forecasts are heavily biased by the economic condition existing at the time they are made. Accordingly forecasts have limited usefulness."[21]

In spite of this critical evaluation of demand studies, the Engineering Manpower Commission has conducted surveys of demand each year since 1951 and has also made periodic surveys of the placement of engineering graduates. These surveys, which focus on demand for engineers with college degrees or the equivalent, provide short-term projections based on employers' reports about current vacancies and plans for the immediate future.

The Bureau of Labor Statistics, with support from the National Science Foundation, has made longer range projections of demand for engineers, the most recent of which are based on overall projections of economic growth and employment and on the distribution by industry of that employment.[22] These projections give a useful picture of probable engineering employment under conditions of relatively full employment and sustained economic growth. Although the BLS estimates of engineering employment include a higher proportion of nondegree personnel among engineers than do the Engineering Manpower Commission surveys, which focus on demand for engineers with college degrees or the equivalent, the observed rate of growth in engineering employment in the 1960 to 1964 period is similar in both estimates.

Table 4.8 presents estimates of growth in the demand for engineers from 1960 to 1966 and projections of demand to 1975, based on the BLS projections. Engineering employment increased at a relatively low rate (3 to 4 per cent a year) in the 1960 to 1963 period, but accelerated to 6 to 7 per cent a year in 1964 and 1965 as a result of increased federal spending. For the decade from 1966 to 1975, the projections indicate employment will grow 4 to 5 per cent a year, a rate intermediate between the lowest and highest rates of the past six years. It is likely, of course, that demand will fluctuate in the next decade, just as it has in the past, because a large part of the *new* demand is generated by federal spending for research, development, and design work. The figures in Table 4.8 show the probable sources of supply for new engineers if employment is to reach the level of 1.59 million engineers by 1975. It was assumed that because of the relatively high level of demand and the above-average salaries

21 Committee for the Analysis of Engineering Enrollment, *Factors Influencing Engineering Enrollment, op. cit.,* p. 12.

22 Bureau of Labor Statistics, *Scientists, Engineers, and Technicians in the 1960's: Requirements and Supply,* National Science Foundation, NSF 63–34; and Commission on Technology, Automation, and Economic Progress, *The Outlook for Technological Change and Employment,* Appendix to Vol. I, 1966. See Chapter 2 of the present report for a more complete description of the BLS model and of the assumptions upon which it bases its projections.

TABLE 4.8. *Projections of Demand and Supply for Engineers*

1960–1965 Estimated	
Growth Requirements (822,000 to 1,100,000)	278,000
Death and Retirement Losses	74,000
Transfer Losses	25,000
Total Requirements	377,000
Supply of Engineer Graduates (214,000 × .85)	182,000
Other College Graduates (est. 7,500 per year)	45,000
Noncollege Graduates Entering Engineering (by subtraction)	150,000
Total Supply	377,000
Percentage of College Graduates Among Entrants	60
1966–1975 Projected	
Growth Requirements (1,100,000 to 1,589,000)	489,000
Death and Retirement Losses	148,000
Transfer Losses	0
Total Requirements	637,000
Low Supply of Engineering Graduates (381,000 × .90)	343,000
High Supply of Engineering Graduates (457,000 × .90)	411,000
Other College Graduates (est. 10,000 per year)	90,000
Noncollege Graduates Entering Engineering: Low No. Grads.	204,000
High No. Grads.	136,000
Total Supply	637,000
Percentage of College Graduates Among Entrants: Low	69
High	79

SOURCES: Projections of employment from Commission on Technology, Automation, and Economic Progress, *The Outlook for Technological Change and Employment*; death and retirement rates and transfer rates, as well as supplies of other graduates entering engineering, from *Scientists, Engineers, and Technicians in the 1960's*, pp. 7–26. High supply of engineering graduates from Table 4.10, low projection based on higher attrition rates assumes .85 of engineering graduates during the period 1960 to 1966 are employed in engineering jobs in 1966; for 1966 to 1975 it is assumed that 90 per cent are employed in engineering jobs. Transfer losses are assumed to be zero in the 1966 to 1975 period. See text for discussion of assumptions. The 1966 employment estimate of 1.1 million was derived by applying the 1964 and 1965 employment growth rates in the Engineering Manpower Commission survey of demand in 1966 to the Bureau of Labor Statistics estimate of 975,000 engineers in 1964.

in engineering, the field will suffer no net transfer losses and 90 per cent of all persons graduating with engineering degrees will be employed in engineering in 1975. These rather optimistic assumptions will probably not be realized unless the high level of demand, with its attendant high salaries, continues.

The 1960 Census indicated that about 55 per cent of the people employed in engineering had attended four or more years of college; and according to the estimates for 1966 and the projections to 1975, the new entrants will have, on the average, only a slight educational advantage over those already in the field (see Table 4.8). About 60 per cent of the 1960 to 1966 entrants and 69 to 79 per cent of the 1966 to 1975 entrants will have college degrees. If such proves to be the case, the overall percentage of employed engineers with four or more years of college would increase only 5 to 10 percentage points (to 60 to 65 per cent) by 1975 (see Figure 4.4).

It should be emphasized again that the noncollege entrants are a residual group in our estimating procedure. If the number of engineers employed in the

FIGURE 4.4 *Actual and Projected Number of Engineers: 1960–1975 (figures in 000's)*

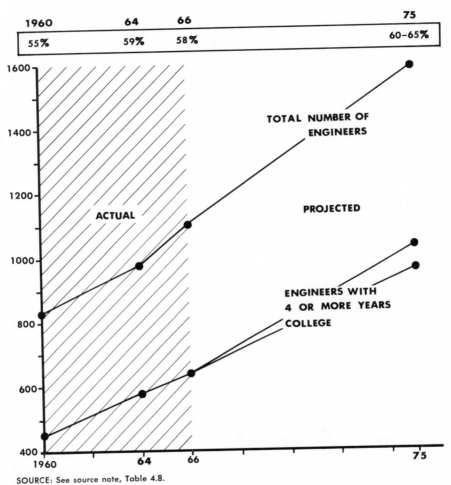

SOURCE: See source note, Table 4.8.

next decade falls short of our projection by about 200,000 (to a total of only 1.8 million), then nearly all the entrants will be college graduates, and the educational level of the occupation will be upgraded further. (Approximately 68 to 73 per cent of this smaller group of engineers would be college graduates.)

Although engineering, broadly defined, has in the past been able to draw on the supply of men who lack a complete college education, the increasing complexity of engineering problems may render this group much less useful as a source of extra manpower in the future. Without more solid information about changes in the skill requirements in specific engineering jobs, we cannot predict precisely how a continuing shortage of engineering graduates will affect the profession. It is possible that even the most highly complicated jobs can be so organized as to apportion those tasks requiring little skill or technical knowledge to persons who do not have degrees in engineering, thus freeing the engineering graduate for the more high-level tasks. The many engineering jobs in sales and management, too, might be filled by men who lack college degrees or who have degrees in other related fields.

But even if more efficient utilization of manpower is achieved in this fashion, it remains clear that, if the demand comes to within 10 per cent of the 1.59 million engineers projected for 1975, engineering graduates will continue to be in short supply. Moreover, this figure does not represent the maximum demand that can be anticipated. It is likely that if a larger supply of engineering graduates were available, the demand for them would expand. As with law and medicine, so with engineering: supply may create demand.

So far, we have been considering demand. If we turn our attention to need— the manpower required to achieve the national goals outlined by the 1960 National Goals Commission, we find that by 1975, over two million engineers will be required, or 440,000 more than was indicated in our demand projections.[23] In this light, the shortage of engineering graduates becomes an even more acute manpower problem.

Mechanisms for Redressing the Balance

What adjustment mechanisms are likely to operate in the future to take up the slack, so to speak, between the supply and demand for engineers? What steps might be taken to redress the balance? Two possibilities are open. The first is to increase the productivity of the engineer, thus assuring that the engineering services required will be delivered even though the actual number of engineering graduates does not increase to the desired level. The second is to increase the number of engineering graduates.

One of the means of increasing productivity—reorganizing specific engineering jobs so that the less skilled personnel take over the routine duties and the highly trained engineer can concentrate on the more complex problems—has already been touched on. Greater utilization of technological advances may offer another means of releasing the engineering graduate for more high-level duties. For instance, engineering computations, which occupy a large part of many engineering jobs, have been greatly speeded up by computers. Other new, unforeseeable innovations may make like contributions to increasing efficiency in the future. The BLS employment projections have an average increase in productivity per worker already built into them; if productivity per engineering

[23] Lecht, Leonard A., *Manpower Needs and National Goals for the 1970's*. Frederick A. Praeger, Inc., New York, 1969.

man year could be increased 2 per cent more than this average, the anticipated 1975 supply of college graduate engineers would be doing enough work to close the gap between supply and demand for engineering services, thus cutting down on the need to employ persons without a college degree.

Another trend that may further increase productivity is the increasing employment of persons with an advanced degree in engineering. To the extent that graduate training adds to skill and effectiveness, the engineering entrants of today and tomorrow should be more productive than those of the past. In 1955, about 20 per cent of the new engineering degree entrants had master's degrees, and about 2 per cent had doctorates; by 1965, a third had master's and 6 per cent had Ph.D. degrees. By 1975, over half the entering engineering graduates may have the master's degree, and about 15 per cent the doctorate. Assuming that the bachelor's graduate can increase his productivity 25 per cent through master's training and 50 per cent through doctorate study, then the rising educational levels alone will add about 7 per cent over the 1965 figure to the productivity of the average engineer entering in 1975. Since there are no good measures of the comparative productivity of engineers at different levels of degree attainment, those percentages are hypothetical. Nonetheless, it is reasonable to assume that graduate training increases the person's potential productivity.

Since these means of increasing productivity are difficult to assess quantitatively, the possibility of relieving demand simply by increasing the numbers of engineering graduates should not be overlooked. We probably cannot do too much more by way of attracting freshman recruits into engineering programs. Already the need for engineers has been publicized widely enough, and salaries and working conditions made attractive enough, that further efforts to provide incentives will net few gains. What can be done, however, is to make sure that, once in engineering programs, more students remain there until graduation rather than transferring to other fields or dropping out of college entirely. If it were possible to increase the output of graduates from the current level of 53 per cent of the entering student to approximately 70 per cent in five years, the output of engineering graduates in 1975 would be boosted approximately 30 per cent above the level of the CHR projections shown in Figure 4.3. If we could anticipate this high a retention rate for the entire 1966 to 1975 period, the number of engineering graduates entering engineering jobs would be increased by 110,000. This increase would greatly reduce the gap between demand and supply of engineering graduates.

How can the retention rate be increased? As was remarked previously, the difficulty is not lack of ability on the part of the entering students, who tend to be an academically bright group relative to entrants to other fields. It seems likely, then, that the difficulty lies in the engineering program itself. Attrition may be influenced by rigorous academic standards, inadequate faculty attention to students, or neglect of the undergraduate program by faculty who spend their time on graduate students and research. Whatever the factors, they deserve to be explored; at present, too little is being done, as the committee on engineering enrollments of the American Society for Engineering Education has remarked: "Very few engineering deans have hard facts concerning the reasons for drop-outs and transfers, and even fewer have indicated that they are planning to investigate the variables which may account for engineering attrition."[24]

The committee goes on to recommend both investigation and action to reduce attrition; we can hope that its report will be influential with the faculties of engineering schools.

Summary

Engineering, which had already received considerable public attention as a shortage field, has in the past made up for the shortage of engineering graduates chiefly through the mechanism of quality substitution: the employment of less well-qualified persons when qualified ones (in this case, engineering graduates) are not available. Projections indicate that demand will continue to grow, and there should be about 1.59 million engineers by 1975, and that, as far as can be predicted from recent trends, engineering schools cannot keep pace with this increase: there will continue to be a tight market for engineering graduates. Although various means may help to increase the average engineer's productivity and thus alleviate the strain, the surest method of bringing the supply into better balance with the demand is to increase the proportion of entering engineering students who obtain the bachelor's degree in engineering. Unfortunately, this manpower adjustment mechanism—since it involves making changes in the educational system—tends to work slowly and to be unwieldy, and the retention will probably not change fast enough to relieve shortages markedly within the next decade. But it is a useful long-range means, and well worth exploring further, if engineering is not to continue indefinitely in its present state of manpower disequilibrium.

ELEMENTARY AND SECONDARY SCHOOL TEACHING

Elementary and secondary school teaching is the largest professional occupation: about one-fifth of all professional workers are teachers in schools below the college level. In 1966–1967 there were slightly more than two million elementary (including kindergarten) and secondary school teachers in public and private schools, about 1,170,000 at the elementary level, of whom about 87 per cent were women, and about 850,000 at the secondary level, of whom about 46 per cent were women. While teaching has been a large profession for a long time, it has also grown every rapidly in the past decade (51 per cent), in response to the rapid increase in the school-age population and in the proportion of youth staying in high school to graduation.

The public has, in recent years, heard a good deal of fairly alarming talk about the "teacher shortage." It appears that the alarm is no longer justified,

[24] *Factors Influencing Engineering Enrollment*, p. 12.

that in the next decade, the supply will not only be equal to the projected demand for teachers, but also to the projected need, as defined by the National Goals Commission.

In this section, we will discuss why the supply of potential entrants is difficult to estimate, how the demand is leveling off in such a way as to produce a surplus of college graduates qualified to teach, what the effects of new educational programs may be on demand, what the characteristics of the group now entering teaching are, and how the forthcoming supply-and-demand situation may change the composition of the group.

Demand has three components: that resulting from the growth of enrollment, that resulting from replacement requirements, and that due to new programs. The first two can be projected quite accurately for at least a decade into the future. In the next decade school enrollment will grow more slowly (22 per cent), and so this part of the demand for teachers will be relatively small (see Table 4.9). The larger component of demand, about two-thirds of the total in the past decade, has been for replacement of teachers dying, or retiring either temporarily or permanently from teaching. One predominant characteristic of occupations that employ a high proportion of women is a high loss rate and thus a large replacement demand, primarily because women leave the labor force to rear families. Moreover, because occupations with large numbers of women employees often offer relatively low salaries, the loss rate for men is raised as well. In the next decade replacement demand, which is projected at a constant 8 per cent a year, will make up nearly 80 per cent of the total demand (see Table 4.9). However, replacement demand will fluctuate with employment conditions, although it is difficult to estimate these fluctuations. Death and retirement due to old age are stable components of replacement demand, but their combined influence makes up only about one-fourth of the 8 per cent total replacement rate. The remaining loss consists of people who enter other jobs, stop work for family reasons, are promoted to administrative positions, or go back to earn an advanced degree.

Most difficult to project is the third component of demand, the effect that new programs will have on future demand. How many more specialist teachers will be added? Will more teachers' aides and subprofessional workers be used, thus holding down the demand for college graduates? Will preschool nursery and kindergarten programs be expanded and made a part of the regular school program? Will new programs of compensatory education for disadvantaged children be launched? While we cannot answer these questions, we can identify the potential that some of these programs have for increasing the size of the profession.

If nursery school and kindergarten programs were expanded over the next decade, the proportion of the three-, four-, and five-year-olds enrolled in school could increase from 25 to 50 per cent of the age group,[25] and such expansion

---

[25] See Schloss, Sam, *Nursery-Kindergarten Enrollment of Children Under Six, October, 1965,* Government Printing Office, Washington, 1967.

TABLE 4.9. *Projected Demand for New Elementary and Secondary Teachers: 1959–1980 (figures in 000's)*

Year	Demand Filled by New College Graduates	Demand Filled by Experienced Returnees	Total Demand	For Enrollment Growth	For Replacement
1959	125	41	166	55	111
1960	134	44	178	63	115
1961	137	46	183	63	120
1962	146	48	194	60	134
1963	156	52	208	80	128
1964	158	52	210	75	135
1965	157	52	209	70	139
Projected					
1966	173	57	230	82	148
1967	170	56	226	70	156
1968	166	55	221	61	160
1969	158	53	211	46	165
1970	161	53	214	46	168
1971	161	54	215	45	170
1972	155	52	207	35	172
1973	157	52	209	35	174
1974	158	52	210	35	175
1975	158	53	211	33	178
1976	147	49	196	15	181
1977	135	45	180	0	180
1978	135	45	180	0	180
1979	135	45	180	0	180
1980	135	45	180	0	180

SOURCE: Projections of replacement needs from U.S. Office of Education, *Projections of Educational Statistics to 1975–76.* Enrollment growth projection from Commission on Human Resources and Advanced Education. Projections include the estimated effect of the Elementary and Secondary Education Act of 1965. Experienced returnees are projected at 25 per cent of total demand.

would mean that between 100,000 and 125,000 additional teachers would be required by 1975, depending on how much the birth rate declines. If the expansion of preschool programs took place at a regular pace, 10,000 to 12,500 additional teachers would be required each year during the next decade.

Improved compensatory education based on more intensive use of professional personnel in slum schools would add 50,000 to 75,000 teachers per billion dollars of added expenditures, depending on salary levels, the nature of the program, and so forth.

The Supply of Potential Entrants

The supply of potential entrants to teaching is more difficult to identify, because of the large numbers of married women employed, who may leave teaching to rear families and then return to jobs after their own children enter school. The returning teacher represents a major source of supply. In two Office of Education surveys in 1958 and 1960,[26] returning teachers constituted 27 and 34 per cent, respectively, of all newly hired teachers. Most of the beginning teachers in the 1963 follow-up NORC survey said they planned a career in teaching, even though they might interrupt their work to rear families. The actual "mix" of experienced returnees and new college graduates will depend on the competition and hiring practices of school systems in thousands of local labor markets; in some, the returning housewife may be the major source of additional supply. Therefore, the projections (shown in Table 4.9) assume that about two-thirds to three-fourths of the teachers who drop out of teaching before retirement will return about a decade later; these figures are consistent with past experience, which indicates that about a fourth of all newly hired teachers will be recruited from among experienced former teachers. If this experience holds true in the future and if the possible demand resulting from new programs is ignored, between 155,000 and 173,000 new college graduates will enter teaching jobs each year between 1965 and 1975.

The supply of college graduates prepared to teach is very large: about one-third of all college graduates in the past five years have been qualified to teach, although not all of them entered teaching directly. Of the college graduates of 1958 who were in the labor force in 1960, 21 per cent of the men and 59 per cent of the women were employed as teachers in the elementary and secondary schools.[27] The figures from the 1963 NORC follow-up of the 1961 college graduate class are very similar; 22 per cent of the men and 61 per cent of the women who were working were employed by a school system.[28] When the number of persons teaching two years after the B.A. is expressed as a percentage of the total college graduate sample—rather than of the total in the labor force— the figures are reduced, because many persons are still in school, are in military service, or have already become housewives. The two surveys are again quite comparable: the 1960 follow-up of 1958 graduates found 47 per cent of the women and 15 per cent of the men teaching full-time (27 per cent for the total); the 1963 follow-up of the 1961 graduates found 43 per cent of the women and 13 per cent of the men teaching full-time (25 per cent for the total).

So far, we have been considering the graduates who are teaching two years after the college degree. If we look at the proportion that enter teaching at some time or other, the figures are even higher: slightly more than one-third (Figure 4.5) of all college graduates in the early 1960's had some teaching

[26] Mason, Ward, and Robert Bain, *Teacher Turnover in the Public Schools, 1957–58,* U.S. Office of Education, Government Printing Office, Washington, 1963, Tables 11 and 15; and Lindenfeld, Frank, *Teacher Turnover in Public Elementary and Secondary Schools 1959–60,* U.S. Office of Education Circular No. 675, Government Printing Office, Washington, 1963, Tables 8 and 11.

[27] Bureau of Social Science Research, *Two Years After the College Degree,* Table 32, p. 46.

[28] Spaeth, Joseph, and Norman Miller, *Trends in the Career Plans and Activities of June 1961 College Graduates.* National Opinion Research Center, Chicago, March, 1965. Mimeographed.

FIGURE 4.5 *Ratio of Recent College Graduates Entering Teaching to Total Number of First-Level Degrees and Total Education Degrees: 1959–1980*

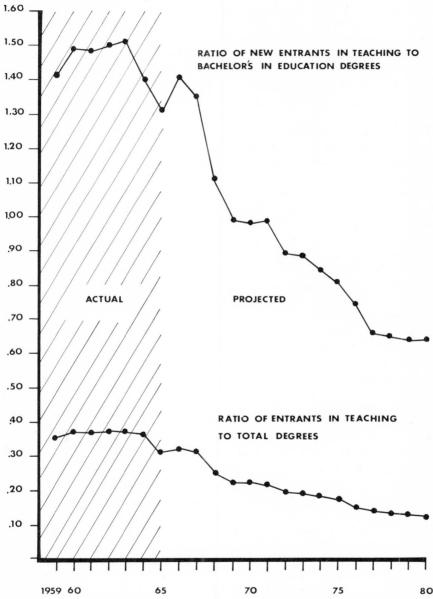

RATIO OF NEW ENTRANTS IN TEACHING TO BACHELOR'S IN EDUCATION DEGREES

ACTUAL   PROJECTED

RATIO OF ENTRANTS IN TEACHING TO TOTAL DEGREES

SOURCE: Commission on Human Resources projections of total and education degrees (see Appendix A). Projection of Education degrees assumes a decline in the percentage of men receiving education degrees from 10 to 8.5 by 1975 and a decline in the percentage of women getting degrees in education from 42 to 37 by 1975.

experience. The difference between the 25 to 27 per cent who were teaching two years after the B.A., and the one-third who had taught is made up of a small group of 2 to 3 per cent who left teaching after the first year to continue their education full-time (but will probably return to teaching), and a larger group who taught only one year (or a part of a year) and then left the profession. About 18 per cent of the women teachers and 13 per cent of the men teachers in the NORC follow-up were in the first-year dropout group. Since four out of five of the women teachers who quit at the end of one year of teaching were mothers, it cannot be assumed that these losses are all permanent.

The Slackening of Demand for Teachers

As the number of bachelor's degree graduates rises during the next decade, the proportion required to fill the demand for teachers will fall from about 33 per cent in 1966 to 22 per cent in 1970. By 1975 the comparable figure will be about 17 per cent and it will probably be less than 15 per cent by 1980. After 1970 the entire demand for new college graduates to enter teaching could be met by individuals who majored in education (Figure 4.6).

Since there are few studies that identify the differences in the preparation of persons with an education major as compared with other majors, and none that links degree field with teaching effectiveness, we cannot say what effect such an employment shift would have on the quality of teaching. Many people regard a decline in the employment of arts and sciences graduates in teaching as undesirable; they feel that the graduate in a subject field is likely to have a better background (especially for secondary teaching) than the education major. However, there is not much difference between the grades of education majors, and those of other majors (see Table 4.10), but grades are only a small part of the comparisons needed, and in our present state of ignorance about teacher quality, we cannot measure the effect of drawing all our teachers from among education majors.

The figures on the relative decline in the demand for new teachers recruited directly from college do not take into account the potential effects of new programs. These effects may be substantial; to illustrate, the Elementary and Secondary Education Act of 1965, according to the U.S. Office of Education estimates,[29] created an additional demand for 50,000 teachers in years 1965 and 1966, or about 12 per cent of all the teachers hired in those two years. If more new programs are developed or if substantial additional federal or state funds to hire additional teachers are made available, the short-run demand may be increased considerably.

Even so, future requirements for teachers are likely to be much smaller than the supply of persons planning a career in teaching. It is for women especially one of the most attractive opportunities to combine a career with marriage and

---

[29] See U.S. Office of Education, *Projections of Educational Statistics to 1975–76,* OE 10030–66, Government Printing Office, Washington, 1966, Table 22.

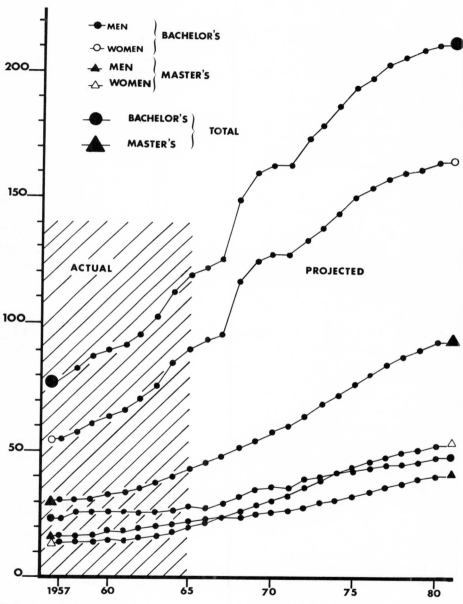

FIGURE 4.6 *Actual and Projected Number of Bachelor's and Master's Degrees in Education, by Sex: 1957–1980 (figures in 000's)*

TABLE 4.10. *Academic Performance Index of Elementary and Secondary Teachers as a Function of Sex, Undergraduate Major Field, and Entry or Departure from the Teaching Profession: 1962– 1964*

Level of Teaching and Entry or Departure	Men Education Major	Women Education Major	Men Other Major	Women Other Major
Secondary				
Stables	1.46	1.83	1.44	1.90
Total Recruits	1.61	1.86	1.54	2.11
Total Defectors	1.53	1.71	1.53	1.71
Recruits from Elementary Education	1.52	1.75	1.37	2.05
Recruits from Nonteaching Jobs	1.64	1.92	1.57	2.13
Defectors to Elementary Education	1.78	1.46	1.50	1.68
Defectors to Nonteaching Jobs	1.45	2.38	1.53	1.84
Elementary				
Stables	1.33	1.70	1.53	1.69
Total Recruits	1.56	1.53	1.39	1.79
Total Defectors	1.56	1.88	1.53	1.88
Recruits from Secondary Education	1.78	1.46	1.50	1.68
Recruits from Nonteaching Jobs	1.24	1.63	1.33	1.86
Defectors to Secondary Education	1.52	1.75	1.37	2.05
Defectors to Nonteaching Jobs	1.65	1.98	1.74	1.43

SOURCE: Special tabulations from NORC 1961 survey and follow-up of college seniors. The Academic Performance Index is a measure based on grades adjusted for differences in college selectivity. It has a range from a low of 1.0 to a high of 3.0.

family. Although a career in teaching is a second choice for many young men unable to qualify for entry to their first-choice occupation, they will change their career objective of teaching only when they can find a more attractive alternative that is open to them. For women, the alternatives will be defined by the working conditions as much as by the pay, while for the men, who are already relatively dissatisfied with the long-run pay prospects, higher pay may be the major attraction needed.

The prospect is that the personnel will be available and opportunities will be open to develop new educational programs for nursery school and kindergarten-age children, and for disadvantaged children who are unsuccessful in the present system. If we assume that nursery and kindergarten enrollment will expand as described earlier and that we develop new programs of compensatory education costing about a half billion dollars a year over a six-year period (for a total additional expenditure of about 3 billion dollars annually when the program is in effect), then a demand for about 40,000 to 50,000 *additional* teachers each year for the six-year period would be created. If all these teachers were drawn from the new college graduates, the proportion of college graduates entering teaching would decline from 33 per cent at present to 23 per cent in 1974. It would be possible to add an average of about 100,000 teachers a year between 1969 and 1975, over and above the normal demand for replacement and growth and to draw all of them from the new college graduate group without taking any larger proportion than have gone into teaching in the past six years. Without the additional demand generated by new programs, the number of teachers will increase about 22 per cent between 1965 and 1975; with the addition of about 600,000 teachers for new programs, the number of teachers would grow about 53 per cent between 1965 and 1975—about the growth rate, which, according to Leonard Lecht's study, will be necessary to achieve the national goals for education stipulated by the National Goals Commission. In elementary and secondary education, it appears that the overall manpower supply will not be a deterrent to the achievement of national goals.[30]

Even if the total supply is adequate, however, certain fields, certain geographical regions, and certain types of schools may experience shortages. Surveys made by the National Education Association show that there are big differences in supply of teachers for different fields, as well as big geographical differences in the distribution of teachers.[31] Increasing the overall supply relative to the demand may do little to resolve the problem of, for instance, inadequately prepared science teachers or of teachers unwilling to teach in slum areas. To reach a decision about the wisdom of expanding the teaching force by, say, 60,000 more than would be needed to meet normal demand, it would be necessary to know what kinds of alternative employment would be available to them. We do not have enough evidence to make reasonable estimates of how the learning of disadvantaged pupils would be affected if we employed from 50,000 to 100,000 additional teachers each year to work with them. Cost-benefit analysis could be applied to the question if we ever develop reasonably adequate estimates of the benefits associated with each additional teacher.

Characteristics of Persons Entering Teaching

It is possible to examine the characteristics of persons who enter teaching now and to make some estimates of how larger supplies of available graduates might bring about changes in the characteristics of teachers as a group. Unfortunately, we have no comprehensive measures of the quality of entering teachers: their knowledge of subject matter, their interest in and motivation toward teaching, and their effectiveness in working with students to promote their learning. The best that is available is a measure of their performance in college, called the Academic Performance Index (API), based on grades adjusted for differences in college selectivity.[32] This measure was used in the NORC survey of 1961 college graduates.

---

[30] Lecht, Leonard A., *Manpower Needs and National Goals for the 1970's.*
[31] See *Teacher Supply and Demand in Public Schools, 1966,* NEA Research Report, 1966–R16.
[32] The information on grades was obtained by the National Opinion Research Center in a survey of 1961 college seniors who were followed up for three years after graduation. Special tabulations of persons who planned to enter teaching, and who actually entered, were provided to the Commission by NORC. See Spaeth and Miller, *Trends in Career Plans and Activities of College Graduates,* for the sample and follow-up procedures.

People who entered teaching had lower grades in college than the people who entered other occupations. Female entrants to teaching had an average API of 1.80 as compared with 1.95 for all other women college graduates, while for men the average was 1.50 as compared with 1.70 for all others. Unpublished tabulations from the Bureau of Social Science Research 1963 follow-up of the 1958 college graduates indicated very little difference between the grades of women who entered teaching and those who did not, but confirmed the NORC survey finding that men who entered were academically inferior to other male college graduates.

There were few differences in the average grades of people who planned to teach and did, who planned to teach but did not, or who did not plan to teach but did (see Table 4.11). Those who changed their plans at the last minute had slightly lower average grades than those who carried through with them, but the differences were very small.

However, once in teaching, it was the brighter men who left the field, lowering further the average academic standing of the group as a whole. For women, the picture was not so consistent; in some cases, the women with lower grades left the field (see Table 4.10). There are few differences in the average API of arts and sciences majors and that of education majors. The largest and most consistent differences were between men and women and between elementary and secondary school teachers. Men who remained in elementary education had the lowest grades, while women who were recruited to secondary education after doing something else had the best academic backgrounds.

About one-third of the men who left teaching went back to graduate school. This group may have much higher API's than other male entrants to teaching, and some of them will probably return to the classroom, although it may be a junior or senior college classroom.

TABLE 4.11. *Academic Performance Index of Persons Who Planned to Enter Teaching, by Sex and Career Destination*

	Planned as Seniors to Teach, and Taught	Did Not Plan, but Taught	Planned to Teach, but Did Not
Men			
Academic Performance Index	1.51	1.50	1.47
Number	(1,517)	(429)	(159)
Women			
Academic Performance Index	1.81	1.79	1.76
Number	(3,001)	(439)	(131)
Total			
Academic Performance Index	1.71	1.65	1.60
Number	(4,518)	(868)	(290)

SOURCE: See Table 4.10. Figures in parentheses indicate the number of sample cases in each cell of the table.

TABLE 4.12. *Percentage of Persons Who Left Teaching Within Three Years, and Type of Post-Teaching Activity, by Sex, Family Status, and Level of Teaching*

Level and Destination	Single Women	Married, No Children	Mothers	Men
Elementary—Percentage Leaving	10.6	16.3	63.5	21.5
Destination—Total	100.0	100.0	100.0	100.0
Other Job	69.2	40.1	8.9	68.2
Student	30.8	5.1	5.6	31.8
Housewife	—	54.8	85.5	—
Secondary—Percentage Leaving	28.1	27.0	73.2	22.6
Destination—Total	100.0	100.0	100.0	100.0
Other Job	66.7	52.3	10.1	70.9
Student	33.3	13.9·	11.2	29.1
Housewife	—	33.8	78.7	—

SOURCE: See Table 4.10. Other job includes college or junior college teaching, but excludes other elementary or secondary teaching jobs.

Loss rates from the profession were high for both men and women in the first three years after graduation (see Table 4.12). The effect of these losses on the composition of the profession with respect to academic performance cannot be estimated precisely from a three-year follow-up, because some proportion of the men who returned to graduate school may go back to the elementary and secondary classroom after receiving an advanced degree (see Table 4.13). As long as these losses occur, however, becoming more selective in the choice of entering teachers seems a futile policy, since it may simply increase the rate of subsequent attrition among men, at any rate. Moreover, a policy that selected applicants for teaching positions on the basis of undergraduate grades would increase the proportion of women in teaching, and that, in turn, would increase the proportion of married women who will drop out of teaching, at least temporarily, to rear families.

These considerations raise a number of interesting social policy questions. The supply-demand equation indicates that some school systems that formerly

TABLE 4.13. *Academic Performance Index of Persons Who Stayed in Teaching or Who Left Within Three Years, by Sex, Family Status, and Level of Teaching*

Sex and Family Status	Elementary		Secondary	
	Quit	Never Quit	Quit	Never Quit
Men	1.47	1.37	1.68	1.52
Single Women	1.78	1.65	1.82	1.86
Married Women, no children	1.67	1.70	1.90	2.03
Married Women, with children	1.79	1.87	1.96	1.88

SOURCE: See Table 4.10.

were not highly selective will have an opportunity to raise their standards for entering teachers in the near future. The question arises, however, is selectivity based almost entirely on academic performance a wise policy? Is the person who made the best grades in college necessarily the best teacher? May not high academic achievement sometimes get in the way of effective teaching, particularly at the elementary level? What other, nonacademic, personal characteristics influence teaching performance? At present, we know too little about these questions to develop effective selection rules. More efforts are needed to appraise teaching effectiveness if we are to get enough information to develop social policies which will be effective in improving the quality of teaching.

Summary of Supply and Demand for Teachers

Teaching is one profession where the number of graduates prepared for entry will probably be more than adequate to the demand in the next decade. The favorable balance of supply to demand should focus attention on the problems of identifying and selecting the best teachers out of the number available. Instead of trying to attract more college students to careers in education or developing new techniques such as television to enable each teacher to teach more pupils (which would be appropriate responses in a shortage situation), attention should be directed to more discriminating selection. In the absence of measures of teaching effectiveness and systematic teacher evaluation and appraisal procedures by school systems, initial selection is likely to be the main method of controlling and improving quality. Study of selection procedures currently used by school systems, especially those relatively affluent suburban school systems that have always been able to choose among several applicants for each position, would provide a factual basis for estimating the kind of person who will be selected in the future if present policies and procedures are continued. Such a study might investigate, for example, whether experience is weighed more heavily than graduate education in choosing among candidates, whether college grades are weighed very heavily in selecting a new teacher, and whether men are given preference over women. The selection of effective teachers will be the major manpower problem facing the teaching profession in the next decade. To deal with it successfully, school administrators need a great deal more information about the nature of effective teaching and about how good teachers can be identified and selected.

THE SOCIAL WELFARE OCCUPATIONS

Social welfare is unique in that it is one profession in which most of the entrants have not obtained a degree in social work prior to entry to the job. Further, the structure of the profession itself promises to change rapidly, perhaps radically in the near future, as public interest in social programs grows. Finally, it shares many of the problems of other woman-dominated professions like nursing, librarianship, and teaching: local labor markets, a rapid turnover, and a large labor reserve. In this section, we will deal with the probable demand for social welfare workers, the profession's competitive position, particularly in relation to teaching, the characteristics of persons entering the field, and their training.

To begin with, the boundaries of the field are indistinct, and the available statistics inadequate to make them clearer. The narrowest definition might include only those professional social workers with master's degrees: about 40,000 people; the broadest might include clergymen, lawyers, labor relations workers, social workers, parole officers, prison attendants, and the clerical, technical, skilled, and unskilled workers associated with them: about 2 per cent of the total experienced civilian labor force. Neither definition is very satisfactory, the first because it excludes many people working at a professional level, and the second because it covers a heterogeneous group, over 60 per cent of whom are not working at the professional level.

The ideal definition depends on the purposes of the policy-maker, administrator, or research analyst. For our purposes we will concentrate on the 116,000 to 135,000 persons working in what the Bureau of Labor Statistics and the Census Bureau, respectively, identified in 1960 as professional-level jobs in social work, group work, recreation work, and a few other related specialties.[33] Before we take a closer look at these occupations, something needs to be said about the limitations of this kind of quantitative analysis.

In the field of social work both need and demand are hard to measure accurately. Changing concepts of demand and changing estimates of the social problems to which social work can make its greatest contributions will probably have a great deal to do with the magnitude of the need and of the demand for social workers.[34] Most of our social problems are so massive, and our resources for dealing with them so inadequate, that new approaches must be found. Social work is now developing such approaches. The answers that they arrive at and apply will have a major impact on future demand. If laws and social institutions are modified, many more social workers may be needed than can now be foreseen. If jobs are reorganized to make better use of the skills of social workers, demand may be altered in ways difficult to predict. In short, in this field, the past is likely to prove a very unreliable guide to the future.

Trends in Social Welfare Employment

With these uncertainties in mind, we can project current trends in welfare occupations into the future and compare the potential supply with the demand. Two points can be established rather easily. The first is that demand generated by new federal programs and by new public concern over social problems will

[33] For a comprehensive discussion of social welfare statistics, with comparisons of different estimates, see Szaloczi, Jean, "Some Conceptual Issues in Social Welfare Manpower Statistics," *Welfare in Review*, vol. 5, March, 1967, pp. 1–12.

[34] Department of Health, Education, and Welfare, *Closing the Gap in Social Work Manpower.* Government Printing Office, Washington, 1966.

increase very rapidly; according to one estimate, about 100,000 additional social workers will be required between 1964 and 1970—a growth rate of about 20 per cent a year.[35] Bureau of Labor Statistics projections indicate that, with a 4 per cent annual economic growth rate, social work employment will increase about 115,000 between years 1965 and 1975, and the total number of professional social workers will be about 330,000 in 1975. To achieve the national goals discussed by Leonard Lecht, an additional 90,000 to 100,000 would be required, for a 1975 total of about 425,000 persons employed at the professional level. These projections indicate very rapid rates of growth in the social work profession.

The second point is that most social welfare positions will continue to be filled by persons who lack a professional master's degree. The output of graduates from social work master's programs has been increasing at an average of 8 to 9 per cent a year since 1957, but even this rate of growth is barely adequate to keep up with the growth of the profession. If this rate of increase continues into the future, the percentage of master's graduates in social work occupations will probably remain stable at about 18 to 21 per cent between 1965 and 1975. Even if schools expand rapidly and stipend support is given to all full-time students enrolled in them, the proportion of social workers trained at the master's level is unlikely to rise above 24 to 25 per cent by 1975 (Table 4.14).

To summarize, shortages of personnel and difficulties in staffing positions with even minimally qualified persons will continue for at least the next decade.

The Competitive Position of Social Welfare

In addition to the supply of graduates available, an important determinant of whether new jobs can be filled is the demand in, and relative attractiveness of, the fields that compete with social welfare. The competing occupational groups include elementary and secondary teachers (the largest group), librarians, clergymen and religious workers, and some of the health professions. Demand in all the health professions will be very high during the next decade, and they may draw away potential entrants to social welfare occupations. The demand for librarians is also likely to remain high, but because it is a relatively small occupation (i.e., fewer than 100,000 persons), it will provide less competition than the health professions. The relatively slow increases in the numbers of clergymen and religious workers may improve the possibilities that potential entrants to this group will choose instead to be social workers. But it is probably from elementary and secondary school teachers that social work will have its greatest opportunities for attracting graduates. Though the demand for teachers will remain at about the same level to 1975 as it has been in the 1955 to 1965 decade, the supply of college graduates prepared for teaching will be much larger, especially in 1968 and after. Therefore, many college graduates planning teaching careers are potential candidates for entry into social work.

[35] *Ibid.* The estimate given is one of mixed need and demand.

TABLE 4.14. *Estimated and Projected Numbers of Social Work Students Enrolled in Professional Programs, and of Master's Degree Output: 1955–1975*

	1955	1960	1965	1970	1975
1. Number enrolled, past trend projection	3,644	5,136	8,400	11,900	16,400
2. Number enrolled, high projection	3,644	5,136	8,400	14,200	20,400
3. Number supported (unduplicated number of students)	2,700	4,300	7,300	12,800	18,400
4. Number with state and federal support	1,600	2,900	6,100	11,200	16,800
5. Percentage supported	74	84	87	90	90
6. Number of master's degrees, past trend projection	1,655	2,087	2,950	4,600	6,500
7. Cumulative total, previous five years	9,100	9,000	12,750	19,800	28,600
8. Number of master's degrees, high projection	1,655	2,087	2,950	5,300	8,000
9. Cumulative total, previous five years	9,100	9,000	12,750	21,200	34,400

SOURCE: Data for 1955 and 1960 from Council on Social Work Education, *Statistics on Social Work Education,* November 1, 1964. Data for 1965 estimated from estimated support and number of students in 1964. The past trend projection is an extrapolation of growth rates from 1958 to 1964. The high projection assumes larger numbers of student stipends. Degree projections are based on and consistent with enrollment projections.

How well social welfare does in the market will depend chiefly on its competitive position, with respect especially to salaries, working conditions, and student interest in and knowledge of the occupation.

The salary structures of the professional occupations that compete with social work are complex. Nationally, social welfare occupations pay about the same annual average salary for people with a bachelor's degree as teaching does. But the comparison is misleading: teachers usually work under more favorable conditions, and most of them work only 36 to 40 weeks for the same salary that social workers receive for 50 to 52 weeks. Moreover, welfare workers are more heavily concentrated in the North and West and in urban areas where living costs are higher. Unless the welfare jobs open to qualified poeple in specific locations can offer incentives comparable to those in other sorts of jobs in the same location, an overall increase in the supply of college graduates will not ease recruitment problems in places where they are most difficult. Social welfare occupations have both a national market and a series of local labor markets. Because about one-third of all social workers are married women whose husbands are also in the labor force, they cannot leave the local area. In short, national statistics may obscure the situation in local labor markets where one community may suffer extreme shortages, while another may have a relatively adequate supply of personnel.

The fact that most social welfare workers are women carries with it certain other problems involving a more rapid rate of turnover. In 1960 there were about 29,000 women who had worked in the social welfare occupations in the previous decade, but who were no longer in the labor force. This figure represents a labor reserve of about 48 per cent the size of the working group. By comparison, in nursing the labor reserve was 55 per cent of the size of the group of active nurses; the comparable figure for elementary teachers was 38 per cent, and for librarians, 37 per cent. For the subcategory of social welfare occupations called recreation and group work, the labor reserve was about two and one-half times the size of the active labor force; as apparently in this field, careers are short, and family responsibilities usually take the women out of recreation work permanently.

As is true in other occupations, conflict between work and family responsibilities is an important factor in the woman social worker's leaving employment, especially if she is trained only at the bachelor's level. Moreover, the statistics suggest that reentry to a career is more difficult for the married woman social worker than for the married teacher. Women social workers remain in the labor reserve longer and tend to be somewhat older than the nonworking teacher. Among working women, 58 per cent of the social workers in the 35 to 44 age group are married; for teachers, the comparable figure is 73 per cent. The differential in percentage married between teachers and social workers is about as great at younger and older ages.

If the potential for additional social workers represented by the women in the labor reserve are to be brought back into the labor force in any substantial numbers, flexible arrangements to facilitate combining a home and a career will be required. If the difference in the proportions of women teachers and of women social workers in the labor reserve can be taken as a measure of the extent that a teaching job is more adaptable to the requirements of family life, then modified job opportunities might be expected to attract almost one-fourth of the women who were formerly social welfare workers back into the labor force. This figure represents a potential expansion of about 12 per cent of the women in the occupation or about 7 per cent of the occupational group as a whole.

Even though the social welfare occupations do depend heavily on women to supply them, the percentage of men in social welfare occupations increased from 31 to 37 per cent between 1950 and 1960, and estimates for 1964 indicate that over 40 per cent of all social workers were men. However, a one-year follow-up of a sample of college graduates of 1961 found over four-fifths of the graduates who went into social work occupations directly after receiving the degree were women[36]—which provides additional evidence of the high attrition rate among women in the field.

As long as salaries remain low, it may be hard to increase the number of men

---

[36] Glockel, Galen, *Silk Stockings and Blue Collars,* NORC Report 114. National Opinion Research Center, Chicago, April, 1966. Computed from Table V.6.

in the profession much above present levels. For women more attractive and flexible working conditions may be more important than higher pay in inducing larger numbers to enter and remain in social welfare occupations.

While the establishment of more undergraduate curricula might focus attention on social welfare as an occupational area and might facilitate recruitment, the evidence that this will occur is inconclusive. It is clear that changes in salaries and working conditions will be required to bring about any fundamental improvement in the recruiting power of social welfare occupations.

Characteristics of Persons Entering Social Welfare Occupations

Several surveys have been conducted to collect information about the characteristics of persons entering social work occupations. One, the Glockel study, was especially valuable because it followed college seniors with career choices of social work for two years after graduation to see who went into social work and who dropped out.[37] This study found, among other things, that persons who had value preferences for people over things and who wanted to help others were drawn to social work, while people who scored high in leadership ability, creativity, and interest in money were defectors from the field. Persons with high college grades tended not to enter social work, and those of them who did enter were more likely to leave. The field recruits more women than men, more only children, and more Negroes than do other fields.

Men who planned careers in social work were especially likely to make lower than average grades; women social workers also scored lower than women entering many fields, and about the same as women planning careers in teaching (see Table 4.15).

The B.A. recipients with higher grades who were planning a career in social work were more likely to go directly to graduate school than were those with

TABLE 4.15. *Average Academic Performance of College Seniors, by Sex and Career Preference*

	Social Work	Social Sciences	Education	Other Fields
Men	1.44	1.88	1.49	1.70
Women	1.77	2.19	1.79	1.94
Male to Female API Ratio	.81	.86	.83	.88

SOURCE: Glockel, Galen, *Silk Stockings and Blue Collars*, NORC Report 114, April, 1966, Table 1.8. Academic Performance Index is based on undergraduate grades, weighted by estimated school selectivity. Index ranges from 3 (high) to 1 (low). Figures above have not been adjusted for differences in grading standards between fields, but an independent analysis suggests that social work, social sciences, and education have similar grading standards, and that the sciences, engineering, and business tend to give persons with equivalent aptitudes lower grades.

---

[37] *Ibid.* Glockel's study was based on the approximately 1,000 persons who chose social work as a career field in a survey of about 57,000 college seniors of the class of 1961. See also Pins, Arnulf, *Who Chooses Social Work, When and Why?* Council on Social Work Education, New York, 1963. Pins' study was based on a survey of all the first-year master's students in 1960.

low grades, but the graduate school entrants to social work still had lower grade averages than did entrants to graduate work in the arts and sciences.[38] The entering graduate students in the humanities, engineering, and the physical sciences had an undergraduate average (unadjusted for school differences) of about 3.3 (where 4.0 is an A), and those in the life sciences and behavioral sciences had an average of about 3.2, whereas social work entrants had an average of only 3.0.

Training in Social Work

One of the most striking characteristics of social work is that instead of making professional training a requirement for entry, it usually provides the major professional education to the person after he has entered the occupation, by allowing him to take leaves for graduate training and, often, subsidizing him. Only 16 per cent of the seniors in the 1961 NORC survey who identified social work as their career field had definite plans to attend graduate school the following fall, though another 12 per cent said they hoped to attend, a very low figure in a field which required a graduate degree for full professional status.[39] Only one-third of the entrants to graduate study in social work in 1963 came directly from undergraduate preparation (as compared with two-thirds of the entrants to arts and sciences fields), and another one-third had been out of college more than five years (compared with 10 to 15 per cent in arts and sciences fields).

The advantage of the educational leave system is that it involves people who have already selected and worked in the occupation and thus have a commitment to the field; such commitment should minimize turnover and loss of personnel. But deferred professional training has disadvantages too. First, it is an expensive system; the subsidies paid people already on the job are almost always higher than those required to attract students just out of college. Second, the average age of persons at the time of professional school graduation under this kind of system is greater, and their professional working life is shorter. Third, students whose occupational advancement depends on educational success are under a great deal of pressure to succeed (which may be good), and the graduate schools they attend are under some pressure not to flunk them. Such pressure may cause some marginal students to succeed who might not have if they had attended under different circumstances. Whether one regards this situation as good or bad depends on the relative weight one gives to the needs for a larger quantity of graduates as compared with a higher academic quality of graduates.

Despite the considerable financial support given for expanding graduate social work education in recent years, the proportion of all social welfare workers with graduate training has increased very little. Figures from the Bureau of Labor

---

[38] Warkov, Seymour, and Galen Glockel, "Career Choice of Undergraduate and Graduate Students: The Case for Social Work," Table 12. Paper given at conference on Research Approaches to Manpower Problems in Social Welfare Services, August 23–26, 1964, University of Minnesota.

[39] *Ibid.*

Statistics surveys and from the 1960 Census suggest that at that time about 20 per cent of all social welfare workers had a graduate degree, and another 15 per cent had a partial graduate education. As was mentioned earlier, this figure is projected to remain fairly steady to 1975. The educational level of social welfare workers as reported in the Census was quite similar to that of librarians, but substantially lower than that of secondary teachers, 53 per cent of whom have some graduate training.

The Council on Social Work Education's statistics on degree output indicate that slightly more than 18,000 persons had received master's degrees between 1950 and 1960. As indicated earlier, the number of active social workers with master's degrees increased by about 8,500 in the same period. If we assume that 2,500 of the graduates in the 1950 to 1960 period were needed to replace people who died or retired, then it took from 15,000 to 16,000 graduates to increase the size of the profession by 8,500. Either the surveys gave us a very defective picture of the profession's growth rate, or the rate of loss during the decade was exceptionally high. If the surveys can be taken at face value, the loss rate, including deaths and retirements, averaged about 8 per cent a year. In a stable population, such a figure means that the average career length is about 12 years; with such a career pattern, very large sums of money must be invested in training just to maintain present levels of professionalization among social workers.

Both the salaries of social workers and the training costs of their education are largely public expenditures. From the public point of view, therefore, it might be wiser to put more money into higher salaries and to reduce the proportion of funds expended on training.

Table 4.14 shows two projections of enrollment and degrees; the first, labeled "past trend projection," is based on the growth in enrollments and degree output in master's programs during the past decade; the second, labeled "high projection," indicates the number of enrollments and degrees that might be expected if all of the planned student support is forthcoming from state and federal sources. The higher level of enrollment may require that schools grow more rapidly than is consistent with recruitment of a well-qualified faculty.

If current projections of demand for social workers are realistic, then even if the high projection of degree output is achieved, and even if departures from the profession can be cut from 8 per cent a year to 3 per cent, little progress can be made in increasing the proportion of persons in the field who have master's degrees. In 1975 social work will still be a profession where only about a fourth will have the degree considered necessary for full professional status. Recognizing the problem, some persons have advocated greatly expanded undergraduate preparation in social work, partly to recruit students and partly to train them in the skills needed for specific jobs.[40] In view of the conservatism of our educational institutions in introducing new programs, it seems unlikely that such a

[40] Department of Health, Education, and Welfare, *Closing the Gap in Social Work Manpower.*

possibility will be realized. Moreover, we have no evidence that those who now enter social welfare occupations after graduating with baccalaureate degrees in the humanities, the social sciences, or education—the three areas from which most entrants to the field are currently drawn—are any less competent than baccalaureate graduates in social welfare would be. Nor do we know that undergraduate curricula in social work would be effective as a recruiting device. Until we have better information on these points, educational policy will continue to be made from an inadequate base.

Summary

Social welfare occupations are growing rapidly and will probably continue to do so during the next decade. The nature of professional tasks is also changing, so that precise estimates of future demand are very difficult, but it seems likely that at least 100,000 professionals will be added to the welfare occupations by 1975.

The supply of college graduates who might be attracted to social welfare occupations will be larger than in the past, but improvements in salaries and working conditions are necessary if a larger proportion of the potential supply is to be drawn into a career in the field.

The available evidence indicates that large numbers of persons leave social welfare occupations each year and that professional careers are relatively short. Until the transfer of men to other occupations and the loss of women from the labor force are slowed down, staffing problems will continue to be severe.

In spite of the large amount of public support for professional education in social work, the next decade's expansion of the numbers of persons with master's degrees seems unlikely to bring about much improvement in the proportion of persons in the welfare occupations who have master's level education.

The answer to personnel problems in social welfare lies more in improving working conditions and salaries and reorganizing jobs so that professionals can provide more service than it does in expanding graduate programs or developing undergraduate curricula. Educational expansion will be necessary, but not sufficient, to provide these occupations with adequately educated personnel.

NURSING

Nursing, the second largest professional occupation for women, presents several marked contrasts with the other professions examined in this chapter. It is almost entirely a woman's occupation, its educational and role requirements have been changing significantly, it must expand rapidly if it is to meet the high demand for nursing care, but at the same time it occupies a relatively unfavorable competitive position in the labor market.

Basic professional nursing programs are of three types: baccalaureate programs requiring four years of study in a college or university; three-year diploma

programs, generally conducted in hospital schools; and two-year associate degree programs, usually offered in junior colleges. In addition, there are shorter
training programs, as well as on-the-job training programs for practical nurses,
nurses' aides, and orderlies. This section will focus primarily on the professional
nurses, although the supply of and demand for auxiliary nursing workers will
also be briefly considered.

FIGURE 4.7 *Proportion of Total Nursing Graduates with Baccalaureate,
Diploma, and Associate Degrees: 1957–1966*

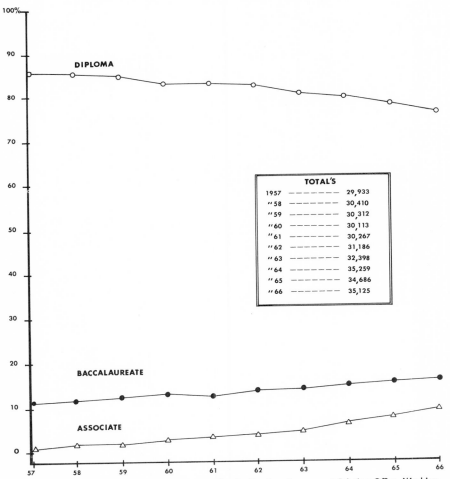

TOTAL'S		
1957	————————	29,933
''58	————————	30,410
''59	————————	30,312
''60	————————	30,113
''61	————————	30,267
''62	————————	31,186
''63	————————	32,398
''64	————————	35,259
''65	————————	34,686
''66	————————	35,125

SOURCES: U.S. Public Health Service, *Toward Quality in Nursing*, Government Printing Office, Washington, February, 1963, p. 62; U.S. Public Health Service, *Health Manpower Source Book*, Section 18, ''Manpower in the 1960's,'' Government Printing Office, 1963, p. 62; and unpublished figures from the U.S.
Public Health Service.

TABLE 4.16. *Students Admitted to Schools Offering Initial Programs in Professional Nursing Who Were Graduated, by Type of Program: 1964–1966, with Projections to 1968*

Year[a]	Total Graduates	Baccalaureate			Diploma			Associate		
		Graduates	Admissions 4 Years Prior	Completion Rate	Graduates	Admissions 3 Years Prior	Completion Rate	Graduates	Admissions 2 Years Prior	Completion Rate
1964	35,259	5,059	7,555	67.0	28,238	38,702	73.0	1,962	2,504	78.4
1965	34,686	5,381	8,700	61.9	26,795	38,257	70.0	2,510	3,490	71.9
1966	35,125	5,498	9,044	60.8	26,278	36,434	72.1	3,349	4,461	75.1
1967 low	36,819	5,835	9,597	60.8	26,555	37,936	70.0	4,429	6,160	71.9
1967 high	38,952	6,430	9,597	67.0	27,693	37,936	73.0	4,829	6,160	78.4
1968 low	39,630	6,244	10,270	60.8	27,726	39,609	70.0	5,660	7,872[b]	71.9
1968 high	42,527	6,881	10,270	67.0	28,914	39,609	73.0	6,732	8,587[b]	78.4

a Projections for 1967 to 1968 based on high and low completion rates of the 1964 to 1966 period.
b Estimated, based on high and low growth rates over prior three years.

SOURCE: Table 4.15 and American Nurses' Association, *Facts About Nursing*, American Nurses' Association, New York, 1966, p. 83.

Recent Trends in Supply and Demand

In the decade 1957 to 1966 the number of graduates each year from all these nursing programs combined increased from about 30,000 to more than 35,000. This is an average annual increase of approximately 2 per cent, or 20 per cent for the entire decade. The increase in the output of nursing graduates was among the lowest of any field; in the same period (1957 to 1966), for example, the number of women college graduates approximately doubled. Over this period the "mix" of graduates from the three types of programs changed, with the proportion of graduates from diploma programs declining from more than 87 per cent in 1957 to less than 75 per cent in 1966. The proportion with associate degrees, on the other hand, increased from less than 1 per cent to almost 10 per cent over the decade, while first-degree graduates of baccalaureate programs increased from 12 per cent to more than 15 per cent of all graduates over the period (Figure 4.7). Current admission statistics indicate that, over the next two years, these trends will continue. In 1968, between 39,500 and 42,500 new nurses will graduate, with almost 16 per cent originating from baccalaureate programs and approximately 15 per cent from associate degree programs (Table 4.16). In the 1970's the training facilities are likely to be increasingly outside hospital programs. These are the trends implied by the data in Figure 4.7 and Table 4.16. The rise in the number of available associate and baccalaureate programs, together with a decrease in the number of hospital programs, also suggests that the future supply of nurses will tend to hold associate and baccalaureate degrees rather than diplomas (Figure 4.8).

Over the 1956 to 1965 decade the number of nurses receiving more than one degree in the field also increased. The number receiving post-R.N. master's degrees about doubled, reaching 1,300 to 1,400 in the mid-1960's. Currently, however, fewer than 30 doctoral degrees are awarded annually; and in the past few years, the number of post-R.N. baccalaureate degrees awarded has stabilized at between 2,250 and 2,500 (Table 4.17).

TABLE 4.17. *Number of Degrees Awarded to Nurses Who Previously Received Professional Qualification: 1956–1965*

Year	Master's and Doctorate	Baccalaureate
1956	554	2,094
1957	728	2,123
1958	1,005	2,072
1959	1,101	2,301
1960	1,203	2,520
1961	1,020	2,456
1962	1,111	2,353
1963	1,162	2,319
1964	1,301	2,445
1965	1,404	2,254

SOURCE: American Nurses' Association, *Facts About Nursing.* American Nurses' Association, New York, 1966, p. 104.

FIGURE 4.8 *Number of Basic Professional Nursing Programs: 1957–1965*

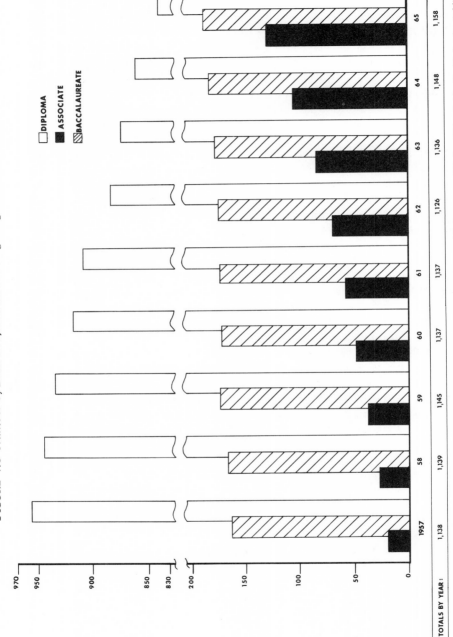

TOTALS BY YEAR:	1957	58	59	60	61	62	63	64	65
	1,138	1,139	1,145	1,137	1,137	1,126	1,136	1,148	1,158

SOURCE: U.S. Public Health Service, *Health Manpower Source Book, Section 2, "Nursing Personnel,"* Government Printing Office, Public Health Service Publication No. 263, Washington, January, 1966, p. 59.

The statistics suggest that nursing is becoming a less popular career. Although the absolute number of graduating nurses increased in the 1956 to 1965 decade, the proportion of high school graduates who subsequently complete nurses' training has, with some minor fluctuations, declined from a 1958 to 1960 high of 4 per cent to a 1963 low of 3.4 per cent. Between 1964 and 1966 this had leveled off to 3.5 per cent a year. In Table 4.18 two projections are given. The first assumes that the current rate of high school graduates who enter nursing will continue. Under this assumption by the year 1975 approximately 50,000 nurses will be graduating annually; by 1980, 55,000 will be graduating annually. The second projection assumes that an increasing proportion of high school graduates will choose nursing as a career. Such an increase based on the 1963 to 1966 trend and assuming a leveling off at 4 per cent, would require a

TABLE 4.18. *Number of Graduating Nurses Attaining First Professional Qualifications: 1958–1966, with Projections to 1980*

Year	Number of Female High School Graduates Three Years Earlier (000's)	Number of First-Degree Graduating Nurses (000's)	
		Low Projection	High Projection
1958	703		30.4
1959	739		30.3
1960	750		30.1
1961	784		30.3
1962	849		31.2
1963	966		32.4
1964	1,013		35.3
1965	984		34.7
1966	991		35.1
1967	1,167	36.8	38.9
1968	1,337	39.6	42.5
1969	1,319	41.9	42.9
1970	1,327	42.2	44.1
1971	1,358	43.2	46.0
1972	1,406	44.7	48.6
1973	1,464	46.6	51.7
1974	1,515	48.2	54.5
1975	1,556	49.5	57.1
1976	1,592	50.6	59.5
1977	1,632	51.9	62.2
1978	1,665	52.9	64.6
1979	1,682	53.5	66.3
1980	1,707	54.3	68.2

SOURCES: Data and projections of high school graduates from U.S. Office of Education, *Projections of Educational Statistics to 1975–76*, O.E.-10030–66, Government Printing Office, Washington, 1966, p. 25; number of nursing graduates from Table 4.15. Projections of new nurses for 1967–1968 from Table 4.16; for 1969–1980, based on number of high school graduates and prepared by the Commission on Human Resources. For assumptions, see text.

large but feasible expansion in training facilities.[41] But even if the higher projection were achieved, the annual number of graduates by the year 1970 will still be 10,000 fewer than the 53,000 which, according to the Surgeon General's Consultant Group on Nursing, would be a "feasible goal."[42] By 1975 the annual output would be 57,000, and by 1980 approximately 68,000.

The total number of nurses in practice increased from about 402,000 in 1954 to about 621,000 in 1966, an average annual increase of 4.5 per cent. The average net loss rate through death, retirement, separation from employment, and the failure of new graduates to enter employment has been less than 2.5 per cent over the period. Such a low loss rate, primarily the result of the large influx of former nurses back to the profession, often in part-time positions,[43] has had the effect of increasing the median age of employed nurses by more than three years between 1950 and 1960.[44] Although probably a short-term phenomenon, this unexpectedly low attrition rate has meant that most projections for recent years have been underestimates,[45] and that alternate models are likely to yield a closer approximation of the future supply of professional nurses.

Figure 4.9 shows two alternate series of projections of practicing nurses to 1980. The low projection assumes that the net loss rate will gradually increase to 4 per cent by 1970, thereafter remaining constant, and that the number of graduating nurses over the period will be the low projection as shown in Table 4.18. The high projection in Figure 4.9 is based on the higher estimate of output of nurses and assumes that the low loss rate (2.6 per cent) of the 1963 to 1966 period will continue to 1970, and thereafter will increase to the 4 per cent level by 1980. Under these sets of assumptions, we can expect from 688,000 to 716,-000 practicing professional nurses by 1970; from 767,000 to 846,000 by 1975; and from 858,000 to 982,000 by 1980. The higher projections would make it possible to achieve the 1975 employment requirement of about 830,000 nurses estimated by the Bureau of Labor Statistics for the National Commission on

---

[41] The Health Facilities Act of 1963 and the Nurse Training Act of 1964, which authorize funds for construction of nursing school facilities, are too recent to account for the increased number of graduates through 1965. In light of this fact, these programs may have the effect of making the higher series of projections possible.

[42] U.S. Public Health Service, *Toward Quality in Nursing*. Government Printing Office, Washington, February, 1963, p. 21.

[43] The number of part-time nurses in practice increased from 40,000 in 1950 to more than 130,000 in 1964. Reported in U.S. Public Health Service, *Health Manpower Source Book*, Section 18, "Manpower in the 1960's," p. 54; and unpublished figures from the U.S. Public Health Service.

[44] In 1950, the median age of female nurses in the active labor force was 35.4 years; in 1960, 39.1 years. Over the same period, the median age of employed male nurses had increased from 38.8 years to 40.4 years. See U.S. Bureau of the Census, *U.S. Census of Population: 1950*, Vol. IV, *Special Reports*, Part 1, Chapter B, Occupational Characteristics, Government Printing Office, Washington, 1956, pp. 69, 75; and U.S. Bureau of the Census, *U.S. Census of Population: 1960, Subject Reports, Occupational Characteristics*, Final Report PC(2)-7A, Government Printing Office, Washington, 1963, pp. 71, 81.

[45] For example, the *Health Manpower Source Book* estimated a net loss rate of 4 per cent annually. In 1966, however, the most recent year for which figures are now available, the number of nurses in active practice was approximately 621,000—as opposed to a projected *Source Book* figure of less than 590,000 derived four years earlier.

FIGURE 4.9 *Actual and Projected Number of Professional Nurses in Practice: 1954–1980 (figures in 000's)*

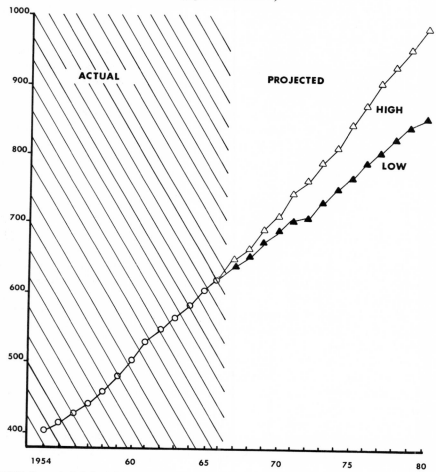

NOTE: Figures include both full-time and part-time nurses.

SOURCES: U.S. Public Health Service, *Health Manpower Source Book,* Section 18, "Manpower in the 1960's," Government Printing Office, Washington, 1964, p. 54; and unpublished figures from U.S. Public Health Service. Projections prepared by the Commission on Human Resources. For assumptions, see text.

Technology, Automation, and Economic Progress,[46] but would fall considerably short of the estimated 1,091,000 that are needed to achieve the health goals of 1975 identified in the National Goals Project.[47]

[46] National Commission on Technology, Automation, and Economic Progress, *The Outlook for Technological Change and Employment,* Appendix to Vol. I. Government Printing Office, Washington, February, 1966, p. 142.
[47] Lecht, Leonard A., *Manpower Needs and National Goals for the 1970's.*

Even under the more optimistic assumptions and projections, however, the anticipated future demand is likely to exceed the supply. In addition to the country's growing population and the increasing numbers of the very young and the elderly (the age groups most needing nursing care), the rising educational and economic level of the population, new federal programs for medical care, the expansion of medical services as a result of advanced medical technology and drugs, the increasing interest in preventive medicine, and a number of other factors will all work to increase demand. Consequently, the demand (the economic means to support employment of nurses) will more closely approximate the need for nursing care, which has been estimated at about 850,000 active professional nurses in 1970.[48] The number of available nurses will be between 135,000 and 160,000 less than these figures and will fall short of the numbers needed to achieve national goals in the year 1975 by between 245,000 and 324,000.

The Competitive Position of Nursing

Professional nursing is almost entirely a female labor market. In 1962 less than one per cent of all employed professional nurses were men, and over the past decade, only about one per cent of the annual enrollment in nursing schools were men.[49] In short, nursing must compete—through its salary scales, working conditions, and attractiveness of "image"—with other professions which employ a large proportion of women.

In general, because of the larger supply of women who will be available for professional occupations and because of the leveling off in demand for elementary and secondary school teachers in the next decade, nursing should be in a much better competitive position than it has been in the past. The demand for librarians and social welfare workers—two other occupational groups that compete for women—will remain high, but the small size of these professions (together they employ only about one-fourth as many women as does professional nursing) may reduce their competitive effect on recruitment of more women into nursing. The projected expansion of about 200,000 nursing jobs in the 1965 to 1975 decade could be filled, and the educational attainment of nurses could at the same time be upgraded considerably, if nursing attracts only one-third of the college graduates who formerly would have entered teaching, but who will not be needed in the next decade.

A number of recent social changes may increase the likelihood that women who make career choices will select nursing or some closely related profession. Among these are the increased subsidization for nursing facilities and nursing education, the greater awareness and emphasis on social services and medical aid, and the publicity that the mass media have given to personnel needs in the

[48] U.S. Public Health Service, *Toward Quality in Nursing*, p. 21.
[49] Computed from American Nurses' Association, *Facts About Nursing*, American Nurses' Association, New York, 1964, pp. 20, 100.

health professions. However, a number of other factors may militate against the probability that a larger proportion of women will choose nursing as a career. Relative to most other predominantly women's professions, particularly teaching, working conditions and salaries have been poor. Teachers work fewer weeks of the year, have working schedules that permit more satisfactory fulfillment of home and family responsibilities, and have in the past received greater compensation for their work. Even when working time is held constant, the major professions that attract women had higher salary levels than nursing did. In 1959, for example, in selected professional occupations, nurses had the lowest median income among women who worked from 40 to 49 weeks during the year. For secondary school teachers, the median income was $5,200; for elementary school teachers, it was $4,900; for librarians, $4,200; for social, welfare, and recreation workers, $3,700; and for professional nurses, $3,200.[50] In the past few years, however, nurses' salaries have been rising substantially, and the salary gap between nursing and other fields may be smaller.

Improvements in working conditions, and particularly in schedules, may also attract more women into nursing. In 1960, about 316,000 professional nurses who had worked in the previous decade were no longer working, a figure that represents about 55 per cent of the number of active professional nurses. By comparison, professional women in the labor reserve were 46 per cent of all working professional women. (See page 118 for comparable figures in other fields.) The statistics suggest that the conflict between work and family may be particularly acute for nurses. If the difference between teaching and nursing, with respect to proportions of women in the labor reserve, reflects the greater adaptability of a teaching job to the requirements of family life, then the modification of working conditions to make them comparable to teaching conditions might be expected to attract one-third of all professional nurses in the labor reserve back into the labor force. This figure represents a potential expansion of about three times the current annual output of nurses from nursing schools.

Greater opportunity for part-time work has helped to relieve the supply-demand imbalance. Over 130,000 nurses now work on this part-time basis—more than three times the number who were working part time in 1950. More efficient utilization of professional nurses and greater utilization of auxiliary personnel may also help to alleviate shortages. Only 60 to 75 per cent of the time spent by hospital nurses is at a level of activity commensurate with their training.[51] If auxiliary personnel were more widely used in hospitals for such tasks as making beds, keeping records, giving routine medication, serving food,

---

[50] U.S. Bureau of the Census, *U.S. Census of Population: 1960,* Final Report PC(2)-7A, *Subject Reports, Occupational Characteristics,* p. 234. Much of this income difference, however, may be attributed to educational differences. The median number of school years completed by women in the experienced civilian labor force in 1960 was 16.8 years for secondary school teachers, 16.4 for elementary school teachers, 16.2 years for librarians, 16.5 years for social and welfare workers, and 13.2 years for professional nurses. *Ibid.,* p. 123.

[51] U.S. Public Health Service, *Toward Quality in Nursing,* pp. 46–47.

and taking temperature, pulse, and blood pressure, the demand for professional nurses would substantially lessen. Since the supply of nurses has been increasing at a slower rate than the supply of auxiliary nursing personnel, this adjustment mechanism seems a sensible one. Between 1950 and 1962, for example, the number of employed professional nurses increased only 47 per cent, from about 375,000 to about 550,000, while employed practical nurses increased 64 per cent, from about 137,000 to about 225,000, and aides, orderlies, and attendants increased 85 per cent, from about 221,000 to about 410,000.[52]

Under the best conditions, if the previously discussed projections were fulfilled and if working conditions were improved to the point of decreasing the proportionate number of nurses in the labor reserve to that of teaching, shortages of nurses would continue to persist, at least in some communities and in some fields of service. As was true with social welfare, nursing constitutes a series of local labor markets rather than a national labor market, and married nurses stay in the locale of their husbands. Further, differences in salary and working conditions make for differences in the market for nurses in general hospital settings, psychiatric hospitals, schools, doctors' offices, private practice, and other sectors.

Summary of Supply and Demand for Nurses

In summary, the supply of nurses in the future will be greater than was anticipated at the time (1963) of the Surgeon General's Consultant Group on Nursing report. By 1970, if present trends continue, there will be about 700,-000 professional nurses in the labor force; and by 1980, between 860,-000 and 980,000. Further, since an increasing proportion of new entrants will come from nonhospital-sponsored programs, large numbers of nurses will have a four-year college background or a junior college education.

More efficient utilization of professional nursing personnel, which would require fuller use of auxiliary personnel, together with higher salaries and improved working conditions, also holds potential for increasing nursing services in the future. Over the next decade, however, demand for professional nurses will almost certainly continue to exceed supply, and within certain subfields of nursing and in some areas of the country, acute shortages may persist.

THE PERFORMING ARTS

Although the problems of the performing arts have received a good deal of attention in recent years,[53] performing artists have generally been ignored by manpower specialists. Their lack of interest is attributable, in part, to there being no apparent shortage of artists—indeed, many of them appear to be under-employed—and, in part, to the fact that even if a shortage exists in some artistic

---

[52] Computed from *Ibid.*, p. 58.

[53] For example, see Baumol, William, and William Bowen, *Performing Arts: The Economic Dilemma,* Twentieth Century Fund, New York, 1966; and the Rockefeller Panel Report, *The Performing Arts,* McGraw-Hill, Inc., New York, 1965.

fields, it does not affect the national economy or security in the way that a shortage of scientists or health professionals does. The lack of systematic attention to manpower issues in the performing arts is reflected in the paucity of data about the size and characteristics of the group. The Census, which provides the most extensive information about professionals in the arts, is the source of most of the analyses that follow.

Under the general heading of professionals in the arts, we have considered five occupational groups: actors, artists, authors, dancers, and musicians. The Census includes dancing teachers, arts teachers, and music teachers in these professionals in the arts are employed in educational activities. About 363,000 occupational groups, and slightly more than 40 per cent of all persons listed as persons were counted in these five groups in 1960, or a little less than 5 per cent of all professional workers in the United States. Designers, general entertainers, and photographers—a total of about 132,000 workers—were excluded from these analyses because they represent too heterogeneous a group of professionals and semiprofessionals in artistic and quasi-artistic endeavors.

The Status of Professionals in the Arts

The fine and performing arts differ considerably from the other professions considered in this chapter. First, formal education is not as important a criterion for entry as it may be in other professions, and as a result, professionals in the arts have, on the average, two years less formal education than professionals in general (see Table 4.19). As might be expected, authors attain the highest levels of education, and dancers the lowest.

Second, unlike other professions, in which unemployment is rare and part-time employment uncommon, the artistic occupations tend to employ people only part time (especially dancers and actors), and to have a high rate of unemployment: it was more than three times as great as the unemployment rate for other professions during 1949, and more than twice as great during 1959 (see Table 4.20).

TABLE 4.19. *Median Years of School Completed by Arts Professionals, by Sex: 1950 and 1960*

Occupation	1950		1960	
	Men	Women	Men	Women
Actors	12.8	13.2	14.1	13.1
Artists	13.0	14.4	13.7	15.1
Authors	15.7	16+	15.6	16.0
Dancers	12.5	12.5	12.5	12.5
Musicians	12.8	14.6	14.9	14.8
All Professional Workers	16+	15.4	16.3	15.7

SOURCES: (1) U.S. Bureau of the Census, *U.S. Census of Population: 1950*, Vol. IV, *Special Reports*, Part 1, Chapter B, Occupational Characteristics. Government Printing Office, Washington, 1956, Table 10, p. 107.

(2) U.S. Bureau of the Census, *U.S. Census of Population: 1960, Subject Reports, Occupational Characteristics*, Final Report PC(2)-7A. Government Printing Office, Washington, 1963, Table 9, p. 116.

TABLE 4.20. *The Employment Status of Male Arts Professionals: 1950–1960*[a]

Occupation	Weeks Worked, 1950					Weeks Worked, 1960				
	Did not work	1 to 13	14 to 39	40 to 49	50 to 52	Did not work	1 to 13	14 to 39	40 to 49	50 to 52
		(Percentages)						(Percentages)		
Actors	4.5	12.3	38.0	11.1	29.0	1.5	15.8	36.5	18.3	27.9
Artists	5.2	3.8	12.1	10.9	63.7	0.9	2.3	9.7	16.2	70.9
Authors	11.3	4.2	9.8	11.6	55.1	1.1	2.1	10.2	12.8	73.8
Dancers	5.9	4.6	29.4	18.3	37.3	2.2	8.1	26.3	26.3	37.1
Musicians	5.6	5.6	24.1	18.3	40.8	1.6	6.5	21.8	28.2	41.9
All Professional, Technical, and Kindred Workers	3.2	2.1	9.4	9.8	71.0	0.6	1.7	8.1	12.6	77.0

[a] Employment status in both 1950 and 1960 is based on "Professional Workers in the Experienced Civilian Labor Force," as defined by the Census Bureau. Table includes the employment status for only the male artists; Percentages for 1950 do not add up to 100 because the nonrespondents were not included.

SOURCES: (1) U.S. Bureau of the Census, U.S. Census of Population: 1950, Vol. IV, Special Reports, Part 1, Chapter B, Occupational Characteristics. Government Printing Office, Washington, 1956, Table 16, p. 159.
    (2) U.S. Bureau of the Census, U.S. Census of Population: 1960, Subject Reports, Characteristics of Professional Workers, Final Report PC(2)-7E. Government Printing Office, Washington, 1964, Table 5, p. 33.

TABLE 4.21. *Arts Professionals Employed, by Specific Occupation: 1940, 1950, and 1960*

Occupation	1940[a] Number Employed	"Employed" as Percentage of "Experienced Workers"	1950 Number Employed	"Employed" as Percentage of "Experienced Workers"	1960 Number Employed	"Employed" as Percentage of "Experienced Workers"
Actors	11,692	64.2	13,530	82.4	9,217	73.2
Artists	51,985	88.7	78,600	96.2	101,689	97.3
Authors	11,806	n.a.	15,390	97.0	27,476	97.3
Dancers	11,213	n.a.	15,120	94.0	19,813	93.3
Musicians	129,256	86.9	154,380	94.9	191,004	97.3
Total	215,952	n.a.	277,020	94.6	349,199	96.2
All Professional, Technical, and Kindred Workers	3,345,048	96.2	4,857,810	98.4	7,223,241	98.6

[a] In 1940, the number of experienced persons here employed is defined by the Census as "Employed Persons and Experienced Workers Seeking Work." The other numbers (for 1950 and 1960) are defined by the Census as "Workers in the Experienced Civilian Labor Force."

SOURCES: (1) U.S. Bureau of the Census, U.S. Census of Population: 1940, Vol. III, The Labor Force, Part 1, United States Summary. Government Printing Office, Washington, 1943, Table 59, pp. 81 and 83.

(2) U.S. Bureau of the Census. U.S. Census of Population: 1950, Vol. IV, Special Reports, Part 1, Chapter B, Occupational Characteristics. Government Printing Office, Washington, 1956, Table 1, p. 15.

(3) U.S. Bureau of the Census, U.S. Census of Population: 1960, Subject Reports, Characteristics of Professional Workers. Final Report PC(2)-7E. Government Printing Office, Washington, 1964, Table 10, p. 126.

The uncertainty of employment is associated with a much lower-than-average rate of growth in the number of employed persons in these occupations, as compared with other professional occupations. During the 1940 to 1950 decade these occupations grew less than two-thirds as rapidly as all professions, with only employment of artists keeping pace with trends for all professionals. In the 1950 to 1960 decade employment grew only half as rapidly in the arts as in all professions. The employment of actors actually declined about 30 per cent; only authors had an employment increase larger than the total for all professionals (Table 4.21).

Concomitant with higher unemployment and lower growth rates, the earnings of arts professionals increased a little more slowly than earnings of other professionals in the 1950 to 1960 decade. The earnings of men in the arts were 79 per cent of the average for all male professionals in 1950, and had risen to 81 per cent by 1960 (Table 4.22). For women arts professionals, earnings were only

TABLE 4.22. *Median Earnings of Arts Professionals: 1949 and 1959*[a]

Occupation	1949		1959		Men Median Percent-age In-crease 1949–1959	Women Median Percent-age In-crease 1949–1959
	Men Median	Women Median	Men Median	Women Median		
Actors	$3,260	$2,167	$5,662	$3,464	73.7	59.9
Artists	3,552	2,214	6,350	3,742	78.8	69.0
Authors	4,033	2,103	6,848	3,189	69.8	51.6
Dancers	2,385	1,347	3,362	1,780	41.0	32.1
Musicians	2,700	1,195	4,738	1,696	75.5	41.9
All Professional, Technical, and Kindred Workers	$3,494	$2,265	$6,846	$3,711	73.4	63.8

[a] The median earnings here for both years are based on "Professional Workers in the Experienced Civilian Labor Force," as defined by the Census Bureau.
SOURCES: (1) U.S. Bureau of the Census, *U.S. Census of Population: 1950*, Vol. IV, *Special Reports*, Part I, Chapter B, *Occupational Characteristics*. Government Printing Office, Washington, 1956, Table 1, p. 183.
(2) U.S. Bureau of the Census, *U.S. Census of Population: 1960, Subject Reports, Characteristics of Professional Workers*, Final Report PC (2)-7E. Government Printing Office, Washington, 1964, Table 10, p. 126.

66 per cent of the earnings for all women professionals, and they had declined to only 60 per cent by 1960. Thus, a small relative rise in the earnings of male artists was counterbalanced by a slightly larger relative decline in female artists' earnings. The important fact that emerges is that—despite the distorted image we have, because of the high earnings of a few leading authors and actors— relative to other professionals, the mass of artists are low paid.

The picture that emerges from these employment statistics is that of a slow-growing, underpaid, and underemployed group of professional fields, quite unlike the high-demand occupations examined in other parts of this chapter. Probably as a result of economic pressures, the proportion of women employed in the arts professions has been rising. In 1940 the arts professions had the same sex distribution as the total of all professional fields, 56 per cent men and 44 per cent women, but by 1960 only 51 per cent were men, compared with 62 per cent men in all professions.

Another aspect of the employment picture is that more professionals are being employed in educational settings and fewer in the recreation and entertainment industry. In 1950 about 37 per cent of all artists were employed in education; the figure increased to 43 per cent by 1960, with a parallel decline in the employment of artists in entertaining services (see Figure 4.10).

Projections of Future Demand

What is the future demand for arts professionals likely to be? Will the rising income and increasing leisure of our society lead to a resurgence in the arts, and to a greater employment demand in these fields? Or will the experience of the 1940's and 1950's continue with low growth rates and low earnings relative to other occupations? While no precise answers to these questions are possible, a reasonable range of possibilities is indicated in lines 2a and 2b of Table 4.23. The low projection is based on population growth and assumes also that the number of arts professionals per million persons will continue to rise slowly,

TABLE 4.23. *Growth of Number of Arts Professionals in Relation to Growth of Population and Recreation Expenditures*

	1940	1950	1960	1970	1975	1980
1. Population, July (in millions)	132.6	152.3	180.7	207	223	242
2. Number of Arts Professionals (in thousands)	216	277	349			
a. Low Projection				424	475	525
b. High Projection				510	600	690
3. Arts Professionals per Million Population	163	182	193			
a. Low Projection				205		217
b. High Projection				246		285
4. Recreation Expenditures (in billions)	7.70	13.47	18.95	31		47
5. Recreation Expenditures per Arts Professional (in thousands)	36	49	54			
a. Low Projection				73		89
b. High Projection				61		68

SOURCES: (1) Population from *Current Population Reports,* Series P-25, No. 345, July 29, 1966, Series B. Projection.

(2) Number of Arts Professionals from Census for 1940, 1950, and 1960 includes entire experienced civilian labor force. Low projection is based on continuation of 1950 to 1960 rate of increase in the number of Arts Professionals per million population. High projection is based on continuation of 1950 to 1960 rate of change in recreational expenditures per Arts Professional.

(3) Recreational expenditures are in 1957–1959 constant dollars. For the period from 1940 to 1960 recreational expenditures have ranged between 3.7 and 3.96 per cent of the GNP; they are projected at 3.88 per cent of GNP, the percentage in 1960 and 1965.

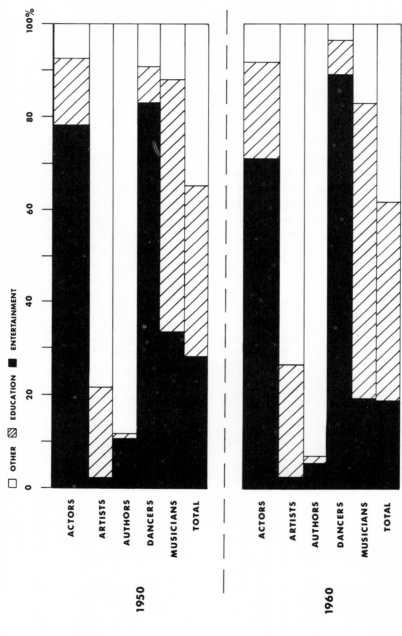

FIGURE 4.10 *Distribution of Arts Professionals, by Industry of Employment: 1950 and 1960*

□ OTHER ▨ EDUCATION ■ ENTERTAINMENT

NOTE: "Entertainment" includes TV and radio, movies and theaters, restaurants, night clubs, and hotels and lodges. "Education" includes educational services; "Other" includes advertising, miscellaneous professional and personal services, free-lancing, and other miscellaneous.

SOURCES: U.S. Bureau of the Census, *U.S. Census of Population: 1960, Subject Reports, Occupations by Industry.* Government Printing Office, Washington, 1963, Table 2, pp. 7–146. U.S. Bureau of the Census, *U.S. Census of Population: 1950, Special Reports, Occupations by Industry.* Government Printing Office, Washington, 1954, Table 2, pp. 12–75.

the rate of increase has been decelerating. Under these conditions, employment will increase about 21 per cent in the 1961 to 1970 decade, less than half the growth anticipated for professional occupations generally.

The high projection is based on the relation of arts professionals to expenditures for all forms of recreation, though this base is not entirely appropriate, since some forms of entertainment do not involve the services of artists. Nevertheless, it includes most of the expenditures for services by artists except educational expenditures, which support about 40 per cent of the artists. Recreational expenditures in constant dollars have increased rapidly—from about $36,000 per artist in 1940 to about $54,000 in 1960, although they represent a fairly stable proportion of GNP (ranging from 3.96 in 1950 to 3.88 in 1965). These rising recreational expenditures per artist, coupled with the slow increases in wage and salary income, indicates that proportionately more money is being spent for sports equipment, television receivers, and so forth. If this trend is projected to 1970 and 1980, recreation expenditures per artist will be $61,000 and $68,000, respectively. Under these conditions, there will be about 510,000 arts professionals in 1970, and about 690,000 in 1980, a rate of growth about equal to the projected growth rates for all professional workers.

While a growth in employment in the arts is possible on the basis of available economic resources, increases in expenditures for mass media entertainment (television, movies, radio, records, and so forth) may bring about a further decline in the proportion of entertainment expenditures used for the salaries of performing artists. The economic problems of the performing arts, which have been described in detail by Baumol and Bowen,[54] do not seem likely to change in a major way unless large government subsidies are spent on the arts.

Although none of the arts can be regarded as typical of the others, a brief account of the history of the theater over the past three decades indicates some of the problems in one artistic field. Internal changes in types of theaters, in number of productions per season, and in the average length of the run account in part for the decline in the number of persons employed in the theater. For example, the number of Broadway productions dropped from 264 productions in the year 1928 to 67 productions during 1965–1966,[55] although the total number of tickets sold did not vary greatly during the 1948 to 1966 period. Apparently, the drop in the number of productions per season has been compensated by longer runs and larger average audiences per production, resulting in steadier employment for fewer actors. The number of touring companies decreased from 560 groups in 1921 to 193 in 1960.[56] A slight countertrend can be found in the increasing number of resident theaters, from 8 in 1959 to 18 by 1964.[57]

[54] Baumol and Bowen, *Performing Arts.*
[55] National Council on the Arts, "Theaters and Community Art Centers," in *State and Local Public Facility Needs and Financing,* Government Printing Office, Washington, 1966, vol. 1, p. 595.
[56] *Ibid.,* p. 598.
[57] Baumol and Bowen, *Performing Arts,* p. 28.

The Supply of Graduates

Although a college degree is not a prerequisite to becoming an artist, the level of education for professionals in the arts has been rising, and possession of a degree will undoubtedly be more common in the future. Figure 4.11 shows the academic major of people who had graduated in 1958 and were employed in 1960 as writers, artists, and musicians. In each of the three fields at least one-fourth had majored in an unrelated field, and only about one-half were employed in the field of their major. During the decade 1956 through 1965 about 3.5 per cent of all bachelor's degrees were awarded in the fine arts (excluding architecture). If we were to include degrees in music education and art education, the percentage rises to about 5 per cent of all bachelor's degrees. It appears that the annual output of degrees in these fields has been relatively stable, in spite of the uncertainty of employment in artistic occupations.

However, the proportion of freshmen aspiring to careers in the arts increased between 1961 (5 per cent) and 1965 (6 per cent), and in 1966, slightly less than 7 per cent of a large national sample of freshmen aspired to artistic careers. Nonetheless, in 1960 only 1.5 per cent of college graduates of 1958 were working as arts professionals. Of those who had majored in the fine and performing arts, 18 per cent were working as fine and performing artists, while a much larger proportion (52 per cent) were employed as elementary, secondary, and college teachers.

If the 290,000 to 300,000 fine arts college graduates during 1960 to 1970 were to find jobs in the arts, they would represent an adequate supply for the high projection of occupational employment (about 510,000) in 1970, a projection that assumes an annual loss of 4 per cent. During the decade 1970 to 1980 an additional 425,000 to 475,000 graduates in fine arts are anticipated, a supply sufficient to provide for the high employment projection in 1980 and for an annual loss rate of 5 per cent. The relationships of anticipated output to growth and replacement demands are not greatly different from the actual number of arts and arts education degree graduates in the 1950 to 1959 period in relation to growth of the arts professions from 1950 to 1960. These figures are misleading, however, since only a small proportion of the college graduates trained in the arts (probably no more than one-fourth) actually became writers or performing artists, and new entrants to these occupations continue to be drawn in large part from people without college degrees, or with degrees in unrelated areas.

Summary of Supply and Demand for Performing Artists

Future employment in the creative and performing arts is difficult to project with any confidence. Although the increasing affluence and leisure of American society provide the potential for increased support of the arts, we cannot be certain enough about the tastes and interests of the American people to say whether the arts will actually receive this greater support. The technology of

FIGURE 4.11 *Undergraduate Degree Field of Arts Professionals*

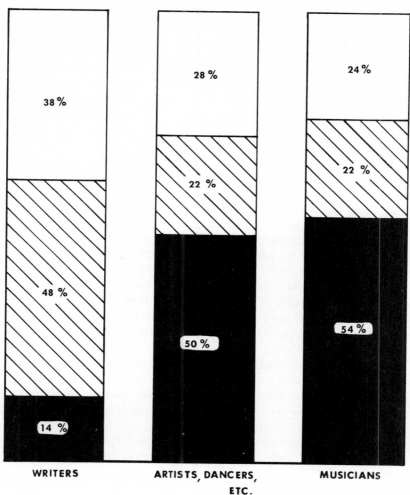

TOTALS: 238   127   67

☐ OTHER
▨ HUMANITIES
■ FINE ARTS OR MUSIC

SOURCE: Bureau of Social Science Research, *Two Years After the College Degree.* NSF 63–26, Government Printing Office, Washington, 1963, Table A–24.

the mass media, which has had a big impact on employment in the recent past, will continue to exert an influence on future employment. Under these conditions, the rather wide range between the high and low projections of employment demand represents the margin of uncertainty for these occupations. Employment in the educational sector of the arts will probably continue to increase, both numerically and as a proportion of the total. There has been no shortage of aspirants to jobs in the arts professions, but as in all other fields, the number of highly original, creative, and gifted performers is limited. No doubt the situation in the future will be the same as in the past, with more persons interested in careers in the creative and performing arts than can find employment in them.

SUMMARY

We have examined seven professional fields, which, along with college teaching and research and development examined in Chapter 3, employ roughly half of all professionals; about 65 per cent of all college graduates go into these fields. More important, these fields illustrate a variety of problems in balancing supply with demand in high-level occupations.

All but two of the seven fields (medicine and the performing arts) are growing more rapidly than is the average white-collar occupation (whose growth rate is about 2.75 per cent a year). Medicine has grown slowly because the professional educational system, which is the only route to entry into the profession, has expanded very slowly. The performing arts have grown slowly because the demand for creative and performing artists has been low; a minority of arts professionals are college graduates, and the colleges are turning out more than enough graduates to supply the field.

Of these seven fields, only in elementary and secondary school teaching and the arts does the output of colleges and universities appear to be adequate to the projected demand for graduates. In the arts fields, there is no evidence that a shortage of graduates has ever existed; in teaching, long considered a shortage occupation, the favorable supply-demand balance now developing will be clearly evident in three or four years. Law provides a special case: since law graduates can perform a wide variety of jobs, no good measures of demand exist. The supply in this field helps to create the demand. If there is a larger supply, they will probably all find employment; if fewer lawyers are produced, the jobs they now perform will be done in other ways.

The analysis of each profession indicates the importance of flexibility in adjusting manpower supply to demand. Every field has experienced periods of rapid growth or shortages of graduates, and each has used some substitute means so that necessary services are provided. These adjustments will continue to be necessary in the future, because of our limited ability to project either the trend of demand or fluctuations in that trend.

The professions analyzed here use different methods of adjusting supply to demand. Teaching and nursing draw former women workers back into the labor force in substantial numbers. The labor reserve of former teachers and former nurses is sufficiently large to provide for a rapid expansion of employment at times when demand is high, if working conditions permit the woman to combine family responsibilities with work. In addition, nursing has increased its supply of subprofessional assistants very rapidly—another method of balancing supply and demand.

Social welfare and engineering, on the other hand, have not adopted this adjustment mechanism; rather, they have met their manpower needs by recruiting persons with subprofessional educational qualifications into professional jobs. In part, the loose definition of the boundaries of these professions permits them to do this. If engineering and social work had more rigidly defined and enforced criteria for membership, they would be smaller professions, and they would have much higher numbers of subprofessional workers associated with them. But as long as engineering technicians can become engineers they will do so, and clearly identifiable engineering subprofessional groups may develop slowly.

Medicine has met the increased demand made on it by increasing the productivity of the average doctor, chiefly through greater use of subprofessionals and more efficient organization of tasks. It has also relied heavily on foreign-trained doctors in recent years.

One of the important features of our manpower supply system is the stability in patterns of degree output over time. In the short run, we have not been able to bring about sharp changes in the proportion of degree graduates in specific fields. Even so, the first thought of persons in a professional field who are confronted by an anticipated shortage is usually that degree output should be stepped up. However, other adjustments are usually quicker and easier to introduce than changes in the proportion of graduates in a field. A better understanding of these other means of meeting demand and of adjusting to short-run variations in demand is needed if manpower planning is to be effective.

Introduction to Section II

THE FIRST section of this report dealt with estimates and projections of the supply of persons with advanced education and the demand for such persons in various high-level professions. In this section we will consider some of the dynamics that help to determine the quantity and quality of that supply. In particular, the personal and background factors that influence the individual's educational progress, career choice, mobility, and professional achievement are explored. Whereas Section I was concerned chiefly with the overall manpower picture for the next ten or fifteen years, Section II inquires into some of the larger causal forces that operate in shaping that picture.

Of first importance in determining the number of highly educated persons who will be available in the future is, of course, the output of our colleges and universities. Chapter 5, "The Flow of Students Through the Educational System," describes how the system works to sort students at different educational levels and into different occupations. Three major stages of educational progress are defined: (1) the point of entry into college; (2) the undergraduate years; and (3) the point of entry into graduate school. Various factors—including ability, socioeconomic status and its correlates, interests, marital status, and so forth—are analyzed in an effort to assess their relative contribution to the student's decision to attend college (since it is at the point of high school graduation that most students drop out of the educational system), his persistence in college, and his decision to enter graduate school. Institutional characteristics—such as degree level, type of control, and selectivity—are examined to determine how they affect the student's educational aspirations and progress. In view of the possibility that the larger proportions of high school graduates now entering college may lower the overall quality of student bodies, the average ability level of today's entering freshmen is compared with that of freshmen in the past. And

144

finally, the chapter explores the important question of whether our national commitment to equal educational opportunity for all, regardless of socioeconomic background, constitutes a realistic and attainable goal.

Not only the overall supply of college graduates, but also their fields of specialization and their career choices, are significant factors in determining the available supply in particular fields. Chapter 6, "Career Plans of High School and College Students," draws from the work of vocational theorists and from analyses of high school and college students to examine the relative stability of career choices in relation to the career chosen and in relation to the characteristics of the students making the choices; recent changes in the popularity of various fields; and identifiable personal and environmental factors that play a role in influencing the individual's career choice. Although students manifest considerable changeability in their career plans during the high school and college years, certain patterns of choice can be predicted with fair accuracy; these patterns and their implications for the supply of talented manpower in various professions are investigated. Consideration is also given to what steps can be taken to recruit students into shortage fields and to how consistent such steps are with the traditional emphasis on free choice and self-determination in the United States.

Just as students frequently change their career plans during the college years, so college graduates continue to manifest considerable flexibility even after receiving the baccalaureate. Chapter 7 deals with various types of mobility exhibited by highly educated persons. The most obvious type, geographical mobility, raises questions about the gains and losses in high-level manpower incurred by the various regions of the country; migration patterns, their relations to the quality of the institutions attended, and their implications for the distribution of our "wealth" of highly educated persons across various areas in the country are therefore analyzed. Other types of mobility—including changes in major field between undergraduate and graduate school, changes in career field after the bachelor's degree, changes in areas of specialization, changes of employer, changes in work function, and changes from one job setting to another —are also discussed, inasmuch as these manifestations of mobility constitute an important and valuable mechanism in adjusting supply to demand in this country.

The nation needs more than just sufficient numbers of persons with the necessary advanced training for high-level occupations; it needs also productive people who will use their training effectively to make positive contributions to their professions. Chapter 8 takes up the subject of professional achievement and rewards (with respect to salary) for professional services. First, it analyzes the difficulties of evaluating performance and describes some of the measures often used as indices of productivity—and, in particular, the citation count, an index that seems to have considerable validity. On the basis of that index, the background factors and occupational factors that affect productivity are discussed. Finally, the chapter inquires into some of the probable determinants of professional income, finding relatively little evidence that salary is closely related to other measures of professional achievement. Although limited to scientists in certain fields, the chapter may have application to professionals in other fields as well.

As a whole, Section II attempts to analyze the larger forces that ultimately determine supply in different fields and to suggest those areas where more research is needed if our knowledge of the factors that influence educational and career choice patterns, mobility, and achievement is to be sufficient to allow manpower specialists and others plan more effectively.

5 The Flow of Students
Through the Educational System

THE COLLEGES and universities of the United States perform the dual function of educating students and of sorting persons for careers. As the college-educated become more sought-after for a wide variety of occupations, the sorting function becomes more important to our society. At the same time, because of the wide variety of our colleges and universities and the great diversity of our students, the process is very complex. This chapter reviews the ways in which our higher educational system sorts students for jobs, the points in the educational process where dropouts occur, and the personal and background factors that influence some students to leave higher education (or never to begin college) and others to continue into graduate and professional schools.

In the past most research has concentrated on the immediate transition from high school to college, and less attention has been given to the effects of ability, socioeconomic status, and other relevant variables on later educational progress. Using the Project TALENT five-year follow-up study, we have attempted to measure the influence of 38 different variables (organized into 10 broad groups; see Appendix B) on five aspects of educational progress: initial college attendance, attendance at a junior or a senior college, dropping out or graduating from college, attendance at a selective college, and graduate school attendance.

Specifically, we have attempted to answer the following questions: Who goes to college? Who goes to what kind of college? Who remains to graduate and who drops out? Who goes on to graduate school? How long does it take to complete graduate training?

ENTRY INTO COLLEGE

The beginning point of our examination is high school graduation. Prior to reaching this point, about one-fourth of the age group has already dropped out of school. However, the proportion dropping out has been decreasing steadily. Figure 5.1 shows the steady increase, which has averaged 1.5 per cent a year since 1955, in the proportion of the age group who graduate from high school. With the current emphasis on compensatory education and on the retention of

FIGURE 5.1 *Actual and Projected Proportions of Eligible Age Group Who Graduate from High School, by Sex: 1955–1975*

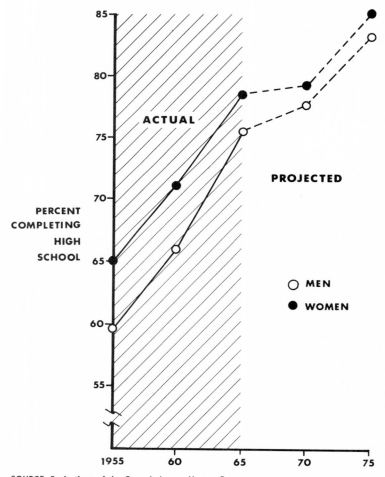

SOURCE: Projections of the Commission on Human Resources.

potential dropouts, there is little reason to suppose that this increase will level off in the immediate future, although it is likely to slow down, averaging about 0.8 per cent a year for boys and 0.6 per cent a year for girls through 1975. Nevertheless, even this lower rate of increase would mean that 83 per cent of the boys and 85 per cent of the girls in 1975 will obtain high school diplomas. In some states the proportion of the age group completing high school is already as high as the national average projected for 1975. Increases beyond this level might occur, especially if special curricula were developed for students who are unable or unwilling to stay in present programs. But even without new special programs, the vast majority of young people will complete high school, and future concern about talent loss and talent development will increasingly focus on education beyond high school.

Estimating Talent Loss

In the foreseeable future, as at present, more young people will leave the educational system after high school graduation than at any other point. In the period after World War II, with its heightened interest in problems of talent loss, a great deal of attention centered on the able high school graduate who did not go to college. This interest stimulated efforts to estimate the magnitude of talent loss, to understand its causes, and to reduce the loss.

One of the important early postwar estimates of talent loss was reported by the first Commission on Human Resources.[1] At that time it was estimated that only about 35 per cent of high school graduates go on to college; intelligence, grades, and a number of other factors were assessed as important influences on subsequent attainment. More recent studies show that higher proportions of high school graduates are now entering college, but these estimates vary because they employ different methods and different sampling procedures. Changes in dropout rates, reentry rates, and graduation rates are even more difficult to determine.

Some of the gaps in our information result from the diversity and decentralization of our educational system, so that different schools define terms like "full-time" and "part-time" student in different ways. Moreover, the progress of students through the educational system is often uneven, and therefore summary statistics on the number of students enrolled do not give an adequate notion of the *flow* of students.

There have been two basic approaches to estimating the percentage of high school graduates who go on to college. The first, based on actual follow-up studies of representative samples of high school graduates, has the advantage of permitting us to relate characteristics of individual students to the fact of college attendance or nonattendance, but it is not always possible to follow up students long enough to get a reasonably complete estimate of the number who eventually attend college. For example, Table 5.1 shows a number of estimates

---

[1] Wolfle, Dael, *America's Resources of Specialized Talent*. Harper and Bros., New York, 1954, Tables V.10 and V.11 and Table VI.3.

TABLE 5.1. *Estimates of the Percentage of High School Graduates Attending College the Year After High School: 1956–1965*

Study	Year of College Entry	Total	Men	Women
		(Percentages)		
National ETS-NSF Sample	1956	32	36	27
National Estimate	1956	37	41	32
Census Current Population Survey	1960	42	46	38
Project TALENT	1960	42	49	35
	1963	48	52	44
Bureau of Labor Statistics Surveys	1963	45	52	39
	1965	53	61	45

SOURCE: The National ETS-NSF Sample and the "National Estimate" are both reported in *The Duration of Formal Education for High Ability Youth*, NSF 61–36, Table 7. Government Printing Office, 1961.

The Census CPS estimate is reported in Census-ERS Series P-27 No. 32.

The Project TALENT data are reported in Chapter 10 of *The American High-School Student*, University of Pittsburgh, Pittsburgh, 1964.

The Bureau of Labor Statistics surveys are reported in U.S. Department of Labor, *Special Labor Force Reports*, No. 41 and No. 47.

of the proportion of youth going directly from high school to college. These studies employed different methodologies, different sampling procedures, and different follow-up procedures. (In fact, the Bureau of Labor Statistics surveys are not based on longitudinal data at all; they are national sample reports about activities of youth in the year following high school completion.) A large part of the variance in the results is due to differences in the surveys, but the data suggest that the proportion of youth going directly from high school to college has been rising about one to one and a half percentage points a year in the past decade.[2]

The second basic approach to estimating the percentage of high school graduates going to college is to compare the total number of high school graduates with the total number of entering college freshmen. Since each series of figures is subject to some reporting errors, and since the Korean and Vietnam conflicts have had some effect on the timing of college attendance, these estimates are also approximate. Because many students delay college entry beyond the first year after high school graduation, the actual proportion of high school graduates who eventually become college freshmen will be higher than the figures shown in Table 5.1. The figures in Table 5.2 indicate that the percentage of high school graduates going on to college has increased about 7 per cent for men and about 10 per cent for women in the last decade.[3]

[2] For a contrary view, see Jaffee, A. J., and Walter Adams, "Trends in College Enrollment," *College Board Review*, Winter, 1964–1965, pp. 27–37. This article, however, is mostly concerned with long-term trends rather than recent (1955–1965) experience.

[3] The smaller increase in the percentage of men going to college shown in Table 5.2 as compared with Table 5.1 is largely attributable to the fact that the proportion of all college

TABLE 5.2. *Proportion of High School Graduates Who Are College Entrants, and Proportion of Eligible Age Group Who Are College Entrants: 1955–1966*

Year	High School Graduates			Eligible Age Group		
	Total	Men	Women	Total	Men	Women
	(Percentages)			(Percentages)		
1955	45.9	56.5	36.1	28.6	33.9	23.4
1956	47.3	58.2	37.2	30.0	35.3	24.7
1957	47.6	58.5	37.6	30.3	35.5	25.0
1958	49.6	60.4	39.5	32.0	37.4	26.7
1959	49.5	60.5	39.3	32.9	38.6	27.2
1960	49.6	60.1	39.8	34.3	40.1	28.6
1961	51.6	61.8	42.1	36.0	41.6	30.4
1962	53.5	63.5	43.9	36.8	42.2	31.3
1963	53.6	63.0	44.6	37.7	43.1	32.3
1964	53.4	62.4	44.8	39.5	45.3	33.6
1965	54.6	63.5	45.8	41.3	47.3	35.3
1966	53.0	64.7	46.7	41.0	46.4	35.5

SOURCE: Based on comparisons between high school graduates of the preceding Spring and entering college freshment (first time in college) as reported in U.S. Office of Education *Projections of Educational Statistics to 1975–1976*, OE, 10030–66, Government Printing Office, Washington, 1966. The "Eligible Age Group" is a construct developed by taking the appropriate percentages of the 17, 18, and 19-year-old population.

Although estimates, both the direct follow-up of students and the trends in the aggregate statistics indicate that in the past decade the proportion of men going on to college has increased between .7 and 1.4 per cent a year and the proportion of women attending college has increased between 1.0 and 1.3 per cent a year. These trends seem likely to continue into the future, and adding these increases to the increases in high school graduates discussed previously, we can safely anticipate continued rapid growth in college enrollments. Three recent trend projections are shown in Table 5.3. Any of them could be realized, but the highest (that of the Commission on Human Resources) is indicative of the potential student demand in the coming decade. This potential demand may not be realized if external conditions (military, economic, or other) put constraints on attendance.

Institutional inability to expand and accept more students could possibly prevent the realization of enrollment potentials. In the more selective private col-

entrants who go directly from high school to college has been rising. In 1956, about 30 per cent of all the male college entrants had finished high school more than a year earlier; by 1960, this figure had decreased to 22 per cent; and by 1966, it was estimated at 15 per cent—only half the level of a decade earlier. The figures for 1956 were undoubtedly affected by the Korean War, although we have tried to eliminate the effects of returning veterans. The Vietnam conflict may have a similar effect in building up a backlog of future college entrants, although this trend may be counterbalanced by the war's influence in causing more young men to go directly from high school to college in order to benefit from a student deferment. For girls, only a small proportion (5 per cent) of those who ever go to college delay entry, although a decade ago the figure was larger (13 to 15 per cent).

TABLE 5.3. *Projections of Fall College Enrollment, Full-Time and Part-Time (figures in 000's)*

Year and Projection	Total	Men	Women
Actual—Fall of 1965	5,526	3,375	2,152
Projected—Fall of 1968			
Commission on Human Resources	6,720	4,058	2,662
Office of Education	6,923	4,184	2,739
Bureau of the Census	6,399	4,053	2,345
Projected—Fall of 1970			
Commission on Human Resources	7,589	4,583	3,006
Office of Education	7,299	4,350	2,949
Bureau of the Census	7,105	4,517	2,588
Projected—Fall of 1975			
Commission on Human Resources	10,158	6,053	4,105
Office of Education	8,995	5,218	3,777
Bureau of the Census	9,120	5,792	3,329

SOURCE: Projections by the Commission on Human Resources. These proportions assume a rise in the percentage of the age group entering college from 46 per cent in 1964 to 51 per cent in 1975.

U.S. Office of Education, *Projection of Educational Statistics to 1975–76*, OE-10030–66; and U.S. Bureau of the Census, *Current Population Reports*, No. 338, May 31, 1966, p. 25.

leges, enrollment growth may be limited by the institution's unwillingness to absorb the additional students. However, when we look at the total capacity of our higher institutions, the increase in the enrollment of all our higher educational institutions was 53 per cent in the 1962 to 1967 period, a figure considerably higher than that anticipated for the 1968 to 1973 period (35 per cent). Colleges are adjusted to accepting a rapid rise in student enrollment and can probably continue to grow as fast as student demand for entry requires them to grow. The major effects of the postwar baby boom will have been felt at the undergraduate level by 1968, and most of the enrollment growth in the remainder of the 1968 to 1980 period will come from the increased proportions of the age group who want to attend college. The *actual number* of additional students added to college rolls in the period from 1968 to 1975 (about 3.5 million) will be larger than the number added in the preceding seven years (3 million from 1961 to 1967); but, as indicated in Chapter 3, the numbers of faculty available to teach these additional students will expand even more rapidly. In short, total institutional capacity to expand is not likely to be a barrier to increased enrollments, although many students may not be able to enter the institution of their choice. If current enrollment trends continue, and if selective institutions continue to grow more slowly than the average, it may be even more difficult to get into these colleges a decade hence than it is at present. As a counter-influence, a number of additional colleges will probably adopt the same admissions standards as our currently most selective colleges. By 1975, if the changes in average selectivity observed in the 1952 to 1965 period continue, the number of highly selective colleges and universities will grow by 50 per cent, and admission to this larger group will probably be no more competitive than it is today.

The rising costs of higher education may thwart the college ambitions of some youth. The greatest unrealized potential for college attendance is among the poor students who rank in the top half of their high school graduating class academically (see below and Chapter 10). Our understanding of the forces that inhibit college attendance is inadequate for precise predictions about how much rising college costs may slow down enrollment increases. Youth who decide not to go to college usually are influenced by several factors in addition to inadequate finances. Since the largest share of future enrollment growth will presumably come from persons of lower socioeconomic background, low-cost access to higher education will be a more important factor in encouraging increased college attendance in the future than it has been in the past.

Factors That Determine College Entry

Out of the vast array of studies of the determinants of college entry and progress,[4] some consistent generalizations have emerged. Nearly all studies have

[4] There is copious literature of the 1940's and 1950's that examines these variables. A number of the references are cited in the following: Sewell, William H., Archie O. Haller, and Murray A. Straus, "Social Status and Educational and Occupational Aspiration," *American Sociological Review*, vol. 22, February, 1957, pp. 67–73; McDill, Edward L., and James Coleman, "High School Social Status, College Plans, and Interest in Academic Achievement," *American Sociological Review*, vol. 28, December, 1963, pp. 905–918; and Sewell, William H., and Vimal P. Shah, "Socioeconomic Status, Intelligence, and the Attainment of Higher Education," *Sociology of Education*, vol. 40, Winter, 1967, pp. 1–23.

A recent review of single factor studies is that by Robert H. Beezer and Howard F. Hjelm, *Factors Related to College Attendance*, OE-54023, Cooperative Research Monograph No. 8, U.S. Office of Education, Washington, 1961. Research in the past five years that has reported on these variables includes the following: Herriott, Robert E., "Some Social Determinants of Educational Aspiration," *Harvard Educational Review*, vol. 33, 1963, pp. 157–177; Berdie, Ralph F., and A. B. Hood, *Trends in Post-High School Plans Over an 11-Year Period*, Cooperative Research Project No. 951/SAE–8976, U.S. Office of Education, Washington, 1963; Turner, Ralph H., *The Social Context of Ambition*, Chandler Publishing Co., San Francisco, 1964; Astin, Alexander W., "Socio-Economic Factors in the Achievements and Aspirations of the Merit Scholar," *Personnel and Guidance Journal*, February, 1964, pp. 581–586; Sewell, William H., "Community of Residence and College Plans," *American Sociological Review*, vol. 29, February, 1964, pp. 24–38; Alexander, C. Norman, Jr., and Ernest Q. Campbell, "Peer Influences on Adolescent Educational Aspirations and Attainments," *American Sociological Review*, vol. 29, August, 1964, pp. 568–575; Bennett, William S., Jr., and Noel P. Gist, "Class and Family Influences on Student Aspiration," *Social Forces*, vol. 43, December, 1964, pp. 167–173; McDill, Edward L., and James Coleman, "Family and Peer Influences in College Plans of High School Students," *Sociology of Education*, vol. 38, Winter 1965, pp. 112–126; Elder, Glen H., Jr., "Family Structure and Educational Attainment: A Cross-National Analysis," *American Sociological Review*, vol. 30, February, 1965, pp. 81–96; Neubeck, Gerhard, and Vivian Hewer, "Time of Marriage and College Attendance," *Journal of Marriage and the Family*, vol. 27, November, 1965, pp. 522–524; Medsker, Leland L., and James W. Trent, *The Influence of Different Types of Public Higher Institutions on College Attendance from Varying Socio-economic and Ability Levels*, Center for the Study of Higher Education, University of California, Berkeley, 1965; Sewell, William H., and J. Michael Armer, "Neighborhood Context and College Plans," *American Sociological Review*, vol. 31, April, 1966, pp. 159–168; Barger, Ben, and Everette Hall, "The Interrelationship of Family Size and Socioeconomic Status for Parents of College Students," *Journal of Marriage and the Family*, vol. 28, May, 1966, pp. 186–187; Warkov, Seymour, and Andrew M. Greeley, "Parochial School Origins and Educational Achievement," *American Sociological Review*, vol. 31, June, 1966, pp. 406–414; Bayer, Alan E., "Birth Order and College Attendance," *Journal of Marriage and the Family*, vol. 28, November, 1966, pp. 480–484; Bayer, Alan E., "Birth Order and Attain-

found academic aptitude and previous school performance to be of prime importance, and also have found that sex and socioeconomic background play a significant role. Because a number of other variables have some influence, our analysis of the national sample of Project TALENT students who completed high school in 1960 necessitated a multivariate approach, in which each factor was studied while other variables were held constant. The results of this analysis are reinforced by findings from other studies. Roughly half the total variance in college attendance was accounted for by the 38 variables (a multiple correlation of .67 for men and .73 for women), about the same degree of correlation found in several other multivariate studies.

College commitment in the senior year of high school—a group of variables that include college plans, parental encouragement, and encouragement by friends—was most highly related to subsequent college entry and explained more of the variance in college attendance than any of the other variables. Other studies have also shown that college plans are an important predictor of actual college entry, a relationship that is not surprising. Commitment was not a good predictor of whether the person would remain in college or drop out ($R = .16$ for men, $.12$ for women), whether he would attend a selective or unselective college ($R = .12$ for men, $.06$ for women), or whether he would go to graduate school ($R = .05$ for men, $.03$ for women). If the high school students had been asked more specific questions about the kind of college they planned to attend and about whether they planned to go to graduate school, their answers might have been quite predictive; but just knowing whether they are planning to go to college does not help us much in predicting their educational progress after they enter.

The ability variables were also important predictors of initial college entry, and in the case of men, they were the best single predictors of the other points of educational progress. For women, educational progress after entry could be predicted about as well from marital and family status as from ability, and

ment of the Doctorate," *American Journal of Sociology,* vol. 72, March, 1967, pp. 540–550; Kriesberg, Louis, "Rearing Children for Educational Achievement in Fatherless Families," *Journal of Marriage and the Family,* vol. 29, May, 1967, pp. 288–301; Greeley, Andrew M., "Religion and Academic Career Plans," *American Journal of Sociology,* vol. 72, May, 1967, pp. 668–672; Flanagan, John C., and William W. Cooley, *Identification, Development and Utilization of Human Talents: Report of the Eleventh-Grade Follow-up Study,* Project TALENT Cooperative Research Project No. 635, University of Pittsburgh, Pittsburgh, 1965; Cooley, William W., and Susan J. Becker, "The Junior College Student," *The Personnel and Guidance Journal,* vol. 44, January, 1966, pp. 464–469; Nam, Charles B., and John K. Folger, "Factors Related to School Retention," *Demography,* vol. 2, 1965, pp. 456–462; Duncan, Beverly, *Family Factors and School Dropout,* Cooperative Research Project No. 2258, University of Michigan, Ann Arbor, 1965; Duncan, Beverly, "Education and Social Background," *American Journal of Sociology,* vol. 72, January, 1967, pp. 363–372; Rehberg, Richard A., and David L. Westby, "Parental Encouragement, Occupation, Education and Family Size: Artifactual or Independent Determinants of Adolescent Education Expectations?" *Social Forces,* vol. 45, March, 1967, pp. 362–374; Berdie, Ralph F., and Albert B. Hood, "How Effectively Do We Predict Plans for College Attendance?" *The Personnel and Guidance Journal,* vol. 44, January, 1966, pp. 487–493.

family factors were more important in predicting dropouts (R = .44 for family factors, R = .28 for ability variables).

Ability variables were more highly correlated with initial entry to college (R = approx .54) than with dropping out (R = approx .31) or going to graduate school (R = approx. .20 for both sexes); in fact, no aspect of subsequent educational progress was as closely related to ability as was the initial entry to college.

Socioeconomic background variables also exerted an independent effect, roughly one-half to three-fourths as great as the influence of academic aptitude, on college attendance and on college progress. Our analysis does not support the idea that socioeconomic influences operate primarily at the point of college entry, and that, once enrolled, the student's progress is primarily determined by ability. While the independent influence of socioeconomic factors was relatively small (partial correlation between .10 and .20 at most educational progress points), the effect of SES at the point of graduate school entry (partial correlation of .12) was almost as large as the relationship (partial correlation of .13) between SES and initial college entry.

All of the relationships of the 38 variables at the point of initial college entry are in Table 5.4. A large number of factors exerted small independent influences on college attendance and college progress, but—unfortunately for the educational planner and the policy-maker—most of them are very difficult to influence. Measured academic aptitude is the result of 16 to 18 years of interaction between native ability and a variety of school and nonschool educational environments; by the student's senior year in high school, it is a "given," hardly amenable to the manipulations of the planner. Variables such as ethnic-religious background, sibling position, or parental encouragement are completely outside the control of educational authorities.

Motivation to go to college, as revealed by college plans and by interest and temperament variables, is a more promising avenue for influencing college attendance. Although planning to attend college was affected by the same variables—academic aptitude, socioeconomic status, intellectual interests—that affected college attendance itself, when these influences are accounted for, the independent influence of "plans" was still substantial. Such plans are based, in part, on career goals that require college and, in part, on general social expectations that a youth from a middle or upper-middle-class family will attend college, just as he has attended high school. Both career plans (see Chapter 6) and college plans are highly changeable during the high school years: more people start high school with career choices that require college attendance than actually get to college, and more people are discouraged (perhaps quite properly) from college aspirations during high school than are encouraged to develop college plans. The key question is whether the process of encouragement works effectively in uncovering the students who have potential for college, and whether those who are discouraged during the high school years really ought to have persisted in their plans. While our knowledge of how the encouragement

TABLE 5.4. *Relationship of Selected Personal and Background Factors to College Attendance or Nonattendance, by Sex*
($R_{male} = .674$, $R_{female} = .733$)

Personal and Environmental Variables	Zero-Order Correlation of Separate Factor with Criterion		Partial Correlation of Separate Factor with Criterion, Partialling-out Effect of Remaining 37 Factors		Partial Correlation of Separate Factor with Criterion, Partialling-out Effect of All Other Factors Not in Same Specified Domain		Multiple Correlation of All Factors in Specified Domain with Criterion		Multiple-Partial Correlation of All Factors in Specified Domain with Criterion, Partialling-out Effect of All Other Factors	
	Male	Female	Male	Female	Male	Female	Male	Female	Male	Female
I Ability Variables										
1. Vocabulary	.432	.458	.012	.021	.190	.224	.531	.553	.279	.302
2. General Information	.485	.507	.065	.083	.225	.261				
3. Creativity	.272	.259	-.041	-.045	.093	.106				
4. Abstract Reasoning	.318	.302	.048	.036	.151	.151				
5. Math Aptitude	.497	.511	.143	.136	.255	.266				
II Interests Variables										
6. Physical Science	.266	.294	-.004	-.008	.013	.020	.336	.377	.101	.098
7. Literary/Linguistic	.273	.338	.044	.034	.087	.071				
8. Social Service	.152	.188	.051	.067	.091	.092				
III Temperament Variables										
9. Sociability	.080	.010	.048	.019	.045	.025	.167	.222	.049	.028
10. Impulsiveness	.016	.073	-.015	-.001	-.006	.003				
11. Mature Personality	.165	.205	-.009	.014	.005	.020				
IV Socioeconomic Variables										
12. Family Income	.214	.224	.029	.015	.071	.066	.366	.438	.133	.164
13. Father's Occupation	.263	.317	.059	.048	.102	.104				
14. Father's Education	.291	.351	.019	.045	.089	.122				
15. Mother's Education	.268	.342	.052	.074	.098	.129				
16. Number of Books in Home	.249	.299	.018	.034	.060	.088				

Variable										
V Ethnic-Religious Variables										
17. Race	.053	.004	−.010	−.063	−.008	−.062	.145	.175	.025	.071
18. Religion I (Jewish/Other)	.134	.154	.010	.023	.006	.026				
19. Religion II (Catholic/Other)	.022	.101	−.023	.007	−.021	.014				
20. Nativity-Parentage	−.002	−.034	.004	−.021	.002	.022				
VI Residence Variables										
21. Region of U.S.	−.004	.007	−.047	−.042	−.048	−.041	.171	.096	.057	.050
22. Size of Hometown	.162	.079	.022	−.004	.024	−.002				
23. Geographic Mobility	.065	.059	−.020	−.028	−.019	−.028				
VII Family of Orientation Variables										
24. Parents' Marital Status	.059	.062	.015	.012	.014	.013	.182	.173	.063	.028
25. Sibship Size	−.169	−.151	−.062	−.014	−.059	−.020				
26. Ordinal Position	.094	.113	−.018	.015	−.002	.021				
VIII High School Variables										
27. Type of High School	.122	.021	.014	−.009	.041	.001	.282	.221	.060	.045
28. Size of Student Body	.107	.084	−.008	−.022	−.020	−.019				
29. Size of Faculty	.121	.089	−.010	−.004	−.027	−.004				
30. Proportion Attending College	.268	.217	.041	.039	.051	.038				
31. Guidance Facilities	.063	.074	−.009	.007	−.015	.007				
IX College Commitment Variables										
32. Individual's College Plans	.539	.581	.320	.339	.359	.367	.546	.590	.362	.373
33. Encouragement by Father	.265	.288	.006	.009	.170	.149				
34. Encouragement by Mother	.260	.289	.021	.025	.178	.160				
35. Encouragement by Peers	.024	.043	−.019	.004	.063	.062				
X Family of Procreation Variables										
36. Age Planning Marriage	.184	.378	.055	.154	.079	.202	.282	.451	.151	.269
37. Marital Status	.176	.235	.041	.060	.107	.171				
38. Parental Status	.247	.354	.084	.123	.134	.211				

SOURCE: See Appendix B.

and discouragement process operates is still fairly rudimentary, we do know that there is a college where a student of almost any ability can be successful if he is persistent. The encouragement or discouragement of talent is only partly affected by school performance; socioeconomic factors have considerable force. For example, the young men from an upper-middle-class family is under substantial pressure to attend college; about half of this group who ranked in the bottom third in academic aptitude attended college, indicating that social background pressures can overcome the effects of marginal high school performance. Only about 15 per cent of the youth who were from low socioeconomic backgrounds and were in the bottom third academically attended college.

Given this complex of social pressures, educational pressures, and other influences that operate to determine college plans, there are a number of ways in which educators and administrators can encourage college attendance among persons with academic potential who do not go to college now. Most of these students come from lower socioeconomic backgrounds, and more of them are women than men. No single prescription is likely to work with all these students, and a detailed study of the development of college plans is needed to determine just which measures will have maximum effect with which subgroups of the population.

The Ability Level of Entering College Students

Some educators have argued that, with the increased proportions of high school students now attending college, the ability level of entering freshmen must inevitably drop and many higher educational institutions become less selective. So far, however, their dire predictions seem to have no basis in fact. In a study covering the period from 1952 to 1959, John Darley found that, for a representative national sample of colleges, the average ability level of entering students did not change much: "For the 1952 entrants to these 167 colleges, the weighted average of the ability measure was 105 and the weighted standard deviation was 27; 53,485 students were included in these statistics. For the 1959 entrants to the same 167 colleges, the weighted average was 109 and the weighted standard deviation was 28; 78,603 students were involved. Thus, even though enrollments had greatly increased, the basic levels of ability had not greatly changed."[5]

To bring the study of institutional selectivity up to date, a sample of 160 institutions that reported College Entrance Examination scores for both 1961–1962 and 1964–1965 were chosen, largely from among the more selective colleges. To provide a more balanced distribution, another 120 schools that participated in the American College Testing Program were added to the sample.[6]

[5] Darley, John G., *Promise and Performance.* Center for the Study of Higher Education, University of California, Berkeley, 1962, p. 34.
[6] Scores were obtained from the *Manual of Freshman Class Profile,* College Entrance Examination Board, New York, 1962 and 1965. Data refer to college entrants in 1961 and 1964. The ACT comparisons covered 1962 to 1965, so that the time period is not identical

After adjusting the sample to be representative of the total population, we find that academic aptitude increased about .17 of a standard deviation unit between 1961 and 1964, a figure comparable to Darley's figure of .15 of a standard deviation unit *covering a seven-year period.* Although the differences in the samples make precise comparisons impossible, there is no evidence that the more rapid expansion of college enrollments in the early 1960's resulted in a lowering of the academic aptitude of the entire freshman class. Indeed, the results suggest the opposite trend.

Nearly all the sample institutions registered an increase in their selectivity; only 11 per cent registered no change or a decrease. Junior colleges as a group changed least (.08 of a standard deviation unit average). The faster-growing institutions tended to have slightly smaller gains than the slow-growing institutions, but the differences were small and not entirely consistent (see Table 5.5). These figures indicate that selectivity was increasing in institutions of all sizes and all growth rates.

As would be expected, schools that were relatively unselective in 1961 had somewhat larger average gains, but the relationship between initial selectivity level and gains in the three-year period was small (correlation −.05). Table 5.6 shows that some fairly selective colleges (SAT average over 600) registered gains in selectivity of .3 or more of a standard deviation unit.

The increased interest in college attendance, when added to the rapid rise in the number of high school graduates in the early 1960's, made it possible for most institutions to enroll more able students. Junior Colleges and Catholic colleges increased their selectivity very little in the three-year period, possibly because of their commitments to provide educational opportunities to practically all applicants; the large Ph.D.-granting institutions had the largest gains in selectivity, and M.A.-level and B.A.-level institutions did not lag far behind.

As another way of examining the effects of increased enrollment on the average ability level of college students, data from the 1956 Educational Testing Service sample study and from several statewide studies were compared with Project TALENT data on students entering college in the fall of 1960. Comparison of these studies indicates that increases in the college attendance of highly able youth were even more rapid in the 1956 to 1960 period than the total attendance increase, as a result the ability level of entering college students was rising during this period.

---

for the two groups, although the length of the period is equivalent. All of the entrance examination scores were converted to a single distribution and the institutions were compared on gains in selectivity in the three-year period, 1961 to 1964 or 1962 to 1965. There were too few unselective colleges in the sample (28 per cent as compared with 50 per cent in the population) and too many highly selective colleges (33 per cent in the sample, 17 per cent in the population). There were also only about half as many Catholic colleges in the sample as in the population; about twice as many doctoral-level institutions in the sample as in the population; and only one-third the proportion of junior colleges in the sample as in the population.

TABLE 5.5. *Average Increase in Selectivity as Reflected in Standard Deviation Scores, by School Size and Rate of Growth: 1961–1964*

Percentage Increase in Enrollment, 1961–1964	Enrollment Size in 1961									
	Less than 1,000		1,000 to 3,499		3,500 to 7,499		7,500 up		Total	
	Number	Average Increase	Number	Average Increase	Number	Average Increase	Number	Average Increase	Number	Average Increase
10 or less	30	.27	46	.29	14	.27	8	—	98	.28
11 to 20	13	.17	22	.19	4	—	5	—	44	.21
21 to 49	27	.22	26	.25	12	.23	10	.33	75	.25
50 up	17	.13	26	.24	11	.17	8	—	62	.26
Total	87	.21	120	.25	41	.22	31	.28	279	.24

SOURCE: Special tabulations of data from a sample of 279 colleges. Average change scores in college selectivity are reported as a fraction of a standard deviation, and all are positive. Means are not shown where there are fewer than 10 institutions per cell. See text and footnote 6 for description of sample.

TABLE 5.6. *Percentage Increases in Selectivity as Related to Initial Selectivity: 1961–1964*

Initial Selectivity Scholastic Aptitude Test or Equivalent	Change in Selectivity During the Three Years (Standard Deviation Units)					Number of Institutions
	Loss or No Change	Gain .01 to .09	Gain .10 to .29	Gain .30 or more	Total	
	Per Cent of Institutions					
Less than 500	10	10	39	41	100	133
500 to 599	12	7	45	36	100	106
600 or more	7	15	51	27	100	41
Total	11	9	43	37	100	280

SOURCE: See Table 5.5. ACT scores were converted to SAT equivalents by using two different anchor measures of each college's selectivity by means of regression equations. See text for description of standardization procedures.

Highly able youth can continue to increase their college attendance rates more rapidly than low ability youth for about a decade; but by that time, nearly all (over 90 per cent) of the academically gifted group will be entering college. After 1975 further increases in the proportion of high school youth attending college will necessarily lead to declining average ability levels among all college entrants. Since about 90 per cent of the high ability youth from high socio-economic backgrounds already attend college, further increases in proportions of talented youth attending college must come primarily from middle and lower socioeconomic groups. Unless scholarship programs are widely available and low tuition schools are accessible to students from low-income backgrounds, the average ability level of entering college students will begin to decline even before 1975.

PATTERNS OF COLLEGE ATTENDANCE

Having dealt with some of the aspects of college entry, we will turn our attention in this section to what happens during the college years. First, the different growth rates of different types of colleges and the distribution of talent are discussed. Second, the relationships between the student's background characteristics and the type of college he attends are analyzed. Third, the institutional and background characteristics influencing college progress—including completing or dropping out of college permanently or temporarily—are considered, and finally, the progress of the transfer student is compared with that of the nontransfer.

Institutional Growth Rates and Selectivity

Our institutions of higher learning, which are both more numerous and more diverse than those of any other nation, are growing at very different rates. The highly selective, private, liberal arts colleges are expanding slowly, whereas the public, unselective "open-door" colleges, both two- and four-year, are growing rapidly. To examine the effects of this growth on different types of colleges, we classified institutions on the basis of four characteristics: size, degree level (junior college, bachelor's degree, master's degree, doctorate, specialized professional, and other), public or private control, and selectivity.[7] These classifications were then used to examine both the growth rates of institutions and the characteristics of students who enroll at different institutions.

The most selective colleges (which enroll students who have an average I.Q. of about 130 or better) are highly visible in the American higher educational system, but they enroll only about 4 per cent of all entering college freshmen. There are about a hundred of these institutions in the United States; most of them are private, and about one-fourth of them (enrolling about half of the 44,000 freshmen who enter selective schools) award the Ph.D. degree. Table 5.7 shows the estimated distribution of freshmen entering different kinds of institutions, categorized by selectivity and level of degree awarded, in 1965. The approximately 180 Ph.D.-granting universities enrolled about two-thirds of all the freshmen who enter selective and very selective institutions; they (rather than the small private liberal arts college) are the dominant institutional type serving students of above-average ability.

Except for junior colleges, the institutions ranking high and very high in selectivity grew more slowly between 1960 and 1965 than did those ranking average or below in selectivity. Of the junior colleges, those that were average in selectivity grew more rapidly than those that were below average. The probable explanation for this finding is that junior colleges with the best students are in metropolitan areas with better-than-average high schools; the rapid population growth in these areas boosts the enrollment growth of the junior colleges that serve them.

The lower growth rates of the more selective colleges illustrates one way that a college can become more selective or can remain selective. A college can become selective by reducing its growth rate as it screens out the less able applicants. Some institutions have so many applicants that they can continue to grow rapidly and still maintain or increase their selectivity, but for others, holding down the growth rate may be the main route to higher selectivity.

As far as distribution of students with respect to ability is concerned, college entrants ranking in the top 20 per cent academically are widely distributed

---

[7] Selectivity was estimated from the average I.Q. scores of Project TALENT sample students entering each college. Colleges enrolling fewer than 25 entering Project TALENT students were not rated. Selectivity scores are available for only 1,204 of the 2,168 institutions listed in the Office of Education *Directory* in 1964–1965: 24 per cent of the junior colleges, 58 per cent of the bachelor's-level institutions, 81 per cent of the master's-level institutions, 100 per cent of the Ph.D.-granting institutions, and 12 per cent of the specialized and professional institutions. The schools with selectivity scores enrolled about 70 per cent of all college freshmen and appear to be distributed by region very much like the total, although they are larger than those without selectivity scores.

TABLE 5.7. *Estimated Distribution of Entering College Freshmen, by College Selectivity and Degree Level: 1965 (figures in 000's)*

Degree Level of Institutions	College Selectivity of Institutions					
	Very High	High	Average	Low	Very Low	Total
Less than Bachelor's Institutions, Total Number of Entering Freshmen	0	1	26	193	36	256
Per cent Growth, 1960–1965, in enrollment in the category	—	33	86	38	24	55
Bachelor's Granting Institution, Total Number of Entering Freshmen	8	39	65	44	14	170
Per cent Growth, 1960–1965, in enrollment in the category	16	20	39	46	58	37
Master's Granting Institution, Total Number of Entering Freshmen	10	61	112	91	19	293
Per cent Growth, 1960–1965, in enrollment in the category	14	33	43	54	54	43
Doctorate Granting Institution	23	214	178	14	2	431
Per cent Growth, 1960–1965, in enrollment in the category	6	33	40	50	67	35
Other Types of Institutions, Total Number of Entering Freshmen	3	6	10	8	11	37
Per cent Growth, 1960–1965, in enrollment in the category	53	16	33	34	53	56
Total, All Types of Institutions Total Number of Entering Freshmen	44	321	390	349	81	1,184
Per cent Growth, 1960–1965, in enrollment in the category	12	31	43	55	60	43

SOURCE: Classification of institutions based on 1,204 colleges that enrolled 25 or more students from Project TALENT. The sample institutions enrolled 70 per cent of all students, but are under-representative of junior colleges (they include only 64 per cent of the 400,000 junior college freshmen) and of small schools generally. Enrollment in schools without selectivity scores is assumed to be distributed like the enrollment in schools with scores. Enrollment data from U.S. Office of Education, first time in college, fall of 1965.

among all selectivity groups of colleges (see Table 5.8). The most highly selective institutions enroll very few students who are not in the top 20 per cent, but because of their small sizes, they enroll only about 12 to 15 per cent of all top ability students who are in college.

Only the least selective group of colleges fails to enroll any appreciable fraction of the most able students, and it is interesting to observe that the proportion of able students in the junior colleges is larger than the proportion in the highly selective baccalaureate and master's-degree institutions. Slightly more than half of all the most capable students are enrolled in the 180 large Ph.D.-granting universities, although these institutions enroll only about 37 per cent of all the students in the sample.

TABLE 5.8. *Enrollment of Students Ranking in the Top Fifth in Academic Aptitude, by College Selectivity and Degree Level*

Institutional Degree Level	College Selectivity					
	High	Medium-High	Medium	Medium-Low	Low	Total
			(Percentages)			
Junior College	—	a	2	6	a	9
B.A.	2	5	5	2	a	14
M.A.	3	8	9	3	a	23
Doctorate	7	29	15	a	a	51
Other	1	1	1	a	a	3
Total	13	43	32	11	1	100

a Less than one-half of 1 per cent.

SOURCE: Special tabulations of data from Project TALENT five-year follow-up survey of 1960 high school seniors. Estimated from distribution of academic aptitude scores within each selectivity group. Total includes 220,000 students, which is only 18.5 per cent, rather than 20 per cent of all college students in the sample.

Factors That Determine the Kind of College Attended

Knowing a student's background characteristics, how successfully can we predict the kind of college that he will attend? To answer this question, the Project TALENT data were analyzed by relating the 38 variables previously mentioned to the student's attending a junior college vs. a senior college and to his attending a selective vs. a nonselective institution.

As Table 5.9 indicates, the variables were not very useful in predicting junior vs. senior college attendance; all 38 combined explained less than 10 per cent of the variance. It might seem odd that attendance at low-cost junior colleges cannot be more accurately predicted from information about the student's socioeconomic background, but the multiple correlation with SES was only .13 for men and .08 for women. Junior colleges attracted many students from lower ability groups, but the multiple correlation with ability was only .20. The explanation for these low correlations is found in the diversity of the student group that attends junior colleges. They attract youth from high socioeconomic levels who have low academic ability and cannot get admitted to more selective colleges, as well as bright youth from low socioeconomic backgrounds who may not be able to afford to go away to college. Thus, we can make only relatively poor predictions of whether a student will enter a junior or a senior college from knowledge of his background characteristics.

Attendance at a selective or an unselective four-year college was somewhat more predictable, because both ability measures and socioeconomic variables yielded moderate multiple correlations (ability .35; socioeconomic status .23) with college selectivity (see Table 5.10). When only the most selective colleges were considered, socioeconomic background was an important factor in attendance for the students who had sufficient academic talent to be admitted. When we compare attendance patterns of the students in the top fifth in ability, we find that a boy from the top fifth group in socioeconomic status was about ten times as likely to attend a highly selective college as a boy from the bottom fifth in SES.

From these facts we can raise new questions about equality of opportunity for higher education. Does equality of opportunity mean only that the student be given a chance to attend some college? Or does it mean he should have the chance to attend a highly selective, intellectually stimulating college or university where he will be given the advantage of easier entry to graduate or professional school? If the latter definition is adopted, access is clearly affected in an important way by socioeconomic status. The principal influence operating may be self-selection. A bright but poor boy's social background and contacts may limit his horizons so that he never applies to a selective college. The higher costs of very selective colleges (most of them private) are also a factor that may restrict attendance. The necessary information is not available to determine how much of the barrier to attendance at selective colleges is self-imposed by the student's own failure to apply, and how much is the result of college costs and other factors within the control of academic administrators.

These questions will become more important to talent development in American society than the simple question of whether a student has a chance to attend college. In the future, opportunities for a good education and for a good chance to enter one of the prestige professions will continue to be partially dependent on the kind of college the student can enter. Career opportunities have always been affected by the kind of college attended, although we do not have the longitudinal data needed to determine whether this effect is getting greater or not. Nor do we have information on whether the person from an economically deprived background is encountering more difficulty now in obtaining admission to a selective college. It is harder to get into the most selective colleges today than it was ten or twenty years ago, but this difficulty may affect the economically advantaged and disadvantaged equally. If we are to assess equality of educational opportunity in the future, we must have the information to answer these questions.

Student Progress in Different Kinds of Colleges

The extensive literature on dropouts has been adequately summarized in other sources,[8] so we will not present a comprehensive review. Knoell summarized existing knowledge as follows:

1. About half the students who enter our colleges as freshmen drop out at some point during the four-year period following their initial enrollment; fewer than 40 per cent graduate four years after admission.

[8] See: Iffert, R. E., and Betty Clarke, *College Applicants, Entrants and Dropouts*, U.S. Office of Education Bulletin No. 29, Government Printing Office, Washington, 1965; Montgomery, James, editor, *College Dropouts*, Cooperative Research Project F–065, University of Tennessee, Knoxville, 1964; Summerskill, John, "Dropouts from College," in Sanford, Nevitt, editor, *The American College*, John Wiley and Sons, New York, 1962.

TABLE 5.9. *Relationship of Selected Personal and Background Factors to Junior College or Senior College Attendance, by Sex*

$(R_{male} = .269, R_{female} = .298)$

Personal and Environmental Variables	Zero-Order Correlation of Separate Factor with Criterion		Partial Correlation of Separate Factor with Criterion, Partialling-out Effect of Remaining 37 Factors		Partial Correlation of Separate Factor with Criterion, Partialling-out Effect of All Other Factors Not in Same Specified Domain		Multiple Correlation of All Factors in Specified Domain with Criterion		Multiple-Partial Correlation of All Factors in Specified Domain with Criterion, Partialling-out Effect of All Other Factors	
	Male	Female	Male	Female	Male	Female	Male	Female	Male	Female
I Ability Variables										
1. Vocabulary	.144	.137	−.011	.004	.083	.103	.202	.196	.148	.171
2. General Information	.175	.160	.044	.035	.111	.125				
3. Creativity	.087	.066	−.024	−.036	.041	.034				
4. Abstract Reasoning	.111	.093	.029	.023	.077	.079				
5. Math Aptitude	.188	.187	.082	.103	.136	.161				
II Interests Variables										
6. Physical Science	.064	.055	−.030	−.071	−.026	−.047	.117	.140	.087	.125
7. Literary/Linguistic	.101	.134	.028	.067	.062	.085				
8. Social Service	.074	.081	.052	.063	.078	.088				
III Temperament Variables										
9. Sociability	.012	−.014	.004	−.000	.018	.002	.090	.071	.042	.005
10. Impulsiveness	.006	.013	.002	.004	.007	.004				
11. Mature Personality	.089	.061	.038	.004	.041	.004				
IV Socioeconomic Variables										
12. Family Income	.056	.020	.006	−.013	.028	.002	.130	.083	.073	.045
13. Father's Occupation	.087	.070	.011	.035	.041	.041				
14. Father's Education	.117	.065	.040	.012	.064	.027				
15. Mother's Education	.104	.049	.027	−.003	.052	.011				
16. Number of Books in Home	.060	.051	−.018	−.002	.008	.010				

V Ethnic-Religious Variables										
17. Race	.023	−.013	−.000	−.046	−.001	−.047	.082	.049	.045	.056
18. Religion I (Jewish/Other)	.045	.037	.024	.014	.020	.010				
19. Religion II (Catholic/Other)	.040	.009	.008	.003	.013	.007				
20. Nativity-Parentage	.048	.021	.040	.029	.037	.028				
VI Residence Variables										
21. Region of U.S.	−.021	.005	−.038	−.009	−.038	−.010	.023	.009	.051	.013
22. Size of Hometown	.004	−.007	−.001	.009	.000	.009				
23. Geographic Mobility	−.008	.001	−.033	−.003	−.033	−.002				
VII Family of Orientation Variables										
24. Parents' Marital Status	.031	−.004	.021	−.008	.021	−.009	.054	.023	.033	.019
25. Sibship Size	−.042	−.023	−.026	−.011	−.025	−.006				
26. Ordinal Position	.028	.004	−.007	−.016	−.000	−.014				
VIII High School Variables										
27. Type of High School	.030	.030	.009	.014	.031	.029	.068	.046	.049	.055
28. Size of Student Body	−.002	.007	−.008	.011	−.026	−.007				
29. Size of Faculty	−.013	−.029	−.032	−.032	−.046	−.047				
30. Proportion Attending College	.064	.001	.003	−.022	.011	−.022				
31. Guidance Facilities	−.004	−.020	.000	−.012	−.014	−.028				
IX College Commitment Variables										
32. Individual's College Plans	.100	.076	.048	.041	.048	.050	.106	.093	.049	.080
33. Encouragement by Father	.018	.028	−.007	−.043	.007	.027				
34. Encouragement by Mother	.016	.049	.005	.058	.011	.053				
35. Encouragement by Peers	−.022	−.008	−.003	.013	.003	.024				
X Family of Procreation Variables										
36. Age Planning Marriage	.027	.117	.000	.065	.007	.082	.072	.172	.050	.139
37. Marital Status	.026	.067	−.007	.007	.018	.067				
38. Parental Status	.070	.143	.047	.098	.050	.122				

SOURCE: See Appendix B.

TABLE 5.10. *Relationship of Selected Personal and Background Factors to Completion of Nonselective or Selective Senior College, by Sex*

(R_{male} = .423, R_{female} = .416)

Personal and Environmental Variables	Zero-Order Correlation of Separate Factor with Criterion		Partial Correlation of Separate Factor with Criterion, Partialling-out Effect of Remaining 37 Factors		Partial Correlation of Separate Factor with Criterion, Partialling-out Effect of All Other Factors Not in Same Specified Domain		Multiple Correlation of All Factors in Specified Domain with Criterion		Multiple-Partial Correlation of All Factors in Specified Domain with Criterion, Partialling-out Effect of All Other Factors	
	Male	Female	Male	Female	Male	Female	Male	Female	Male	Female
I Ability Variables										
1. Vocabulary	.289	.274	.055	.052	.167	.163	.352	.320	.237	.225
2. General Information	.296	.271	.030	.030	.168	.163				
3. Creativity	.128	.102	−.053	−.059	.042	.032				
4. Abstract Reasoning	.165	.132	.026	−.004	.091	.065				
5. Math Aptitude	.314	.277	.140	.131	.212	.202				
II Interests Variables										
6. Physical Science	.117	.057	−.006	−.056	−.005	−.055	.164	.148	.033	.077
7. Literary/Linguistic	.105	.075	.031	.032	.032	.004				
8. Social Service	−.017	−.092	−.005	−.052	.012	−.048				
III Temperament Variables										
9. Sociability	−.039	−.086	−.019	−.053	.006	−.036	.139	.145	.069	.064
10. Impulsiveness	.033	.053	.029	.027	.031	.018				
11. Mature Personality	.111	.068	.061	.047	.060	.033				
IV Socioeconomic Variables										
12. Family Income	.164	.195	.067	.091	.094	.130	.193	.232	.107	.153
13. Father's Occupation	.126	.146	.031	.027	.072	.096				
14. Father's Education	.137	.172	.007	.032	.061	.102				
15. Mother's Education	.108	.132	.023	−.002	.058	.069				
16. Number of Books in Home	.122	.154	.002	.036	.035	.087				

Variable										
V Ethnic-Religious Variables										
17. Race	.060	.091	.017	.005	.018	.007	.109	.169	.077	.106
18. Religion I (Jewish/Other)	.083	.141	.063	.096	.066	.101				
19. Religion II (Catholic/Other)	.000	.009	−.018	−.010	−.009	.004				
20. Nativity-Parentage	−.059	−.071	−.029	−.032	−.039	−.046				
VI Residence Variables										
21. Region of U.S.	.133	.150	.091	.090	.091	.092	.171	.167	.091	.098
22. Size of Hometown	.098	.073	.004	−.020	−.002	−.029				
23. Geographic Mobility	.050	.041	.007	−.027	.006	−.030				
VII Family of Orientation Variables										
24. Parents' Marital Status	.025	.006	.009	−.014	.009	−.014	.046	.062	.018	.026
25. Sibship Size	−.032	−.062	.003	−.020	.007	−.021				
26. Ordinal Position	.028	.022	−.014	.003	−.015	.009				
VIII High School Variables										
27. Type of High School	.046	.042	.026	.049	.024	.049	.197	.166	.144	.121
28. Size of Student Body	.021	.049	−.113	−.100	−.100	−.096				
29. Size of Faculty	.147	.119	.071	.069	.048	.022				
30. Proportion Attending College	.101	.120	−.027	−.001	−.015	.000				
31. Guidance Facilities	.128	.080	.049	−.012	.064	−.000				
IX College Commitment Variables										
32. Individual's College Plans	.060	.009	.026	−.008	.016	−.011	.123	.066	.042	.045
33. Encouragement by Father	−.044	−.039	.001	−.002	−.029	−.029				
34. Encouragement by Mother	−.059	−.057	−.015	−.015	−.032	−.031				
35. Encouragement by Peers	−.082	−.020	−.009	.031	−.014	.024				
X Family of Procreation Variables										
36. Age Planning Marriage	.107	.073	.043	.051	.049	.051	.123	.084	.060	.055
37. Marital Status	.072	−.002	.026	−.007	.038	.006				
38. Parental Status	.060	.038	.011	.021	.030	.022				

SOURCE: See Appendix B.

2. The average rate of attrition has been found to be quite stable over the past 40 years in a considerable number and variety of studies; however, a considerable amount of variability has been found among different types of colleges studied at any one time. . . .[9]

Eckland, following a cohort of male entrants to the University of Illinois for a period of ten years, found that over 80 per cent of them eventually completed college somewhere, a much higher completion rate than has been found in most other studies.[10] In the 1965 Project TALENT five-year follow-up of 1960 high school seniors, 45 per cent of the men and 47 per cent of the women who had ever attended college had obtained a bachelor's degree, a figure consistent with the four-year completion rates of about 40 per cent estimated by Knoell on the basis of a number of studies. In a follow-up study of a sample of all Wisconsin high school graduates seven years after high school graduation, Sewell and Shah found that 50 per cent of the male college entrants and 47 per cent of the women college entrants had graduated from college.[11] All these studies indicate the importance of the distinction between immediate completion rates and cumulative completion rates.

It is also possible to estimate completion rates by comparing the number of first-time college students to the number of bachelor's degrees awarded four years later.[12] While this figure will fluctuate as a result of changes in the proportion of youths who delay college completion for military service or other reasons, when averaged over several years, it should give a reasonable approximation of the percentage of college entrants who complete college. During the 1960 to 1964 period the proportion of men averaged 51 per cent, and the proportion of women averaged 49 per cent, figures consistent with the sample results obtained in the Project TALENT and Wisconsin longitudinal surveys noted above. The much higher rates found by Eckland undoubtedly reflect the different educational patterns of the more select and more highly motivated entrants to the University of Illinois and the longer period (ten years) of follow-up.

Further evidence about dropouts is provided in a study of Panos and Astin,[13] who reported that 65 per cent of a national sample of four-year college freshmen in 1961 had completed four or more years of college by 1965. This figure is similar to the Project TALENT estimate that 60 per cent of four-year college

[9] Knoell, Dorothy, "Needed Research on College Dropouts," in Montgomery, James, editor, *op. cit.*

[10] Eckland, Bruce K., "Social Class and College Graduation: Some Misconceptions Corrected," *American Journal of Sociology,* vol. 70, July, 1964, pp. 36–50.

[11] Sewell, William H., and Vimal P. Shah, "Socioeconomic Status, Intelligence, and the Attainment of Higher Education," *Sociology of Education,* vol. 40, Winter, 1967, pp. 1–23. See especially Table 5.

[12] First professional degrees that usually follow a bachelor's degree (such as M.D., L.L.B., and so forth) have been excluded.

[13] Panos, Robert J., and Alexander W. Astin, "Attrition Among College Students." Paper presented at the Annual Meeting of the American Educational Research Association, New York, February, 1967.

entrants received a bachelor's degree within five years, even though the two studies are not completely comparable. These studies show that completion rates are much higher among entrants to degree-granting colleges than among entrants to junior colleges.

To examine the progress of students who attend different kinds of colleges, we divided students into several college progress groups.[14] Junior college enrollees were separated from enrollees in degree-granting institutions, and this latter group was divided into those who did all their work at one institution, and those who transferred between senior colleges. Each of these three groups was broken down further into dropouts, students still enrolled, and graduates. The graduates were subdivided into those who had enrolled in graduate school the year following the bachelor's degree and those who had not. If a student went directly from high school to college, made normal progress in a four-year degree program, and went directly from college into graduate school, he would be a first-year graduate or professional degree student by the time of the five-year follow-up. The student who delayed entering college or completing a degree program would probably not have received a degree and may have dropped out of college. Some of the dropouts will reenter college at a later date and may complete a degree. Of the students enrolled in or graduated from college five years after high school graduation, 14 per cent were freshmen, 18 per cent were sophomores, 11 per cent were juniors, 11 per cent were seniors, 23 per cent were in graduate school, and the remaining 23 per cent had completed a B.A. degree and were not enrolled.[15]

Students who enrolled in junior colleges were much less likely to complete a degree within five years of high school graduation than were students in any kind of four-year college. The male student who did all his college work at one institution was more likely to complete a degree than was the man who transferred from one college to another; but there was practically no difference between the women transfers and nontransfers. Students who attended highly selective colleges were more likely to complete college, and less likely to drop out, than were students at medium or low selectivity colleges (see Table 5.11). When selectivity and transfer status were controlled, women were more likely than men to have dropped out or to have graduated (as opposed to being still enrolled) except at the most selective colleges.

Students who attend selective colleges are more likely to graduate, and are also more likely to attend graduate school (Figure 5.2). Men who attended very selective colleges were about twice as likely to complete college as men who attended unselective colleges; for women, the differences were only a little smaller. The influence of college selectivity on graduate school attendance in

[14] Based on the five-year follow-up of the 1960 high school seniors in the Project TALENT sample.

[15] Information about the point of dropout for persons in the sample who were no longer enrolled is not available, but national sample studies indicate that most dropouts occur in the first year of college enrollment. See references cited in note 8.

FIGURE 5.2 *College Graduation and Graduate School Attendance in 1965, by College Selectivity (High–Low) and Sex: 1960 High School Seniors Who Attended College*

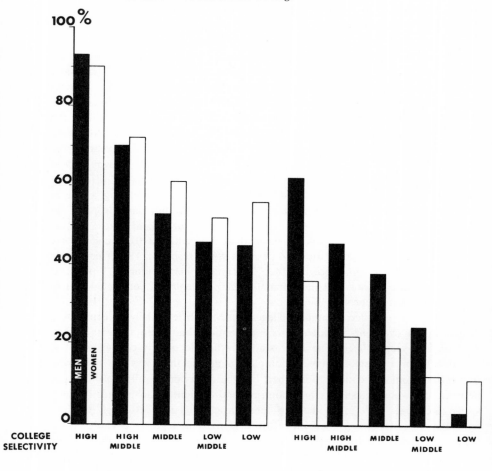

SOURCE: Special tabulations from the Project Talent five-year follow-up of 1960 high school seniors. Data exclude the junior college transfers into senior institutions.

the year after college completion was even more marked. The selective colleges are heavily oriented toward preparing their students for graduate and professional school attendance, and this emphasis pays off for the students both in graduate school attendance and in advanced degrees awarded.

The student's progress through the educational system is affected to a con-

TABLE 5.11. *College Progress, by College Type and Selectivity and by Sex*

College Type and Sex	Total	College Progress		
		Bachelor's Graduates	Still Enrolled	Dropped Out
		(Percentages)		
Males				
Junior College Transfer	100	20.5	(79.5)[a]	
Senior College Transfer				
Low and Low-Medium Selectivity	100	50.6	22.7	26.7
Medium Selectivity	100	45.4	31.8	22.7
High-Medium and High Selectivity	100	61.0	21.6	17.5
Senior College Nontransfer				
Low and Low-Medium Selectivity	100	45.4	23.2	31.4
Medium Selectivity	100	54.6	20.9	24.6
High-Medium and High Selectivity	100	76.8	11.6	12.0
Females				
Junior College Transfer	100	22.7	(77.3)[a]	
Senior College Transfer				
Low and Low-Medium Selectivity	100	62.7	10.2	27.1
Medium Selectivity	100	61.4	10.2	28.4
High-Medium and High Selectivity	100	73.5	12.9	13.5
Senior College Nontransfer				
Low and Low-Medium Selectivity	100	52.4	6.5	41.1
Medium Selectivity	100	60.8	7.4	31.8
High-Medium and High Selectivity	100	74.3	4.0	21.7

[a] Figures on junior college graduates are comparable with senior college figures, but other figures cannot be separated into the dropped-out and still enrolled groups.

SOURCE: Special tabulations from the five-year follow-up survey of Project TALENT. Selectivity refers to college attended at the time of the five-year follow-up on bachelor's graduates. Two top selectivity groups have been combined, as have the two bottom groups.

siderable extent by his ability (Table 5.12). Nevertheless, the fact that about a third of the lowest fifth in ability among high school seniors who went to college had completed a college degree, and that 8 per cent of the men and 3 per cent of the women in this group went on to graduate school is evidence that there is a college for practically every high school graduate in the United States, no matter what his or her academic aptitude.[16]

Can these major differences be explained entirely or mostly by the fact that different colleges attract students of differing ability? If not, what other influences are involved?

The most striking difference in college completion rates (defined as receipt of a baccalaureate degree) is between students who begin their education in a junior college and those who begin their education in a four-year college or

[16] These estimates may be affected by the follow-up sample obtained by Project TALENT. Only about 40 per cent of the original sample responded to the follow-up questionnaire, and they were the more successful members of the group. While the tabulations above are based on the weighted sample, which included a follow-up of a representative subsample of nonrespondents, the sample may still not be entirely representative of the less successful. To the extent that it is not, the differences discussed are probably underestimates of the differences between high and low ability students.

TABLE 5.12. *College Progress, by Academic Aptitude and Sex*

Sex and Academic Aptitude	Total	Now in Graduate or Professional School	College Graduate Only	Still Enrolled	Dropouts
		(Percentages)			
Men					
High	100	32	38	17	13
High-Middle	100	20	35	22	23
Middle	100	10	27	33	30
Low-Middle	100	9	20	34	37
Low	100	8	22	24	46
Women					
High	100	17	57	9	17
High-Middle	100	11	49	9	31
Middle	100	7	42	11	40
Low-Middle	100	4	33	12	51
Low	100	3	30	14	53

SOURCE: Special tabulations from Project TALENT five-year follow-up survey; figures exclude students who originally enrolled in a junior college.

university. About half the junior college entrants in the sample reported that they had been enrolled only in a junior college, 22 per cent had transferred and graduated, about 17 per cent had transferred and subsequently dropped out, and the remainder (8 per cent of the women and 19 per cent of the men) were still enrolled. The 22 per cent completion rate compares with a 60 per cent rate of completion for entrants to four-year colleges.

In a major national sample study of junior college transfers to senior institutions, Dorothy Knoell and Leland Medsker found that "forty-five percent of the students who transferred after two years in junior college received their baccalaureate degree about two years later. . . . Slightly more than half the students who did not graduate (31 percent of the total group) were still enrolled at the end of two years. . . ."[17]

The figures from the Project TALENT five-year follow-up were similar: 40 per cent of the junior college transfers graduated from a four-year college, 32 per cent dropped out after transferring, and 28 per cent were still enrolled (Table 5.13).

Grades earned in junior college affected the type of college to which students transferred. Knoell found that students who made the best grades in junior college tended to transfer to private universities, major state universities, and technical institutions, where they made lower grades in their last two years than the "native" nontransfer students. Students with intermediate grades in junior college tended to transfer to state colleges, while the students with the lowest

[17] Knoell, Dorothy M., and Leland Medsker, *Factors Affecting the Performance of Transfer Students From Two to Four Year Colleges.* U.S. Office of Education, Cooperative Research Project No. 1133, University of California, Berkeley, 1964, p. 177.

TABLE 5.13. *Academic Progress of Junior College Transfers to Senior Institutions, by Academic Aptitude and Sex*

Academic Aptitude and Sex	Weighted Number of Cases	Total	Graduated	Still Enrolled in 4-Year Institution	Dropout from 4-Year Institution
			(Percentages)		
Men					
Low and Low-Middle	36,600	100	24	38	38
Middle	35,700	100	39	43	18
High-Middle and High	97,500	100	41	30	29
Total	169,300	100	37	35	28
Women					
Low and Low-Middle	17,400	100	26	13	61
Middle	18,200	100	44	18	38
High-Middle and High	66,600	100	52	17	31
Total	102,200	100	47	16	37

SOURCE: Special tabulations from the Project TALENT five-year follow-up survey.

grades tended to transfer to teachers colleges, where they made grades very similar to those of the "native" students. The relative difference in grading standards between the junior college and major universities was about .5 of a grade point (where 4 = A, 3 = B, 2 = C, and so forth); in state colleges it was .3 of a grade point; and in teachers colleges about .1 of a grade point, with the grading standards of the four-year colleges being higher in every case.[18]

Academic aptitude is related to completion rate for transfer students, although motivation, finances, and other factors are involved, too. While most of the selection takes place before transfer, even when the transfers in the top two-fifths of the total group of high school seniors are considered, graduation rates for the students who begin in junior college are still only about 40 per cent.

When only the high-ability and above-average-ability groups are considered, the proportion of junior college entrants who have graduated is less than half the percentage of senior college entrants of comparable ability who have graduated (see Tables 5.14 and 5.15). When we recall that more high ability students attend junior colleges than highly selective colleges, it becomes obvious that the talent loss among these able junior college students is high. The low completion rates of junior college enrollees may result, in part, from inadequate motivation or uncertainty about the value of college—factors that may have led them to enroll in a junior college in the first place—and, in part, from inadequate financial resources that made an interrupted study pattern necessary.

One study showed that "only three-fourths of the two-year college students, compared with nine-tenths of the four-year college students, had plans for

[18] *Ibid.*, Table 67.

TABLE 5.14. *Proportion of Students Receiving Bachelor's Degrees Among
Senior and Junior College Entrants with Similar Academic
Aptitude, by Sex*

Academic Aptitude and SES by Type of College	Per Cent Graduating from College Men	Per Cent Graduating from College Women
Academic Aptitude		
High		
Senior College	70	74
Junior College	31	40
High-Medium		
Senior College	55	60
Junior College	19	20
Socioeconomic Status		
High		
Senior College	67	70
Junior College	21	26
High-Medium		
Senior College	57	63
Junior College	23	21

SOURCE: Special tabulations from Project TALENT five-year follow-up survey.

TABLE 5.15. *Socioeconomic Background of High Ability (Top Fifth) Students, by Type of College Entered and Sex, with Percentage
Completion of Senior College*

| Socioeconomic Status | Men | | Women | |
	Junior College	Senior College	Junior College	Senior College
Low	6.9 (a)	4.5 (62)	4.2 (a)	3.8 (66)
Low-Middle	13.6 (29)	9.9 (69)	14.2 (26)	8.2 (72)
Middle	36.6 (28)	24.2 (65)	26.2 (31)	24.8 (68)
High-Middle	22.2 (33)	19.8 (70)	22.2 (42)	21.4 (72)
High	20.7 (32)	41.5 (78)	33.1 (52)	41.8 (79)
Total	100 (31)	100 (70)	100 (40)	100 (74)
Weighted Number	69,700	683,200	54,100	514,000

a Number of cases completing college too small to permit computation.
SOURCE: Special tabulations from the Project TALENT five-year follow-up totals include students who enrolled and subsequently dropped out, are currently enrolled, or have graduated. Junior college figures include all persons who initially enrolled in a junior college, even if they subsequently transferred to a senior college. Figures in parentheses indicate the percentage of each group that had completed college in 5 years. Percentage not shown when base is less than 50 unweighted (actual) cases.

college early in their high school senior year."[19] Moreover, relative to highly able four-year college students, a large proportion of highly able junior college students came from low socioeconomic backgrounds (see Tables 5.14 and 5.15). But even when ability and socioeconomic factors were controlled, men in junior

[19] Folger, John K., and Charles B. Nam, *Education of the American Population.* Government Printing Office, Washington, 1967, p. 63.

colleges were less than half as likely to finish college as were their counterparts in senior institutions. A disproportionate number of junior college enrollees also delayed entry to college. If high school seniors were followed up for ten years, the differences between junior colleges and degree-granting institutions might be substantially reduced. We have suggested that inadequate motivation and financial limitations are probably important reasons for the lower graduation rates of junior college entrants, but the data at hand are inadequate to pinpoint the precise causes of this large talent waste.

In our study of the factors affecting college dropout, ability was the most important predictor of dropping out for men, while marital and family status was the best predictor for women. High socioeconomic background, high scores on a personality scale that measured maturity and interests in nonscience fields exerted smaller independent influences on progress through and completion of college. Persons with scientific interests were more likely to drop out or to be delayed in completing college than were persons with literary-linguistic or social service interests, perhaps because of the greater rigor of science curricula.

As would be expected, girls tend to drop out when they marry ($r = .23$) and have children ($r = .40$), but for men, getting married has almost no effect on dropout rates ($r = .07$), and becoming a parent (which may mean losing the wife's earnings) has only a small influence ($r = .18$). Tables 5.16 and 5.17 give the figures for each of the 38 variables.

Very little information is available about how transferring affects the flow of students through the system of higher education, although almost one out of every three students does transfer during his college career. In the Project TALENT sample, 30 per cent of the men and 28 per cent of the women attended more than one institution. Approximately half of the students who enrolled initially in a junior college attended more than one institution; approximately 22 per cent of the students who enrolled in a four-year institution transferred. About 5 per cent attended three or more institutions during the five-year period following high school graduation.

The Project TALENT one-year and five-year follow-ups were used to classify students who transferred between four-year colleges according to the selectivity of the colleges they were attending one year after high school and at the time of college graduation or undergraduate attendance five years after high school. Thus, we were able to examine the college progress of students who attended colleges of different selectivity levels. Because only 4 and 7 per cent of the institutions in the sample were in the highest and lowest selectivity groups, respectively, it was necessary to combine the selectivity groups into a low and low-medium level, a middle level, and a high-medium and high level. The percentage of transfers from each selectivity level was fairly similar. Twenty-four per cent of the students initially in the high group, and 21 per cent of those initially in each of the other two groups transferred. Most of these students

TABLE 5.16. *Relationship of Selected Personal and Background Factors to Dropping Out or Completing Senior College, by Sex*

($R_{male} = .432$, $R_{female} = .532$)

Personal and Environmental Variables	Zero-Order Correlation of Separate Factor with Criterion		Partial Correlation of Separate Factor with Criterion, Partialling-out Effect of Remaining 37 Factors		Partial Correlation of Separate Factor with Criterion, Partialling-out Effect of All Other Factors Not in Same Specified Domain		Multiple Correlation of All Factors in Specified Domain with Criterion		Multiple-Partial Correlation of All Factors in Specified Domain with Criterion, Partialling-out Effect of All Other Factors	
	Male	Female	Male	Female	Male	Female	Male	Female	Male	Female
I Ability Variables										
1. Vocabulary	.238	.194	−.003	−.017	.144	.120	.339	.281	.264	.199
2. General Information	.269	.239	.057	.072	.179	.164				
3. Creativity	.109	.115	−.048	−.027	.051	.061				
4. Abstract Reasoning	.145	.124	.005	.019	.093	.086				
5. Math Aptitude	.324	.266	.187	.102	.253	.180				
II Interests Variables										
6. Physical Science	.085	.150	−.077	−.015	−.076	.006	.139	.189	.108	.116
7. Literary/Linguistic	.118	.148	.035	.046	.061	.081				
8. Social Service	.061	.078	.041	.082	.070	.106				
III Temperament Variables										
9. Sociability	.006	−.041	.014	−.020	.038	−.005	.174	.157	.108	.079
10. Impulsiveness	−.035	−.033	−.043	−.031	−.030	−.035				
11. Mature Personality	.162	.133	.093	.071	.099	.067				
IV Socioeconomic Variables										
12. Family Income	.093	.051	.008	−.008	.034	.022	.161	.135	.101	.101
13. Father's Occupation	.122	.105	.036	.025	.063	.063				
14. Father's Education	.134	.124	.023	.065	.063	.090				
15. Mother's Education	.125	.090	.055	.020	.075	.056				
16. Number of Books in Home	.070	.069	−.049	−.034	−.016	.006				

V Ethnic-Religious Variables										
17. Race	.014	.020	−.028	−.020	−.025	−.020	.122	.096	.079	.048
18. Religion I (Jewish/Other)	.117	.090	.049	.041	.047	.043				
19. Religion II (Catholic/Other)	−.008	.040	−.050	.009	−.042	.015				
20. Nativity-Parentage	−.047	−.031	−.028	.001	−.037	−.005				
VI Residence Variables										
21. Region of U.S.	.027	.003	−.025	−.045	−.026	−.044	.076	.042	.058	.069
22. Size of Hometown	.069	.001	.012	.003	.012	.005				
23. Geographic Mobility	−.018	−.042	−.051	−.053	−.051	−.051				
VII Family of Orientation Variables										
24. Parents' Marital Status	.030	.043	.019	.027	.019	.027	.071	.103	.042	.064
25. Sibship Size	−.064	−.093	−.035	−.056	−.031	−.051				
26. Ordinal Position	.029	.011	−.021	−.031	−.012	−.015				
VIII High School Variables										
27. Type of High School	.042	−.012	−.005	−.013	.025	−.006	.133	.060	.051	.051
28. Size of Student Body	.056	.051	−.021	.014	−.033	.005				
29. Size of Faculty	.049	.005	−.026	−.025	−.039	−.028				
30. Proportion Attending College	.128	.022	.024	−.030	.028	−.033				
31. Guidance Facilities	.034	−.011	−.001	−.018	−.012	−.027				
IX College Commitment Variables										
32. Individual's College Plans	.142	.107	.073	.064	.081	.071	.156	.123	.082	.085
33. Encouragement by Father	.032	.051	.001	.032	.037	.055				
34. Encouragement by Mother	.022	.033	.006	−.012	.038	.046				
35. Encouragement by Peers	−.047	−.025	.002	.008	.016	.018				
X Family of Procreation Variables										
36. Age Planning Marriage	.105	.164	.042	.068	.062	.119	.197	.437	.153	.412
37. Marital Status	.067	.226	−.044	.062	.027	.227				
38. Parental Status	.182	.422	.138	.343	.141	.402				

SOURCE: See Appendix B.

TABLE 5.17. *Relationship of Selected Personal and Background Factors to Delayed Completion of Senior College or Completion of Senior College in Five Years, by Sex*

$(R_{male} = .341, R_{female} = .343)$

Personal and Environmental Variables	Zero-Order Correlation of Separate Factor with Criterion		Partial Correlation of Separate Factor with Criterion, Partialling-out Effect of Remaining 37 Factors		Partial Correlation of Separate Factor with Criterion, Partialling-out Effect of All Other Factors Not in Same Specified Domain		Multiple Correlation of All Factors in Specified Domain with Criterion		Multiple-Partial Correlation of All Factors in Specified Domain with Criterion, Partialling-out Effect of All Other Factors	
	Male	Female	Male	Female	Male	Female	Male	Female	Male	Female
I Ability Variables							.228	.168	.197	.146
1. Vocabulary	.168	.093	.012	−.001	.119	.067				
2. General Information	.184	.111	.037	.016	.137	.081				
3. Creativity	.078	.037	−.036	−.041	.037	.008				
4. Abstract Reasoning	.080	.080	−.003	.024	.058	.066				
5. Math Aptitude	.215	.163	.133	.105	.187	.139				
II. Interests Variables							.091	.068	.116	.068
6. Physical Science	.025	.043	−.095	−.031	−.094	−.025				
7. Literary/Linguistic	.085	.046	.021	.000	.046	.018				
8. Social Service	.063	.050	.046	.060	.067	.061				
III Temperament Variables							.133	.055	.086	.021
9. Sociability	−.007	−.001	−.023	−.018	−.008	−.014				
10. Impulsiveness	−.045	.018	−.042	.014	−.042	.011				
11. Mature Personality	.117	.050	.076	.008	.069	.003				
IV Socioeconomic Variables							.120	.108	.070	.068
12. Family Income	.077	.058	.023	.007	.039	.026				
13. Father's Occupation	.086	.073	.025	.000	.042	.031				
14. Father's Education	.074	.086	−.008	.028	.028	.052				
15. Mother's Education	.101	.094	.047	.040	.056	.059				
16. Number of Books in Home	.050	.028	−.023	−.021	−.001	.007				

V. Ethnic-Religious Variables										
17. Race	.018	.034	−.034	−.011	−.033	−.011	.064	.068	.050	.027
18. Religion I (Jewish/Other)	.057	.039	.032	.020	.027	.017				
19. Religion II (Catholic/Other)	.020	.045	−.023	−.014	−.015	−.011				
20. Nativity-Parentage	.010	.013	.012	.011	.007	.009				
VI. Residence Variables										
21. Region of U.S.	−.003	−.007	−.033	−.033	−.031	−.029	.015	.055	.051	.061
22. Size of Hometown	−.012	−.054	−.010	−.043	−.010	−.042				
23. Geographic Mobility	−.008	−.008	−.038	−.030	−.038	−.031				
VII. Family of Orientation Variables										
24. Parents' Marital Status	.054	.028	.040	.009	.039	.008	.095	.088	.087	.069
25. Sibship Size	−.077	−.082	−.074	−.069	−.066	−.065				
26. Ordinal Position	.066	.012	−.042	−.022	−.024	−.001				
VIII. High School Variables										
27. Type of High School	.035	−.046	.003	−.028	.040	−.036	.094	.056	.077	.053
28. Size of Student Body	.001	.010	−.008	.006	−.035	.013				
29. Size of Faculty	−.037	−.005	−.060	.005	−.075	.014				
30. Proportion Attending College	.078	.005	.014	−.034	.022	−.037				
31. Guidance Facilities	−.006	−.020	.007	−.017	−.018	−.012				
IX. College Commitment Variables										
32. Individual's College Plans	.156	.194	.111	.170	.113	.182	.166	.214	.114	.200
33. Encouragement by Father	.023	.109	.007	.050	.022	.096				
34. Encouragement by Mother	.013	.087	−.012	−.024	.019	.080				
35. Encouragement by Peers	−.034	.044	−.003	.045	.009	.062				
X. Family of Procreation Variables										
36. Age Planning Marriage	.049	.097	.020	.077	.020	.074	.102	.186	.090	.155
37. Marital Status	−.040	−.083	−.083	−.107	−.058	−.063				
38. Parental Status	.055	.094	.064	.117	.033	.090				

SOURCE: See Appendix B.

(56 per cent of the men and 62 per cent of the women) transferred to institutions of the same selectivity level as the college in which they had initially enrolled. About 16 per cent transferred up to a more selective institution, and about 24 per cent transferred down to a less selective institution. The person who transfers down might be expected to enhance his chances for completing college, because he faces competition that is not so stiff, but it does not work out that way. Transferring between institutions of the same selectivity level was more conducive to college graduation (60 per cent graduated in five years) than either transferring up (50 per cent graduated) or down (only 40 per cent graduated). Apparently the unselective colleges attract transfers whose motivation and career plans are like those of the native nontransfer students.

Compared with nontransfers at the destination college (see Table 5.11), transfers to the low selectivity colleges had a slightly better chance of graduating. Men transferring to the medium and high selectivity institutions were somewhat less likely to complete college than were nontransfer students, but for women, these differences did not occur. Transfers to each of the three selectivity groups had a higher proportion of students still enrolled than the nontransfers, probably because the transfer process often involves taking some time out of college or losing credit or both. If the students in this sample were followed for a longer time period, probably half or more of the differences in degree completion between the nontransfers and transfers would be overcome. These data suggest strongly that the process of transferring between senior colleges does not lead to any major talent loss, although it may slow down the progress of some students. For the majority of students who transferred between colleges at the same selectivity level, the rates of completion (60 per cent) in five years and of dropping out (20 per cent) were almost identical with those of the entire *senior college* sample (60 per cent and 23 per cent, respectively).

Graduate School Attendance

The percentage of college graduates who go on to graduate or professional school has been rising rapidly in recent years. The proportion just about tripled in the fourteen years from 1951 to 1965, with the percentage of college graduates going directly to graduate school increasing about 2 per cent a year, a slightly greater rate of increase than the percentage of high school graduates who went on to college.

The estimates of immediate post-college graduate school attendance are shown in Table 5.18. It should be remembered that because many students delay entry to graduate school for several years, the figures will rise for a number of years after college graduation. For example, two follow-up surveys of 1958 college graduates, one in 1960 and the other in 1963, revealed that in the three-year period the proportion of students who were enrolled for a graduate degree rose from 29 to 34 per cent, the proportion who had enrolled for courses

TABLE 5.18. *Proportion of Bachelor's Graduates Going On for Graduate Study: 1951–1965*

Time Period and Sample	Total	Men	Women
	(Percentages)		
1951 College Graduates Followed in 1952			
Full-Time Students	13.8	16.1	8.1
1958 Graduates Followed in 1960			
Total	45.1	48.1	40.0
Enrolled in a Degree Program	28.6	33.8	19.6
Enrolled for Courses Only	16.5	14.2	20.3
1961 Graduates Followed in:			
1962—Enrolled in a Degree Program	35.1	42.1	25.1
1963—Enrolled in a Degree Program	35.6	42.1	26.5
1964 Graduates Followed in 1965			
Enrolled for an Advanced Degree	41.4	50.3	30.4

SOURCE: 1951 sample—*Education and Employment Specialization in 1952 of June, 1951 College Graduates,* National Science Foundation, 1955, Tables B1-3. Based on a 60 per cent response to a mail survey; includes about 10 per cent of all college graduates of 1951.

1958 sample—Bureau of Social Science Research, *Two Years After the College Degree,* National Science Foundation 63–26, Table 15. Based on a 64 per cent response to a mail survey; includes about 10 per cent of all college graduates of 1958.

1961 sample—Spaeth, Joseph, and Norman Miller, *Trends in the Career Plans and Activities of June, 1961 College Graduates,* National Opinion Research Center, University of Chicago, March, 1965, Table 1.4. Based on a 76 per cent and 71 per cent response in 1962 and 1963 respectively; respondents are about 7 to 8 per cent of all 1961 college graduates.

1964 sample—Five-year follow-up survey of Project TALENT. Percentages are derived by dividing the graduate enrollees by the entire group of B.A. recipients, some of whom may have received the degree too recently to enroll in graduate school. Tabulations are based on weighted sample which includes a sample of nonrespondents to the mail questionnaire.

increased only from 17 to 24 per cent, and the total increased from 45 per cent to 58 per cent.[20]

One of the major problems in assessing the flow of students into graduate institutions is the large number of part-time graduate students. While part-time undergraduate enrollment remained stable at 28 per cent from 1960 to 1965, between 56 and 60 per cent of graduate enrollment has been part-time. Full-time graduate enrollment is concentrated among the younger age groups—22 to 29. Less than 10 per cent of the full-time students are over age 30. By contrast, about 60 per cent of the part-time graduate students are over age 30. Many students are not enrolled for degrees, though their status may shift from year to year between full- and part-time enrollment and from course enrollment to pursuit of a degree. In a two-year follow-up of the 1961 college graduates, Spaeth reports that "one-third of the men were enrolled for both years (1962 and 1963), 8 per cent left school by the end of the first year, and another 8 per cent entered for the first time in the second year. Among the women, a sixth

[20] The 1963 figures are from Sharp, Laure M., *Five Years After the College Degree: Part I, Graduate and Professional Education,* NSF Contract C299, Bureau of Social Science Research, Washington, June, 1965, p. 3 (mimeographed). The 1960 figures are from Bureau of Social Science Research *Two Years After the College Degree,* NSF 63–26, Government Printing Office, Washington, 1963.

(16 per cent) were enrolled both years with 9 per cent leaving and 10 per cent entering."[21]

The 1965 figures in Table 5.18 may overestimate the percentage of college graduates going on to graduate school, because the cohort of graduate entrants was drawn from students who had made normal or accelerated progress in undergraduate programs, and these students are more likely to go on to graduate school than are students who make slower than normal progress. Men were about twice as likely to enroll as women, but the gap between the sexes is narrowing slightly. The rise in the graduate enrollment of women, however, has not led to any increase in the proportion of women who obtain master's degrees. As the Bureau of Social Science Research (BSSR) 1958 survey shows, women are more likely than men to enroll part-time for courses rather than to enroll for degrees, and some of the apparent gains in the proportion of women enrolled for advanced degrees may result from part-time course enrollments being reported as degree enrollments.

One consequence of these varied patterns has been a substantial delay between initial enrollment and receipt of a degree. In the BSSR five-year follow-up mentioned above, it was found that nearly half the nonprofessional degree graduate students had only taken courses; of those who were enrolled for a graduate degree, only 62 per cent had received either a master's or a Ph.D. degree. By contrast, 83 per cent of the professional degree candidates had received a degree in the same time period.

When the overall figures on graduate degrees awarded are compared with the total graduate enrollment, it is clear that graduate education is a rather loose and inefficient process. The combined number of master's and doctor's degrees awarded each year is less than one-fourth of the total graduate enrollment, and since graduate enrollment has been growing more rapidly than degree output, the ratio has been declining. However, it is possible to make some estimates of the proportion of graduate student entrants who eventually receive degrees. If degrees are converted to years of enrollment on the basis of one and a half years of full-time equivalent enrollment for each master's degree and four years of full-time equivalent enrollment for each doctor's degree, and if part-time students are assumed to be half-time on the average, then the ratio of enrollment years required to complete graduate degrees (as output of graduate degrees) to full-time-equivalent enrollments is about .53 and has declined from .56 five years earlier. This figure suggests that the completion rate for graduate degrees is not too different from the completion rate for bachelor's degrees, although the patterns of enrollment in graduate school are more irregular than in undergraduate education.

[21] Spaeth, Joseph, and Norman Miller, *Trends in the Career Plans and Activities of June, 1961 College Graduates.* National Opinion Research Center, University of Chicago, March, 1965, p. 10.

Factors Affecting Graduate School Entry

The 38 predictors used earlier to assess college entry and undergraduate progress accounted for only about 13 per cent of the variances in graduate attendance (see Table 5.19). The relatively small influence of academic aptitude (multiple correlations of about .2) is a reflection of the great variety of students and the varying admissions standards at different graduate schools. Socioeconomic status, interests, and marital status for women exerted a small influence, but prediction of graduate school attendance from background factors is much less adequate than prediction of initial college entry.

There have been several efforts to study the attrition of graduate students by following longitudinal cohorts, usually Ph.D. students. Allan Tucker and associates conducted the most comprehensive of these studies, which was based on a national sample utilizing the records of 24 universities and following post-master's arts and sciences graduate students from 1950–1953 to 1962.[22] About 62 per cent of the students completed a doctorate in the 9- to 12-year period, but completion rates in different fields and in the same field at different schools varied widely; they ranged from a low of 14 per cent noncompletion at a small highly prestigious university to 67 per cent noncompletion at a big urban commuter university that was below average in prestige.[23]

Tucker divided the universities in his sample into three quality or "prestige" groups (on the basis of ratings by Keniston and of number of degrees awarded) and found that student attrition from graduate school was influenced almost as much by the quality of the program (29 per cent attrition from top-quality, 42 per cent from intermediate-quality, and 52 per cent from low-quality universities) as attrition from undergraduate schools is affected by institutional selectivity. Attrition was also affected by field of study, being greatest among students in the humanities and lowest for students in the sciences.

The post-master's attrition described by Tucker came after the initial screening of candidates in the first year of graduate school had already occurred, so it is an underestimate of the total attrition in the Ph.D. program. Studies of graduate students in physics, for example, indicate that about 35 per cent of the entrants are eliminated in the first year without receiving any degree, and half of the remainder do not obtain a Ph.D. degree.[24]

A recent study of Woodrow Wilson Fellowship winners of 1958–1960 found that, even among this highly select group, less than half (about 42 per cent) had completed a Ph.D. degree six to eight years later.[25] National statistics on the

[22] Tucker, Allan, David Gottlieb, and John Pease, *Attrition of Graduate Students,* Final Report on Cooperative Research Project No. 1146. Publication No. 8, Michigan State University, East Lansing, 1964.

[23] *Ibid.,* Table 3.5.

[24] American Institute of Physics, *Physics Manpower, 1966.* American Institute of Physics, New York, p. 47.

[25] Mooney, Joseph, "Attrition Among Ph.D. Candidates: An Analysis of a Cohort of Recent Woodrow Wilson Fellows." Department of Economics, Princeton University, Table 1. Unpublished paper.

TABLE 5.19. *Relationship of Selected Personal and Background Factors to Termination of College with Baccalaureate or Continuation with Graduate School, by Sex*

$(R_{male} = .360, \quad R_{female} = .336)$

Personal and Environmental Variables	Zero-Order Correlation of Separate Factor with Criterion		Partial Correlation of Separate Factor with Criterion, Partialling-out Effect of Remaining 37 Factors		Partial Correlation of Separate Factor with Criterion, Partialling-out Effect of All Other Factors Not in Same Specified Domain		Multiple Correlation of All Factors in Specified Domain with Criterion		Multiple-Partial Correlation of All Factors in Specified Domain with Criterion, Partialling-out Effect of All Other Factors	
	Male	Female	Male	Female	Male	Female	Male	Female	Male	Female
I Ability Variables							.231	.182	.138	.105
1. Vocabulary	.182	.155	−.000	.008	.081	.064				
2. General Information	.202	.156	.031	.017	.102	.073				
3. Creativity	.099	.071	−.002	−.021	.051	.018				
4. Abstract Reasoning	.108	.062	.012	−.003	.058	.031				
5. Math Aptitude	.210	.161	.087	.071	.129	.100				
II. Interests Variables							.201	.161	.154	.102
6. Physical Science	.075	.082	−.009	−.013	−.011	.006				
7. Literary/Linguistic	.187	.148	.066	.092	.127	.101				
8. Social Service	.117	.008	.088	.008	.140	.045				
III Temperament Variables							.122	.127	.066	.072
9. Sociability	−.045	−.065	−.034	−.054	−.021	−.035				
10. Impulsiveness	−.023	.031	−.024	.018	−.026	.009				
11. Mature Personality	.094	.079	.059	.060	.048	.047				
IV Socioeconomic Variables							.183	.104	.120	.059
12. Family Income	.072	.060	−.029	.018	.016	.014				
13. Father's Occupation	.124	.010	.030	−.055	.077	−.035				
14. Father's Education	.161	.070	.060	.025	.106	.015				
15. Mother's Education	.116	.051	.030	.006	.078	.010				
16. Number of Books in Home	.133	.075	.022	.016	.058	.018				

Variable										
V Ethnic-Religious Variables							.162	.158	.089	.092
17. Race	.012	.025	−.014	−.013	−.013	−.014				
18. Religion I (Jewish/Other)	.162	.154	.087	.083	.085	.089				
19. Religion II (Catholic/Other)	.026	.022	−.023	.020	−.008	.033				
20. Nativity-Parentage	−.039	−.060	.001	−.008	−.012	−.020				
VI Residence Variables							.109	.102	.051	.052
21. Region of U.S.	.084	.090	.044	.034	.045	.037				
22. Size of Hometown	.059	.055	−.018	−.036	−.020	−.039				
23. Geographic Mobility	.037	−.001	.019	−.008	.017	−.010				
VII Family of Orientation Variables							.040	.089	.018	.069
24. Parents' Marital Status	−.007	.001	−.001	−.005	−.001	−.003				
25. Sibship Size	−.027	−.080	.002	−.043	−.002	−.057				
26. Ordinal Position	.034	.062	.018	.038	.018	.053				
VIII High School Variables							.168	.154	.044	.078
27. Type of High School	.020	.037	.006	.063	.013	.054				
28. Size of Student Body	.121	.124	.026	.034	.022	.025				
29. Size of Faculty	.076	.071	−.008	.010	−.002	.005				
30. Proportion Attending College	.132	.096	.028	.017	.032	.027				
31. Guidance Facilities	.062	.073	.013	.027	.013	.027				
IX College Commitment Variables							.049	.031	.015	.024
32. Individual's College Plans	.026	.014	−.006	−.007	−.007	−.004				
33. Encouragement by Father	−.018	−.005	−.005	.011	−.009	.019				
34. Encouragement by Mother	−.024	−.015	.001	−.003	−.008	.016				
35. Encouragement by Peers	−.031	−.013	.011	.012	.008	.015				
X Family of Procreation Variables							.127	.171	.077	.171
36. Age Planning Marriage	.044	.048	−.012	.015	−.001	.034				
37. Marital Status	.133	.158	.053	.140	.070	.164				
38. Parental Status	.095	.106	.030	.046	.055	.095				

SOURCE: See Appendix B.

number of full-time entrants to graduate study in relation to the number of Ph.D.'s awarded seven years later indicate that no more than one-fourth to one-third of the full-time entrants complete a doctor's degree. If part-time students were included, these attrition estimates would be even higher.

Graduate school attrition is much higher than attrition in medical school (which has been about 10 per cent in the past decade), and the attrition of doctoral-level students is higher than attrition among law students (which has been about 40 per cent in recent years). The lower attrition in medical schools may be partly attributed to the academic ability of their entrants, although entering graduate science students differ very little from entering medical students in ability and undergraduate performance. In fact, the best graduate departments attract students with better undergraduate grades than do medical schools (see next section). The lower attrition of medical schools seems to be a result of the much greater structure of the medical program, which is organized in a definite four-year period of full-time study. Attrition rates in graduate programs will probably remain high as long as departments permit so many of their students to study part-time and to interrupt their graduate work. The pressure on students to complete a medical program is also much greater, because two years of medical school does not allow entry to the profession, whereas some graduate education, even without a degree, will improve employment opportunities in most arts and sciences fields and in education.

The Ability of Entering Graduate Students

As was indicated earlier, academic aptitude is an important factor in initial entry to college, and it continues to be important to persistence in college and completion of a baccalaureate degree. The point of entry to graduate and professional school constitutes an additional screening of applicants on criteria of academic performance. We have also shown that colleges differ considerably in the kind of students they attract. Do these differences persist to graduation, and what effect do they have on entry to graduate school?

The average academic aptitude test scores of students who had graduated from college but had not yet attended graduate school were compared with the test scores of students who went to graduate school. As Table 5.20 shows, the academic aptitude of students going on to graduate school was generally higher than that of students who did not go on, but the differences were small for most selectivity groups of colleges. The large variation in the selectivity of undergraduate institutions, which continues to graduation, is reflected in the proportion of students that each stratum sent on to graduate school. The graduates of unselective schools were generally low in average academic aptitude, and relatively few of them went on to graduate school (see column 3 of Table 5.20). The average ability level of all entering graduate students was raised by the selection process because most of the entrants were drawn from the top three undergraduate selectivity strata which include the schools with average and

TABLE 5.20. *Average Academic Aptitude of Bachelor's Graduates Who Did and Did Not Enter Graduate School, by Undergraduate Selectivity and Sex*

Undergraduate College Selectivity and Sex	Average Academic Aptitude Test Score		Sample Number (in 000's) Going to Graduate School
	B.A., No Graduate Work	B.A. and Graduate Work	
Men			
High	737	728	43
High-Medium	671	692	156
Medium	632	647	109
Low-Medium	594	632	17
Low	508	526	2
Women			
High	718	734	13
High-Medium	668	686	58
Medium	639	647	45
Low-Medium	599	618	7
Low	498	559	2

SOURCE: Special tabulations from the five-year follow-up survey of Project TALENT. Averages are for the Academic Aptitude Composite Score (C-002) in the Project TALENT Test Battery which is described in Appendix B of *The American High-School Student.* The sample number (col. 3) excludes all the nonrespondents of college selectivity and graduate school attendance. See Appendix B of this report for a discussion of the numbers of nonrespondents to these items. The academic aptitude measure has a mean of 500 and a standard deviation of 100 for all high school students.

above-average selectivity. This upgrading exerted a greater influence on graduate school entrants and nonentrants in each stratum. The students who went to graduate school from a given stratum usually had lower aptitude test score averages than the students from the next higher stratum who did not go to graduate school. In other words, the graduates from the best colleges who do not go to graduate school are superior in academic aptitude to most of the graduate school entrants from the poorer schools.

In order to examine the relationships between the quality of the graduate school and the academic ability of its entrants, we tabulated the undergraduate Academic Performance Index scores of entrants to different graduate programs in different quality strata.[26] This analysis indicates that the quality of an institution's graduate program has a strong influence on the kinds of students attracted to the program. The top-quality Ph.D.-granting universities enroll students who are much better academically than the average college graduate; in the physical and social sciences and in medicine, their entering graduate students

[26] API scores were obtained from the National Opinion Research Center's follow-up of its 1961 college senior sample. Quality ratings were based on Allan M. Cartter's *Assessment of Quality in Graduate Education,* American Council on Education, Washington, 1966. This study rated engineering and arts and sciences departments, so overall institutional ratings based on these scores may be less appropriate for professional schools like law, medicine, and education.

TABLE 5.21. *Average Undergraduate Academic Performance Index Scores for Students Enrolled in Different Graduate School Strata, by Field and Sex*

Graduate Field and Sex	Quality of Ph.D.-Granting Graduate School				Non-Ph.D. Graduate School
	High	Medium-High	Medium-Low	Low	
Men					
Physical Sciences	2.75	2.54	2.14	1.99	1.62
Biological Sciences	2.31	1.98	1.77	2.15	1.47
Social Sciences	2.71	2.52	2.20	1.85	1.59
Humanities	2.59	2.23	2.27	2.00	1.82
Engineering	2.51	2.45	2.21	1.92	1.70
Medicine	2.68	2.75	2.58	2.09	a
Law	2.58	2.24	1.98	1.73	1.56
Education	2.14	1.90	1.76	1.59	1.48
Business	2.13	1.91	1.92	1.78	1.51
Total	2.49	2.29	2.09	1.84	1.57
Women					
Physical Sciences	a	a	a	2.34	a
Social Sciences	2.67	a	a	2.17	a
Humanities	2.85	2.50	2.35	2.42	2.10
Education	2.24	2.32	2.08	1.87	1.79
Total	2.54	2.36	2.22	2.14	1.83

a Number of cases too small to permit computation.

SOURCE: Special tabulations of follow-up survey of 1961 senior sample. Quality classes were developed by the National Opinion Research Center from Cartter quality ratings. Mean API for male seniors was 1.67, for female seniors 1.88. Scores range from 1 = low to 3 = high. Biological sciences include forestry and agriculture. Psychology is grouped with the social sciences.

from medium-selectivity undergraduate schools have an A average, and those from selective schools have a B+ average. At the other extreme, typical students entering graduate programs in institutions that do not offer the Ph.D. are below the average of the entire college senior population (Table 5.21). In other words, there are unselective graduate schools that attract the average and below-average undergraduate performer, just as there are unselective colleges that take average and below-average high school graduates.

The students who enter different graduate fields differ substantially in undergraduate achievement, too, and approximately the same ranking of fields occurs in each quality stratum.[27] In general, fields within a given quality stratum differ less than do fields in schools from different quality strata. In his study of graduate education, Berelson found that the best universities recruited their students from the best undergraduate institutions.[28] Our analysis confirms the belief that attendance at a selective undergraduate institution is an asset to getting into graduate

[27] Project TALENT data were used. The test that was administered in 1960, when the students were seniors in high school, is a composite of several tests of mathematical and verbal skills and knowledge. It has a mean of 500 and a standard deviation of 100.

[28] Berelson, Bernard, *Graduate Education in the United States.* McGraw-Hill, Inc., New York, 1960.

school and that recruitment to graduate school is a selective process that continues the sorting of students by ability that was so pronounced a feature of undergraduate institutions.

Trends in the Length of Doctoral Training

One of the recurring suggestions for increasing supplies of Ph.D.-level manpower is to shorten the average period that elapses between the receipt of the bachelor's degree and the receipt of the Ph.D. If the time span could be shortened, each year "saved" would represent a year added to a person's professional career, at a point where he should be highly productive. This section examines some of the factors that cause delay in receipt of the doctoral degree. Alternative possibilities for reducing the average length of training are examined.

Doctoral training is still a lengthy affair, despite the rapid increase in the absolute number and the slight increase in the proportion of students who hold fellowships and traineeships, types of support which should in theory reduce the time required to complete the degree. While there are a number of ways in which the length of Ph.D. training can be measured, we will concentrate on the time that elapses between graduate school entry and Ph.D. completion, which averages about eight and one-half years for all fields combined.[29] The total period from entry to degree receipt can be subdivided into full-time study (three to four years), part-time study (two to seven years, depending on the field), and time spent not enrolled (two to five years in different fields). See Table 5.22.

Earlier trends have been summarized by Harmon and Soldz,[30] who showed that, when the fluctuations due to World War II are eliminated, the B.A.-Ph.D. time lapse increased slightly over the entire 1920 to 1961 period. The time required to obtain a Ph.D. was shortest in the physical sciences, next shortest in biological sciences, intermediate in the social sciences, longer in arts and humanities, and longest in education. Differences among fields were generally stable in the two prewar decades but widened slightly in the postwar decade.

Kenneth Wilson's *Of Time and the Doctorate*[31] assesses the effects of a number of factors on the rate of Ph.D. completion of about two thousand graduates of the 1950 to 1958 period. Wilson shows that such factors as outside employment, employment as a teaching assistant, clarity of goals at the beginning of graduate study, dissertation requirements, and other aspects of curricular structure operate to shorten or lengthen the period of Ph.D. study. The problems of length are also discussed by Berelson in *Graduate Education in the*

[29] The data are taken from the Doctoral Files of the National Academy of Sciences—National Research Council, a virtually complete compilation (99.5 per cent) of the earned doctorates (including the Ed.D. and other professional doctorates, as well as the Ph.D.) awarded by U.S. institutions.

[30] Harmon, Lindsey R., and Herbert Soldz, compilers, *Doctorate Production in United States Universities, 1920–62.* National Academy of Sciences-National Research Council, Publication No. 1142, Washington, 1963.

[31] Wilson, Kenneth M., *Of Time and the Doctorate.* Southern Regional Education Board, Research Monograph No. 9, Atlanta, Ga., 1965.

United States.[32] From these discussions and from an examination of the data for the 1957 to 1964 period, certain key problems and issues emerge.

Interruptions in graduate school attendance and part-time study are largely responsible for the long period of time that elapses between a student's receiving the B.A. and Ph.D. degrees. As Table 5.22 shows, the average amount of full-time study ranged from two to four years. When full-time and half of part-time study are added together, the total number of full-time equivalent years spent studying (shown in the last column of Table 5.22) is fairly similar for all fields,

TABLE 5.22. *Average Number of Years from Graduate School Entry to Award of the Doctorate, by Field: 1957–1964*

Field	Total	Full-Time Study	Part-Time Study	Not En-rolled	Full-Time Plus One-Half Part-Time
Mathematics	7.3	3.2	2.5	1.6	4.5
Geology	7.6	3.6	1.7	2.3	4.5
Physics	6.9	4.0	1.9	1.0	5.0
Chemistry	5.9	3.9	1.1	0.9	4.5
Engineering	7.1	2.7	2.9	1.5	4.2
Biology	7.4	3.7	2.0	1.7	4.6
Psychology	8.0	3.4	2.7	1.9	4.8
Social Sciences	9.6	3.4	2.6	3.6	4.9
Arts and Humanities[a]	10.3	3.4	3.1	3.8	5.0
Education	12.7	2.0	5.5	5.2	4.7

[a] Arts and Humanities also include other professional doctorates (such as doctor of business administration, doctor of music, and so forth).

SOURCE: National Academy of Sciences-National Research Council special tabulations of time from graduate school entry to Ph.D. Tabulations based on 84,908 cases. Data are available for 96 per cent of all doctorates awarded in the period. Years are calendar years.

ranging from 4.2 years in engineering to 5.0 in physics and humanities. If all students went full-time and did not interrupt their studies at all, the average time lapse could be cut in half: in chemistry, the saving would be one and a half years; in education, eight years. Curricular reform and changes in the nature of the dissertation might reduce the length of programs by as much as one to two years (the difference between the expectations stated in some catalogues and the actual average amount of full-time-equivalent study).

Relative to other fields, the sciences have a much higher percentage of students who go straight through full-time, but only in physics and chemistry do as many as three-fourths of them follow this pattern, which is typical of both undergraduate education and most professional schools. In the 1957 to 1964 period, the amount of full-time study increased about .4 of a year in all graduate fields combined, but this trend was partly counterbalanced by a decrease of about .2 to .3 of a year in part-time study. The increases in full-time study

[32] Berelson, Bernard, *Graduate Education in the United States.*

occurred in every field except education; they were greatest in mathematics and the physical sciences (except chemistry) and smallest in the arts and humanities. The increased support available in the science fields may have been the principal determinant of the shift to greater amounts of full-time study. The small decrease (about .3 of a year) in interrupted study during the 1957 to 1964 period cannot be explained by the greater support given to students, since the decreases were greatest in the arts and humanities, education, and the social sciences, fields in which support for graduate students is less readily available.

When the student changes major fields from undergraduate to graduate study (for example, from an undergraduate major in mathematics to graduate work in psychology), the length of his graduate training increases from about a half-year in biology, chemistry, and geology to about a year in mathematics and psychology. Between 10 and 35 per cent of students shift fields between undergraduate and graduate study, and though this shifting is a necessary part of adjusting individual career goals, it adds to the length of time students must remain in the educational system. (See Chapter 7 for a further discussion of the effects of field changes.)

Bypassing the master's degree has the effects of shortening the average period of graduate study about .8 of a year and of shortening the average period of interrupted study by about .9 of a year, for a total average saving of 1.7 years. In chemistry, half the Ph.D. graduates bypass the M.A., and in physics, a third bypass the M.A. In all of the other fields, less than 20 per cent of the students go straight through to the doctorate without getting a master's degree. If more students in other fields bypassed the M.A., the overall savings in time spent on the Ph.D. would be substantial. The effect of bypassing the master's degree on the value of graduate training is difficult to measure, and it undoubtedly varies in different fields and for different individuals. For the able students the average of an extra 1.7 years seems a high price to pay for the educational benefits involved. However, there does not appear to be any increase in recent years in the proportion of students who bypass the M.A. in the humanities, the social sciences, or education.

Predominant opinion on graduate faculties holds that students going on for the Ph.D. should shift to another institution after the B.A., and between 67 and 80 per cent, depending on the field, do so. The student who does not change institutions shortens the length of his graduate study slightly, but the time lost in shifting schools is probably compensated by the benefits that accrue from diversity of educational experience.

Identification of the stages where doctoral training potentially could be shortened is only the first step in bringing about changes. The present patterns of interrupted study and part-time attendance have existed for several decades, and the average B.A.-Ph.D. time lapse has remained remarkably stable over a several-decade period when graduate education expanded enormously and when many new institutions began to offer graduate education and many new graduate programs were developed. Powerful forces will have to change if the time lapse is to be substantially reduced.

The factors that promote drawn-out graduate programs include admission of weak and poorly prepared students, the employment of graduate students on activities unrelated to their educational goals, a widespread permissiveness toward part-time and discontinuous study, and a lack of sufficient stipend support to enable students to complete an entire degree program in one continuous period of residence. In addition, a student who has completed only part of a program can often get a good job and can obtain professional status.

The factors listed above are interrelated in important ways, so that merely pouring more money into the system, or changing faculty attitudes, or raising standards for admission will not by themselves have much effect. In addition, the rapid entry of new institutions into graduate education will make it difficult to develop common standards for the admission of students or the operation of programs. In spite of these formidable barriers to reduction of time lapse, the advantages to both the individual and society justify a substantial effort to structure graduate programs more efficiently. When doctoral degree production comes closer to meeting the needs for new research personnel and college teachers, some of the pressures to employ people before they have earned a degree will be eased, and students may have more incentive to complete graduate work. The job market may prove more effective in encouraging continuity in graduate work than any of the internal reforms that graduate schools initiate.

SUMMARY

The size and diversity of our educational system is an important asset to American society because it provides widely available opportunities for college attendance and for subsequent entry into the occupations in which a college background is required or expected. There is a substantial amount of student mobility in the present system of higher education; in general, the system is flexible enough, and institutions similar enough so that students can transfer without major loss of time or without sharply increasing the likelihood that they will drop out. In view of the many different career and job opportunities in our society, the mobility permitted by our present system of higher education represents a necessary and desirable feature.

The system is rapidly growing larger and will continue to do so (although at a lower rate) for at least the next 10 to 15 years, barring major wars or economic collapse. It does not seem to be growing more diverse, but it may be growing more stratified and specialized. The highly selective colleges are, by definition, attracting students who are academically talented and relatively homogeneous on ability measures, and they also tend to come from relatively high socioeconomic backgrounds. These colleges, despite the efforts of some to diversify their student bodies, are likely to continue to be an elite stratum, serving only a small fraction of the college students, nearly all of whom will go on to graduate or professional school. Although a few more colleges will enter this group, a smaller proportion of all college students in 1975 will be educated in institutions of this type than in 1965. Those students who attend these institutions will be at least as select academically a decade hence as they are today.

The largest and most dominant group of institutions is composed of the large, complex, and usually publicly supported Ph.D.-granting universities, which range in selectivity from high to average. They are growing at a slightly greater than average rate. While they have much more diverse student bodies than do the very selective schools, they enroll about half of all the students in the higher one-fifth in ability, and they provide most of the graduate and professional training in America. In the next decade they will probably continue to grow rapidly, to increase in number, and to become more selective in admissions. Our big universities are likely to play an even more significant role in the total process of talent development in the next decade because of the rapid rise of enrollments in graduate and professional programs.

The most diverse group of institutions consists of other degree-granting colleges and universities; they can be divided into many subcategories, but they have in common a tendency to enroll students who represent a fairly wide spectrum of abilities and interests. The statistics of the past decade indicate that many of these schools have been able to recruit more academically able students, especially during the 1960's, when rapid enrollment growth characterized most schools. Only the poorest of them do not enroll any high ability students. Most of these institutions—except for a few that have special purposes and serve special student groups—aspire to become either a big university or a highly selective liberal arts college. A few of them may achieve one of these ambitions in the next decade, but the remainder will continue in some intermediate category, part way between the open-door colleges and the more select universities and colleges. In some states (such as California), this intermediate status is formalized in public policy, but in a majority of cases, tradition and the availability of student applicants and financial resources determine rates of progress toward either the university or elite college model.

The final category is the open-door college, typified by the junior college, but represented also by a number of degree-granting colleges and universities that are committed to this admissions policy. These institutions, the most rapidly growing of all, are not increasing in selectivity, although, in general, the academic aptitude of their students has not been decreasing. The open-door colleges are likely to continue to be the most rapidly growing part of higher education, and the next decade may see some actual declines in the average ability level of their entering students. A given institution may not change its admissions policies much, but the overall average may decline if the schools that recruit students with lower average aptitude grow more rapidly or if new open-door colleges attract students with lower academic aptitude than the average for existing colleges of this type.

The evidence we have been able to assemble shows that the bright student who enters the junior college is much less likely to complete a college degree than his counterpart who enters a four-year institution and that the entrant to an unselective college is less likely to graduate than the entrant to a more selective college. The reasons for these institutional influences are not understood well enough to enable us to say how much these differences are related to aspects of the selection process which the institution cannot easily modify, and how much they are related to institutional practices that can be controlled or modified.

If the selectivity gap between our major universities and our open-door colleges widens further, however, students who initially enter the open-door colleges may find it difficult to make the transition to the major universities, which largely control access to the prestige professions. If it were simply a matter of sorting students into institutions on the basis of ability and motivation, there would be no cause for great concern, but the choice of a college is also determined by economic and social background factors. These factors will loom even larger in the next decade when the academically able students who do not go to college, or do not complete college, seem likely to be chiefly persons from impoverished backgrounds.

Data which show that the costs of attending college are rising no faster than average family income may suggest that the financial barriers to college attendance are getting no higher, but the real problem is to lower them for the group of poor but able students who represent the largest potential for further development of talent in our society. If equal opportunity for higher education means that persons similar in academic ability have an equal probability of receiving a bachelor's or advanced degree and of getting a first-rate education, then we are a long way yet from having a system that is equitable.

6 Career Plans of High School and College Students*

MANPOWER problems and needs give impetus to theory and research in occupational choice and vocational counseling. Conversely, knowledge about vocational development aids the work of the manpower specialists greatly, since it centers around the issue of how the supply for various fields is produced. It involves such questions as how career decisions are made, the kinds of careers that young people plan to enter, the points at which critical vocational decisions take place, and the ways in which vocational plans are implemented.

The different theories of vocational choice—formulated by psychologists, sociologists, and economists—have provided researchers with a set of important conceptualizations for exploring and understanding the determinants of specific career choices and the patterns of career choices. Some of the questions that have interested vocational theorists are whether career decisions can be predicted and if so, whether the environment can be manipulated so as to influence or change career choices. Consequently, most of the research on occupational behavior has centered on the personal characteristics—for example, abilities, values, interests—of people in different occupations and on the characteristics of a person's environment—for example, his parents, peers, and other significant people in his life; his social and educational opportunities; the availability of occupational information; the prerequisites for entry into different occupations; and supply and demand in the occupational world.

* An earlier version of parts of this chapter appeared in *Personnel and Guidance Journal*, vol. 45, 1967, pp. 541–546, and vol. 46, 1967, pp. 75–79, under the titles "Patterns of Career Choices Over Time" and "Factors Associated with the Participation of Women Doctorates in the Labor Force." Both articles were written by Helen S. Astin and copyrighted by the *Personnel and Guidance Journal*.

Vocational research studies have generally been of two types: those that seek to predict individual career choices and those that seek to predict the career patterns of groups of people. The first type is valuable in that it aids the work of vocational counselors, parents, teachers, and persons making vocational decisions and plans. It is helpful also to manpower specialists and policy-makers: for instance, studies of the effect of institutional factors on career decisions may provide information about variables that are amenable to change—educational curricula, guidance and counseling, teaching practices, and so forth—and that thus may be manipulated to benefit society. The second type—patterns in career plans of large groups of people—are also important to manpower theory and research because they provide information about the trends that may affect future supplies in different fields.

In general, the second kind of study has been more useful for manpower planning than the first: the career patterns of groups of people show considerable uniformity and stability over time. It is less easy to predict individual choices than patterns of group choice, primarily because there is a great deal of similarity in the characteristics of people who enter different but related professions. The categorizations of occupations and personal characteristics differ from one study to another, which makes it more difficult to determine when generalizations about individuals can be established.

Since the youth of today constitute the supply for different fields in the future, it is important to examine the career plans and aspirations of high school and college students. The Commission of Human Resources staff carried out such a study to investigate the probable future supplies to the different fields, the existence of any trends regarding popular or often-chosen occupations, and shifts in students' career plans.

Stability and Change in Career Choice

Although our understanding of career stability and career change is still rather limited, recent studies have produced some provocative findings. Research so far suggests that both personal characteristics and environmental influences are important in changing career plans of college students. For example, students who tend to be more dependent and who come from permissive homes are more likely to change from their initial career choice.[1] Also, if a student's initial career choice is atypical to his or her sex role (as in the case of a freshman girl choosing engineering or a freshman boy choosing elementary school teaching), the student is more likely to make another career choice later on.[2]

---

[1] Holland, John L., and Robert C. Nichols, "Explorations of a Theory of Vocational Choice-III, A Longitudinal Study of Change in Major Field of Study," *Personnel and Guidance Journal*, 1964, vol. 43, pp. 235–242; and Holland and Nichols, "The Development and Validation of an Indecision Scale: The Natural History of a Problem in Basic Research," *Journal of Counseling Psychology*, vol. 11, 1964, pp. 27–34.

[2] Davis, James, *Undergraduate Career Decisions*. Aldine Publishing Co., Chicago, 1965, pp. 34–40.

The type of college the student attends also affects his career choice. For example, a student who initially aspires to become an engineer is more likely to maintain this career plan if he attends a technological college than if he attends a liberal arts college.[3] In our exploration of the career expectations of high school and college students we were concerned with the questions: What proportions of young people plan to enter the natural sciences, social sciences, arts and humanities, and other professions? What has happened to these initial plans by the time they complete high school and by the time they terminate college? What occupations do young people of the 1960's prefer? Are there any observable trends in the changes of preferred occupations over time? The data and analyses that follow deal with the career plans of men; a discussion of career development of women is included in Chapter 9. Aspects of career development during the graduate school years and subsequent to college graduation are discussed in Chapter 7 and Chapter 8.

In order to examine the career preferences of ninth-grade high school students and to evaluate changes in these preferences during the high school years, the career expectations of 19,362 male subjects from Project TALENT[4] were analyzed. These students were assessed in 1960 as ninth-graders and followed up in 1964 when they had been out of high school for a year. One of the items of information obtained at both dates was the subject's expected career choice. On the basis of the 31 career alternatives included in this item an 11-group classification was developed.[5] Table 6.1 presents the distribution of career choices over these 11 categories in the ninth grade and one year after high school. Those ninth-graders who made normal progress were graduates, others were dropouts or still in high school.

When these high school freshmen were asked to indicate their expected career choice, about one-third indicated a preference for careers in engineering and natural science, but only one-eighth still indicated these preferences after they had been out of high school for a year. Students who initially aspired to business or to skilled and technical careers were less likely to change than were those who had indicated a preference for one of the nine other occupational

---

[3] Astin, Alexander W., "Effect of Different College Environments on the Vocational Choices of High Aptitude Students," *Journal of Counseling Psychology,* vol. 12, 1965, pp. 28–34.

[4] The data source of these analyses was obtained from the tables presented in Chapter 8 of Flanagan, John C., and William W. Cooley, *Project Talent One-Year Follow-up Studies,* Cooperative Research Project No. 2333, University of Pittsburgh, School of Education, Pittsburgh, 1966.

[5] The 11-group classification for the career expectations of high school students was as follows: Natural Sciences (mathematician, physical scientist, and biological scientist); Engineering (all types); Business (businessman, accountant, and salesman); Health Professions (physician and dentist); Law (lawyer); Clergy (clergyman); Arts (writer, artist, and entertainer); Teaching (elementary, secondary, and college teacher); Skilled/Technical (engineering or scientific aide; aviator; skilled, structural, or protective worker; medical technician, farmer, barber, office worker, armed forces personnel); Social Science/Social Service (social worker, psychologist, and sociologist); Other (unclassified, pharmacist, nurse, government worker).

TABLE 6.1. *Career Choice Distribution in the Ninth Grade and One Year After High School—Males*

Field	1960 Ninth Grade		1964 One Year After High School		Net Gains and Losses in Percentage Points	Stability Rate[a]
	Number	Per Cent	Number	Per Cent		
1. Natural Sciences	2,008	10.4	879	4.5	− 5.9	12.4
2. Engineering	4,359	22.5	1,746	9.0	−13.5	20.0
3. Business	1,158	6.0	2,710	14.0	+ 8.0	35.1
4. Health—M.D. and D.D.S.	1,233	6.4	819	4.2	− 2.2	26.3
5. Law	793	4.1	659	3.4	− 0.7	20.9
6. Clergy	392	2.0	291	1.5	− 0.5	28.8
7. Arts	382	2.0	621	3.2	+ 1.2	25.4
8. Teaching	864	4.5	1,790	9.2	+ 4.7	27.0
9. Skilled and Technical	5,176	26.7	4,374	22.6	− 4.1	34.0
10. Social Sciences and Services	167	1.0	367	1.9	+ 0.9	3.0
11. Other	2,830	14.6	5,106	26.4	+11.8	33.0

[a] The stability rate is the percentage of the initial group who had the same career choice at the initial and follow-up period.

SOURCE: Flanagan, John C., and William W. Cooley, *Project Talent One-Year Follow-up Studies,* Cooperative Research Project No. 2333. University of Pittsburgh, School of Education, 1966, Table 8–3, p. 175. (Data in table based on a total of 19,362 cases.)

groups shown in Table 6.1. Very few high school freshmen expect to engage in the social sciences or social service occupations, and the proportion remaining stable in this choice is only 3 per cent of the total group.

Most of the high school students who changed their career preference (see Table 6.2) shifted to skilled/technical occupations, business, or teaching. Clergy, arts, social sciences and services, and the health professions, on the other hand, were the least popular careers among those who changed their initial preference. Changes in career choices tended to be into fields allied to the initial choice: those who shifted out of natural sciences tended to go into engineering; those who shifted from engineering tended to go into business; defectors from health and law also shifted into business; clergy and arts defectors shifted into teaching. Since students who prefer engineering or law are more likely to have "entrepreneurial" interests, it is not surprising that they shift to business, whereas students with initial preferences in clergy or arts are apt to shift to teaching.[6]

In summary, career plans of high school freshmen are rather unstable. Two-thirds of the high school ninth-grade students changed their initial career choice to another four years later. These changes reflect some of the developmental aspects of career choice. Ginzberg in his developmental scheme characterized the early adolescent years (13 to 16) as the "tentative choice" period in indi-

[6] Holland, John L., "A Theory of Vocational Choice and Achievement: II, A Four-Year Prediction Study," *Psychological Reports 1963,* vol. 12, 1963, pp. 547–594.

TABLE 6.2. *Proportion of High School Boys Shifting from Each Field Between the Ninth Grade and One Year After High School*

Field Choice in the Ninth Grade	Number	Field Choice One Year After High School (Percentages)										
		1	2	3	4	5	6	7	8	9	10	11
1. Natural Sciences	2,008	12.4	10.7	9.7	6.4	3.4	1.0	3.4	10.4	15.2	3.8	23.5
2. Engineering	4,359	5.0	20.0	13.0	3.0	3.0	1.0	2.0	8.0	21.0	1.0	23.0
3. Business	1,158	3.7	3.6	35.1	1.9	2.6	1.2	2.3	8.1	16.0	1.4	24.0
4. Health—M.D. and D.D.S.	1,233	2.4	5.6	12.7	26.3	5.4	0.6	2.2	8.3	14.4	3.2	18.8
5. Law	793	2.0	4.0	16.0	4.0	20.9	2.0	3.0	11.0	13.0	2.0	21.9
6. Clergy	392	3.1	3.1	8.9	3.1	5.1	28.8	3.1	11.0	12.0	4.1	17.9
7. Arts	382	1.6	1.8	10.2	1.3	1.8	1.0	25.4	11.5	13.6	3.7	28.0
8. Teaching	864	3.0	3.0	13.0	3.0	2.0	1.0	3.0	27.0	17.0	4.1	23.9
9. Skilled/Technical	5,176	3.1	5.8	12.6	1.5	1.7	0.6	2.0	7.0	34.0	1.5	30.2
10. Social Sciences and Services	167	3.6	1.8	13.8	1.8	5.4	1.8	3.0	6.0	20.3	3.0	39.5
11. Other	2,830	4.0	6.0	14.0	2.0	2.0	1.0	5.0	9.0	23.0	1.0	33.0

SOURCE: Flanagan, John C., and William W. Cooley, op. cit., chap. 8 (Data in table based on a total of 19,362 cases.) See Source Note, Table 6.1.

vidual occupational planning.[7] Super also characterizes the adolescent years (15 to 17) as the "Tentative Substage" of the "Exploration Stage" of career development.[8] While these descriptive labels do not fit all young people nor do all youth pass through these stages of career planning at the same time, the titles of these stages indicate the uncrystallized nature of career choices at the beginning of high school. The studies of vacational development lead us to anticipate a lot of career change between the beginning of high school and the beginning of college, and our results verify this expectation.

The Commission staff also examined the career aspirations of college students.[9] A high proportion of them (about two-thirds) also changed their career plans at least once during their college years, but their anticipated careers were rather different from those of high school students. Twice as many college freshmen as high school freshmen aspired to teaching and business careers (see Table 6.3). Less than one-fourth of the college freshmen aspired to careers in science or engineering, as compared to one-third of the ninth-grade high school students.

While engineering, natural science, and health professions were popular with high school freshmen, engineering, teaching, and business were the three most popular preferences among college freshmen. Furthermore, over one-half of the college freshmen aspiring to business and teaching careers proved loyal to these choices four years later. As with the high school students, those college freshmen who aspired to natural science and social science fields have the lowest rates of stability. Social science/social service remained unpopular with college freshmen (only 1 per cent aspired to those careers). Although the proportion of expected careers in social science/social service doubled by 1965, the time of college graduation, it was still small (2 per cent). Because 14.6 per cent of the students *majored* in social science or social work, it appears that most of the

[7] Ginzberg, Eli, S. W. Ginsberg, S. Axelrod, and J. L. Herma, *Occupational Choice: An Approach to a General Theory*. Columbia University Press, New York, 1951, pp. 55–66.

[8] Super, D. E., and P. E. Bachrach, *Scientific Careers and Vocational Developmental Theory*. Teachers College Bureau of Publications, New York, 1957, pp. 40–41.

[9] The sample includes 20,677 male students who were surveyed in the fall of 1961 as freshmen and followed up in the fall of 1965. The career choice item in this longitudinal study was an open-ended question. The subjects' indicated career choices on this item, originally coded into 49 categories, were collapsed into 11 major groups somewhat comparable to those used with the Project TALENT data discussed previously. The 11-group classification for the college sample was: Natural Sciences (biologist, chemist, mathematician, physicist, college researcher, geologist); Engineering (engineer, engineering executive); Business (accountant, businessman, business executive, business administrator, advertising man); Health Fields (physician and dentist); Law (Lawyer); Clergy (clergyman, missionary); Arts (actor, artist, decorator, journalist, architect, musician); Teaching (college professor and teacher); Social Science/Social Service (social worker, sociologist, anthropologist, psychologist); Skilled/Technical (nurse, pilot, military personnel, skilled worker, farmer, diplomat, lab technician, home economist, therapist, veterinarian, interpreter, government worker, pharmacist, secretary or clerical worker, housewife, housewife +); Other (unclassified, no response).

The data from this longitudinal study were provided by the Office of Research of the American Council on Education. For further information on this sample, see Astin, Alexander W., *Who Goes Where to College?* Science Research Associates, Chicago, 1965.

TABLE 6.3. *Career Choice Distribution in the Freshman and Senior Years of College—Males*

Field	1961 College Freshmen		1965 College Seniors		Net Gains and Losses in Percentage Points	Stability Rate[a]
	Number	Per Cent	Number	Per Cent		
1. Natural Sciences	1,299	6.3	875	4.2	—2.1	25.2
2. Engineering	2,846	13.8	1,679	8.1	—5.7	36.5
3. Business	2,178	10.5	4,161	20.1	+9.6	52.0
4. Health—M.D. and D.D.S.	1,978	9.6	1,097	5.3	—4.3	33.9
5. Law	1,002	4.8	1,311	6.3	+1.5	40.8
6. Clergy	275	1.3	272	1.3	0.0	40.7
7. Arts	713	3.4	679	3.3	—0.1	38.1
8. Teaching	2,321	11.2	3,512	17.0	+5.8	52.6
9. Skilled/Technical	1,570	7.6	1,655	8.0	+0.4	32.4
10. Social Sciences and Services	208	1.0	422	2.0	+1.0	22.1
11. Other	6,287	30.4	5,014	24.2	—6.2	28.8

[a] The stability rate is the percentage of the initial group who had the same career choice at the time of the follow-up.

SOURCE: Unpublished data of the American Council on Education, Office of Research. A Longitudinal Study of 1961 College Freshmen. (Data in table based on a total of 20,677 cases.)

students majoring in these fields either define their careers as "teacher" rather than "social scientist," or plan to enter other occupations rather than becoming social workers or social scientists. The three initially most favored careers— business, teaching, and engineering—remained popular with these students four years after entering college.

Table 6.4 shows the proportions of college students who shifted from their initial preference to one of the ten other occupational groups.

Business, teaching, and law were chosen most often as careers by those who changed from their initial career preference, and social science/social service, clergy, arts, and the health professions were chosen least often. The popularity of business and teaching careers with those who change their career plans was also observed in another study which reported on four different samples.[10] Although these samples varied, not only in age and educational attainment but also in scholastic ability, the patterns of change were very similar for all four (see Table 6.5).

The patterns in shifts in career choice—which result in net gains and losses to various occupational groups—appear to reflect to some extent the maturational nature of career development. That is, the student perceives a given career differently at different stages in his educational and occupational development, partly because he gains in self-awareness and in his knowledge about

[10] For further details of this study, see Astin, Helen S., "Patterns of Career Choices Over Time," *Personnel and Guidance Journal*, vol. 45, 1967, pp. 541–546.

TABLE 6.4. *Proportion of College Males Shifting from Each Field Between Freshman and Senior Years of College*

Field Choice (Freshman Year)	Number	Field Choice (Senior Year)										
		1	2	3	4	5	6	7	8	9	10	11
		(Percentages)										
1. Natural Sciences	1,299	25.2	8.3	11.4	3.8	2.8	0.7	2.5	17.3	4.5	1.8	21.5
2. Engineering	2,846	4.3	36.5	18.4	1.1	2.5	0.4	1.0	7.5	6.4	1.3	20.5
3. Business	2,178	0.4	1.9	52.0	0.8	5.8	0.1	1.5	7.7	4.2	1.0	24.6
4. Health—M.D. and D.D.S.	1,978	3.9	1.4	12.9	33.9	7.5	0.7	1.4	10.2	4.8	3.2	20.1
5. Law	1,002	0.9	0.3	16.0	1.1	40.8	0.6	1.2	11.1	5.5	1.7	20.9
6. Clergy	275	0.4	1.1	5.1	2.2	1.5	40.7	6.8	17.5	5.8	3.6	20.4
7. Arts	713	1.4	2.5	12.2	0.6	3.4	0.4	38.1	13.0	5.0	0.4	22.9
8. Teaching	2,321	1.8	1.5	9.6	0.9	1.5	1.2	2.5	52.6	5.7	1.5	21.1
9. Skilled/Technical	1,570	2.5	2.3	14.5	2.4	4.5	0.3	1.1	11.3	32.4	1.4	27.3
10. Social Sciences and Services	208	0.0	0.5	11.5	6.3	4.8	1.4	1.9	14.9	7.7	22.1	28.8
11. Other	6,287	3.8	5.8	21.7	3.7	6.0	1.3	3.0	16.3	7.3	2.2	28.8

SOURCE: American Council on Education, 1961–1965 Longitudinal Study of College Students. (Data in table based on a total of 20,677 cases.)

TABLE 6.5. *Net Percentage Change in the Career Plans of Students Over Time in Four National Samples*

Sample	Occupational Groups					Total Number
	Business	Engineering	Sciences	Education	Other Professions	
Astin Ninth–Twelfth Grade (1960–1963)	+7.7	− 4.7	− 2.9	+ 7.2	−1.8	650 (Males)
Flanagan Ninth–One Year After High School (1960–1964)	+7.1	−13.4	− 4.4	+ 4.5	−3.3	19,352 (Males)
Davis Freshman–Senior Year in College (1957–1961)	+5.5	− 6.1	+ 0.9	+ 7.9	−2.0	49,817 (Males and Females)
Nichols Freshman–Senior Year in College (1957–1961)	+3.2	−17.2	−13.9	+12.3	+3.1	4,474 (Males)

SOURCES: The ninth–twelfth grade data are based on special tabulations from the Project TALENT sample, described in Astin, Helen S., "Patterns of Career Choices Over Time," *Personnel and Guidance Journal*, vol. 45, 1967, pp. 541–546. The ninth–one year after high school follow-up is described in Flanagan, John C., and William W. Cooley, *Project Talent One Year Follow-up Studies*, University of Pittsburgh, School of Education, 1966, chap. 8. The Davis college sample is described in Davis, James, *Undergraduate Career Decisions*, Aldine Publishing Co., Chicago, 1964. The Nichols sample is described in Nichols, Robert C., "Career Decisions of Very Able Students," *Science*, June 12, 1964.

what is involved in preparing for a career, and partly because he has different personal needs at different developmental stages. Some "changers" may merely be expressing their original choice in different terms: as they grow older, they take into consideration the setting or the institution in which they will work, and they decide to be, let us say, scientists in a business setting, rather than in an academic institution.

Another possible interpretation is that these consistent patterns can be explained on the basis of the environmental, cultural, and educational influences that determine career development. It could be that our high school curricula and teaching methods encourage students to take up pragmatic and applied careers (business and education) rather than theoretical and research-oriented careers. In the case of medicine, dentistry, law, and engineering, which are also applied fields, the need for early commitment and highly specialized training may discourage students from aspiring to these careers, or they may simply recognize that they do not have the aptitudes and achievements required for these careers.

In considering the educational environment and its effect on career decisions, one should also examine the overall cultural and social forces that may be operating. All the samples included here were assessed during the late 1950's and early 1960's, and thus the shifts to choices of careers in education may reflect the increasing needs for teachers at all levels, and the concomitant efforts expended to persuade students to take up careers in education. During the same period (the late 1950's and early 1960's) there was at least an equal and perhaps greater emphasis on recruitment of students to careers in science and engineering. This recruitment effort was unsuccessful in increasing the proportion of youth graduating with degrees in engineering, or in slowing the decline in career choices of engineering among young men during the high school and college years.

The increasing demand in the job market and publicity about needs for recruits to teaching led to changing career choices, but in engineering the same efforts did not markedly affect the patterns of choice. The role of the college curricula in discouraging the less able aspirants to engineering is probably quite important. In education, by contrast, the curriculum and teaching methods do not appear to have the effect of discouraging the less able students from becoming teachers.

Trends in Career Plans

So far, we have considered patterns of career choice, particularly with regard to the career stability and career change within the same samples of students. To find out more about the emerging supplies for different fields and to discover how societal and cultural needs and expectations shape the anticipated careers of young persons, we examined the career choices of a sample of freshmen entering college in the fall of 1961 and those of another sample entering college in the fall of 1965; our primary aim was to see if there were any changes in the most popular career choices among a more recent freshman class as compared to the choices of the 1961 freshmen.[11] While the trends may not be fully representative of the entire population of college freshmen, they are probably not too dissimilar.[12]

An examination of Figure 6.1 suggests that the health professions (M.D. and D.D.S.), law, social sciences/social service, arts, and teaching have become more popular, while the natural sciences and engineering have become less popular since 1961. This finding is consistent with trends for successive samples of National Merit semifinalists as reported by Nichols. His results show that there were progressive decreases between 1957 and 1963 in the proportions of Merit semifinalists who preferred physical sciences and engineering and increases in the proportions preferring humanities and social sciences. With regard to career expectations, teaching, law, and medicine showed increases, while science and engineering showed decreases.[13] These trends suggest that students have been moving away from technical and scientific careers—which received a great deal of publicity in the 1950's—and toward careers in the artistic and social fields. The interest in social science and teaching may be, in part, a result of the emergence of new government programs such as the Peace Corps, VISTA, Head Start, and so forth.

Personal and Environmental Determinants of Career Outcomes

Studies of the determinants of vocational choice are primarily aimed at developing predictors of career outcomes. If we could predict which students in the ninth grade would be planning different types of careers four years later, or if we could identify the students who would be likely to change their career plans over time, our educational and other training institutions would be better prepared to meet future student demands for different fields and our manpower planning would be facilitated. Furthermore, our ability to assess early a student's personal characteristics as they relate to eventual career choice and stability would help guidance counselors to aid students more efficiently in their educational choices and long-range career plans.

As we have seen, although career plans during the high school and even

[11] These data were obtained from the research files of the Office of Research of the American Council on Education. The data on the career plans of entering freshmen of 1961 were collected as part of a national survey of all entering freshmen at 246 institutions. The data for 1965 entering freshmen were obtained as part of a pilot study of entering freshmen at 61 institutions. Forty-five institutions were common to the two samples.

[12] Further characteristics of these 45 institutions are described by Alexander W. Astin in "Trends in the Characteristics of Entering College Students, 1961–1965," paper presented at the 1966 meeting of the Association for Institutional Research, in Boston. The career choices of all entering freshmen in the same 45 institutions in 1961 and 1965 were the data used in the analysis of trends presented in Figure 6.1. Compared with all higher educational institutions, these 45 institutions enroll students who tend to be more intellectual and masculine and to come from higher socioeconomic backgrounds. The sample of institutions is also somewhat more selective and wealthier than the general institutional population.

[13] Nichols, Robert C., "Career Decisions of Very Able Students," *Science,* June 12, 1964.

FIGURE 6.1 *Career Plans of Entering College Male Freshmen: 1961 and 1965*

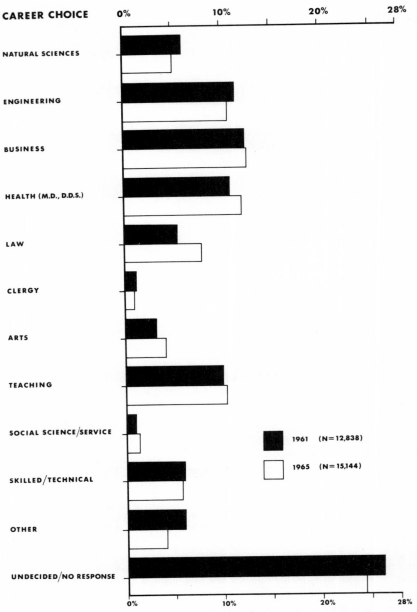

SOURCE: Special tabulations provided by the American Council on Education—Office of Research.

during the college years are rather unstable (at least one-half of the students change their plans), and often unrealistic, certain predictable patterns do exist. Certain careers, such as business and teaching, attract more people than they lose. Moreover, certain career groups have greater stability rates than others. For example, high school and college students who initially aspired to careers in business, teaching, and as clergy were more likely to maintain the same career plans over time than were students who had aspired initially to careers in natural sciences or social sciences.

If we accept the postulate that people choose careers for which they think they possess the necessary skills and interests for success, these observed career changes during the preparatory years (high school and college) are essential in the sorting-out process of occupational development. As people become more aware of themselves and of the unique requirements and rewards of different occupations, they will change their plans if their self-concept seems to be inconsistent with the careers they have been considering. Therefore, one would expect that students who are unlike most of the other students with the same initial career plans to be more likely to change their plans. Davis[14] and Werts,[15] who have studied career changes among college students, both report that students who deviate in ability and socioeconomic status from the majority of students with the same initial career plan are more likely to change their career plans over time. Thus, because of career decisions and changes in plans during the college years, occupations become more differentiated with respect to the characteristics of people aspiring to them.

Occupations that are more often chosen by men become more male dominated over time, whereas occupations that are considered feminine tend to increase the proportion of women in them as the result of career shifts. Occupations that initially attract better students academically tend to lose students who have less academic ability. Occupations that require longer training (for example, medicine, law) not only initially attract students from higher socioeconomic backgrounds, but also emerge with a greater proportion of students from high socioeconomic backgrounds.[16]

Another staff study, based on a sample of 16,773 male subjects from the Project TALENT who were initially tested in 1960 when they were in the ninth grade and followed up in 1964, also indicates similar patterns.[17]

One of the test items administered to the TALENT sample at both times was a question regarding expected career choice. A 10-group classification system

[14] Davis, James, *op. cit.*

[15] Werts, Charles E., *Career Choice Patterns: Ability and Social Class.* National Merit Scholarship Corporation Research Reports, 1966, No. 3, Evanston, Ill.

[16] Davis, James, *op. cit.*, pp. 73–77.

[17] Most of the analyses reported herein are based on the 16,733 unweighted number of cases. However, the flow chart of career plan changes, the stability rates, and the overall gains and losses in the career groups are based on a weighted number of 19,353 cases adjusted for nonrespondent biases.

was used to classify the student's initial and final choices.[18] Each subject was then classified as a "Stable," or as a "Defector" from one group and a "Recruit" to another. Thus, if he chose a career in business when he was in the ninth grade and again when he was followed up one year after high school, he was classified as a business Stable. If, on the other hand, he shifted to another choice, he was counted as a business Defector, but as a Recruit to the career group he chose in the follow-up assessment.

On the basis of these classifications, the sample was divided into 30 groups. (See Appendix C for the number in each of the 30 subgroups.) The subjects classified either as Stables, Defectors, or Recruits in any of the 10 career groups were compared on scores from different aptitude, achievement interest, and personality measures that they had provided when they were tested as ninth-graders in 1960.

Furthermore, to determine how the shifts that took place during the four-year span affected the composition of the group, the ten career groups were compared at the two points of time on the basis of their means and standard deviations on five selected aptitude measures.

The mean differences obtained in seven (natural sciences, engineering, business, health professions, law, clergy, and teaching) of the nine groups examined (see Tables C.1 through C.9 in Appendix C) indicate that the Defectors of each group score significantly lower than do the Stables on the aptitude measures (35 out of the 42 t-tests performed yielded significant p values at the 0.05 level or greater); with regard to cumulative grade point average, five out of the seven t-tests were significant; on the interest measures, four out of seven mean differences were significant; and on a temperament scale designed to measure mature personality, four out of seven mean differences were significant. Five out of the seven mean differences on socioeconomic status were significant; one would expect students from lower socioeconomic backgrounds to change their plans as they realize that some careers require a longer time in educational preparation and greater expenses. All of the remaining mean differences were in the predicted direction: The Stables were superior on the measures employed.

The other two occupational groups (arts and skilled/technical) did not exhibit these patterns. The three subgroups (Stables, Defectors, and Recruits) of the arts career groups did not differ from one another in any significant way. The Defectors from the skilled/technical group scored significantly higher than the Stables of that group on every measure employed.

The Recruits to business, health, law, clergy, teaching, and skilled/technical

---

[18] The 10-group classification was as follows: Natural Sciences (mathematician, physical scientist, and biological scientist); Engineering (all types); Business (businessman, accountant, and salesman); Health Professions (physician and dentist); Law (lawyer); Clergy (clergyman); Arts (writer, artist, and entertainer); Teaching (all levels); Skilled/Technical (engineering or scientific aide; aviator; skilled, structural or protective worker; medical technician; farmer; barber; office worker; and military personnel); Other (unclassified, pharmacist, social worker, psychologist, sociologist, nurse, and government worker.)

did not make significantly different scores from the Stables of these groups on the aptitude measures employed. The Recruits to engineering and to natural sciences, on the other hand, scored significantly lower in aptitude than the Stables of those two groups.

Furthermore, the Recruits to the career groups did not resemble the Stables of those groups in their scores on the interest measures or on the temperament scale. The Recruits tended to score significantly lower than the Stables on the mature personality scale.

Over the four-year span, practically all the groups (with the exception of skilled/technical, arts, and other) seem to have increased in aptitude and to have become more homogeneous (see Table 6.6). The composition of the arts group, however, did not change, a finding which may be attributable to the types of measures employed. One might, indeed, find differences between Stables, Recruits, and Defectors in this group if one were to compare them on non-intellective measures such as artistic ability. The final composition of the skilled/technical group shows a decrease in aptitude. Although the means of the group that included other occupations increased, the standard deviations also increased, indicating that the group composition became more heterogeneous over the four-year span. The health professions, law, and teaching groups show the greatest mean increases.

The shifts that took place during the high school years resulted in each of the groups becoming more homogeneous in aptitude (Table 6.6). Moreover, the pool of talent (as reflected in the measure of academic aptitude) was more evenly distributed four years later. The Defectors from science and engineering tended to raise the mean score of the career groups to which they were recruited.

Although some groups did better than others, the mean aptitude scores for all the professional and business/managerial occupational groups were higher four years later, primarily because the fields which the brighter students initially chose (natural sciences and engineering) tended to lose more subjects than they recruited. Therefore, the fields that recruited the Defectors from these two fields raised their mean aptitude scores.

The finding that the less intellectually able students are more likely to change their plans suggests that brighter students make appropriate choices earlier, thus demonstrating a greater degree of career stability over time. That is, the more academically capable students are probably better aware of their aptitudes, skills, and interests and of career requirements and opportunities, and thus can choose careers that are more realistic and congruent with their personal qualities. The intellectually less capable, on the other hand, tend early to make unrealistic career plans which they change as they grow older in the direction of greater realism.

Another possible interpretation of these changes in career plans is that they result from maturational changes. That is, young students tend to base voca-

TABLE 6.6. *Means and Standard Deviations on Selected Aptitude Measures of the Initial Group Choosing Each Career Field and Final Group Choosing Each Career Field*

Field		R-100 (Grand Total)		R-230 (English Total)		R-250 (Reading Comp.)		R-290 (Abstract Reas.)		R-340 (Total Math)	
		M	SD	M	SD	M	SD	M	SD	M	SD
Natural Sciences	I	232.68	49.35	82.99	11.39	33.85	9.51	9.93	2.73	25.73	8.10
	F	235.72	44.21	84.19	10.84	34.40	8.89	10.20	2.60	26.69	7.81
Engineering	I	219.92	47.15	80.71	10.71	31.49	9.30	9.72	2.66	24.14	7.36
	F	231.27	43.01	83.33	9.44	33.36	8.38	10.39	2.35	26.45	7.21
Business	I	194.57	48.98	77.15	12.43	27.71	9.89	8.84	2.98	21.47	7.29
	F	200.36	43.20	78.11	10.73	28.43	9.10	8.92	2.65	21.21	6.55
Health	I	221.53	46.55	81.99	10.62	32.37	9.06	9.47	2.57	23.74	7.60
	F	240.89	38.94	85.40	8.98	35.59	7.66	10.19	2.39	26.34	7.03
Law	I	216.69	49.28	80.92	12.63	32.15	9.85	9.06	2.79	22.85	7.60
	F	234.89	42.73	84.01	9.96	35.20	8.19	9.81	2.45	24.99	7.41
Clergy	I	214.61	45.46	84.16	12.79	32.87	9.23	9.71	2.57	24.41	7.15
	F	224.07	44.95	85.40	9.49	33.75	8.73	9.93	2.34	25.51	6.55
Arts	I	208.10	48.67	79.16	13.03	30.25	10.64	9.33	2.78	20.71	7.29
	F	209.16	50.32	79.77	13.01	30.15	10.14	9.30	2.78	21.10	7.09
Teaching	I	201.41	54.60	77.84	13.95	28.94	11.01	8.55	3.01	21.82	7.48
	F	215.17	43.75	80.87	10.30	31.45	9.13	9.36	2.69	22.96	7.10
Skilled/ Technical	I	189.24	45.85	74.63	11.57	25.85	9.77	8.60	2.84	19.61	6.46
	F	181.46	47.15	72.53	12.28	24.37	9.80	8.21	2.99	18.77	6.44
Other	I	195.49	46.21	76.67	11.71	27.54	9.71	8.77	2.80	20.41	6.79
	F	202.68	51.15	77.59	12.20	28.86	10.35	8.98	2.86	21.51	5.93

I = Initial composition of career group in the ninth grade.

F = Final composition of career group one year after high school graduation.

SOURCE: Special tabulations from the ninth-grade one-year follow-up file of the Project TALENT Data Bank.

tional decisions primarily on their interests, but as they mature, they take into account the abilities required for success in different occupations. Therefore, they change their career plans in order to make them more consistent with their own aptitudes. If this is so, then it would be desirable to explore measured interests in greater detail to determine whether and how interests are modified with maturation. For instance, are high school students more interested in social service when they finish high school than they are when they first enter? The finding that the Recruits to the different groups did not score as high as the Stables or the Defectors of that group on the interest measures employed suggests that a number of the students in the Defector group would show changes in their interest patterns if they were to be retested. As partial support for this hypothesis, Cooley reports that students who had the same career plans between the ninth and twelfth grade in high school also remain more stable in their measured interests.[19]

Thus, the analysis of career plan changes and of the characteristics of students who are likely to change indicates that there are predictable patterns of change over time among high school and college students. Another very important question in studies of career development is whether one can predict future career plans if one knows about certain characteristics of the student and of the environment of the high school or college he attends. One of the main aims of a longitudinal study of college freshmen, conducted by the American Council on Education's Office of Research staff, was to explore this question, by attempting to predict the future career plans of freshmen entering college in the fall of 1961 who were followed up four years later (fall of 1965). Of the 85 separate personal variables employed, 29 variables, in addition to initial career expectation and intended major, were significant predictors of career outcomes.[20] Initial career expectation and intended major were the best predictors. These two variables accounted for about two-thirds of the weight in the prediction equation. Other variables, too, contributed to the prediction of different career plans. For instance, students who came from larger high schools were more likely to plan future careers in bioscience and college teaching. The student who had high scholastic achievement in high school tended to choose careers in the natural sciences, medicine, law, and college teaching. The higher the father's income, the more likely the son was to plan a career in either law or business. The student's level of aspiration, as measured by his future plans for advanced edu-

[19] Cooley, William W., "Vocational Interests." Paper read at the Annual Meeting of the American Educational Research Association, New York, February 18, 1965.

[20] A 13-group career classification was employed (Biosciences, Business, Clergy, College Teaching, Engineering, Health Professions—non-M.D., Law, Arts, Physical Sciences, Medicine and Dentistry, Social Sciences, Teacher, and Other). The stepwise multiple regression technique was the method of analysis employed. The personal variables that entered the prediction equation were: size of high school; grade-point average in high school; achievements in high school (science, art, music, leadership, writing); sex; father's income; father's occupation; mother's education; level of aspiration; race; and religion.

cation and the highest degree he sought, predicted careers in social sciences and college teaching. Sons were inclined to choose a career in the same field as the father.

The two institutional characteristics that proved to be the most important predictors in this study were the type of institution the student attended and the type of student-teacher interaction he experienced. Students increased their chances of planning engineering careers if they attended technological institutions. Furthermore, students who planned careers in college teaching were more likely to remain stable in their choice if they attended colleges in which the interactions between students and teachers were described as familiar and friendly. This effect, in conjunction with the importance of father's occupation as a predictor of a like occupational choice for the son, suggests that a strong identification with authority-figures (father or teacher) influences significantly the career plans of some young people.

Because the high school years are so important in career development and because decisions made during that time may determine one's occupational role later in life, the Commission on Human Resources conducted a study to investigate whether the career plans of high school seniors could be predicted from information about the subjects when they were in the ninth grade and from information about the types of high schools they attended. There are two critical decision points that confront high school students. The first comes during the freshman year in high school, when most students choose the type of high school curriculum they intend to take. The second occurs during the twelfth grade, at which time the student must decide whether to pursue higher education or vocational education, to enter the military service, or to find a job.

This study was designed with two main goals in mind: to identify some of the ninth-grade student's personal characteristics that would predict his career choice three years later as he was about to terminate high school and to identify any institutional factors and other environmental experiences that might influence certain occupational outcomes.[21]

The results of the discriminant analyses performed indicated that twelfth-grade boys with different career choices can be differentiated on the basis of several characteristics they exhibited three years earlier in the ninth grade.

---

[21] The sample for this study consisted of 650 male subjects from the Project TALENT Data Bank, all of whom were originally tested in 1960. It was limited to high school seniors (as of 1963) who had taken the Student Information Blank (SIB) during the 1963 retesting, because the SIB contains the criterion item: "Stated career choice in the senior year of high school."

A 7-group a priori classification of occupations was employed (Sciences, Engineering, Teaching, Professions, Business, Non-college Careers, and Unclassified). From the Project TALENT battery of tests, 26 measures of the students' personal characteristics in the ninth grade and three measures of high school environmental characteristics were selected (see description of variables and method of analysis in Appendix C).

For further details, see Astin, Helen S., "Career Development During the High School Years," *Journal of Counseling Psychology*, vol. 14, 1967, pp. 94–98.

Their measured interests and their initial career choices appeared to be the most potent ninth-grade predictors of the twelfth-grade career choice. In general, the twelfth-grade career choice is best predicted from similar choices and interests expressed three years earlier. Flanagan and Cooley,[22] in a study of the career plans of students after they had been out of high school for a year, found that measured interests at the ninth grade were better predictors of later plans than abilities were. However, the student's career plans in the ninth grade were an even better predictor of future plans than were measured interests or abilities.

When the three high school predictor variables (size of high school, high school mean on reading comprehension, and proportion of students who go to college) were included in a second analysis, the predictive value of the test battery was somewhat improved.[23] The results of this second analysis suggest that the larger high schools and those that have students who score higher on reading comprehension tended to influence students toward careers in the professions and away from careers in teaching and engineering. Although it is not possible to generalize this finding adequately without better data on the environments of the larger and more intellectually stimulating high schools, we can say that the characteristics of the high school play an important role in shaping the careers of some students.

In summary, these analyses indicated that knowing a student's interests and other personal orientations at the ninth grade increased the probability of predicting his career choice when he was about to terminate high school by 25 per cent better than chance. In brief, the engineering aspirants showed an earlier interest in physical science, tended to choose college preparatory curricula, possessed mathematical information, and were likely in the ninth grade to choose engineering as a career. Seniors choosing careers in the sciences showed an earlier interest in physical science and literature-linguistics, and they tended to obtain higher reading comprehension scores than did those subjects aspiring to other occupations. Seniors aspiring to the professions tended as ninth-graders to score high on the mature personality temperament scale, to possess more information about literature, and to come from larger high schools and from high schools in which the school mean on reading comprehension is higher.

The business group tended earlier to score high on the business or management scale, to receive low scores on literature-linguistics interest and literature information, and to score high on the English variables. For the teaching group, interests in social service and literature-linguistics appeared to be the best predictors. High scores on physical science interests and mathematics information and a career choice of engineering in the ninth grade were negative predictors of a twelfth-grade career choice of teaching.

[22]Flanagan, John C., and William W. Cooley, *Project TALENT One-Year Follow-up Studies,* chap. 9.

[23] When we added the three high school variables, Wilk's λ decreased by three units, bringing the equivalent χ^2 value from 532 to 576. Wilk's λ can be viewed as an inverse multivariate generalization of the F statistic in Analysis of Variance.

Summary and Conclusions

Our examination of career development during the high school and college years shows that the career plans of students go through a great deal of change and modification. More than two-thirds of the high school students changed their plans during high school, and about 50 per cent of college freshmen report different career plans four years later when they terminate their college experience. In spite of this instability in individual career plans, however, there are predictable patterns in the type of career changes that take place and in the characteristics of students who change their plans over time.

When students are high school or college freshmen, they tend to prefer careers in the sciences or engineering, but at the termination (or shortly after) of their high school or college education, they choose careers in business and teaching. Students who initially plan careers in sciences, engineering, the professions, or teaching and who change those plans tend to score lower on measures of academic aptitude than do students who maintain the same plans over time. On the other hand, students with higher scores on measured aptitudes change from choices of technical and skilled occupations to choices of careers that require more education and specialized training. As a result of these shifts, occupational groups become more homogeneous with respect to the characteristics of their members; at the same time, the pool of talent (with respect to measured academic ability) increases for each of the professional fields.

A trend analysis of the career plans of two different college freshmen classes, one in 1961 and one in 1965, indicates that the popularity of different careers changes over time. More students are now aspiring to careers in social sciences and humanities, whereas science and engineering have become somewhat less popular in the four-year period.

One primary concern of manpower specialists is whether the supply will be adequate to meet future demands in a number of specialized fields: Are people making vocational choices and receiving training for fields that are appropriate to society's needs? If not, can choices be influenced to ensure that the necessary supply of trained talent will be available? These concerns about adequate manpower supplies should be tempered, however, with a recognition that there are a variety of mechanisms for adjusting to an ever-changing world of work: the interrelationships of occupations, the overlapping interests and abilities of people in different occupations, the adaptability of individuals to changing environmental demands, and so forth.

Furthermore, the longitudinal studies reported in this chapter indicate that, although our ability to predict the career plans of individuals during the pre-college and college years is meager, certain characteristics of the high school and college environment do affect career outcomes. These findings and other research may be useful in the development of guidance and counseling techniques as well as in the development of innovative curricula.

7 The Mobility of
High-Level Manpower*

THE CAREERS of highly educated persons in the United States are characterized by a great deal of mobility, which takes several different forms. For instance, as the preceding chapter indicates, students as they mature may change their major fields and their career choices to make them more congruent with their personal characteristics. Many of these changes occur early in the student's educational experience and shifts in occupational plans continue through the undergraduate college years.

Even subsequent to completion of the undergraduate degree, persons continue to exhibit mobility of various kinds. The most obvious kind is geographic mobility, which often begins after completion of high school. The proportion of students who leave home (often for the first time) to attend college has always been substantial,[1] and by the end of the past decade more than two-thirds of all undergraduate students in American colleges and universities did *not* live with their parents or with other relatives.[2] Among college seniors, only about one-fourth live with parents or relatives.[3] Moreover, many students migrate to other states or regions of the country for their education. Approxi-

---

* An earlier version of parts of this chapter appeared in *Sociology of Education,* vol. 41, 1968, pp. 88–102, under the title "Interregional Migration and the Education of American Scientists," by Alan E. Bayer.
[1] A fairly comprehensive historical review is presented by H. Theodore Groat in "Internal Migration Patterns of a Population Subgroup, College Students 1887–1958," *American Journal of Sociology,* vol. 64, January, 1964, pp. 383–394.
[2] Computed from U.S. Bureau of the Census, *U.S. Census of Population: 1960, Subject Reports, School Enrollment,* Final Report PC (2)–5A, Government Printing Office, Washington, 1964, p. 74.
[3] *Ibid.*

mately one out of every six undergraduate students attends a college outside his home state, and even among junior and community college students, one out of ten crosses state lines to attend. More than one-third of the students enrolled in professional schools and about one-fourth of those in graduate schools migrate to other states for their advanced training.[4] After formal education is completed, the flow of manpower across state and regional boundaries persists. Although a person becomes less likely to migrate the longer he has been in the labor market, a large proportion of the highly educated remain geographically mobile throughout their careers. The first section of this chapter explores the extent and effects of this geographic mobility, particularly with respect to interregional migration flows of those who hold doctoral degrees.

A second type of mobility manifested by highly trained persons in the United States is mobility from one career field to another or from one area of specialization to another. The high degree of technical training often required for entrance into a high-level occupation and the pressure on the adult to get on with his career restricts to some extent this type of mobility. Nevertheless, stability of career choice beyond the undergraduate years is not universal, and the second section of this chapter focuses on some of the changes that occur.

Closely related to mobility between fields are the less dramatic changes that may occur after a person has entered the labor force. Such changes include switches from one sector of the economy to another—from employment in a college or university to employment in an agency of the federal government, for example—and changes of employer, for example, shifts from one university to another. The third section of the chapter discusses the vertical and horizontal occupational mobility of highly educated persons, particularly those who hold doctoral degrees.

The long period of formal education required for entry to most professions and their higher degree of specialization leads to lower rates of occupational mobility for the professions. A variety of surveys of occupational mobility made between 1940 and 1966 indicate that job shifts in and out of the professions are only at about two-thirds the average rate for all occupations.[5] Annual occupational mobility rates for the professions ranged from a high of 8 per cent in 1946 (a period of postwar adjustment) to a low of about 4 per cent in 1966.

By contrast, geographic mobility for professional occupations is about 60 to 70 per cent *higher* than the average migration rates for all occupations. These

[4] Folger, John K., and Charles B. Nam, *Education of the American Population,* Government Printing Office, Washington, 1967, chap. 2; American Association of Collegiate Registrars and Admissions Officers, *Home State and Migration of American College Students, Fall 1958,* March, 1959.
[5] Average annual rates for 1940 to 1950 can be computed from Gladys Palmer's *Labor Mobility in Six Cities,* Social Science Research Council, New York, 1954, p. 115. Two national sample surveys of the Census Bureau collected information on occupational mobility. The first of these was based on the August, 1946, sample survey of the Bureau of the Census, *Current Population Reports,* Labor Force Series, P-50, No. 1, July 11, 1947, and the second from the January, 1966, sample survey, *Special Labor Force Reports, Occupational Mobility of Employed Workers.*

figures are for the young adult ages when migration is at a maximum; because professionals remain mobile longer, their rates are even more above the average at older ages. Recurring sample surveys of the Census have indicated an annual average geographic mobility rate of about 10 per cent for professionals in the past decade.[6] Although we have fewer measures of occupational mobility, the available comparisons suggest that geographic mobility rates among professional workers are about twice as large as occupational mobility rates, and geographic mobility is more important in distributing and redistributing workers to jobs.

In all but the most rapidly growing professions the number of people who migrate to new jobs in the same profession, and the number who move from one type of job to another each year exceed the new entrants to the profession; these figures underline the importance of mobility processes in the total picture of manpower supply and demand.

Geographic Mobility and Regional Gain and Loss of Educated Persons

Change of residence is often required for college attendance; indeed, it is the mode. Few college students live at home with their parents. Large numbers of them cross state and regional boundaries to attend institutions of higher education, and the proportion who migrate tends to increase as the level of education sought increases. Of those going on for doctoral degrees, almost one-half make a major geographic change—from one region of the United States to another. Moreover, this high level of geographic mobility has existed over the past several decades since 1930.[7]

Subsequent to completion of education, too, we find that the more highly educated a person is, the greater his geographic mobility tends to be. In Shryock and Nam's[8] recent report of a comprehensive analysis of interregional migration over the last quarter of a century, it is shown that interregional migration tends to be most frequent among the better educated. In practically all interregional migration streams, both whites and nonwhites of all age groups who have some college background are overrepresented, as compared with persons who have completed elementary school or high school. Among those who have had varying amounts of college education, geographic mobility increases as degree level becomes higher. Among doctorate recipients of the past few decades, approximately one-half leave the region of their doctoral training for their first post-

[6] The most recent survey report is *Current Population Reports, Population Characteristics,* Series P-20, No. 156, December 9, 1966, Table 10, which indicated that 10.5 per cent of professional workers migrated during the year.
[7] Based on the nine regional divisions employed by the Bureau of the Census and computed from Harmon, Lindsey R., and Herbert Soldz, compilers, *Doctorate Production in United States Universities: 1920–1962,* National Academy of Sciences–National Research Council, Publication No. 1142, Washington, 1963, pp. 188–201.
[8] Henry S. Shryock, Jr., and Charles B. Nam, "Educational Selectivity of Interregional Migration," *Social Forces,* vol. 43, March, 1965, pp. 299–310.

doctoral position.[9] As the length of time in the labor market increases, however, less interregional migration takes place.[10] Nevertheless, one-sixth of all full-time college faculty were serving their first year on a new job in 1964–1965, and even if the nation is divided into only four regions, one-half of the new faculty who are scientists had migrated across regional boundaries.[11]

This extensive interchange of high-level manpower during both the training and the employment periods has been of continuing interest and concern to educators and others, particularly to those whose regions experience a net loss. It is felt that some regions get more than their fair share of highly educated manpower. The recent call for a more "equitable" regional distribution of federal funds for higher education and for research exemplifies a similar concern at the national level.

What Is Regional "Gain" or "Loss"?

Until recently, "gain" and "loss" have been defined quantitatively, as the net numerical distribution and redistribution of high-level manpower in the regional labor force. A "gain" or "loss" in a region is proclaimed if there is an imbalance either in (a) the ratio of the number of living "natives" (defined on the basis of place of birth, place of high school graduation, or place of undergraduate education) who eventually attain the doctorate to the number of doctor recipients in the regional labor force, or (b) the ratio of the number of doctorate recipients annually produced in the region's educational institutions to the number of doctorate recipients annually entering the regional labor force. The first employs the "native" pool of intellectually and culturally able (as defined by attainment of the doctorate) as a referent; the second employs the amount of graduate education provided in the region as a referent. The first type of imbalance may be referred to as the "untrained brain gain (loss)"; the latter as the "trained brain gain (loss)." Other quantitative approaches may use as their basis the absolute number of doctorates in a region relative to the absolute number within another region; or the number of doctorates per unit of population in the region relative to that in other regions.

Regardless of how "gain" and "loss" are measured, however, the quantitative definition is inadequate for an accurate assessment of "regional equity." The *qualitative* component in the interregional migration of doctorates is just as important—and probably more so—in assessing a region's "wealth" of doctorate-level manpower as is the sheer numbrs. Indeed, a region may experience a net numerical loss and at the same time a qualitative gain (in the ability level, edu-

[9] Hollis, Ernest V., *Toward Improving Ph.D. Programs,* American Council on Education, Washington, 1945, pp. 42–54; and Harmon, Lindsey R., *Profiles of Ph.D.'s in the Sciences,* National Academy of Sciences–National Research Council, Publication No. 1293, Washington, 1965, pp. 7–14.
[10] Harmon, Lindsey R., *op. cit.*
[11] Brown, David G., and Jay L. Tontz, *The Mobility of Academic Scientists.* National Science Foundation, Washington, 1966, pp. 79, 133.

cational experience, or achievement of the incoming doctorate recipients), and the converse holds true also.

In a recent report Abbott Ferriss compares qualitative and quantitative regional imbalances in the concentration of graduate students in science.[12] Quantitatively, the Pacific, New England, and the East North Central Census Divisions are big gainers in numbers of science graduate students (relative to the number of students in graduate school who received their high school education in the region). The Middle Atlantic Division is a big loser, while the West North Central and South Atlantic regions lose moderately. The other three Census divisions about hold their own. Qualitatively, however, the picture is somewhat different. If we consider the academic potential (as defined by the undergraduate grade-point average of the students going to graduate schools in the region), we find that the South Atlantic, which experiences a quantitative loss, has a moderate qualitative gain. The Pacific, New England, and the East North Central Divisions gain in graduate student quality (as well as quantity). Only the Middle Atlantic and West North Central regions lose "academic potential" through student migration.

Another approach to assessing the qualitative regional distribution of American doctorates is taken by John Creager, in his study of more than 1,500 National Science Foundation graduate fellowship candidates.[13] Assuming that, among fellowship candidates, awardees as a group are more able than nonawardees, Creager assesses a region's wealth in terms of the percentage of awardees that it attracts for employment. New England and the Midwest emerge as having the most advantageous positions; whereas the Middle Atlantic area experiences the most adverse balance. The South and West attract approximately equal proportions of awardees and nonawardees.

To explore further the regional distribution of "wealth" (assessed on a qualitative rather than a quantitative basis), the Commission on Human Resources analyzed the migration flows of high-level talent. The analysis was confined to persons who had received their doctoral degrees in selected science disciplines in the period 1957 to 1960 and who reported their place of employment four to seven years after completion of the degree to the 1964 National Register of Scientific and Technical Personnel.[14] The measure of "quality" used was the quality of graduate education that the subject had received, judged on the basis

[12] Ferriss, Abbott L., "Characteristics of Migrating Graduate Students." Paper presented at the Annual Meeting of the American Sociological Association, Miami Beach, Florida, August 30, 1966.

[13] Creager, John A., *Some Characteristics of Former Fellowship Applicants Six to Nine Years Later,* National Academy of Sciences-National Research Council, Technical Report No. 20, Washington, May 15, 1962, pp. 11–15. For a further discussion of these data, see Harmon, Lindsey R., *Fourteen Years of Research on Fellowship Selection,* National Academy of Sciences–National Research Council, Publication No. 1420, Washington, 1966, pp. 24–25.

[14] For a further discussion of the sample, see Appendix D and Alan E. Bayer's "Interregional Migration and the Education of American Scientists," paper presented at the Annual Meeting of the Southern Sociological Society, Atlanta, Georgia, April, 1967.

of Allan Cartter's ratings[15] of degree of excellence of the graduate department attended: there were seven categories, with "1" denoting the highest quality departments and "7" the lowest.[16] The seven regions considered in the analysis correspond to the nine regional divisions employed by the Bureau of the Census, except that the "Southeast" combines the South Atlantic and East South Central Census Divisions, and the "West" includes both the Mountain and West South Central Census Divisions.[17] The remainder of this section reports the results of this analysis.

A Migration Paradigm

Looking at migration flows across regional boundaries over three points in time—from home region (place of high school) to graduate school region (place of Ph.D.) to region of employment in 1964—we find that persons fall into five distinct categories, on the basis of the migration pattern they exhibit (Figure 7.1).

The *Returnee* (Ia) leaves the home region for his Ph.D. work, but returns upon completion of the degree to employment in the home region. The *Unattached* (Ib) exhibits the most mobile pattern of the five. He leaves the home region for his Ph.D. education and then enters a third region for his employment. The *Recruit* (II) also leaves the home region, but secures his employment in the same region as that in which he received his doctoral education. The *Defector* (III), on the other hand, remains in the home region through the completion of his graduate education, but then goes to another region for employment. The *Loyalist* (IV) has the most stable pattern; he does not migrate to another region at all.

The quality of Ph.D. education received of these five types were compared, in order to explore a number of questions regarding the regional interflow of

FIGURE 7.1 *A Typology of Interregional Migration Patterns*

Home (High School) to Ph.D.	Ph.D. to Employment	
	Migration	No Migration
Migration	(Ia) Returnee (Ib) Unattached	(II) Recruit
No Migration	(III) Defector	(IV) Loyalist

FIGURE 7.2 *Type of Employment in 1963 of New College Science Faculty in 1964–1965, by Subject Matter Specialty*

[15] Cartter, Allan M., *An Assessment of Quality in Graduate Education*. American Council on Education, Washington, 1966.

[16] These ratings have high face validity and modest predictive validity as demonstrated by the positive and statistically significant correlations between this measure and other "qualitative" measures, including measured intelligence and citations to scientific papers.

[17] These two larger regional classifications were used because of the small sample N in each of these Census divisions. For the specification of states included in each regional category, see U.S. Bureau of the Census, *U.S. Census of Population: 1960*, Vol. I, *Characteristics of the Population*, Government Printing Office, Washington, 1961, S2.

high-level manpower. For instance, are those who move away from the home area attracted by—and do they thus receive—a higher quality education than those who do not move, as Ferriss suggests?[18] Further, if those who move for their Ph.D. education are likely to move again after their education, as Lee and others suggest,[19] are they also those with higher quality training? The following questions were explored:

(1) Do those who migrate from the home region receive a higher quality education than those who do not migrate?

(2) Do those who migrate after completing their education receive higher quality Ph.D. training than those who do not migrate subsequent to completing their Ph.D.?

(3) Does the most mobile group (the Unattached) receive a higher quality graduate education than those with any of the other migration patterns?

(4) Does the least mobile (the Loyalists) receive the lowest quality of education?

Migration Patterns and Educational Quality of Doctoral Training

For the total sample in all fields, 52 per cent of those who received science doctorates in the 1957 to 1960 period migrated from their high school region to another region of the United States for their doctoral study. From completion of the Ph.D. degree to employment four to eight years later, 57 per cent migrated to another region. In both migration periods, the likelihood of migration increased consistently as the quality of doctorate education increased (Table 7.1). Both within each major field and for the total of all fields, those who migrated had indeed attended departments of significantly higher average quality (Table 7.2).[20]

The most mobile group (the Unattached), which represented 21.3 per cent of the sample, consistently exhibited an average educational quality higher than that of any of the other four migration groups (Table 7.3). With the exception of two cases (the bioscience Returnees and Defectors), these differences were statistically significant ($p < .05$). Conversely, the most stable group (the Loyalists) consistently exhibited the lowest average educational quality of all five groups, and these differences were in all cases statistically significant ($p < .05$).

In summary, we found that: (1) Those who migrated to another region for

[18] Ferriss, Abbott L., "Characteristics of Migrating Graduate Students," *op. cit.*; and Ferriss, "Predicting Graduate Student Migration," *Social Forces*, vol. 43, March, 1965, pp. 310–319.

[19] Lee, Everett S., "The Theory of Migration," *Demography*, vol. 3, 1966, p. 54. See also the brief review of this point by Henry S. Shryock, Jr., and Elizabeth A. Larmon in "Some Longitudinal Data on Internal Migration," *Demography*, vol. 2, 1965, pp. 579–592.

[20] This and subsequent findings reported herein generally hold for all field distinctions. Similar analyses were undertaken using the finer 9-field classification (Mathematics/Statistics, Physics, Chemistry, Earth Sciences, Biosciences, Biochemistry, Psychology, Sociology, Economics), but the results differed very little from the results reported by major field areas.

TABLE 7.1. *Proportion Changing Region for Doctorate Education and Employment, by Quality of Doctorate Education and Field: 1957–1960 Doctorate Recipients*

Period of Migration and Field	High Quality		Middle Quality		Low Quality		Total, All Quality Groups	
	Total Number	Per Cent Changing Region	Total Number	Per Cent Changing Region	Total Number	Per Cent Changing Region	Total Number	Per Cent Changing Region
High School to Ph.D.								
Physical Sciences	2,730	57.0	1,299	47.7	684	42.4	4,713	52.3
Biological Sciences	1,172	54.3	892	48.6	343	47.6	2,407	51.2
Social Sciences	1,541	54.2	915	48.7	551	48.6	3,007	51.5
Total	5,443	55.6	3,106	48.3	1,578	45.7	10,127	51.8
Ph.D. to Employment								
Physical Sciences	2,730	63.4	1,299	57.3	684	52.3	4,713	60.1
Biological Sciences	1,172	62.0	892	55.8	343	49.3	2,407	57.9
Social Sciences	1,541	55.2	915	49.5	551	47.3	3,007	52.1
Total	5,443	60.8	3,106	54.8	1,578	49.9	10,127	57.2

SOURCE: See Appendix D for description of sample. Quality groups are based on Allan M. Cartter's An Assessment of Quality in Graduate Education, American Council on Education, Washington, 1966.

TABLE 7.2. *Mean Quality of Doctorate Education by Regional Migration Status and Major Field Area: 1957–1960 Doctorate Recipients*

| Field Area | High School to Ph.D. | | | | | | Ph.D. to Employment | | | | | |
| | Migrant | | | Nonmigrant | | | Migrant | | | Nonmigrant | | |
	Number	Mean Qual.	Stnd. Dev.	Number	Mean Qual.	Stnd. Dev.	Number	Mean Qual.	Stnd. Dev.	Number	Mean Qual.	Stnd. Dev.
Physical Sciences[a]	2,467	2.46	1.50	2,246	2.82	1.60	2,832	2.51	1.51	1,881	2.81	1.62
Biological Sciences[a]	1,233	2.84	1.39	1,174	3.03	1.46	1,394	2.79	1.33	1,013	3.12	1.54
Social Sciences[a]	1,550	2.82	1.60	1,457	3.07	1.58	1,565	2.81	1.58	1,442	3.08	1.60
Total[a]	5,250	2.65	1.52	4,877	2.95	1.56	5,791	2.66	1.49	4,336	2.97	1.60

[a] In all cases, test of difference between means is significant (p. < .001).
SOURCE: See Table 7.1. A low score indicates higher quality training.

TABLE 7.3. *Mean Quality of Doctorate Education, by Migration Pattern and Major Field Area: 1957–1960 Doctorate Recipients*

| Field Area | Returnee | | | Unattached | | | Recruit | | | Defector | | | Loyalist | | |
	No.	Mean Qual.	Stnd. Dev.	No.	Mean Qual.	Stnd. Dev.	No.	Mean Qual.	Stnd. Dev.	No.	Mean Qual.	Stnd. Dev.	No.	Mean Qual.	Stnd. Dev.
Physical Sciences	771	2.50	1.52	1,032	2.34	1.43	664	2.59	1.57	1,029	2.70	1.54	1,217	2.93	1.63
Biological Sciences	325	2.85	1.41	542	2.72	1.29	366	3.00	1.49	527	2.83	1.30	647	3.19	1.57
Social Sciences	413	2.93	1.66	587	2.66	1.59	550	2.91	1.55	565	2.88	1.50	892	3.19	1.62
Total	1,509	2.70	1.55	2,161	2.52	1.46	1,580	2.79	1.56	2,121	2.78	1.48	2,756	3.08	1.61

SOURCE: See Table 7.1. The lower the score, the higher the quality rating of graduate training.

their education attended better institutions than those who did not migrate; (2) those who migrated away from the region where they received their Ph.D. education had attended better institutions than those who did not migrate; (3) the most mobile group attended the best institutions; and (4) the least mobile group had attended the poorest institutions.

Whether these patterns will persist in the future can only be a matter of speculation; but as long as we have a national system of graduate schools, attracting and recruiting students from all parts of the country, and giving their graduates a national visibility in the job market, these patterns of mobility seem likely to persist.

Regional Gain and Loss Through Migration

Looking more closely at how migration flows affect the "human capital" of various regions, we find that in terms of untrained brain gain (that is, the number of students who migrated to a region for their Ph.D. training as compared with the number of "natives" who received the Ph.D. in the same time period), the East North Central region has the largest net quantitative gain in the biological and social sciences. In the physical sciences, New England was the region with the largest net numerical gain. In all fields, the Pacific region had the second highest proportionate number of students entering the region for Ph.D. training relative to the number attending high school in the region who received Ph.D.'s in the time period. The high correlation between the weighted aggregate quality of the graduate departments in the region and the net numerical gain in the number of doctorates entering the region for training suggests the obvious fact that high institutional quality is a major factor in attracting graduate students to a region.[21]

With respect to the trained brain gain (that is, the number of doctorate recipients who enter the region for employment over the number who received their Ph.D. training in the region), a number of different relationships emerge. In all three major field areas, the greatest proportionate numerical losses were incurred by the East North Central and the West North Central Census Divisions (Table 7.4). The largest numerical gains for the physical and biological sciences occurred in the Southeast and the West. In the social sciences, the Southeast, followed by the Pacific and the Southwest and Mountain regions, had the only quantitative trained brain gain.

In all fields, the East North Central region lost both quantitatively and qualitatively. In the West North Central region, on the other hand, quantitative losses were coupled with qualitative gains in the physical and biological sciences, and in the social sciences, the qualitative loss was slight.

---

[21] In the physical sciences, the rank-order correlation coefficient between aggregate quality of doctorate education in the regions and the net numerical gain in the proportion inflow of students for Ph.D. training relative to the number of Ph.D.'s originating in the regions is .86; in the biological sciences, .68; and in the social sciences, .69.

...essional Gains and Losses in 1951–1960 Doctorate Recipients from Ph.D. to Employment

Field/Region	Per Cent Gain or Loss Over Period		Mean Educational Quality				Qualitative Gain or Loss	Significance of Difference in Mean Qual. between In- and Out-migrants
	High School to Ph.D.	Ph.D. to Employment	Ph.D. Training in Region	Out-migrants for Employ. After Ph.D.	In-migrants for Employ. After Ph.D.	Employed in Region		
Physical Sciences								
New England	+53.9	− 34.7	1.79	1.66	2.71	2.52	(−)	.001
Middle Atlantic	−32.9	+ 26.9	2.66	2.57	2.36	2.52	(+)	.05
E. N. Central	+19.3	− 37.6	2.24	2.16	2.78	2.59	(−)	.001
W. N. Central	+ 3.6	− 44.1	3.14	3.16	2.26	2.57	(+ −)	.001
Southeast	+ 3.7	+ 50.2	4.14	4.11	2.51	3.10	(+ +)	.001
Southwest and Mtn.	−45.5	+107.7	4.28	4.23	2.55	2.91	(+ +)	.001
Pacific	+42.7	+ 15.1	1.94	1.92	2.49	2.24	(−)	.001
Biosciences								
New England	−27.1	+ 15.2	2.76	2.65	2.80	2.86	(−)	n.s.
Middle Atlantic	−32.4	+ 9.3	2.96	2.69	2.77	2.98	(−)	n.s.
E. N. Central	+38.0	− 40.9	2.32	2.29	2.86	2.60	(−)	.001
W. N. Central	+19.3	− 18.6	3.22	3.23	2.80	2.94	(+ −)	.01
Southeast	+14.5	+ 59.0	4.09	3.84	2.73	3.28	(+ +)	.001
Southwest and Mtn.	−47.2	+ 51.3	4.77	4.85	2.91	3.35	(+ +)	.001
Pacific	+35.8	+ 3.0	2.13	1.99	2.76	2.50	(−)	.001
Social Sciences								
New England	+ 4.7	− 15.2	2.26	1.91	2.72	2.78	(−)	.001
Middle Atlantic	−24.5	+ 6.1	2.97	2.87	2.45	2.83	(+ −)	.001
E. N. Central	+38.6	− 32.4	2.44	2.33	3.08	2.80	(−)	.001
W. N. Central	+ 6.5	− 20.7	2.97	2.99	3.13	3.05	(−)	n.s.
Southeast	+ 2.1	+ 76.5	4.18	4.15	2.75	3.20	(+ +)	.001
Southwest and Mtn.	−21.7	+ 25.2	5.36	5.35	2.95	3.66	(+ +)	.001
Pacific	+21.9	+ 58.1	2.51	2.29	2.82	2.74	(−)	.01
Total								
New England	+18.5	− 21.7	2.07	1.86	2.74	2.68	(−)	.001
Middle Atlantic	−30.1	+ 11.9	2.83	2.69	2.46	2.70	(+)	.001
E. N. Central	+29.3	− 36.9	2.32	2.24	2.89	2.66	(−)	.001
W. N. Central	+ 4.0	− 29.8	3.11	3.13	2.73	2.86	(+ −)	.001
Southeast	+ 6.2	+ 59.0	4.13	4.04	2.64	3.17	(+ +)	.001
Southwest and Mtn.	−39.9	+ 66.2	4.77	4.77	2.72	3.20	(+ +)	.001
Pacific	+35.5	+ 22.1	2.12	2.01	2.65	2.45	(−)	.001

SOURCE: See Table 7.1. A low score indicates high quality of graduate school training.

The Southeast and the Southwest had large gains in the number of doctorate recipients who entered for employment, even though the two regions ranked lowest in the aggregate quality of Ph.D. training offered. They also had large and significant qualitative gains in the pool of science doctorates employed in those regions. The Pacific region, which employed more doctorates than it produced but offered a relatively high quality of doctoral training, suffered significant qualitative employment losses in all fields.

In summary, the regions that had relatively greater net numerical losses in Ph.D.'s employed in the region, as against Ph.D.'s trained there, were those regions that generally offered a higher than average quality of graduate education.[22]

Table 7.5 shows regional gains and losses over another time interval: from place of high school to place of employment four to seven years after completion of the Ph.D. Numerical gains (the number of doctorate recipients employed in the region over the number of 1957–1960 doctorate recipients who had gone to high school there) were most marked in the Southeast and the Pacific regions. Numerical losses were greatest in the West North Central region for the physical sciences and in the Middle Atlantic region for the biological and social sciences.

An assessment of qualitative gains and losses (based on the educational quality of those who *left* the region for employment but had graduated from high school there versus those who *entered* the region for employment but had not graduated from high school there) had a somewhat different outcome than did the quantitative analysis. In the physical sciences, the West North Central region, which had the largest numerical loss, gained significantly. The Southeast had virtually no qualitative changes in the physical sciences, while the Pacific region, which gained the most numerically and which offered the highest aggregate educational quality, experienced a significant net qualitative loss. In the biological sciences, there was no significant qualitative regional redistribution from place of high school to place of employment, although the directions of the changes were similar to those in the physical sciences.

For the social sciences, the proportionate numerical loss from high school to employment was greatest for the Middle Atlantic region, but that region exhibited the only significant qualitative gain. Conversely, the Pacific and Southeast regions, the only two regions with quantitative gains, experienced a slight, though statistically not significant, loss in the average educational quality of those who entered relative to those who left the region. In the Southeast, however, while those who left the region were of slightly higher educational quality than those who entered after high school, those who entered the region for

---

[22] In the physical sciences, the rank-order correlation coefficient between aggregate quality of doctorate education in the regions and the net numerical gain in the proportion inflow of Ph.D.'s for employment relative to the number trained in the regions is −.54; in the biological sciences, −.64; and in the social sciences, −.53.

employment were qualitatively superior to those who stayed in the region for employment; moreover, three times as many entered the region for employment as left it. The net result was, therefore, a slight qualitative gain of those employed in the region over those who went to high school there, even though those who left were slightly superior to those who entered.

To generalize from these particular findings, the results of geographic migration are, first, that regions which offer high quality education tend to experience greater numerical losses of Ph.D. recipients from training to employment than do other regions and, second, that those who attend the better graduate institutions and, presumably, receive a better education, tend to form a national labor market, while those who attend the poorer schools more generally form a local (regional) labor market. As a result of the operation of these two kinds of labor markets, regions generally tend to retain for employment scientists whose educational background is inferior to that of scientists who leave the region, and at the same time they attract scientists of superior educational background. Because regions differ widely from one another in institutional excellence, however, the quality of those who enter the region for employment versus those who leave it (from high school or from doctorate training) is usually not in balance.[23] Moreover, although the relationship between the quantitative and qualitative redistribution of American scientists within a region is largely a function of the quality of the region's graduate education, quantitative gains do not necessarily imply qualitative gains. Nor are numerical losses for employment the sole determinant of the quality mix of those who remain in or enter the region for employment. The New England, East North Central, and Pacific regions have the best overall institutional quality, but all lose qualitatively in regional interchange from doctorate training to employment. From high school to employment, however, New England experiences a slight qualitative gain, though the East North Central and Pacific regions again lost. While New England and the East North Central regions also generally lose numerically from high school to employment, however, the Pacific states consistently experience quantitative gains. On the other hand, the regions whose overall institutional quality is poorest (Southeast and West) gain considerably, both quantitatively and qualitatively, from Ph.D. training to employment. From high school to employment, however, the West experiences qualitative losses in all fields.

Migration does, indeed, exert a significant influence in equalizing the distribution of talent in the United States. Were it not for these migration flows, regions that start at a low level would become more and more disadvantaged and those of generally high educational quality would grow steadily more superior. But the geographic mobility of highly educated manpower prevents rigid stratification: those areas where graduate education is poorest and where little doctoral training is offered gain in Ph.D.'s who enter the region for employment, whereas

[23] For a further treatment of the regional variation in institutional quality, see Allan M. Cartter's *An Assessment of Quality in Graduate Education,* especially pp. 109–111.

TABLE 7.5. *Regional Gains and Losses in 1957–1960 Doctorate Recipients from High School to Employment*

Field/Region	Per Cent Gain or Loss Over Period		Mean Educational Quality				Qualitative Gain or Loss	Significance of Difference in Mean Quality Between In- and Out-migrants
	High School to Ph.D.	High School to Employment	High School Origin in Region	Out-migrant for Employ. After High School	In-migrant for Employ. After High School	Employed in Region		
Physical Sciences (N = 4,713)								
New England	+53.9	+ 0.5	2.73	2.55	2.26	2.52	(+)	.05
Middle Atlantic	−32.9	−14.9	2.58	2.55	2.40	2.52	(+)	n.s.
E. N. Central	+19.3	−25.6	2.41	2.33	2.65	2.59	(−)	.001
W. N. Central	+ 3.6	−42.0	2.86	2.86	2.38	2.57	(+)	.01
Southeast	+ 3.7	+55.8	3.23	2.86	2.85	3.10	(+)	n.s.
Southwest and Mtn.	−45.5	+13.2	2.87	2.58	2.68	2.91	(−)	n.s.
Pacific	+42.7	+64.3	2.09	2.11	2.33	2.24	(−)	.05
Biosciences (N = 2,407)								
New England	−27.1	−16.0	3.02	2.96	2.71	2.86	(+)	n.s.
Middle Atlantic	−32.4	−26.1	3.01	2.91	2.75	2.98	(+)	n.s.
E. N. Central	+38.0	−18.4	2.56	2.60	2.70	2.60	(−)	n.s.
W. N. Central	+19.3	− 2.9	3.02	2.96	2.84	2.94	(+)	n.s.
Southeast	+14.5	+82.0	3.56	3.12	2.99	3.28	(+)	n.s.
Southwest and Mtn.	−47.2	−20.2	3.09	2.95	3.28	3.35	(−)	n.s.
Pacific	+35.8	+39.9	2.36	2.32	2.56	2.50	(−)	n.s.

Social Sciences
(N = 3,007)

Region							
New England	+ 4.7	−11.2	2.83	2.70	2.60	2.78	(+) n.s.
Middle Atlantic	−24.5	−29.1	2.91	2.82	2.43	2.83	(+) .001
E. N. Central	+38.6	− 6.3	2.86	2.84	2.73	2.80	(+) n.s.
W. N. Central	− 6.5	−25.9	3.00	2.94	2.98	3.05	(−) n.s.
Southeast	+ 2.1	+80.2	3.23	2.78	3.02	3.20	(−) n.s.
Southwest and Mtn.	−21.7	− 2.0	3.26	2.86	3.48	3.66	(−) .01
Pacific	+21.9	+92.7	2.73	2.61	2.71	2.74	(−) n.s.

Total
(N = 10,127)

Region							
New England	+18.5	− 7.2	2.83	2.70	2.46	2.68	(+) .01
Middle Atlantic	−30.1	−21.8	2.78	2.72	2.48	2.70	(+) .001
E. N. Central	+29.3	−18.4	2.57	2.53	2.69	2.66	(−) .01
W. N. Central	+ 4.0	−27.0	2.95	2.91	2.74	2.86	(+) .01
Southeast	+ 6.2	+68.8	3.32	2.90	2.94	3.17	(−) n.s.
Southwest and Mtn.	−39.9	− 0.1	3.03	2.76	3.01	3.20	(−) .01
Pacific	+35.5	+65.4	2.32	2.29	2.50	2.45	(−) .01

SOURCE: See Table 7.1.

[231]

those regions that have offered the highest quality graduate education over the past several decades[24] suffer losses of the doctorate recipients they produce. Thus, a more equitable distribution of talent is produced.

Nevertheless, the ranking of regions on the basis of quality of those originating, trained, and employed in the area is remarkably consistent. Moreover, while qualitative differences between migrant and nonmigrant groups are significant, the qualitative differences among regions are at present even larger. Migration is a significant force in exerting a "strain toward balance" in the geographic distribution of American scientists, but it will not eliminate all qualitative differences. Unless there are further changes in the rate of flow of talent, and in the quality of education offered in each region, qualitative differences will persist.

Changes in Career Field After the Baccalaureate Degree

A second type of mobility that characterizes highly educated manpower involves major changes in field following completion of the baccalaureate degree. For instance, a person may enter a career field different from the field he majored in as a college student; or he may change major fields when he enters doctoral study. And even after he received the Ph.D. degree in a specialized field, he may switch specializations.

Many college graduates who enter the labor force go into occupations that do not require degrees in the particular field in which they received their bachelor's or master's degree (Table 7.6). Of those men with the baccalaureate degree

TABLE 7.6. *Proportion of College Graduates in Selected Major Fields Who Were Employed Full-Time in the Same Field Five Years After Graduation, by Sex: 1958 B.A. and M.A. Recipients*

Major Field of Degree	Bachelor's Degree		Master's Degree	
	Men	Women	Men	Women
Natural Sciences	25.5	11.6	52.3	27.1
Engineering	77.3	17.4	75.3	a
Social Sciences	4.2	3.2	23.5	17.0
Education	75.9	90.8	87.6	82.6
Business/Commerce	58.7	20.8	64.9	a

a Too few cases to compute percentage.

SOURCE: Sharp, Laure M., and Rebecca B. Krasnegor, *Five Years After the College Degree: Part II—Employment*. Bureau of Social Science Research, Washington, March, 1966, pp. 17–21, 104–105.

[24] *Ibid.*, chap. 3, pp. 15–77, reports comparisons of the top-rated departments in 1925, 1957, and 1964. General consistency in relative institutional and regional rankings is evident over this period. Regional consistencies in net numerical gains and losses over the past several decades may be assessed by comparing the regional ratios of total doctorate employment to total doctorate production, as reported by Ernest Hollis in *Toward Improving Ph.D. Programs*, pp. 43–45, for the pre-World War II period with those ratios reported in Table 7.4 of the present study. For the seven regions, the rank-order correlation coefficient between the net proportional regional gain in the two periods, for all fields combined, is .82.

who were employed full-time five years after college graduation, only about three-fourths who were engineering majors reported being employed as engineers; about the same proportion who majored in education reported that they were employed as teachers. Only one-fourth of the natural science majors worked in that field; slightly over half of the business majors were in business or commerce; and less than 5 per cent of the social science majors had positions as social scientists. Women with the bachelor's degree tend to be even less likely than men to go into the occupational field that corresponds to their undergraduate field, although a large proportion of the women with majors in all fields reported that five years after college they held teaching positions, and probably many of them are teaching in the field in which they received the degree, although the data are classified so that we cannot determine how often this occurs.

Although a larger proportion of M.A. recipients than of B.A. holders tend to go into occupations that are the same as the major field in which they received the master's degree, many do not. About 10 per cent of the men who had received a master's degree in business, for example, reported that they were engineers five years after college; more than 7 per cent of the humanities majors reported their occupation as engineering; and more than 4 per cent of the humanities majors and of the engineering majors reported that they were engaged in business and managerial occupations.[25]

Similarly, those persons who continue school for graduate education leading to the doctoral degree often report changes in major field. One-fourth of all recent doctoral degree recipients had changed into an entirely new area between the baccalaureate degree and the doctoral degree. Approximately 6 per cent of the doctoral degrees in the physical sciences were awarded to those who had a baccalaureate degree in some other field; in the biological sciences, the figure was 23 per cent; in social sciences, 24 per cent; in the arts and humanities, 19 per cent; and in education, 66 per cent (Table 7.7). Moreover, about 15 per cent make minor field changes from A.B. to Ph.D. (for example, from physics to chemistry or from psychology to sociology).[26] Thus, only 60 per cent of recent doctoral degree recipients majored in the same field for both the first college degree and for the doctoral degree.

Following completion of the doctoral degree, changes in field of specialization continue to be made. Of the 1957–1962 U.S.-born doctorate recipients in selected fields who reported to the 1964 National Register of Scientific and Technical Personnel, 10 per cent said that they had received their doctoral degree in a field (that is, chemistry, mathematics, psychology) different from the one they currently identify themselves with. As compared with other scientists, those con-

[25] Sharp, Laure M., and Rebecca B. Krasnegor, *Five Years After the College Degree: Part II—Employment.* Bureau of Social Science Research, Washington, March, 1966, p. 104.
[26] Computed from Harmon and Soldz, compilers, *Doctorate Production in United States Universities: 1920–1962*, pp. 210–211.

TABLE 7.7. *Major Field of Baccalaureate and of Doctoral Degrees: 1957–1961 Doctorate Recipients*

Field of Baccalaureate Degree	Field of Doctoral Degree									
	Physical Sciences		Biological Sciences		Social Sciences		Arts and Professions		Education	
	Number	Per Cent	Number	Per Cent	Number	Per Cent	Number	Per Cent	Number	Per Cent
Physical Sciences	13,216	94.2	1,238	15.1	398	4.0	234	3.6	597	7.7
Biological Sciences	322	2.3	6,329	77.1	382	3.9	70	1.1	381	5.0
Social Sciences	50	0.4	94	1.1	7,023	75.6	642	9.8	1,477	19.2
Arts and Professions	326	2.3	294	3.6	1,646	17.4	5,326	81.2	1,858	24.1
Education	120	0.9	249	3.0	468	10.4	283	4.3	3,392	44.0
Total	14,034	100.0	8,204	100.0	9,917	100.0	6,555	100.0	7,705	100.0

SOURCE: Harmon, Lindsey R., and Herbert Soldz, compilers, *Doctorate Production in United States Universities: 1920–1962*. National Academy of Sciences-National Research Council, Publication No. 1142, Washington, 1963, p. 34.

sidering themselves social scientists in 1964 were most often drawn from other disciplines and those identifying themselves as physical scientists in 1964 were most likely to have received the doctoral degree in the same field (Table 7.8). The longer the time spent in the labor force, the greater is the tendency of doctorate-trained manpower to change field of specialization. Of those who have been in the labor force two to seven years, slightly more than three-fourths have *not* switched fields since degree completion; the figure decreases to 70 per cent for those who have been in the labor force 8 to 17 years, and to less than 60 per cent for those in the labor force 18 years or more (Table 7.9). Table 7.9 also shows that retention rates are highest in the social and physical sciences; intermediate in the arts, humanities, and the professions; and lowest in the biosciences.

In summary, even the highly trained persons move across career fields and lines of specialization as well as geographically. Although changes in field tend to decrease as educational level increases, a great deal of field switching takes place not only during the educational process but also throughout virtually the whole working history. The extent of these major changes in career partially reflects current labor market conditions. When job opportunities are greatest, people will be drawn into the field from adjacent fields, and when they are relatively limited, there will be an outflow of trained personnel to adjacent fields. The names we give to specialties and the differing breadth of specialized fields make comparison of rates of field shifting inconclusive, but the field mobility of physical scientists is generally lower than in the social sciences and humanities, which reflects, in part, the greater technical content of the scientific specialties. But even where job opportunities are great, and the technical background required for the occupation is high, as in engineering, a substantial number of persons move out of the occupation. This mobility is partly into even more attractive scientific jobs, is partly a question of nomenclature (is a manager of an engineering related activity still an engineer?), and is partly a reflection of the individual interests and values that lead people to change jobs for personal reasons. The important point is that occupational mobility is extensive and occurs in nearly every occupation.

The Occupational Mobility of College Graduates

Even after they have embarked on their careers, recent college graduates continue to be occupationally mobile in various ways. They may change occupations; they may turn from full-time to part-time work; they may stay in the same field but change employers; they may alter their work functions; or they may move from one job setting to another (for instance, from a college or university setting to a business or industry setting).

Of those receiving B.A.'s in 1958, one-fourth of the men and 17 per cent of the women who were employed full-time during the 1960 to 1963 period were *not* engaged in the same occupation in 1963 as they had been in 1960 (Table

TABLE 7.8. *Reported Major Field of Study at Time of Receipt of the Doctoral Degree and in 1964: 1957–1962 U.S.-Born Doctorate Recipients in Selected Sciences*

Major Field Reported at Time of Doctoral Degree Completion	Major Field Reported in 1964									Total
	Mathematics/ Statistics	Physics	Chemistry	Earth Sciences	Biological Sciences	Bio-chemistry	Psychology	Sociology	Economics	
Mathematics/Statistics	1,131	2	—	—	—	—	—	—	—	1,133
Physics	3	2,253	13	1	2	—	—	—	—	2,272
Chemistry	—	10	4,081	1	34	16	1	—	—	4,143
Earth Sciences	1	3	4	785	1	—	1	—	—	795
Biological Sciences	24	14	32	12	3,193	31	1	—	—	3,307
Biochemistry	—	1	84	—	49	759	—	—	—	893
Other Natural Sciences	23	63	61	5	201	12	1	2	23	391
Psychology	2	3	1	—	2	—	2,903	109	2	3,022
Sociology	—	—	—	—	—	—	2	625	1	628
Economics	3	1	—	2	—	—	—	1	1,025	1,029
Other Social Sciences	19	7	10	—	5	—	6	14	27	69
Education	44	3	2	—	6	—	516	23	12	617
Arts and Professions	10	—	—	—	—	—	49	14	204	288
Total	1,260	2,360	4,288	806	3,493	818	3,480	788	1,294	18,587
Per Cent Reporting Same Field at Both Times	89.8	95.5	95.2	97.4	91.4	92.8	83.4	79.3	79.2	90.1

SOURCE: See Appendix D.

TABLE 7.9. *Percentage Remaining in the Same Field from Doctoral Degree to Employment Position in 1962: Selected 1935–1960 Doctorate Recipients*

Field of Doctoral Degree	Year of Doctoral Degree			Total, All Years
	1935–1940	1945–1950	1955–1960	
Physiology	30.7	49.4	67.3	51.5
Pharmacology	22.5	40.4	77.3	51.6
Biochemistry	30.0	51.9	71.5	55.7
Microbiology	46.0	73.8	78.0	68.4
Botany	39.8	39.3	52.5	44.7
Genetics	31.4	40.7	59.7	47.1
Zoology	39.9	47.7	50.5	46.5
Other Biological Sciences	22.6	a	45.5	40.5
Medical Sciences	74.3	66.7	77.7	74.0
Agricultural Sciences	64.9	78.0	72.8	72.2
Psychology	70.8	81.9	89.5	81.0
Sociology	62.2	65.6	79.0	69.9
Economics	67.6	70.1	77.7	72.2
Political Science	68.2	74.8	81.4	75.7
History/Geography	68.4	75.3	85.1	77.3
Mathematics/Statistics	82.4	89.3	91.3	88.2
Physics	64.3	76.4	89.9	76.8
Chemistry	63.7	80.4	84.1	75.9
Geological Sciences	89.7	85.4	92.8	89.4
Engineering	79.7	86.8	92.3	86.8
Language/Literature	75.2	82.3	89.0	82.3
Arts/Humanities	53.3	70.4	82.4	69.4
Miscellaneous Professions	62.6	68.4	80.4	72.1
Education	65.6	75.7	81.0	75.5
Total	58.8	70.6	76.9	69.8

a Too few cases to compute percentage.

SOURCE: Harmon, Lindsey R., *Profiles of Ph.D.'s in the Sciences.* National Academy of Sciences-National Research Council, Publication No. 1293, Washington, 1965, pp. 113–116.

7.10). Moreover, 9 per cent of the men and more than one-half of the women who were employed in 1960 were not employed full-time three years later.[27] Presumably, many of the men had gone on to graduate study, and many of the women had terminated employment in order to take on home and family responsibilities. (See Chapter 9 for a more detailed discussion of the labor force participation and occupational mobility of women.)

As Table 7.10 also shows, more than 45 per cent of the men and 46 per cent of the women changed employers during the 1960 to 1963 period, although more than half of those who changed employers remained in the same occupation.

In view of the large number of changes in employer during this brief time-span, it seems probable that the overwhelming majority of college graduates

[27] Sharp and Krasnegor, *Five Years After the College Degree*, pp. 30–59.

TABLE 7.10. *Proportion of Full-Time Employed 1958 B.A. Recipients Who Changed Occupation, Employer, or Both, Between 1960 and 1963, by Field of B.A. and Sex*

Undergraduate Major	Men						Women					
	Total Full Time Employed		Both Same	Same Occup.; Diff. Employer	Diff. Occup.; Same Employer	Diff. Occup.; Diff. Employer	Total Full Time Employed		Both Same	Same Occup.; Diff. Employer	Diff. Occup.; Same Employer	Diff. Occup.; Diff. Employer
	Number	Per Cent					Number	Per Cent				
Total	12,563	100.0	51.1	23.0	3.2	22.7	3,988	100.0	51.2	31.7	2.3	14.8
Natural Sciences	1,605	100.0	46.0	26.5	3.2	24.2	345	100.0	44.9	28.4	2.6	24.1
Engineering	2,656	100.0	57.3	22.4	4.8	15.5	23	100.0	69.6	17.4	4.3	8.7
Social Sciences	2,138	100.0	44.0	23.9	3.7	28.4	545	100.0	45.3	31.9	2.2	20.5
Humanities and Arts	1,195	100.0	39.4	31.0	3.4	26.2	804	100.0	40.3	33.8	4.2	21.6
Health	253	100.0	45.5	45.1	0.8	8.7	266	100.0	49.2	34.6	2.6	13.5
Business and Commerce	2,815	100.0	54.9	15.5	2.5	27.0	198	100.0	55.0	26.8	2.0	16.2
Education	1,476	100.0	60.1	23.8	1.4	14.8	1,586	100.0	60.2	31.7	1.4	6.7
Agriculture (Men); Home Economics (Women)	366	100.0	47.3	17.8	3.6	31.4	197	100.0	45.2	31.0	2.0	21.8
General Courses	59	100.0	42.3	33.9	5.0	18.6	24	100.0	66.7	25.0	—	8.3

SOURCE: Sharp, Laure M., and Rebecca B. Krasnegor, *Five Years After the College Degree: Part II—Employment*, p. 58.

will also change their job setting at some time during their careers. However, major occupational changes are not as likely. More than 80 per cent of the men and over 70 per cent of the women with B.A. degrees indicate a continuing commitment to the occupation in which they were currently working, although there are wide variations from one field to another (Table 7.11).

TABLE 7.11. *Proportion of 1958 B.A. Recipients Intending to Change or Not to Change Current Occupation During Major Part of Working Life, by Current Occupation and Sex*

Occupation in 1963	Men			Women		
	Plan Change	Do Not Plan Change	Expect to Leave Labor Force, or No Response	Change Plan	Do Not Plan Change	Expect to Leave Labor Force, or No Response
Natural Sciences	11.3	87.4	1.3	9.3	59.3	31.5
Engineering	14.2	84.7	1.1	—	93.3	6.7
Social Sciences	13.6	85.2	1.2	12.5	50.0	37.4
Arts/Humanities	10.4	87.6	1.9	12.3	65.4	22.4
Health	13.6	84.8	1.6	6.7	77.5	15.7
Teaching	14.7	83.2	2.1	5.4	75.6	19.1
Business/Managerial	13.7	85.3	1.0	7.8	70.6	21.6
Other Professions	12.0	87.3	0.6	14.9	63.6	21.6
Semiprofessional	34.8	60.9	4.3	12.3	53.3	34.5
Clerical and Sales	20.2	78.0	1.8	26.1	31.5	42.4
Other Nonprofessional	35.3	61.8	2.9	31.9	55.3	12.8
Total	15.0	83.2	1.9	8.2	70.8	21.2

SOURCE: Sharp, Laure M., and Rebecca B. Krasnegor, *Five Years After the College Degree: Part II—Employment*, p. 60.

Many of those people who received a master's degree in 1958 have completed additional graduate or professional work since that time, especially if they are in the natural sciences and social sciences; over one-third of those in the natural sciences and one-fifth of those in the social sciences had actually earned a Ph.D. by 1963. Over all fields, more than one-fourth of the 1958 M.A.'s had undertaken additional graduate or professional training in the ensuing five years, although fields vary considerably.[28] Table 7.12 indicates that such graduate training is conducive to job mobility within an occupation. The decreases in employment of men in elementary school, high school, and junior college were offset by the increases in employment by colleges and universities. Among women, the decrease in elementary school teaching was balanced by the increase in high school teaching and the decrease in junior college teaching by the increase in colleges and universities. The increases in employment in higher

[28] See *Ibid.*, pp. 95–171, for a more detailed discussion of these fields in regard to the additional advanced training and mobility of master's degree recipients.

TABLE 7.12. *Job Setting in 1960 and in 1963, by Sex: 1958 M.A. Recipients Employed Full-Time*

Type of Employer	Men		Women	
	1960	1963	1960	1963
	(Percentages)		(Percentages)	
Business/Industry	34.1	32.3	4.3	2.5
Elementary School	8.5	7.3	32.2	27.9
High School	23.1	21.2	23.8	28.8
Junior College	2.0	1.2	5.1	0.6
College/University	14.1	18.5	12.6	14.5
Nonprofit Institution	4.2	4.8	11.6	11.7
Federal Government	6.7	7.3	2.0	2.6
State/Local Government	6.3	5.2	7.1	7.8
Other and no Response	1.1	2.3	1.3	3.7
Total	100.0	100.0	100.0	100.0
Number of Cases	2,974	3,260	1,278	1,115

SOURCE: Sharp, Laure M., and Rebecca B. Krasnegor, *Five Years After the College Degree: Part II—Employment*, pp. 124–128.

educational institutions partially reflect the additional advanced training received between 1960 and 1963. For some persons, employment in noneducational settings was probably a stopgap measure intended to tide them over while they gained the training necessary to qualify them for employment in higher education.

M.A. recipients who were employed both in 1960 and in 1963 were less likely to have changed occupations than were B.A. recipients. Less than 16 per cent of the M.A. recipients had changed occupations in the three-year period. Moreover, generally fewer M.A. than B.A. recipients, particularly among women, said that they intended to switch from their current occupation during their working life. Approximately 87 per cent of the men and 85 per cent of the women who received the master's degree in 1958 and were currently working said they intended to remain in their current occupation throughout the major part of their working life (Table 7.13).

Turning to doctorate recipients, we find, as was noted previously, that about two-fifths have in the past changed major fields some time during their post-B.A. career. A more common type of mobility for this group is, of course, changes of employer. Approximately one-half of all Ph.D. graduates changed employers within the first five years after graduation, and this rate has remained relatively steady over the last three decades. As careers mature, job stability increases, but changes are not uncommon throughout the careers of Ph.D.'s (Table 7.14). Those in the social science fields tend to change jobs most frequently over each successive five-year period; the natural scientists are also highly mobile, whereas persons with Ph.D.'s in the biological sciences and the arts are inclined to have the lowest rate of job mobility.[29]

[29] For a further discussion of these points, see Harmon, Lindsey R., *Profiles of Ph.D.'s in the Sciences*, especially pp. 47–52.

TABLE 7.13. *Proportion of 1958 M.A. Recipients Intending to Change or Not to Change Current Full-Time Occupation During Major Part of Working Life, by Current Occupation and Sex*

Occupation in 1963	Men (N = 3,445)			Women (N = 1,229)		
	Plan Change	Do Not Plan Change	Expect to Leave Labor Force, or No Response	Plan Change	Do Not Plan Change	Expect to Leave Labor Force, or No Response
Natural Sciences	16.3	82.0	1.7	6.9	86.2	6.8
Engineering	13.3	84.4	2.3	—	—	—
Social Sciences	23.2	75.9	0.9	9.5	81.0	9.5
Arts/Humanities	11.4	80.9	7.6	9.5	82.4	8.3
Health	42.2	51.1	6.7	5.4	86.5	8.1
Teaching	8.6	90.3	1.0	1.8	93.5	4.7
Business/Managerial	11.4	82.8	5.7	—	—	—
Other Professional	28.4	66.6	4.9	8.9	83.0	8.1
Semiprofessional	16.7	83.3	—	12.5	37.5	50.0
Clerical and Sales	3.4	82.8	13.8	—	—	—
Other Nonprofessional	18.2	78.8	3.0	—	—	—
Total	12.6	84.5	2.9	5.2	86.5	8.3

SOURCE: Sharp, Laure M., and Rebecca B. Krasnegor, *Five Years After the College Degree: Part II—Employment*, pp. 145–146.

Work functions also may change over time. New Ph.D.'s tend to engage primarily in either research or teaching. With increasing time in the labor force, they tend to devote significantly less time to research, slightly less time to teaching, and considerably more time to administrative activities (Table 7.15).

Changes in Job Setting

Most persons who change employment move from one employer to another *within* the same job setting rather than from one type of setting to another. In the 1964–1965 academic year, for example, 34 per cent of the newly appointed

TABLE 7.14. *Percentage of Doctorate Recipients with No Job Changes During Successive Five-Year Work Periods, by Year of Receipt of the Doctoral Degree*

Postdoctoral Work Period	Year of Ph.D.				
	1935	1940	1945	1950	1955
1936–1940	53.4				
1941–1945	55.7	41.0			
1946–1950	61.1	51.2	45.1		
1951–1955	80.6	75.2	71.8	54.8	
1956–1960	83.4	78.4	78.0	66.1	52.2

SOURCE: Harmon, Lindsey R., *Profiles of Ph.D.'s in the Sciences*, p. 47.

TABLE 7.15. *Type of Major Work Activity in 1960, by Number of Years Since Receipt of the Doctoral Degree*

Number of Years Since Receipt of Doctoral Degree	Type of Major Work Activity[a]		
	Teaching	Research	Administration
	(Percentages)		
1 to 10	34	46	12
11 to 20	31	31	27
21 to 30	30	25	32

[a] More than 50 per cent of time spent in defined function.

SOURCE: Harmon, Lindsey R., *Profiles of Ph.D.'s in the Sciences*, p. 19.

NOTE: Percentages do not add to 100 because some of the subjects split work among all three activities.

science faculty in American colleges and universities came from other educational institutions; only one-fourth were from business, government, or other job settings; the largest proportion (43 per cent) being new college graduates (Figure 7.2). It is the mobility of high-level manpower from one sector of the economy to another that has the greatest effect in allocating human resources throughout the nation, the remainder of this section focuses primarily on these

FIGURE 7.2 *Type of Employment in 1963 of New College Science Faculty in 1964–1965, by Subject Matter Specialty*

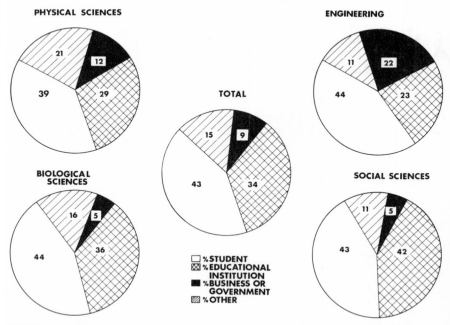

SOURCE: Brown, David G., and Jay L. Tontz, *The Mobility of Academic Scientists*. Report to the National Science Foundation, April, 1966, p. 103.

changes, from one *kind* of employer to another, among recent recipients of doctoral degrees in science.

Of the 17,836 male science doctoral degree recipients of 1957–1962 who reported to the 1964 National Register of Scientific and Technical Personnel that they were employed full-time and who had records in the National Academy of Sciences, Office of Scientific Personnel Doctoral Files, about 5 per cent (858) had no formal plans in regard to employment at the time they left the doctoral degree-granting institution.[30] Of the 16,978 who reported postdoctoral employment plans, 12 per cent (2,100) said they had a postdoctoral fellowship, 45 per cent (7,582) were going into colleges and universities, 23 per cent (3,953) were going into business or industry, 8 per cent (1,350) were going into a federal government setting, and the remaining 12 per cent (1,993) were going into other work settings, including secondary schools, nonprofit organizations, state or local government, and military service. By 1964, more than one-fifth (23 per cent) of the total sample had changed into another employment setting: 19 per cent had made this change within three years after completion of college; 24 per cent had changed within four to five years; and over one-fourth had switched job settings within six to seven years (Table 7.16). Social scientists

TABLE 7.16. *Doctoral Degree Recipients in 1957–1962 Changing Employment Setting Between Receipt of the Doctoral Degree and 1964, by Field*

| Field | Year of Doctoral Degree | | | |
	1957–1959	1959–1960	1961–1962	Total 1957–1962
	(Percentages)			
Physical Sciences	23.0	22.7	17.2	20.9
Biological Sciences	26.6	21.0	15.6	21.2
Social Sciences	31.5	28.9	22.4	27.1
Total	26.3	24.2	18.6	22.9

SOURCE: See Appendix D.

(psychologists, sociologists, economists) are more likely to change employment settings than are the bio-scientists (anatomists, biochemists, biophysicists, botanists, ecologists, entomologists, geneticists, microbiologists, nutritionists, pathologists, pharmacologists, physiologists, phytopathologists, virologists, and zoologists) or the physical scientists (chemists, physicists, mathematicians/statisticians, and earth scientists—including meteorologists and oceanographers).

Table 7.17 shows what the first postdoctoral employer setting had been for Ph.D.'s who, by 1964, were employed in colleges and universities. Of those who received the Ph.D. degree in 1957 or 1958 and were employed in colleges and universities in 1964, more than one-fifth of the physical scientists, 14 per cent of the biological scientists, and 17 per cent of the social scientists did *not*

[30] See Appendix D for description of the sample.

TABLE 7.17. *Job Setting of First Position After Doctorate, by Major Field and Year of Doctorate: Men Employed in Colleges and Universities in 1964[a]*

Year of Ph.D. and Field	Job Setting of First Position											
	College/ University		Business/ Industry		U.S. Government		Post-doctoral Fellowship		Other		Total	
	Number	Per Cent	Number	Per Cent	Number	Per Cent	Number	Per Cent	Number	Per Cent	Number	Per Cent
1957 and 1958												
Physical Sciences	673	68.5	129	13.1	36	3.7	108	11.0	36	3.7	982	100.0
Biological Sciences	567	72.8	34	4.4	36	4.6	105	13.5	37	4.7	779	100.0
Social Sciences	637	79.9	21	2.6	31	3.9	25	3.1	83	10.4	797	100.0
1959 and 1960												
Physical Sciences	845	65.2	145	11.2	42	3.2	222	17.1	42	3.2	1,296	100.0
Biological Sciences	542	65.6	22	2.7	29	3.5	201	24.3	32	3.9	826	100.0
Social Sciences	787	80.4	16	1.6	44	4.5	52	5.3	80	8.2	979	100.0
1961 and 1962												
Physical Sciences	992	63.8	89	5.7	35	2.2	365	23.4	75	4.8	1,556	100.0
Biological Sciences	552	63.0	13	1.5	12	1.4	272	31.0	27	3.1	876	100.0
Social Sciences	986	82.6	19	1.6	29	2.4	64	5.4	96	8.0	1,194	100.0

[a] Excludes all cases in which there is no collation, no response to employment question, or the subject was in military service in either period.

SOURCE: See Appendix D.

have a postdoctoral fellowship and were *not* employed in a college or university for their first position. Comparable figures for the 1959 and 1960 doctorate recipients employed in colleges and universities in 1964 are: 18 per cent in physical sciences, 10 per cent in biological sciences, and 14 per cent in social sciences. Of the 1961 and 1962 doctorate recipients, comparable proportions are: 13 per cent in physical sciences, 6 per cent in the biological sciences, and 12 per cent in the social sciences.

Of those persons who had received their Ph.D.'s in 1957 and 1958 and who were employed in business and industry in 1964, approximately 76 per cent had taken their first postdoctoral position in the same job setting. Physical scientists were the least mobile group in this respect: four-fifths who were in business/industry in 1964 had been in the same setting two to seven years previously. In the biological and social sciences, a greater proportion (between one-third and one-half) were drawn into business or industrial employment after starting out in some other work setting several years earlier (Table 7.18).

Persons in a federal government organization in 1964 were more likely than either those in college/university or those in business/industry to have been drawn from a different earlier work setting. Only slightly more than one-half of the 1957–1958 doctorate recipients who were in a U.S. government setting in 1964 were employed by the U.S. government for their first postdoctoral position (Table 7.19). Even among the more recent graduates (1961–1962), only three-fifths to two-thirds of those working in U.S. government organizations in 1964 were in similar settings two to three years earlier.

As a result of these large interchanges of manpower between different employer types, government organizations, and business and industry tend to lose doctorate personnel even though their salary levels are slightly higher (see Chapter 8). Colleges and universities, nonprofit organizations, and other employment categories (which include persons who are self-employed) gain in highly educated personnel, although there are a number of exceptions dependent upon field of specialization (Table 7.20).

The Employment of Postdoctoral Fellowship Recipients

A fairly large proportion of the 1957–1962 doctorate recipients in science reported that they had received a postdoctoral fellowship or its equivalent immediately after receiving their degrees. Of all the fields included, biochemistry had the largest proportion—one-third—of doctorate recipients who had been awarded a postdoctoral fellowship. In both chemistry and the biosciences (including anatomy, botany, ecology, entomology, genetics, microbiology, nutrition, pathology, pharmacology, physiology, phytopathology, virology, zoology, and biophysics), more than 15 per cent of recent doctoral recipients received such fellowships. Physics had 11 per cent, followed by mathematics/statistics with 7 per cent, and the earth sciences with 6 per cent. Least likely to receive

TABLE 7.18. *Job Setting of First Position After Doctorate, by Major Field and Year of Doctorate: Men Employed in Business and Industry in 1964*[a]

Year of Ph.D. and Field	Job Setting of First Position											
	College/University		Business/Industry		U.S. Government		Postdoctoral Fellowship		Other		Total	
	Number	Per Cent	Number	Per Cent	Number	Per Cent	Number	Per Cent	Number	Per Cent	Number	Per Cent
1957 and 1958												
Physical Sciences	101	9.4	867	80.6	31	2.9	56	5.2	21	2.0	1,076	100
Biological Sciences	38	20.9	99	54.4	14	7.7	16	8.8	15	8.2	182	100
Social Sciences	16	21.3	44	58.7	5	6.7	0	0.0	10	13.3	75	100
1959 and 1960												
Physical Sciences	96	8.0	954	79.8	31	2.6	83	6.9	31	2.6	1,195	100
Biological Sciences	30	17.5	111	64.9	7	4.1	15	8.8	8	4.7	171	100
Social Sciences	17	15.7	66	61.1	11	10.2	1	0.9	13	12.0	108	100
1961 and 1962												
Physical Sciences	57	5.1	896	80.3	13	1.2	111	9.9	39	3.5	1,116	100
Biological Sciences	19	12.2	109	69.9	3	1.9	13	8.3	12	7.7	156	100
Social Sciences	10	11.8	50	58.8	5	5.9	3	3.5	17	20.0	85	100

[a] Excludes all cases in which there was no collation, no response to employment question, or the subject was in military service in either period.

SOURCE: See Appendix D.

TABLE 7.19. *Job Setting of First Position After Doctorate, by Major Field and Year of Doctorate: Men Employed by U.S. Government in 1964*[a]

Year of Ph.D. and Field	College/University		Business/Industry		Work Setting of First Position U.S. Government		Postdoctoral Fellowship		Other		Total	
	Number	Per Cent	Number	Per Cent	Number	Per Cent	Number	Per Cent	Number	Per Cent	Number	Per Cent
1957 and 1958												
Physical Sciences	15	11.3	34	25.5	72	54.1	7	5.3	5	3.8	133	100.0
Biological Sciences	44	30.1	6	4.1	76	52.1	10	6.8	10	6.8	146	99.9
Social Sciences	35	27.8	1	0.8	71	56.4	3	2.4	16	12.7	126	100.1
1959 and 1960												
Physical Sciences	38	20.9	29	15.9	79	43.4	27	14.8	9	4.9	182	99.9
Biological Sciences	26	19.5	4	3.0	79	59.4	17	12.8	7	5.3	133	100.0
Social Sciences	37	27.8	2	1.5	74	55.6	0	0.0	20	15.0	133	99.9
1961 and 1962												
Physical Sciences	21	9.5	19	8.6	130	58.8	45	20.4	6	2.7	221	100.0
Biological Sciences	18	10.7	6	3.6	104	61.5	31	18.3	10	5.9	169	100.0
Social Sciences	27	17.5	3	1.9	103	66.9	8	5.2	13	8.4	154	99.9

[a] Excludes all cases in which there was no collation, no response to employment question, or the subject was in military service in either period.

SOURCE: See Appendix D.

TABLE 7.20. *Net Change in Number of 1957–1962 Doctorate Recipients in Selected Job-Setting Categories Between First Position and 1964, by Field[a]*

Field of Doctoral Degree	College/University		Business/Industry		U.S. Government		Other Government		Nonprofit Organization		Other Employer	
	Number First Position	Per Cent Net Change by 1964	Number First Position	Per Cent Net Change by 1964	Number First Position	Per Cent Net Change by 1964	Number First Position	Per Cent Net Change by 1964	Number First Position	Per Cent Net Change by 1964	Number First Position	Per Cent Net Change by 1964
Mathematics/ Statistics	775	+ 2.7	224	− 6.3	55	−32.7	20	−35.0	33	+48.9	8	+ 25.0
Physics	979	+ 6.6	622	−28.8	206	−23.8	23	−91.3	94	+19.1	36	+450.0
Chemistry	840	+13.1	2,226	− 6.9	125	+10.4	26	−30.8	80	+11.2	24	+125.0
Earth Sciences	342	+ 0.9	196	−10.2	113	+10.6	37	− 8.1	19	−10.5	9	+111.1
Biological Sciences	1,659	+ 1.3	316	+10.8	334	0.0	88	−31.8	85	− 4.7	37	− 62.2
Biochemistry	234	− 4.7	103	+ 3.9	44	+27.3	15	−26.7	49	− 2.0	8	0.0
Psychology	1,244	+ 6.6	174	+ 0.6	325	−16.9	349	−24.1	217	+10.7	242	+ 12.4
Sociology	523	+ 2.1	11	+ 9.1	23	+26.1	22	−36.4	40	− 7.5	21	− 33.3
Economics	972	− 0.3	76	− 1.3	105	− 1.9	27	−40.7	47	+ 8.5	8	+162.5
Total	7,568	+ 4.0	3,948	− 8.3	1,330	− 6.1	607	−28.7	664	+ 9.5	393	+ 55.2

[a] Excludes all cases in which there was no information on either first job or job in 1964, the subject received a postdoctoral fellowship, or did not respond to the employment question, or was in military service in either period.

SOURCE: See Appendix D.

TABLE 7.21. *Proportion of 1957–1962 Doctorate Recipients Engaged Primarily in Research and in Academic Settings in 1964, by Postdoctoral Fellowship Status and Field[a]*

	Per Cent of Total in Research		Per Cent of Total in Academic Settings	
Field	Former Post-doctoral Fellows	Non-Fellows	Former Post-doctoral Fellows	Non-Fellows
Mathematics/ Statistics	59.8	37.6	80.4	83.9
Physics	73.2	61.2	66.5	52.6
Chemistry	65.8	63.0	59.6	30.0
Earth Sciences	57.7	41.3	53.8	47.9
Biosciences	67.2	51.6	76.0	64.8
Biochemistry	79.8	73.4	71.5	48.1
Psychology	51.4	20.6	61.4	50.1
Total[b]	66.9	45.9	67.3	53.3

[a] Number of cases on which percentages are based shown in Figure 7.3.
[b] Includes Sociology and Economics.
SOURCE: See Appendix D.

postdoctoral fellowships were those in the social sciences—psychology, 6 per cent; sociology, 4 per cent; and economics, less than 1 per cent (Figure 7.3).

In every field, prior postdoctoral fellowship holders are more likely than others to be found engaged primarily in research activities.[31] This is so even though the postdoctoral fellowship awardees are also more likely than others, with the exception of mathematicians/statisticians, to be in college or university settings, where research activity as the primary responsibility is less likely than in other settings (Table 7.21). Within each work setting, the proportion of those who reported a postdoctoral fellowship and subsequent activity primarily research is from 5 per cent to more than 50 per cent greater than those who had not received a fellowship (Table 7.22).

Summary and Conclusions

The major conclusion to be drawn from the preceding discussion is that U.S. high-level manpower is highly flexible and capable of responding to the demands of the society within fairly wide limits. If geographic barriers exist, they are easily penetrated; for many people, specialized training is not so narrow that it precludes the possibility of their switching to another career field or area of specialization; and highly trained persons appear to be able to move easily from one sector of the economy to another, as changes in individual desires, institutional requirements, or national needs may warrant.

From the standpoint of the individual, mobility probably helps to optimize

[31] Additional comparisons between the productivity and salaries of those who receive postdoctoral fellowships and those who do not is presented in Chapter 8.

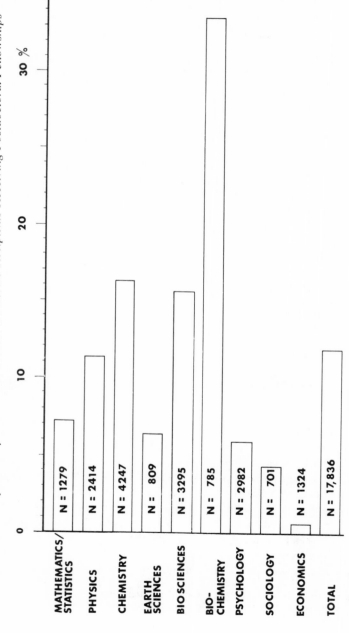

FIGURE 7.3 *Proportion of 1957–1962 Science Doctorate Recipients Receiving Postdoctoral Fellowships*

NOTE: N's show total collated cases, both postdoctoral and nonpostdoctoral fellows.

SOURCE: See Appendix D.

TABLE 7.22. *Proportion of 1957–1962 Doctorate Recipients Engaged Primarily in Research in 1964, by Postdoctoral Fellowship Status, Work Setting, and Field*

	College/University		Business/Industry		Other		Total	
	Total Number	Per Cent in Research	Total Number	Per Cent in Research	Total Number	Per Cent in Research	Total Number	Per Cent in Research
Mathematics/Statistics								
Postdoctoral Fellow	74	51.4	7	85.7	11	100.0	92	59.8
Not Postdoctoral Fellow	837	27.0	222	66.2	128	57.0	1,187	37.6
Total	911	29.0	229	66.8	139	60.4	1,279	39.2
Physics								
Postdoctoral Fellow	181	63.5	39	89.7	52	94.2	272	73.2
Not Postdoctoral Fellow	1,126	45.8	482	78.2	534	78.5	2,142	61.2
Total	1,307	48.3	521	79.1	586	79.9	2,414	62.6
Chemistry								
Postdoctoral Fellow	412	49.3	182	90.6	97	89.7	691	65.8
Not Postdoctoral Fellow	1,031	26.5	2,170	77.6	355	79.7	3,556	63.0
Total	1,443	33.0	2,352	78.6	452	81.8	4,247	63.4
Earth Sciences								
Postdoctoral Fellow	28	32.1	7	57.1	17	100.0	52	57.7
Not Postdoctoral Fellow	363	17.1	183	58.5	211	68.3	757	41.3
Total	391	18.2	190	58.4	228	70.6	809	42.4
Biosciences								
Postdoctoral Fellow	390	61.5	27	66.7	96	90.6	513	67.2
Not Postdoctoral Fellow	1,802	41.5	378	61.4	602	75.7	2,782	51.6
Total	2,192	45.0	405	61.7	698	77.8	3,295	54.0
Biochemistry								
Postdoctoral Fellow	188	77.1	14	92.9	61	85.2	263	79.8
Not Postdoctoral Fellow	251	67.3	120	78.3	151	80.0	522	73.4
Total	439	71.5	134	79.9	212	81.1	785	75.5
Psychology								
Postdoctoral Fellow	110	49.1	4	100.0	65	52.3	179	51.4
Not Postdoctoral Fellow	1,404	21.2	197	33.0	1,202	17.8	2,803	20.6
Total	1,514	23.2	201	34.3	1,267	19.6	2,982	22.4

SOURCE: See Appendix D.

job satisfaction and career advancement. Career progress is closely associated with geographic mobility, and willingness to change employers and job settings. The reward system and the possibility of progress in a professional career, which act as strong incentives in encouraging these types of mobility, are explored in the next chapter.

The figures presented above indicate that most highly educated persons are mobile. They move between regions of the country, they move from one job to another within a field, they change types of employers, and some of them change their field of specialization. The professional person who makes no moves or job changes of any kind is in a distinct minority. While the self-employed professionals who serve the public (doctors, dentists, lawyers) are relatively immobile after they establish a practice, salaried professionals of all types are much more likely to move from one part of the country to another than persons in other occupations. The salaried professions that require advanced training beyond the bachelor's degree (such as college teaching) have, in varying degrees, a national job market, and persons in these fields are highly mobile over a large part of their professional careers and often they move long distances.[32]

Mobility, both geographic and occupational, is essential to adjustment of supply and demand in a dynamic economy. While there are many imperfections in our professional labor markets, where imperfections are defined in the economists' sense of barriers to the free flow of labor between jobs; a great deal of mobility does take place, and in most professional occupations it appears to be the principal method of adjusting supply and demand for personnel. (Other methods are described in Chapter 12.)

From the point of view of the individual, mobility in most occupations is essential to realization of career goals, and it is also an important way of increasing job satisfaction and job rewards.

The mobility processes that have been described in this chapter are very complex and vary in different professional occupations as a function of the organization of the job market and the kinds of career progression that are possible within the occupation. Our models of these processes have been oversimplified; in addition, we do not have sharply defined criteria for assessing the effectiveness or lack of effectiveness of either geographic or occupational mobility. Useful models of future supply and demand in high level occupations must include assumptions about occupational mobility and projections for regions or other geographic subdivisions of the nation, and must also include assumptions about geographic mobility. Better information about mobility is a key requirement for improved forecasting of future supply and demand for personnel; most assumptions that have been used in past projections have been based on inadequate information about mobility processes and amounts.

[32] A more detailed discussion of the implications of the mobility of high-level manpower, with particular reference to mobility from one educational institution to another, is presented by Abbott L. Ferriss in "A Hypothesis on Institutional Mobility of Teachers in Higher Education," *College and University,* Fall, 1966, pp. 13–28.

8 Determinants of
Professional Achievement and
Rewards Among Scientists

WHILE IT IS important to know whether or not a particular occupation is attracting a sufficient number of persons, it is even more important to know whether the entrants are of the "right" quality. Even though this is a central question, our ability to provide even approximate answers is very limited. Occupational performance, especially at the professional and managerial levels is very complex, and in many occupations the components of effective performance have not been defined or measured satisfactorily. For example, although there is an extensive literature on the components of effective teaching performance,[1] generally agreed-on criteria are lacking and measures of teaching performance for adequate national samples of college, high school, or elementary school teachers are nonexistent.

Faced with this unsatisfactory state of affairs, manpower specialists have tried to use various indices and indirect measures that would provide some evidence about the quality of the personnel. Income or salary received is one of the most widely used indices of effective performance; data are available about salaries in many occupations, and in a market economy they should give a measure of a man's effectiveness, at least relative to other persons who are employed in the field.

---

[1] See Walter C. Eells' bibliography *College Teachers and College Teaching* (with two supplements), Southern Regional Education Board, Atlanta, 1957, for a sample of the recent (postwar) literature on this subject. See also McKeachie, W. J., "Procedures and Techniques of Teaching, A Survey of Experimental Studies" in Sanford, Nevitt, editor, *The American College*, John Wiley and Sons, New York, 1962, chap. 8.

Another indirect assessment is possible by use of educational attainment, test score results, and other characteristics of entrants to an occupation as a proxy for the quality of performance. If the characteristics being measured are closely related to effective performance in the occupation then information about changes in the characteristics of entrants to the particular profession or occupation gives at least an indirect estimate of the quality changes among personnel in the field. For example, in Chapters 2, 3, and 4 the changes in the educational level of a number of occupations are described; these changes are assumed to be related to the quality of performance in the occupation. A number of manpower studies have used the level of education of engineers, college teachers, or some other occupational group as an indication of changes in the quality of personnel in the field.

Although educational level and salary paid, as well as several other measures discussed below, have been widely used in manpower studies, there have been a limited number of efforts to relate these indirect measures of effectiveness to more direct measures such as teaching effectiveness, research publications, honors and awards. In most of these studies relatively low relationships were found between any single characteristic and any criterion of effectiveness.[2]

The Commission on Human Resources made a study of factors affecting scientific performance, as one important aspect of this problem. The results illustrate both the complexities of research on this problem and the limitations of background characteristics as indirect measures of the quality of personnel in a professional field.

To explore more fully the determinants of professional achievement, the Commission on Human Resources undertook a study of recent recipients of a doctoral degree in science. Several of the same factors explored in the preceding chapters were employed as predictors of these two indicators of success in science, scholarly output and salary. Among them are ability, motivation, and educational experience, as well as certain occupational characteristics—including job setting, work activity, and field of specialization—that may influence the criteria. Special attention was given to the influence of a postdoctoral fellowship on subsequent career development.

The sample, which was drawn from the basic 1964 National Register file of recent doctorates, consisted of approximately 6,300 1957–1959 doctorate recipients in selected sciences. (See Appendix D.) The National Register also provided information on several background and employment characteristics. Additional information was drawn from the National Academy of Sciences' Doctoral Files. For example, the number of years that elapsed between the time a person got his baccalaureate degree and the time he received his doctoral degree, obtained from the Doctoral Files, was used as a crude proxy for his

---

[2] See, for example, Hoyt, Donald, "The Relationship Between College Grades and Adult Achievement: A Review of the Literature," *American College Testing Program Research Report*, No. 7, September, 1965. See also the references in notes 5 through 8 below.

"drive" or "motivation." Job settings in 1964 were divided into four main categories: colleges (which employed 12 per cent of the doctorate recipients in the sample), universities (25 per cent), business and industry (30 per cent), and the federal government (8 per cent). A fifth residual category, which included roughly one-fourth of the sample, comprised persons in secondary school systems, nonprofit organizations, state or local governments, consulting firms, and other miscellaneous work settings. The emphasis on research in a particular work setting was assessed on the basis of subjects' own reports about the first and second most important kinds of activity, in terms of working time, in their jobs. If a subject said research was the most important, it was counted as the "primary activity"; if it was checked as second most important, it was counted as the "secondary activity." Of the total sample, 48 per cent reported that research was their primary activity, but there is considerable variation among fields: 38 per cent of the mathematicians, 59 per cent of the physicists, 60 per cent of the chemists, 75 per cent of the biochemists, and 19 per cent of the psychologists said it was the activity to which they devoted the most time.

In addition, scores on ability measures were available for 45 per cent of the sample.[3] These scores, from various intelligence tests, have been converted to equivalent standard scores with a general population mean of 50 and a standard deviation of 10. Of those in the sample for whom scores were available, the mean ability score was 69 in mathematics/statistics; 69 in physics; 65 in chemistry; 65 in biochemistry; and 66 in psychology. Since the high school rather than the individual was responsible for reporting these ability scores, the non-response bias was small as related to the criterion variable and to educational experience and work activity variables. For each of these variables, there were no statistically significant differences between those for whom ability measures were available and those for whom they were not.

The subject's educational experience was assessed through ratings of the quality of the graduate program at the university from which he received his doctorate.[4] In mathematics, 81 departments were evaluated; in physics, 86; in chemistry, 96; in biochemistry, 75; and in psychology, 88. The combined quality scores ranged from 0.00 (lowest quality) to 5.00 (highest quality). The ratings were made in 1964, five to seven years after those in the sample had received the doctoral degree, but there is considerable evidence that the relative ranking of departments changes slowly, so that a measure of institutional quality made at an earlier date would probably have correlated highly with these ratings.

Finally, information was available on the first employment position held after

[3] Harmon, Lindsey R., "High School Backgrounds of Science Doctorates," *Science,* vol. 133, March 10, 1966, pp. 679–688; and Harmon, *High School Ability Patterns: A Backward Look at the Doctorate,* Scientific Manpower Report No. 6, National Academy of Sciences-National Research Council, Office of Scientific Personnel, Washington, August, 1965.

[4] Cartter, Allan M., *An Assessment of Quality in Graduate Education.* American Council on Education, Washington, 1966.

receipt of the doctoral degree for 5,277 *male* doctoral degree recipients employed in 1964 in the five fields. Of these, 455 (9 per cent) reported that they had been awarded a postdoctoral fellowship.

Criterion Measures of Scientific Productivity

Of the various types of measures used to assess scientific accomplishment,[5] the commonest have been bibliographic counts. Sometimes these have consisted of a simple count of number of publications,[6] and sometimes various weighting procedures have been attempted,[7] though the researchers usually have not had any empirical basis for their choice of weights. A number of people—including those who have used bibliographic counts themselves—have criticized this method of assessing productivity on the grounds that it gives an advantage to the "operator" who produces quantity rather than to the scholar who produces quality.

A better measure of the quality of scientific achievement can probably be obtained by use of ratings (votes) by peers, although such ratings may be influenced by the personality of the scholar being judged or by the prestige of the institution that employs him.[8]

Another approach is the use of citation counts. Until recently, citation counts were not often employed because of the time and expense involved in obtaining the necessary information. But now, the *Science Citation Index* (SCI)[9] has greatly simplified the task. Indexing its entries by cited senior author and by citing author, this publication gives information about the media in which the cited work appeared, the form of the work (journal article, book, abstract, book review, editorial, thesis, unpublished paper, personal correspondence, and so forth), and other pertinent publication information. First compiled to cover 1961 journals, the most recent complete compilation covers journals published in 1964 and 1965 and includes 1,100 such journals, selected on the recom-

---

[5] An extended review of many of the criterion measures that have been used is included in Taylor, Calvin W., and Frank Barron, editors, *Scientific Creativity: Its Recognition and Development*, John Wiley and Sons, New York, 1963, especially Section 1, "The Criterion," pp. 5–98. See also Bayer, Alan E., and John K. Folger, "Some Correlates of a Citation Measure of Productivity in Science," *Sociology of Education*, vol. 39, Fall, 1966, pp. 381–390.

[6] See, for instance, Roe, Anne, "Changes in Scientific Activities with Age," *Science*, vol. 150, October 15, 1965, pp. 313–318.

[7] For examples of attempts to weight various types of publications, see Maris, Jerome G., "Some Academic Influences upon Publication Productivity," *Social Forces*, vol. 29, March, 1951, pp. 267–272; Meltzer, Bernard, "The Productivity of Social Scientists," *American Journal of Sociology*, vol. 55, July, 1949, pp. 25–29; Crane, Diana, "Scientists at Major and Minor Universities: A Study of Productivity and Recognition," *American Sociological Review*, vol. 30, October, 1965, pp. 699–714; Wilson, Logan, *The Academic Man: A Study in the Sociology of a Profession*, Octagon Books, Inc., New York, 1964, p. 110; and "A Review of Selected Disciplines," in Allan M. Cartter; *An Assessment of Quality in Graduate Education*, pp. 78–105.

[8] Clark, Kenneth E., *America's Psychologists: A Survey of A Growing Profession*. American Psychological Association, Washington, 1957, pp. 54–57.

[9] Institute for Scientific Information, *Science Citation Index*, Institute for Scientific Information, Philadelphia, 1961, 1964, and 1965. The SCI was compiled and published under the sponsorship of the National Science Foundation and the National Institutes of Health.

mendation of advisory boards in each of the fields covered (mathematics, physical sciences, biological and medical sciences, engineering, and psychology) and after subsequent evaluation by the staff of the Institute for Scientific Information.

Although a work may be cited for a variety of reasons, it seems reasonable to assume that the much-cited work is one that has had an impact on scientific knowledge. It has been influential inasmuch as it has been noticed and reacted to. As Creager and Harmon put it, "Where a particular reference or a particular author is frequently cited, there is some presumptive indication of his influence on the scientific enterprise and some presumption that this influence is positively, if not perfectly, correlated with the quality of the cited work."[10] Citation counts provide what may be called a "natural weighting" of written and accessible scholarly works. The frequency with which a scholar is cited by others is perhaps the best single measure of his known scientific achievement;[11] at least, it is consistent with the customs and standards of the scientific community.

The validity of a citation index is attested by its ability to distinguish, for example,[12] persons awarded Nobel prizes in physics, chemistry, and medicine from nonwinners. For all scientists included in the SCI in these fields, the mean number of references cited was 3.4, and the mean number of citations per author was 5.5; for the Nobel Prize winners, the mean number of references cited was 58.1 and the mean number of citations per author was 169.0. Similar additional evidence has been reported by the Coles,[13] who found that when there is an inconsistency between quantity and quality (citation frequency) of work, quality is the more significant correlate of the amount of recognition accorded physicists as demonstrated by their receiving honorific awards, being appointed to top-ranking departments, and having their research widely known in the national community of physicists. Moreover, Clark[14] found that the number of votes a person received from his peers has a higher correlation with citation counts ($r = .67$) than with any other measure investigated, including bibliographic counts, total professional income, number of professional offices held, and number and quality of Ph.D. students studying under the scholar.

Citation data on the present sample were derived from the 1964 and the 1965

[10] Creager, John A., and Lindsey R. Harmon, *On the Job Validation of Selection Variables,* National Academy of Sciences–National Research Council, Office of Scientific Personnel, Washington, 1966, p. 54. The authors note that some works are cited because they are bad examples or because they are being criticized, but such instances represent only a small proportion of total citations.

[11] Further discussion of this measure is presented by J. Margolis in "Citation Indexing and Evaluation of Scientific Papers," *Science,* vol. 155, March 10, 1967, pp. 1213–1219.

[12] Sher, Irving H., and Eugene Garfield, "New Tools for Improving and Evaluating the Effectiveness of Research." Paper presented at the Second Conference on Research Program Effectiveness, Washington, D.C., July 27–29, 1965.

[13] Cole, Stephen, and Jonathan R. Cole, "Scientific Output and Recognition: A Study in the Operation of the Reward System in Science." Paper presented at the Annual Meeting of the American Sociological Association, Miami, Florida, August, 1966.

[14] Clark, Kenneth E., *America's Psychologists,* pp. 54–57.

SCI.[15] All citations to works by those in the samples were counted, regardless of the media in which they appeared. The mean number of citations received by those in the mathematics sample was 2.7; in physics, 18.8; in chemistry, 10.0; in biochemistry, 26.1; and in psychology, 2.1. The striking differences among fields are largely the result of their differing emphases on research and publication and of differences in the absolute number of professionals in the field, although the SCI's uneven coverage may also have some influence. All subsequent analyses, therefore, maintain the field of specialization as a control variable.

An independent check was available on the validity of the citation measure for the 1957–1959 doctorate sample. As a part of another project the names of the 1957–1959 doctorate recipients had been sent to the appropriate department chairmen at the institution granting the doctoral degree. The chairmen were asked to nominate those of their former students on the roster who, in their opinion, had demonstrated sufficient scientific competence to provide effective service on a technical panel of the National Research Council. Rosters were returned for about one-fifth of the 1957–1959 doctorate recipients included in the present sample, and approximately 14 per cent of them were nominated. Although the heterogeneity of the responding institutions tends to diminish the differences between those nominated and those not nominated, marked significant differences in citation frequency were found; in all fields, a far greater proportion of those who were nominated had had their published works cited. Among mathematicians/statisticians, those nominated had a mean of 8 citations, as compared with a mean of fewer than 2 citations for those not nominated; among physicists, the comparable means were 36 and 14; for chemists, 26 and 10; for biochemists, 31 and 18; and for psychologists, 6 and 1 (Table 8.1).

Background Factors Affecting Citation Frequency

Although it is generally assumed that ability, motivation, and quality of graduate education all influence subsequent accomplishment in science, the relative contribution of each factor is largely unknown. Crane, noting that scientists trained at major universities are more productive than those who graduate from minor universities, suggests that this pattern might be explained by the superior ability of Ph.D. graduates of the major universities, but has no data on ability differentials for her sample group.[16] Clark comes to the same conclu-

[15] Only those who received their doctorates in 1957–1959 were included, to ensure that enough time had elapsed to permit publication of research and citation of these works by 1964–1965. The sample was further limited to mathematics/statistics, physics, chemistry, biochemistry, and psychology because some of the other field categories were too heterogeneous for detailed analysis, or because the relevant literature was not included at all or was not thoroughly covered in the *Science Citation Index*. The psychology reference journals included in the SCI are primarily those in clinical and experimental psychology. Nevertheless, since a majority of psychologists work in these fields and since we wanted to include social science, psychology was not omitted.

[16] Crane, Diana, "Scientists at Major and Minor Universities," p. 704.

TABLE 8.1. *Citation Frequency of Those Nominated and Those Not Nominated for a National Research Council Technical Panel: 1957–1959 Doctorate Recipients in Selected Fields*

Field of Doctoral Degree	Nominated for NRC Technical Panel			Not Nominated for NRC Technical Panel		
	Number	Per Cent with No Citations	Mean Number of Citations	Number	Per Cent with No Citations	Mean Number of Citations
Mathematics/Statistics	16	25.0	8.4	79	57.0	1.8
Physics	40	2.5	35.7	223	23.3	13.9
Chemistry	54	20.4	26.2	478	30.1	9.7
Biochemistry	16	0.0	30.5	47	21.3	18.2
Psychology	52	34.6	5.8	300	.69.3	1.2

SOURCE: Special tabulations of the Commission on Human Resources described in Appendix D, and special information on National Research Council technical panel nominations furnished by the Office of Scientific Personnel of the National Academy of Sciences.

sion, though he, too, lacks the data to test this hypothesis.[17] The present data showed statistically significant correlations, ranging from .14 to .27, between measured ability in high school and quality of doctorate education. In all fields, graduate department quality and citation frequency were positively and significantly correlated, with coefficients ranging from .13 in mathematics/statistics and psychology (fields in which more than one-half of the doctorates had no citations) to .20 in chemistry[18] (Table 8.2). The relationship between the proxy motivation variable (time lapse between receipt of B.A. and of Ph.D.) and citation count ranged from a correlation coefficient of −.14 to −.18, and all coefficients were statistically significant (Table 8.3). The stronger the motivation (as reflected in the subject's taking a relatively short time to get the Ph.D.), the higher the citation count. The relationship between measured ability and

TABLE 8.2. *Relationship Between Citation Count and Educational Quality, by Field*

Field	Per Cent with No Citations		Correlation Coefficient: Quality with Citation Count
	Low Quality	High Quality	
Mathematics/Statistics (N = 601)	60.8	49.3	.13
Physics (N = 1,220)	18.6	16.2	.17
Chemistry (N = 2,295)	39.6	29.2	.20
Biochemistry (N = 448)	15.9	7.1	.15
Psychology (N = 1,727)	71.1	60.6	.13

SOURCE: See Table 8.1. Quality refers to the Cartter rankings of graduate departmental quality. Low quality is below 3.0 on the Cartter scale, and high quality is above 3.0.

[17] Clark, Kenneth E., *America's Psychologists*, p. 230.
[18] Since a high proportion of 1957–1959 doctorate recipients in some fields had no citations listed in the SCI, the correlation coefficients were somewhat reduced.

TABLE 8.3. *Relationship Between Citation Count and B.A.-Ph.D. Time Lapse, by Field*

Field	Per Cent with No Citations		Correlation Coefficient: Lapse with Citation Count
	Time Lapse Less Than 5 Years	Time Lapse More Than 5 Years	
Mathematics/Statistics (N = 601)	41.1	61.2	—.17
Physics (N = 1,220)	16.1	19.1	—.14
Chemistry (N = 2,295)	29.8	38.4	—.18
Biochemistry (N = 448)	8.1	14.8	—.14
Psychology (N = 1,727)	44.9	70.2	—.18

SOURCE: See Table 8.1.

citation count is consistently less marked than are the relationships mentioned above, and are, except in the case of physics, statistically insignificant (Table 8.4).

The interrelationships of measured ability, institutional quality, and B.A.-Ph.D. time lapse, all tend to be statistically significant (Table 8.5). As a result, when all of the variables above were employed simultaneously to predict citation counts, the ability measure lost almost all of its predictive power in determining citation frequency. Taken together, however, institutional quality and the proxy motivation variable B.A.-Ph.D. time lapse had greater predictive power than either one taken separately.

Occupational Factors Affecting Citation Frequency

Scientists in different employment settings differed greatly in scientific achievement as assessed through citation counts. Scientists employed in universities generally had the highest citation counts. Those working for the federal government also had relatively high citation counts and, indeed, in mathematics/statistics and in biochemistry, tended to exceed scientists in a university setting

TABLE 8.4. *Relationship Between Citation Count and Measured Ability, by Field*

Field	Per Cent with No Citations		Correlation Coefficient: Ability with Citation Count
	Ability Score Less Than 60	Ability Score More Than 60	
Mathematics/Statistics (N = 250)	55.0	50.0	.04
Physics (N = 495)	22.6	15.9	.10
Chemistry (N = 1,111)	40.0	30.9	.07
Biochemistry (N = 207)	11.7	8.8	.04
Psychology (N = 750)	72.0	58.2	.07

SOURCE: See Table 8.1. Ability score is based on tests given during high school, and have a mean of 50 and a standard deviation of 10.

TABLE 8.5. *Intercorrelations and Multiple Correlations of Predictor Variables and Citation Count, by Field*

Variables Entering Regression Equation[a]	Mathematics/ Statistics (N = 250)	Physics (N = 495)	Chemistry (N = 1,111)	Biochemistry (N = 207)	Psychology (N = 750)
Zero-Order Correlation:					
r_{q1}	−.27	−.20	−.23	−.17	−.05
r_{qa}	.27	.24	.19	.14	.15
r_{1a}	−.23	−.13	−.03	−.07	−.09
First-Order Multiple:					
$R_{c.q1}$	.19	.20	.24	.19	.22
$R_{c.qa}$	.13	.18	.20	.15	.14
$R_{c.1a}$	.17	.16	.19	.14	.19
Second-Order Multiple:					
$R_{c.q1a}$	.19	.21	.24	.19	.22

[a] Where c denotes citation count, q denotes Cartter quality rating, l denotes B.A.-Ph.D. time lapse, and a denotes measured ability in high school.

SOURCE: See Table 8.1.

(Table 8.6). The citation counts of those in college settings were among the lowest: they averaged only one-fifth to one-half the figure for all doctorates in the same field.

Although scientists in universities consistently had higher citation rates than the total group of scientists in the same discipline, the rated quality of the university further differentiated scientists with regard to citation counts. Scientists in major high-quality universities are cited more frequently than are scientists in the lower quality universities (Table 8.7).[19]

The suggestion[20] that those who receive their doctorates from the better graduate schools generally go into universities rather than into other work set-

TABLE 8.6. *Mean Citation Count, by Field and Type of Employer*

Type of Employer	Mathematics/ Statistics (N = 601)	Physics (N = 1,220)	Chemistry (N = 2,295)	Biochemistry (N = 448)	Psychology (N = 1,727)
Private Industry/Business	2.4	21.3	6.9	10.3	1.1
College	0.4	3.7	5.9	5.7	1.2
University	3.3	23.5	20.6	30.6	3.9
Federal Government	4.3	15.8	13.0	34.6	2.2
Other	3.4	17.1	13.8	29.3	1.5
Total	2.7	18.8	10.0	26.1	2.1

SOURCE: See Table 8.1.

[19] The quality of the employer university is based on an average of the Cartter quality ratings of institutional department in the fields herein considered. High-quality employers have an overall average of 3.00 or more on Cartter quality in these fields.

[20] See Marcson, Simon, *The Scientist in American Industry: Some Organization Determinants in Manpower Utilization*, Harper and Bros., New York, 1960, pp. 54–55; Berelson, Bernard, *Graduate Education in the United States*, McGraw-Hill, Inc., New York, 1960, p. 115.

TABLE 8.7. *Citation Count of Those Employed in Universities, by Field and Quality of University Employer*

Field and Quality of University Employer[a]	Number of Citations			
	Total	None	1 to 10	11 or more
Mathematics/Statistics		(Percentages)		
High Quality (N = 194)	100	37.6	50.6	11.8
Low Quality (N = 108)	100	59.3	37.0	3.7
Physics				
High Quality (N = 256)	100	9.8	35.9	54.3
Low Quality (N = 129)	100	23.3	46.5	30.2
Chemistry				
High Quality (N= 188)	100	14.9	31.3	53.8
Low Quality (N = 187)	100	21.9	38.0	40.1
Biochemistry				
High Quality (N = 59)	100	3.4	32.2	64.4
Low Quality (N = 25)	100	8.0	36.0	56.0
Psychology				
High Quality (N = 253)	100	47.0	39.6	13.4
Low Quality (N = 190)	100	57.9	34.2	7.9

[a] Based on average Cartter quality rating of institutional departments within fields under analysis. High-quality university employers have an overall average of over 3.00 on Cartter quality in these fields.
SOURCE: See Table 8.1.

tings for subsequent employment was supported by our data. In all fields except physics, universities employed a higher proportion of doctorates from high-quality institutions than did any other employer category (Table 8.8). The previously reported relationship between quality of the degree-granting graduate department, B.A.-Ph.D. time lapse, and the scientific accomplishment criterion held true for each field and each category of job setting (Table 8.9).

Not surprisingly, the type of work activity was also related to the criterion measure. Of the scientists reporting that their research activity is minimal, 81 per cent of the psychologists, 78 per cent of the mathematicians, 47 per cent of the chemists, 31 per cent of the physicists, and 29 per cent of the biochemists had no citations; the proportion of those who reported that their primary activity was research and who had no citations ranged from one-third to two-thirds of these figures (Table 8.10).

Although the amount of research activity accounted for a substantial part of variation in citation counts, it did not adequately account for the differences among the categories of job setting. For instance, scientists in university settings had higher than average citation counts in all fields, and yet a lower than average proportion of them, with the exception of psychologists, were primarily engaged in research (Table 8.11). On the other hand, of the scientists in college settings, who consistently had among the lowest average citation rates, a very small proportion reported research as their primary activity.

Receiving a postdoctoral fellowship seems to stimulate scholarly output. In

TABLE 8.8. *Quality of Doctorate-Granting Institution, by Field and Type of Employer in 1964*

Type of Employer in 1964	Mathematics/Statistics (N = 601)		Physics (N = 1,220)		Chemistry (N = 2,295)		Biochemistry (N = 448)		Psychology (N = 1,727)	
	High Quality	Low Quality	High Quality	Low Quality	High Quality	Low Quality	High Quality	Low Quality	High Quality	Low Quality
Private Industry/Business	59.0	41.0	47.9	52.1	48.9	51.1	44.0	56.0	41.1	58.9
College	56.6	43.4	41.3	58.7	51.7	48.3	21.1	78.9	43.8	56.2
University	59.6	40.4	52.5	47.5	64.5	35.5	56.0	44.0	61.9	38.1
Federal Government	45.4	54.6	41.2	58.8	40.7	59.3	31.6	68.4	32.9	67.1
Other	59.0	41.0	55.2	44.8	46.0	54.0	44.3	55.7	47.6	52.4
Total	58.4	41.6	50.2	49.8	51.1	48.9	43.8	56.2	48.2	51.8

SOURCE: See Table 8.1.

TABLE 8.9. *Relationship Between Citation Count, Quality of Degree-Granting Department, and B.A.-Ph.D. Time Lapse, by Field and Type of Employer*[a]

Type of Employer in 1964	Mathematics/Statistics			Physics			Chemistry			Biochemistry			Psychology		
	r_{cq}	r_{cl}	$R_{c.ql}$	r_{cq}	r_{cl}	$R_{c.ql}$	r_{cq}	r_{cl}	$R_{c.ql}$	r_{cq}	r_{cl}	$R_{c.ql}$	r_{cq}	r_{cl}	$R_{c.ql}$
Private Industry/Business	.31	−.28	.36	.21	−.13	.25	.15	−.10	.17	.17	.18	.27	.09	−.08	.14
College	.31	−.09	.31	.23	−.05	.24	.21	−.21	.27	b	b	b	−.03	−.31	.32
University	.13	−.20	.22	.20	−.18	.23	.26	−.27	.32	.38	−.05	.39	.12	−.21	.24
Federal Government	b	b	b	.10	−.30	.32	.10	−.23	.24	.11	−.44	.44	.17	−.10	.19
Other	.25	.15	.28	.12	−.18	.19	.20	−.15	.21	.10	−.05	.11	.16	−.11	.19
Total	.13	−.17	.19	.17	−.16	.20	.20	−.16	.24	.15	−.10	.19	.13	−.18	.22

[a] Where c denotes citation count, q denotes Carter quality rating, and l denotes B.A.-Ph.D. time lapse.
b Statistic not computed; fewer than 20 cases.

SOURCE: See Table 8.1.

TABLE 8.10. *Proportion of Sample with No Citations, by Field and Work Activity*

Research Activity	Mathematics/Statistics		Physics		Chemistry		Biochemistry		Psychology	
	Number	Per Cent with No Citations	Number	Per Cent with No Citations	Number	Per Cent with No Citations	Number	Per Cent with No Citations	Number	Per Cent with No Citations
Research Primary	225	38.7	724	10.5	1,385	32.3	337	9.5	332	38.9
Research Secondary	250	56.0	345	25.5	604	32.4	62	12.9	396	51.0
Research Minor	126	77.8	151	31.8	306	47.4	49	28.6	999	81.0
Total	601	54.1	1,220	17.4	2,295	34.3	448	12.1	1,727	66.0

SOURCE: See Table 8.1.

TABLE 8.11. *Proportion of Sample with Research as Primary Work Activity, by Field and Type of Employer*

Type of Employer	Mathematics/Statistics		Physics		Chemistry		Biochemistry		Psychology	
	Number	Per Cent Research Primary	Number	Per Cent Research Primary	Number	Per Cent Research Primary	Number	Per Cent Research Primary	Number	Per Cent Research Primary
Private Industry/Business	117	57.3	284	72.5	1,308	74.3	75	77.3	117	29.9
College	99	8.1	109	1.8	271	3.3	19	0.0	265	3.8
University	302	33.8	385	47.0	375	38.9	84	71.4	443	25.9
Federal Government	22	72.7	107	76.6	113	82.3	60	78.3	179	24.6
Other	61	52.4	335	75.5	228	72.4	210	81.9	723	17.7
Total	601	37.4	1,220	59.3	2,295	60.3	448	75.2	1,727	19.2

SOURCE: See Table 8.1.

each field, the 1957–1959 male doctorate recipients who had received a post-doctoral fellowship had about twice as many recent citations to their work as did those who were nonrecipients, and these proportions held true (except for psychologists engaged primarily in research) regardless of primary job activity (Table 8.12). Of course, those who received such a fellowship were more likely than others to engage primarily in research in their 1964 jobs and to be employed in college or university settings (see Chapter 7); but even when these factors are held constant, the former postdoctoral fellowship holders tended to have higher citation counts than did their colleagues. Similarly, controlling for work setting (five to seven years after the Ph.D. degree was received) does not change the relative magnitude of citation counts for the former postdoctoral fellowship holders (Table 8.13).

Summary of Determinants of Scientific Productivity

A person's scientific accomplishment can be at least partially assessed through a measure that indicates how aware other scientists are of his work. The relative merit of a scholar's work can be inferred from the frequency with which his colleagues cite it in scholarly reports, professional journals, and so forth. No other single measure gets at a person's contribution to science as directly as does citation frequency.

Using citation frequency as the criterion, we found that earlier research which reported a low correlation between college grades (a proxy for ability) and later achievement was substantiated.[21] Although measured ability was related to attendance at a selective graduate school (institutional quality) and to motivation (the rate of progress through graduate school), it had virtually no relationship to subsequent scientific accomplishment (citation frequency) of doctorate recipients in science except what was mediated through the two other variables. Though students who enter graduate school and complete doctoral training vary rather widely in measured ability levels, the influence of ability on subsequent productivity was overshadowed by other influences. A person's motivation and the quality of his graduate education were related both to the type of employment setting he moved into and, even more closely, to his subsequent accomplishment in science, whatever his employment setting. Undoubtedly, these two factors were also important in determining whether he received a postdoctoral fellowship. Although it is not possible to say how much of the postdoctoral fellowship holder's scientific productivity was a function of these and other selection factors and how much was a function of his additional training or of his richer opportunities to do publishable research, the data make it clear

---

[21] See, for example, Taylor, Calvin W., William A. Smith, and Brewster Ghiselin, "The Creative and Other Contributions of One Sample of Research Scientists" in Taylor and Barron, editors, *Scientific Creativity*, pp. 53–76. A comprehensive review of the research in this area is presented by Donald P. Hoyt in "The Relationship Between College Grades and Adult Achievement: A Review of the Literature."

TABLE 8.12. *Mean Citation Count, by Postdoctoral Fellowship Status, Major Work Activity in 1964, and Field: 1957–1959 Male Doctorate Recipients*

Field of Doctoral Degree	Postdoctoral Fellowship Holder						Not Postdoctoral Fellowship Holder					
	In Research		Not in Research		Total, All Work Activities		In Research		Not in Research		Total, All Work Activities	
	Number	Mean Citation Count	Number	Mean Citation Count	Number	Mean Citation Count	Number	Mean Citation Count	Number	Mean Citation Count	Number	Mean Citation Count
Mathematics/Statistics	16	6.63	13	3.23	29	5.00	177	4.53	323	1.68	500	2.69
Physics	56	44.71	28	24.14	84	37.86	532	21.37	396	10.89	938	16.72
Chemistry	127	19.93	73	17.00	200	18.86	1,041	10.84	723	7.38	1,764	9.42
Biochemistry	66	37.74	20	28.40	86	35.57	217	26.67	75	12.40	292	23.00
Psychology	21	4.86	35	3.71	56	4.14	248	6.01	1,080	1.48	1,328	2.33

SOURCE: See Table 8.1.

TABLE 8.13. *Mean Citation Count, by Postdoctoral Fellowship Status, Type of Work Setting in 1964, and Field: 1957–1959 Male Doctorate Recipients*

Field of Doctoral Degree	Postdoctoral Fellowship Holder						Not Postdoctoral Fellowship Holder					
	In College or University Setting		Not in Academic Setting		Total, All Work Settings		In College or University Setting		Not in Academic Setting		Total, All Work Settings	
	Number	Mean Citation Count	Number	Mean Citation Count	Number	Mean Citation Count	Number	Mean Citation Count	Number	Mean Citation Count	Number	Mean Citation Count
Mathematics/Statistics	23	3.70	6	9.98	29	5.00	341	2.60	159	2.88	500	2.69
Physics	53	45.40	31	24.97	84	37.86	472	15.03	466	18.43	938	16.72
Chemistry	108	24.39	92	12.37	200	18.86	518	13.85	1,243	7.59	1,764	9.42
Biochemistry	59	40.96	27	23.77	86	35.57	140	26.32	152	19.94	292	23.00
Psychology	33	5.88	23	1.65	56	4.14	655	3.30	673	1.38	1,328	2.33

SOURCE: See Table 8.1.

that postdoctoral fellowship holders were considerably more productive than were those who had not been awarded a fellowship.

Occupational factors, too, appear to be important determinants of the scientist's professional achievement. The differential citation rates of scientists in different job-settings may reflect the varying conditions existent in different sectors of the economy. For instance, competition between corporations or considerations of national security may preclude release and publication of some scientific findings. A large, rigidly structured bureaucracy or the use of a team approach may obscure individual contribution.

More obvious is the fact that the differential citation rates were partly a function of the amount of time available for scientific research as opposed to other tasks, such as teaching, administration, and counseling. Thus, those in college settings, where available research time is limited because of heavy teaching duties, had among the lowest citation rates. College employment virtually eliminates the opportunity to pursue research for most scientists in this setting.[22] Scientists in universities, on the other hand, generally had the highest citation rates. Ferriss has recently suggested some of the reasons for these differences among academic institutions:

> The academician may value teaching alone or teaching and research. While institutions may not all be uniquely classifiable according to this dichotomy, they tend to emphasize one or the other. Universities and technological institutions are much more likely than other types of institutions to emphasize teaching and research. Conversely, junior colleges undoubtedly emphasize teaching. State colleges probably lie closer to the teaching-research end of the continuum than do liberal arts colleges, but any single case examined might be in a state of transition from one category to another. In addition, the role of teaching graduate students requires that research interests be stimulated, that the teacher himself be actively engaged upon some "front" of knowledge, whereas the role of teaching undergraduates, particularly in a liberal arts college, requires that broad intellectual interests be stimulated, that the teacher have command of the results of scholarship and research. Thus, the institutional function dictates the role requirements of its faculty.[23]

Even among universities, however, significant differences emerged. Those in the better universities had considerably higher citation rates than those in the lower quality universities. The amount of research time available cannot entirely explain these differences. Storer points to some other possible explanations:

> It is by no means proven . . . that the "best" men are always hired by the top ten or twenty universities in the country or by a select group of industries and government agencies, although the representation of these institutions on government panels and in the leadership of professional societies would certainly

---

[22] It is also probable that doctorate recipients in science who choose a college setting for employment have also made the prior choice to restrict their research activities.
[23] Ferriss, Abbott L., "A Hypothesis on Institutional Mobility of Teachers in Higher Education," *College and University*, Fall, 1966, p. 23.

suggest this. It may be that the young scientist who is hired by one of these institutions is somehow encouraged to do better work than he might have done at a second- or third-rate institution, so that the institution makes the man rather than vice versa. Or it may be that his affiliation will give him more direct access to journals and in receiving greater opportunity to demonstrate his abilites.[24]

Although the case of college-employed doctorate recipients in the sample makes it clear that an almost complete lack of research time will probably result in a lack of scientific achievement, the converse does not follow. Scientists whose primary activity is research will not necessarily and automatically manifest high scientific achievement. Nor is it likely that innate differences in ability are of significant influence in differentiating among the scientifically productive and the unproductive. Rather, strong motivation and a high-quality educational experience appear to be among the primary determinants of scientific achievement.

Determinants of Professional Income

The relations between various levels of educational attainment and salaries have been analyzed and demonstrated by a number of researchers.[25] There exist, even among those who have the same amount of education, large differences in the earnings of people in different fields and different work settings.[26] Of the 1957–1962 Ph.D.'s in the major scientific disciplines who reported their salaries to the 1964 National Register of Scientific and Technical Personnel, average annual difference of more than $2,000 were not uncommon between fields, even within the same kind of work setting. Holders of doctoral degrees in economics, physics, and mathematics/statistics generally receive unusually high salaries relative to all Ph.D.'s, while those in the biosciences generally receive lower than average salaries (Table 8.14). Table 8.14 also shows salary differences among work settings. In general, annual gross income tends to be lowest in colleges and universities, highest in business and industry, and intermediate in governmental and other job settings.

What accounts for these differences? It might seem that those currently in the work force who had received a postdoctoral fellowship would receive additional financial rewards. Surprisingly enough, however, this was not the case. Rather, the former fellowship holders had an average income below that of their cohorts who had not received a fellowship. With only one exception (the 1957–1958 bioscientists in colleges and universities), this generalization

[24] Storer, Norman W., *The Social System of Science.* Holt, Rinehart and Winston, Inc., New York, 1966, p. 149.

[25] See, for example, Glick, Paul C., "Educational Attainment and Occupational Advancement," *Transactions of the Second World Congress of the International Sociological Association,* Liege, Belgium, 1953 (published in London, 1954); Miller, Herman P., "Annual and Lifetime Income in Relation to Education, 1939–1959," *American Economic Review,* vol. 50, 1960, pp. 962–986; and Hansen, W. Lee, "Total and Private Rates of Return to Investment in Schooling," *Journal of Political Economy,* April, 1963, pp. 128–140.

[26] A comprehensive review of these differences is presented in Vetter, Betty M., and Eleanor L. Babco, compilers, *Salaries of Scientists, Engineers, and Technicians,* Staff Report 67–1, Scientific Manpower Commission, Washington, June, 1967.

TABLE 8.14. *Mean 1964 Gross Annual Professional Income, by Job Setting in 1964, Year of Ph.D., and Field of Ph.D.*

Employer Type in 1964 and Year of Ph.D.	Mathematics/ Statistics	Physics	Chemistry	Earth Sciences	Biological Sciences	Biochemistry	Psychology	Sociology	Economics
College/University									
1957	$13,434	$13,750	$12,004	$12,465	$11,111	$10,769	$13,009	$12,388	$13,356
1958	13,182	12,758	10,944	11,918	11,175	11,449	12,881	12,281	14,131
1959	12,023	12,695	10,760	11,078	10,517	11,176	12,007	11,055	13,206
1960	11,834	11,981	10,064	10,435	9,818	10,720	11,659	11,150	12,431
1961	11,279	11,572	10,110	9,989	9,613	10,324	10,912	10,820	11,903
1962	10,800	10,423	9,627	9,397	9,318	9,310	10,465	10,111	11,288
Business/Industry									
1957	17,733	17,161	14,349	13,476	14,546	15,767	18,357	a	22,150
1958	20,417	16,604	13,687	12,800	13,598	14,681	16,617	a	22,482
1959	17,917	15,859	13,379	12,859	13,180	12,694	15,239	a	19,060
1960	15,450	15,409	13,090	12,674	13,369	11,872	15,517	a	19,927
1961	15,991	14,911	12,401	12,338	12,593	11,500	14,732	a	19,209
1962	15,011	14,099	12,080	10,890	11,398	11,715	13,455	a	a
U.S. Government									
1957	a	15,465	12,991	12,808	11,765	12,033	14,367	a	14,780
1958	a	14,071	12,550	13,259	11,668	12,591	13,470	a	15,850
1959	a	13,426	11,987	12,000	11,595	a	13,686	a	13,728
1960	a	13,173	12,348	10,635	12,523	12,220	12,934	a	13,272
1961	a	12,496	11,711	10,971	10,571	a	12,110	a	12,411
1962	a	11,850	10,948	9,959	10,089	a	11,652	a	12,547
Other									
1957	a	16,350	12,552	18,754	11,935	12,100	17,372	12,700	16,283
1958	a	15,593	13,759	a	11,733	12,500	15,643	a	19,527
1959	17,617	16,046	13,869	13,082	11,020	12,930	14,761	12,383	a
1960	16,692	15,096	12,055	12,660	14,963	12,800	15,151	a	16,740
1961	a	14,516	11,973	10,269	11,857	a	13,928	15,279	15,620
1962	13,460	12,794	12,111	a	10,527	a	12,649	11,640	12,467
Total, All Employers									
1957	14,446	15,107	13,597	13,711	11,719	12,125	14,856	13,054	14,422
1958	14,915	14,280	12,869	12,308	11,566	12,543	13,998	12,698	15,213
1959	13,965	14,126	12,501	11,883	11,032	11,820	13,325	11,520	13,695
1960	13,011	13,366	12,157	11,140	10,968	11,479	13,267	11,815	13,369
1961	12,321	12,748	11,639	10,870	10,257	10,603	12,159	11,438	12,615
1962	11,766	11,653	11,351	9,909	9,829	10,214	11,393	10,267	11,538

a Fewer than 10 cases.   SOURCE: See Table 8.1.

was true even when 1964 work setting was held constant (Table 8.15). Those scientists in research who did not hold a postdoctoral fellowship made a consistently higher average income than the awardees who are also engaged primarily in research, though there was less consistency in salary differences among those in other primary work activities (Table 8.16).

This rather surprising finding can be explained by the fact that the persons included in the sample were relatively recent Ph.D.'s. Those who took a year or two as postdoctoral Fellows had been employed for a shorter period of time and had less opportunity for earning either automatic increases based on length of employment, or merit increases that depend on sufficient tenure to allow for publication records and evidence about teaching ability to become known. Since the postdoctoral Fellows had more published works and citations than their non-postdoctoral colleagues; these figures suggest that time on the job has more to do with salary level than scholarly accomplishment at the beginning of a career. In later stages of career development the reverse may be true, and the man with a record of research accomplishment may have higher earnings than his colleague who has one or two years more tenure.

Other factors that have been suggested as determinants of earnings include ability, motivation, and various institutional and situational variables.[27] Some economists have attributed differences in lifetime incomes to variations among occupations in the supply of and demand for manpower. They assert, for example, that the high salaries of engineers in research and development are an index of a shortage in that field.[28] The costs of entering different professions and the differences in educational requirements are usually taken into account in comparing lifetime earnings, but other factors, such as ability, productivity, activity in the profession, and so on, are generally neglected.

The Commission on Human Resources analyzed eleven of these factors to assess the relative influence of each on the income levels of the 1957–1959 doctorate recipients.[29] In addition to the sample employed in the preceding section of this chapter, those who responded to the 1964 National Register survey and received the doctoral degree in 1957–1959 in the earth sciences (including meteorology and oceanography) or in other biological sciences in addition to biochemistry (including anatomy, biophysics, botany, ecology, entomology, genetics, microbiology, nutrition, pathology, pharmacology, physiology, phytopathology, virology, and zoology) were also included in the following analyses.

---

[27] See, for example, Duncan, Otis Dudley, and Robert W. Hodge, "Education and Occupational Mobility: A Regression Analysis," *American Journal of Sociology*, vol. 68, May, 1963, pp. 629–644; Barber, Bernard, "Social-Class Differences in Educational Life Chances," *Teachers College Record*, vol. 63 November, 1961, pp. 102–113; and Anderson, C. Arnold, "A Skeptical Note on the Relation of Vertical Mobility to Education," *American Journal of Sociology*, vol. 66, May, 1961, pp. 560–570.

[28] Hansen, W. Lee, "The Economics of Scientific and Engineering Manpower," *Journal of Human Resources*, vol. 2, Spring, 1967, pp. 191–215.

[29] For a fuller discussion of the variables and the regression equation employed, see Appendix D.

TABLE 8.15. *Mean 1964 Gross Annual Professional Income, by Postdoctoral Fellowship Status, Type of Work Setting, Year of Ph.D., and Major Field of Degree*

Year of Ph.D. and Major Field of Degree	Postdoctoral Fellowship Holder						Not Postdoctoral Fellowship Holder					
	In College Setting		Not in College Setting		Total, All Work Settings		In College Setting		Not in College Setting		Total, All Work Settings	
	Number	Mean Income	Number	Mean Income	Number	Mean Income	Number	Mean Income	Number	Mean Income	Number	Mean Income
1957 and 1958												
Physical Sciences	102	$12,038	72	$13,715	174	$12,732	928	$12,513	1,293	$14,709	2,221	$13,792
Biosciences	100	11,487	39	12,092	139	11,657	720	11,117	420	12,992	1,140	11,808
Social Sciences	24	12,817	17	14,917	41	13,688	815	13,034	547	16,293	1,362	14,343
1959 and 1960												
Physical Sciences	217	11,106	127	13,094	344	11,840	1,098	11,387	1,396	13,879	2,494	12,782
Biosciences	195	10,128	54	11,147	249	10,349	631	10,298	375	12,419	1,006	11,089
Social Sciences	51	11,267	17	13,359	68	11,790	932	12,018	595	14,810	1,527	13,106
1961 and 1962												
Physical Sciences	351	9,351	198	11,322	549	10,062	1,239	10,582	1,428	12,533	2,667	11,627
Biosciences	267	8,716	94	9,088	361	8,813	611	9,458	391	10,928	1,002	10,032
Social Sciences	61	10,064	40	10,758	101	10,339	1,137	10,939	614	13,043	1,751	11,677

SOURCE: See Table 8.1.

TABLE 8.16. *Mean 1964 Gross Annual Professional Income, by Postdoctoral Fellowship Status, Major Work Activity, Year of Ph.D., and Major Field of Degree*

Year of Ph.D. and Major Field of Degree	Postdoctoral Fellowship Holder								Not Postdoctoral Fellowship Holder							
	In Teaching		In Research		In Other		Total, All Work Activities		In Teaching		In Research		In Other		Total, All Work Activities	
	Num-ber	Mean Income	Num-ber	Mean Income	Num-ber	Mean Income	Num-ber	Mean Income	Num-ber	Mean Income	Num-ber	Mean Income	Num-ber	Mean Income	Num-ber	Mean Income
1957 and 1958																
Physical Sciences	49	$11,208	113	$13,119	12	$15,310	174	$12,732	598	$12,006	1,156	$13,846	467	$15,945	2,221	$13,762
Biological Sciences	34	11,459	90	11,532	15	12,855	139	11,657	339	10,887	637	11,603	164	14,508	1,140	11,808
Social Sciences	10	11,060	16	12,894	15	16,286	41	13,688	490	12,456	286	14,336	586	15,924	1,362	14,343
1959 and 1960																
Physical Sciences	118	11,175	198	12,159	28	12,386	344	11,840	698	10,916	1,407	13,160	389	14,763	2,494	12,782
Biological Sciences	65	10,111	166	10,340	18	11,291	249	10,349	308	10,123	555	11,115	143	13,068	1,006	11,089
Social Sciences	25	11,164	31	11,026	12	15,067	68	11,790	591	12,003	378	12,212	558	14,879	1,527	13,106
1961 and 1962																
Physical Sciences	137	9,624	400	10,141	12	12,429	549	10,062	764	10,332	1,600	11,964	303	13,112	2,667	11,627
Biological Sciences	62	9,035	284	8,745	15	9,182	361	8,813	326	9,405	554	10,134	122	11,244	1,002	10,032
Social Sciences	23	10,161	60	10,043	18	11,553	101	10,339	757	10,765	403	11,696	591	12,832	1,751	11,677

SOURCE: See Table 8.1.

The resulting sample consisted of 3,506 doctorate recipients of 1957–1959 who had reported their 1964 professional income and for whom complete data on the eleven variables were available. The dependent variable in the analysis was annual income for 1964. The other variables were field, major work activity (research, teaching, and administration), region of employment (East, South, West, or Central), years of employment, sex, B.A.-Ph.D. time lapse, measured ability, citation count, quality of Ph.D.-granting department, age, and type of job setting (business setting, federal government setting, academic setting).

TABLE 8.17. *Factors Associated with the 1964 Annual Income of 3,506 Scientists Who Received the Doctoral Degree Between 1957 and 1959*

Variables	Partial	Coefficient of Determination[a] r^2	Significance Level
Field		.082	.01
Activity		.040	.01
Region		.005	.05
Years of Employment		.012	.01
Sex		.041	.01
B.A.-Ph.D. Time Lapse		.007	.01
Measured Ability		.002	.01
Citation Count		.017	.01
Quality of Ph.D. Department		.000	n.s.
Age		.000	n.s.
Job Setting		.053	.01
		$R = .5411$	
		$R^2 = .2928$	

[a] The coefficient of partial determination is the square of the partial correlation coefficient. Thus, a partial correlation coefficient of .20 would have a coefficient of partial determination of .04.
SOURCE: See Table 8.1.

As Table 8.17 indicates, the variables accounted for approximately 29 per cent of the variation in income among the 3,500 Ph.D.'s. When one considers the number of factors that influence annual income, this result is encouraging. The finding that field was the most important variable in explaining the variation of income in the sample can be interpreted in several ways. First, it may reflect disequilibrium in the labor market. If that is so, then the variations among fields would disappear as more people entered the fields that offered higher earnings. All other factors remaining the same, the increase in supply would cause incomes to fall. Second, income variations may be compensated for by nonpecuniary differences among fields. For example, high prestige associated with some fields may balance its lower salaries. Finally, lack of information about specific occupations and differences in the amount of on-the-job training might also account for variations in income by field.

The importance of type of work setting can be explained in much the same way. However, the fact that field was in the regression equation suggests that nonpecuniary elements of employment may be a factor in the importance of this variable in explaining variation in annual income.

Sex explained about 4 per cent of the variation in income. While this finding may indicate that women are discriminated against in the labor market, it may also indicate that there are certain costs associated with employing women. For example, a higher rate of turnover and absenteeism among women may work to the financial disadvantage of the employer.

Even though citation count explained only about 2 per cent of the variation in income, this is sufficient to suggest that financial rewards are associated with productivity. This variable may grow more important the longer the person has been in the profession, since differences in productivity become more apparent as persons remain in a profession longer.

The relatively weak influence of region of employment and of quality of the Ph.D.-granting institution deserves special mention. That region accounted for so little of the variation in income suggests that the market for professionals is truly national, as one would expect. (See Chapter 7 for a more detailed discussion of regional variations.) It is surprising, however, that the quality of the Ph.D.-granting department was not more important in explaining variations in income. Nevertheless, Shane Hunt obtained similar results in his study of the incomes of some 9,000 graduates from four-year colleges. It may be, as Hunt suggests, that when other factors are accounted for, the quality of the institution makes no difference.[30] Of course, one cannot discount the possibility that the lack of significance of this variable was attributable to interaction among the independent variables. But the zero-order correlations among the independent variables were very low. In addition, when the four variables that contain sets of dummy variables were excluded from the regression equation one at a time, this variable did not become significant; this finding does not exclude the possibility of interaction, but it is evidence against it.

Table 8.18 shows the results of a similar analysis for Ph.D.'s in academic settings only.[31] Rank explained the greatest amount of variation in the income of those in the academic world. Rank can be interpreted as evidence that the individual has been effective in his work environment. Presumably, high rank means that one has shown himself to be a productive member of the academic world. In this case, of course, the measures of productivity are numerous, and they are evaluated by one's colleagues. Therefore, since rank and income are both part of the same reward system, one would expect rank to be correlated with annual income.

The results shown in Table 8.18 indicate at least one characteristic of colleges

---

[30] Hunt, Shane, "Income Determinants for College Graduates and the Return to Educational Investment," *Yale Economic Essays*, Fall, 1963, pp. 305–357.

[31] Two variables, academic rank and type of employing school, were added in this analysis, and the variable "type of employment" was, of course, excluded. This reduced the sample size to approximately 1,460, and the coefficient of multiple correlation fell to .21.

TABLE 8.18. *Factors Associated with the 1964 Annual Income of 1,464 Scientists in Colleges and Universities Who Received the Doctoral Degree Between 1957 and 1959*

Variables	Coefficient of Partial Determination r^2	Significance Level
Field	.029	.01
Activity	.017	.01
Region	.004	n.s.
Years of Employment	.005	.01
Sex	.020	.01
B.A.-Ph.D. Time Lapse	.010	.01
Measured Ability	.004	.05
Citation Count	.017	.01
Quality of Ph.D. Department	.000	n.s.
Age	.001	n.s.
Academic Rank	.061	.01
Type of Employing School	.023	.01
	$R = .4626$	
	$R^2 = .2139$	

SOURCE: See Table 8.1.

and universities: they usually have wage schedules that set maximums and minimums by rank. Such a practice almost certainly has the effect of reducing the variation in earnings by field and sex. As can be seen by comparing Tables 8.17 and 8.18, sex and field explained less of the income variation among those in academic settings than among all Ph.D.'s. The reduction in salary variation attributable to field and the fixed salary schedule make it difficult for universities to recruit in fields where the supply of manpower is short. The results in Table 8.18 also suggest that the academic market place is a national market, and, surprisingly, that citation count is not any better in explaining the variation in income among academic Ph.D.'s than it was in explaining the variation for all Ph.D.'s.

Summary of Determinants of Professional Income

Although the analysis should be helpful to those interested in professional labor markets, it certainly does not explain even a major fraction of the variation observable in the incomes of professionals.

These studies underline the need for caution in using characteristics of entrants to a profession as measures of effectiveness of performance. Even if we project a slight drop in the average I.Q. of scientists in the next decade as more people enter scientific careers, our studies indicate that a change in average I.Q. of less than five points probably would have little if any measurable effect on either the amount or quality of output of scientific literature.

The low relationship between salaries and measures of scientific accomplishment also indicate caution in the use of salary data as a measure of effectiveness. The lower average salaries paid to postdoctoral fellowship holders emphasize the importance of seniority and time of service as factors in salary determination. The low correlations between salaries and citation measures are undoubtedly partly a result of the short career service of our sample; if a longer career service sample were available it might show that higher salaries are paid both for effective research service, and for administration and other activities. If a man does not receive a salary increase for research, he will move into another field where he can get financial rewards for other kinds of activity. All of these analyses show the necessity of multiple criteria of effectiveness, and development of studies which employ a number of predictors if further progress is to be made in assessing the changes in the quality of professional performance in our society.

Introduction to Section III

In the two preceding sections we have, among other things, touched on some of the considerations that make it difficult to predict what the future supply of high-level talent will be. In this section, we will focus on three special groups that constitute important, though not always predictable, sources of supply. In the past, two of these sources—women and persons from lower socioeconomic levels—have been underutilized; definite steps must be taken if the potential talent in these groups is not to be wasted in the future. The third group—the foreign-born or foreign-educated—have long made substantial contributions to the manpower pool in the United States, and with the removal of immigration barriers, they will doubtless continue to grow in importance. The chapters in this section deal with some of the issues that arise in connection with each of these three groups and make policy recommendations regarding their appropriate utilization.

In three of the occupations discussed in Chapter 4—elementary and secondary school teaching, social welfare, and nursing—a sizable proportion of the workers are women. As was pointed out in that chapter, this fact makes it particularly difficult to predict the adequacy of supply in these fields. We can say that if these (or other women-dominated) occupations become shortage fields, then they may draw on the labor reserve of women trained in the occupation but not currently working. The transformation of this labor reserve into an active labor force represents an important adjustment mechanism in our economy. Chapter 9 describes trends in the educational and career patterns of women, pointing out that women who once dropped out of the labor force permanently in order to rear families are now tending to return to employment after their children are in school. The chapter concentrates, in particular, on the labor force participation of women doctorate recipients, most of whom are employed in colleges and universities, and compares the academic rank and salary of men and women and the work activities and scholarly productivity of women doctorates in different fields. Some of the barriers to the career development of women are also touched upon. Finally, recommendations are made as to what steps should be taken in order to make better use of the abilities of women.

The nation provides employment for nearly all of the highly able middle-class men and nearly all of them will be college graduates for the foreseeable future. If the quality of personnel in various fields is not to be diluted in the future, further attempts must be made to tap the resources of the lower socio-economic groups. Today, much attention is being directed to the potential of persons in these groups, and national programs have been initiated to help such persons overcome the disadvantages imposed by their backgrounds. Chapter 10 attempts to assess the magnitude of talent loss among lower socioeconomic groups and to relate socioeconomic status to ability, college attendance, enrollment at a selective college, retention in college, and career plans. The probable effects of increased financial support to disadvantaged students and of special programs to remedy motivational handicaps and other SES-related obstacles to full development of potential are also considered. Obviously, these problems have far-reaching implications relating to the ability of this country to fulfill its commitment to provide a college education for all who are capable of absorbing it, and unless we can arrive at a definite understanding of the issues involved and of the policies that should be followed, we will fall short of our ideals as a nation.

The international interchange of talented persons, whether trained or untrained, is a complex phenomenon that deserves close scrutiny from several angles. As Chapter 11 indicates, the foreign-born and foreign-educated have made substantial contributions to the pool of high-level manpower in this country, particularly in the field of medicine. But this "brain gain" to the United States represents only one aspect of the migration flow. The chapter covers other components of gain and loss: the numbers of foreign students trained in this country, at both the undergraduate and graduate levels, and the proportion of these persons who become a permanent part of the U.S. labor force; the number of American students who receive at least some of their advanced training in a foreign college or university; the number of talented persons born and trained in this country who subsequently go abroad to work in foreign countries. An attempt is made to assess the net talent gain (or loss) resulting from these migration streams and to evaluate the costs and benefits that derive to American society from the interchange. In particular, it is emphasized that the advantage that this country may have in attracting high-level manpower may be offset, in part, by the international ill will that results from the siphoning off of talent from underdeveloped countries sorely in need of highly trained manpower. It is also pointed out that initiative in preventing this "brain drain" must be taken by the foreign countries themselves, with the United States playing a cooperative rather than a controlling role.

In short, manpower specialists must take a long and conscientious look at the potential offered by these three special groups, if they are to come to an understanding of when and how they may best be utilized and of what programs should be undertaken for the benefit not only of our society but of the talented individual himself.

9 The Educational and
Vocational Development of Women

ALTHOUGH STUDIES of and concerns about manpower needs have often been limited to only one-half of the nation's population—the men, the revolution in the employment of women makes it imperative that we also come to a better understanding of the educational and career aspirations of women. Increases in the proportion of women in the labor force and changes in their employment patterns have outmoded the skepticism sometimes expressed about the advisability of training women for the professions and specialized occupations.

The revolution in women's participation in the labor force has been taking place over the past several decades. In 1920, women constituted 20 per cent of the working population; today, they make up more than 32 per cent. Some of the reasons for this increased participation are obvious. As a result of the nation's economic and technological growth, new jobs and more job opportunities in traditional fields have opened up for women and at the same time the burden of housework has been lightened, thus affording them greater freedom to choose and develop a career. Furthermore, employers' attitudes toward hiring women have grown more favorable, even though some discrimination may still exist.[1]

The postwar years have seen changes not only in the numbers of women who work outside the home, but also in the characteristics of working women with respect to marital status and age. Before the 1940's, women tended to

---

[1] For a more extensive discussion of the possible reasons for the observed increases of all women in the labor force, see Ginzberg, Eli, and others, *Life Styles of Educated Women*, Columbia University Press, New York, 1966, chap. 1.

leave the labor force once they were married and never return to it. But the pattern has changed. Women now may interrupt their careers for about a decade in order to be at home with their growing children, but they return to work later on. Until 1960, women in their early twenties had the highest rate of employment. But the supply of young and unmarried women has been on the decline, partly because of the lower birth rates during the depression years and partly because more women tend to take advanced training and thus are unavailable for employment during their early twenties. On the other hand, the percentage of married women who work after marriage has grown steadily: in 1962, 60 per cent of the women in the labor force were married, as compared with only 23 per cent in 1920,[2] and increases have been greatest among those in the 45- to 54-year-old age category. About 40 per cent of this group were part of the labor force in 1960, whereas in 1950 the comparable figure was only 23 per cent. This increase was over three times as great as the increase (5 per cent) for single women in the same age category.[3]

Figure 9.1 indicates some of the relationships between educational attainment and labor force participation among women. Although the greatest increases in employment for all three age groups shown in the figure occurred among women who had only an elementary school education, still it is clear that the more education a woman has, the more likely she is to be in the labor force. For instance, in the 25- to 34-year-old age group, over two-thirds of the women who had five or more years of advanced education were in the labor force in 1960, as compared with 44 per cent of the women who had only a high school education. One partial explanation for this difference is that more highly educated women are more likely to be single.[4] Moreover, they have a greater investment and interest in a career.

But in certain fields, even the better-educated women remain poorly represented: for instance, less than 1 per cent of engineers are women,[5] and less than 2 per cent of the doctoral degrees in physical sciences are awarded to women.[6]

Factors Affecting the Education of Women

The educational attainment of women is considerably lower than that of men, even though the sexes do not differ significantly in intelligence or academic

[2] Report of the President's Commission on the Status of Women, *American Women*. Government Printing Office, Washington, 1963.

[3] Oppenheimer, Valerie K., "The Female Work Force in the United States: Factors Governing Its Growth and Changing Composition." Doctoral dissertation, University of California, Berkeley, 1966.

[4] Ginzberg, Eli, and others, *op. cit.*; and Astin, Helen S., "The Woman Doctorate in America: Family and Career Characteristics of Professional Women," *Women's Education*, vol. 7, March, 1968.

[5] Rossi, Alice S., "Women in Science: Why So Few?", *Science*, vol. 148, 1965.

[6] Harmon, Lindsey R., and Herbert Soldz, *Doctorate Production in United States Universities 1920–1962*. National Academy of Sciences–National Research Council, Publication No. 1142, Washington, 1963.

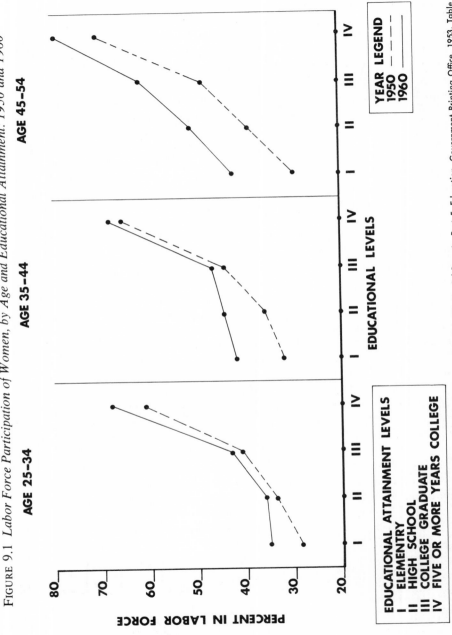

FIGURE 9.1 *Labor Force Participation of Women, by Age and Educational Attainment: 1950 and 1960*

AGE 25-34   AGE 35-44   AGE 45-54

PERCENT IN LABOR FORCE

EDUCATIONAL LEVELS

YEAR LEGEND
1950 — — —
1960 ————

EDUCATIONAL ATTAINMENT LEVELS
I   ELEMENTRY
II HIGH SCHOOL
III COLLEGE GRADUATE
IV FIVE OR MORE YEARS COLLEGE

SOURCES: U.S. Bureau of the Census, U.S. Census of Population: 1950. Vol. IV, Special Reports, Part 5, Education, Government Printing Office, 1953, Table 10, p. 83; and U.S. Bureau of the Census, U.S. Census of Population: 1960, Subject Reports, Educational Attainment. Final Report PC (2)-5B, Government

ability.[7] The proportion of women completing each degree level is smaller than the proportion of men, and the difference is greater at each successive level (see Table 9.1). Over the ten-year span 1955 to 1965, the proportions of master's degrees and doctoral degrees awarded to women remained remarkably consistent, and the proportion of baccalaureates awarded to them increased slightly. For both sexes, the absolute numbers of advanced degrees awarded in 1965 were about twice as great as the numbers awarded in 1955; still, only one woman in a hundred with a bachelor's degree attains the doctorate, as compared with one in every ten or eleven of the male bachelor's degree recipients.

A number of factors account for these inequalities in the educational attainment of men and women. Most parents have different expectations for their daughters from those they have for their sons, in the extent to which they encourage and support the child in obtaining a higher education. When differences in academic ability are controlled, girls from lower socioeconomic backgrounds are not as well represented in higher educational institutions as are boys from the same backgrounds.[8] Since advanced education is a requirement for entry into most professional, business, and managerial occupations, one can easily understand why parents are more concerned with the education of their sons than of their daughters; a man's status in our society is usually determined by his occupational achievement, whereas a woman's status often depends on the kind of man she marries, her home, and her children. Very early in life, most women come to feel that whatever else they may do, their societal role will be (and ought to be) that of wife and mother. Therefore, they place less value on formal education that will prepare them for careers.

The conflict that women often experience over these role expectations is manifested in their attitudes toward the working mother. A study by Hewer and Neubeck, for example, showed that freshman women tended to favor the traditional wife-mother role for women and to have a negative attitude toward the working mother.[9] Rossi's findings also support the view that women experience ambivalence and conflict about their vocational and other roles in life. Although Rossi's sample of women college graduates expressed more admiration for women who had achieved intellectually and professionally, they tended to anticipate and to accept the traditional role of wife and mother for themselves.[10]

---

[7] The underlying assumption in intelligence test construction is that both sexes are equal on I.Q. and therefore an I.Q. of 100 represents the average for both sexes. For further discussion of this, see Terman, L. J., and Maud A. Merrill, *Measuring Intelligence*, Houghton Mifflin Co., Boston, 1937; and Wechsler, David, *The Measurement of Adult Intelligence*, Williams and Wilkins Co., Baltimore, 3rd ed., 1944.

[8] See Folger, John K., "Expanding Higher Education Opportunities—Some Problems and Issues," unpublished manuscript of the Commission on Human Resources, 1966; and Werts, Charles E., "Sex Differences in College Attendance," unpublished manuscript of National Merit Scholarship Corporation, Office of Research, 1966.

[9] Hewer, Vivian H., and Gerhard Neubeck, "Attitudes of College Students Toward Employment Among Married Women," *Personnel and Guidance Journal*, vol. 42, no. 6, 1964.

[10] Rossi, Alice S., "Women in Science: Why So Few?"

TABLE 9.1. *Degree Attainment, by Sex: 1955–1965 (figures in 000's)*

	Bachelor's Degrees					Master's Degrees					Doctoral Degrees				
	Men		Women		Total	Men		Women		Total	Men		Women		Total
Year	Number	Per Cent	Number	Per Cent	Number	Number	Per Cent	Number	Per Cent	Number	Number	Per Cent	Number	Per Cent	Number
1955	163	62	101	38	264	39	67	19	33	58	8.0	90	.9	10	8.9
1956	180	62	109	38	289	39	66	20	34	59	7.7	91	.8	9	8.5
1957	202	64	114	36	316	41	66	21	34	62	7.6	88	1.0	12	8.6
1958	221	65	119	35	340	44	68	21	32	65	7.9	89	1.0	11	8.8
1959	232	65	127	35	359	47	68	22	32	69	8.4	90	1.0	10	9.4
1960	233	63	136	37	369	51	68	24	32	75	8.9	89	1.1	11	10.0
1961	233	62	142	38	375	54	69	24	31	78	9.6	89	1.2	11	10.8
1962	236	60	155	40	391	59	69	26	31	85	10.4	89	1.2	11	11.6
1963	247	59	172	41	419	63	69	28	31	91	11.4	89	1.4	11	12.8
1964	272	58	198	42	470	69	68	32	32	101	13.0	89	1.5	11	14.5
1965	290	57	215	43	505	76	68	36	32	112	14.7	89	1.8	11	16.5

SOURCE: Prepared for the Commission on Human Resources by Donald S. Bridgman from data of the National Science Foundation, the Office of Education, and the National Academy of Sciences, Office of Scientific Personnel.

It is often maintained that discrimination against women—operating, for example, in admissions to graduate school or in the awarding of financial aid—is another factor that hinders their educational and vocational development. But the evidence does not seem to support this view. Women applicants have fared about as well as men applicants with respect to acceptance for admission to medical schools during recent years. For example, during the academic year 1964–1965, 47 per cent of the male applicants were accepted, as compared with 48 per cent of the women applicants.[11] There is no evidence that it is harder for women to be admitted to and continue in the high-quality graduate programs than the average or lower quality programs. Among 1961 doctorate recipients, 52 per cent of the men were trained in either "distinguished" or "strong" departments, as compared with 51 per cent of the women.[12]

It appears that women doctoral students receive about as much financial aid as men doctoral students: 57 per cent of the 1957 and 1958 women doctorate recipients held either an assistantship or a fellowship during their graduate training, as compared with 58 per cent of 1955 men doctorate recipients.[13] Since different years were examined, however, these figures may obscure a difference favoring men, inasmuch as such funds were probably more available in the later years. Moreover, the fields typically studied by women—humanities and education—are not as well subsidized as other fields.

These data suggest that personal decisions not to attend graduate or professional school, rather than discrimination, may account for the low proportion of women with advanced degrees. It could be argued, of course, that since women applicants to graduate school are a more highly selected group than are men applicants,[14] a higher proportion of women applicants would be accepted if admissions practices were truly nondiscriminatory. On the other hand, attrition rates in medical schools are greater among women than among men (16 per cent as compared with 8 per cent), probably because of the uncertainty and conflict involved in combining such a demanding career with marriage. In addition, Mooney reports that a large proportion of women graduate students with Woodrow Wilson Fellowships interrupt or discontinue their graduate training:

[11] Association of American Medical Colleges, *Datagrams*, vol. 7, no. 8, 1966.

[12] To perform this analysis, we divided the institutions attended by 1961 Ph.D. recipients into six categories on the basis of the quality of the department awarding the degree. Quality ratings were based on Allan M. Cartter's *An Assessment of Quality in Graduate Education*, American Council on Education, Washington, 1966.

[13] See Appendix 8 in Lindsey R. Harmon's *Profiles of Ph.D.'s in the Sciences*, National Academy of Sciences-National Research Council, Publication No. 1293, Washington, 1965. There were 57.8 per cent of the 1955 doctorate recipients in Harmon's sample who had either assistants or fellowships, and 60.5 per cent in 1960. On the basis of a .5 per cent increase per year, we would estimate that about 59 per cent of the doctorate recipients in 1957 had this type of financial assistance as compared with 57 per cent reported by the 1957–1958 women doctorate recipients in our study sample.

[14] See Bernard, Jessie, *Academic Women*, Pennsylvania State University Press, University Park, 1964, p. 78, for a discussion of differences between academic men and academic women with regard to test-intelligence.

of the women Woodrow Wilson Fellows, only 17 per cent had received their Ph.D. degrees six to eight years after they entered graduate training, as compared with 42 per cent of the men.[15]

The differences observed in the educational attainment of women and men seem to reflect differences in career interests and aspirations rather than discriminatory practices. Figure 9.2 shows clearly that women are likely to choose careers that do not require advanced training: nursing, teaching (primarily on the elementary school level), and office work. About half of the women high school graduates plan careers in one of these fields. A similar proportion of women college graduates expect either to teach or to be employed in one of the health fields (as medical technicians, dietitians, and so forth). Conversely, careers that required training beyond the baccalaureate—for example, medicine, law and many of the scientific fields—attract only about 4 per cent of all women college graduates.

FIGURE 9.2 *Career Expectations of Women High School Graduates of 1960 and Women College Graduates of 1965*

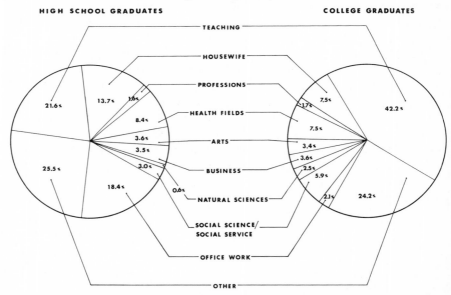

SOURCE: High school graduate figures from Flanagan, John C., and William W. Cooley, *Project Talent One-Year Follow-up Studies,* Cooperative Research Project No. 2333, School of Education, University of Pittsburgh, 1966, Table 8–3, p. 175. College graduate figures are based on unpublished data of the American Council on Education 1965 follow-up survey of 1961 college freshmen.

---

[15] Mooney, Joseph D., "Attrition Among Ph.D. Candidates: An Analysis of a Cohort of Recent Woodrow Wilson Fellows." Unpublished manuscript of the Department of Economics, Princeton University, 1967.

The Career Plans of Women

Not only are there marked differences in the educational attainment of men and women, there are even greater differences in their career plans. The factors that influence these career plans also differ between the sexes; for example, socioeconomic background is more important for girls than for boys in determining college completion and entry to a professional occupation.

Girls who in the ninth grade chose a college preparatory curriculum, scored high on mathematical aptitude, came from high socioeconomic backgrounds, and received some counseling about their college plans were more likely than other girls to report, at the time of high school graduation, that they planned careers in the sciences, the professions, or teaching. Of this group, those who scored highest on aptitude and achievement measures were more likely to maintain these career plans over time.[16] In contrast, the antecedent variables that best predicted the career plans of boys at the time of high school graduation were measured interests and career plans in the ninth grade. (See Chapter 6.)

Thus, it appears that career outcomes of boys are closely related to their early career plans and their interest in the activities involved in those careers, while the career outcomes of girls depend upon certain preparatory activities in high school. Since girls tend to score lower than boys on mathematical aptitude tests, the relation between their mathematical aptitude and their career choices suggests that girls who at an early age resemble boys in these aptitudes and interests are more likely to aspire to careers in the sciences, the professions, and teaching rather than in office work or homemaking.

Women were more career-oriented as college freshmen than they were four years later. While 6 per cent of all entering college freshman women planned careers in the natural sciences or the professions (law, medicine, dentistry, and so forth), only 4 per cent of the group anticipated such careers four years later. Furthermore, "housewife" as a future career was specified by less than 2 per cent of the freshman women; four years later, however, 8 per cent indicated that they expected to be housewives. These changes may indicate that women are uncertain about marriage when they enter college, but that they develop specific marriage plans during the four-year period.

With regard to stability and change in career plans, women planning to go into teaching, health fields, and social science or social service as freshmen tended to indicate that they had similar career plans at the termination of college; women who initially chose careers in the natural sciences or the traditional professions, on the other hand, were much more likely to alter their career plans.

---

[16] Data on the career plans of high school and college students were obtained from the Project TALENT Data Bank and from the American Council on Education, Office of Research. The data on ability levels of men and women are based on the high school graduates of 1960. The data on career plans of college men and women are based on a national sample of 1961 entering college freshmen. For further information on career development of high school girls, see Astin, Helen S., "Stability and Changes in the Career Plans of Ninth Grade Girls," *Personnel and Guidance Journal*, vol. 46, 1968, pp. 961–968; and Astin, Helen S., "Career Development of Girls During the High School Years," *Journal of Counseling Psychology*, vol. 15, 1968, pp. 536–540.

These findings suggest that when women deviate somewhat from the feminine role by aspiring to careers that are primarily favored by men, the likelihood of their carrying through with those plans is dim. It is not clear, however, whether these changes result from poor initial planning or from social pressures on women to conform to traditional career roles. High school girls who altered their initial plans to pursue careers in one of the sciences or the professions tended to score significantly lower on measures of aptitude and achievement than did girls who continued with career plans in the sciences or professions one year after they had completed high school. Conversely, girls who initially said that they planned to become housewives but later indicated that they planned a career tended to score significantly higher on achievement and aptitude tests than girls who remained stable in their choice of "housewife" over four years.

Apparently many girls change their career plans during high school because they come to a more realistic recognition of their own abilities. Nonetheless, there remains a sizable proportion of women capable of pursuing scientific or professional careers who do not do so. For instance, although the men and women attending four-year colleges during the early 1960's were equal in ability (32 per cent of the men and 31 per cent of the women came from the upper quintile in ability among all high school graduates), in 1961 only 2 per cent of the women aspired to carrers in science and only 2 per cent to medical careers. Of the men, however, 7 per cent planned careers in the sciences and 12 per cent in medicine or dentistry.

A disproportionately large number of women still choose teaching, nursing, and clerical careers, but the evidence suggests that more and more are aspiring to professional careers. For instance, in a sample of 45 institutions, less than 2 per cent of the freshman women entering college in 1961 aspired to careers in medicine or dentistry, whereas over 2.5 per cent of 1965 entering freshman women aspired to these careers in 1965. The proportion of entering freshman women who planned law careers, though very small, had just about doubled between 1961 (.59 per cent) and 1965 (.94 per cent). On the other hand, the proportion of women anticipating teaching careers decreased by 1 per cent from 1961 to 1965.

Labor Force Participation of Women Doctorate Recipients

Women doctorate recipients constitute a unique minority among women, but a knowledge of their career patterns, their scholarly productivity, and the problems of and barriers to their career development are essential if we are to understand better the future of women in highly specialized occupations. Therefore, in 1965, a follow-up survey of all the women who received doctoral degrees in 1957 and 1958 was undertaken. (See Appendix E for a detailed description of the sample and procedures.) The primary goals of this inquiry were: (a) to

determine how the talents of highly trained women are utilized; (b) to investigate the patterns of career development of women doctorate recipients; and
(c) to assess the woman doctorate recipients' career interests, commitment to
work, and professional contributions. We were also interested in identifying the
factors that influence the highly educated woman to combine a career with
marriage and the conditions that facilitate or hamper her career development.
Finally, the women doctorate recipients were compared with other groups of
women on various occupational characteristics.

The work experience of the 1957 and 1958 women doctorate recipients was
quite impressive. Only 9 per cent of these highly trained women were not in
the labor force at the time of the survey (see Figure 9.3). Even if we correct
these proportions to allow for nonrespondents' bias (that is, 18 per cent of the
nonrespondents whom we made contact with by telephone were not in the labor
force), the proportion of the total sample in the labor force decreases by only
1 per cent. Not surprisingly, single women participated in the labor force more
fully than married women (see Figure 9.4). The lowest participation in the
labor force among married women occurred in the natural sciences.[17] Marital
status had the greatest impact on the working patterns of women in the natural
sciences and in psychology. For psychologists, the principal effect of marriage
on employment status was to increase the percentage of women who work part
time. The working patterns of married and single women in the fields of education and humanities are very similar.

A small number of the 1957 and 1958 women doctorate recipients (less than
2 per cent of the total sample) had never been employed since receiving the
degree, and another 2 per cent had retired and did not plan to resume their professional careers. Of the 1,214 women with doctoral degrees who were fully
employed in 1965, 79 per cent had never interrupted their careers, and 18 per
cent reported career interruptions of 11 to 15 months, with 14 months being
the median.

Despite the withdrawals and career interruptions, the rate of employment
among these educated women was double that of women in general. Among
women of comparable age groups in the general population, only 45 per cent
work,[18] as compared with 91 per cent in our sample.

Participation in the labor force depends to a large extent on fields of specialization. Women in the natural sciences, for example, withdrew from the labor
force in greater proportion than women in other fields, a finding supported by

[18] U.S. Bureau of the Census, *Census of Population: 1960*, Vol. I, Part 1. Government
zations of the subjects: natural sciences (physical sciences and biosciences); social sciences
(all social sciences except psychology); humanities (the language specialties and the arts);
education (all subspecialties within education); and psychology (all the subspecialties
within psychology).

[18] U.S. Bureau of the Census, *Census of Population: 1960*, Vol. I, Part 1. Government
Printing Office, Washington, 1963.

FIGURE 9.3 *Employment Status of 1957–1958 Women Doctorate Recipients, by Field: 1965*

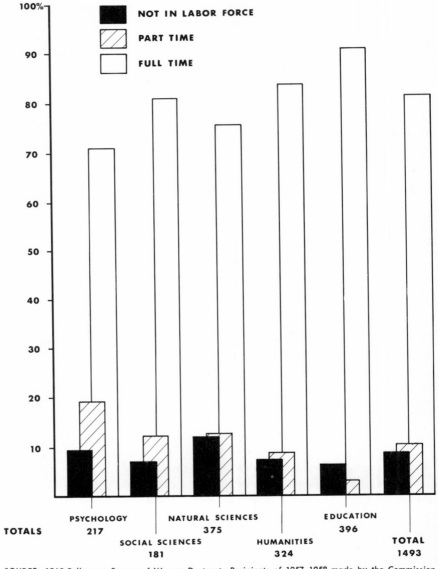

SOURCE: 1965 Follow-up Survey of Women Doctorate Recipients of 1957–1958 made by the Commission on Human Resources. See Appendix E.

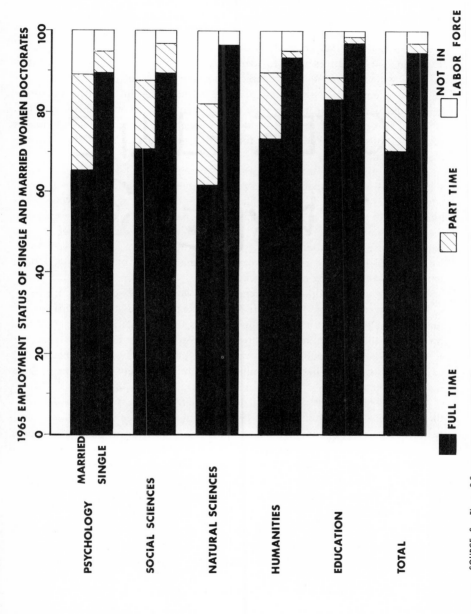

1965 EMPLOYMENT STATUS OF SINGLE AND MARRIED WOMEN DOCTORATES

■ FULL TIME   ▨ PART TIME   □ NOT IN LABOR FORCE

PSYCHOLOGY — MARRIED / SINGLE

SOCIAL SCIENCES

NATURAL SCIENCES

HUMANITIES

EDUCATION

TOTAL

SOURCE: See Figure 9.3.

Rossi.[19] A recent survey reveals that women engineers had a high rate (47 per cent) of withdrawal from the labor force.[20]

In order to investigate more fully the factors other than fields that are associated with the participation of women with doctoral degrees in the labor force, a series of regression analyses were performed, utilizing 47 different personal and environmental variables descriptive of the women doctorate recipients. The principal objectives were to identify some of the personal characteristics of those women with doctoral degrees who later work full time, holding constant the effects of such relevant personal variables as intelligence, doctorate field, and age, to investigate how their employment status is affected by marriage, children, size of city or town of residence, and other environmental experiences and conditions. (See Appendix E for a description of variables and methodology.)

Although the field of the doctorate, by itself, was related to employment status, it was not an important variable when other personal characteristics were considered (see Figure 9.4 and Table 9.2). For example, women psychologists tended not to work on a full-time basis as often as did other women doctorate recipients, partly because a greater proportion of them were married. Those women who married after receiving the doctoral degree were less likely to be working full-time seven or eight years later than were women who had been married before or during graduate school.

Women who had working mothers during their childhood were more likely to be employed full time in 1965. It is interesting to speculate what this finding may reveal about the psychodynamic processes that operate in the career development of the woman doctorate recipient. Perhaps the child who sees her mother handling the double roles of housewife and career woman is better able as an adult to resolve her own conflicts and thus to accept and manage these dual roles herself.

Women who held assistantships during their graduate training were more likely to be working full time in 1965 than were women who did not have assistantships. One explanation for this finding is that the woman who is able to pursue graduate studies and at the same time to work as a graduate assistant has the high degree of energy and the strong motivation required to work full time and to be a wife and mother as well. Another explanation is that the type of woman doctoral student selected for an assistantship is one with a greater career commitment.

Several environmental variables relating to aspects of the 1965 situation were also examined to see what influence they had on the woman doctorate recipient's work status. After the influence of personal characteristics was controlled statis-

---

[19] Rossi, Alice, "Women in Science: Why So Few?". Rossi's study utilized data from the 1960 Census.
[20] Data were obtained from a preliminary unpublished report of the 1964 survey of women engineering graduates by the Society of Women Engineers.

TABLE 9.2. *Full-Time Employment of Women Doctorate Recipients as a Function of Personal and Environmental Variables* (N = 1,547)

Variables	Multiple R	Partial r with Residual Criterion	Beta Coefficient
Birth Date	.200	—.200**	—.000
Measured Intelligence	.226	—.108*	—.041*
Mother Worked While Subject Was Growing Up	.260	+.028	+.058**
Early Marriage	.288	—.124**	+.128**
Is Currently Married	.410	—.300**	—.266**
Is Retired	.454	—.213**	—.192**
Assistantship as a Graduate Stipend Source	.457	+.038	+.057*
Preschool Children (Some vs. None)	.511	—.254**	—.255**
First Job after the Doctorate Was Full-Time	.551	+.238**	+.187**
Husband's Income	.562	—.135**	—.135**
Postdoctoral Fellowship	.570	+.078**	+.062**
Husband's Occupation in Law or Business Administration	.572	+.059*	+.058**
College or Older Age Children (Some vs. None)	.574	+.058*	+.057*
Husband's Occupation in the Social Sciences	.576	+.055*	+.050*
Size of Town Where She Lives	.578	+.057*	+.046*
Number of Children She Has	.582	—.051*	—.135**

* p < .05, ** p < .01.

NOTE: "Partial r is a Pearson product-moment r between two sets of residuals from both of which variance associated with the same set of individual variates has been eliminated." See DuBois, Philip H., *Multivariate Correlational Analysis*, Harper and Bros., New York, 1957, p. 192.
"Beta coefficient is the proportion of variance of a residual variate that is represented by the covariance between such a variate and the criterion." DuBois, op. cit., p. 188.
The variables entered the regression equation on a step-wise fashion in the order indicated in this table. "Birth date" became an insignificant predictor of full-time employment when the variable of preschool children entered the regression equation.
"Is retired" does not correlate 1.0 with the criterion of full-time employment because a number of Ss that scored 1 on "retired" had a score of 2 on a third dichotomous variable—"part-time employment."

tically, nine of the 19 environmental variables related significantly to her being employed full time. As might be expected, having preschool children was the greatest deterrent to full-time work. The husband's educational attainment and present earnings were also factors in the woman doctorate recipient's decision to hold a full-time job. If she was married to a highly educated man who earned a high income, she was less likely to work; if she did work, she was more likely to hold a part-time position.

The career behavior of the woman doctorate recipient immediately after she received the Ph.D. degree was closely related to her later career commitment, independent of other environmental factors. If she worked full time in the year after earning the doctorate or if she was a postdoctoral Fellow, she was more likely to be working full time seven or eight years later. Although women who go through graduate training and receive a doctoral degree are—almost by definition—highly motivated, the data indicate that intensity of commitment to a career still varies considerably. These variations, which can be observed almost as soon as graduate training is completed, tend to persist for some years.

The husband's occupation, independent of his education and income, was also related to the employment status of the woman having a doctoral degree. Women who married lawyers, businessmen, or social scientists were more likely to be working than were women whose husbands were in other occupations. It may be that women with a greater commitment to their careers tend to marry men in these fields or that men in these occupations are more likely to accept and to encourage their wives' work and career activities. Another possible explanation is suggested by the finding that the larger the town in which the woman doctorate recipient lived, the more likely she was to be in the labor force. Perhaps those women who marry men employed in law, business, or social science are more likely to live in large towns or in cities, where there is greater opportunity for both full-time and part-time employment.

In summary, although the personal and environmental variables employed in this study had a multiple correlation of .58 with the criterion of full-time employment, their differential contributions (see Table 9.2) help us understand some of the factors that affect a woman doctorate recipient's decision to participate in the labor force.

The employment settings, job activities, and professional activities that characterized the women doctorate recipients who were employed full time show that the woman doctorate recipient who worked full time, as compared with the one who did not, tended to participate more frequently in professional meetings and to be an active member of a number of professional organizations. Because she was likely to employ a full-time housekeeper, she spent less time in domestic activities, and thus could devote more time to her professional work. Judging by the number of her articles and books published in her field of specialization, she was more productive in scholarly endeavors. She also earned a good deal more income, but more often claimed that her employer discriminated against women.

Finally, women with doctorates who worked full time, as compared with those who either did not work or who worked only part time, were more likely to be engaged in research or administrative activities and to be employed by government agencies.

Employment Conditions of Women Doctorate Recipients

Women doctorate recipients seem to change jobs about as often as men do. Of the 1957–1958 women doctorate recipients employed in 1965, 45 per cent had been with the same employer since receiving the doctorate, and another 30 per cent had changed jobs only once, figures comparable to the rates of job mobility for men reported by Harmon, who found that 52 per cent of his sample of 1955 males had stayed on the same job for five years, and another 33 per cent had changed only once.[21]

The greatest proportion (70 per cent) of women with doctorates were employed in colleges and universities. Junior colleges and public school systems absorbed another 10 per cent. Approximately 6 per cent were employed by the federal government, 5 per cent by nonprofit organizations, 4 per cent worked in clinical settings and 3 per cent in industry; about 3 per cent were self-employed. Harmon reports similar results for women doctorate recipients of 1955 and 1960; he found that 70 per cent were employed in colleges and universities, 11 per cent in industry and government, and 19 per cent in other settings. Of his sample of male doctorate recipients from the same two years, 61 per cent were employed in colleges and universities and 22 per cent in industry and government.[22]

The aggregate of women doctorate recipients in all employment settings combined spent about half their working time in teaching and about one-fourth in research, with the remaining one-fourth almost equally divided between administration and services to clients and others (see Table 9.3). In contrast, men

TABLE 9.3. *Average Percentage of Time Spent in Each Type of Activity Within Colleges and Universities and in All Work Settings Combined*

Types of Activity	Total	Psychology		Social Sciences		Natural Sciences		Humanities		Education	
		1	2	1	2	1	2	1	2	1	2
Teaching	50	57	31	65	58	49	36	68	66	58	48
Research	25	16	15	16	22	41	51	8	8	8	7
Administration	12	13	18	14	13	7	9	17	18	26	32
Services to Clients and Others	13	14	35	5	7	3	4	7	8	7	13

NOTE: "1" indicates colleges and universities and "2" indicates all work settings combined.
SOURCE: Special Survey of Women Doctorate Recipients. See Appendix E for details.

doctorate recipients devoted a greater proportion of time to research and administration: research (41 per cent), teaching (31 per cent), administration (20 per cent), and other (8 per cent).[23] For women doctorate recipients employed in academic settings (who spent most of their time teaching, whatever their field), research ranks as the next most important activity among natural scientists, whereas administration is second in importance among women with doctorates in education or the humanities.

In a recent survey of academic men and women, the National Education Association reported that women who are now working in universities (excluding

[21] Harmon, Lindsey R., *Profiles of Ph.D.'s in the Sciences.*
[22] *Ibid.*
[23] *Ibid.*

colleges) do not hold high academic ranks (professor or associate professor) as often as do men: 33 per cent of the instructors but only 9 per cent of the professors were women. Since fewer of the women than of the men in the NEA sample had doctoral degrees, however, it is not surprising that they were under-represented in the high ranks.[24] Of the 1957 and 1958 women doctorate recipients in our sample, slightly over half held one of the two upper academic ranks (see Figure 9.5). Women in the humanities and education appeared to fare best, whereas the greatest proportion of those in the natural sciences held ranks at the level of assistant professor or lower, perhaps because there may be greater competition for positions and ranks at the institutions that employ them.

In contrast to the NEA study reported above, an examination of the academic ranks of a sample of men and women natural and social scientists drawn from the National Register of Scientists revealed no significant sex differences with respect to academic ranks.[25] Women tended to start at somewhat higher ranks than men, but five to six years later, the men in social science held higher ranks than either the women in social science or the men in natural science. On the other hand, female natural scientists emerged with somewhat higher ranks than male natural scientists.

The median annual income of all the women doctorate recipients employed full time in 1965 was $11,330. Since 52 per cent of the academic women in the sample held positions as associate or full professors, their median salary appears to be equivalent to salary figures reported by the NEA for both sexes, who at the rank of professor had a median salary of $12,953; at associate professor, $10,058; and at assistant professor, $8,417. When salary differences among fields were examined (see Table 9.4), the women doctorate recipients in psychology and education fared the best, whether they worked in academic institutions or in other employment settings. Women in education—who spent a greater proportion of their time in administrative activities—also received higher salaries, whereas the women in the humanities, who engaged primarily in teaching, reported the lowest incomes, relative to women doctorate recipients in other fields.

Harmon reported similar trends for all doctorate recipients. He found that doctorate recipients devoting at least half their time to administration received the highest salaries.[26] The relatively high salaries of women psychologists may be partly explained by the fact that academic psychologists often provide psychological services to students. The implication is that these services are more highly valued, at least with respect to financial rewards, than teaching is.

Women doctorate recipients who do a great deal of administrative or service work may earn more money because they are typically employed on a twelve-

[24] National Education Association, *Research Bulletin*, May, 1966.

[25] Bayer, Alan E., and Helen S. Astin, "Sex Differences in Academic Rank and Salary Among Science Doctorates in Teaching," *Journal of Human Resources*, vol. 3, 1968, pp. 191–200.

[26] Harmon, Lindsey R., *Profiles of Ph.D.'s in the Sciences.*

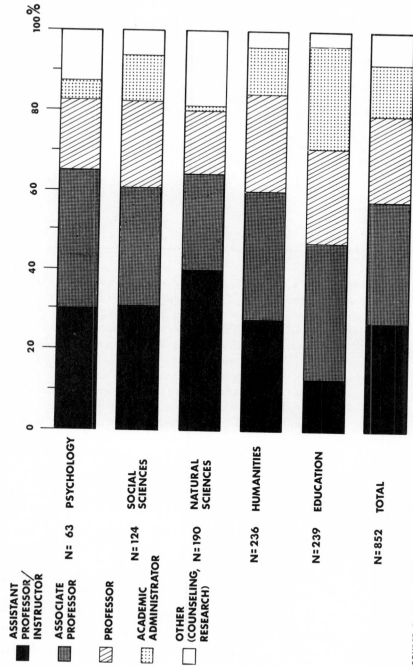

FIGURE 9.5 *Academic Rank of Women Doctorate Recipients Employed Full-Time in Colleges and Universities, by Field*

SOURCE: See Appendix E.

TABLE 9.4. *Differences in Salary, by Field of Doctorate and by Work Setting for Women Doctorate Recipients*

Work Setting	Psychology	Social Sciences	Natural Sciences	Humanities	Education
All Work Settings					
Number of Cases	136	119	250	232	331
Mean Salary	$11,940	$10,380	$10,160	$10,030	$11,510
Significance of Difference Between Psychology and Other Fields		.001	.001	.001	—
College and University Employment					
Number of Cases	56	101	164	206	223
Mean Salary	$10,880	$ 9,980	$ 9,190	$ 9,920	$11,310
Significance of Difference Between Psychology and Other Fields		.05	.001	.01	—

SOURCE: See Appendix E.

month rather than a ten-month basis. Differences in measured intelligence did not appear to account for the differences in salaries.[27] Women with doctorates in education received the highest salaries in academic settings, yet tended to obtain lower intelligence scores than did women in other fields. The mean measured intelligence was 63.3 in education, 66.8 in social sciences, 68.2 in natural sciences, 67.3 in humanities, and 68.6 in psychology.

In the natural and social sciences, women received a significantly lower average income than men in academic settings.[28] Their mean salary was only 84 per cent of the mean salary reported by men in the natural sciences. The discrepancy was somewhat smaller in the social sciences, but the men still had higher average salaries.

This sample study indicates that academic men and women were given nearly equal title and rank, but the women were not paid as well.

The Scientific and Scholarly Productivity of Women Doctorate Recipients

Judged on the basis of scientific or scholarly productivity,[29] women doctorate recipients do not seem to do as well as men, although Jessie Bernard's review

[27] The measured intelligence scores referred to in this study were the scores that these subjects attained when they were in high school. The scores have been converted to AGCT equivalent scores and normalized with a mean of 50 and a standard deviation of 10. For further explanation, see Lindsey R. Harmon's *High School Ability Patterns: A Backward Look from the Doctorate*, National Academy of Sciences-National Research Council, Scientific Manpower Report No. 6, Washington, August, 1965.

[28] Bayer, Alan E., and Helen S. Astin, "Sex Differences in Academic Rank and Salary Among Science Doctorates in Teaching."

[29] A person's scientific or scholarly productivity was defined as the absolute number of articles published in one's field of specialization.

of the existing literature suggests that if all other relevant variables were controlled, sex differences in scholarly productivity would be reduced to insignificance.[30] Institutional affiliation seems to account for most of the observed differences. Regardless of sex, people employed at universities tend to have more works published than people employed in colleges. (See Chapter 8.) Women more often join college faculties—chiefly because they prefer teaching to research—whereas most academic men are employed by universities. Thus, the higher overall productivity of academic men is at least partially explained by the basic differences in the career interests of the two sexes.

Among women doctorate recipients, as among men, field of specialization seems to be the most important determinant of scientific and scholarly productivity: those in the natural sciences are far more productive than those in other fields (see Table 9.5).

Table 9.6 shows other personal and environmental variables associated with productivity. Independent of field, the quality of the doctoral institution attended by the woman doctorate recipient was related significantly to her productivity.[31] Women who obtained their doctorates at distinguished institutions were more likely to have produced three or more scientific or scholarly publications than were women doctorate recipients trained at mediocre institutions. Bayer and Folger[32] and Buswell and McConnell[33] report similar findings.

Being married and having children were negatively related to scholarly productivity. Somewhat puzzling is the finding that the woman doctorate recipient's

TABLE 9.5. *Productivity of Women Doctorate Recipients as Measured by Articles Published in the Field of Specialization*

	All Work Settings (Median) (Number of Articles)	Colleges and Universities (Median) (Number of Articles)	No Articles Published (Percentage)	Eleven or More Articles Published (Percentage)
Psychology	2.88	4.00	26.3	9.8
Social Sciences	3.40	3.08	25.3	10.7
Natural Sciences	5.80	6.00	7.8	24.3
Humanities	1.30	1.50	33.6	10.4
Education	2.52	2.99	32.3	7.3
Total	3.26	3.54	24.7	13.0

SOURCE: See Appendix E.

[30] Bernard, Jessie, *Academic Women*, pp. 146–163.

[31] A stepwise multiple regression method was used to analyze these data. The criterion of productivity was dichotomized as three or more articles published in one's field of specialization versus two or fewer articles published. The 28 personal variables and the 19 environmental variables employed were the same measures used in the analysis of factors associated with full-time employment. (See Appendix E for a description of the variables.)

[32] Bayer, Alan E., and John K. Folger, "Some Correlates of a Citation Measure of Productivity in Science," *Sociology of Education*, vol. 39, 1966, pp. 381–390.

[33] Buswell, Guy T., and T. R. McConnell, *Training for Educational Research*, Cooperative Research Project No. 51074. University of California, Berkeley, 1966.

TABLE 9.6. *Scientific and Scholarly Productivity as a Function of Selected Personal and Environmental Variables*
(N = 1,547)

Variables	Multiple R	Partial r of Entering Variable with Residual Criterion
Biological Sciences	.208	.208**
Physical Sciences	.237	.116**
Mother's Occupation	.253	—.062*
Institutional Quality	.286	—.088**
Is Currently Married	.298	—.065*
Postdoctoral Fellowship	.322	.070**
Number of Children	.328	—.066*
First Job, Full-Time Employed	.335	.048*

* $p < .05$.
** $p < .01$.
SOURCE: See Appendix E.

scientific and scholarly productivity tended to be higher if her mother had worked in one of the unskilled or semiskilled occupations (as opposed to one of the professions) while the woman doctorate recipient was growing up. Apparently, low socioeconomic status of the parents, particularly of the mother, plays some part in developing the daughter's interest in producing scientific and scholarly work, but our understanding of the factors associated with motivation to achieve is too limited to explain just how the mother's low occupational status affects the woman doctorate recipient's perception of herself, need to achieve, and need for status.

After the personal and environmental variables were controlled statistically, certain variables associated with the employment situation yielded significant relationships with the criterion of productivity. The highly productive woman doctorate recipient was usually employed in a research position ($r = .13$) and spent most of her time in research activities ($r = .11$). Compared to the unproductive woman doctorate recipient, she was more active professionally ($r = .14$), had been honored more often for her professional achievements ($r = .14$), earned above the median income ($r = .11$), but was more likely to feel that women are discriminated against in salaries ($r = .09$).

Barriers to the Career Development of Women Doctorate Recipients

Only 14 per cent of the women doctorate recipients who were not in the labor force in 1965, or who worked only part time, said that they did not intend to return to part-time or full-time employment. The remaining 200 women said they planned to return to part-time or full-time jobs within a year or so. The difficulty of finding adequate domestic help to take care of the children and to handle other domestic responsibilities was reported as the major reason for nonparticipation in the labor force: 60 per cent of the 1957 and 1958 women doctorate recipients who were not working or were working only part-time felt that if they could find adequate domestic help, they would more quickly return to the labor force or take full-time jobs. These women also reported that if more jobs with flexible hours were available, their return to the labor force would be facilitated.

The second most important barrier to the career development of these highly educated women was employer bias, perceived or actual. Some examples of discriminatory practices mentioned, and the proportions of women who reported each, were: (a) prejudices against hiring a woman, 25 per cent; (b) lower salaries for women, 40 per cent; (c) stricter policies regarding tenure and promotions for women, 33 per cent; and (d) unwillingness to delegate authority to professional women employees, 33 per cent. A number of women doctorate recipients said also that antinepotism policies handicapped their career development by forcing them to accept jobs not commensurate with their training or to commute great distances because the universities or colleges where their husbands were employed were located in small towns that offered women few professional opportunities beyond academic employment.

Women Doctorate Recipients as Compared with Other Groups of Women

Women doctorate recipients tend to participate more fully in the labor force than do women who have only a baccalaureate.[34] The proportion employed part-time—10 per cent—was the same for both the college graduates and the women doctorate recipients, but the proportion of women with baccalaureate degrees who worked full time fell far below the proportion of women doctorate recipients: 39 per cent as compared with 81 per cent. One explanation of this difference is that women doctorate recipients were older (median age of 44) than the college graduates (median age of 28) who were studied. Moreover, 81 per cent of the college graduates were married (and so less likely to work full time) at the time of the survey, whereas only 45 per cent of the women doctorate recipients were married. About two-thirds of the employed college graduates reported that their services were educational, a proportion not too much smaller than the proportion of women doctorate recipients (81 per cent) who reported being employed by educational institutions or school systems.

Seven to eight years after receiving the degree, women with doctorates earned twice as much as women with only bachelor's degrees. Mean salaries were $11,034 for women doctorate recipients and $5,947 for women college graduates.

The labor force participation of women with doctorates corresponds more closely to that of other professional women. Of all women physicians who received their M.D. degrees between 1931 and 1956, only 9 per cent were not

[34] *College Women Seven Years After Graduation: Survey of Women Graduates, Class of 1957*, Government Printing Office, Washington, 1966.

employed in 1964,[35] and the women lawyers who received their degrees between 1956 through 1965, only 13 per cent were not employed.[36]

Summary and Conclusions

Several conclusions and tentative recommendations are suggested by these findings. First, the steady increases in the proportion of women in the labor force indicate that gainful employment has now become an important experience in the life of the typical American woman. Parents and educators face the responsibility of helping the young woman to prepare for this experience in the best possible way. But the lower educational attainment of women as compared with men and the limited number of careers they choose indicate that at present there are still values and attitudes which inhibit the equal participation of women in the occupational world.

Moreover, if the increased career expectations of women are to be fulfilled, they will have to enter new fields, for the traditional fields of elementary and secondary teaching, which have been employing 40 to 50 per cent of the women college graduates, will require only 20 to 30 per cent of the women college graduates of the next decade. (See Chapter 4.) The academic standards necessary for entry into school teaching will probably continue to rise, but there will be a substantial proportion of young women graduating from college who will find employment in other occupations. Since a sizable number of the teachers who return to graduate school plan to take up new activities, such as guidance and counseling, administration, or other specialized roles in the schools, new jobs are being created in the field that will absorb some of the additional teachers; but despite these trends, greater diversity of employment will characterize the young women who graduate from college in the future.

Because the number of girls who aspire to graduate education is increasing, new generations of women college graduates will be educated to enter new types of careers. Scientific and professional careers—which women have avoided in the past, partly because of the long and involved training they require—may become more popular as education beyond the baccalaureate attracts a larger fraction of girls.

Finally, we must recognize that employment patterns have changed over the past few decades. Nowadays, a woman's career typically involves two phases, the first being initial entry and the second being reentry after children have grown up and domestic responsibilities have lightened. Therefore, more efforts should be made to provide continuing education, retraining opportunities, and counseling services for adult women.

The study of women doctorate recipients illustrates that opportunities for

[35] Powers, Lee, Harry Wiesenfelder, and Rexford C. Parmelee, "Practice Patterns of Women and Men Physicians." Preliminary report, October, 1966.
[36] White, James J., "Women in the Law," *Michigan Law Review*, vol. 65, 1967, pp. 1051–1122.

meaningful and satisfying employment are open to highly educated women and that they constitute an important source of supply for filling the demand for specialized talent that exists in a technologically advanced and expanding economy. Perhaps most important, the data indicate that a woman can successfully combine the role of homemaker and mother with the role of scientist or professional. Obviously, traditional role expectations, which often create conflicts that obstruct the educational and career development of women, are changing and should lead more women to enter professional careers.

If the potential contributions of highly trained women are to be realized fully, conditions at work and at home must be made more conducive to part-time employment. Perhaps the tendency of women to leave the labor force, permanently or temporarily, when they take on family responsibilities can be counterbalanced by offering more part-time positions and more jobs with flexible hours. In addition, if qualified domestic help and well-staffed child care centers were more readily available, highly educated women who want to combine marriage and family life with a career might be greatly encouraged to remain in the labor force.

Our studies of the process of attraction of women to high-level professional occupations emphasize the importance of self-selection in reducing the number of women who seek to enter these fields. Indications of overt discrimination against women in the admissions process, in the award of stipends, and in their subsequent employment exist, but they are slight and cannot explain the low proportion of women in occupations like college teaching, medicine, and law; the major influence may be the lack of encouragement on the part of teachers, parents, and counselors, which affects the girls' own self-images and drastically reduces the number of capable women who enter the advanced professions, especially those that demand a full-time career commitment.

National attitudes have changed about women combining careers and marriage, and about the reentry of mothers to the labor force after their children are in school. Attitudes about women pursuing full-time careers and entering high-level occupations may be shifting, too, so that the next decade or two will find more girls aspiring to professions which require a high level of commitment, and more of them being encouraged in this direction by parents and other advisers. The increasing number of mothers who are working outside the home may provide an extra push to their daughters who go to college to seek a challenging career and to weigh the values of career as high or higher than the values of home and family.

There will be role conflict for many women who want both a family and a career; successful resolution of these conflicts so that more women will enter high-level professional careers will require changes in values and attitudes about the performance of the wife and mother role, *and* changes in the values and attitudes about the "proper" performance of a professional career. In professions where there are strong traditions of total commitment to the professional life, such as medicine, law, the ministry in certain churches, and university teaching, and where professional membership in general is tightly controlled, the kind of changes that will attract more women to the profession will be slower in coming.

Accurate prediction of future change in the percentage of women employed in the professions will require careful analysis, occupation by occupation, of the professional values that affect the acceptability of part-time work, interruptions in careers, and other changes that will make it possible for women to enter the occupation in greater numbers. The economic impact of additional women professionals on the income level in each occupation is also involved, as well as the general level of demand for additional persons in the occupation, and the length and rigor of educational preparation required.

When changes in the professions can be related to more specific information about the goals and career aspirations of different groups of women, we will be able to assess the likelihood of a greater proportion of women entering any particular career.

10 Talent

Development Among Low

Socioeconomic Groups

IN THE PRECEDING CHAPTERS the United States is characterized as an open-class society in which the predominant philosophy is that one's achievement should be commensurate with one's talents and skills, and independent of social origin and family background. The educational system is one of the principal social institutions through which this philosophy is manifested; it is the primary institution for talent development and an increasingly important channel for upward social and occupational mobility. The great diversity of the system allows it to accommodate persons of various talents, values, and financial means.

In spite of the prevailing national philosophy, however, and in spite of the rapid expansion of colleges and universities to absorb the increased numbers of young people who seek higher education, there still remains a large proportion of youth who do not go beyond high school. Even though the situation today represents an improvement over previous decades (see Chapter 5), more young people leave the educational system after high school than at any other point in the educational process. Many of them have the intellectual skills necessary to continue their education, although often they lack interest, motivation, or finances. These people are a "loss" to society in that they do not receive the level of training consistent with their talent. Not only does society suffer from this loss, but the individual, too, is often robbed of the opportunity for full self-development.

This definition of talent loss—as the proportion of young people who do not receive as much education as they would seem, on the basis of their academic ability, to have the potential for—is but one way of defining the problem. It may be important for our economy to have a number of bright and talented people working in occupations that do not require advanced education. Many students who never consider going to college, much less to graduate or professional school, may nonetheless find it personally rewarding to become experts in a skilled trade. Moreover, from the standpoint of society, these people may make as valuable or more valuable a contribution as the college graduate who is working as a salesman or a local government official.

Nonetheless, even though we grant that the relation between formal education and a productive career is far from perfect, it is clear that the more education a person has, the more numerous the job alternatives that are open to him. Although our definition of talent loss as the failure to enter or complete a collegiate program may be limited, it offers one important way of assessing how well we are doing in talent development.

This definition of talent loss is based on the assumption that a nation needs and can utilize all of its intellectually talented citizens who are suitably trained. In some underdeveloped countries today, societal demand for high-level manpower in some fields is very small, and positions are not available for people trained in some specialized fields and occupations. In the United States, by contrast, the economy is developed to a level where there is continuing demand for highly educated manpower. For the indefinite future, job opportunities in a wide range of fields will continue to be open to people with an advanced education. If the amount of talent loss were reduced, more of these jobs could be filled by qualified persons.

In Chapter 5 we noted that many factors besides ability have an impact on whether a person receives any education beyond high school. In that chapter it was also pointed out that if the average ability of future college students—and thus of future personnel in high-level occupations—is not to be lowered, larger proportions of bright but disadvantaged youth must receive college and graduate education. The special concern of our society today for this group of young people is evidenced by the recent development of Upward Bound, Talent Search, the Job Corps, VISTA, and other national programs intended to help the culturally deprived and economically disadvantaged. The increased emphasis on redeveloping urban areas, raising the quality of the nation's school systems, and allotting larger funds for educational scholarships and loans to able but needy students also reflects the national interest in more equal opportunities.

All of these social policies reflect a desire to compensate for the disadvantages that talented young people may suffer if they come from low socioeconomic backgrounds. Usually, socioeconomic status (SES) is defined in terms of parental income, occupation, and education. As such it is a composite measure that conceals many variations that can be important in determining college attendance. SES is also correlated with other personal traits and characteristics—interests, motivation, personality, values, race, residence, and so forth—that may be influential in educational and career development. (See Chapter 5.) This chapter focuses on SES as it is related to academic attainment and career aspirations. It seeks to answer the following questions: How does SES affect the proportions of able students who enter college, complete college, and go to graduate school? What influence does SES exert on a person's choice of a college? How does it influence his choice of a career? What can be done to minimize the adverse effects of low SES so as to provide the best possible training to the potential pool of high-level manpower in the years ahead?

Socioeconomic Status and Measured Ability

One of the correlates of socioeconomic status is ability. Appendix B shows the intercorrelations between a number of ability measures (vocabulary, general information, creativity, abstract reasoning, and mathematical aptitude) and socioeconomic measures (family income, father's occupation, father's education, mother's education, and number of books in the home); the coefficients range from .10 to .32 for all high school students. Generally speaking, these statistically significant coefficients indicate that higher socioeconomic status is related to higher scores on ability measures, but the relatively modest relationships allow for a good deal of individual variance. Even overall composite measures of socieconomic status and of aptitude yielded only slightly higher relationships: .33 for female high school graduates and .38 for male high school graduates.[1] In their study of a large sample of Wisconsin high school graduates, Sewell and Shah found quite similar relationships, .29 for males and .32 for females.[2] From this finding it is clear that large numbers of young people from relatively low socioeconomic backgrounds have the academic potential to further their education beyond high school.

Among recent high school graduates, 68 per cent of the boys and 61 per cent of the girls who ranked in the upper two-fifths of SES also ranked in the upper two-fifths on measured aptitude; a much lower proportion of those in the lower two-fifths on SES were in the top two-fifths on measured aptitude, 33 per cent

---

[1] The overall socioeconomic index includes nine separate items regarding family income, father's occupation, educational level of parents, and the number of specified family possessions. This item is referred to in the Project TALENT reports as P-801 and is described by Marion F. Shaycoft in *The High School Years: Growth in Cognitive Skills*, Report No. 3, American Institutes for Research, Pittsburgh, 1967, Appendix E. The general I.Q. composite score is referred to in the Project TALENT reports as C-002 and comprises vocabulary, reading, reasoning, and mathematics measures, as described by John C. Flanagan and others in *The American High-School Student*, American Institutes for Research, Pittsburgh, 1964, Appendix B. All correlations and distributions reported in this chapter are based on unpublished tabulations employing these variables.

[2] Sewell, William H., and Vimal P. Shah, "Socioeconomic Status, Intelligence, and the Attainment of Higher Education," *Sociology of Education*, vol. 40, Winter, 1967, pp. 1–23.

TABLE 10.1. *Ability Level and Socioeconomic Status of Twelfth-Grade Students, by Sex: 1960*

Sex and Academic Aptitude	Low	Low Middle	Middle	High Middle	High
			Socioeconomic Status		
Boys			Percentages		
Low	35.3	18.6	11.6	8.0	4.2
Low Middle	21.8	19.5	16.4	12.8	7.0
Middle	17.8	20.5	18.4	18.7	12.5
High Middle	16.1	21.1	25.0	25.0	23.6
High	8.9	20.3	28.5	35.5	52.7
Total	100.0	100.0	100.0	100.0	100.0
Girls					
Low	33.0	17.7	13.0	8.8	4.6
Low Middle	26.3	23.6	19.1	15.8	9.5
Middle	19.5	22.9	23.7	22.5	16.6
High Middle	14.3	21.3	25.0	26.5	27.5
High	6.8	14.4	19.2	26.3	41.8
Total	100.0	100.0	100.0	100.0	100.0

SOURCE: Special tabulations from the Project TALENT one-year follow-up of twelfth-grade students. Data are based on an actual sample size of approximately 50,000 students, with frequencies weighted to approximate population parameters of twelfth-grade students. For a further discussion of the sample and weighting procedures, see Flanagan, John C., and William W. Cooley, *Project Talent One-Year Follow-up Studies*, Cooperative Research Project No. 2333, University of Pittsburgh, Pittsburgh, 1966.

for boys and 29 per cent for girls (Table 10.1).[3] But to the extent that aptitude and intelligence tests are not culture-free or culture-fair, these distributions understate the intellectual levels of youth from low socioeconomic backgrounds.

Although it is not possible to determine precisely how much of the apparent lower academic aptitude of low SES students is due to test biases, how much to environmental influences, and how much to genetic factors, there is ample evidence that all three components are involved. Many efforts have been made to measure their relative strength, and in a recent review of the literature on this subject, Eckland states:

. . . roughly 70 percent of the variance within families in intelligence has been attributed to genetic heredity. Moreover, the findings have been remarkably consistent despite differences in the methods used to construct the heritability coefficients, differences in the types of intelligence tests, differences in the age structure, ethnic composition, or socioeconomic character of the samples. . . . Yet, no research has demonstrated that the cultural component in these tests "explains" as much as 50 percent of the inter-individual variance; while, at the same time, no research has ever found that the genetic component "explains" less than 50 percent of the variance. On the other hand the evidence must be interpreted cautiously, not because it is wrong but because to ask how much behavior is determined by heredity and how much by environment is not a very sensible

[3] The distributions in Table 10.1 and subsequent tables and in Figure 10.1 are based on approximate quintile cutting points as derived from weighted Project TALENT sample distributions of all high school seniors.

approach. Heredity and environment should not be set against each other in this way; . . . the problem is far more complex.[4]

The importance of genetic factors in achievement levels does not mean that achievement potentials are not affected in important ways by environmental conditions. There is substantial evidence that changes in learning conditions can lead to substantial changes in academic performance for nearly all persons within the normal range of intelligence. There is no basis for inferences that socioeconomic differentials in achievement are permanent or unchangeable; on the contrary, there is evidence that some individuals can overcome the handicaps of an unfavorable background. Our purpose is to examine the socioeconomic differentials that do exist, so that there will be a better basis for planning changes in them.

In the analyses that follow, the focus is on the students from low socioeconomic backgrounds who score high in academic aptitude on the tests used. Necessarily excluded are students who might have been in this "college potential" group if other means of assessing talent had been available. The reader should remember that these figures understate, to some extent, the magnitude of the problem.

Socioeconomic Status and College Attendance

Many studies based on substantial samples have documented the fact that the person from a low socioeconomic background is less likely to go to college than the person from a high socioeconomic background.[5] In a recent comprehensive report on Wisconsin high school graduates, for example, Sewell and Shah found that only about one-half of the boys and one-fourth of the girls in the highest ability quartile but the lowest SES quartile eventually attended college, while more than 90 per cent of the boys and over three-fourths of the girls in the high ability and high SES quartiles eventually attended college.[6] Somewhat similar results were indicated in estimates derived from the Project TALENT one-year follow-up of a national sample of 1960 high school seniors (Table 10.2). Low socioeconomic status seems to have a particularly adverse effect on the college attendance of girls: at all ability levels, the proportion of high SES girls who attended college was very similar to the proportion of men, whereas

[4] Eckland, Bruce, "Genetics and Sociology: A Reconsideration," *American Sociological Review*, vol. 32, April, 1967, p. 178.

[5] Sewell, William H., Archie O. Haller, and Murray A. Straus, "Social Status and Educational and Occupational Aspirations," *American Sociological Review*, vol. 22, February, 1957, pp. 67–73; Berdie, Ralph F., and A. B. Hood, *Trends in Post-High School Plans Over an 11-Year Period*, Cooperative Research Project No. 951/SAE–8976, Department of Health, Education, and Welfare, Office of Education, Washington, 1963; Medsker, Leland L., and James W. Trent, *The Influence of Different Types of Public Higher Institutions on College Attendance from Varying Socioeconomic and Ability Levels*, Cooperative Research Project No. 438, Center for the Study of Higher Education, University of California, Berkeley, 1965.

[6] Sewell, William H., and Vimal P. Shah, "Socioeconomic Status, Intelligence, and the Attainment of Higher Education," *Sociology of Education*, vol. 40, Winter, 1967, p. 13.

TABLE 10.2. *Percentage of High School Graduates Who Went To College the Following Year, by Academic Aptitude, Socioeconomic Background, and Sex: 1960*

Sex and Academic Aptitude	Socioeconomic Status					
	Low	Low Middle	Middle	High Middle	High	Total
Boys						
Low	10	13	15	25	40	14
Low Middle	14	23	30	35	57	27
Middle	30	35	46	54	67	46
High Middle	44	51	59	69	83	63
High	69	73	81	86	91	85
Total	24	40	53	65	81	49
Girls						
Low	9	9	10	16	41	11
Low Middle	9	10	16	24	54	18
Middle	12	18	25	40	63	30
High Middle	24	35	41	58	78	49
High	52	61	66	80	90	75
Total	15	24	32	51	75	35

SOURCE: See source note, Table 10.1.

among high ability-low SES groups, only 52 per cent of the girls went to college, as compared with 69 per cent of the boys. Parents of low SES youth may be financially unable to send more than one of their children to college, and in this situation they more often favor the son. Finances apart, a college education is regarded as more important for boys than for girls. A girl from a low socioeconomic background is expected to marry, and her job and career are secondary to her role as wife and mother, but for the man, college attendance is relatively more crucial to career advancement. The data on women's career plans presented in Chapter 9 indicate that these traditional definitions of the woman's role are changing, and this trend will probably have the effect of raising the educational aspirations of bright girls from lower-middle-class and working-class backgrounds.

While about 90 per cent of the high school graduates in the high ability-high SES quintiles attended college, only about 10 per cent of those in the low ability-low SES quintiles attended college. More important, when aptitude was held constant, college attendance increased with increasing SES score (Table 10.2). Only about two-thirds of those who were in the upper 20 per cent in ability but who came from disadvantaged backgrounds went to college, for example, as against about 90 per cent of high ability-high SES youth. Thus, if steps were taken to lessen the influence of socioeconomic background so that low SES young people were more highly motivated and had the opportunity to attend college on a par with their higher SES peers, we could expect about 20 to 30 per cent more college attendance among talented high school students in the lowest fifth of their class economically. Present talent losses appear even larger numerically, though not in percentages, if students of medium ability are included in these figures.

There are several factors involved in the lower college attendance of students from low socioeconomic backgrounds. Briefly, the low SES student may not value education so much, he may not be as strongly motivated to achieve, or he may not have adequate financial means. Inadequate finances are probably the easiest of these handicaps to eliminate, and greater financial assistance to students is one of the principal mechanisms that educators and public officials can employ to increase the proportions of low SES youth who enter college. In the Project TALENT follow-up, one-fourth of the students who discontinued their college studies reported that lack of funds was one of their reasons for doing so.[7] Of course, financial hardships and blocks can be partially removed by scholarship aid. For those students already in college, 28 per cent of the entering freshmen boys in the low SES group received some form of scholarship aid, as compared with 17 per cent of those in the high SES group. For girls, the comparable figures are 36 per cent and 20 per cent, respectively (Table 10.3). Nevertheless, the proportion of low SES college students who received scholarship aid in 1961, even after control of academic ability, was very low: only two-fifths of the high ability-low SES college males, and a little more than one-half of the comparable group of college girls get scholarship aid. The development of federal programs

TABLE 10.3. *Percentage of Students Attending the First Year of College Who Received Some Form of Scholarship Aid, by Sex, Academic Aptitude, and Socioeconomic Status: 1961*

Sex and Academic Aptitude	Socioeconomic Status					
	Low	Low Middle	Middle	High Middle	High	Total
Boys						
Low	*	*	10	4	16	16
Low Middle	18	12	12	12	9	12
Middle	17	17	14	10	8	13
High Middle	31	18	16	14	7	15
High	41	36	35	30	24	30
Total	28	24	23	20	17	21
Girls						
Low	*	*	*	9	5	14
Low Middle	*	*	13	11	5	13
Middle	24	16	16	15	10	15
High Middle	41	30	24	21	15	22
High	56	51	51	44	28	40
Total	36	31	30	28	20	27

* Base for percentages less than 100 unweighted cases.

SOURCE: See source note, Table 10.1.

[7] Flanagan, John C., and William W. Cooley, *Project Talent One-Year Follow-up Studies.* University of Pittsburgh, Pittsburgh, 1966, Appendix B.

of work-study assistance and educational opportunity grants, as well as increased private and institutional programs of student assistance, have probably increased these percentages substantially in the last four or five years.

These surveys suggest that somewhere between one-fourth to one-half of all high ability-low SES students who do not now attend college might do so if financial barriers could be eliminated by scholarships, work-study programs, lower tuition, or other means. If a scholarship program that covered most of the costs of college education and was open to all low SES students in the top half in ability were established, it might attract approximately 4 per cent more high school graduates to college. For about half these students, the scholarship program would probably make immediate and full-time college attendance a possibility; without financial support, these students would necessarily delay entry to college, and even when they did attend they would probably have to attend on a part-time basis. Numerically, such a percentage increase means that an additional 100,000 students would have entered college in 1966, and that an additional 115,000 would enter in 1970.

Removal of the financial barriers to college attendance for bright youth would have the same quantitative effect on enrollment as continuation for three or four more years of recent rates of "normal" increase in the percentage of high school graduates going on to college (between 1 and 1.5 per cent per year). The effects on the ability level of college students would be decidedly favorable, however, since much of the "normal" increase occurs among low ability groups.

Whereas financial problems can partially be remedied, some of the other obstacles that prevent lower SES persons from furthering their education are harder to remove. By the time of high school graduation, the student's family background has already affected his level of aspiration and his educational prep-aration, both of which are important determinants of his attending college. High school students from lower socioeconomic backgrounds are more likely to select vocational courses than college preparatory courses in mathematics, English, and languages.[8] Better early counseling may help some of these students to plan a high school curriculum that would prepare them more adequately for college.

Socioeconomic background and ability are important determinants not only of whether high school graduates decide to go on to college, but also of where they go to college. Figure 10.1 reports the proportions of men and women college students from the five SES quintiles who attended different types of colleges, categorized by degree level. While low SES students distributed them-selves about equally across the four major types of institutions, only about 10 per cent of the high SES high school graduates attended junior colleges. Almost three-fourths of the high SES students were undergraduates in institutions that had master's or Ph.D. programs. The high proportion of low SES youth who attend junior colleges is understandable because of the lower costs of attendance

[8] Shaycoft, Marion F., *The High School Years: Growth in Cognitive Skills,* chap. 8.

FIGURE 10.1 *Type of College Attended by Entering College Freshmen, by Sex and Socioeconomic Background*

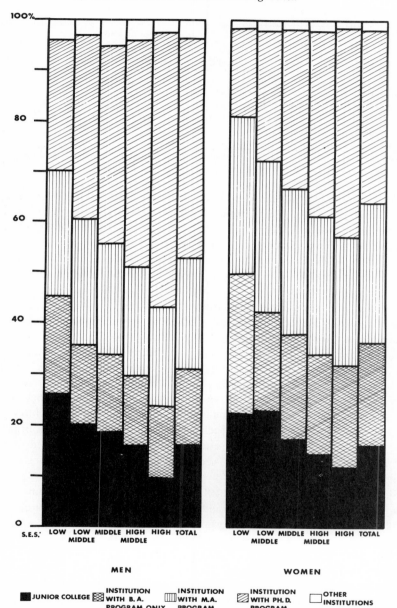

SOURCE: See source note, Table 10.1.

TABLE 10.4. *Percentage of Entering College Freshmen Who Attended* Selective *Colleges, by Socioeconomic Status, Sex, and Academic Aptitude: 1961*

Sex and Academic Aptitude	Socioeconomic Status				
	Low	Low Middle	Middle	High Middle	High
Boys					
High Middle	0	0.4	0.5	0.8	0.2
High	2.4	4.7	5.0	8.0	18.6
Girls					
High Middle	0	0	0.4	0.2	2.0
High	1.9	1.5	2.2	4.8	12.9

SOURCE: See Table 10.1. The most selective colleges include about 100 institutions and enroll a little more than 4 per cent of all college students.

at these institutions. Students who attend a junior college are less likely to complete a college degree. (See Chapter 5.) Since a high percentage of low SES students attend junior colleges, this reduces their chances of obtaining a degree.

Table 10.4 shows the percentage of highly able entering freshmen from the various SES levels who attended the more selective colleges.[9] Only about 2 per cent of the high ability-low SES men attended selective institutions, compared with 19 per cent of the high ability-high SES men. The small proportion of bright but poor freshmen at the selective institutions is perhaps a function of both inadequate finances and a class-related value system. That is, the bright student from a low socioeconomic background may value going to college, but he and his family are not as concerned about whether the institution is mediocre or distinguished or he may be discouraged from attending because he feels that the most selective institutions (nearly all of which are private and have relatively high tuitions) would simply be too expensive. Most selective colleges have extensive scholarship aid available, and many of them have active programs to recruit more students from disadvantaged backgrounds. But these recruitment programs have mostly been developed since the data reported here were collected (1961); so a new survey would be needed to see if they have changed the socioeconomic composition of the selective colleges to any important degree.

Since bright youth from lower SES background usually come from families that have no tradition of college attendance, their below-average rates of enrollment in selective colleges may be primarily a result of their failure to apply to these colleges. Colleges that are attended by few of the student's friends and that appear to be too expensive, too tough academically, and too exclusive socially are less likely to attract the bright but poor student. Moreover, his high school teachers and counselors may be just as unfamiliar with these selective colleges as he, and so may suggest the state university, a local college, or a junior college

---

[9] The selectivity of various colleges was assessed on the basis of the mean score on academic aptitude of entering freshmen. See Chapter 5.

as the "right" place for him. The net effect of these influences is that the selective colleges have been socially as well as intellectually elitist, serving chiefly the sons and daughters of the high-middle and high classes. Since attendance at a selective college enhances the student's chances of entering and completing graduate and professional school (see Chapter 5), it adds to the other advantages that a high SES background gives a youth in getting a good job and advancing his career opportunities.

The influence of SES on college opportunities is substantial, but it should not be overemphasized. Ability is a more influential factor in initial college entry and type of college attended. Almost all of the entrants to selective colleges are high school graduates from the top quintile in ability, and if a student's academic achievement places him in the lower three-fourths of the group, he has virtually no chance of attending a selective college, regardless of his socioeconomic background.

TABLE 10.5. *Percentage of College Completion by 1965 of 1960 High School Seniors, by Aptitude, Socioeconomic Status, and Sex*

Sex and Academic Aptitude	Socioeconomic Status				
	Low	Low Middle	Middle	High Middle	High
Males					
Low	0.5	1.2	3.1	5.9	2.9
	(74,390)	(33,669)	(37,639)	(12,449)	(10,519)
Low Middle	2.2	4.0	5.5	6.3	19.1
	(31,080)	(27,114)	(37,439)	(13,545)	(12,742)
Middle	9.2	14.0	16.0	20.7	32.4
	(20,808)	(24,791)	(33,329)	(20,743)	(16,108)
High Middle	27.4	17.7	26.8	38.4	42.2
	(16,271)	(14,358)	(46,048)	(23,226)	(26,189)
High	39.4	34.7	49.1	54.4	63.8
	(7,371)	(18,779)	(41,416)	(33,832)	(56,321)
Total	6.8	11.9	20.7	32.0	45.3
Weighted Number of Cases	(149,920)	(118,711)	(195,870)	(103,796)	(121,879)
Females					
Low	2.6	0.6	3.4	5.4	1.4
	(61,425)	(29,353)	(40,821)	(12,723)	(6,946)
Low Middle	1.2	4.9	4.6	9.5	14.5
	(39,370)	(38,641)	(41,005)	(19,256)	(17,465)
Middle	7.0	4.7	8.7	15.9	28.0
	(28,055)	(30,728)	(55,661)	(21,521)	(19,979)
High Middle	15.9	17.2	17.7	21.7	42.6
	(18,823)	(22,373)	(45,412)	(25,197)	(35,800)
High	34.1	37.9	38.2	46.9	70.2
	(7,394)	(15,866)	(32,662)	(29,515)	(44,900)
Total	5.8	9.2	13.6	23.1	42.8
Weighted Number of Cases	(155,067)	(136,961)	(215,562)	(108,212)	(125,091)

SOURCE: Special tabulations from the Project TALENT five-year follow-up. Tabulations are based on a total of 35,235 cases which have been weighted to a total of 1,631,000 based on original sampling ratios and differential weights assigned to mail respondents and direct interview follow-up of a subsample of non-respondents.

Socioeconomic Status and Educational Progress

Socieconomic background is also influential in determining college persistence and completion and enrollment in graduate school. In a study of college drop-outs, Panos and Astin report that students who did not complete four years of college within nine semesters tended to make lower grades in high school, did not plan graduate or professional education, and came from relatively low socio-economic backgrounds.[10] Sewell and Shah also report that both socioeconomic status and intelligence have direct effects on college plans, college attendance, and college progress.[11]

Utilizing Project TALENT data from the five-year follow-up study, the Commission on Human Resources staff examined the effects of SES on college completion.

The rate of college completion in five years for the entire cohort of 1960 high school seniors was 22 per cent for males and 17 per cent for females. (See Table 10.5.) If we consider only the students who entered college the first year after high school, 45 per cent of the boys, and 49 per cent of the girls had graduated from college by 1965. While there are some differences, these national totals are similar to the data reported from the eight-year follow-up of Wisconsin high school graduates by Sewell and Shah.[12]

[10] Panos, Robert J., and Alexander W. Astin, "Attrition Among College Students," ACE Research Reports, vol. 2, no. 4, 1967.
[11] Sewell, William H., and Vimal P. Shah, "Socioeconomic Status, Intelligence, and the Attainment of Higher Education."
[12] Sewell's data definitely show greater SES differences than the Project TALENT data. Adjusting the TALENT data to a quartile basis, and comparing *only* the high ability quartiles, we have the following ranges:

	Low SES	High SES	Percentage Point Difference
College Entry			
Males			
Sewell	52	91	39
Talent	59	87	28
Females			
Sewell	27	76	49
Talent	41	85	44
College Completion			
Males			
Sewell	20	64	44
Talent	30	50	20
Females			
Sewell	14	51	37
Talent	26	46	20

These differences may be the result of:
(a) The very high percentage of Wisconsin youth who complete high school, so that for Wisconsinites, SES selectivity occurs post-high school. In the national sample, more of the low SES students have already been eliminated before reaching the twelfth grade.
(b) This does not explain the even larger differences among the college completion group. The Sewell data cover a longer follow-up, and thus more time for SES differentials to develop, a second possible difference.
(c) Sewell's follow-up survey had a smaller percentage of nonrespondents and although Project TALENT followed up a small subsample of nonrespondents intensively and fairly completely, the weighting procedures may have biases. Since nonrespondents are almost always of lower status and less successful than respondents, it seems likely that the differences

Socioeconomic influences affect both the kind of college attended, and the probability of completion for those attending each type. If the whole group attending college is considered, the boys from high-status backgrounds are almost twice as likely to complete college as the boys from low-status backgrounds (55 per cent college completion for the former group, 29 per cent for the latter group). See Table 10.6. For girls the comparable differences are smaller, but still substantial (40 per cent college completion for low-status girls, 57 per cent for high-status girls). Part of this difference is due to the different distribution of measured ability among high and low SES youth, but even when ability is controlled, substantial differences attributable to socioeconomic influences remain. Table 10.6 compares college completion rates by socioeconomic status in the Project TALENT five-year follow-up and in the eight-year follow-up of Wisconsin high school graduates. The comparisons are limited to the students who are in the upper half of the ability distribution, but they show clearly that the chances of college graduation, among students of comparable academic aptitude, increase from about 15 to more than 30 percentage points as we move from low to high socioeconomic status.

For both boys and girls who have entered college, the independent effects of academic aptitude on college graduation chances are greater than the effects of socioeconomic status, but the independent effect of socioeconomic status remains substantial. For the Wisconsin sample, the independent path coefficients indicate that academic aptitude is about twice as important as socioeconomic status in determining college graduation.[13]

The findings from these large samples, which include persons attending a variety of institutions, indicate that socioeconomic background affects, in an important way, college completion as well as college entry. These findings are in contrast to a number of studies made in individual institutions which indicate that socioeconomic factors have little or no influence on college completion. For example, Eckland[14] reviews 24 studies that used 33 measures of social class influence, 20 of these socioeconomic measures were unrelated to college progress, the other 13 showed a positive relation to college progress.

The apparent inconsistency in these findings from national and state samples on the one hand, and institutional studies on the other hand can be explained primarily by the fact that socioeconomic status is an important determinant of

---

may be the result in survey procedures and in the weighing of nonrespondents in the TALENT follow-up. This seems to be the most likely cause of the differences, but there is no basis for concluding that the weighting of TALENT nonrespondent follow-up was inadequate. Because of the known demographic differences between the Wisconsin population and the national population it is not clear which set of data provides a better national estimate of the effects of SES on college completion.

[13] Sewell, William H., and Vimal P. Shah, *op. cit.*, Figure 1. For those who attended college the path coefficient for SES on college graduation was .13 for both males and females, the path coefficients for intelligence on college graduation were .28 for males and .27 for females.

[14] Eckland, Bruce, *op. cit.*, Table 1, p. 41.

TABLE 10.6. *Percentage of College Entrants Graduating, by Sex, Ability, and Socioeconomic Status: Project TALENT National Sample and Wisconsin Sample*

Project TALENT Five-Year Follow-up

SES Level and Sex	Intelligence Level			Total[a]
	Middle	High Middle	High	
Males				
Low	30	*	57	29
Low Middle	40	35	47	30
Middle	35	46	60	40
High Middle	39	55	63	50
High	48	51	70	55
Females				
Low	*	*	*	40
Low Middle	27	48	62	37
Middle	36	41	57	43
High Middle	40	38	59	45
High	44	55	78	57

Wisconsin High School Graduates Eight-Year Follow-up

SES Level and Sex	Intelligence Level		Total[a]
	High Middle	High	
Males			
Low	39	38	37
Low Middle	39	58	42
High Middle	47	65	49
High	52	71	57
Females			
Low	29	50	32
Low Middle	37	57	37
High Middle	39	52	40
High	54	67	56

[a] Total includes lower intelligence levels, as well as those shown in the preceding columns.

* Too few cases to provide reliable percentages.

SOURCE: Project TALENT data from the one-year follow-up (shown in Table 10.2) and the five-year follow-up (shown in Table 10.5). Wisconsin data from Sewell, William H., and Vimal P. Shah, "Socioeconomic Status, Intelligence, and the Attainment of Higher Education," *Sociology of Education*, vol. 40, Winter, 1967, pp. 1–23, Table 5.

where people go to college, and different colleges have very different completion rates. The bright low-status youth is likely to enter a junior college where his chances of transfer and subsequent college completion are not so great as if he enters a senior college. (Table 10.7.) If he enters a senior college, it is not likely to be a selective college where dropout rates are low, but is more likely to be an unselective state college or urban commuter college with a relatively high drop-out rate. Eckland states this same idea as a "diversity hypothesis" ". . . the rate of dropout at a college or university varies inversely with the class composition of its student population."[15] The data from these national and state samples which include entrants to the complete spectrum of colleges and universities in this country confirm the "diversity hypothesis" and show how socioeconomic status continues to affect graduation chances by affecting the kind of college that students enter.

There is another way in which socioeconomic status affects college completion rates, which is called the "persistence hypothesis" by Eckland. He is able to show that studies which follow students for a longer period are more likely to find socioeconomic differences in completion rates than are studies that have shorter follow-ups.[16] High-status youth with average or below-average aptitude are likely to have difficulty in completing college, but they are more likely to have the motivations and parental pressures to keep on going, as well as the financial resources which enable them to persist in college until they finally get through. By contrast, the low-status youth with average or below average ability will not have the resources to keep trying to finish college, nor is he likely to have the same family and other social pressures to stay in college. Thus, a disproportionate share of the students who have been in college for one, two, or three years beyond the normal completion time are from higher status backgrounds. With a longer follow-up the socioeconomic differential in college completion is likely to be greater. Comparison of the eight-year follow-up of the Wisconsin high school graduates with the five-year follow-up of Project TALENT does not indicate any marked difference in the size of the socioeconomic differentials in college completion among men except at the highest ability level, where the Wisconsin data show larger differentials. The data also indicate larger differentials among women in the Wisconsin study than in the Project TALENT follow-up. Since there were substantial differences in the samples, in the follow-up procedures, and in other aspects of the two studies, it is not possible to draw any firm conclusions from these comparisons.

Paradoxically, the community colleges appear to have increased college opportunities for low-status youth, and at the same time to have increased the socioeconomic differentials in college completion. They have been successful in getting low-income youth into college, but have not increased their chances of getting a degree nearly as much. This is illustrated indirectly by examination

---

15 *Ibid.*, p. 37.
16 *Ibid.*, Table 1, p. 41.

of socioeconomic differentials in college completion among students who did all their work in degree-granting institutions; that is, they never attend a junior college.

The overall rate of college completion (five years after high school graduation) for all ability groups who entered a degree granting college or university was 58 per cent for boys and 63 per cent for girls. This compares with the earlier reported 45 per cent for boys and 49 per cent for girls among the entire group who entered college. More than three-fourths of the entrants from the high ability-high SES group completed college. Among the high ability-low SES students, on the other hand, less than two-thirds (62 per cent of the boys and 65 per cent of the girls) completed college within five years after high school. While college completion rates for bright youth from low SES backgrounds were slightly above those of all entrants who completed college, and much higher than those of low ability-high SES students who completed college (where the rate drops to 21 per cent for boys and 15 per cent for girls), they were still 10 to 15 percentage points lower than high SES youth of comparable ability. For those students who enter a four year college, ability is a much more important determinant of college completion than socioeconomic status, but each exerts an independent influence. Table 10.7 summarizes information about the educational progress of highly able college students from different socioeconomic levels. The completion rate of the high ability-low SES students was about 15 percentage points lower than the high ability-high SES students.

Furthermore, almost twice as many high ability-high SES students were in graduate school. The number of high SES girls who entered graduate school was two-and-one-half times as large as the number of low SES girls. The lower rate

TABLE 10.7. *The Effect of Socioeconomic Status on College Completion and Graduate School Attendance Among High Ability Students Who Entered Degree Granting Institutions, by Sex*

SES	Percentage Graduating From College		Percentage of College Entrants Enrolled in Graduate or Professional School	
	Men	Women	Men	Women
Low	61.6	65.6	24.5	8.2
Low Middle	68.6	71.8	26.1	17.8
Middle	64.9	68.0	27.8	15.0
High Middle	70.0	71.7	32.7	15.7
High	77.6	79.0	41.9	20.1
Total	71.4	73.7	34.3	17.3

SOURCE: Special tabulations from the Project TALENT five-year follow-up of 1960 twelfth-grade students. Percentages are based on the sample weighted to the approximate population parameters. High ability students include approximately the top fifth of the high school population in ability. Entrants to junior colleges are excluded from these figures, which include only students who did all of their college work in a degree-granting institution. Sixteen per cent of the high ability men nongraduates and 9 per cent of the women nongraduates were still enrolled in college at the end of the five-year follow-up, and might graduate later.

of enrollment in post-baccalaureate programs among low SES youth reflects in part their initial enrollment in programs in which continuation in graduate or professional school is uncommon and unnecessary for professional success: business, education, and engineering—all vocationally oriented curricula—rather than arts and sciences, medicine, and law. Financial limitations on graduate school entry are also more likely to exist for low SES youth, since most of the money for graduate student support is distributed without explicit consideration of the student's SES background. Although most graduate students are part of family units that are independent of their parents, having well-to-do parents to fall back on and being able to finish the undergraduate program without incurring debts for education, give the high SES student an advantage over the low SES student in graduate and professional school entry. The financial problems are most pronounced for the low SES student who wants to go into law or medicine, and entry into these fields is affected more by SES background than is entry into other post-baccalaureate programs.

Socioeconomic Status and Career Aspirations

So far, the discussion has centered on how a person's socioeconomic background affects his educational plans and progress. But socioeconomic status is important to his occupational aspirations and plans as well. Werts, for instance, found that low SES male college freshmen aspired to careers in teaching, engineering, chemistry, and accounting, whereas high SES male college freshmen aspired to careers in medicine, law, and the academic profession.[17] Similarly, Davis, in his study of college graduates, reported that while engineering and education careers were favored by low SES graduates, medicine, law, humanities, and social sciences were chosen more frequently by high SES college graduates.[18] He explains these differential career preferences on the basis of educational costs. That is, students of low SES do not choose careers in medicine, law, or dentistry because they do not have the finances to carry on their training through professional schools. Werts, on the other hand, suggests that low SES students tend to choose lower-level careers more often than do other students not only because of their different value system, lower measured academic aptitude, and inadequate finances, but also because sons in general tend to over-choose their father's occupation.[19]

Summary and Conclusions

We can summarize the effects of SES on educational progress by comparing two cohorts of 100 male 1960 high school graduates, one from the top quintile in SES background and the other from the bottom quintile. Each cohort comes

---

[17] Werts, Charles E., "Social Class and Initial Career Choice of College Freshmen," *Sociology of Education*, vol. 39, Winter, 1966, pp. 74–85.

[18] Davis, James A., *Great Aspirations*, Aldine Publishing Co., Chicago, 1964, pp. 141–238; and Davis, *Undergraduate Career Decisions*, Aldine Publishing Co., 1965, pp. 78–191.

[19] Werts, Charles E., *op. cit.*

from the top fifth of his age group in academic aptitude. There is very little talent loss from this highly able group prior to high school graduation; virtually all of the dropouts occur after the diploma has been received.

Of the high SES-high ability group of 100 male high school graduates:
      9 did not go to college
      9 went to a junior college
         3 of these also finished senior college
    82 went to a senior college
        63 of these graduated from senior college

Of the 66 who received a bachelor's degree:
    36 continued immediately in graduate or professional school

Of the low SES-high ability group of 100 male high school graduates:
    31 did not go to college
    17 went to a junior college
        5 of these also finished senior college
    52 went to a senior college
        32 of these graduated from senior college

Of the 37 who received a bachelor's degree:
    15 continued immediately in graduate or professional school

Thus, in the early 1960's, a bright but poor boy had only about 55 per cent as much chance of completing college within five years as his well-to-do counterpart, and only about 40 per cent as much chance of entering advanced training.

To return to an earlier question: How much of this gap can be closed by giving greater financial support to low SES students? We cannot give an accurate answer to this question, but we can choose a set of assumptions which indicate a probable maximum effect of removing financial barriers. Let us assume that between one-fourth and one-half of their lower college attendance rate, half of their higher junior college attendance rate, and half to three-fourths of their lower college completion rate are directly related to their limited financial resources. By relieving these burdens, we could presumably raise the proportion of poor but bright youth who complete college from 37 per cent to between 42 and 46 per cent, and the proportion of those who enter advanced training from 15 per cent to between 18 and 20 per cent.

Unfortunately, these assumptions are vastly oversimplified, and even the relatively feasible solution of increasing financial support could have unforeseen consequences opposed, or at any rate irrelevant, to the intended objectives. For example, any large scholarship or loan program or any major reduction in tuition and other college costs would probably affect the student's (and his parents') perceptions of the possibility of college attendance. Thus, average-ability students from medium-high SES levels, suddenly changing their college aspirations, might profit from these financial support programs more than would the poor but bright student whom they were intended to encourage. Furthermore, a student's college aspirations will be affected by changes in his perception of the educational opportunities available to him. The establishment of a nearby junior college—or any other new educational opportunity highly visible to the local community—may lead more students from all SES levels to plan college attendance. In short, the interactions of such factors are complex, and our understanding of them and of how they affect college attendance rates is imperfect. To assume that simply by increasing financial support and opening up new educational opportunities, we will automatically enable all bright but poor youth to attend college, is naive.

The causative effects of SES are often indirect, because socioeconomic differences are related to differences in the values, motivations, and aspirations of youth, and these in turn affect college attendance, career plans, and achievement. Consequently, although loan and scholarship programs to assist in financing the post high school education of disadvantaged youth are necessary, they are not sufficient. If we are to solve the problem of filling society's needs for talented persons in high-level positions, we must intervene much earlier in the developmental history of the individual; by the time of graduation from high school motivations and academic ability are well structured and much more difficult to modify than at early stages of intellectual development. Effective programs are needed for early identification of the many different facets of talent.

In spite of environmental handicaps, 9 per cent of the boys, and 7 per cent of the girls from the lowest fifth in socioeconomic background scored in the top quintile in academic aptitude and were generally successful in elementary and secondary school. They are the easiest part of the undeveloped talent in this country to encourage toward more education, because their potential has been assessed and they do not suffer the stigma of ineffective performance. If we cannot devise programs to enable these youth to overcome the handicaps of their background, we will probably be even less successful in coping with the more complex problems of talent development among individuals whose potentials have not been adequately assessed and who may be encumbered with the stigma arising from ineffective academic performance.

The fact that socioeconomic influences in college completion rates within colleges tend to be rather small indicates that individual colleges' efforts to eliminate the differentials are likely to have rather limited results. For every bright poor boy or girl specially recruited to one of the Ivy League colleges through an expensive talent search, probably 10 to 20 others just enroll on their own in a hometown community college, urban university, or other nearby public institution. The former student is likely to get a great deal of assistance in completing college, the others must have similar attention if we are to reduce substantially the socioeconomic differentials in college completion. National programs and national policies are needed to help the open door, low budget, commuter colleges, where high proportions of the lower SES students enroll, to improve their educational programs and their institutional environment, and to develop programs which are oriented to the special needs of students from lower SES families.

The effectiveness of colleges in modifying socioeconomic differentials occurs within a broader framework of social interest and concern with the same problem. One of the major changes in our colleges since the first Commission on Human Resources study has been the increase in the percentage of able students going on to college. A large proportion of these gains has come from the lower socioeconomic groups who are now entering college, and completing college at much higher rates than formerly. Many people evaluate this progress unfavorably, however, because our expectations about equality of opportunity have changed even more than the reality of expanding opportunity. In the past two decades our colleges have become more important as the determinants of occupational entry and as institutions for classifying and providing credentials necessary for an increasing fraction of the jobs in our occupational structure. At the same time they have done a great deal to expand educational opportunities for all classes in society. Because a college education is believed to be more important to success, and because we are more concerned about equal opportunities than ever before, our colleges and universities find themselves admitting more students from the lower classes than ever before, and being criticized more than before because their efforts are insufficient.

It could be argued that the talent losses we have been discussing are proportionately rather small, and from some points of view they are overshadowed by our successes in expanding educational opportunity at the college level. If we could hold constant ability differences, and eliminate all the socioeconomic influences that operate during the college years, the number of bachelor's degrees awarded would be increased by only 60,000 to 75,000, or about 2.5 to 3 per cent of the 18-year-old population in 1960.

But if all socioeconomic groups equaled the rates of the highest socioeconomic group in college entrance rates, in type of college attended, and in college completion rates, then the number of college graduates in 1965 would have been increased by more than 50 per cent. This would have added more than a quarter million college graduates to the approximately half million who graduated in 1965. While these differences are caused by many factors, some of which cannot be eliminated by changes in social policy or economic costs of college attendance, it is clear that the reduction of socioeconomic differences represents important unfinished business for our society.

11 The Effect of
International Interchange of
High-Level Manpower on
the United States *

IMMIGRATION has been an important source of high-level manpower throughout the history of the United States. In recent years the number of immigrants reported as being professional, technical, and kindred workers has grown rapidly. In the half-century from 1900 to 1950, an average of more than 8,000 such workers were admitted annually; in the decade 1951 to 1960, this figure jumped to 18,000 annually; and the number has been increasing steadily from 22,000 in 1960 to 29,000 in 1965.[1] In 1960, as a result of this continued influx of professionally and technically trained immigrants, there were 287,000 foreign-born male and 129,000 foreign-born female profession, technical, and kindred workers in the experienced civilian labor force. These figures represent 6.8 per cent of the total male population and 4.6 per cent of the total female population in this occupational group in the labor force.[2]

---

* This chapter is a revision of an article under the same title by Alan E. Bayer which appeared in *Social Forces*, vol. 46, 1968, pp. 465–477.

[1] Computed from U.S. Bureau of the Census, *Historical Statistics of the United States: Colonial Times to 1957*, Government Printing Office, Washington, 1960, p. 60; U.S. Bureau of the Census, *Statistical Abstract of the United States*, Government Printing Office, Washington, 1966, p. 95.

[2] Computed from U.S. Bureau of the Census, *U.S. Census of Population: 1960, Subject Reports, Occupational Characteristics*, Final Report PC(2)–7A, Government Printing Office, Washington, 1963, pp. 111–115.

The proportion of foreign stock contributing to the pool of highly educated manpower—defined as those who have completed four or more years of college—is similar to the foreign stock composition in professional, technical, and kindred occupations (not surprisingly, since the two groups overlap to a considerable degree). Of the 4,626,000 men in the 1960 U.S. population who were age 25 or over and had completed four or more years of college, 308,000 (6.7 per cent) were foreign born. Of the 2,991,000 women in the comparable group, 136,000 (4.6 per cent) were foreign born.[3]

While small in relation to the number of native born, the absolute number of persons of foreign origin who are in the U.S. pool of high-level manpower is still considerable. Moreover, in particular disciplines, immigrants have provided the numbers and have been of the quality necessary to advance significantly the standard of living and to further technological and scientific development in the United States. In medicine, for example, our ability to sustain and improve health care has been substantially augmented through the employment of foreign-born or foreign-trained manpower. In the recent three-year period 1963 to 1965, over one-fourth of all medical interns and residents in the United States were from foreign medical colleges.[4] Among all physicians and surgeons in the United States, 15 per cent (14 per cent of the men, 27 per cent of the women) are foreign born.[5] As an index of how much immigrants have contributed to the advancement of American science: of the 40 U.S. Nobel Prize winners in physics and chemistry between 1907 and 1961, 15 were of foreign origin. In addition, a number of Nobel Prize winners born in the United States undertook part of their training in foreign institutions.[6] Conversely, some of the foreign Nobel Laureates had part of their training in the United States.

This chapter explores in further detail the contribution of foreign sources of manpower to the high-level occupations in this country. Such an analysis necessarily focuses on several different components. Foreign high-level manpower may be divided into two main sectors: the "trained brain gain," those who receive advanced education prior to their immigration to the United States; and the "untrained brain gain," those who travel to the United States for advanced education and remain in the country after graduation. In the case of the first group, the foreign country has incurred a significant portion of the costs of advanced training; in the case of the latter, the United States has often absorbed considerable training costs. A third "gain" is the aggregate of U.S. born who received advanced education abroad—often with considerable expense to the host country—and who subsequently return to the U.S. manpower pool.

---

[3] Computed from U.S. Bureau of the Census, *U.S. Census of Population: 1960, Special Reports, Educational Attainment,* Final Report PC(2)–5B, Government Printing Office, Washington, 1963, pp. 1–4.

[4] Computed from Association of American Medical Colleges, "Physician Manpower: Foreign Trainees," *Datagrams,* vol. 8, December, 1966.

[5] Computed from U.S. Bureau of the Census, *Occupational Characteristics.*

[6] National Science Foundation, *Scientific Manpower from Abroad,* NSF 62–24. Government Printing Office, Washington, 1962, p. 25.

The three components of "loss" are: (1) foreign nationals who receive advanced training in the United States and then leave; (2) scientists born and trained in the United States who subsequently emigrate ("trained brain drain"); and (3) U.S.-origin scientists who were neither trained in nor reside in the United States, and who are not employed by U.S. firms abroad ("untrained brain drain").

If the parameters of these migration streams are ascertained, we can assess in absolute numbers the net gain or loss of highly trained individuals and make an estimate of how much the international interchange benefits the United States, economically and otherwise. Many of the societal benefits and costs cannot be easily quantified, however, and measurable gains may be offset by losses that cannot be measured. For example, the United States may gain economically, but lose through a depreciation in international good will. On the other hand, the pool of high-level talent is to some degree an international resource as well as a national one; new discoveries and advancements in scientific knowledge are readily transmitted across political boundaries.

This chapter focuses on what is currently known about the numbers of high-level manpower involved in the international interchange. The discussion concerns the net numerical gain (or loss) to the U.S. pool of high-level manpower, how this figure compares with the levels we might expect today if migration had not been operative, what the probable magnitude of the contribution of foreign high-level manpower will be in the future, and what implications these findings have for policy.

Immigration of High-Level Manpower

Immigration to the United States reached a peak in the first decade of this century, exceeding more than one million immigrants per year for the first time in 1905. The annual number of immigrants fluctuated around this figure until the beginning of World War I. In 1918, the last year of the war, only about 110,000 immigrants were admitted. With the end of the war, however, the number again began to raise, reaching a high of about 805,000 in 1921 and thereafter generally declining. Since 1925, annual immigration has not exceeded 350,0000, and during the depression and World War II years, it was less than 100,000. In the past five years, the average annual number of immigrants has been around 288,000 (Table 11.1).

Over this period, the occupational distribution of immigrants has changed significantly, with the influx of high-level talent growing in recent decades. In the past half-century, the proportion of professional, technical, and kindred workers in the total immigrant stream has increased eightfold (Table 11.2).[7]

[7] These figures are only crude historical approximations of the occupational characteristics of immigrants. Over the years there have been changes in the definitions of occupations, changes in classification schemes, and variations in the completeness and accuracy of the data. Changes in the demographic composition of immigrants are such that the growth rate and proportions in professional, technical, and kindred occupations are actually

TABLE 11.1. *Average Number of Immigrants per Year, by Decade: 1911–1964*

Decade	Average Number of Immigrants per Year
1911–1920	573,580
1921–1930	410,720
1931–1940	52,840
1941–1950	103,500
1951–1960	251,550
1961–1964	288,400

SOURCE: U.S. Immigration and Naturalization Service, *Annual Report, 1964.* Government Printing Office, Washington, 1964, p. 19.

Figures on immigrants who are natural scientists and engineers have likewise reflected an increased contribution to the total flow of new natural scientists and engineers entering the U.S. labor market, although there are large fluctuations from year to year. In the period 1949–1950 immigrants constituted 1 per cent of the pool of new natural scientists and engineers, while in the most recent period for which data are available, 1963–1964, immigration added 6 per cent to this pool (Table 11.3).

The new immigration laws enacted in 1965, which will end the national quota system by the middle of 1968, will result not only in an estimated increase of about 50,000 in the annual immigration stream, but also in an increase in the proportion of high-level manpower. Under this legislation, visa priority is awarded to "immigrants who are members of the professions, or who because of their exceptional ability in the sciences or the arts will substantially benefit

TABLE 11.2. *Proportion of Immigrants in Professional, Technical, and Kindred Occupations, by Decennial Years: 1910–1965*

Year	Proportion in Professional, Technical and Kindred Occupations
1910	0.9
1920	2.4
1930	3.6
1940	9.6
1950	8.2
1960	8.3
1965	9.7

SOURCE: Computed from U.S. Bureau of the Census, *Historical Statistics of the United States, Colonial Times to 1957,* Government Printing Office, Washington, 1961, p. 60; and U.S. Bureau of the Census, *Statistical Abstract of the United States, 1966,* 87th Edition, Government Printing Office, Washington, 1966, p. 95.

higher than herein reported if dependents are excluded and only those immigrants likely to enter the active U.S. labor force are considered. From 1910 to 1960, the proportion of men in the total immigrant stream decreased from 70 per cent to 44 per cent, and the proportion of minors (defined as persons age 16 or under) increased from about 13 per cent in 1910 to approximately 23 per cent in 1960.

TABLE 11.3. *Contributions of Immigrants to the Pool of New Natural Scientists and Engineers in the United States: 1949–1964*

Year	(1) Number of Domestic Graduates in Natural Science and Engineering[a]	(2) Number of Immigrant Natural Scientists and Engineers	Group (2) as Percentage of Group (1)
1949–1950	209,179	2,753	1.3
1951–1952	166,409	4,765	2.9
1953–1954	118,717	5,918	5.0
1955–1956	119,600	6,652	5.6
1957–1958	151,271	11,013	7.3
1959–1960	175,917	9,407	5.3
1961–1962	183,439	8,027	4.4
1963–1964	196,697	11,181	5.7

[a] Includes bachelor's degrees.

SOURCE: National Science Foundation, *Scientific Manpower from Abroad*, NSF 62-24, Government Printing Office, Washington, 1962, p. 5; and National Science Foundation, *Scientists and Engineers from Abroad: 1962–64*, NSF 67-3, Government Printing Office, Washington, 1967, p. 3.

prospectively the national economy, cultural interests, or welfare of the United States"; their priority status is exceeded only by the status of the spouses or unmarried children of U.S. citizens or of permanent U.S. residents.[8]

Foreign Student Inflow

The number of "untrained brains" who come to the United States for education has grown dramatically over the past several decades. Foreign student enrollment in American colleges and universities is increasing at a far more rapid rate than overall student enrollment. Between 1930 and 1953, for example, the number of foreign students increased 300 per cent, while the enrollment of U.S. students increased only about 120 per cent.[9] In the past decade foreign student enrollment in U.S. graduate schools increased from about 12,000 in 1955 to more than 36,000 in 1965; this is an average increase of about 20 per cent annually, as opposed to an estimated 11 to 12 per cent annually for total graduate enrollment over the same period.[10] Although foreign graduate students represented only about 4 to 5 per cent of the total U.S. graduate enrollment in the mid-1950's, by the mid-1960's they constituted about 7 per cent of the total enrollment in U.S. graduate schools.[11]

A large proportion of foreign graduate students are doctoral degree students. In the 1960 to 1966 period 13 per cent of all doctorates awarded by U.S. uni-

[8] U.S. Congress, *Amendments to the Immigration and Nationality Act*, Public Law 89-236. 89th Congress, H.R. 2580, October 3, 1965, p. 3.

[9] Dubois, Cora, *Foreign Students and Higher Education in the United States*. American Council on Education, Washington, 1956.

[10] Institute of International Education, *Open Doors, 1954–55*, and *Open Doors, 1966*, Institute of International Education, 1955 and 1966, New York; U.S. Office of Education, *Projections of Educational Statistics to 1973–74*, Government Printing Office, Washington, 1964, p. 8.

[11] Computed from *Ibid.*

versities were to students who had received the bachelor's degree in a foreign institution (though not all of these were foreign born, of course), as compared to less than 6 per cent in the period 1920 to 1939. Moreover, in particular fields, the proportion of doctoral degree recipients of foreign baccalaureate origin is considerably larger, being 20 per cent in the biological sciences and 16 per cent in the physical sciences (Figure 11.1).[12] Since a number of foreign nationals receive both their baccalaureate and doctoral degrees in the United States, these proportions tend to be underestimates of the actual number of foreign doctorate recipients trained in the United States. While the relative rank of the proportion of foreign doctorates by major field remains the same when citizenship status rather than baccalaureate origin is employed as the criterion, recent data indicate that the proportion defined as being of foreign origin is generally larger when citizenship is used as the criterion. These data also show that the proportion of all U.S. doctoral degrees awarded to those of foreign origin is continuing to increase. In 1959–1960, 12 per cent of all doctorate recipients were not U.S. citizens, and this figure grew to 13 per cent in 1961–1962, to 14 per cent in 1963–1964, and to 15 per cent in 1965–1966 (Table 11.4).

TABLE 11.4. *Proportion of Non-U.S. Citizens Receiving U.S. Doctoral Degrees, by Major Field and Year of Degree: 1959–1966*[a]

Major Field of Doctoral Degree	1959 and 1960	1961 and 1962	1963 and 1964	1965 and 1966	Total, 1959–66
	(Percentages)				
Physical Sciences[b]	15.8	17.0	17.5	18.4	17.4
Biological Sciences	18.4	18.8	20.7	22.2	20.3
Social Sciences	10.2	11.1	11.5	12.2	11.4
Arts and Professions	7.2	8.2	9.0	10.3	8.9
Education	4.8	5.7	5.3	4.9	5.2
Total	12.0	13.0	13.6	14.5	13.5

[a] Excludes all cases with citizenship not reported.
[b] Includes engineering.
SOURCE: Unpublished tabulations, National Academy of Sciences–National Research Council Doctoral Files.

There is some indication that doctoral students of foreign origin tend to concentrate in the higher quality universities. The graduate institutions identified in the Cartter study[13] as outstanding produce between 20 and 30 per cent of all doctorates and enroll a greater proportion of foreign-origin students in all fields than do the less outstanding universities (Table 11.5).

Little information is available on the proportion of those students of foreign origin who receive a terminal degree in the United States and then remain in

[12] Harmon, Lindsey R., and Herbert Soldz, compilers, *Doctorate Production in United States Universities, 1920–1962*. National Academy of Sciences–National Research Council, Publication No. 1142, Washington, 1963, p. 30.
[13] Cartter, Allan M., *An Assessment of Quality in Graduate Education*. American Council on Education, Washington, 1966, p. 108.

FIGURE 11.1 *Proportion of U.S. Doctoral Degrees Awarded to Those of Foreign Origin, by Field and Decade of Degree*

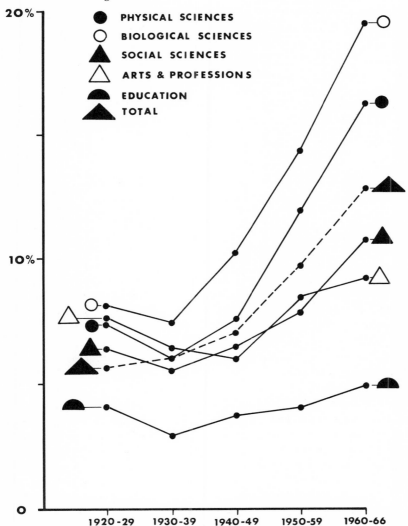

NOTE: "Foreign origin" is defined by place where the baccalaureate was received. Physical Sciences include engineering.

SOURCES: Harmon, Lindsey R., and Herbert Soldz, compilers, *Doctorate Production in United States Universities, 1920–1962*, National Academy of Science—National Research Council, Publication No. 1142, Washington, 1963, p. 30; and unpublished tabulations, National Academy of Sciences—National Research Council Doctoral Files.

TABLE 11.5. *Baccalaureate Origins of U.S. Doctorate Recipients, by Area of Study and Quality of Doctoral Institutions: 1960–1966*

Major Area of Doctoral Degree[a]	Doctoral Degree from "Leading University"[b]		Doctoral Degree from Other University		Total, All Doctoral Degrees, 1960–1966	
	Number	Per Cent with Foreign Baccalaureate	Number	Per Cent with Foreign Baccalaureate	Number	Per Cent with Foreign Baccalaureate
Physical Sciences	5,261	14.3	15,107	13.3	20,368	13.6
Biological Sciences	3,106	20.1	12,354	19.3	15,460	19.5
Social Sciences	5,244	11.8	12,840	10.2	18,084	10.7
Engineering	2,811	24.6	7,500	20.0	10,311	21.2
Arts and Humanities	2,878	11.3	8,593	8.5	11,471	9.2

[a] Excludes 17,004 doctorate recipients with degrees in Business or Education, and 165 with baccalaureate origin unknown.
[b] Based on highest aggregate faculty quality rating in area of study as reported by Allan M. Cartter in *An Assessment of Quality in Graduate Education*, American Council on Education, Washington, 1966 p. 107. Nine institutions are included in the "leading university" category in the Physical Sciences, 9 in the Biological Sciences, 9 in the Social Sciences, 5 in Engineering, and 6 in the Arts and Humanities.
SOURCE: Unpublished tabulations from the National Academy of Sciences—National Research Council Doctoral Files. Data based on fiscal years 1960–1966.

this country, or return here at some later date, for full-time employment. In the 1965–1966 academic year approximately 11,000 of the foreign students (both graduate and undergraduate) stated that they intended to stay in the United States after completing their education; about 83,000 said that they planned to return home. In the previous year, fewer than 7,000 had stated that they planned to remain in this country after completing their training. The change indicates a probable rise in the future retention rate of foreign students for employment in the United States.[14] How closely these stated intentions correspond with actual behavior is unknown. Undoubtedly, a large proportion do leave the United States, and, indeed, many foreign students are granted visas which stipulate that they must leave after receiving their degree. Virtually all who stay or who eventually return to reside permanently in the United States would, however, be included in the immigration figures reported previously. As a result, the two components, the "untrained brain gain" and the "trained brain gain," cannot be adequately factored out of the totals of immigrant flow.

Some indication of the "trained brain" gain (or loss) is given in data from follow-up studies[15] of all graduates (both U.S.-origin and foreign-origin graduates) who received their doctoral degrees from U.S. universities. Four per cent of the 1935–1940 cohort, 5 per cent of the 1945–1950 cohort, and 7 per cent of the 1955–1960 cohort reported that they took their first postdoctoral position

[14] Institute of International Education, *Open Doors, 1966*, p. 4.
[15] Harmon, Lindsey R., *Profiles of Ph.D.'s in the Sciences*. National Academy of Sciences–National Research Council, Publication No. 1293, Washington, 1965, p. 7.

outside the United States. Comparable estimates of more recent cohorts indicate that the proportion of doctorate recipients going abroad for their first postdoctoral employment is continuing to increase. In the 1959–1960 cohort, 8 per cent planned to leave the United States for their first postdoctoral position; and 9 per cent of the 1961–1962 cohort and 8 per cent of the 1963–1964 cohort planned to do likewise.[16] Since these proportions are consistently lower than the proportions of U.S. doctoral degrees awarded to those of foreign origin (see Figure 11.1 and Table 11.4), the United States has experienced a net gain throughout the past half-century. In the recent six-year period 1959 to 1964, about 9,000 doctoral degrees were awarded to those of foreign origin, whereas fewer than 6,000 of the doctorate recipients of this period reported that they took the first postdoctoral position outside the United States (Table 11.6). These

TABLE 11.6. *Place of First Postdoctoral Position, by Citizenship: All U.S. Doctorate Recipients, 1959–1964*

Place of First Postdoctoral Position	U.S. Citizen		Non-U.S. Citizen		Total, All Doctorates	
	Number	Per Cent	Number	Per Cent	Number	Per Cent
United States	49,623	82.0	3,570	39.5	53,193	76.5
Non-United States	1,941	3.2	3,794	42.0	5,735	8.2
Unknown	8,921	14.7	1,667	18.5	10,588	15.2
Total	60,485	100.0	9,031	100.0	69,516	100.0

SOURCE: Unpublished tabulations, National Academy of Sciences–National Research Council Doctoral Files.

figures are difficult to interpret because some of the increase in postdoctoral employment abroad represents the short-term employment of U.S. citizens who go abroad. The net balance of interchange clearly favors the United States, but changes in the retention rate of foreign-born, U.S.-trained Ph.D.'s cannot be determined accurately from these figures.

The region of origin of foreign students in the United States in 1964 who were working on the doctoral degree is as follows: 18 per cent from the Americas, 8 per cent from Africa, 12 per cent from Europe, and 62 per cent from Asia and Australasia.[17] Assuming that this distribution has remained constant over the past six years, only Africa and the Americas gain more in "trained brain" than they contribute to the foreign doctoral student pool in the United States. One-half of the non-U.S. citizens who went abroad for their first position went to Asia and Australasia, 10 per cent went to Europe, 10 per cent to Africa, and 30 per cent to the Americas (Figure 11.2). These cross-sectional statistics

[16] Unpublished tabulations of the National Academy of Sciences–National Research Council Doctoral Files. Estimates are based on all doctorate recipients who reported taking a postdoctoral position at the time of completing their doctorate. Approximately 15 per cent of the doctorate recipients of this period (15 per cent of U.S. citizens, 19 per cent of non-U.S. citizens) did not reply to this question.

[17] Computed from Institute of International Education, *Open Doors, 1965,* Institute of International Education, New York, 1965, pp. 16–21.

[334]

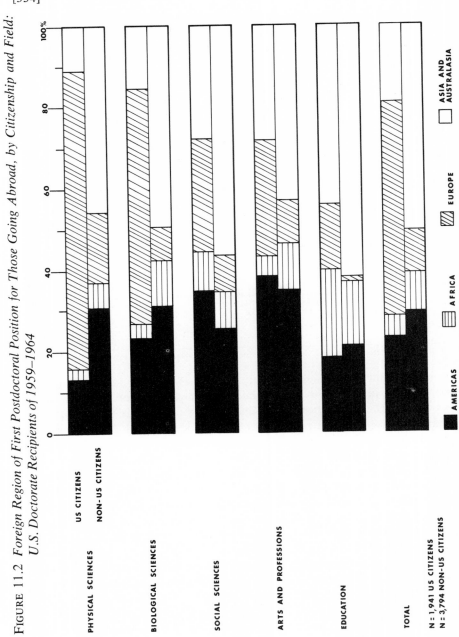

FIGURE 11.2 *Foreign Region of First Postdoctoral Position for Those Going Abroad, by Citizenship and Field: U.S. Doctorate Recipients of 1959–1964*

SOURCE: Unpublished tabulations, National Academy of Sciences—National Research Council Doctoral Files.

do not provide an adequate picture of the impact of international migration on different parts of the world, inasmuch as an underdeveloped country may suffer more from a small loss of talent than a Western European nation does from a relatively large loss.

U.S. Students Abroad

Little information is currently available on the number of U.S. citizens enrolled abroad in higher education, the kind of institution in which they are enrolled, or the characteristics of these students. In 1960, the U.S. Bureau of the Census reported that approximately 13,700 U.S. civilians of age 18 and over were enrolled in schools abroad, with almost one-half (48 per cent) being women (Table 11.7). No additional information on level of education is available,

TABLE 11.7. *U.S. Citizens Age 18 and Over Enrolled in Schools Outside the United States, by Sex: 1960*

Age Group	Men		Women		Total	
	Number	Per Cent	Number	Per Cent	Number	Per Cent
18 to 19	1,370	49.2	1,416	50.8	2,786	100
20 to 24	1,803	49.4	1,846	50.6	3,649	100
25 and over	4,012	55.1	3,266	44.9	7,278	100
Total	7,185	52.4	6,528	47.6	13,713	100

SOURCE: U.S. Bureau of the Census, *U.S. Census of Population: 1960, Selected Area Reports, Americans Overseas,* Final Report PC(3)–1C. Government Printing Office, Washington, 1964, pp. 4, 11, 51, 67, 79.

although virtually all in this age group are probably enrolled for post-high school education, and many are graduate students.

The Institute of International Education (IIE) gives a somewhat larger estimate for the same period. In the academic year 1959–1960, a survey of 1,392 responding foreign institutions of higher education indicated that there were more than 15,000 U.S. students studying abroad.[18] Since many people are probably missed in a worldwide enumeration, both this estimate and that of the Census Bureau are probably underestimates, although the IIE figures appear to be closer to the true figure. Neither source reports the degree level of U.S. students abroad, although the IIE does report the host country and the major field of study of U.S. students.

In 1959–1960, France and Canada were the countries hosting the largest number of U.S. students. By far the largest number were in Europe (69 per cent), followed by the Americas (24 per cent). In the more recent academic year 1964–1965, there were more than 18,000 U.S. students enumerated as studying abroad, with Canada and France continuing to receive more U.S. stu-

[18] Institute of International Education, *Open Doors, 1961.* Institute of International Education, New York, 1961, pp. 17–20.

dents than any other foreign country. Again, Europe enrolled the largest number (58 per cent), followed by the Americas (26 per cent).

Enrollment of U.S. students abroad in the past five years has been growing more slowly than enrollment of U.S. students in the United States, but at about the same rate as enrollment of foreign students in the United States. The basic difference in orientation of Americans studying abroad and foreign students coming to the United States is revealed by the fields of study of the two groups: American students abroad are heavily concentrated in the humanities, while foreign students in this country are concentrated in the sciences and professional areas. This difference indicates that cultural understanding is an important aspect of American study abroad, while preparation for a career and profession motivates foreign students to study in America.[19]

U.S. High-Level Manpower Abroad

In 1960, 50,300 U.S. civilians abroad were reported as employed in professional, technical, and kindred occupations. By educational level, 74,500 U.S. civilians abroad had finished four or more years of college.[20] These figures represent less than .6 per cent of the U.S. pool of professionally and technically trained persons, and only 1.6 per cent of the U.S. pool of persons with a college education.

Figure 11.2 shows that U.S. citizens with the doctoral degree who go abroad for their first position distribute themselves differently from the non-U.S. citizen who leaves the United States after his doctoral training. Over one-half of the U.S. citizens go to Europe, about one-fourth go to the Americas, one-fifth go to Asia or Australasia, and 6 per cent go to Africa. Furthermore, the major field of the U.S. citizen is a factor in determining which region he goes to. While physical and biological scientists who go abroad are most likely to go to Europe, the social scientists and those in the arts and professions are most likely to go to the Americas, and the educators are most likely to go to Asia and Australasia.

The U.S. "Brain Gain"

So far, the data indicate that the international interchange of high-level manpower favors the United States. Our actual net gain of doctorates is even larger than these figures would suggest for several reasons. First, many—probably most—of the U.S. citizens who go abroad after receiving the Ph.D. degree do so for only a short period of time, often to undertake postdoctoral study or to take positions with U.S. firms that have foreign offices. Thus, they are a "loss" to this country only by geographical definition. Few renounce U.S. citizenship. A second reason that these gain figures are conservative is that some of the non-

---

[19] *Open Doors, 1961; Open Doors, 1966.*

[20] U.S. Bureau of the Census, *U.S. Census of Population: 1960, Selected Area Reports, Americans Overseas,* Final Report PC(3)–1C. Government Printing Office, Washington, 1964, pp. 4–6.

U.S. citizens who leave eventually return to the United States for employment. They come back as immigrants after their two years of residence outside the United States, required for those students with J visas, has expired. A third factor making for an underestimate of the "untrained brain gain" of students who later complete doctorates in the United States is that many students of foreign origin attain U.S. citizenship prior to completion of the doctoral degree. Of those 1957–1961 doctorate recipients who were born in a foreign country and received their secondary education abroad, 1,050 (16 per cent) were U.S. citizens at the time they received the doctorate.[21] Undoubtedly, some of these people were U.S. citizens by birth, but some were not.

On the other hand, many foreign students are allowed to remain in the United States for a short period of time to take a postdoctoral position that allows them additional experience in their field prior to their departure from this country. Statistics on first job after the degree may mistakenly identify these foreign post-doctoral Fellows as employees who will remain in the United States permanently.

Some notion of how many foreign persons with doctoral degrees make a longer-term commitment to a career in the United States may be derived from a study that attempts to cover all people in selected natural and social science fields who are considered a permanent part of U.S. manpower.[22] Of the 20,965 doctorate recipients who have been in the labor force from two to eight years (that is, received the doctoral degree between 1957 and 1962), 1,143 (5 per cent) received the doctoral degree outside the United States. Of the 19,882 who received the Ph.D. degree from a U.S. institution, 738 (4 per cent) held a foreign bachelor's degree. As a consequence of these inflows of foreign manpower, the proportion of doctorate recipients entering the fields of mathematics/ statistics, physics, chemistry, and biochemistry has increased more than 10 per cent; the increase has been less than 5 per cent in psychology and sociology, with an overall average of 9 per cent in all fields considered (Table 11.8). In contrast, during the same period 12 per cent of all U.S. doctoral degrees in the same selected disciplines were awarded to those holding a foreign bachelor's degree.

These figures suggest that about one-third of the foreign graduate students who received a natural or social science Ph.D. from a U.S. institution have either remained in the United States or returned here within two to six years after receiving the degree. The loss of foreign graduates who leave the United States after receiving a Ph.D. is also partly counterbalanced by the immigration of persons who have received a doctorate abroad. While the statistics are inadequate to make a precise estimate, it appears that the inflow of foreign-trained doctorate recipients—"the trained brain gain"—is between one-half and three-

[21] Harmon and Soldz, *Doctorate Production in United States Universities, 1920–1962*, p. 27.
[22] The study of recent doctorates is included in the 1964 National Register of Scientific and Technical Personnel in the United States. See Appendix D.

TABLE 11.8. *Number of 1957–1962 Doctorate Recipients in the 1964 National Register, by Place of Baccalaureate and Doctoral Degree: Selected Sciences*

Field	(1) U.S. B.A., U.S. Ph.D.	(2) Foreign B.A., U.S. Ph.D.	(3) Foreign Ph.D.	Total	(2) +(3) as Percentage of Total
Mathematics/Statistics	1,290	84	92	1,466	12.0
Physics	2,396	112	334	2,842	15.7
Chemistry	4,414	163	372	4,949	10.8
Earth Sciences	817	23	32	872	6.3
Biological Sciences	3,583	132	149	3,864	7.3
Biochemistry	846	52	77	975	13.2
Psychology	3,608	62	51	3,721	3.0
Sociology	809	27	9	845	4.3
Economics	1,321	83	27	1,431	7.7
Total	19,048	738	1,143	20,965	9.0

SOURCE: See Appendix D.

fourths of the outflow of U.S.-trained foreign doctorate recipients who leave the United States.

We train moie foreign students at the doctoral level than we gain foreign doctorates (whether trained here or abroad) as permanent residents. We also gain far more in international interchange than we lose in U.S. citizens with the doctoral degree who go abroad to work.

Estimated Costs and Benefits of International Student Exchange

At present, the number of foreign students who enter the United States for study is five times as great as the number of U.S. students going abroad for study. Only 7 per cent of these foreign students in the United States receive support from their own government; less than 40 per cent are self-supporting. The remainder—more than one-half—depend on U.S. sources for financial support.[23] In addition, the educational costs not covered by student fees—such as those for laboratory equipment and computers—are paid entirely by U.S. sources. The total cost to the United States for supporting foreign students is estimated at more than $173 million for the academic year 1963–1964.[24] Moreover, U.S. citizens going abroad for study also depend to a substantial degree on U.S. economic support. The foreign contribution to U.S. students abroad is estimated at $30 million.[25] In addition, the United States incurs considerable noneconomic costs, which have not been adequately measured. For instance, in graduate programs in which student spaces are limited, foreign students may displace American students, or at least force them to forego attendance at their first-choice

[23] *Open Doors, 1966*, p. 10.
[24] Grubel, Herbert G., and Anthony D. Scott, "The Cost of U.S. College Student Exchange Programs," *Journal of Human Resources*, vol. 1, Fall, 1966, pp. 81–98.
[25] *Ibid.*

institution. Similarly, they may be given teaching assistant and research assistant assignments that would otherwise go to American students.

With regard to the education of foreign students in U.S. colleges and universities, the United States probably bears a short-term economic loss. The proportion of foreign students who are retained in the United States ranges between 12 per cent (based on IIE reports of foreign students intending to stay in the United States subsequent to training) and 40 per cent (based on the proportion of foreign-origin recipients of U.S. doctorates who take the first postdoctoral position in the United States). If the United States is assumed to support 80 per cent of U.S. students abroad (14,560) and 53 per cent of foreign students in the United States (49,660), the United States pays the educational costs for 64,220 students. If all U.S. students now studying abroad (18,200) remain in the U.S. manpower pool, and if 40 per cent (37,480) of all foreign students enter the U.S. manpower pool—a high estimate for all degree levels combined—the United States has gained 55,680 trained persons through international exchange. However, it has borne the cost for educating 64,220—an additional 15 per cent. Thus, the immediate costs probably represent a loss to the United States; but the long-term benefits, as measured by lifetime earnings or other indices of career contribution, far outweigh the incurred educational costs.

Moreover, the combination of the untrained and the trained brain gain to the United States, as reflected in immigration, yields an even more substantial numerical boost to the pool of high-level manpower, a boost not balanced by comparable outflows of U.S. citizens to other countries. The brain drain from the United States is small[26] in relation to this inflow of high-level manpower to the United States. The absolute number of U.S. citizens abroad is not substantial and represents only a very small proportion of the highly trained manpower pool residing in the United States. In 1960, only about 50,000 U.S. professional, technical, and kindred workers lived outside the United States. In 1960, more than 20,000 immigrants of professional, technical, and kindred occupations entered the United States for permanent residence. At this rate of entry each year, in just two and one-half years, the inflow of high-level talent to the United States would exceed the *total* existing number of U.S. high-level manpower working abroad.[27]

Manpower Gains Through the Second Generation

While the primary focus of this chapter is on the relatively immediate gains in U.S. manpower through immigration, it should also be noted that the first-

[26] More than 50 per cent of American civilians, age 25 and over, who are overseas have been abroad for three years or less. More than 70 per cent of the total number of civilians abroad are employees of the U.S. government or dependents of federal employees. Computed from U.S. Bureau of the Census, *Americans Overseas.*

[27] Whatever small loss the United States may incur can be a very important gain to recipient countries. Even though most U.S. manpower abroad is temporary, it can provide valuable training to the recipient countries.

TABLE 11.9. *Percentage of Employed Men in Professional, Technical, and Kindred Occupations, by Birthplace of Parents and Age: 1960*

Age Cohort	Native White	Foreign or Mixed Parentage	Foreign-Born
25 to 34	15.0	18.6	19.7
35 to 44	12.0	12.7	14.9
45 to 54	8.9	10.2	8.6
55 to 64	8.9	9.1	6.4
65 and over	9.2	9.8	6.4

SOURCE: U.S. Bureau of the Census, *U.S. Census of Population: 1960, Subject Reports, Nativity and Parentage*, Final Report PC(2)–1A, Government Printing Office, Washington, 1965, pp. 13–15.

generation offspring of immigrants make significant contributions to the high-level manpower pool. With respect to occupational achievement, the sons of immigrants are more likely to be employed in professional, technical, and kindred occupations than are the sons of native-born Americans for all comparable age cohorts (Table 11.9). With the exception of the oldest group (age 65 and over), the sons of the foreign born have greater average educational attainment than the sons of native parentage. In all age groups between 25 and 64, the proportion of men of foreign or mixed parentage who have completed four or more years of college is equal to or greater than the proportion of native white males who have attained this educational level (Table 11.10).[28]

Summary and Discussion

To summarize, in recent years, U.S. gains from immigration of high-level manpower have been equal to less than 5 per cent of the output of all U.S. institutions of higher learning. The proportionate addition to the U.S. high-level manpower pool and to the U.S. economy is thus small. For many foreign coun-

[28] If the total native group (both white and nonwhite) is taken as the base for comparison, the contribution of foreign stock is even more pronounced. It appears more valid to compare foreign stock with white natives only, however, as only a small proportion of the foreign stock is nonwhite (only 5 per cent of the foreign-born and 2 per cent of the second generation, but 13 per cent of the native-born are nonwhite).

TABLE 11.10. *Percentage of Men with Four or More Years of College, by Birthplace of Parents and Age: 1960*

Age Cohort	Native White	Foreign or Mixed Parentage	Foreign-Born
25 to 34	15.2	17.8	19.2
35 to 44	12.3	12.3	14.6
45 to 54	8.8	9.6	8.7
55 to 64	7.1	7.1	5.4
65 and over	5.3	4.7	2.8

SOURCE: U.S. Bureau of the Census, *U.S. Census of Population: 1960, Subject Reports, Nativity and Parentage*, Final Report PC(2)–1A, Government Printing Office, Washington, 1965, pp. 13–15.

tries, however, losses through migration to the United States represent substantial fractions of their current output of high-level manpower. The annual number of scientists and engineers from Canada who immigrate to the United States, for example, represents about one-third of that country's annual output of science and engineering graduates; from Switzerland, 17 per cent; from Norway, 16 per cent; from the Netherlands, 15 per cent; and from Greece, 10 per cent.[29]

In some of the less well-developed countries, even larger proportions of their trained manpower have emigrated to the United States. In 1962, for example, more than one-third of the Dominican Republic's stock of new physicians entered the United States, and more than two-thirds of the country's new engineering graduates came to the United States. Colombia lost 15 per cent of its physicians and 18 per cent of its scientists; Brazil lost more than one-fifth of its scientists; and Chile lost one-fifth of its engineers and more than 10 per cent of its annual output of scientists to the United States.[30]

Insofar as immigration policy is concerned, the response of the United States to the plight of these countries experiencing a serious brain drain has long been either to adopt a laissez-faire attitude or to encourage emigration to the United States. Cattell and Brimhall, writing in 1921—the same year that the immigration quota system was enacted to reduce the inflow of "undesirables"—state succinctly the prevailing attitude almost a half-century ago:

> We could and should see to it that the foreigners coming to the United States contribute their share of men of performance. From the point of view of national selfishness nothing could be more profitable than to add to the community as many foreign men of distinction . . . and as many young men of promise as would come. . . . Such men we can obtain from abroad free of cost beyond the payment for their living, which must be paid equally to those who are educated and selected at our own expense. Not only the men themselves, but their descendants also are assets to the country of incalculable value. From the point of view of the world at large, it is probably an advantage to bring men of distinction and of promise to this country, as this tends to promote friendly international relations and good-will, and because, the wealth being greater here and the competition less we should be able to give better opportunity to the men.[31]

The present U.S. position with regard to the immigration of high-level manpower is very similar to that stated a half-century ago by Cattell and Brimhall, although there is more general concern about America's responsibilities to the

[29] Friedwald, E. M., "The Research Effort of Western Europe, the U.S.A., and the USSR," *The OECD Observer*, special issue on science, February, 1966, p. 15. Special caution is enjoined in regard to the emigration figures for Canada. Many foreign citizens enter Canada for employment with the intention of subsequently gaining easier access to the United States.

[30] U.S. House of Representatives, *The Brain Drain into the United States of Scientists, Engineers, and Physicians*, Staff Study for the Research and Technical Programs Subcommittee of the Committee on Government Operations, 90th Congress, 1st session. Government Printing Office, Washington, Publication No. 81–176, July, 1967, pp. 7–8.

[31] Cattell, J. McKeen, and Dean R. Brimhall, editors, *American Men of Science: A Biographical Directory*, Third Edition. Science Press, Garrison, N.Y., 1921, pp. 782–783.

world community. Now, because international good will is being threatened, a laissez-faire policy, or a policy that encourages foreign students and foreign manpower to remain in or migrate to the United States, regardless of circumstances in the country of origin, is not likely to endure much longer. The future path is, however, unclear. While the democratic ideals of the Western World make undesirable the enactment of rigid laws or quota limitations that would substantially reduce the number of nonreturning students or the inflow of foreign talent, there exist a number of other possibilities that would lead to a more harmonious balance between domestic manpower policies and foreign assistance programs. The productivity of American medical schools and of colleges and universities could be stepped up so as to come closer to meeting domestic needs for high-level manpower, limitations on foreign student enrollment and higher entrance requirements for foreign nationals could be instituted, American education could be geared more closely to the needs of foreign countries, additional programs could be adopted on college campuses to keep the foreign student involved in his own culture, the number of years an exchange visitor must wait before he can apply for readmission to the United States could be extended, and more assistance could be given to upgrade academic institutions abroad. Incentive programs could be formulated by the United States. Return scholarships, for example, could be offered to foreign students completing their education in the United States. Many positions in the U.S. government and U.S. business abroad could be made available to those students who would return to their home country and to those citizens of other countries who are presently residing outside the United States and who might otherwise tend to leave the home country.

Regardless of what steps the United States may take in the future, if it is decided that American foreign policy requires measures to curtail the immigration of high-level manpower or to encourage the return of foreign nationals to their homeland, major initiative will also have to be taken by the countries that are losing talent. As long as social and economic conditions in the home countries thwart the development of professional and scientific careers, there will be continuing pressures to emigrate. When the difference between a career in the home country and in the United States is not great, the loss of talent can be slowed or halted entirely. Many losing countries could retain more of their talented manpower if they offered higher salaries, modernized their educational systems, made available necessary research equipment, gave greater emphasis to merit in their promotion policies, and instituted other methods to improve career opportunities.

The recent alarm expressed by many of the countries that have been losing high-level manpower suggests that corrective actions will probably be undertaken. The role of the United States should be to support these actions and to cooperate with whatever legislation foreign governments formulate to curtail their manpower losses, provided that such measures do not reduce domestic sources for fulfilling U.S. manpower needs, that such policy is consistent with democratic principles, and that the programs are supportive of the welfare and progress of men throughout the world. Indeed, the most effective role for the United States is probably a cooperative rather than a restrictive and legislative one. It is the individual countries now suffering manpower losses that are best qualified to initiate policy consistent with their specific national needs and their particular level of development.

What these measures will be, and how effective their impact will prove, depends in large part upon how complete our knowledge is on the international interchange of high-level manpower. Additional information about the components of the various migration streams discussed in this chapter and further study of the personal, economic, political, and social dynamics involved in the emigration and immigration of high-level manpower will be needed if countries are to develop effective programs to limit their talent loss. The United States can play a useful role by undertaking such studies at home and supporting such efforts abroad.

Section IV

12 Manpower

Planning and Manpower

Market Operations

THROUGHOUT THIS BOOK we have been concerned with the "goodness of fit" between the demands of society for highly trained individuals and the career choices of American youth and adults. This chapter reviews the various ways in which manpower market mechanisms operate to adjust supply to demand and examines the effectiveness of efforts to plan better adjustments.

As earlier chapters have indicated, a person's career choice is strongly affected by such factors as sex, genetic potential, socioeconomic status, and geographic origin; but even among persons who share similar background characteristics there is considerable variability not only in the choice of specific jobs, but also in general career choice. Moreover, the United States is ideologically committed to allowing the individual freedom in selecting his career and work setting. Any discussion of manpower planning to adjust supply and demand must begin with a recognition of that commitment.

We must recognize, too, that manpower planning in our society is diverse and decentralized. The federal government—through such legislation as the National Defense Education Act, the Manpower Development and Training Act, and the Health Professions Act, and through its draft deferment policies—exerts a heavy influence, but state and local agencies, as well as professional societies and other groups, are also deeply involved in manpower planning activities. There is no American counterpart to the highly centralized planning models being developed for certain European countries under the auspices of the Organization for Economic Cooperation and Development (OECD).[1] In the United States, the educational institutions that prepare the manpower supply and the employing institutions that create the demand tend to plan independently and are eager to maintain their autonomy. The problems connected with expanding medical schools offer but one good example among many of the difficulties of implementing plans to change the supplies of graduates entering a field; to make such changes, it is necessary to enlist the support of many independent institutions, professional organizations, and agencies of government.

Manpower Adjustment Mechanisms

Among the mechanisms that operate to adjust supply to demand, those that have been chiefly relied upon in the United States are the expansion and change of the educational system, and attempts to attract students into high-demand occupations. Other mechanisms include drawing on the labor reserve to fill demands, changing requirements for entrance to particular occupations or leaving entry standards flexible, using subprofessional personnel so that the professional can provide more or better services, use of retired persons, and fostering geographic and occupational mobility. In the rest of this section, each of these mechanisms will be discussed and its effectiveness evaluated.

Adjustments in the Educational System

It is ironic that in our attempts to alleviate manpower shortages, we have devoted so much attention to expanding the flow of persons through the educational system and attracting people into high-demand occupations, because these are among the slowest and in many ways least effective methods for relieving manpower shortages. The difficulties of timing educational expansion so that the supply is available when the demand arises are formidable. For one thing, the time required in higher education to prepare a person to enter a given professional occupation is usually lengthy, varying from a minimum of two to three years in a field like nursing, computer science, or business to a maximum of ten to twelve years in a field like medicine. Thus, simply expanding the supply of graduates helps little, if at all, to alleviate short-run changes in demand. Such changes, arising from fluctuations in business conditions, changes in military manpower requirements, and legislative enactment of new programs for space exploration, pollution control, the alleviation of poverty, and so forth, cannot be predicted with much accuracy. They are part of the uncertainty of life in a complex and rapidly changing world.

For coping with the long-range and relatively predictable changes in demand

---

[1] See Organization for Economic Cooperation and Development, *Forecasting Educational Needs for Economic and Social Development,* and *Planning Education for Economic and Social Development,* OECD Bureau of Publications, Paris, 1963. A brief exposition of this approach to planning can be found in Gottfried Bombach's "Manpower Forecasting and Education Policy," *Sociology of Education,* vol. 38, no. 5, 1965, pp. 343–374.

that result from population growth and distribution, technological development, and overall economic expansion, educational expansion mechanisms may be more effective. But even when changes in demand can be predicted a decade or more in advance, as was the case with elementary and secondary school teaching, it is difficult to expand the supply or to cut off this expansion at the right time. A hypothetical illustration may make this problem clearer.

Consider a profession whose entrants are recruited from college graduates in a particular major field. If the profession has 100,000 members, mostly male, and an average career length of 33 years, 3,000 new entrants per year will be required to maintain a stable size. If we assume that the population growth of the group that is served by this profession will require a 50 per cent expansion of the profession over a ten-year period and that then the profession will level off at the new larger size (150,000), it follows that the number of entrants must expand from 3,000 to 8,000 a year (almost tripling in size) for a ten-year period and then must drop back to 4,500 a year to maintain the profession at a constant size.

One of the difficulties in adjusting the supply to demand inheres in the conservative nature of our educational system. If the high-demand occupation is one that requires expensive educational facilities and highly specialized faculty, higher education may not be able to provide the necessary training even when a sufficient pool of applicants exists. Furthermore, once facilities are expanded, educators may be unwilling to cut back on programs when the demand levels off at the end of the ten-year period.

Another difficulty is that we know very little about how to attract students into the high-demand fields. The rate of change in the percentages of people majoring in different fields is relatively slow, making it impossible to increase the number of graduates rapidly enough when they are needed and to cut off the expansion at the proper time. The democratic belief in individual self-determination dictates that changes in choice of major field and career be voluntary. We cannot coerce people into entering or dropping a particular major field, but must rely on providing incentives. But up to now there is little evidence that the steps commonly taken to persuade students to enter particular fields—offering scholarships and fellowships, trying to change the "image" of a profession, providing information about specific careers—have had much impact on patterns of career choice. For instance, Rossi, reviewing NORC studies of the effects of financial aid programs on career choice, concludes: "Although it is extremely difficult to assess the effectiveness of fellowships and scholarships in shifting about the attention of graduate and professional students to one or another topic, it is certainly apparent that such programs hardly affect the distribution of students among broad career fields."[2]

Different fields encounter different problems in their efforts to ensure a suffi-

[2] Rossi, Peter H., "Career Patterns: Trends and Prospects." Paper given at Manpower and Mental Health Symposium, Airlie House, June 28–30, 1967, p. 25.

cient supply of qualified graduates. For some, the problem is not in attracting people, but rather in keeping them in the major field until graduation. In medicine, the physical sciences, and engineering, for example, the number of students who aspire to the field as college freshmen is greater than the demand, but each of these fields loses students during the college years, usually because of the strenuous academic demands of the program or because of limitations in the capacity of educational facilities. The flow into medicine, for example, is determined by the number of spaces available for entrants into medical school. In the physical sciences and engineering, the standards of instruction and the nature of the curriculum may account for high dropout rates from the program. If the demand for scientists and engineers continues to grow (and there is every evidence that it will), then it may be necessary to change undergraduate programs in these fields by making standards less rigid, by modifying the curriculum and methods of instruction, or by improving student and faculty relationships. Since such changes must be made by many faculty members in the individual departments of many different institutions, they are likely to be slow in occurring.

A second situation obtains in career fields where the number of students initially aspiring to the field falls short of the demand; social work and library science are examples. Frequently, such fields do not have a highly technical content or rigorous academic standards, and dropout rates are lower than in the sciences and engineering. The problem is to attract more people into the field during the college years. The most effective method for obtaining the necessary supply may be to keep these occupations open to people who have majored in other fields (as has been done with elementary and secondary teaching).

Given the difficulties of inducing students to enter high-demand occupations and of making the educational system more responsive to short-range changes, our principal approach to expanding the supply of college graduates in specific fields has been to expand the total educational system. The rapid expansion of higher education has led to enrollment growth in most fields, but in some of the fields of greatest demand, such as engineering and medicine, enrollment growth has been far below average. This procedure is essentially wasteful, since it may produce an oversupply of graduates in some fields. This oversupply, however, can be absorbed into other occupations where a college degree is important chiefly as a measure of intelligence and motivation, and an indication of possession of a set of appropriate values and attitudes. In some fields, like the social sciences, overall expansion of the educational system has already helped to increase the supply of educated manpower and will have an even greater impact in the future. But in other high-demand fields, general expansion has not increased the supply. In medicine, for instance, its effect has been to raise the quality of entering students slightly in the last few years, thus reducing the rate of attrition. Similarly, in the physical sciences and engineering, the effect has been to make these already selective fields even more selective, and there has been a much lower than average increase in the number of graduates. A high percentage of baccalaureate-holders in these fields are going on to graduate study, and in this respect, the general increase in undergraduate enrollment and the quality of undergraduate students have encouraged a rapid expansion of graduate degree output.

To summarize, our knowledge of how to influence young people to enter high-demand fields is inadequate; we do not even have evidence that the forces that inhibit or stimulate enrollment growth in general are any more amenable to planned change than are the forces that influence choice of major field and occupation.[3] Moreover, expanding the supply to the total educational system is an inefficient means of dealing with both short-range unpredictable changes and long-range foreseeable changes in demand. The college enrollment increases that have occurred were not planned to meet the requirements of the economy. Rather, they resulted from increased student demand attributable to population growth and to the increased numbers of high school graduates. Expressed in another way, had it been thought a desirable social policy to restrain the growth of higher education over the past two decades, we would have been hard put to do so.

Educational planners, particularly at the state and institutional level, have not paid enough attention to demands for graduates in specific fields (with the exception of medicine). A review of a number of recent state education plans and state-sponsored studies of higher education reveals that, although such plans usually pay their respects to the general need for college-trained manpower, they focus chiefly on future student demand for education and on problems of finance, organization, and educational program development.[4] Their consideration of

[3] For a somewhat different analysis of the same issue, see C. Arnold Anderson's "The Adaptation of Education to a Mobile Society," *Journal of Human Resources,* vol. 2, 1967, pp. 221–248.

[4] Following is a list of the master plans that were examined. They are felt to be representative of current state plans in higher education, since they represent all sections of the country and come from states of different sizes with different systems of state higher education.

California Coordinating Council for Higher Education, *Dental Education and Manpower,* No. 1015, December, 1964. A supply and demand study.

California Coordinating Council for Higher Education, *Faculty Recruitment in California Higher Education,* No. 1017, March, 1965. A supply and demand study.

California Coordinating Council for Higher Education, *Medical Education in California,* No. 1001, January, 1963. A supply and demand study.

Study Commission on Higher Education, *Higher Education in Connecticut.* Vol. 2, *Summary, Conclusions, and Recommendations,* December, 1964. Contains no enrollment or manpower projections.

Illinois Board of Higher Education, *College Enrollments.* Report of Master Plan Committee A, December, 1963. One of a number of reports on the aspects of higher education. Contains no data on manpower requirements.

Provisional Master Plan for Public Higher Education in Ohio. Ohio Board of Regents, Columbus, April, 1965, chaps. 1 and 2. Contains *national* estimates of fields of study needed.

Higher Education Opportunities and Needs in Oklahoma. Oklahoma State Regents for Higher Education, Oklahoma City, September, 1965, chap. 7. Contains occupational projections and needs to 1975. (Methods are not identified.)

Russell, J. D., *Higher Education in Michigan.* Michigan Legislative Study Committee, Lansing, September, 1958. Contains enrollment projections but no estimates of requirements for graduates.

manpower needs is used chiefly as a justification for planned expansion rather than as a basis for estimating the kinds and the extent of the educational programs that will be required.

Obviously, if manpower planning is to be more effective in the future, we cannot merely rely on general expansion of the educational system or on efforts to induce students to enter high-demand fields. Other approaches are needed to supplement the slow changes that occur through modification of higher education.

The Labor Reserve

The labor reserve includes those persons who are trained and qualified to work in an occupation and who last worked in that occupation but are not currently employed. Occupations in which a high percentage of the employees are women—teaching, nursing, and social work—are likely to have a large labor reserve; in 1960, Census reports indicated that women in the labor reserve constituted over a third of the total number employed in each of these three fields. Nearly all members of the labor reserve in the professions are married women who leave the labor force when they have children and often return to it after the children are in school. In periods of high demand or in situations where the family income is limited, the woman may reenter sooner, sometimes taking only a brief maternity leave. For example, the proportion of women teachers who leave the labor force when they have a child is much lower among Negro women than among white women because the Negro woman's contribution to family income is more critical.

It is useful to distinguish between two types of women in the labor reserve. The first is career-oriented and definitely plans to go back to work as soon as family responsibilities will let her. The proportion of college women with this orientation seems to have risen substantially since World War II, although accurate historical statistics to measure these changes are lacking. The second type of woman, who accepts the more traditional role of wife and mother, may not reenter the labor force unless there is a strong pull in the form of an attractive job or a strong push in the form of family financial needs. The career-oriented woman averages 25 to 30 years in the labor force between college graduation and age 65; this represents a career contribution of 60 to 70 per cent

Minnesota Governor's Committee on Higher Education, *Minnesota's Stake in the Future, Higher Education, 1956–70,* Minneapolis, December, 1956.

North Carolina Governor's Commission, *Education Beyond the High School,* Raleigh, 1962. Contains data on enrollments; needs for graduates are not discussed.

New York State Department of Labor, *Technical Manpower in New York State,* vols. 1 and 2, December, 1964.

Advisory Panel Joint State Government Commission, *Higher Education in Pennsylvania,* University of Pittsburgh, Pittsburgh, 1959. Contains population and enrollment projections but no projections of demands.

Texas Commission on Higher Education, *Public Higher Education in Texas, 1961–71,* Austin, March, 1963. Contains enrollment projection; needs are discussed only in terms of student demand.

of the total possible if she had been employed constantly. These women can help to adjust supply to demand by timing their departure from and return to the labor force. In periods when demand is high, they may postpone the birth of the first child, or they may accelerate their reentry into the labor force. In the case of the more traditionally oriented woman, a high level of labor demand may provide incentives of money or appeals to professional loyalty that will cause her to return to the labor force. Obviously, these basic patterns vary, and we know too little about the characteristics of women in the labor reserves of the professions to construct a good model of the flow in and out under different circumstances.

For a nearly all-female profession such as nursing, the labor reserve offers the potential for a very rapid (one to two-year) adjustment of 5 to 10 per cent in the size of the occupation. To expand the profession that much by increasing the number of graduates—assuming that funds, faculty, and students were available—would probably take three to five times as long. Even in a field where only one-fourth of the employees are women, the labor reserve has the potential for expanding the occupation at least 2 or 3 per cent in a year's time, a figure that is roughly equivalent to half or more of the year's graduating entrants. The system works the other way, too: in periods of low demand, more women will remain in the labor reserve.

The extent to which the labor reserve can provide a balance for short-run fluctuations in the demand for professionals depends, in part, on our ability to provide conditions of work that allow the woman to combine employment with family responsibility. (See Chapter 9.) While salary incentives have some effect in encouraging the woman to return to a job, they are probably less important than offering part-time work arrangements and work schedules that fit with children's school schedules.

Even though the labor reserve is an important aspect of supply and demand adjustment, it has received little study; planners usually ignore it in their calculations. For example, from 1950 to 1965 the National Education Association's annual reports on the supply and demand for teachers made no effort to identify the magnitude of or flow into and out of the labor reserve.[5] In view of its potential, the labor reserve merits a good deal more attention from manpower specialists and educational planners.

Changing the Age of Retirement

Extending the working life by delayed retirement is a special case of using the labor reserve to meet manpower demand. The potential for meeting short-run requirements for additional professionals by delayed retirement is substantial, although the additional years of active service from each worker will be fairly short on the average. In occupations like law and medicine, formal retire-

---

[5] The Association's 1966 report does not include a discussion of the teacher reserve and the effect of reentries.

ment is uncommon; doctors and lawyers just reduce the amount of service they provide as they get older. In these occupations the potential for additional service among retirees is small. In an occupation like teaching, the opportunities for part-time or full-time work after normal retirement age are substantial, but the pool of able and willing retirees is far smaller than the size of the labor reserve in women's occupations (retirees are only one-tenth to one-fourth the size of the labor reserve in elementary and secondary teaching, for example), and the problems of fitting retired people to jobs is more complex than is the case for women in their thirties and forties.

Although there has been considerable publicity about the importance of employing retired persons, and registers of retired professionals have been established in several fields (such as teaching and engineering) to assist in the placement of these individuals, the percentage of all employed professionals who were over 65 remained constant at 4 per cent between 1950 and 1960, a period when there was a decline from 4.9 to 4.6 per cent in the proportion of all employed workers over 65. Thus, there is some tendency for professional workers not to follow the general trend toward earlier retirement, although there is no indication that efforts to obtain better utilization of retired persons have had any major impact on employment trends.

Entry Standards and Quality Substitution

The labor reserve provides a way of adjusting supply and demand only in those occupations where significant numbers of women are employed. In engineering, law, medicine, the physical sciences, and other professions where the proportion of men is 90 per cent or more, different methods of adjustment are required. In some occupations—for instance, college teaching, elementary and secondary education, and engineering—adjustments are commonly made by changing the educational standards required for entry or by leaving them flexible.

David Brown has given a detailed account of the way in which quality substitution works in academic employment.[6] When a person with a Ph.D. degree in the proper field is unavailable, the position will be filled temporarily, or perhaps permanently, by a person who has less education in the same field. The percentage of all faculty members who do not have a doctorate is about the same now as it was ten years ago and similar to the percentage of doctorates on the faculties in the 1930's.[7] Thus, employment of persons with less than a doctorate is not simply a short-run method of adjustment during periods of high demand; it reflects in addition the wide variability in the requirements for teaching jobs in

---

[6] Brown, David, *The Market for College Teachers,* University of North Carolina Press, Chapel Hill, 1965; and *Academic Labor Markets, Vol. 2,* a report to the Office of Manpower, Automation and Training, U.S. Department of Labor, September, 1965.

[7] Hollis, E. V., *Toward Improving Ph.D. Programs,* American Council on Education, Washington, 1945, Table 7. For a review of changes in the postwar period, see Allan M. Cartter's "The Supply and Demand for College Teachers" in Social and Economic Statistics Section: *Proceedings, 1965,* American Statistical Association, Washington.

higher education. In junior colleges and in some four-year colleges, the master's degree is the usual educational standard for entry. In Ph.D.-granting universities, on the other hand, the doctorate is the entry standard, and deviations indicate either that the employed nondoctorate-holder is unusually competent or that qualified doctorate recipients are not available.

Hansen has shown that a similar substitution occurs in engineering: about 40 per cent of the entrants to the profession, as defined in the Census, have not obtained a college degree.[8] The upgrading of persons without a complete college education to the status of engineers is not merely an adjustment to a sudden increase in demand; it appears to have been going on for a long time and seems likely to continue for a decade or more. Like college teaching, engineering covers a very wide spectrum of activities that take place in many different work settings. While licensed professional engineers are nearly all college graduates or advanced degree-holders, as are the engineers employed by research and development projects, in many other situations men trained on the job perform engineering functions and call themselves engineers.

The substitution of persons with lesser educational qualifications will probably occur in any occupation that includes a wide variety of jobs and employment settings, that has flexible or undefined educational standards for job performance, and that does not control entry requirements rigidly. When these conditions exist, the presence of less well-educated persons in the occupation does not necessarily imply a temporary imbalance in supply and demand; it may reflect the diversity of the occupation. Nonetheless, even in occupations ordinarily filled by people drawn from several different educational levels or from schools of different quality, the substitution of better-qualified and more highly educated people for the less well-qualified, and vice versa, is an important way of adjusting supply to demand fluctuations. A similar process operates in licensed professions that have formal and rigid entry requirements, but the use of subprofessional assistants provides the primary means for quality substitution.

Using Subprofessional Personnel to Expand Professional Services

In the traditional professions where entry is controlled by licensing, relatively rigid educational requirements, or both, subprofessional assistants may be used or some new intermediate professional occupation introduced as a means of adjusting supply to demand. For example, the number of dentists in private practice has been growing much more slowly than the amount of dental service (as measured by patient visits) provided; while there are several factors responsible, the growth in the number of dental assistants and hygienists per dentist is probably a major one.[9] In the 1950 to 1960 decade the number of dentists

[8] Hansen, W. Lee, unpublished paper prepared for the Commission on Human Resources.
[9] For a discussion of the situation in medicine and dentistry, see Rashi Fein's *The Doctor Shortage: An Economic Diagnosis,* The Brookings Institution, Washington, 1967, pp. 111–122.

increased 17 per cent, the number of dental assistants increased 50 per cent, and the number of dental hygienists increased over 75 per cent.[10]

In some cases, the addition of assistants and intermediate-level professionals enables the professional to concentrate his attention on provision of professional services, thus increasing his efficiency. In others, the job itself may be reorganized, and activities previously performed by the professional will be taken over by another worker; for example, in dentistry the cleaning of teeth is now usually done by a dental hygienist.

The introduction of subprofessionals usually involves long-run changes in the work situation, and thus represents a relatively permanent kind of adjustment. Because of the shorter training time and generally lower skill requirements for subprofessionals, it is easier to increase their numbers than to increase the numbers of professionals to fill demands. In recent years a good deal of attention has been paid to the reorganizing of occupations so that more subprofessionals can be utilized. Whether the jobs will be differentiated within a broad occupational category (as in engineering or teaching), or organized hierarchically into professional layers with different titles (as in medicine, with physicians, registered nurses, and practical nurses), depends on licensure and other forces that create and maintain sharp boundaries between occupations. Neither teacher aides nor engineering aides have become a major part of the manpower supply within their respective fields; on the other hand, nearly all the licensed professions have developed a group of subprofessional occupations that are related to the central professional occupation, and many of these are growing very rapidly.

Although job differentiation and the introduction of subprofessionals are recognized as important ways of expanding professional services, we have a very rudimentary knowledge of how new specialties are developed or of the conditions under which they operate successfully. This lack of information makes it difficult for the planner, the administrator, and the policy-maker to encourage the development of a new subspecialty or to modify an existing one. In addition, no single organization or government agency controls enough of the situation to be able to determine whether a new specialization will be developed; it will emerge only if a large number of individuals and organizations (including both the provider and the consumer of services) want it to emerge.

Geographic and Occupational Mobility

In the short run, the mobility of highly educated persons is a primary mechanism for adjusting supply to demand. Geographic mobility—migration from one region of the country to another—is fairly well understood. A less obvious type of mobility—changing from one occupation to another or from one employment setting to another—also operates, even in fields that require long training and specialized knowledge. The physician can become a research scientist or an

---

[10] *Ibid.,* Table IV-3.

administrator or a teacher. The engineer can become a manager, and the businessman a college teacher. At the boundaries, an occupation attracts people from or loses them to related fields. New fields often depend almost entirely on cross-occupational mobility for personnel. Until recently, for example, computer programmers, systems analysts, and computer engineers were almost entirely trained in other disciplines.

Unfortunately, occupational mobility is often ignored in planning for professional occupations, and the phenomenon is not clearly understood. We need to know whether occupational mobility is adequate to adjust supply to demand and what its effects are on the quality of persons in both the recruiting and the losing fields. In addition, we need to know whether it is practical for the planner and the manager to influence the flow of manpower from one occupation to another, whether incentives such as higher salaries and greater prestige attract talented people, and how far such incentives can be controlled.

Some tentative evidence about these questions is available. Several studies attest to the imperfections of professional labor markets; inadequate information about occupations, inflexible salary schedules, and other factors restrict the extent to which the market can allocate its manpower resources.[11] Movement from one job setting (academic institutions, federal government, business and industry) to another within an occupation is not greatly affected by small differences in salaries; in the past few years, there has been a small net flow into academic employment, even though such jobs usually pay less than jobs in industry and government. An occupation or an employer type that offered a much higher salary would probably attract people, but only a few employers are able to provide large differentials in salary. Many professional jobs are in the public sector or in large bureaucratic organizations that are unable to make rapid and "nonstandard" salary adjustments.

The evidence suggests, too, that providing more information about job characteristics or attempting to improve the "image" of an occupation have little effect on a person's evaluation of occupations. Hodge, Siegel, and Rossi have shown that rankings of occupations on the basis of prestige are highly stable over time and are rated in a similar way by persons from widely varied backgrounds.[12]

Even if potential entrants had a perfect knowledge about the occupation and employers had complete freedom to adjust salaries, the interoccupational flow would still encounter the barriers of professional licensing practices and of the need for technical and specialized knowledge to perform certain jobs.

Since interoccupational mobility is so significant an adjustment mechanism, and even where it occurs chiefly at the subprofessional level it can have impor-

---

[11] See, for example, David Brown's *Placement Services for College Teachers and Academic Labor Markets,* Report to Department of Labor, 1965, (mimeographed); and Kershaw, Joseph A., and Roland N. McKean, *Teacher Shortages and Salary Schedules,* McGraw-Hill, Inc., New York, 1962.

[12] Hodge, Robert W., Paul M. Siegel, and Peter H. Rossi, "Occupational Prestige in the United States, 1925–63," *American Journal of Sociology,* vol. 70, 1964, pp. 286–302.

tant consequences for overall supply in a field, a great deal of additional information is needed. Current measures of mobility rates and of the characteristics of mobile persons are inadequate. Berelson's review of the defects of the measure of mobility in and out of teaching illustrates a problem common to most high-level occupations;[13] for many occupations, we have only guesses, indirect estimates, and assumptions to go by. Until we have better measures, we will be in a poor position to know how to influence interoccupational flows or how to take advantage of them as they occur.[14]

The Effectiveness of Manpower Planning

Any review of manpower planning must conclude that we know much less than we should if we are to be successful in our efforts to divert the flows of highly educated manpower into those occupations where they will be most needed. The future is always uncertain, and we have often made errors in predicting the direction and rate of development of both short- and long-range changes. Moreover, our knowledge of how manpower adjustment mechanisms work and of how they can be influenced is far from exact. In our efforts to ensure that high-demand fields will have an adequate supply of trained personnel, we have relied too much on the inefficient expedient of expanding the entire educational system. We need to explore more fully how to improve communication so as to facilitate mobility, how to attract those in the labor reserve back into the active force when they are needed, and how to augment professional services by introducing new technology, using subprofessional assistants, and reorganizing jobs.

Two other factors that complicate our efforts to plan are inherent in our society and our political beliefs. First, the resources, decision-making power, and planning activities necessary to make changes in manpower flows are decentralized, and it is often difficult for the many agencies and institutions involved to work together or even to agree upon goals. Second, our national commitment to allowing the individual freedom in his career decisions, coupled with our ignorance of how to influence career choice, makes planning difficult.

Given these conditions, can manpower planning be effective? Is it wise even to undertake such planning? One view holds that it is not, that our ability to forecast the future is so poor and our knowledge of adjustment mechanisms so inadequate that any planned intervention is about as likely to have an unwanted outcome as a result that was intended. A proponent of this point of view, C. Arnold Anderson, argues persuasively that what we should try to do is to ensure as much flexibility as possible by allowing entry into a career at many different points, by providing general rather than highly specialized education, and by enabling the market to operate freely.[15]

[13] Berelson, Bernard, *Graduate Education in the United States.* McGraw-Hill, Inc., New York, 1960.
[14] For a fuller discussion of geographic and occupational mobility, see chapter 7.
[15] Anderson, C. Arnold, *op. cit.*

Nonetheless, though our ability to foresee the future is limited, we can make some predictions with fair certainty; for example, we know that the growth of scientific programs and the impetus of our technology will keep the demand for scientists and engineers high, that the continued growth in educational enrollment at all levels will increase the demand for teachers, and so forth. We need not have precise knowledge in order to make policy decisions. Consequently, at the present time, we are combining planning with efforts to allow for flexibility so that adjustment mechanisms can operate freely, antithetical though these notions may seem.

Through long-range projections of demand, manpower specialists, government officials, educators, and others concerned with manpower problems can better order their priorities and more effectively direct their efforts to institute new educational programs and to provide alternative career opportunities. Moreover, planning has the value of focusing our attention upon ultimate goals, pushing us to define them more sharply and to examine them more critically. Such cloudy verbalizations as "the full realization of human potential of every citizen," or "equality of opportunity for higher education," or "a medical profession of the highest possible quality" become much more clear and meaningful when they are translated into specific planning goals. For instance, does our commitment to equal opportunity mean that everyone should have the chance to attend a junior college or does it mean that everyone should have the chance to attend a selective liberal arts college? In plotting the steps necessary to develop a long-range plan, we can better identify and evaluate the issues that are important in making good use of our human resources. The planning process seems to be one of the most advantageous ways of directing public attention to these issues, because it necessitates consideration of goals in relation to the problems that prevent their accomplishment and calls attention to the procedures through which they can be achieved.

13 Research Needed
on Talented Manpower

IT IS ALWAYS possible to conclude any discussion of manpower problems with a call for more research. Our knowledge of educational and manpower processes is always incomplete, and the possible problems for study are endless. Out of all these possibilities for study some are of key importance for better planning and administration, while others may be critical to a better understanding of social processes and individual career development. While the important questions to the administrator are not always congruent with the important questions that will fill in the gaps in our knowledge of human behavior, there is a substantial overlap. Both the social scientist and the administrator are concerned with understanding social processes and human behavior; the latter's interest is more sharply focused on the effects of certain changes he can introduce on the achievement of goals he is trying to accomplish, but in the field of manpower research there are many studies that will make a key contribution to both scientific and practical interests.

A first need for both scientific and administrative purposes is for a more effective system of statistics to measure occupational entry and occupational mobility. Longitudinal sample studies have given us baseline data on the patterns of career shifts that occur as students move through high school and college and out into the world of work. Some of these studies have been retrospective: What were you doing five years ago? What are you doing now? Others have followed groups of students for a number of years. Both types of studies present some difficult methodological problems. Longitudinal follow-ups are expensive and the nonrespondents who are lost from such samples are almost always different in important ways from the respondents. Retrospective data rely on the memory of respondents, and comparisons with records at earlier periods indicate that substantial response errors are involved. The actual follow-up of groups of youth as they pass through the years when career plans are formulated and occupations are entered have the greatest promise for providing useful information for both administrators and social scientists, provided they are supported well enough so that complete follow-ups can be made. The administrator's complaint about this type of research is that it takes too long to produce data; the follow-up of the 1957 Wisconsin high school graduating class by Sewell and his associates, and the Project TALENT five-year follow-up of the 1960 high school graduation class were providing useful information for administrators from 7 to 10 years after the students left high school. Administrators must ask themselves, have conditions changed so much in the intervening decade that the findings cannot be applied to current graduating classes?

A useful system of data collection could partly avoid this problem by providing for a biennial or triennial sample survey and follow-up of cohorts who were (a) entering high school, (b) finishing high school, (c) entering college, and (d) finishing college. If each of the cohorts (a) through (d) were followed for three years, it would provide a new longitudinal picture of the career development and entry years every two or three years. This type of data collection has been used effectively by Cooley (for a small sample), and a variation on this plan is being followed by Project TALENT. We have had past sample surveys of each of the cohorts (a) through (d) above; although they have used different samples, collected different information, and had differing success in complete follow-up. Currently the American Council on Education is collecting information on a sample of cohort (c), the college entrants, and the National Merit Scholarship Corporation is collecting information about part of cohort (b), the high school juniors. What is needed is financing for a coordinated data collection (possibly carried out by various organizations with the capability of handling large-scale surveys) that could provide comparable information over a period of a decade on the processes of talent flow and talent development in our society.

Whether a continuing survey of cohorts of youth is carried out by government survey agencies such as the Bureau of the Census or the Bureau of Labor Statistics, or by other organizations with government support, or by some combination of the two, is important primarily because it is necessary for the studies to be coordinated and to be repeated periodically.

It should be noted that certain parts of the needed human resources data system already exist. The Office of Scientific Personnel of the National Academy of Sciences has a basic file on doctorate recipients that provides an excellent base for longitudinal studies. The American Council on Education has begun periodic sample surveys of entering college freshmen who can be followed up at later points in their educational careers. The National Science Foundation is in the process of developing a "longitudinal register" of scientists in selected fields. Although this register is incomplete in its coverage, it has great potential for furnishing information about the later careers of scientists. The National Merit Scholarship Corporation collects periodic information on a very large proportion of the more able high school graduates in the United States. It would probably be more effective to coordinate the data collection of these existing organizations (which have proved to be highly effective in both collecting data and reporting their results), and fill in the gaps with other surveys, instead of trying to duplicate their work with one comprehensive survey covering all the different groups.

The rapid social and occupational changes occurring now will continue into the future. Formal education is increasingly important as an entry route into jobs and careers. Both of these changes make new social indicators of the processes of education and occupational entry very important. We have already shown that socioeconomic background affects the chances of college entry and completion, even for youth who are in the top quarter in academic aptitude; further monitoring is required of the extent to which our society provides opportunity for full talent development to all citizens. We have also shown that there will be a number of important shifts in occupational opportunities; a smaller proportion of college graduates will be needed in teaching; larger proportions will be needed in science and technology and the health professions. Unless we have a system for monitoring the development of educational and career plans we will be in a poor position to advise students or to plan the needed changes in recruitment policies or educational program developments. With an annual investment of more than 50 billion dollars in education, the cost of maintaining an adequate accounting of both the quantitative and qualitative aspects of our human resource development would probably cost less than one one-hundredth of one per cent of our annual investment in education.

The minimum requirements for a data collection "system" have been indicated above: it should cover, in overlapping longitudinal surveys the years from the beginning of high school to a point two or three years beyond the completion of graduate and professional school; it should include samples of persons *not* in the educational system as well as those enrolled, and it should provide information about the characteristics of persons that have been shown in previous research, much of which has been reviewed in earlier chapters of this volume, to be important determinants of both occupational entry and effective occupational performance. The kind of information to be collected at different points in career development would be somewhat different—but a common core of items would be collected from each cohort, for example, academic aptitude, socioeconomic background, sex, family characteristics, and performance at the previous stage of educational and/or occupational endeavor.

The system of data collection should have the flexibility to accommodate changing research interests, as well as a continuing core of "social indicators." While it is beyond the scope of this book to outline such a data system in detail, it would be an essential base for effective research or administrative planning activities.

Without a coordinated manpower data system, we will have to continue to rely on sample surveys of part of our human resources, and the relatively inadequate inferences that can be drawn from cross-sectional surveys. We have already had enough experience with longitudinal surveys to know that a human resource or manpower data system can be developed; both the survey methodology and the knowledge of which social indicators should be included are adequate to begin the system, and there is a great need for the information it will produce.

In addition to the recurring surveys of the educational development phases of careers described above, we need periodic information on occupational mobility for a number of professional careers. There was a national sample study of occupational mobility in a number of scientific and technical occupations, covering the 1960 to 1962 period, and utilizing the 1960 Census as a sampling framework. There is also the national register of scientists, and registers in medicine and some other professions, that have the potential of generating occupational mobility data. There have also been periodic current population surveys that have collected occupational mobility data for broad occupational categories (professionals, managers, clerical, skilled workers, and so forth). These initial efforts at the development of national occupational mobility statistics have identified some of the problems of collecting reliable and meaningful national information on occupational mobility. Briefly these are:

(1) The boundaries of many occupations are imprecise, and the terms used to define occupations are not uniform. As a result, the response reliability for occupational questions is rather low. Response errors can exceed the magnitude of annual occupational mobility rates, making it very difficult to draw firm conclusions from the reported statistics.

(2) To be useful in planning for high-level manpower requirements information is needed for detailed occupations, and sometimes these need to be further subdivided by employer type. To collect useful figures on the many very small specialized occupations, either a large sample survey is required, or a register approach must be used. Each of these approaches is relatively expensive and presents complicated problems in assuring the quality of data collected.

(3) Rates of occupational mobility vary with changing economic conditions, changes in the relative supplies of graduates, and other influences. Periodic surveys of job mobility, using similar data collection procedures, or a register that can provide information at any particular point in time are required if the mobility is to be linked or related to the social and economic conditions that bring it about.

In the area of occupational mobility statistics we have sufficient knowledge of methods of conducting surveys, and also can define the important questions that should be included in such surveys to enable us to begin a series of recurring national surveys of occupational mobility. Without periodic information about mobility, we will continue to make gross errors in estimating both the nature and magnitude of supply and demand problems.

A statistical system that provides periodic information on both the development of talent in the educational system and on the subsequent occupational mobility and career development in the specialized occupations represents the minimum in social indicators necessary for planning and policy making. Such a statistical system would also provide the basis for many more detailed research inquiries necessary to our understanding of the processes by which people are educated, enter jobs, or change occupations as their careers develop.

Research on the Quality of Human Resources

At a number of points in the preceding chapters we have indicated that while our information about numbers was sufficient, our information about the quality dimension was very poor or nonexistent. As the possession of bachelor's and advanced degrees becomes more commonplace in the future and as employers seek new and more useful evidence about potential accomplishment of tomorrow's college graduates, there will be more emphasis on the quality of our human resources.

In addition, some of the criteria now in use for separating the successful from the unsuccessful in the educational system seem to have limited utility in predicting the more important criteria of job or career success. The prediction of success in the educational system has been developed to the point where we can make reasonably good estimates of the success of students at one level of education from information about their performance at the preceding level, plus other background characteristics and ability measures. Our prediction of success in undergraduate education is considerably better than our predictions of success in graduate school. Grades, tests, and other measures of academic ability typically show relatively low relationships with subsequent measures of professional and managerial career performance. This is true even for those aspects of performance like research publication and citations that are similar to academic activities. It is obvious that effectiveness in complex professional roles cannot be predicted satisfactorily from one or two measures based on the educational record of the individual. The readily available predictors of performance, for example, grades and estimates of institutional quality, need to be supplemented by other measures that differentiate the person who is effective in his career from the ineffective professional. The whole field of assessment of complex job performance has been studied extensively, particularly in military settings, and in other large organizations that have been interested in more rational personnel selection and development procedures. In spite of voluminous literature on the topic, we do not have any group of measures with demonstrated validity that can be used to assess "quality" or "effectiveness" in all or even most of the specialized occupations. In fact, what we have learned from studies of specialized occupations is that the chances of developing a few all-purpose measures of "quality" appear to be very slim. The complexity of professional performance and the differential influence of different factors in different jobs suggest that even within a single occupation such as chemist, the variety of job requirements is large. Persons who will be effective in teaching roles will have different characteristics from those who will be successful as industrial research chemists, although they will also have much in common.

From the point of view of national and state planning we need measures of quality of human resources that can be applied to large aggregates—for example, will the expansion of engineering technician training draw personnel from the same quality pool as engineering itself? Will the expansion of engineering and engineering technician training lead to a decline in the quality of personnel entering the health professions, especially the professionals and subprofessionals who assist the doctors? How will the quality of entering teachers change, if at all, as a result of the greater selectivity that school systems will have in the next decade? If we can apply some of the assessment and prediction methods that have been used within companies in the past, to the prediction problems for whole occupations and industries, we should be able to get better measures of quality.

In spite of the difficulties involved, additional research on the qualitative dimensions of human resources is a priority need. Some of the new program budgeting systems currently under development assume that valid performance criteria exist or can be developed for functions now being performed by specialized personnel. Other budget and personnel management systems make implicit assumptions about the identification of "merit" or effective performance. As further efforts are made to rationalize investments in education and training by states and the federal government, the need for information about the quality of our human resources will grow. In many cases the alternatives may be to use quality measures with low demonstrated validity (such as the score on a single standardized test), or to continue on the basis of common sense and historical tradition. For many administrators, the issue will not be whether we can measure the quality of human resources with great accuracy, but whether the relatively crude measures that are available now will enable us to make better decisions than we could make without them. The importance of research on the dimensions of quality should be more and more apparent in the next few years.

Research on the Development of New Specialties and Subprofessional Roles

Another important area for research is the process by which new occupations emerge, and the ways in which occupational requirements change as a result of the impact of technology and the increasing size and complexity of organizations. The recent National Commission on Technology, Automation, and Economic Progress sponsored a number of explorations of these processes. Although the Commission was able to show that some of the alarming prophesies about wholesale technological unemployment are exaggerated, at least in terms of developments that have occurred up to this time, there is still a great deal of information needed about the way in which technological changes are changing professional roles today, and how they are likely to change these roles in the future. Related to the impact on existing professional occupations is the question of whether new subprofessional roles will emerge, and if so, how they will affect the demand for professionals. In nearly every profession where a shortage of personnel is felt to exist, there have been proposals to extend the work of the professionals by adding subprofessional assistants and by greater use of technology. In some professions, such as medicine, dentistry, and research sciences, there have been very large changes in the use both of assistants and of more complex and sophisticated equipment. In other professions such as elementary and secondary teaching, the influence of these factors has been slight, in spite of the efforts of a number of groups to introduce them. Research is needed not only on the manpower implications of technology and organizational change for specific professions, but also on the conditions under which the use of lesser-trained personnel and new technology are likely to affect a profession, and the conditions under which they are not likely to have much impact.

Closely related to the question of the impact of technology in creating new professions, and the acceptance of technology by a profession, is the impact of technology and the advancement of knowledge on professional obsolescence. Are there adequate mechanisms for self-renewal and updating of knowledge and skills for the profession? Every profession has ways to provide for the updating of knowledge among its members, but are these adequate to the more rapid pace of change? Viewed another way, the problem of preventing professional obsolescence is just a part of the problem of maintaining quality and of measuring the level of quality of the members of the specialized occupation. Because knowledge is growing, and technology and organizational change are proceeding at a very rapid rate, there is a greater need for adequate means for assessing the self-renewal of each specialized occupation. In the future the problem of keeping up to date will be even more pressing. Some of the methods of assuring currency of skills used by professions may be much more effective than others; it would be valuable to compare professions in the way they deal with the problem. It might be possible to induce organizational changes in professions that would increase the pressure on persons to keep up to date and perform effectively. For example, one of the potential benefits of group medical practice is that diagnoses and other professional decisions are made in a situation where they are readily subject to professional review. Any reorganization of work that moves the practice of a profession from a private unobserved activity to one that receives regular surveillance from other professionals is likely to put a premium on the possession of current knowledge and skills. Studies of other changes in incentive systems, provisions for continuing education, and other ways in which professionals can keep themselves currently informed represent an important area for research.

Another way of examining the question of the operation and organization of professions and the effectiveness of their numbers is in terms of the utilization of manpower. Research on utilization asks how well professional talents are being employed now, and whether we have personnel who are underutilized in relation to their experience and training. Research on utilization depends on the availability of measures of effectiveness. Where such measures are lacking, research can focus on the way in which jobs are organized and the effects of incentive systems on job performance as they affect the way people are likely to be utilized. For example, even without good measures of effectiveness, we can study the problems of limiting geographic and occupational mobility to the extent that it would produce major problems of utilization. We may be able to determine whether a particular occupational system or specialized profession has enough mobility opportunities to allow for movement that will make more effective utilization of manpower possible, even if we cannot measure the actual level of utilization very accurately.

Whether research begins with the question of whether people have adequate skills and knowledge for the job (the obsolescence issue) or with the question of whether there are people whose skills and knowledge are not being adequately used on the job, the "fit" between job requirements and personal qualifications must be ascertained. This is another way of looking at the measurement of quality and effectiveness in professional performance. These measurement problems present complicated and important research questions that will (and should) be the subject of more study.

Because the ultimate question of measuring professional effectiveness is so complex, we should also support more research on the intermediate questions of organizational arrangements and incentive systems that are likely to encourage effective utilization of professionals, and are likely to encourage professionals to keep their knowledge and skills current. Similarly, we can encourage further research on the costs and benefits of using persons with subprofessional training, or persons with less than optimum educational qualifications. This type of research will be especially important in those occupations where the supply of fully qualified persons is likely to continue to be inadequate, or where the costs of full professional staffing would be so high as to reduce the demand for service far below the estimates of need for it. Useful answers to some of these intermediate level questions may be forthcoming even in specialized occupations where the measures of professional performance are very rudimentary.

Research on the Processes of Occupational Choice and Educational Effects

There has been a substantial amount of research on the way in which individuals choose their occupations, and in the prediction of future occupational choices at early points in the individual's career, where intervention might affect the outcomes. From the point of view of manpower research, these studies of the individual choice process are important in helping us to understand the behavior of aggregates—for example, what percentage of college entrants will choose engineering programs? If the number expected to choose engineering is insufficient, what can be done about it?

For the specialized occupations in particular, study of the interaction between the educational system and the percentages of youth choosing different occupations is of key significance. College graduation is already the expected entry route in many of these occupations, and for some it is the required route. We know that there are substantial shifts in the aggregate percentages choosing different occupations during the high school and college years, and that these shifts occur in definite, patterned ways. We have less comprehensive information about the way different kinds of educational experiences affect these patterns of choices. This represents an important area for further study. For example, we know that a bright student from a selective college is much more likely to graduate from college, and to go on to graduate school, than is a student with equal academic aptitude who enters an open-door junior college. Given these facts, what policy suggestions are appropriate? Is it feasible to modify the student climate, the curriculum, or the guidance and counseling activities in the junior colleges so that the talented students they attract will be more likely to continue on to a career in one of the occupations where an advanced degree is needed? Or is the poorer record of the junior college primarily a measure of the lesser motivation of the entrants to these colleges, motivations that have been largely determined by the time of college entry? The challenge for research is that these are not really either/or questions—family background and motivation, as well as the nature of the college experience, affect career plans. The research problem is to determine their relative importance, and to provide some more precise measures of the probable effects of changes in educational environments on the future distribution of career choices. Many of the needed research tools, in the form of aptitude and interest scales, scales to assess the college environment, and measures of aptitude and ability, are already available or are in an advanced stage of development.

This area of research will be even more important in the future than it has been in the past. The separation of the home from work is much greater than it used to be, and as bureaucracy and metropolitan life both become more prominent features of our society, our youth will have less contact with actual work experience that is relevant to their career plans and goals, especially if these are professional or managerial career plans. The school and college is becoming more important as an institution where different career alternatives can be explored, at least in the form of courses and majors. Research on the impact of college on patterns of career choice should also consider whether or not there are more effective ways that college can bridge the gap between childhood and the world of work.

The opportunity to enter specialized occupations without a college education has been decreasing rapidly, and for many jobs college is now a prerequisite for entry. The way in which persons are selected for college, the way their progress is assessed, and the effects of the college experience on career plans and on the chances for career entry thus becomes an even more important area for research. When a society depends to so large a degree on a social institution like college, research is needed to assess its current impact on the development and channeling of human resources, as well as to indicate ways in which institutional modifications can help us to better achieve the number and kinds of specialists our society needs.

Research on the Development of Human Resources Investment Models

In the past two decades economists have shown an increasing interest in the question of the value of investment in the training and education of our human resources. The interest of economists has included the question of the economic returns that society gets from educational investments, as well as the alternative way of putting the same question: How can we assess demand for educated manpower to meet economic growth targets? Mary Jean Bowman[1] has given an excellent account of the development of economic thought on this problem. Recently, the emphasis has been on the development of more complex planning models in which economic investment criteria are only some of the variables required to reach decisions about educational expansion or manpower demands. The use of models that employ more than economic variables is a response to one of the chief criticisms of past analyses of educational investment by economists; namely, that they have dealt with educational goals that can be only partly measured in economic terms, and have made assumptions about the allocation of costs and benefits that are unrealistic.

One area of needed research is the question of how much of the greater earnings of college-educated as compared to high school-educated persons ought to be allocated to their educational difference, and how much to other factors such as differences in motivation, aptitude, and family connections. The same question can be asked about the differences in income of persons graduating from different colleges. A few surveys have found big differences between the incomes of persons who graduate from different colleges. Can part of these differences be attributed to the differences in the quality of education received, and are there other factors? One important cause of differences in earnings will be the occupations which graduates choose—a college that sends a high proportion of its graduates on to medical school will have alumni with a higher average income

---

[1] Bowman, Mary Jean, "The Human Investment Revolution in Economic Thought," *Sociology of Education*, vol. 39, 1966, pp. 111–137.

than a college that prepares its graduates for teaching. There will be other institutional differences in selectivity, too, that complicate any efforts to attribute income differentials to differences in the quality and amount of education received. The situations in which valid inferences can be drawn about the relationship between education and income must be carefully delineated, which is another way of saying that a number of other variables must be analyzed and controlled before useful conclusions can be drawn about educational investment alternatives.

Economists' attention to questions of educational and human resources investment has been extremely valuable in the past decade because their studies have focused attention on the need for clear definition of goals, and on the quantitative expression of both costs and benefits of education. Further progress in this area of research is likely to come as we develop more adequate quantitative measures of the value of different kinds of education not only for the individual (the direct benefits) but also for the society (the indirect benefits).

Specialized manpower markets do not conform very closely to the ideals of competition and the assumption that salary and wages reflect the principal differences between jobs. Past economic analysis of manpower flows has often ignored these limitations and assumed that the basic conditions were reasonably well met. In particular, comparative analysis of income in different professions (such as engineering or teaching) has been used to draw conclusions about the demand for personnel, or the existence or absence of relative shortages, which have ignored or glossed over problems of substitution of less well-qualified personnel, differences in the way in which wage rates reflect changing market conditions, and similar problems. Future research utilizing economic analysis of manpower flows needs to concentrate on the measurement and control of those variables that affect the way the market actually operates—for example, if quality substitution is more prevalent than price substitution in employment decisions, this fact needs to be built into the analytic procedures. An important strategy is to set up research analyses in such a way that the economic model "fits" the situation being studied. Although this is obviously desirable, it needs more attention in future economic analyses of manpower markets.

Summary and Conclusions

These suggested directions for future research are not presented as a comprehensive inventory, but rather as an indication of some of the work that the authors feel needs attention. Whichever problems are studied, the methods of research on manpower problems and the standards of good research are changing rapidly. Studies will increasingly require well-selected national samples. Multivariate procedures will be required for most research, and studies will increasingly be concerned with systems of variables, rather than the study of one or a few variables.

In the future, more of the specialized manpower research questions will require the methods and concepts from several disciplines. Manpower research is already interdisciplinary in nature, involving the cooperation of demographers, psychologists, economists, and sociologists, and it seems likely to continue to require work from a number of perspectives.

There are already a few interdisciplinary manpower research programs, but additional research groups are needed in which the skills of persons from different disciplinary backgrounds can be brought to bear on manpower problems. A close relation needs to be developed between research groups and the operation of manpower data systems (as described earlier in this chapter). The maximum use of data for research, as well as planning and administrative purposes, will make it desirable to have continuing relationships between research scholars and the sources of data. If improved opportunities are developed for work by research scholars from different disciplines, and if they have effective access to the data systems that are developed to provide information on our human resources, the benefits will be substantial in increased understanding of manpower development in America.

Appendices

Appendix A: Projections of Enrollments and Degrees

Donald S. Bridgman reviewed existing projections of enrollment and degrees for the Commission, and prepared an independent set of projections based on past trends in the ratio of enrollments to population, and to degrees at lower levels. The approach used was to calculate, from Census data, the contribution of each age group to the enrollment and degrees at a particular level. Rather than base the projections on a single age group—such as 18 to 21 for college enrollment, or 17 and 18 for college entrants—the projections are based on a broader group of ages which include the ages that supply most of the students. This approach is used by the Census Bureau in projecting enrollments, but the Census enrollment concept differs in the reported totals from the Office of Education reported total enrollments, and all figures were adjusted to conform to the Office of Education concept of student.

Mr. Bridgman added some other refinements to the projections by subdividing the total enrollment into full-time and part-time, undergraduate, graduate, and advanced professional (law, medicine, and so forth—all of the post-baccalaureate professional degrees). Degrees awarded were also separated into bachelor's, advanced professional, master's, and doctor's degrees.

The projections of total enrollment and total degrees are both higher than those developed by either the Census Bureau or the Office of Education. The difference between the Census and these projections comes from the different definitions of a college student and from higher projected enrollment rates of women in the Commission's projections. For example, about a quarter of a million of the difference between the Census and these projections is due to the exclusion of persons over 35 from the Census enrollment totals.

The main difference between these projections and those of the Office of

Education is the broader age base used for the projections. The size of the age groups over 21 will increase more rapidly than the 18 to 21-year-old age group during the 1970's, and a substantial (and increasing) percentage of all college students is drawn from these age groups. The projections of advanced degrees are based on the number of bachelor's graduates (by field) in each field in recent years, rather than on the changes in the size of the underlying age group. Since the number of bachelor's degrees has been increasing rapidly, as well as the proportion of all degree recipients who go on to graduate school, the combination of these trends produces an expansion of advanced degrees that is somewhat greater than that produced by the Office of Education method of relating advanced degrees to the underlying age group.

All of the projections of enrollments and degrees are extrapolations of the past trends in the underlying population, enrollments, and degrees awarded at lower levels. While most of the projections are linear extrapolations, some of them are adjusted to slow down the rate of change in the rates.

In the past, trend projections have generally been underestimates of actual enrollments and degrees. It is quite possible that these projections, even though they are based on underlying rates of change in population and college attendance and completion rates, will also prove to have a substantial margin of error. Changes in social and economic conditions, and other influences might affect these totals by 10 to 20 per cent within a decade. The projections are not tied to any specific set of social or economic conditions because (a) the relationship between changes in enrollment rates and changes in social and economic indicators is only moderate, and (b) our ability to predict future social and economic conditions is also imperfect.

The refinements introduced into the projection methods by Mr. Bridgman should eliminate projection errors that are associated with inappropriate selection of the demographic base, or failure to account for changes in the number of graduates completing the next lower level of education; but they are just as subject to other types of fluctuation as any of the other projections.

PROJECTED OPENING FALL ENROLLMENTS IN ALL INSTITUTIONS OF HIGHER EDUCATION: UNITED STATES 1966–1975

This part of Appendix A presents projected opening fall, degree-credit enrollments in United States institutions of higher education for each year from 1966 through 1975. These are shown in Tables A-3 through A-7. The second part of this Appendix presents projections of degrees.

A single projected enrollment figure derived from one set of assumptions is presented for each subgroup shown and corresponding figures from other projections by the Bureau of the Census and the U.S. Office of Education are shown to permit ready comparisons.

The projected figures are designed to be consistent generally with past and current figures reported by the Office of Education, which represent as nearly exact a count of actual enrollments as can be obtained. As indicated in Table A-7, however, the classifications of (a) undergraduate and first professional and (b) graduate enrollments used by the Office of Education will be altered to (a) undergraduate, (b) graduate, and (c) advanced professional (professional students with preprofessional college training as in law, medicine, theology, and so forth) and other sources of data required to accomplish this subdivision are utilized. In addition to the pertinent population data of the Bureau of the Census to be used with the Office of Education data, the Bureau's figures on school enrollments by age group are employed to supplement the Office of Education figures. Although, as will be shown later, these Census figures obtained from individuals in a sample population differ somewhat (and in certain subgroups they differ substantially) from those of the Office of Education, they have been considered most valuable for the purposes used. By definitions and the timing of their collection, they appear closely representative of the Office of Education enrollments.

Table A-1 gives pertinent Office of Education college enrollment figures for the base years to be employed and its projection for 1970 and 1975 as shown in its publication, *Projections of Educational Statistics to 1975–76*, 1966 Edition, with estimates of the sex breakdowns of those for the full-time and part-time enrollments at all levels combined. The sex breakdowns for the full-time and part-time enrollments at each level, revised as indicated above, will be presented later.

The projection method used by the Office of Education employs ratios of enrollment to the population 18 to 21 years of age. The actual age distributions of college enrollments obtained from the Census bulletins on school enrollments raise a serious question as to whether the 18 to 21 population provides an adequate base for projections, since only about 55 per cent of the male enrollment and 70 per cent of the female enrollment fall within these age limits. The weight of the several age groups included also varies in different years, particularly among the men. The proportion of all college enrollment from the 18 to 19 year group varies from 27 per cent to almost 35 per cent and that from the 25 to 29 year group drops from 21 per cent to 13 per cent in the 1959 to 1965 period. Much of this shift was due to the after-effects of the Korean War but, as indicated by the corresponding but smaller shift in the distribution of female enrollments, the relative size of the age groups also had a substantial effect.

The suggested distributions to be used for the projections are approximations of the more recent years and have been used to construct other population bases which are artificial but more representative of the populations from which the enrollments come than the 18 to 21-year-old group. This process is admittedly an approximation, but suggests that the Office of Education enrollment projections are too low.

Table A-2 compares the Bureau of Census enrollments and the Office of

Education enrollments for the period 1960 to 1965 and indicates the percentages that the Office of Education figures are of those reported by the Census Bureau. The Census figures for total male enrollments, with some exceptions, and for full-time enrollments for each sex are higher than those of the Office of Education, while they are lower than the latter for female enrollments and markedly lower for part-time enrollments of each sex.

The contrast between the full-time and part-time comparisons presumably is due, in part, to a more exacting classification of full-time students by the Office of Education, but also results from failure to include significant numbers of part-time students in the Census count, in particular those of more than 34 years of age who are excluded from it. An attempt to approximate the number of older college students is included as a part of these projections.

Tables A-3, A-4, A-5, and A-6 carry on the process described through the projected years 1966–1975. Table A-7 presents the projected enrollments obtained in this paper and the comparable ones from the Office of Education. Comparisons of projected enrollments with those of the Office of Education show this total enrollment projection for 1970 is some 500,000 or about 7 per cent higher than that of the Office of Education, and for 1975 it is about 1,400,000 higher or some 16 per cent. Generally, the widening difference between these projections between 1970 and 1975 seems in large part due to the more rapid growth of the 22 to 34-year-old population during that period, from which a significant part of the enrollment is drawn, about 21 per cent as compared with 11.5 per cent for the 17 to 21-year-old population. As suggested earlier, the Office of Education projections do not give due weight to the significant contribution of these older age groups.

As compared with the latest projection of male enrollments by the Bureau of the Census, the figure in this Appendix is slightly lower in 1966, is 300,000 higher than the Census Bureau's Series 1 figure and 100,000 higher than its Series 2 in 1970. In 1975, this projection is 300,000 higher than that of the Census Bureau's Series 1 and 800,000 higher than Series 2. As previously stated, the Bureau's Series 2 figures are quite close to those of the Office of Education. The 1970 and 1975 differences between these projections of male enrollments and those of the Census Bureau as published in Series P-25, No. 338, are somewhat higher, and that bulletin's Series B-2 is below that of the Office of Education. Actually the Census bulletin contains two sets of projections, the second set based on lower projected fertility rates, but for the college age groups up to 1975, the two sets are identical. Even the higher of the Census projections of female enrollments is well below that of the Office of Education for the entire 1966 to 1975 period and, of course, even further below that of this Appendix. By 1975, that projection is 900,000 or over 20 per cent below this Appendix figure and 400,000 or over 10 per cent below that of the Office of Education. Such differences arise naturally from the fact that, except for 1965, the Census female enrollment figures were consistently below those of the Office of Education in all recent years used as a projection base.

PROJECTION OF BACHELOR'S, MASTER'S, AND DOCTOR'S DEGREES

Bachelor's degrees were projected from a base of the age group 21 to 25, which provides the bulk of college graduates. The percentage of the age group obtaining a bachelor's degree has increased about .6 of one per cent a year during the past decade for both men and women; and the projections assume this annual rate of increase for the next decade. The degree projections were also compared with the separately projected entering college freshmen four years earlier; this check indicated that the two projections were consistent with each other. The first-level degree projections presented here differ from those of the Office of Education because professional degrees that usually follow the bachelor's degree (law, social work, medicine, and so forth) are excluded from the first-level degree group, although the Office of Education classifies them as first professional degrees and counts them as first-level degrees. This means that an individual obtaining a first-level degree and then a first professional degree gets counted twice as a first-level degree recipient by the Office of Education.

The projected total number of bachelor's degrees was subdivided into fields by projecting the trend in the percentage of degrees awarded in each field and applying these percentages to the projected total enrollment. The classification of fields generally follows the Office of Education system, with exceptions as noted in the tables.

At the master's degree level the projections are based on the output of bachelor's degrees in the appropriate preceding years. The definition of "appropriate" is the key problem, since the persons completing an advanced degree in any particular year will have started their graduate work from one to as much as 20 or 30 years earlier.

Actual distributions of year of completion of the bachelor's degree for a given year's master's degree graduates was used to develop weights to apply to each year's bachelor's graduates, proportional to the contribution of that year's graduates to the master's degrees of a given year. In this way a bachelor's degree base made up of parts of the graduating classes of several years is developed. To this weighted base is applied a percentage to allow for the proportion of graduates who go on to graduate school and subsequently complete an advanced degree. These completion proportions are shown for master's degrees in Tables A-18 and A-19; and for doctorates in Table A-23. The number of years that go into the base vary from field to field. For example, at the master's level in psychology, about 10 per cent of the M.A. graduates come from B.A.'s of the previous year, about 50 per cent come from the graduates two years previously, and another 20 per cent are drawn from the graduates three years earlier. Thus, 80 per cent of the graduates come from the preceding three years. In education,

TABLE A–1. *Opening Fall Degree-Credit Enrollments in Institutions of Higher Education (figures in 000's)*

Enrollment	1959	1960	1961	1962	1963	1964	1965	1970	1975
Total	3,377	3,583	3,861	4,175	4,495	4,950	5,526	7,299	8,995
Male	2,161	2,257	2,409	2,588	2,773	3,033	3,375	4,351	5,218
Female	1,216	1,326	1,452	1,588	1,722	1,917	2,152	2,949	3,777
Full-Time Total	2,314	2,466	2,714	2,902	3,068	3,418	3,911	5,116	6,269
Male	(1,503)	(1,570)	(1,711)	(1,807)	(1,896)	(2,096)	(2,410)	(3,081)	(3,660)
Female	(811)	(896)	(1,003)	(1,095)	(1,172)	(1,322)	(1,501)	(2,035)	(2,609)
Part-Time Total	1,063	1,117	1,147	1,273	1,426	1,532	1,615	2,183	2,725
Male	(658)	(687)	(698)	(781)	(870)	(920)	(950)	(1,271)	(1,550)
Female	(405)	(430)	(449)	(492)	(556)	(612)	(665)	(912)	(1,175)
Undergraduate Total	3,046	3,227	3,474	3,753	4,031	4,433	4,945	6,473	7,905
Male	1,924	2,004	2,135	2,290	2,446	2,670	2,966	3,774	4,464
Female	1,122	1,223	1,339	1,463	1,585	1,764	1,969	2,700	3,441
Full-Time Total	2,183	2,323	2,552	2,725	2,881	3,204	3,656	4,753	5,787
Part-Time Total	863	904	922	1,028	1,151	1,229	1,289	1,721	2,118
Graduate Total	331	356	386	422	464	517	582	826	1,090
Male	237	253	273	298	327	363	409	577	754
Female	94	103	113	124	137	154	173	249	336
Full-Time Total	131	143	162	177	188	214	254	363	482
Part-Time Total	200	213	224	245	276	303	328	462	608

SOURCE: Office of Education, *Projections of Educational Statistics, 1966 Edition*, Tables 4, 11, and 12. Full-time and part-time by sex (in parentheses), estimated from Comprehensive Report on Enrollments in Institutions of Higher Education, 1959–60; *Resident and Extension Enrollment in Institutions of Higher Education, Fall, 1961*; and for 1962–65 from *Opening Fall Enrollment—Higher Education, 1965*, Table 1; 1970 and 1975 consistent with these figures and sex breakdown of total enrollments for these years.

by contrast, less than 15 per cent of the graduates received their bachelor's degrees in the preceding three years.

The construction of these degree "bases" was done separately for each field. At the doctoral level, the necessary information on B.A.-Ph.D. time lag was obtained from the Doctoral Files of the National Academy of Sciences. At the master's level, the 1958 college graduate survey data of the Bureau of Social Science Research was used, and was checked for reasonableness against other surveys of the National Opinion Research Center. The broad base for the projections assures that the increases in the size of the base are not simply the "heaping" of candidates which will be followed by a decline in a year or two. The use of this technique shows how the expansion of our graduate schools has provided a great increase in the number of degree candidates, and the degree statistics are only now beginning to reflect this increased pool of students.

TABLE A–2. *College Enrollments as Reported by the Census Compared with Reports by the Office of Education (figures in 000's)*

Source and Group	1960	1961	1962	1963	1964	1965
Census,[a] Total	3,570	3,731	4,208	4,336	4,643	5,675
Office of Education,[b] Total	3,583	3,861	4,175	4,495	4,950	5,526
Census, Male	2,339	2,356	2,742	2,742	2,888	3,503
Office of Education, Male	2,257	2,409	2,588	2,773	3,033	3,375
Census, Female	1,231	1,375	1,466	1,594	1,755	2,172
Office of Education, Female	1,326	1,452	1,588	1,722	1,917	2,152
Census, Total, full-time	2,681	2,902	3,237	3,260	3,556	4,414
Off. of Ed., Total, full-time	2,466	2,714	2,902	3,068	3,418	3,911
Census, Male, full-time	1,713	1,796	2,022	2,048	2,187	2,748
Off. of Ed., Male, full-time	1,570	1,711	1,807	1,896	2,096	2,410
Census, Female, full-time	968	1,106	1,215	1,212	1,369	1,666
Off. of Ed., Female, full-time	896	1,003	1,095	1,172	1,322	1,501
Census, Total, part-time	887	830	971	1,076	1,087	1,261
Off. of Ed., Total, part-time	1,117	1,147	1,273	1,426	1,532	1,615
Census, Male, part-time	625	559	720	694	701	755
Off. of Ed., Male, part-time	687	698	781	870	920	950
Census, Female, part-time	262	271	251	382	386	506
Off. of Ed., Female, part-time	430	449	492	556	612	665
Ratio of Census to Office of Education						
Male, full-time	91.5	95.3	89.0	92.5	95.8	87.7
Female, full-time	92.6	90.7	90.0	97.7	96.6	90.0
Male, part-time	110.0	125.0	108.5	125.4	131.2	126.0
Female, part-time	164.0	165.0	196.0	146.0	159.0	131.0
Total, Male	96.4	102.3	94.4	101.3	105.0	96.3
Total, Female	107.7	106.0	108.3	108.0	109.2	99.2
Total	100.4	103.5	99.2	103.7	106.6	97.4

[a] Census P-20—School Enrollments (generally Table 7).
[b] Office of Education, *Projections of Educational Statistics*, 1966 Edition. Full-time and part-time and sex breakdown from Table 1.

382 / *Projections of Enrollments and Degrees*

TABLE A–3. *Projections of Full-Time Male Enrollments (figures in 000's)*

Age	1966	1967	1968	1969	1970	1971	1972	1973	1974	1975
17										
Population	1,787[a]	1,793	1,843	1,898	1,959	2,002	2,048	2,071	2,115	2,125
Percentage	6.70[b]	6.82	6.94	7.06	7.18	7.30	7.42	7.54	7.66	7.78
Enrollment	120	122	128	134	141	146	152	156	162	165
18 to 19										
Population	3,667	3,584	3,587	3,642	3,748	3,863	3,967	4,056	4,125	4,192
Percentage	29.4	30.2	31.0	31.8	32.6	33.4	34.2	35.0	35.8	36.6
Enrollment	1,080	1,080	1,110	1,160	1,220	1,290	1,355	1,420	1,475	1,530
20 to 21										
Population	2,947	3,409	3,675	3,593	3,595	3,651	3,756	3,871	3,975	4,064
Percentage	23.40	24.05	24.70	25.35	26.00	26.65	27.30	28.05	28.70	29.35
Enrollment	90	785	905	910	935	975	1,028	1,088	1,140	1,190
22 to 24										
Population	4,264	4,312	4,475	4,840	5,222	5,384	5,407	5,459	5,569	5,734
Percentage	10.4	10.8	11.2	11.6	12.0	12.4	12.8	13.2	13.6	14.0
Enrollment	445	465	500	560	627	668	692	722	755	800
25 to 29										
Population	5,834	6,111	6,460	6,735	6,983	7,271	7,777	8,103	8,484	8,864
Percentage	3.5	3.7	3.9	4.1	4.3	4.5	4.7	4.9	5.1	5.3
Enrollment	204	224	255	275	300	327	365	396	433	470
30 to 34										
Population	5,433	5,448	5,518	5,612	5,700	5,879	6,154	6,500	6,771	7,019
Percentage	0.71	0.72	0.73	0.74	0.75	0.76	0.77	0.78	0.79	0.80
Enrollment	39	39	40	42	43	45	47	51	54	56
Total Enrollment	2,578	2,715	2,938	3,081	3,266	3,451	3,639	3,833	4,019	4,211

[a] Unpublished Census tabulations.
[b] This percentage is the 1964–1965 average plus one and one-half times the increment.

TABLE A–4. *Projections of Full-Time Female Enrollments (figures in 000's)*

Age	1966	1967	1968	1969	1970	1971	1972	1973	1974	1975
17										
Population	1,730[a]	1,735	1,785	1,835	1,900	1,935	1,980	2,000	2,042	2,060
Percentage	6.9[b]	6.9	6.9	6.9	6.9	6.9	6.9	6.9	6.9	6.9
Enrollment	119	120	123	127	131	134	137	138	141	142
18 to 19										
Population	3,580	3,500	3,496	3,540	3,650	3,760	3,870	3,950	4,000	4,065
Percentage	25.5	26.5	27.5	28.5	29.5	30.5	31.5	32.5	33.5	34.5
Enrollment	910	938	960	1,010	1,073	1,145	1,220	1,280	1,340	1,400
20 to 21										
Population	2,900	3,340	3,600	3,510	3,510	3,560	3,670	3,770	3,880	3,970
Percentage	16.0	17.0	18.0	19.0	20.0	21.0	22.0	23.0	24.0	25.0
Enrollment	473	568	648	667	702	747	807	870	930	992
22 to 24										
Population	4,235	4,275	4,425	4,780	5,160	5,320	5,350	5,400	5,500	5,650
Percentage	2.67	2.85	3.03	3.21	3.39	3.57	3.75	3.93	4.11	4.29
Enrollment	113	122	134	153	175	190	204	212	226	242
25 to 29										
Population	5,865	6,145	6,450	6,720	6,970	7,255	7,760	8,140	8,415	8,790
Percentage	0.55	0.59	0.63	0.67	0.71	0.75	0.79	0.83	0.87	0.91
Enrollment	32	36	41	45	50	55	62	68	73	80
30 to 34										
Population	5,500	5,520	5,573	5,668	5,757	5,938	6,216	6,535	6,805	7,055
Percentage	0.26	0.27	0.28	0.29	0.30	0.31	0.32	0.33	0.34	0.35
Enrollment	14	15	16	16	17	18	20	21	23	25
Total Enrollment	1,661	1,799	1,922	2,018	2,148	2,289	2,450	2,589	2,733	2,881

[a] Unpublished Census tabulations for males adjusted to female populations according to Series P-25, No. 345, Table 4.

[b] This percentage generally is the 1964–1965 average plus one and one-half times the increment.

TABLE A–5. *Projections of Part-Time Male Enrollments (figures in 000's)*

Age	1966	1967	1968	1969	1970	1971	1972	1973	1974	1975
17										
Population	1,787[a]	1,793	1,843	1,898	1,959	2,002	2,048	2,071	2,115	2,125
Percentage	0.60[b]	0.60	0.60	0.60	0.60	0.60	0.60	0.60	0.60	0.60
Enrollment	11	11	11	11	12	12	12	12	13	13
18 to 19										
Population	3,667	3,584	3,587	3,642	3,748	3,863	3,967	4,056	4,125	4,192
Percentage	2.5	2.6	2.7	2.8	2.9	3.0	3.1	3.2	3.3	3.4
Enrollment	92	93	97	102	109	116	123	130	136	142
20 to 21										
Population	2,947	3,409	3,675	3,593	3,595	3,651	3,756	3,871	3,975	4,064
Percentage	4.10	4.35	4.60	4.85	5.10	5.35	5.60	5.85	6.10	6.35
Enrollment	121	148	169	174	183	195	210	226	242	258
22 to 24										
Population	4,264	4,312	4,475	4,840	5,222	5,384	5,407	5,459	5,569	5,734
Percentage	5.9	6.3	6.7	7.1	7.5	7.9	8.3	8.7	9.1	9.5
Enrollment	252	272	300	343	392	425	449	475	506	545
25 to 29										
Population	5,834	6,111	6,460	6,735	6,983	7,271	7,777	8,103	8,484	8,864
Percentage	5.0	5.1	5.2	5.3	5.4	5.5	5.6	5.7	5.8	5.9
Enrollment	292	312	336	356	377	400	435	461	492	524
30 to 34										
Population	5,433	5,448	5,518	5,612	5,700	5,879	6,154	6,500	6,771	7,019
Percentage	3.60	3.77	3.94	4.11	4.28	4.45	4.62	4.79	4.96	5.13
Enrollment	195	205	217	231	244	257	286	311	336	360
35+										
Enrollment	84	88	92	96	100	105	110	115	120	125
Total Enrollment	1,047	1,129	1,212	1,313	1,417	1,510	1,625	1,730	1,845	1,967

[a] Unpublished Census tabulations.
[b] This percentage is the 1964–1965 average plus one and one-half times the increment.

TABLE A–6. *Projections of Part-Time Female Enrollments (figures in 000's)*

Age	1966	1967	1968	1969	1970	1971	1972	1973	1974	1975
17										
Population	1,730[a]	1,735	1,785	1,835	1,900	1,935	1,980	2,000	2,042	2,060
Percentage	0.55[b]	0.56	0.57	0.58	0.59	0.60	0.61	0.62	0.63	0.64
Enrollment	10	10	10	11	11	12	12	12	13	14
18 to 19										
Population	3,580	3,500	3,496	3,540	3,650	3,760	3,870	3,950	4,000	4,065
Percentage	2.63	2.66	2.69	2.72	2.75	2.78	2.81	2.84	2.87	2.90
Enrollment	94	93	94	96	100	104	109	112	115	118
20 to 21										
Population	2,900	3,340	3,600	3,510	3,510	3,560	3,670	3,770	3,880	3,970
Percentage	4.25	4.55	4.85	5.15	5.45	5.75	6.05	6.35	6.65	6.95
Enrollment	127	152	174	181	191	205	222	239	258	277
22 to 24										
Population	4,235	4,275	4,425	4,780	5,160	5,320	5,350	5,400	5,500	5,650
Percentage	3.28	3.40	3.52	3.64	3.76	3.88	4.00	4.12	4.24	4.36
Enrollment	139	145	156	174	194	206	214	222	232	246
25 to 29										
Population	5,865	6,145	6,450	6,720	6,970	7,255	7,760	8,140	8,415	8,790
Percentage	2.70	2.86	3.02	3.18	3.34	3.50	3.66	3.82	3.98	4.14
Enrollment	158	175	194	214	232	254	284	310	335	362
30 to 34										
Population	5,500	5,520	5,573	5,668	5,757	5,938	6,216	6,535	6,805	7,055
Percentage	1.77	1.89	2.01	2.13	2.25	2.37	2.49	2.61	2.73	2.85
Enrollment	97	104	112	121	130	141	155	171	186	201
35+										
Enrollment	84	88	92	96	100	108	116	124	132	140
Total Enrollment	709	767	832	893	958	1,030	1,112	1,190	1,271	1,364

[a] Unpublished Census tabulations for males adjusted to female populations according to Series P-25, No. 345, Table 4.
[b] This percentage generally is the 1964–1965 average plus one and one-half times the increment.

TABLE A–7. *Projected Total Fall Enrollments in Institutions of Higher Education Compared with U.S. Office of Education Projections: 1966–1975 (figures in 000's)*

Enrollment	1966	1967	1968	1969	1970	1971	1972	1973	1974	1975
					This Study					
Total	5,995	6,410	6,904	7,305	7,789	8,280	8,826	9,342	9,868	10,423
Male	3,625	3,844	4,150	4,394	4,683	4,961	5,264	5,563	5,864	6,178
Female	2,370	2,566	2,754	2,911	3,106	3,319	3,562	3,779	4,004	4,245
Full-Time Total	4,239	4,514	4,860	5,099	5,414	5,470	6,089	6,422	6,752	7,092
Male	2,578	2,715	2,938	3,081	3,266	3,451	3,639	3,833	4,019	4,211
Female	1,661	1,799	1,922	2,018	2,148	2,289	2,450	2,589	2,733	2,881
Part-Time Total	1,756	1,896	2,044	2,206	2,375	2,540	2,737	2,920	3,116	3,331
Male	1,047	1,129	1,212	1,313	1,417	1,510	1,625	1,730	1,845	1,967
Female	709	767	832	893	958	1,030	1,112	1,190	1,271	1,364
					Office of Education[a]					
Total	6,055	6,541	6,923	7,050	7,299	7,604	7,976	8,335	8,684	8,995
Male	3,700	3,975	4,184	4,237	4,351	4,504	4,698	4,885	5,063	5,218
Female	2,355	2,566	2,379	2,813	2,949	3,099	3,278	3,450	3,621	3,777
Full-Time Total	4,265	4,602	4,866	4,948	5,116	5,323	5,577	5,823	6,059	6,269
Male	(2,640)[b]				(3,081)					(3,660)
Female	(1,625)				(2,035)					(2,609)
Part-Time Total	1,790	1,939	2,057	2,102	2,183	2,280	2,399	2,512	2,625	2,725
Male	(1,060)				(1,271)					(1,550)
Female	(730)				(912)					(1,175)

[a] *Projections of Educational Statistics to 1975–76*, 1966 Edition, Table 4.
[b] Estimated.

TABLE A–8. *Enrollments for First Professional Degrees Requiring Pre-professional Training (figures in 000's)*

Enrollment	Estimated Actual							Projected[d]	
	1959	1960	1961	1962	1963	1964	1965	1970	1975
Total[a]	133	135	139	145	151	161	171	207	243
Male[b]	116	118	122	127	132	141	149	180	211
Female[b]	17	17	17	18	19	20	22	27	32
Full-Time Total[c]	100	102	104	109	113	121	128	155	182
Male	88	89	91	95	99	106	112	135	159
Female	12	13	13	14	14	15	16	20	24
Part-Time Total[c]	33	33	35	36	38	40	43	52	61
Male	28	29	31	32	33	35	37	45	53
Female	5	4	4	4	5	5	6	7	9

[a] Sum of such enrollments (1959–1965) in law, medicine, theology, library science, social work, and business and commerce plus 10 per cent for other fields (health, education, and so forth). This sum for 1963 is 137.5 as compared with 151, or 10 per cent more, reported by the Office of Education (*Digest of Educational Statistics*, 1965 Edition, Table 55, p. 79), and this difference has been used for other years. Sources of these data for the first-named fields are *Review of Legal Education, 1964 to 1966; Journal of American Medical Association*, Nov. 21, 1966, Table 23, p. 68; *Dental Students' Register, 1961 to 1966* (one half of total given to exclude undergraduates); tabulations of American Association of Theological Schools and Dept. of Education; National Catholic Welfare Conference (basis of estimates); and *Summary Report, Students Enrolled for Master's and Higher Degrees*, Fall, 1964 (basis of estimates using also master's degree trends in library science, social work, and business administration).
[b] The 1963 sex breakdown reported in *Digest, op. cit.* (87.5 per cent male, 12.5 per cent female) has been used for other 1959–1965 years. It corresponds well with that estimated from specific field data.
[c] Estimated from data and general characteristics of students in specific fields as 75 per cent, full-time; 25 per cent, part-time.
[d] Straightline projection of 1960–1965 increments (rounded) in each series shown.

TABLE A–9. *Projected Full-Time and Part-Time Degree-Credit Enrollments, by Level of Study (figures in 000's)*

Enrollment	1966	1967	1968	1969	1970	1971	1972	1973	1974	1975
					Male					
Total	3,636	3,929	4,204	4,448	4,759	5,044	5,341	5,649	5,962	6,309
Full-Time	2,575	2,777	2,955	3,116	3,324	3,516	3,703	3,903	4,107	4,334
Part-Time	1,061	1,150	1,249	1,332	1,435	1,528	1,638	1,746	1,855	1,975
Undgr. Total	3,033	3,271	3,495	3,665	3,899	4,114	4,347	4,587	4,826	5,089
Full-Time	2,231	2,406	2,562	2,683	2,850	2,988	3,158	3,324	3,481	3,660
Part-Time	802	865	933	982	1,049	1,126	1,189	1,263	1,345	1,429
Grad. Total	448	495	541	609	680	744	802	863	931	1,009
Full-Time	227	250	271	302	334	368	400	433	472	515
Part-Time	221	245	270	307	346	376	402	430	459	494
Advcd. Prof. Total	155	161	168	174	180	186	192	199	205	211
Full-Time	117	121	126	131	135	140	145	149	154	159
Part-Time	39	40	42	43	45	46	48	49	51	53
					Female					
Total	2,371	2,565	2,762	2,920	3,122	3,319	3,555	3,774	4,007	4,242
Full-Time	1,666	1,791	1,930	2,021	2,165	2,300	2,449	2,600	2,749	2,904
Part-Time	705	774	832	889	957	1,019	1,106	1,174	1,258	1,338
Undgr. Total	2,166	2,340	2,516	2,651	2,829	3,004	3,212	3,406	3,611	3,818
Full-Time	1,589	1,704	1,834	1,947	2,050	2,172	2,312	2,454	2,595	2,740
Part-Time	577	636	682	714	779	832	900	952	1,016	1,078
Grad. Total	182	201	221	243	266	287	314	338	365	392
Full-Time	60	69	78	89	95	107	116	123	131	141
Part-Time	122	132	143	154	171	180	198	215	234	252
Advcd. Prof. Total	23	24	25	26	27	28	29	30	31	32
Full-Time	17	18	18	19	20	21	21	22	23	24
Part-Time	6	7	7	7	7	8	8	8	8	9

SOURCE: Total from Table A-7, advanced professional from Table A-8; projections are straightline trend projections.

TABLE A–10. *Summary: Projected Degree-Credit Enrollments in Institutions of Higher Education (figures in 000's)*

Enrollment	1966			1970			1975		
	Total	Male	Female	Total	Male	Female	Total	Male	Female
Total—CHR	6,007	3,636	2,371	7,881	4,759	3,122	10,551	6,309	4,242
Office of Educ.	6,055	3,703	2,352	7,299	4,351	2,949	8,995	5,218	3,777
Bur. of Census	—	—	—	7,105	4,517	2,588	9,120	5,792	3,329
Full-Time—CHR	4,241	2,575	1,666	5,489	3,324	2,165	7,238	4,334	2,904
Office of Educ.	4,265	(2,640)	(1,625)	5,116	(3,081)	(2,035)	6,269	(3,665)	(2,604)
Part-Time—CHR	1,766	1,061	705	2,392	1,435	957	3,313	1,975	1,338
Office of Educ.	1,790	(1,063)	(730)	2,183	(1,271)	(912)	2,725	(1,553)	(1,173)
Undergrad.—CHR	5,199	3,033	2,166	6,728	3,899	2,829	8,907	5,089	3,818
Office of Educ.	5,230	3,092	2,138	6,266	3,594	2,673	7,662	4,253	3,409
Graduate—CHR	630	448	182	946	680	266	1,401	1,009	392
Office of Educ.	647	456	191	826	577	249	1,090	754	336
Adv. Prof.—CHR	178	155	23	207	180	27	243	211	32
Office of Educ.	—	—	—	—	—	—	—	—	—
Undrg.-F.T.—CHR	3,820	2,231	1,589	4,900	2,850	2,050	6,400	3,660	2,740
Office of Educ.	3,849	(2,304)	(1,545)	4,598	(2,669)	(1,929)	5,605	(3,145)	(2,460)
Undrg.-P.T.—CHR	1,379	802	577	1,828	1,049	779	2,507	1,429	1,078
Office of Educ.	1,381	(788)	(593)	1,669	(925)	(744)	2,057	(1,108)	949
Grad.-F.T.—CHR	288	227	60	434	329	95	656	515	941
Office of Educ.	283	(217)	(66)	363	(274)	(90)	482	(356)	(126)
Grad.-P.T.—CHR	342	221	122	512	341	171	745	494	251
Office of Educ.	364	(239)	(125)	462	(303)	(159)	608	(398)	(210)
Adv. Prof.-F.T.—CHR	133	117	17	155	135	20	182	159	24
Office of Educ.	—	—	—	—	—	—	—	—	—
Adv. Prof.-P.T.—CHR	45	39	6	52	45	7	61	53	9
Office of Educ.	—	—	—	—	—	—	—	—	—

SOURCE: Previous tables except Office of Education figures by sex in parentheses, which are estimated.
CHR stands for Commission on Human Resources.
F.T. means full-time and P.T., part-time.

TABLE A–11. *First-Time Enrollments—Male, Compared with High School Graduates and Age Groups (000's omitted)*

Year	(a) First-Time Enrollments	(b) High School Graduates	(c) Per Cent (a)/(b)	(d) Average of 17 and 18-Year-Olds, on Oct. 1	(e) Per Cent (a)/(d)	(f) Composite of 30%—17, 50%—18, and 20%—19-Year-Olds	(g) Per Cent (a)/(f)
1954	354[a]	615	57.6	1,081	32.7	1,074	32.8
1955	366	648	56.5	1,111	33.0	1,081	34.0
1956	397	682	58.3	1,142	34.8	1,124	35.3
1957	407	696	58.5	1,163	34.9	1,148	35.5
1958	440	729	60.5	1,210	36.4	1,177	37.4
1959	478	790	60.5	1,301	36.7	1,238	38.5
1960	540	898	60.2	1,410	38.3	1,348	40.1
1961	592	958	61.8	1,433	41.2	1,424	41.5
1962	598	941	63.4	1,405	42.5	1,418	42.2
1963	604	959	62.9	1,466	41.0	1,402	43.0
1964	706	1,121	63.0	1,698	41.7	1,546	45.8
1965	835	1,315	63.5	1,824	45.8	1,752	47.6
				Projected			
1966	809	1,334	60.5	1,777	45.5	1,803	47.8
1967	810	1,341	60.2	1,781	45.5	1,775	49.1
1968	823	1,353	60.7	1,806	45.5	1,785	50.3
1969	857	1,384	61.9	1,857	46.1	1,822	51.6
1970	902	1,450	62.2	1,913	47.2	1,877	52.8
1971	945	1,512	62.4	1,962	48.1	1,930	54.1
1972	984	1,569	62.5	2,004	49.0	1,978	55.3
1973	1,018	1,619	63.8	2,035	50.0	2,014	56.6
1974	1,052	1,669	63.1	2,065	51.0	2,045	57.8

[a] Adjusted for Korean War veterans 1954–1959. See "Projections of Earned Degrees and Graduate Enrollments." NSF, 1962 unpublished Appendix Table 2.

SOURCE: Age groups, from Census *Current Population Reports*, Series P-25, No. 310 and No. 286. High School Graduates, from Office of Education *Projections of College Enrollments to 1975–76*.

TABLE A–12. *First-Time Enrollments—Female, Compared with High School Graduates and Age Groups (000's omitted)*

Year	(a) First-Time Enrollments	(b) High School Graduates	(c) Per Cent (a)/(b)	(d) Average of 17 and 18- Year-Olds, on Oct. 1	(e) Per Cent (a)/(d)	(f) Composite of 30%—17, 50%—18, and 20%— 19-Year-Olds	(g) Per Cent (a)/(f)
1954	243	667	36.4	1,070	22.5	1,063	22.8
1955	254	703	36.2	1,096	23.2	1,084	23.4
1956	275	739	37.2	1,136	25.1	1,113	24.7
1957	282	750	37.6	1,142	24.6	1,129	25.0
1958	310	784	40.1	1,188	26.1	1,164	26.6
1959	334	849	39.4	1,274	26.2	1,227	27.2
1960	384	966	40.0	1,379	27.8	1,343	28.4
1961	426	1,013	42.0	1,400	30.5	1,402	30.4
1962	432	984	44.0	1,371	31.5	1,379	31.4
1963	442	991	44.6	1,428	31.0	1,370	32.2
1964	528	1,169	45.1	1,647	32.0	1,555	33.8
1965	618	1,353	45.6	1,768	35.0	1,736	35.6
				Projected			
1966	621	1,366	45.5	1,725	36.0	1,738	36.0
1967	630	1,369	46.0	1,726	36.5	1,721	37.1
1968	647	1,378	47.0	1,751	36.8	1,735	38.2
1969	671	1,402	47.9	1,802	37.2	1,777	39.3
1970	712	1,464	48.6	1,860	38.2	1,833	40.4
1971	754	1,525	49.4	1,910	39.5	1,889	41.5
1972	792	1,575	50.5	1,947	40.7	1,932	42.6
1973	824	1,618	50.9	1,977	41.5	1,963	43.7
1974	859	1,663	51.6	2,011	42.6	1,996	44.8

SOURCE: See Table A–11.

TABLE A–13. *Estimated Distributions of Male College Entrants, by Intelligence Test Score Ranges in 1953 and 1973 for Two Different Assumptions About Enrollment Rates (figures in 000's)*

	Population of College Entry Age		Actual Entrants			Projected College Entrants					
			1953—33 Per Cent of Age Gr. Entrants			Low			High		
						1973—50 Per Cent of Age Gr. Entrants			1973—55 Per Cent of Age Gr. Entrants		
	Number	Per Cent of Total	Number	Per Cent of Age Gr.	Per Cent of C.E.	Number	Per Cent of Age Gr.	Per Cent of C.E.	Number	Per Cent of Age Gr.	Per Cent of C.E.
Total	2,035	100	680	33	100	1,020	50	100	1,120	55	100
AGCT Score											
less than 95	815	40	70	9	10	100[a]	12	10	110[a]	14	10
95 +	1,220	60	610[a]	50	90	920	75	90	1,010	83	90
95 to 102	305	15	90	30	13	90	30	9	190	62	17
102 to 117	530	26	240	45	35	450	85	44	450	85	40
118 +	385	19	280	73	41	370	95	36	370	95	33

[a] *America's Resources of Specialized Talent*, Appendix G2. Percentages of age groups attending college applied to 1973 population to provide total estimated entrants. These estimated total entrants can be compared with the 1,024,000 first-time-in-college students in Table 5 of *Projections of Educational Statistics to 1976–77*, U.S. Office of Education, OE 10030-67, Government Printing Office, Washington, 1968. Ability distribution of college entrants based on assumptions that 10 per cent of male college entrants will fall below a score of 95 on the Army General Classification Test (AGCT, which was the Intelligence Test used) as in 1953, but that 95 per cent of the AGCT group 118 and above and 85 per cent of those 102 to 117 will enter college. C.E. means College Entrants.

SOURCE: For projected age group data, see Bureau of the Census, *Current Population Reports*, Series P-25, No. 388.

TABLE A-14. *Estimated Distributions of College Graduates Intelligence Test Score Ranges in 1955, 1975, and 1985, by Sex (figures in 000's)*

| | Population of College Graduation Age | | College Graduates | | | | | | | | |
| | | | 1955 | | | 1975 | | | 1985 | | |
	Number	Per Cent of Total	Number of Grads.	Per Cent of Age Group	Per Cent of All Grads.	Number of Grads.	Per Cent of Age Group	Per Cent of All Grads.	Number of Grads.	Per Cent of Age Group	Per Cent of All Grads.
Males											
Total	1,890[a]	100	284	15[a]	100	510	27[a]	100	622	33[a]	100
AGCT Score											
Less than 100	945	50[b]	23	2	8[b]	41[c]	4[c]	8[c]	50[c]	5[c]	8[c]
100 to 109	360	19	48	13	17	90	25	18	156	43	25
110 to 119	283	15	71	25	25	142	50	28	170	60	27
120 to 129	170	9	68	40	24	119	70	23	128	75	21
130 +	132	7	74	56	26	118	90	23	118	90	19
Females											
Total	1,870[a]	100	187	10[a]	100	410	22[a]	100	513	28[a]	100
AGCT Score											
Less than 100	935	50[b]	15	2	8[b]	33[c]	4[c]	8[c]	41[c]	4[c]	8[c]
100 to 109	355	19	32	9	17	96	31	23	126	35	25
110 to 119	280	15	47	17	25	112	40	27	140	50	27
120 to 129	168	9	45	27	24	84	50	20	101	60	20
130 +	131	7	49	37	26	85	65	21	105	80	20

[a] Age group numbers from Tables 8a and 8b, column (e) also (rounded) percentages of total college graduates within the age group for 1955 and 1975 and as further projected for 1985 (annual increment 0.6 per cent).

[b] America's Resources of Specialized Talent, Appendix Table G2 with percentages applied to 1975 population group (21- to 25-year-olds). Percentage distributions for combined sexes from that table assumed to apply to both males and females in age group, among college graduates. The Intelligence Test used is the Army General Classification Test.

[c] The figures in these columns are based on the assumption that the percentage of college graduates with AGCT scores below 100 will remain constant at 8 per cent of their total but that the percentages of graduates from the 110 to 119, 120 to 129, and 130+ ranges within the corresponding ranges of the age group were increased to the levels shown for 1975 and 1985, leading to the numbers and percentages of the graduates' total in the adjoining columns. The numbers and percentages of the graduates for the 100 to 109 range then are those remaining.

TABLE A–15. *First-Level Degrees—Males (figures in 000's)*

Year	Total[a]	Engrg.	Math.	Phys. Sci.[b]	Bio. Sci.[c]	Agric. and For.	Soc. Sci.	Psych.	Arts[d] and Hum.	Educ.[e]	Bus. and Comm.	Other
1956	178	26.2	3.1	11.1	10.1	6.0	27.3	3.1	20.8	19.9	36.6	14.2
1957	200	31.1	3.8	12.4	11.3	6.5	30.4	3.5	22.4	23.3	41.1	14.2
1958	219	35.2	5.0	14.1	12.0	6.7	33.8	4.1	22.3	25.6	45.4	14.8
1959	230	38.0	6.5	15.3	12.3	6.7	34.4	4.5	22.9	26.3	47.0	16.1
1960	230	37.7	8.3	15.8	12.6	6.2	35.2	4.8	24.0	26.2	45.7	13.7
1961	230	35.7	9.5	15.1	12.7	5.6	36.9	5.1	24.3	25.7	44.8	14.4
1962	236	34.6	10.4	15.5	13.1	5.8	39.4	5.8	25.6	26.3	46.0	13.1
1963	247	33.3	11.2	15.9	14.8	5.9	44.1	6.5	28.3	26.2	47.5	13.7
1964	272	35.1	12.7	17.1	17.4	6.1	51.5	7.8	32.0	26.7	52.2	13.0
1965	290	36.7	13.1	17.7	18.9	6.6	55.9	8.7	35.0	28.2	55.6	13.8
						Projected						
1966	295	36.6	13.3	17.7	19.8	6.5	59.0	8.9	36.0	28.0	56.1	13.3
1967	314	36.4	14.4	18.8	21.7	6.8	64.7	9.8	38.9	29.2	59.3	13.8
1968	361	39.7	17.0	21.6	25.6	7.6	75.8	11.6	45.5	32.9	67.9	15.2
1969	398	43.4	19.1	23.9	28.7	8.2	85.2	13.2	50.5	35.4	74.4	16.3
1970	418	45.1	20.5	25.1	30.1	8.4	90.3	14.2	53.5	36.4	77.7	16.7
1971	422	45.6	21.1	25.3	30.8	8.2	92.0	15.1	54.4	36.3	78.1	15.2
1972	464	50.1	23.2	27.8	33.9	8.8	101.6	16.9	60.3	39.4	85.4	16.7
1973	476	51.4	23.8	28.6	35.2	8.8	104.7	17.6	61.9	40.5	87.1	16.7
1974	499	53.9	25.0	29.9	36.9	9.0	110.3	18.7	64.9	41.9	90.8	17.5
1975	518	55.9	25.9	31.1	38.9	9.3	115.0	19.7	67.3	43.5	93.8	17.6

[a] First-level degrees include bachelor's and first professional degrees except professional degrees in such fields as law, medicine, and so forth, which actually are second-level degrees granted to persons previously counted in the bachelor's and first professional degree figures. This adjustment affects the columns for Social Sciences (social work degrees), Business and Commerce (M.B.A. degrees), and Other (degrees in medicine, law, and so forth).

[b] Includes geography and one-half Science-General Program in Office of Education reports.

[c] Includes one-half Sciences-General Program in Office of Education reports.

[d] Includes English and Journalism, Fine Arts, Architecture, Foreign Languages, Philosophy, Arts General Program, and Arts and Sciences General Program in Office of Education annual degree reports.

[e] As shown in Office of Education annual degree reports, which include education majors in certain special fields counted instead within those fields in its *Projections of Educational Statistics.*

SOURCE: Projections of degrees described in the text.

TABLE A–16. *First-Level Degrees—Females (figures in 000's)*

Year	Total[a]	Math.	Phys. Sci.[b]	Bio. Sci.[c]	Soc. Sci.	Psych.	Arts[d] and Hum.	Educ.[e]	Bus. and Comm.	Health	Other
1956	109	1.5	1.8	3.1	11.5	2.6	19.9	50.7	4.1	7.2	6.4
1957	115	1.7	1.9	3.3	11.2	2.7	20.6	54.4	3.9	7.8	7.2
1958	120	2.0	1.9	3.4	12.8	2.9	21.2	57.3	4.0	8.3	6.0
1959	127	2.5	2.1	3.8	13.5	2.9	22.8	61.8	4.1	8.6	4.7
1960	136	3.1	2.4	4.2	14.8	3.3	24.3	64.0	3.9	8.9	6.9
1961	143	3.6	2.4	4.5	15.4	3.4	27.2	66.7	3.8	8.9	6.6
1962	155	4.3	2.6	5.1	17.9	3.8	30.8	71.3	4.0	8.9	6.3
1963	172	5.0	2.7	5.7	21.5	4.6	35.7	76.6	4.2	9.3	6.4
1964	198	6.0	3.0	6.8	25.6	5.5	42.6	85.8	4.6	10.4	7.7
1965	215	6.4	3.2	7.8	28.6	6.0	47.4	91.0	5.1	11.5	8.1
					Projected						
1966	227	6.8	3.3	8.6	31.3	6.5	51.1	94.4	5.3	11.4	8.2
1967	236	7.1	3.4	9.2	33.5	6.9	54.3	96.5	5.4	11.3	8.3
1968	290	8.8	4.1	11.5	42.3	8.7	67.9	116.6	6.5	13.6	9.9
1969	315	9.6	4.4	12.8	46.9	9.6	75.0	124.7	6.9	14.5	10.7
1970	326	9.9	4.6	13.4	49.6	10.1	78.9	127.1	7.0	14.7	10.8
1971	331	10.1	4.6	13.7	51.0	10.5	81.1	127.4	7.0	14.9	10.6
1972	352	10.7	4.9	14.7	54.9	11.3	87.3	134.1	7.3	15.5	11.3
1973	368	11.2	5.2	15.5	58.1	11.9	92.4	138.7	7.5	16.2	11.8
1974	389	11.9	5.4	16.5	61.9	12.7	98.4	145.1	7.9	17.1	12.1
1975	409	12.5	5.7	17.4	65.4	13.5	104.3	151.3	8.2	18.0	12.7

SOURCE: See Table A–15 for explanation of notes.

[396]

TABLE A–17. *First-Level Degrees—Total (figures in 000's)*

Year	Total[a]	Engrg.	Math.	Phys.[b] Sci.	Bio.[c] Sci.	Agri. & For.	Soc. Sci.	Psych.	Arts[d] & Hum.	Educ.[e]	Bus. & Comm.	Health	Other
1956	287	26.2	4.6	12.9	13.2	6.0	38.8	5.7	40.7	70.6	40.7	7.2	20.6
1957	315	31.1	5.5	14.3	14.6	6.5	41.6	6.2	43.0	77.7	45.0	7.8	21.4
1958	339	35.2	7.0	16.0	15.4	6.7	46.6	7.0	43.5	82.9	49.4	8.3	20.8
1959	357	38.0	9.0	17.4	16.1	6.7	47.9	7.4	45.7	88.1	51.1	8.6	20.8
1960	366	37.7	11.4	18.2	16.8	6.2	50.0	8.1	48.3	90.2	49.6	8.9	20.6
1961	373	35.7	13.1	17.5	17.2	5.6	52.3	8.5	51.5	92.4	48.6	8.9	21.0
1962	391	34.6	14.7	18.1	18.2	5.8	53.3	9.6	56.4	97.6	50.0	8.9	19.4
1963	419	33.3	16.2	18.6	20.5	5.9	65.6	11.1	64.0	102.8	51.7	9.3	20.1
1964	470	35.1	18.7	20.1	24.2	6.1	77.1	13.3	74.6	112.5	56.8	10.4	20.7
1965	505	36.7	19.5	20.9	26.7	6.6	84.5	14.7	82.4	119.2	60.7	11.5	21.9
Projected													
1966	522	36.6	20.1	21.0	28.4	6.5	90.3	15.4	87.1	122.4	61.4	11.4	21.5
1967	550	36.4	21.5	22.2	30.9	6.8	98.2	16.7	93.2	125.7	64.7	11.3	22.1
1968	651	39.7	25.8	25.7	37.1	7.6	118.1	20.3	113.4	149.5	74.4	13.6	25.1
1969	713	43.4	28.7	28.3	41.5	8.2	132.1	22.8	125.5	160.1	81.3	14.5	27.0
1970	744	45.1	30.4	29.7	43.5	8.4	139.9	24.3	132.4	163.5	84.7	14.7	27.5
1971	753	45.6	31.2	29.9	44.5	8.2	143.0	25.6	135.5	163.7	85.1	14.9	25.8
1972	816	50.1	33.9	32.7	48.6	8.8	156.5	28.2	145.6	173.5	92.7	15.5	28.0
1973	844	51.4	35.0	33.8	50.7	8.8	162.8	29.5	154.3	179.2	94.6	16.2	28.5
1974	888	53.9	36.9	35.3	53.4	9.0	172.2	31.4	163.3	187.0	98.7	17.1	29.6
1975	927	55.9	38.4	36.8	56.3	9.3	180.4	33.2	171.6	194.8	102.0	18.0	30.3

SOURCE: See Table A–15 for explanation of notes.

TABLE A–18. *Percentage That Master's Degrees Are of First-Level Base of Degrees in the Field—Males*

Year	Engrg.	Math.	Phys. Sci.	Bio. Sci.	Agri. & For.	Soc. Sci.	Psych.	Arts. & Hum.	Educ.	Bus.[a] & Comm.	Other[b]	Combined Fields
1957	19.3	24.0	23.3	13.7	14.3	11.7	23.2	16.1	76.7	8.9	7.1	20.3
1958	21.7	30.0	25.8	14.4	14.3	12.8	26.2	18.3	77.1	10.5	5.2	22.3
1959	24.7	34.0	27.1	15.2	15.4	13.0	25.2	19.5	80.1	11.0	5.9	24.4
1960	24.6	36.0	27.2	16.0	15.9	13.1	26.0	20.4	86.2	11.3	5.9	25.9
1961	26.4	37.0	28.4	17.1	16.6	13.5	28.6	21.5	86.9	11.1	5.2	26.8
1962	27.4	38.0	28.6	18.9	19.0	14.6	28.4	22.4	88.5	12.1	5.0	28.2
1963	28.5	39.0	29.0	19.3	18.6	15.8	27.8	24.8	88.0	12.7	4.8	29.0
1964	31.9	37.0	31.4	21.6	20.4	16.6	25.1	25.5	89.0	13.7	4.9	30.4
1965	34.2	37.0	32.9	21.8	21.2	17.0	24.7	26.2	90.5	15.7	5.4	32.1
Projected												
1966	36.7	37.0	34.3	22.7	22.0	17.6	24.3	27.0	91.0	16.5	5.3	33.1
1967	39.2	37.0	35.7	23.6	22.8	18.4	24.0	27.8	91.4	17.3	5.3	34.0
1968	41.5	37.0	36.8	24.3	23.4	18.9	24.0	28.4	91.7	17.9	5.3	34.8
1969	43.8	37.0	37.9	25.0	24.0	19.4	24.5	29.0	91.9	18.5	5.3	35.5
1970	45.9	37.0	38.7	25.5	24.4	19.8	25.0	29.4	92.0	18.9	5.3	36.1
1971	48.0	37.0	39.5	26.0	24.8	20.2	25.5	29.8	92.0	19.3	5.3	36.6
1972	49.9	37.0	40.0	26.3	25.1	20.5	26.0	30.1	92.0	19.6	5.3	37.0
1973	51.8	37.0	40.5	26.6	25.4	20.8	26.5	30.4	92.0	19.9	5.3	37.3
1974	53.5	37.0	40.8	26.8	25.6	21.0	27.0	30.6	92.0	20.1	5.3	37.5
1975	55.2	37.0	41.1	27.0	25.8	21.2	27.5	30.8	92.0	20.3	5.3	37.6

[a] As reported by Office of Education. If all M.B.A. degrees are included, percentages would be 13.2 for 1957; 22.2 for 1965; and projected to 28.0 for 1970 and 30.4 for 1975.

[b] Percentage of other fields to all fields total, 1957–1965 average of 5.3 projected.

SOURCE: Commission projections. First-level base is made up of cohorts of bachelor's graduates from several earlier years.

TABLE A-19. *Percentage That Master's Degrees Are of First-Level Base of Degrees in the Field—Females*

Year	Percentages of First-Level Base						Percentages of Male Master's Degrees			Basis as Noted	
	Bio. Sciences	Social Sciences	Psych.	Arts & Humanities	Educ.	All Fields	Math.	Phys. Sciences	Bus. & Comm.	Health[a]	Other[b]
1957	10.6	7.8	12.7	11.2	48.9	20.2	24.2	9.2	3.9	—	4.55
1958	12.0	7.9	15.4	11.9	46.2	20.5	24.2	10.6	3.7	—	6.10
1959	14.4	8.0	14.8	13.5	43.1	20.7	26.2	10.7	3.7	10.4	5.10
1960	14.6	8.1	15.4	14.8	41.7	21.0	24.1	11.4	3.7	10.0	5.15
1961	16.2	8.3	18.6	16.4	38.0	20.7	26.4	10.9	3.3	8.6	5.43
1962	18.2	10.6	18.1	17.8	37.7	21.4	23.1	11.3	3.4	7.8	5.29
1963	19.8	11.1	17.3	18.5	37.4	21.9	24.6	12.2	3.8	9.7	4.47
1964	20.0	11.3	18.6	20.2	38.2	23.0	23.4	10.8	3.2	11.4	5.35
1965	21.3	11.3	17.0	20.7	39.0	23.8	24.2	12.4	3.3	12.5	5.28
Projected											
1966	22.2	11.5	17.0	21.5	39.6	24.5	24.5	12.7	3.3	13.3	5.30
1967	23.1	11.5	17.3	22.3	40.2	25.2	24.8	13.0	3.3	14.1	5.30
1968	23.9	11.6	17.3	22.9	40.7	25.7	25.1	13.3	3.3	14.7	5.30
1969	24.7	11.6	17.6	23.5	41.2	26.2	25.4	13.6	3.3	15.3	5.30
1970	25.3	11.7	17.6	23.9	41.6	26.5	25.7	13.9	3.3	15.7	5.30
1971	25.9	11.7	17.9	24.3	42.0	26.8	26.0	14.2	3.3	16.1	5.30
1972	26.4	11.7	17.9	24.6	42.3	27.0	26.3	14.5	3.3	16.4	5.30
1973	26.9	11.8	18.2	24.9	42.6	27.2	26.6	14.8	3.3	16.7	5.30
1974	27.5	11.8	18.2	25.1	42.8	27.3	26.9	15.1	3.3	16.9	5.30
1975	27.7	11.8	18.5	25.3	43.0	27.4	27.2	15.4	3.3	17.1	5.30

[a] Percentage of first-level three years earlier.
[b] Percentage of numbers (female) in all fields.

SOURCE: See Appendix D.

TABLE A-20. *Master's Degrees—Males (figures in 000's)*

Year	Engrg.	Math.	Phys. Sci.	Bio. Sci.	Agri. & For.	Soc. Sci.	Psych.	Arts & Hum.	Educ.	Bus.[a] & Comm.	Other	Total
1957	5.2	0.8	2.7	1.5	1.1	3.5	0.8	3.8	16.5	3.2	2.4	41.5
1958	5.8	1.0	3.0	1.5	1.1	4.0	0.8	4.2	16.5	3.9	2.3	44.1
1959	6.8	1.2	3.2	1.7	1.2	4.3	0.9	4.4	16.9	4.2	2.8	47.6
1960	7.2	1.4	3.4	1.8	1.2	4.6	1.0	4.6	18.1	4.5	3.0	50.8
1961	8.2	1.8	3.8	2.0	1.2	5.0	1.1	4.9	18.7	4.5	2.8	54.0
1962	8.9	2.2	4.0	2.3	1.3	5.7	1.3	5.2	19.8	5.1	2.9	58.7
1963	9.6	2.7	4.2	2.4	1.2	6.5	1.4	5.9	20.4	5.6	3.0	62.9
1964	10.8	2.9	4.7	2.8	1.3	7.3	1.4	6.4	21.9	6.2	3.4	69.1
1965	12.0	3.3	5.1	3.1	1.3	8.2	1.5	7.1	23.0	7.3	4.1	76.0
Projected												
1966	13.1	3.8	5.6	3.5	1.4	9.3	1.7	7.9	23.6	8.0	4.2	82.1
1967	14.1	4.1	6.0	4.0	1.4	10.6	1.9	8.8	24.0	8.7	4.7	88.3
1968	14.8	4.5	6.3	4.4	1.4	11.9	2.1	9.6	24.6	9.4	5.0	94.0
1969	15.9	4.9	6.8	5.1	1.6	13.4	2.3	10.8	25.4	10.2	5.5	101.9
1970	17.3	5.4	7.6	5.8	1.7	15.4	2.6	12.1	26.4·	11.1	6.0	111.4
1971	18.9	5.9	8.5	6.6	1.8	17.4	3.1	13.5	27.6	12.3	6.6	122.2
1972	20.4	6.3	9.0	7.2	1.8	19.1	3.4	14.5	28.8	13.2	7.1	130.8
1973	22.2	6.9	9.6	7.7	1.9	21.0	3.8	15.7	30.3	14.2	7.7	141.0
1974	24.2	7.3	10.3	8.3	2.0	22.6	4.2	16.9	31.8	15.2	8.0	150.8
1975	26.1	7.8	10.9	8.9	2.1	24.4	4.6	18.0	33.4	16.4	8.8	161.4

[a] As reported by Office of Education. If other M.B.A. degrees are included, number would be 4.8 for 1957; 9.5 for 1965; 13.8 for 1970; and 21.0 for 1975.

SOURCE: Based on application of percentages of Table A–18 to the number of bachelor's degrees in the field for base years.

TABLE A–21. *Master's Degrees—Females (figures in 000's)*

Year	Math.	Phys. Sci.	Bio. Sci.	Soc. Sci.	Psych.	Arts & Hum.	Educ.	Bus. & Comm.	Health	Other	Total
1957	0.19	0.25	0.38	0.97	0.33	2.50	14.50	0.12	0.49	0.94	20.67
1958	0.24	0.32	0.42	1.00	0.40	2.60	14.60	0.15	0.38	1.30	21.41
1959	0.31	0.34	0.50	1.06	0.40	2.90	14.70	0.16	0.75	1.13	22.25
1960	0.34	0.39	0.52	1.12	0.43	3.20	15.40	0.17	0.79	1.21	23.54
1961	0.47	0.42	0.60	1.21	0.54	3.60	15.10	0.15	0.71	1.31	24.11
1962	0.50	0.46	0.71	1.65	0.56	4.10	16.10	0.18	0.67	1.38	26.31
1963	0.66	0.52	0.82	1.87	0.57	4.60	17.10	0.21	0.86	1.67	28.48
1964	0.68	0.52	0.90	2.12	0.69	5.50	18.80	0.20	1.01	1.72	32.14
1965	0.81	0.64	1.05	2.42	0.73	6.40	20.80	0.24	1.11	1.90	36.10
Projected											
1966	0.93	0.71	1.23	2.82	0.85	7.50	22.60	0.26	1.23	2.15	40.28
1967	1.01	0.78	1.48	3.19	0.94	8.80	24.70	0.29	1.47	2.40	45.06
1968	1.12	0.84	1.69	3.58	1.06	10.00	26.70	0.31	1.69	2.65	49.63
1969	1.23	0.92	1.96	4.08	1.18	11.70	29.00	0.34	1.75	2.98	55.14
1970	1.38	1.06	2.30	4.75	1.39	13.50	31.40	0.37	1.78	3.34	61.27
1971	1.53	1.21	2.67	5.33	1.58	15.20	33.40	0.40	2.19	3.70	67.21
1972	1.66	1.30	2.97	5.75	1.70	16.80	36.20	0.43	2.38	4.02	73.21
1973	1.82	1.42	3.22	6.37	1.84	18.50	39.30	0.47	2.46	4.30	79.70
1974	1.96	1.56	3.47	6.90	1.97	19.70	42.00	0.50	2.52	4.60	85.18
1975	2.12	1.68	3.76	7.40	2.10	21.50	44.50	0.54	2.66	4.90	91.21

SOURCE: Based on application of percentages of Table A–19 to the bachelor's degree base or to the number of male M.A. degrees.

TABLE A-22. *Master's Degrees, by Field—Total*

Year	Engrg.[a]	Math.	Phys. Sci.	Bio. Sci.	Agr. &[a] For.	Soc. Sci.	Psych.	Arts & Hum.	Educ.	Bus. & Comm.	Health[b]	Other	Total
1957	5.2	1.0	3.0	1.9	1.1	4.5	1.1	6.3	31.0	3.3	0.5	3.3	62.2
1958	5.8	1.2	3.3	1.9	1.1	5.0	1.2	6.8	31.1	4.1	0.4	3.6	65.5
1959	6.8	1.5	3.5	2.2	1.2	5.4	1.3	7.3	31.6	4.4	0.8	3.9	69.9
1960	7.2	1.7	3.8	2.3	1.2	5.7	1.4	7.8	33.5	4.7	0.8	4.2	74.3
1961	8.2	2.3	4.2	2.6	1.2	6.2	1.6	8.5	33.8	4.7	0.7	4.1	78.1
1962	8.9	2.7	4.5	3.0	1.3	7.4	1.9	9.3	35.9	5.3	0.7	4.3	85.0
1963	9.6	3.4	4.7	3.2	1.2	8.4	2.0	10.5	37.5	5.8	0.8	4.3	91.4
1964	10.8	3.6	5.2	3.7	1.3	9.4	2.1	11.9	40.7	6.4	1.0	5.1	101.2
1965	12.0	4.1	5.7	4.2	1.3	10.6	2.2	13.5	43.8	7.5	1.1	6.0	112.1
						Projected							
1966	13.1	4.7	6.3	4.7	1.4	12.1	2.6	15.4	46.2	8.3	1.2	6.4	122.4
1967	14.1	5.1	6.8	5.5	1.4	13.8	2.8	17.6	48.7	9.0	1.5	7.1	133.4
1968	14.8	5.6	7.1	6.1	1.4	15.5	3.2	19.6	51.3	9.7	1.7	7.7	143.6
1969	15.9	6.1	7.7	7.1	1.6	17.5	3.5	22.5	54.4	10.5	1.8	8.5	157.0
1970	17.3	6.8	8.7	8.1	1.7	20.2	4.0	25.6	57.8	11.5	1.8	9.3	171.7
1971	18.9	7.4	9.7	9.3	1.8	22.7	4.7	28.7	61.0	12.7	2.2	10.3	189.4
1972	20.4	7.9	10.3	10.2	1.8	24.9	5.1	31.3	65.0	13.6	2.4	11.1	204.0
1973	22.2	8.7	11.0	10.7	1.9	27.4	5.6	34.2	69.6	14.7	2.5	12.0	220.7
1974	24.2	9.3	11.9	11.8	2.0	29.5	6.2	36.6	73.8	15.7	2.5	12.6	236.0
1975	26.1	9.9	12.6	12.7	2.1	31.8	6.7	39.5	77.9	16.9	2.7	13.7	252.6

[a] Male only—small number of females included in "Other."
[b] Female only—males included in "Other" (some, e.g., in clinical medical sciences more properly third level).
SOURCE: Based on Tables A–20 and A–21.

TABLE A–23. *Percentage That Doctoral Degrees Are of First-Level Base of Degrees in the Field—Males*

Year	All Fields	Engrg.	Math.	Phys. Sci.	Bio. Sci.	Agri. & For.	Soc. Sci.	Psych.	Arts & Hum.	Educ.	Bus. & Comm.[a]	Other[b]
1958	4.28	2.04	7.30	13.70	8.4	3.34	6.10	12.60	5.00	12.00	—	—
1959	4.31	2.44	8.21	15.30	7.9	3.96	5.92	14.10	5.00	10.70	—	—
1960	4.38	2.68	8.55	15.90	9.2	4.82	5.75	14.60	4.80	9.70	—	—
1961	4.65	3.22	9.35	16.90	9.0	5.18	5.85	15.60	4.90	9.65	3.84	3.20
1962	5.13	4.05	9.80	17.30	10.25	5.73	5.47	17.50	4.73	10.15	4.57	3.50
1963	5.75	4.43	10.60	18.50	11.35	5.96	5.75	18.20	5.07	10.30	4.22	3.80
1964	6.55	5.30	11.30	18.00	12.60	7.85	6.30	19.70	5.45	11.00	4.27	4.10
1965	7.24	6.40	10.50	19.80	14.70	7.80	6.65	16.70	5.92	11.90	4.90	4.30
						Projected						
1966	7.80	7.20	10.80	20.50	14.70	8.50	6.95	18.20	6.37	12.70	4.90	4.65
1967	8.30	8.00	11.10	21.20	15.70	9.20	7.25	18.80	6.87	13.50	5.10	4.90
1968	8.75	9.00	11.35	21.80	16.70	9.80	7.50	19.40	7.42	14.20	5.30	5.10
1969	9.15	10.00	11.60	22.40	17.60	10.40	7.75	19.90	8.02	14.90	5.48	5.30
1970	9.50	10.90	11.80	22.90	18.50	10.90	7.95	20.40	8.57	15.50	5.66	5.45
1971	9.80	11.80	12.00	23.40	19.30	11.40	8.15	20.80	9.07	16.10	5.82	5.60
1972	10.00	12.60	12.15	23.80	20.10	11.80	8.30	21.20	9.52	16.60	5.98	5.70
1973	10.35	13.40	12.30	24.20	20.80	12.20	8.45	21.50	9.92	17.10	6.12	5.80
1974	10.55	14.10	12.40	24.50	21.40	12.50	8.55	21.80	10.27	17.50	6.26	5.85
1975	10.75	14.80	12.50	24.80	22.00	12.80	8.65	22.00	10.57	17.90	6.38	5.90

[a] Percentage of doctorates to M.B.A. five years earlier.
[b] Percentage of doctorates to "Other" bachelor's five years earlier.

SOURCE: Based on the ratio of doctorates to the number of bachelor's degree graduates for a period several years earlier, the weights of each year vary, and their sum corresponds to a moving average of earlier bachelor's degrees awarded in the field.

TABLE A–24. *Percentage of Female to Male Doctorates, by Field*

Year	Total	Engrg.	Math.	Phys. Sci.	Bio. Sci.	Agr. & For.	Soc. Sci.	Psych.	Arts & Hum.	Educ.	Bus. & Comm.	Other
1957–59	12.0	0.31	5.9	4.1	12.3	2.3	10.2	18.3	23.2	24.8	0.6	12.5
1960–62	11.8	0.45	6.0	4.0	12.6	1.0	10.7	21.4	24.6	24.6	1.0	13.0
1963–65	12.0	0.54	7.2	4.7	13.6	2.1	10.8	24.8	24.6	24.2	2.3	14.1
						Projected						
1966	12.3	0.60	8.0	5.1	14.2	2.5	11.0	26.2	25.0	25.0	2.9	14.7
1967	12.6	0.60	8.4	5.3	14.5	2.7	11.1	26.8	25.0	25.0	3.2	15.0
1968	12.9	0.60	8.8	5.5	14.8	2.9	11.2	27.4	25.0	25.0	3.5	15.3
1969	13.2	0.60	9.2	5.8	15.4	3.1	11.3	28.0	25.0	25.0	3.8	15.6
1970	13.5	0.60	9.6	6.1	16.0	3.3	11.4	28.6	25.0	25.0	4.1	15.9
1971	13.8	0.60	10.1	6.4	16.6	3.6	11.5	29.2	25.8	25.7	4.4	16.2
1972	14.1	0.60	10.6	6.7	17.2	3.9	11.6	29.8	26.6	26.0	4.7	16.5
1973	14.4	0.60	11.1	7.0	17.8	4.2	12.0	30.4	27.4	27.1	5.0	17.2
1974	14.7	0.60	11.6	7.3	18.4	4.5	12.5	31.0	28.2	27.8	5.3	17.9
1975	15.0	0.60	12.1	7.6	19.0	4.8	13.0	31.6	29.0	28.5	5.6	18.6

SOURCE: 1957 to 1965 Office of Education, Reports of Earned Degrees.

TABLE A–25. *Number of Doctorates, by Field—Males*

Year	Engrg.	Math.	Phys. Sci.	Bio. Sci.	For. & Agric.	Soc. Sci.	Psych.	Arts & Hum.	Educ.	Bus. & Comm.	Other	Total
1957	595	236	1,650	996	331	998	460	770	1,240	93	442	7,811
1958	643	232	1,629	987	334	1,010	488	750	1,300	104	501	7,978
1959	713	267	1,789	939	368	1,069	537	810	1,290	134	455	8,371
1960	783	285	1,840	1,088	433	1,117	544	840	1,280	133	458	8,801
1961	937	327	1,968	1,055	446	1,233	567	920	1,380	170	460	9,463
1962	1,203	372	2,089	1,179	463	1,224	632	950	1,540	221	504	10,377
1963	1,367	454	2,344	1,283	441	1,374	700	1,080	1,670	244	491	11,448
1964	1,686	567	2,405	1,432	545	1,607	757	1,220	1,890	268	578	12,955
1965	2,114	623	2,775	1,705	516	1,806	688	1,360	2,180	315	600	14,682
						Projected						
1966	2,440	745	2,940	1,735	545	1,980	820	1,510	2,500	310	650	16,175
1967	2,750	882	3,150	1,930	570	2,150	936	1,640	2,830	382	650	17,870
1968	3,140	1,030	3,360	2,190	595	2,380	1,083	1,780	3,130	406	700	19,794
1969	3,540	1,172	3,600	2,520	640	2,620	1,242	1,930	3,360	450	700	21,774
1970	3,900	1,305	3,800	2,820	674	2,860	1,416	2,110	3,560	540	750	23,735
1971	4,250	1,450	4,000	3,100	710	3,140	1,600	2,300	3,740	582	750	25,622
1972	4,610	1,620	4,290	3,680	760	3,490	1,819	2,510	3,900	632	800	28,111
1973	5,070	1,800	4,650	4,220	815	3,890	2,062	2,800	4,080	700	900	30,987
1974	5,550	1,980	5,110	4,800	880	4,310	2,328	3,110	4,280	784	950	34,082
1975	6,120	2,160	5,490	5,400	940	4,770	2,495	3,430	4,550	875	1,000	37,230

SOURCE: Based on the application of the percentages in Table A–23 to the moving average of bachelor's degrees in the field, with appropriate time lag to allow for completion of the degree.

TABLE A–26. *Number of Doctorates, by Field—Females*

Year	Engrg.	Math.	Phys. Sci.	Bio. Sci.	For. & Agric.	Soc. Sci.	Psych.	Arts & Hum.	Educ.	Bus. & Comm.	Other	Total
1957	1	13	73	112	10	100	90	190	290	—	60	939
1958	4	15	65	138	6	96	84	160	340	1	55	964
1959	1	15	67	112	8	118	98	190	320	1	59	989
1960	3	18	66	119	7	120	97	230	310	—	58	1,028
1961	6	17	73	140	4	122	136	200	360	—	54	1,112
1962	4	24	91	159	2	141	149	235	363	5	72	1,245
1963	11	36	99	176	8	162	144	249	403	6	80	1,374
1964	7	29	119	193	10	172	182	285	456	7	75	1,535
1965	10	59	133	232	13	185	159	366	529	6	82	1,774
						Projected						
1966	13	60	150	246	14	218	215	378	625	9	96	2,004
1967	17	74	166	280	15	238	251	410	708	12	98	2,269
1968	19	91	185	329	17	267	297	445	783	14	106	2,553
1969	21	108	208	389	20	296	348	485	840	17	109	2,851
1970	24	125	232	451	22	326	405	528	890	22	119	3,144
1971	25	147	256	515	26	361	467	593	965	26	121	3,502
1972	27	172	287	634	30	405	542	670	1,030	30	132	3,959
1973	30	200	324	753	34	467	627	770	1,104	35	154	4,498
1974	33	230	374	885	39	539	722	875	1,190	42	170	5,099
1975	37	262	417	1,025	45	620	788	995	1,300	49	186	5,724

SOURCE: Based on the application of the percentages of Table A–24 to the figures in A–25 for the appropriate years.

TABLE A–27. *Number of Doctorates, by Field—Total*

Year	Engrg.	Math.	Phys. Sci.	Bio. Sci.	For. & Agric.	Soc. Sci.	Psych.	Arts & Hum.	Educ.	Bus. & Comm.	Other	Total
1957	596	249	1,723	1,108	341	1,098	550	960	1,530	93	502	8,750
1958	651	247	1,694	1,125	340	1,106	572	910	1,640	105	552	8,942
1959	715	282	1,856	1,051	376	1,187	635	1,000	1,610	135	513	9,360
1960	789	303	1,906	1,207	440	1,237	641	1,070	1,590	133	513	9,829
1961	949	344	2,041	1,195	450	1,355	703	1,120	1,740	170	508	10,575
1962	1,207	396	2,180	1,338	465	1,365	781	1,185	1,903	226	576	11,622
1963	1,378	490	2,443	1,459	449	1,536	844	1,329	2,073	250	571	12,822
1964	1,693	596	2,524	1,625	555	1,779	939	1,505	2,346	275	653	14,490
1965	2,124	682	2,908	1,937	529	1,991	847	1,726	2,709	321	682	16,456
						Projected						
1966	2,453	805	3,090	1,981	559	2,198	1,035	1,888	3,125	319	746	18,199
1967	2,767	956	3,316	2,210	585	2,388	1,187	2,050	3,538	394	748	20,139
1968	3,159	1,121	3,545	2,519	612	2,647	1,380	2,225	3,913	420	806	22,347
1969	3,561	1,280	3,808	2,909	660	2,916	1,590	2,415	4,200	467	809	24,625
1970	3,924	1,450	4,032	3,271	696	3,185	1,821	2,638	4,450	572	869	26,879
1971	4,275	1,597	4,256	3,615	736	3,501	2,067	2,893	4,705	608	871	29,124
1972	4,637	1,792	4,577	4,314	790	3,895	2,361	3,180	4,930	662	932	32,070
1973	5,100	2,000	4,974	4,973	849	4,357	2,689	3,570	5,184	735	1,054	35,485
1974	5,583	2,210	5,484	5,685	919	4,849	3,050	3,985	5,470	826	1,120	39,181
1975	6,157	2,422	5,907	5,817	985	5,558	3,283	4,425	5,850	924	1,186	42,954

SOURCE: Tables A–25 and A–26.

Appendix B: Studies
Utilizing the Project
TALENT Data Files

The Data File

In 1960 the American Institutes for Research and the University of Pittsburgh, with support from the U.S. Office of Education, initiated Project TALENT, a nationwide study of American youth. A two-day battery of tests and questionnaires was administered to approximately 100,000 students in the twelfth grade in more than 1,300 public, private, and parochial schools in all parts of the United States. This survey yielded about 2,000 items of information about each student and includes aptitude and achievement scores; activities, preferences, and interest inventories; and extensive personal background information. In addition, 1,000 items of data on the high schools were also compiled, including information on school policy, school size, guidance and counseling programs, and financial support.[1]

In 1965, five years after completion of high school, a follow-up of the initial twelfth-grade sample was undertaken. A four-page questionnaire was mailed to all those in the original sample and included comprehensive information on employment, education, and marital history for the five years that had elapsed since the initial data were collected. Approximately one-third (31,474) of the original subjects responded to the several waves of mailing of the five-year ques-

---

[1] An extensive discussion of Project TALENT sampling design and the testing instruments is presented in Flanagan, John C., and others, *Design for a Study of American Youth,* Houghton Mifflin and Co., Boston, 1962. Approximately 100,000 students from each grade, 9 through 12, were tested initially in 1960. Most of the work of the Commission utilized the twelfth-grade sample.

tionnaire and personal follow-up of a subsample of nonrespondents. The subsample was weighted to represent the entire group of nonrespondents.

The Sample

In Chapter 5, thirty-eight personal and environmental variables are analyzed as they relate to post-high school educational attainment. These variables were obtained from three Project TALENT sources—the twelfth-grade student test battery, the school questionnaires, and the five-year follow-up survey. These variables were selected on an *a priori* basis after consideration by the staff of the Commission on Human Resources or because they had been included in other studies of educational attainment.

The inclusion of so large a number of items has a substantial effect in reducing the number of respondents to the five-year follow-up survey who have complete information on all the variables. One variable alone (estimated total 1959 income of the student's family) was not available for 11,000 individuals in the five-year follow-up sample. Approximately 4,900 had information missing on one or more of the other personal and environmental variables. A resulting total of 15,540 individuals with complete information is employed in the analysis. This number includes 8,746 males and 6,794 females.

The large shrinkage in sample size that results from nonresponse to the follow-up survey and from incomplete reporting of information yields a *non-representative sample* that should not be used to estimate parameters. Negroes, females, and those of low socioeconomic background are, for example, underrepresented. The proportions of students who go on to college are overrepresented. Sampling bias has thus resulted in a generally more homogeneous sample with respect to personal and environmental characteristics than would be expected from a random sampling of this age cohort in the general population. This also usually results in more modest background differences between educational attainment aggregates[2] and more conservative correlations between variables than would generally be attained with the use of completely random samples.

The Analysis

While the lack of representativeness of the sample yields obvious restrictions in the data as noted above, the data are sufficient for the purposes of Chapter 5. In this chapter the emphasis is not on the distribution of these various personal and environmental characteristics among the aggregates with differing levels of educational attainment, but rather on the interrelationships and the interaction

[2] Compare, for example, Appendix Tables B-1, B-2, and B-3 with the approximate parameters reported by John C. Flanagan and William W. Cooley in *Project Talent One-Year Follow-up Studies*, University of Pittsburgh, Pittsburgh, 1966, pp. 91–156; and by Alexander W. Astin, Robert J. Panos, and John A. Creager in "National Norms of Entering College Freshmen—Fall, 1966," American Council on Education *Research Reports*, vol. 2, No. 1, 1967.

of these variables as they operate to influence subsequent educational attainment. The homogeneity of the sample does, however, tend to yield lower correlation coefficients than would be expected in the general population and thus the data in Chapter 5 tend to reflect conservative estimates of the impact of the various factors on educational attainment.

The analytical procedure employed in the analysis is least-squares multiple and partial regression. The criterion variable (educational attainment) is always a dichotomized variable. The independent (predictor) variables are also, in some cases, dichotomized dummy variables and, in other cases, continuous or quasi-continuous variables. In the former, the reported zero order correlations are analogous to the phi coefficient; and in the latter; analogous to the point biserial r. While these statistics tend to be conservative estimates of the "true" product-moment correlation coefficients, they allow the exploration of the effects of intercorrelations among the factors through multiple-partial regression analyses. By observing the amount and direction of change in the coefficients obtained for a given factor as other factors are, in turn, added to or deleted from the regression equation or as the criterion is altered, it can be ascertained which intercorrelations mask the underlying relationship between the dependent variable and the criterion and which factors emerge as the primary correlates of various levels of educational attainment. The theoretical foundations of such an analysis are discussed by Coleman,[3] Melichar,[4] Morgan,[5] and Suits,[6] among others. The work of Astin,[7] Morgan and others,[8] and Orcutt and others,[9] are illustrative of the application of dummy variables in multivariate analysis.

The Criterion Variables

Of the 8,746 males in the sample, 513 (5.9 per cent) reported they had attended a junior college and had not subsequently attended a senior college within five years since high school. Sixty-two per cent (5,416) reported they had attended a senior college or university. The remaining 2,768 (31.6 per cent) had not attended college (a four-year college or junior college) since leaving high school. Among the 6,794 girls, 242 (3.6 per cent) had attended a junior

---

[3] Coleman, James S., *Introduction to Mathematical Sociology*. The Free Press, New York, 1964, especially pp. 189–268.

[4] Melichar, Emanuel, "Least-Squares Analysis of Economic Survey Data" in *Business and Economic Statistics Section: Proceedings, 1963*, American Statistical Association, Washington, 1966.

[5] Morgan, James N., *A Note on the Interpretation of Multiple Regression Using Dummy Variables*. Survey Research Center, Institute for Social Research, University of Michigan, April 28, 1964.

[6] Suits, Daniel B., "Use of Dummy Variables in Regression Equations," *Journal of the American Statistical Association*, vol. 52, December, 1957, pp. 548–551.

[7] Astin, Alexander W., "Personal and Environmental Factors Associated With College Dropouts Among High Aptitude Students," *Journal of Educational Psychology*, vol. 55, no. 4, 1964, pp. 219–227.

[8] Morgan, James N., Martin H. David, Wilbur J. Cohen, and Harvey E. Brazer, *Income and Welfare in the United States*. McGraw-Hill Inc., New York, 1962.

[9] Orcutt, Guy H., Martin Greenberger, John Korbel, and Alice M. Rivlin, *Microanalysis of Socioeconomic Systems: A Simulation Study*. Harper and Row, New York, 1961.

college only, 268 (3.9 per cent) had enrolled in a three-year nursing program, and 3,172 (46.7 per cent) had attended a senior college or university. Forty-six per cent (3,112) had not attended college or nursing school.

In the total sample of those who had attended a senior college within five years after high school graduation, 1,849 (21.5 per cent) had not completed a degree and were not currently enrolled in 1965. While some will undoubtedly finish college at some later time, they are all included in the category of "college dropouts" in the analysis. An additional 1,534 (17.9 per cent) had also not completed a degree but were enrolled in college in 1965. These are described as "delayed potential senior college graduates." The remaining 5,184 men and women (60.4 per cent) had completed the baccalaureate degree within five years after completion of high school.

Of the more than 1,250 senior colleges and universities in the United States, more than 1,050 had students who are included in the Project TALENT sample. Based on the aggregate I.Q. composite scores of the Project TALENT sample attending each of these institutions, approximately 380 institutions were rated as either selective or highly selective.[10] Among those in the sample who had completed the baccalaureate degree by 1965, one-half had graduated from one of these selective or highly selective institutions.

Those who had completed a senior college are also divided into two groups, depending upon whether they had gone on to graduate school since completion of the baccalaureate degree. Forty-four per cent (2,316) of the sample who had completed college reported they had enrolled for graduate work by five years after high school. The remaining 2,938 had terminated their current studies with receipt of the baccalaureate degree.

These levels of educational attainment five years subsequent to high school graduation comprise the dichotomous sets of criterion variables for analysis in Chapter 5. These are defined below:

    (I) Noncollege—College

   (II) Nursing School—Senior College (for females only)[11]

  (III) Junior College—Senior College

  (IV) Senior College Dropout—Completed Senior College[12]

   (V) Delayed Potential Senior College Graduate—Completed Senior College

  (VI) Completed Nonselective Senior College—Completed Selective Senior College

 (VII) Terminated with Bachelor's Degree—Continued with Graduate School

---

[10] See Chapter 5 for a further discussion of this college selectivity measure. In the current analysis selective institutions refer to those which are rated either 1 or 2 on the 5-point scale.

[11] The analysis of this grouping is not reported in Chapter 5. A detailed report based on these data is presented in Bayer, Alan E., and Lyle F. Schoenfeldt, "Student Interchangeability in Three-Year and Four-Year Nursing Programs," *Journal of Human Resources*, 1969.

[12] A more detailed analysis and discussion of this grouping than is presented in Chapter 5 is reported in Bayer, Alan E., "The College Dropout: Factors Affecting Senior College Completion," *Sociology of Education*, vol. 41, Summer, 1968, pp. 305–316.

The Independent Variables

The 38 independent variables are distributed in ten different factor domains, each of which includes from three to five variables.[13] The first set of elements includes five *ability* factors. All are derived from the high school test battery and all are continuous variables. Included are the following:

(1) Vocabulary—knowledge of word meanings (30 questions)

(2) General Information—a wide breadth of knowledge in 37 areas including literature, music, social studies, mechanics, home economics, art, and health (395 questions)

(3) Creativity—ability to derive ingenious solutions to a variety of practical problems (20 questions)

(4) Abstract Reasoning—ability to determine logical relationships or progressions among elements of a complex nonverbal pattern (15 questions)

(5) Mathematics—a wide range of mathematical skills, from simple arithmetic reasoning and algebra to geometry, trigonometry, and introductory calculus (54 questions)

The second set of variables are selected *interest* inventories. The following three variables are included; all are derived from the high school test battery, and all are continuous variables:

(6) Physical Science Interests (16 questions)

(7) Literary/Linguistic Interests (16 questions)

(8) Social Service Interests (12 questions)

A third domain is comprised of three personality traits defined as *temperament*. These measures are derived from the Student Activities Inventory of the high school test battery and all are continuous variables. Included are the following:

(9) Sociability—the tendency to like and to relate to others (12 questions)

(10) Impulsiveness—the tendency to make snap decisions and to act on impulse (9 questions)

(11) Mature Personality—the ability to get things done, willingness to accept and discharge responsibilities, and desire to cooperate and help others (24 questions)

Five *socioeconomic* variables are incorporated into the fourth factor domain. All are derived from the Student Information Blank of the high school test battery and all are coded as continuous variables:

[13] With the exception of those variables based on the five-year follow-up survey, further specification of the variables may be found in one of the following three reports: Flanagan, John C., and others, *The Project Talent Data Bank*, University of Pittsburgh, Pittsburgh, March, 1965; Flanagan, John C., and others, *Studies of the American High-School*, University of Pittsburgh, Pittsburgh, 1962; and Flanagan, John C., and others, *The American High-School Student*, University of Pittsburgh, 1964.

(12) Family Income (total estimated 1959 income coded in five increments)

(13) Father's Occupation (coded in five categories from unskilled and semi-skilled worker to professional and technical occupations)

(14) Father's Education (coded in ten increments)

(15) Mother's Education (coded in ten increments)

(16) Books in Home (coded in six categories)

The fifth factor domain involves the *ethnic-religious background.* Four variables are included, all are dummy variables, and the first three are derived from the five-year follow-up questionnaire. The last is derived from the Student Information Blank of the initial high school test battery. Included are the following:

(17) Race (dummy variable with Negro coded 0, other coded 1)

(18) Religion I (dummy variable with Jewish coded 1, other coded 0)

(19) Religion II (dummy variable with Catholic coded 0, other coded 1)

(20) Ethnic Background (dummy variable coded 1 if both parents born in the United States, otherwise 0)

Three variables, all derived from the high school test battery, are included in the *residence* domain. All are coded as dummy variables as follows:

(21) Region of Origin (based on residence at twelfth grade and coded 0 if South—W. Va., Va., Ky., Tenn., N.C., S.C., Ga., Fla., Ala., Miss., La., Ark.—otherwise, coded 1)

(22) Size of Hometown (based on residence at twelfth grade and coded 0 if rural area or place of less than 50,000 population, otherwise coded 1)

(23) Geographic Mobility (dummy variable coded 0 if student had not changed state of residence between birth and twelfth grade, otherwise coded 1)

The *family of orientation* background includes the following three variables derived from the high school test battery:

(24) Family Status (dummy variable coded 1 if unbroken home, otherwise 0)

(25) Sibship Size (continuous variable)

(26) Ordinal Position (dummy variable coded 1 if first-born, otherwise 0)

Five variables are selected as *high school characteristics.* All are derived from the school questionnaires:

(27) Type of High School (dummy variable coded 0 if public, other coded 1)

(28) Size of Student Body (continuous variable based on the total number of enrolled twelfth-grade students)

(29) Size of Faculty (continuous variable based on number of senior high school teachers)

(30) Proportion of Graduates Going On to College (continuous)

(31) Guidance Facilities (dummy variable coded 1 if high school has a guidance program, otherwise coded 0)

Four dichotomized *college commitment* variables are derived from the high school test battery. They are the following:

(32) Individual's College Plans (coded 0 if he doesn't plan to go or plans are indefinite at twelfth grade, otherwise coded 1)

(33) College Encouragement by Father (coded 1 if father strongly supports college consideration, otherwise coded 0)

(34) College Encouragement by Mother (coded 1 if mother strongly supports college consideration, otherwise coded 0)

(35) College Encouragement by Peers (coded 1 if friends strongly support college consideration, otherwise coded 0)

The last specified domain includes variables relevant to the *family of pro-creation.* All are dichotomized variables, with the first one extracted from the Student Information Blank of the high school test battery and the latter two derived from the five-year follow-up questionnaire:

(36) Age Planning Marriage (coded 0 if while in high school stated expectations of marrying by age 20, otherwise coded 1)

(37) Marital Status (coded 1 if not married by five years after high school, otherwise coded 0)

(38) Parental Status (coded 0 if, by five years after high school, individual had children; if no children, coded 1)

The specification of each of these variables and the direction in which they are coded allows general interpretation of Table B-1. This table shows the correlations among each of the 38 independent variables employed in the analysis for the total sample of 8,746 males and 6,794 females. The correlations to the right of the diagonal are those for the males; underscored to the left of the diagonal are the analogous correlations for the females. Almost two-thirds of the correlation coefficients are less than ±.10. Several coefficients are ±.005, and only two coefficients exceed .80 (that between college encouragement by mother and college encouragement by father and between vocabulary score and general information score).

The Distribution of the Independent Variables Among Criterion Groups

Tables B-2 and B-3 show for males and females, respectively, the composition of each educational attainment category with regard to the 38 independent variables. While Chapter 5 employs many of these variables as continuous variables for regression analysis, all are shown in these tables as dichotomous variables for ease in interpretation. While these distributions are suggestive of the simple relationships between each of the independent variables and the criterion measures, the reader is again cautioned that the distributions are based on a nonrandom subsample derived from Project TALENT and do not represent parameters that may be directly translated to apply to the general population.

TABLE B–1. *Correlations Among Selected Personal and Environmental Variables: 1960 High School Students*[a]

	1	2	3	4	5	6	7	8
I *Ability Variables*								
1. Vocabulary	—	.88	.57	.45	.65	.32	.27	.00
2. General Information	.88	—	.63	.50	.74	.41	.29	.01
3. Creativity	.56	.61	—	.45	.48	.28	.16	—.03
4. Abstract Reasoning	.47	.50	.43	—	.54	.29	.15	.00
5. Math Aptitude	.64	.73	.47	.51	—	.48	.21	.04
II *Interests Variables*								
6. Physical Science	.31	.38	.24	.24	.43	—	.29	.14
7. Literary/Linguistic	.36	.39	.24	.18	.29	.44	—	.55
8. Social Service	.05	.06	.03	.04	.11	.24	.45	—
III *Temperament Variables*								
9. Sociability	—.10	—.11	—.04	—.05	—.09	—.07	.02	.19
10. Impulsiveness	.13	.14	.09	.04	.06	.05	.15	—.04
11. Mature Personality	.22	.24	.18	.12	.26	.19	.22	.21
IV *Socioeconomic Variables*								
12. Family Income	.18	.19	.10	.12	.18	.04	.10	.02
13. Father's Occupation	.25	.27	.15	.18	.25	.10	.16	.03
14. Father's Education	.30	.32	.17	.19	.29	.13	.19	.06
15. Mother's Education	.28	.32	.17	.19	.27	.10	.16	.04
16. Number of Books in Home	.26	.29	.16	.18	.24	.17	.23	.08
V *Ethnic-Religious Variables*								
17. Race	.17	.19	.17	.16	.13	—.04	—.02	—.04
18. Religion I (Jewish/Other)	.12	.10	.03	.05	.14	.07	.12	.01
19. Religion II (Catholic/Other)	.04	.08	.00	.02	.05	.00	.04	.03
20. Nativity-Parentage	—.01	.01	.02	.00	—.02	—.04	—.03	.00
VI *Residence Variables*								
21. Region of U. S.	.14	.15	.12	.12	.07	.01	—.01	—.04
22. Size of Hometown	.13	.08	.04	.08	.06	.03	.06	.04
23. Geographic Mobility	.12	.12	.06	.06	.07	.04	.08	—.01
VII *Family of Orientation Variables*								
24. Parents' Marital Status	.07	.08	.04	.06	.07	.02	.02	.01
25. Sibship Size	—.21	—.19	—.12	—.10	—.13	—.03	—.07	.01
26. Ordinal Position	.18	.17	.10	.07	.11	.02	.07	.02
VIII *High School Variables*								
27. Type of High School	.03	.02	.02	.04	.05	.03	—.01	.01
28. Size of Student Body	.12	.08	.05	.07	.07	.03	.08	.00
29. Size of Faculty	.15	.11	.05	.08	.06	.00	.06	.01
30. Proportion Attending Col.	.20	.19	.09	.12	.18	.03	.10	.02
31. Guidance Facilities	.12	.10	.04	.06	.07	.04	.05	.02
IX *College Commitment Variables*								
32. Individual's College Plans	.32	.36	.18	.20	.37	.24	.30	.18
33. Encouragement by Father	.13	.14	.07	.09	.16	.10	.13	.14
34. Encouragement by Mother	.11	.13	.07	.08	.15	.10	.13	.14
35. Encouragement by Peers	—.11	—.11	—.07	—.07	—.08	—.01	.02	.06
X *Family of Procreation Variables*								
36. Age Planning Marriage	.22	.24	.09	.13	.25	.20	.18	.08
37. Marital Status	.11	.12	.05	.03	.12	.20	.09	.01
38. Parental Status	.19	.21	.08	.10	.22	.15	.15	.06

[a] Based on a selected sample of 8,746 males and 6,794 females who responded to the 1965 Project TALENT five-year follow-up and reported complete information. Correlations for males not underscored; those for females are underscored.

TABLE B–1. (*cont.*)

9	10	11	12	13	14	15	16	17	18	19
—.04	.05	.16	.19	.23	.27	.24	.26	.16	.13	.04
—.03	.06	.19	.20	.26	.31	.28	.30	.17	.12	.08
—.01	.04	.13	.12	.16	.18	.17	.18	.14	.03	.06
—.03	—.03	.08	.10	.16	.18	.16	.18	.11	.05	.03
—.03	—.01	.21	.18	.24	.29	.25	.24	.12	.15	.06
.01	—.02	.21	.03	.06	.11	.07	.12	—.02	.05	.03
.06	.05	.15	.10	.10	.15	.13	.22	—.08	.11	.03
.16	—.03	.16	—.01	—.01	.02	.02	.06	—.08	.03	—.02
—	.21	.35	.08	.03	.02	.01	.02	.00	.04	—.04
.16	—	.13	.06	.04	.04	.03	.06	.01	.01	.01
.28	.06	—	.06	.07	.06	.06	.10	.01	.06	—.01
.06	.08	.05	—	.37	.36	.29	.29	.08	.12	.02
.05	.08	.10	.36	—	.49	.35	.29	.09	.14	.09
.04	.08	.08	.36	.50	—	.54	.39	.04	.12	.12
.03	.11	.10	.30	.36	.53	—	.35	.03	.06	.14
.01	.09	.11	.29	.32	.42	.37	—	.05	.11	.07
.02	.01	.00	.06	.08	.06	.05	.02	—	.03	—.05
.03	.05	.04	.16	.18	.18	.10	.14	.04	—	.15
—.05	.00	.02	.04	.12	.13	.15	.10	—.05	.14	—
.01	.01	.02	—.03	.01	.00	.04	—.05	—.02	—.17	.05
—.02	.02	.00	.10	.00	.06	.05	.04	.12	.09	—.16
.02	.04	.01	.18	.05	.14	.08	.15	—.02	.14	—.13
—.02	.04	.02	.10	.10	.17	.13	.07	.04	—.01	.05
.01	—.01	—.01	.12	.04	.04	.03	.03	.10	.02	—.01
—.02	—.03	—.04	—.13	—.12	—.16	—.15	—.07	—.12	—.10	—.06
.02	.04	.06	.05	.06	.13	.10	—.01	.04	.03	.01
.01	.02	.02	.01	.02	.04	.01	.01	.03	—.03	—.30
.01	.04	.01	.19	.12	.15	.08	.16	.01	.41	.02
.00	.04	.00	.20	.07	.16	.11	.18	.03	.15	.03
.03	.06	.05	.25	.24	.27	.21	.19	.10	.31	.08
.00	—.01	.03	.11	.05	.10	.08	.10	.01	.07	.00
.04	.07	.18	.20	.28	.28	.27	.24	.00	.13	.11
.09	.04	.13	.16	.20	.21	.17	.13	—.01	.05	.10
.10	.04	.12	.14	.18	.18	.17	.12	—.01	.05	.10
.10	.05	—.01	.05	.06	.06	.03	.02	—.04	.05	.07
—.03	—.01	.08	.08	.12	.14	.14	.15	—.04	.04	—.05
—.08	—.01	.01	.02	.04	.07	.07	.08	—.06	.05	—.06
—.04	—.01	.07	.09	.13	.14	.14	.13	—.01	.12	.04

TABLE B–1. *(cont.)*

	20	21	22	23	24	25	26	27
I Ability Variables								
1. Vocabulary	.02	.09	.20	.13	.07	—.19	.18	.08
2. General Information	.04	.10	.18	.14	.08	—.20	.19	.07
3. Creativity	.06	.05	.10	.09	.07	—.12	.12	.04
4. Abstract Reasoning	.02	.10	.13	.06	.05	—.10	.07	.05
5. Math Aptitude	.01	.08	.15	.08	.08	—.14	.12	.06
II Interests Variables								
6. Physical Science	.00	—.04	.07	.03	.02	.04	.06	.00
7. Literary/Linguistic	—.02	—.03	.12	.08	—.02	—.04	.03	.05
8. Social Service	—.01	—.02	.02	—.01	—.02	.04	—.04	.04
III Temperament Variables								
9. Sociability	.01	—.02	.00	—.02	.04	—.03	.01	.03
10. Impulsiveness	.00	.01	.03	.02	—.01	—.03	.03	.01
11. Mature Personality	.01	.03	.02	.00	.02	—.03	.06	.03
IV Socio-economic Variables								
12. Family Income	.00	.05	.18	.10	.13	—.11	.04	.12
13. Father's Occupation	.02	—.02	.06	.10	.04	—.10	.06	.09
14. Father's Education	.04	.01	.14	.16	.02	—.12	.10	.10
15. Mother's Education	.07	.01	.07	.12	.02	—.11	.08	.07
16. Number of Books in Home	—.02	.02	.16	.09	.04	—.06	.01	.11
V Ethnic-Religious Variables								
17. Race	—.01	.10	.00	.00	.08	—.10	.03	.04
18. Religion I (Jewish/Other)	—.18	.09	.15	—.02	.03	—.12	.03	—.06
19. Religion II (Catholic/Other)	.07	—.15	—.14	.04	.01	—.10	.01	—.34
20. Nativity-Parentage	—	—.09	—.08	—.01	.05	.02	.07	—.02
VI Residence Variables								
21. Region of U. S.	—.10	—	.06	.00	.04	—.03	.00	.00
22. Size of Hometown	—.10	.09	—	.07	—.01	—.16	.08	.20
23. Geographic Mobility	.00	.01	.05	—	—.01	—.03	.09	—.01
VII Family of Orientation Variables								
24. Parents' Marital Status	.01	.04	.00	—.01	—	—.04	.04	—.01
25. Sibship Size	.00	—.06	—.16	—.02	—.05	—	—.29	.04
26. Ordinal Position	.06	.02	.07	.09	.06	—.33	—	.00
VIII High School Variables								
27. Type of High School	—.02	.04	.13	—.07	.01	.04	—.01	—
28. Size of Student Body	—.16	.16	.46	.02	.00	—.18	.06	—.19
29. Size of Faculty	—.10	.13	.62	.08	.01	—.17	.07	—.28
30. Proportion Attending Col.	—.07	.01	.30	.09	.04	—.14	.07	.09
31. Guidance Facilities	—.05	.17	.32	.05	.01	—.10	.06	—.09
IX College Commitment Variables								
32. Individual's College Plans	—.02	—.01	.04	.08	.04	—.13	.09	.00
33. Encouragement by Father	.02	—.04	—.01	.04	.08	—.10	.07	.01
34. Encouragement by Mother	.03	—.04	—.01	.04	.05	—.09	.05	.00
35. Encouragement by Peers	.00	—.04	.00	.00	.00	—.02	.00	—.04
X Family of Procreation Variables								
36. Age Planning Marriage	—.04	.04	.08	.01	.04	—.05	.03	.05
37. Marital Status	—.08	.02	.07	—.04	.01	—.04	.01	.04
38. Parental Status	—.07	.01	.08	—.02	.05	—.11	.03	.01

TABLE B–1. (*cont.*)

28	29	30	31	32	33	34	35	36	37	38
.15	.20	.25	.12	.33	.10	.09	−.13	.17	.13	.17
.14	.19	.25	.11	.38	.13	.12	−.12	.18	.14	.19
.06	.10	.14	.06	.21	.08	.07	−.11	.09	.04	.07
.09	.14	.16	.09	.23	.08	.07	−.09	.11	.06	.10
.14	.17	.26	.09	.39	.15	.13	−.10	.16	.12	.18
.06	.07	.07	.02	.24	.13	.13	.00	.09	.04	.07
.10	.10	.14	.04	.24	.10	.10	.02	.09	.10	.11
−.01	−.01	.03	−.01	.17	.11	.12	.07	.02	.02	.03
−.02	−.04	.00	−.04	.13	.15	.14	.14	−.05	−.08	−.04
.01	.01	.00	−.02	.04	.03	.03	.05	−.04	−.03	−.04
.00	−.01	.03	−.02	.20	.11	.11	.01	.02	.01	.04
.13	.16	.28	.10	.16	.12	.10	.02	.06	.03	.06
.07	.04	.25	.05	.19	.12	.10	.02	.05	.05	.09
.10	.14	.28	.08	.22	.14	.12	.04	.09	.08	.12
.04	.08	.20	.06	.20	.10	.10	.01	.07	.08	.10
.12	.16	.23	.11	.19	.09	.07	.00	.10	.09	.11
.00	.01	.06	.05	.03	.01	.00	−.04	−.02	−.03	.00
.43	.17	.26	.07	.10	.06	.05	.01	.07	.11	.12
.05	.05	−.02	−.03	.02	.04	.04	.04	−.05	−.07	−.01
−.14	−.09	−.08	−.05	−.01	.00	.00	.01	−.03	−.06	−.05
.14	.10	−.03	.15	−.01	−.03	−.03	−.04	.03	.06	.04
.43	.60	.34	.30	.10	.03	.02	−.04	.11	.10	.12
.01	.07	.07	.04	.07	.01	.01	−.01	.03	.01	.04
.03	.01	.02	.02	.03	.11	.07	−.01	.03	.02	.03
−.18	−.18	−.12	−.09	−.12	−.10	−.09	−.01	−.06	−.04	−.08
.06	.07	.05	.04	.09	.08	.06	−.01	.04	.01	.05
−.22	−.21	.39	−.02	.10	.03	.02	−.01	.05	.06	.03
—	.53	.21	.22	.07	.04	.03	−.01	.10	.11	.12
.54	—	.19	.43	.07	.03	.02	−.02	.12	.10	.11
.29	.26	—	.13	.20	.09	.08	.01	.09	.11	.12
.25	.46	.16	—	.03	.03	.01	−.01	.11	.07	.06
.07	.06	.18	.04	—	.42	.42	.15	.12	.08	.16
.00	.00	.12	.02	.35	—	.90	.29	.07	.02	.08
−.01	−.01	.11	.01	.37	.90	—	.30	.06	.02	.06
.02	.03	.08	−.01	.12	.21	.22	—	−.01	−.01	.00
.04	.07	.06	.06	.29	.13	.13	.01	—	.18	.23
.05	.05	.03	.04	.13	.04	.04	−.01	.27	—	.56
.10	.10	.11	.06	.24	.11	.11	.02	.32	.53	—

	Total Sample (N = 8,746)		Total Attending College (N = 5,978)	
Personal and Environmental Variables	Noncollege (N = 2,768)	College (N = 5,978)	Jr. College (N = 513)	Sr. College (N = 5,416)
	Per cents			
I *Ability Variables*				
1. Low Vocabulary	61.1	23.5	37.4	22.2
2. Low General Information	58.2	16.9	34.3	15.3
3. Low Creativity	56.1	31.4	42.1	30.4
4. Low Abstract Reasoning	64.3	36.3	50.7	35.0
5. Low Math Aptitude	66.0	19.7	40.7	17.7
II *Interests Variables*				
6. Low Physical Science	34.9	18.8	21.6	18.5
7. Low Literary/Linguistic	68.1	43.5	56.5	42.3
8. Low Social Service	70.2	56.6	66.7	55.7
III *Temperament Variables*				
9. Low Sociability	49.7	41.8	43.1	41.7
10. Low Impulsiveness	83.1	82.1	82.7	82.0
11. Low Mature Personality	52.8	38.3	49.1	37.3
IV *Socio-economic Variables*				
12. Low Family Income (< $6,000)	41.7	24.7	29.4	24.2
13. Father's Occupation: Professional/Technical/Managerial	31.4	55.8	41.3	57.1
14. Father's Education < College	91.1	68.3	85.4	66.7
15. Mother's Education < College	92.4	74.1	86.5	72.9
16. Few Books in Home (<100)	70.5	48.5	55.9	47.8
V *Ethnic-Religious Variables*				
17. Negro	2.6	1.1	1.9	1.1
18. Jewish	1.5	8.6	4.5	9.0
19. Catholic	26.7	24.6	30.2	24.1
20. Both Parents U.S. Natives	88.0	87.8	82.7	88.3
VI *Residence Variables*				
21. Home in Southeast U.S.	15.0	15.3	12.9	15.5
22. Small Hometown (<50,000)	36.3	21.0	21.6	21.0
23. No Residence Change Through High School	65.4	58.6	57.3	58.7
VII *Family of Orientation Variables*				
24. Unbroken Home	91.4	94.5	92.2	94.7
25. Small Family (≤3 Children)	55.1	68.7	62.2	69.3
26. First Born	44.1	54.2	49.7	54.6
VIII *High School Variables*				
27. Attended Public High School	94.5	86.2	89.7	85.9
28. Large Number of Students (>360 Seniors)	22.1	30.8	29.0	30.9
29. Large Faculty (>20 Teachers)	63.9	74.5	77.0	74.3
30. Majority of Graduates Attend College	17.7	40.8	30.4	41.8
31. No Guidance Program	9.9	6.3	6.0	6.4
IX *College Commitment Variables*				
32. Individual Not Planning College	57.3	8.1	16.9	7.2
33. College Plans Encouraged by Father	40.3	68.3	65.5	68.5
34. College Plans Encouraged by Mother	43.2	70.4	68.0	70.6
35. College Plans Encouraged by Peers	24.4	26.6	29.8	26.3
X *Family of Procreation Variables*				
36. Plan Early Marriage (Before Age 21)	20.3	7.6	9.9	7.3
37. Not Married by Age 23	38.1	57.1	52.8	57.5
38. Not Parents at Age 23	61.6	84.0	75.6	84.8

Environmental Factors, by Educational Attainment 5 Years After High School

	Total Attending Senior College (N = 5,416)			Total Completed Sr. College (N = 3,188)		Total Completed Sr. College (N = 3,188)	
	Sr. College Dropout (N = 1,048)	Delayed Potential Sr. College Graduate (N = 1,229)	Completed Sr. College (N = 3,118)	Completed Nonselective Sr. College (N = 1,530)	Completed Selective Sr. College (N = 1,658)	Terminated with Bachelor's Degree (N = 1,567)	Continued with Graduate Study (N = 1,621)
Per cents							
	34.1	28.2	15.9	24.4	8.1	20.9	11.1
	26.2	19.5	10.1	15.0	5.6	13.5	6.8
	36.9	34.4	26.7	30.7	22.9	30.1	23.4
	44.4	37.7	30.8	37.2	25.0	34.4	27.4
	31.1	23.7	11.0	16.9	5.6	14.5	7.6
	22.1	17.2	17.8	20.1	15.7	20.0	15.7
	50.7	46.0	38.0	42.3	34.1	45.6	30.7
	58.8	58.7	53.5	53.5	53.5	58.5	48.7
	42.1	41.8	41.5	40.5	42.5	40.3	42.7
	80.0	79.5	83.6	84.4	82.9	83.2	84.0
	46.9	41.9	32.4	36.0	29.0	35.0	29.8
	27.9	26.9	22.0	26.3	18.0	23.2	20.8
	48.7	52.5	61.7	55.5	67.3	56.9	66.3
	76.9	68.9	62.5	68.3	57.1	69.0	56.1
	80.6	77.1	68.9	72.8	65.2	74.0	63.8
	51.1	51.1	45.5	51.5	39.9	51.4	39.7
	1.2	1.3	0.9	1.5	0.4	1.0	0.8
	3.4	7.5	11.3	8.6	13.9	6.1	16.4
	23.1	25.7	23.8	23.9	23.8	24.9	22.8
	91.2	87.1	87.8	89.8	85.9	89.1	86.5
	17.4	14.9	15.1	20.1	10.5	18.2	12.1
	26.5	18.9	20.0	24.1	16.2	22.4	17.6
	57.3	58.4	59.3	61.8	56.9	61.1	57.5
	94.1	92.9	95.6	95.0	96.1	95.7	95.4
	66.0	64.0	72.4	71.6	73.2	70.7	74.1
	52.1	54.7	55.4	53.9	56.7	53.7	57.1
	88.1	87.4	84.7	86.4	83.1	85.4	84.0
	25.9	33.0	31.8	29.5	33.9	27.3	36.1
	69.2	78.0	74.6	68.1	80.5	71.3	77.7
	33.5	39.0	45.6	42.7	48.3	39.7	51.3
	8.0	5.8	6.1	9.3	3.1	7.6	4.6
	11.5	12.3	3.9	5.1	2.8	4.4	3.4
	66.3	67.4	69.7	71.8	67.8	70.6	68.9
	69.0	70.1	71.3	74.1	68.7	72.4	70.3
	29.5	28.0	24.7	28.4	21.3	26.0	23.4
	11.8	8.2	5.5	8.1	3.2	6.6	4.6
	50.3	62.3	57.9	54.2	61.3	52.3	63.4
	73.5	84.5	88.6	86.6	90.4	85.5	91.5

TABLE B–3. *Female High School Seniors Exhibiting Selected Personal and*

Personal and Environmental Variables	Total Sample (N = 6,794)		Total Attending College (N = 3,682)		
	Noncollege (N = 3,112)	College (N = 3,682)	Jr. College (N = 242)	Nursing School (N = 268)	Sr. College (N = 3,172)
I *Ability Variables*			Per cents		
1. Low Vocabulary	64.8	25.0	42.1	28.7	23.4
2. Low General Information	74.7	29.0	54.1	32.1	26.8
3. Low Creativity	61.6	39.5	49.2	43.3	38.4
4. Low Abstract Reasoning	62.9	38.2	49.6	43.3	36.9
5. Low Math Aptitude	77.2	30.6	59.5	32.5	28.2
II *Interests Variables*					
6. Low Physical Science	76.0	53.5	60.7	46.3	53.6
7. Low Literary/Linguistic	37.6	14.8	28.1	22.8	13.1
8. Low Social Service	23.2	13.4	26.4	5.6	13.1
III *Temperament Variables*					
9. Low Sociability	38.7	37.6	35.9	32.8	38.1
10. Low Impulsiveness	82.8	76.8	77.3	81.3	76.3
11. Low Mature Personality	40.0	26.5	33.5	28.3	25.8
IV *Socio-economic Variables*					
12. Low Family Income (< $6,000)	45.4	29.7	30.2	42.5	28.5
13. Father's Occupation: Professional/Technical/Managerial	27.1	57.3	47.1	37.3	59.7
14. Father's Education < College	91.3	64.3	74.4	83.6	61.9
15. Mother's Education < College	93.5	71.3	78.5	89.9	69.1
16. Few Books in Home (<100)	72.3	46.6	56.6	63.4	44.5
V *Ethnic-Religious Variables*					
17. Negro	2.3	2.2	1.7	0.7	2.4
18. Jewish	1.9	9.1	5.8	0.7	10.1
19. Catholic	28.2	19.6	19.8	32.5	18.5
20. Both Parents U.S. Natives	89.3	87.1	84.3	90.3	87.0
VI *Residence Variables*					
21. Home in Southeast U.S.	16.2	15.7	16.5	13.4	15.8
22. Small Hometown (<50,000)	29.4	22.5	21.1	27.2	22.2
23. No Residence Change Through High School	64.0	58.3	57.9	66.0	57.7
VII *Family of Orientation Variables*					
24. Unbroken Home	92.3	95.2	95.5	96.6	95.1
25. Small Family (≤3 Children)	57.3	70.0	67.3	61.2	70.9
26. First Born	45.5	56.9	55.8	60.4	56.7
VIII *High School Variables*					
27. Attended Public High School	94.2	93.2	96.3	88.1	93.4
28. Large Number of Students (>360 Seniors)	28.1	33.6	36.8	17.5	34.7
29. Large Faculty (>20 Teachers)	68.8	76.4	81.8	69.0	76.6
30. Majority of Graduates Attend College	19.2	36.8	37.2	23.5	37.9
31. No Guidance Program	10.3	6.3	4.5	6.3	6.4
IX *College Commitment Variables*					
32. Individual Not Planning College	62.9	7.9	11.6	41.0	4.9
33. College Plans Encouraged by Father	37.0	65.9	62.0	54.1	67.1
34. College Plans Encouraged by Mother	39.2	68.0	60.7	55.6	69.6
35. College Plans Encouraged by Peers	18.0	21.5	23.1	15.7	21.8
X *Family of Procreation Variables*					
36. Plan Early Marriage (Before Age 21)	51.0	15.7	31.8	8.6	15.0
37. Not Married by Age 23	19.7	41.6	30.6	28.3	43.6
38. Not Parents at Age 23	41.8	76.5	56.2	61.2	79.4

	Total Attending Senior College (N = 3,172)			Total Completed Sr. College (N = 2,066)		Total Completed Sr. College (N = 2,066)	
Sr. College Dropout (N = 801)	Delayed Potential Sr. College Graduate (N = 305)	Completed Sr. College (N = 2,066)	Completed Nonselective Sr. College (N = 1,089)	Completed Selective Sr. College (N = 977)	Terminated with Bachelor's Degree (N = 1,371)	Continued with Graduate Study (N = 695)
				Per cents			
35.2	27.9	18.1	25.2	10.3	20.6	13.2
40.8	32.8	20.5	28.1	12.1	23.0	15.5
46.8	40.0	34.9	39.1	30.2	36.3	32.1
44.2	42.3	33.3	38.3	27.6	35.2	29.3
44.8	36.7	20.5	27.6	12.6	23.9	13.8
62.3	55.7	49.9	52.5	47.0	52.4	45.0
18.7	16.4	10.5	11.4	9.4	12.0	7.3
14.9	15.7	11.9	9.6	14.5	12.1	11.7
34.7	38.7	39.4	35.9	43.2	37.5	43.0
76.4	78.4	76.0	78.4	73.4	77.5	73.2
31.6	27.9	23.2	25.3	20.9	24.7	20.3
30.7	34.4	26.8	32.7	20.3	27.6	25.3
53.2	51.1	63.5	57.2	70.5	64.0	62.6
70.0	68.2	57.9	64.2	50.9	60.3	53.1
74.9	75.1	66.0	69.3	62.3	67.1	63.9
48.9	45.9	42.5	49.6	34.6	44.1	39.3
2.7	3.6	2.1	3.3	0.7	2.3	1.6
5.9	8.2	11.9	7.6	16.8	8.4	19.0
20.6	22.3	17.1	17.4	16.8	17.7	16.0
88.9	85.2	86.6	88.9	84.0	88.0	83.7
16.1	15.1	15.8	21.0	10.0	18.2	11.2
22.8	16.1	22.8	25.7	19.5	24.4	19.6
54.3	57.7	58.9	60.9	56.8	58.9	59.0
93.7	94.1	95.8	95.7	95.9	95.8	95.8
65.9	62.3	74.1	72.1	76.5	72.1	78.1
55.9	55.4	57.1	56.1	58.2	54.9	61.4
93.3	90.5	93.9	94.9	92.8	94.5	92.7
31.6	37.0	35.6	33.4	38.1	33.5	39.9
75.7	78.4	76.7	71.9	82.0	74.4	81.1
36.2	35.1	39.0	33.1	45.5	36.4	44.0
6.1	5.2	6.7	8.6	4.6	8.0	4.2
7.2	14.1	2.6	2.7	2.5	2.8	2.3
64.7	54.7	69.9	71.6	68.1	70.1	69.6
68.3	59.7	71.6	74.0	68.9	72.1	70.6
24.1	16.4	21.7	22.5	20.9	22.1	21.0
23.7	20.3	10.9	13.0	8.5	12.0	8.8
23.8	61.0	48.6	48.8	48.5	43.0	59.7
51.7	81.0	89.9	88.8	91.1	87.6	94.4

Appendix C: Career Plan Studies

The Project TALENT Data Bank was used to select a sample of cases from the ninth-grade cohort. A subsample of this group was tested three years later when they were still enrolled in high school. A number of predictor variables were used to predict twelfth-grade career choice using a multiple discriminant method of analysis. The variables used in this study are listed below, with their name and Project TALENT number given. A more detailed description of these variables can be found in Project TALENT.[1]

Information Scores
   R-103 (Literature)
   R-106 (Mathematics)
   R-112 (Mechanics)
   R-131 (Art)
   R-100 (Grand Total Information)

Aptitude and Achievement Scores
   R-230 (English Total)
   R-250 (Reading Comprehension)
   R-260 (Creativity)
   R-270 (Mechanical Reasoning)
   R-340 (Mathematics Total)

Temperament Measure
   R-610 (Mature Personality)

Interest Measures
   P-701 (Physical Science)

[1] See Flanagan, John C., and others, *The American High-School Student,* University of Pittsburgh, Project TALENT, Cooperative Research Project No. 635, 1964.

P-704 (Literary-Linguistic)
P-705 (Social Service)
P-710 (Business/Managerial)
Ninth-Grade Career Choice (SIB 211)
  Sciences
  Professions
  Teaching
  Engineering
  Business
  Noncollege
SIB 91—High School Curriculum
SIB 113—Cumulative Grade Point Average
SIB 118—Guidance Experience Regarding College Plans
SIB 119—Guidance Experience Regarding Occupational Planning
P-801—Socioeconomic Status of the Student
High School Variables
  1. High School Size
  2. High School Mean on R-250 (Reading Comprehension)
  3. Percentage of graduating seniors who go to college from the student's high school

Method of Analysis

Multiple discriminant analysis was used primarily because it permits an assessment of the degree to which an individual's characteristics resemble those of others in each of several occupational groups on the basis of certain predictor or antecedent variables. In addition, discriminant analysis procedures summarize the predictive value of the antecedent variables more parsimoniously by reducing them to a smaller number of discriminant functions. Since these functions are designed to separate each group maximally on the basis of its centroid (group mean vector) and dispersion (group variance), the unique personal qualities associated with different occupational choices are revealed in the variables that define each function.[2]

The method of analysis required that data be available for all subjects on all of the variables listed above. This restriction greatly reduced the number of sample cases, so that the discriminant analysis was performed on 650 cases.

Changes in Career Choice

Another much larger sample was drawn from the ninth-grade group that was tested one year after high school. This larger sample was used to compare the "stables" (persons who had the same career choice at the initial and follow-up

[2] For a more extensive discussion of this method, see Cooley, W. W., and P. R. Lohnes, *Multivariate Procedures for the Behavioral Sciences,* John Wiley and Sons, New York, 1962, chaps. 6 and 7.

periods), "recruits" (those who entered each broad occupational group), and "defectors" (those who left each group). Since there were 10 broad occupational groups, there were 30 subgroups involved in this analysis. The number of cases in each of the 30 subgroups is indicated below:

Natural Sciences: Stables (N = 161); Defectors (N = 885); Recruits (N = 363)

Engineering: Stables (N = 499); Defectors (N = 1,716); Recruits (N = 515)

Health Professions (M.D. and D.D.S.): Stables (N = 197); Defectors (N = 431); Recruits (N = 284)

Law: Stables (N = 99); Defectors (N = 305); Recruits (N = 274)

TABLE C–1. *Mean Differences Among the Natural Sciences Career Choice Subgroups on Measures of Ability, Personality, and Interest*

Measure	Group	Mean	Standard Deviation
R-100 (Grand Total)	Stables	254.27*	39.97
	Defectors	228.75	49.92
	Recruits	227.50	43.62
R-230 (English Total)	Stables	87.94*	8.85
	Defectors	82.09	11.58
	Recruits	82.53	11.25
R-250 (Reading Comprehension)	Stables	37.71*	7.60
	Defectors	33.14	9.66
	Recruits	32.94	9.04
R-290 (Abstract Reasoning)	Stables	10.78*	2.42
	Defectors	9.78	2.76
	Recruits	9.94	2.64
R-340 (Total Mathematics)	Stables	29.29*	6.90
	Defectors	25.08	8.14
	Recruits	25.54	7.93
R-260 (Creativity)	Stables	11.40*	3.65
	Defectors	9.79	3.94
	Recruits	9.76	3.64
R-610 (Mature Personality)	Stables	12.75	5.39
	Defectors	11.78	5.46
	Recruits	11.90	5.52
SIB-113 (Grades)	Stables	4.40*	1.01
	Defectors	4.06	1.15
	Recruits	4.01	1.13
P-801 (Socioeconomic Index)	Stables	103.67*	8.23
	Defectors	100.73	9.50
	Recruits	100.12	9.43
P-701 (Physical Science Interest)	Stables	29.68*	6.19
	Defectors	26.92*	7.39
	Recruits	24.56*	8.47

* Mean is significantly different from each of the other two at the 1 per cent level.
SOURCE: Special tabulations of Project TALENT data.

Clergy: Stables (N = 71); Defectors (N = 141); Recruits (N = 80)
Teaching: Stables (N = 137); Defectors (N = 314); Recruits (N = 895)
Arts: Stables (N = 56); Defectors (N = 125); Recruits (N = 265)
Business: Stables (N = 223); Defectors (N = 354); Recruits (N = 1,342)
Skilled: Stables (N = 984); Defectors (N = 1,452); Recruits (N = 1,398)
Other: Stables (N = 400); Defectors (N = 1,250); Recruits (N = 1,557)

The measures that differentiated stables, defectors, and recruits were different for the different occupations, even though there were many measures (such as reading ability, abstract reasoning ability, and so forth) which discriminated for most of the occupations. Means and standard deviation on the important measures for nine of the groups ("Other" was omitted because it is a heterogeneous category) are shown in Tables C-1 through C-9.

TABLE C–2. *Mean Differences Among Engineering Career Choice Subgroups on Measures of Ability, Personality, and Interest*

Measure	Group	Mean	Standard Deviation
R-100 (Grand Total)	Stables	238.85*	39.89
	Defectors	214.42*	47.69
	Recruits	223.92*	44.70
R-230 (English Total)	Stables	84.76*	8.28
	Defectors	79.54*	11.05
	Recruits	81.95*	10.28
R-250 (Reading Comprehension)	Stables	34.16*	7.80
	Defectors	30.71*	9.56
	Recruits	32.59*	8.86
R-290 (Abstract Reasoning)	Stables	10.61*	2.37
	Defectors	9.47*	2.69
	Recruits	10.18*	2.32
R-340 (Total Mathematics)	Stables	27.51*	7.10
	Defectors	23.16*	7.15
	Recruits	25.43*	7.18
R-260 (Creativity)	Stables	10.76*	3.57
	Defectors	9.33	3.78
	Recruits	9.60	3.62
R-610 (Mature Personality)	Stables	12.52*	5.50
	Defectors	11.39	5.34
	Recruits	11.69	5.49
SIB-113 (Grades)	Stables	4.18*	0.99
	Defectors	3.81*	1.12
	Recruits	4.01*	1.10
P-801 (Socioeconomic Index)	Stables	101.55*	9.05
	Defectors	99.68	9.44
	Recruits	99.78	8.76
P-701 (Physical Science Interest)	Stables	28.94*	6.28
	Defectors	25.59	7.31
	Recruits	25.75	7.39

SOURCE: See Table C–1.

TABLE C–3. Mean Differences Among Business Career Choice Subgroups on Measures of Ability, Personality, and Interest

Measure	Group	Mean	Standard Deviation
R-100 (Grand Total)	Stables	201.11	42.65
	Defectors	190.45*	52.28
	Recruits	200.24	43.33
R-230 (English Total)	Stables	79.77	10.95
	Defectors	75.49*	13.04
	Recruits	77.83	10.67
R-250 (Reading Comprehension)	Stables	29.07	9.13
	Defectors	26.85*	10.27
	Recruits	28.33	9.09
R-290 (Abstract Reasoning)	Stables	9.13	2.76
	Defectors	8.66	3.11
	Recruits	8.89	2.63
R-340 (Total Mathematics)	Stables	22.38	7.22
	Defectors	20.90	7.30
	Recruits	21.01	6.42
R-260 (Creativity)	Stables	8.61	3.41
	Defectors	8.00	3.60
	Recruits	8.48	3.50
R-610 (Mature Personality)	Stables	10.86	5.05
	Defectors	10.33	5.08
	Recruits	10.74	5.25
SIB-113 (Grades)	Stables	3.72	1.13
	Defectors	3.69	1.11
	Recruits	3.70	1.16
P-801 (Socioeconomic Index)	Stables	101.13*	10.78
	Defectors	97.96	10.96
	Recruits	99.14	9.59
P-710 (Business-Managerial Interest)	Stables	22.36	6.74
	Defectors	21.34	7.46
	Recruits	19.82*	7.25

SOURCE: See Table C–1.

TABLE C–4. *Mean Differences Among the Health Professions (M.D., D.D.S.) Career Choice Subgroups on Measures of Ability, Personality, and Interest*

Measure	Group	Mean	Standard Deviation
R-100 (Grand Total)	Stables	244.09	37.87
	Defectors	211.23*	46.60
	Recruits	238.67	39.65
R-230 (English Total)	Stables	86.06	8.40
	Defectors	80.13*	11.03
	Recruits	84.95	9.37
R-250 (Reading Comprehension)	Stables	36.33	7.19
	Defectors	30.55*	9.26
	Recruits	35.08	7.95
R-290 (Abstract Reasoning)	Stables	10.13	2.41
	Defectors	9.17*	2.59
	Recruits	10.24	2.38
R-340 (Total Mathematics)	Stables	26.56	7.15
	Defectors	22.46*	7.47
	Recruits	26.19	6.96
R-260 (Creativity)	Stables	10.31	3.38
	Defectors	8.97*	3.72
	Recruits	10.45	3.58
R-610 (Mature Personality)	Stables	13.71	5.45
	Defectors	12.47	5.13
	Recruits	13.10	5.53
SIB-113 (Grades)	Stables	4.46	1.00
	Defectors	3.96*	1.13
	Recruits	4.31	1.12
P-801 (Socioeconomic Index)	Stables	107.17	8.98
	Defectors	102.55*	10.51
	Recruits	104.50	9.06
P-705 (Social Services)	Stables	16.97	6.83
	Defectors	16.89	6.99
	Recruits	16.55	7.37

SOURCE: See Table C–1.

TABLE C–5. *Mean Differences Among the Law Career Choice Subgroups on Measures of Ability, Personality, and Interest*

Measure	Group	Mean	Standard Deviation
R-100 (Grand Total)	Stables	234.81	39.88
	Defectors	210.81*	50.73
	Recruits	234.92	43.86
R-230 (English Total)	Stables	84.71	10.18
	Defectors	79.69*	13.13
	Recruits	83.82	9.91
R-250 (Reading Comprehension)	Stables	36.17	7.92
	Defectors	30.85*	10.08
	Recruits	34.85	8.29
R-290 (Abstract Reasoning)	Stables	9.56	2.58
	Defectors	8.90	2.84
	Recruits	9.90	2.40
R-340 (Total Mathematics)	Stables	25.72	7.74
	Defectors	21.92*	7.34
	Recruits	24.72	7.30
R-260 (Creativity)	Stables	8.95	3.41
	Defectors	8.89	3.65
	Recruits	9.98	3.77
R-610 (Mature Personality)	Stables	12.70	5.37
	Defectors	11.49	5.62
	Recruits	11.76	5.53
SIB-113 (Grades)	Stables	4.22	1.07
	Defectors	3.95	1.19
	Recruits	4.09	1.14
P-801 (Socioeconomic Index)	Stables	106.74	9.03
	Defectors	100.72*	10.23
	Recruits	104.84	9.08
P-704 (Literature-Linguistics)	Stables	20.81	8.50
	Defectors	19.59	7.62
	Recruits	18.22	7.84

SOURCE: See Table C–1.

TABLE C–6. *Mean Differences Among the Clergy Career Choice Subgroups on Measures of Ability, Personality, and Interest*

Measure	Group	Mean	Standard Deviation
R-100 (Grand Total)	Stables	227.96	38.09
	Defectors	207.89	47.62
	Recruits	220.63	50.50
R-230 (English Total)	Stables	88.31*	8.68
	Defectors	82.06	14.04
	Recruits	82.81	9.53
R-250 (Reading Comprehension)	Stables	35.54	6.83
	Defectors	31.52	10.01
	Recruits	32.16	9.95
R-290 (Abstract Reasoning)	Stables	10.30	1.99
	Defectors	9.41	2.78
	Recruits	9.60	2.60
R-340 (Total Mathematics)	Stables	26.56	5.71
	Defectors	23.33	7.59
	Recruits	24.58	7.16
R-260 (Creativity)	Stables	9.27	3.55
	Defectors	9.11	3.38
	Recruits	9.58	3.81
R-610 (Mature Personality)	Stables	13.00	5.55
	Defectors	10.75	5.19
	Recruits	11.53	5.29
SIB-113 (Grades)	Stables	4.42	1.01
	Defectors	3.97	1.05
	Recruits	4.21	1.20
P-801 (Socioeconomic Index)	Stables	100.30	7.69
	Defectors	99.55	9.37
	Recruits	101.79	10.31
P-705 (Social Services)	Stables	25.49	6.56
	Defectors	23.00	6.91
	Recruits	18.05*	7.74

SOURCE: See Table C–1.

TABLE C–7. *Mean Differences Among the Arts Career Choice Subgroups on Measures of Ability, Personality, and Interest*

Measure	Group	Mean	Standard Deviation
R-100 (Grand Total)	Stables	204.29	49.53
	Defectors	209.82	48.59
	Recruits	210.18	50.61
R-230 (English Total)	Stables	79.45	12.97
	Defectors	79.03	13.17
	Recruits	79.83	13.17
R-250 (Reading Comprehension)	Stables	29.88	10.61
	Defectors	30.42	10.73
	Recruits	30.20	10.08
R-290 (Abstract Reasoning)	Stables	9.43	2.78
	Defectors	9.29	2.80
	Recruits	9.27	2.79
R-340 (Total Mathematics)	Stables	20.43	7.29
	Defectors	20.84	7.35
	Recruits	21.24	7.06
R-260 (Creativity)	Stables	9.50	3.67
	Defectors	9.30	3.83
	Recruits	9.08	3.65
R-610 (Mature Personality)	Stables	10.54	5.62
	Defectors	10.24	5.53
	Recruits	11.11	5.10
SIB-113 (Grades)	Stables	3.68	1.25
	Defectors	3.61	1.10
	Recruits	3.76	1.17
P-801 (Socioeconomic Index)	Stables	97.36	8.59
	Defectors	100.18	10.81
	Recruits	100.07	9.92
P-704 (Literature-Linguistics)	Stables	18.02	8.91
	Defectors	19.38	9.82
	Recruits	17.67	8.12

SOURCE: See Table C–1.

TABLE C–8. *Mean Differences Among the Teaching Career Choice Subgroups on Measures of Ability, Personality, and Interest*

Measure	Group	Mean	Standard Deviation
R-100 (Grand Total)	Stables	214.58	39.82
	Defectors	195.66*	59.13
	Recruits	215.26	44.36
R-230 (English Total)	Stables	81.25	8.76
	Defectors	76.35*	15.49
	Recruits	80.81	10.52
R-250 (Reading Comprehension)	Stables	31.91	8.61
	Defectors	27.65*	11.70
	Recruits	31.39	9.22
R-290 (Abstract Reasoning)	Stables	8.93	2.74
	Defectors	8.38	3.19
	Recruits	9.42*	2.68
R-340 (Total Mathematics)	Stables	22.65	6.46
	Defectors	21.45	7.88
	Recruits	23.01	7.20
R-260 (Creativity)	Stables	8.82	3.40
	Defectors	8.16	3.76
	Recruits	9.10	3.60
R-610 (Mature Personality)	Stables	11.15	5.37
	Defectors	10.81	4.96
	Recruits	11.24	5.31
SIB-113 (Grades)	Stables	3.91	1.00
	Defectors	3.89	1.17
	Recruits	3.82	1.06
P-801 (Socioeconomic Index)	Stables	98.77	9.23
	Defectors	98.81	10.03
	Recruits	99.16	9.21
P-705 (Social Services)	Stables	23.71*	5.95
	Defectors	21.20*	6.90
	Recruits	17.69*	7.00

SOURCE: See Table C–1.

TABLE C–9. *Mean Differences Among the Skilled/Technical Fields Career Choice Subgroups on Measures of Ability, Personality, and Interest*

Measure	Group	Mean	Standard Deviation
R-100 (Grand Total)	Stables	179.71	44.47
	Defectors	195.70*	45.68
	Recruits	182.70	48.95
R-230 (English Total)	Stables	72.38	11.33
	Defectors	76.15*	11.49
	Recruits	72.63	12.91
R-250 (Reading Comprehension)	Stables	23.90	6.69
	Defectors	27.17*	9.61
	Recruits	24.70	9.87
R-290 (Abstract Reasoning)	Stables	8.22	2.90
	Defectors	8.87*	2.78
	Recruits	8.20	3.05
R-340 (Total Mathematics)	Stables	18.42	6.10
	Defectors	20.41*	6.58
	Recruits	19.01	6.66
R-260 (Creativity)	Stables	7.77	3.53
	Defectors	8.20*	3.51
	Recruits	7.74	3.69
R-610 (Mature Personality)	Stables	9.03*	4.56
	Defectors	10.05	5.06
	Recruits	9.92	4.82
P-801 (Socioeconomic Index)	Stables	94.46	8.75
	Defectors	96.91*	9.62
	Recruits	95.38	9.68
SIB-113 (Grades)	Stables	3.41*	1.19
	Defectors	3.61	1.14
	Recruits	3.57	1.17

SOURCE: See Table C–1.

Appendix D: The National Register—Doctoral Files Collated Data Tape and Estimated Coverage of the National Register

COLLATION OF THE FILES AND DEVELOPMENT OF A WORK TAPE

Since 1954, the National Science Foundation, through the National Register of Scientific and Technical Personnel, has collected biennial data on the education, employment, specialization, and other characteristics of U.S. scientists. In recent years complete coverage has been attempted for all of those U.S. citizens professionally identified in most of the major physical and social sciences. In addition, a one-in-six sample of engineers has recently been added to the Register. In 1962, the total number in the Register was 215,000. In 1964, 224,000 scientists were included.[1]

The National Science Foundation provided a tape file to the Commission on Human Resources containing information for 20,965 doctorate recipients in the 1964 National Register of Scientific and Technical Personnel. This tape included all of those who reported receiving the doctoral degree in the period from 1957

---

[1] For a further description of the 1964 National Register File, see National Science Foundation, *American Science Manpower*, 1964, NSF 66–29, Government Printing Office, Washington, 1966.

to 1962 in any of the following fields: Mathematics/Statistics; Physics (including astronomy); Chemistry; Earth Sciences (including meteorology and oceanography); Biological Sciences (including anatomy, biophysics, botany, ecology, entomology, genetics, microbiology, nutrition, pathology, pharmacology, physiology, phytopathology, virology, and zoology); Biochemistry; Psychology; Sociology; and Economics.

This tape was matched against the complete National Academy of Sciences, Office of Scientific Personnel (OSP) Doctoral Files, which contain information on virtually all the earned doctorates granted by U.S. institutions. The matching process was carried out by computer, matching on name, birth date, year of doctorate, institution of doctorate, and field of doctorate. All machine non-matches were hand-checked, using the additional items of the B.A. institution and year of B.A. as matching criteria.

Of the 20,965 cases reported in the National Register, 1,143 (5.4 per cent) reported receiving the doctoral degree from a foreign university. Of the 19,822 reporting a U.S. doctorate, 19,292 (97.3 per cent) were located in the Office of Scientific Personnel Doctoral Files.[2] These collated cases form the base data for the tabulations reported in sections of Chapters 7 and 8.

In addition to the data on employment and education derived from the collation of the two basic data files, several additional items of information were added for a number of those in the sample. Ability measures, collected through the high schools attended by the Ph.D.'s as part of a research study by Lindsey R. Harmon,[3] were read into the data files for about 45 per cent of the cases.

The quality of the institutional department from which the individual received the doctoral degree was also added to the basic information file. These quality scores are based on a study by Allan M. Cartter in which over 150 scholars within each of the disciplines evaluated the departmental programs of all major institutions.[4]

The third major set of additional information included in the data file is citation counts based on references in the *Science Citation Index*. All of the 1957–1959 doctorate recipients in the collated file who had majored in mathematics/statistics, physics, chemistry, earth sciences, biosciences, and psychology were matched by hand with the listings in the 1964 and 1965 *Science Citation Index*. All citations to the works by those in the sample were counted, regardless of

[2] The completeness of coverage in the National Register of the recent Ph.D. scientists varies from about two-thirds in some fields to about four-fifths in others. See the following section of this Appendix for a further discussion of the completeness in coverage.

[3] See Harmon, Lindsey R., "High School Backgrounds of Science Doctorates," *Science*, vol. 133, March 10, 1963, pp. 679–688; and Harmon, *High School Ability Patterns: A Backward Look from the Doctorate*, Scientific Manpower Report No. 6, National Academy of Sciences–National Research Council, Washington, August, 1965. For a further description of the ability measure, see Chapter 8.

[4] See Cartter, Allan M., *An Assessment of Quality in Graduate Education*, American Council on Education, Washington, 1966. In some cases these ratings were combined for several allied disciplines, and occasionally were recoded for analytical and presentation purposes. For a further description of these adjustments, see Chapter 8.

the type of media in which the publications appeared. An interjudge reliability of .95 between citation counts was determined for a random sample of 200 cases, and all citation frequencies were entered into the basic data file.[5]

The merged file, with the additional items that were added, was used in the analysis of factors affecting scientists' productivity, reported in Chapter 8. Most of the statistical analyses were multiple and partial correlations of factors affecting the number of citation counts, which was the criterion variable in the first part of the analyses. In the second part of the chapter, income was used as the criterion measure of accomplishment. The results of these two analyses of criteria of effectiveness are presented in Chapter 8.

For the income analysis, a sample of 3,506 doctorate recipients of 1957–1959 was used. All of these individuals had reported their 1964 professional income and had complete data on 11 additional variables noted below. A regression model was employed to determine the extent that these independent variables are related to the income criterion, with the categorical predictor variables converted to sets of "dummy" variables. This resulted in a final regression equation including 22 independent variables and the dependent variable. In the analysis, the coefficient of multiple determination and the coefficients of partial determination are presented.

The regression equation takes the form

$$X_1 = a + b_2X_2 + b_3X_3 + \ldots\ldots\ldots\ldots + B_{12}X_{12}$$

The variables included in the analysis are defined as follows:

Income X_1—Annual income in 1964 for the 3,506 individuals who received their Ph.D. between 1957 and 1959. This is the dependent variable. The following independent variables were used:

Field X_2—Field is a set of "dummy" variables including mathematics/statistics, physics, chemistry, earth sciences, biosciences, and psychology. The reason for including this variable is that, even after all other factors influencing income are considered, differences in income according to field might be expected to reflect disequilibrium in the labor market. That is, no differences among fields would be found when all factors were accounted for and individuals made occupational adjustments to bring the system into equilibrium.

Activity X_3—The type of work that an individual does within his field can be expected to affect his income. To the extent that certain jobs have unpleasant attributes, such as unusual psychological pressures, differential incomes will be necessary to compensate for these attributes. Again, even when such compensating factors and all personal attributes are taken into account, disequilibrium in the labor market would lead to income differences by activity. The "dummy" variables reflecting activity are research, teaching, and administration.

Region X_4—This set of variables included a variable for employment in the

---

[5] For a further description of this citation measure, see the extended discussion in Chapter 8.

East, the South, the West, and the Central part of the United States. Income differences between areas of the United States have existed for a long time.

Years of Employment X_5—This variable is included as a proxy for experience or on-the-job training, which should result in income differences.

Sex X_6—If women are discriminated against in the labor market, this will be reflected through the relationship of income to this variable. Of course, to the extent that women cause the employer to endure costs from excessive absenteeism or labor turnover, this would also influence the relationship between sex and income. The variable is also a dichotomous "dummy" variable.

B.A.-Ph.D. Time Lapse X_7—The number of years between the B.A. degree and the Ph.D. degree is included in the analysis to measure the influence of need for achievement. Of course, as noted in the Chapter 8 discussion, it is only a crude proxy for "drive" or motivation, which may influence the income that one earns.

Measured Ability X_8—To the extent that individuals with the same level of education have different amounts of "natural ability," one would expect their incomes to differ. That is, all other things remaining the same, one would expect the system to reward differences in manifest ability.

Citation Count X_9—While this index of productivity has its limitations, as noted in Chapter 8, it has the advantage of including a quality dimension that is missing in the other independent variables herein employed.

Quality of Ph.D. Department X_{10}—This variable, based on Cartter's index of quality in graduate education, is a continuous variable recoded with a range of zero for low quality to five for high quality.

Age X_{11}—This variable would reflect any favoritism due to the age, or the influence of sagacity that might accompany age.

Type of Employment X_{12}—This variable is included to see how much of the variation in income among professionals could be explained by the nature of the institution employing the professional. This variable included three categories: business employment, federal government employment, and academic employment. Difference in earnings in different types of employment, after considering the other independent variables, could be due to variations in nonpecuniary aspects of different types of employment. For example, the greater security associated with government employment might allow government agencies to pay lower wages. Of course, there are a number of other reasons for difference in earnings in different types of employment even when the labor market is in equilibrium. In any case, this variable is almost certain to explain some of the variation in income among professionals.

THE COVERAGE OF SCIENCE DOCTORATES IN THE NATIONAL REGISTER

The National Register is an important source of information about the scientific manpower resources of the United States, with data from the Register used for both administrative and research purposes well beyond the studies reported in this volume. Plans are currently being developed to use the Register for a number of longitudinal studies of scientific careers, which should even further enhance its value as a data source. However, even though a large number of cases are in the Register files, little is known in regard to the completeness of coverage or the response biases involved. This is partly the result of the method employed for establishing contact with American scientists for inclusion in the National Register. The professional societies assume the primary responsibility for establishing contact with individuals. There is overlapping membership in the societies and not all individuals eligible for the Register are society members, so that it is not possible to tell whether a nonrespondent should have been included or not.[6] In addition, while there is a universal criterion that eligibility be based on "full professional standing" in the particular scientific field, there is still a good deal of variation in the definitions of persons eligible for inclusion, since these definitions are made independently by each participating society. In some fields a doctoral degree, or a doctorate *plus* several years of professional experience, is required for inclusion in the Register, while in other disciplines the highest degree required is a bachelor's or its equivalent. This may not seriously affect the results when analyses are focused on the interrelationship between variables within a single discipline, but when cross-field comparisons are undertaken or generalizations to the universe of scientists are attempted, the question of coverage and response bias are of primary importance. Most of the reports based on the National Register data that have been issued include both cross-field comparisons and within-field analyses. For example, comparisons of degree levels and salaries across fields, and sex, age, and geographic distributions within fields, are found in most reports.[7] One report, that on the economists, attempts a comparative analysis of characteristics that relates the National Register data with Census data. However, an assessment of the coverage and reliability of the National Register is not possible from these comparisons. One

---

[6] An attempt is made to get in touch with those who may be eligible for inclusion, but are not members of the societies, through several means, including state or local professional society membership lists, lists of persons attending professional conferences, requests to those who receive several questionnaires to give duplicates to others who they think may be eligible but did not receive a questionnaire, and so forth. In addition, the magnitude of duplication of mailing lists is largely unknown, although the number of duplicates returned, which are subsequently eliminated, is reported not to be too large. The net result is that the magnitude of the two classes of nonrespondents, those who are defined as eligible but do not reply to the questionnaires and those who are functionally eligible but who are not included on any roster, is indeterminable from the returns.

[7] See, for example, National Science Foundation, *American Science Manpower: 1962*, NSF 64–16, Government Printing Office, Washington, 1964; National Science Foundation, *American Science Manpower: 1964*, NSF 66–29, Government Printing Office, Washington, 1966; Committee on the National Science Foundation Report on the Economics Profession, "The Structure of Economists' Employment and Salaries, 1964," *American Economic Review*, vol. 55, December, 1965, Part 2, Supplement; Hopper, Janice A., "Sociologists in the 1964 National Register of Scientific and Technical Personnel," *The American Sociologist*, vol. 1, February, 1966, pp. 71–78; and Henderson, Bonnie C., "Earth Scientists in the 1966 National Register," *Geotimes*, vol. 12, April, 1967, pp. 16–17.

of the criteria for an economist being included in the National Register is an advanced degree that cannot be identified in the Census. Additional comparisons that have been made with the data have likewise encountered similar difficulties.[8]

As a byproduct of the studies of career outcomes discussed previously in this Appendix, it was possible to develop some estimates of the coverage of doctorate recipients in the National Register and to make some estimates of nonresponse bias.

Compatibility of the Files

In order to make an adequate estimate of the coverage, it is necessary to make comparisons between groups that are as nearly comparable as possible. The National Academy of Sciences–Office of Scientific Personnel Doctoral Files (subsequently abbreviated to NAS) includes over 99 per cent of all doctorates awarded *in the United States*, regardless of the subsequent location of the recipients.[9] It does not include doctorates awarded outside the United States and possessions.

The National Register, on the other hand, includes only those who are considered in the U.S. manpower pool at the time of the survey. Those who are not U.S. citizens are included only if they are presently located in the United States and an attempt is made to include U.S. citizens even if they were not working in the United States at the time of the survey. Some of these people, in both groups, received the doctoral degree in a foreign institution (Table D-1).[10]

The basic analysis of coverage is limited primarily to the group that had obtained both the B.A. and the Ph.D. in the United States. More than 98.5 per cent of this group were U.S. citizens at the time of receipt of the Ph.D., and for purposes of analysis it is assumed that all of the U.S. B.A.-U.S. Ph.D. cases in the NAS files in the fields included are eligible for inclusion in the National Register. Therefore, the denominator for coverage estimates is the NAS U.S. B.A.-U.S. Ph.D. scientists in the fields of science under consideration who were counted at the time of the Ph.D., while the numerator is the National Register U.S. B.A.-U.S. Ph.D. scientists in the same fields in 1964. Actually, the National Register scientists were matched against the *entire* NAS file, so that, for example, an educational psychologist whose degree was reported in the NAS file as in

---

[8] See, for example, the brief treatment in *American Science Manpower: 1964*, pp. 2–3.

[9] Graduation lists of doctorate recipients are obtained by the National Academy of Sciences from universities that award the degrees and recipients are included in the files whether they submit a questionnaire or not. When a list for a given year is completed, it is returned to every school of graduation for double checking. More than 99 per cent of all doctorate recipients are probably included.

[10] Of the 29,098 individuals in the NAS files who were graduates of U.S. institutions between 1957 and 1962 in the selected fields, 3,457 (11.9 per cent) received the B.A. outside the United States. Among the 20,965 doctorate recipients of the same years in the National Register, 1,143 (5.4 per cent) received the doctorate in a foreign country. Of those receiving the doctorate in the U.S., 738 (3.7 per cent) reported receipt of the B.A. outside the United States (Table D-1).

TABLE D-1. *Number of 1957–1962 Doctorates in NAS Doctoral Files and National Register, by Selected Field and Place of Baccalaureate*

Field	Number in Doctoral Files			Number in National Register			
	U.S. B.A.	Foreign B.A.	Total	U.S. B.A., U.S. Ph.D.	Foreign B.A., U.S. Ph.D.	Foreign Ph.D.	Total
Mathematics/Statistics	1,579	278	1,857	1,290	84	92	1,466
Physics	3,027	404	3,431	2,396	112	334	2,842
Chemistry	5,876	636	6,512	4,414	163	372	4,949
Earth Sciences	1,173	217	1,390	817	23	32	872
Biosciences	5,548	911	6,459	3,583	132	149	3,864
Biochemistry	1,272	251	1,523	846	52	77	975
Psychology	4,548	247	4,795	3,608	62	51	3,721
Sociology	903	109	1,012	809	27	9	845
Economics	1,715	404	2,119	1,321	83	27	1,431
Total	25,641	3,457	29,098	19,084	738	1,143	20,965

education, but who reported his field in the National Register as Psychology, would be included as a match in the numerator, but would not appear in the denominator. The effect of this procedure will be to overestimate slightly overall coverage, but will minimize the extent to which field changes are identified as coverage problems.

National Register Cases Located in NAS Files

Of the 19,084 U.S. doctorate recipients with a U.S. B.A. in the National Register, 18,587 (97.4 per cent) were located in the NAS files. Across fields, Psychology and Biochemistry, with slightly under 97 per cent matched, were low; Physics, Economics, and Earth Sciences were high, with over 98 per cent of the cases matched (Table D-2).

TABLE D-2. *Number and Percentage of National Register U.S. Doctorates Located in NAS Doctoral Files, by Field and Place of Baccalaureate*

Field	U.S. B.A.		Foreign B.A.		Total	
	Number	Per Cent	Number	Per Cent	Number	Per Cent
Mathematics/Statistics	1,260	97.7	84	100.0	1,344	97.8
Physics	2,360	98.5	108	96.4	2,468	98.4
Chemistry	4,288	97.1	154	94.5	4,442	97.1
Earth Sciences	806	98.7	21	91.3	827	98.5
Biosciences	3,493	97.5	126	95.5	3,619	97.4
Biochemistry	818	96.7	51	98.1	869	96.8
Psychology	3,480	96.5	56	90.3	3,536	96.3
Sociology	788	97.4	26	96.3	814	97.4
Economics	1,294	98.0	79	95.2	1,373	97.8
Total	18,587	97.4	705	95.5	19,292	97.3

The nonmatches may reflect some misreporting of honorary degrees as earned degrees in the National Register, coding and punching errors, name changes between Ph.D. and the 1964 Register, or failure of the NAS file to completely cover the universe of doctorates awarded in the United States. The effect of name changes is likely to be the largest factor. Among the 18,587 U.S. B.A.-U.S. Ph.D. cases that were located as matches, 1,252 (6.7 per cent) were women. Of the 497 U.S. B.A.-U.S. Ph.D. cases that were nonmatches, 160 (32.2 per cent) were women, the majority of whom have probably married and changed their name since the NAS data were compiled.

Coverage of Foreign B.A.'s Who Receive a Doctorate in the United States

Of those with a foreign B.A. and a U.S. Ph.D. in the NAS files, only about one-fifth were located in the National Register. This low proportion of matches is primarily the result of a high proportion of the people returning to their own country to work after obtaining the doctorate (the percentage who remain in the United States as estimated by inclusion in the National Register ranges from a low of 10 per cent in Earth Sciences to over one-fourth in the Physical Sciences). As indicated above, the foreign B.A.-U.S. Ph.D. cases are excluded from the analysis of coverage because only a minority of them appear to meet National Register criteria for inclusion.

Coverage of U.S. Doctorates

For all nine fields combined, 72.5 per cent of the 1957–1962 U.S. B.A. doctorates in the Doctoral Files were located in the National Register. By fields, National Register coverage ranges from a high of 87.3 per cent in Sociology to a low of 62.9 per cent in the Biosciences. Mathematics and Statistics, with 79.8 per cent covered, and Physics with 78.0 per cent covered, are next highest; Biochemistry is almost as low as the Biological Sciences (Table D-3). When age specific death rates are used to estimate losses through death from the time of the doctorate to 1964, when the National Register survey was undertaken, coverage is increased slightly (about .6 of one per cent in each field). If we assume that the nonmatches of National Register U.S. B.A.-U.S. Ph.D. cases are key-punching errors or name changes that precluded matching and should therefore be added to the National Register totals, then the adjusted totals of the last column of Table D-3 would be boosted by about 2 per cent overall.

There is a much smaller year-to-year fluctuation than field-to-field difference. Coverage is lowest for doctorate recipients of 1957 (about 70 per cent) and rises to more than three-fourths in 1960, thereafter declining slightly. The coverage in initial and terminal years may be more affected by errors in reporting year of completion of the degree than by variation in response rates across the years covered in this analysis. Since most of these errors would probably involve misstatements of one year in time of completion of degree, some of the 1957 and 1962 graduates may have been excluded from the tape furnished by NSF, although some additional cases, graduates of 1956 and 1963, may also be included as a result of misstatement of degree year.

Discrepancies in the reported year of doctorate in the two files can be partly attributed to variation in interpretation of questions at different points in time. In regard to the year of doctorate, for example, the NAS data are usually collected some time prior to the awarding of the degree itself, but after all doctorate requirements are met. Thus, the year of doctorate may sometimes be reported to NAS as the year in which all requirements were met, not necessarily when the degree itself was awarded. On the other hand, the retrospective nature of this question in the National Register survey may elicit a response in terms of the year in which the doctoral degree was actually awarded.

Table D-4 shows the discrepancies in reported major field of the doctorate for those matched cases with a U.S. B.A. Overall, 90 per cent report the same major field area, with the social scientists generally showing lower agreement

TABLE D–3. *Proportion of NAS Doctorates in National Register, by Field, Place of Baccalaureate, and Year of Ph.D.*

Field	Percentage of U.S. Ph.D.'s with Foreign B.A.'s Located in National Register	Percentage of U.S. Ph.D.'s with U.S. B.A.'s Located in National Register							Adjusted[a] Percentage of U.S. Ph.D.'s with U.S. B.A.'s Located in National Register
		1957	1958	1959	1960	1961	1962	Total	
Mathematics/Statistics	30.2	67.1	73.5	85.7	81.8	75.7	89.4	79.8	80.4
Physics	26.7	74.3	75.7	75.1	81.7	82.8	77.1	78.0	78.6
Chemistry	24.2	67.5	73.8	70.6	77.9	73.6	74.3	73.0	73.6
Earth Sciences	9.7	62.5	67.5	70.4	69.9	73.5	66.7	68.7	69.2
Biosciences	13.8	64.0	64.1	59.9	65.4	64.3	60.3	62.9	63.5
Biochemistry	20.3	62.1	67.0	69.5	61.2	66.1	61.4	64.3	64.8
Psychology	22.7	74.4	70.4	75.8	79.5	75.1	83.1	76.5	77.1
Sociology	23.8	77.7	77.3	78.2	97.9	92.8	96.1	87.3	87.9
Economics	19.5	71.5	71.9	76.5	77.7	71.8	82.3	75.5	76.0
Total	20.4	68.7	70.6	71.4	75.5	73.4	74.5	72.5	73.1

[a] Adjusted for deaths only, based on a death rate of 1.8 per 1,000 per year.

TABLE D–4. *Major Field of Doctorate in National Register and NAS Doctoral Files, All Matched Cases with U.S. B.A.'s*

NAS Field of Doctorate	National Register Field of Doctorate									
	Mathematics/ Statistics	Physics	Chemistry	Earth Sciences	Biosciences	Biochemistry	Psychology	Sociology	Economics	Total
Mathematics/ Statistics	1,131	2	—	—	—	—	—	—	—	1,133
Physics	3	2,253	13	1	2	—	—	—	—	2,272
Chemistry	—	10	4,081	1	34	16	1	—	—	4,143
Earth Sciences	1	3	4	785	1	—	1	—	—	795
Biosciences	24	14	32	12	3,193	31	1	—	—	3,307
Biochemistry	—	1	84	—	49	759	—	—	—	893
Other Natural Sciences	23	63	61	5	201	12	1	2	23	391
Psychology	2	3	1	—	2	—	2,903	109	2	3,022
Sociology	—	—	—	—	—	—	2	625	1	628
Economics	3	—	—	—	—	—	—	1	1,025	1,029
Other Social Sciences	19	1	—	2	—	—	6	14	27	69
Education	44	7	10	—	5	—	516	23	12	617
Arts and Professions	10	3	2	—	6	—	49	14	204	288
Total	1,260	2,360	4,288	806	3,493	818	3,480	788	1,294	18,587
Per cent	89.8	95.5	95.2	97.4	91.4	92.8	83.4	79.3	79.2	90.1

and the physical scientists showing the highest agreement. However, many of the larger areas of disagreement can be readily explained: (1) Almost all of those who reported one of the Biosciences in the National Register but are shown to be in "other Natural Sciences" in the NAS field distribution were in Agricultural Sciences, some of which were classified as Biosciences in the National Register definition employed in this study. (2) Many of those who reported Education as the major field in NAS but Psychology in the National Register are probably educational psychologists. (3) The majority of those not reporting Sociology in both files have reported Psychology in the NAS file and Sociology in the National Register; most are probably social psychologists. If the social psychologists were considered Psychology matches rather than Sociology matches, they would raise the estimated coverage of psychologists from 77 to 81 per cent, and reduce the estimated coverage of sociologists from 88 to 79 per cent. It would, of course, have no effect on the overall estimate of coverage. (4) The NAS Arts and Professions category includes business, which explains the shift of a number of them to Economics in the National Register. If these four situations are considered to be agreements in the major field report to both files, then only about 4 per cent of the cases can be considered discrepant.

The field-by-field comparisons suggest that between 900 and 1,200 of the matched National Register cases are drawn from fields in the NAS files that are not represented in the denominator of the coverage estimate. This suggests an overestimate of coverage of 5 to 7 per cent. However shifts into the numerator would be counterbalanced to an unknown extent by shifts out of the numerator that are not subtracted from the denominator (that is, a psychologist who now considers himself primarily an educator, or a chemist who considers himself a nonprofessionally identified administrator). Because science fields generally have higher prestige than nonscience fields, and because the percentage of Ph.D.'s who give up their professional identification within ten years of receipt of the degree is extremely small, there is probably more inflow to the numerator than outflow from it, leading to an overestimate of the Register coverage, but we have assumed that the two flows counterbalance each other.

Investigation for Biases in the National Register

In all fields, the proportion of female U.S. B.A.-U.S. Ph.D. doctorate recipients in the total NAS files is considerably higher than that of the matched cases. Across all the included fields, 8.7 per cent of the total number of doctorates in NAS files are female; of the matched cases from the National Register, 6.7 per cent are female. The residual distribution includes 13.7 per cent female cases (Table D-5). This is partially a function of the unmatched cases being largely the result of name changes of women as noted previously. But the total percentage of women in the National Register is smaller (7.4 per cent) than the total of doctorates awarded to women in these fields (8.7 per cent). A field-by-field comparison indicates that Physics, Earth Sciences, and Sociology in the National

TABLE D–5. *Percentage of Female U.S. Ph.D.'s with U.S. B.A.'s in NAS Doctoral Files and National Register, by Field*

Field	Total, Doctoral Files		Matched Cases		Residual "Unmatched Cases"		Total, National Register	
	Number Female	Per Cent Female	Number Female	Per Cent Female	Number Female	Per Cent Female	Number Female	Per Cent Female
Mathematics/ Statistics	84	5.3	51	4.0	33	10.3	60	4.6
Physics	47	1.6	28	1.2	19	2.8	34	1.4
Chemistry	269	4.6	152	3.5	117	7.4	172	3.9
Earth Sciences	18	1.5	11	1.4	7	1.9	13	1.6
Biosciences	629	11.3	277	7.9	352	17.1	311	8.7
Biochemistry	164	12.9	74	9.0	90	19.8	84	9.9
Psychology	810	17.8	509	14.6	301	28.2	574	15.9
Sociology	132	14.6	108	13.7	24	20.9	120	14.8
Economics	69	4.0	42	3.2	27	6.4	44	3.3
Total	2,222	8.7	1,252	6.7	970	13.7	1,412	7.4

Register are close to the sex distribution of the NAS files, while the remaining National Register fields included in this analysis have a considerable under-representation of women, which suggests that fewer women retain their professional identification than men.

In the study of women doctorate recipients from the 1957–1958 cohort, reported in Chapter 10, it was noted that a very high proportion (91 per cent) were working full- or part-time in their field of study. About 10 per cent of them were working part-time, and may be harder to include in the National Register.

Two additional measures are employed to assess qualitative differences between the matched cases and the unmatched cases in the Doctoral Files. The first of these is an ability measure, available for about one-half of the sample. These data were collected from the high school that had been attended by the doctorates as part of a research study by Lindsey R. Harmon.[11] The test scores, from various intelligence tests, have been converted to equivalent standard scores with a population mean of 50 and a standard deviation of 10. The approximately 12,000 NAS doctorate recipients in the present study sample who had intelligence scores available have a mean of 65.5 and a standard deviation of 8.6. Across all fields, no difference in the mean or variance of this ability measure for the matched and for the unmatched cases is evident. Within fields, only Sociology and Economics emerge as having a large difference between the matched cases and the residual, with matched National Register doctorates in Sociology having a higher ability level than the residual unmatched cases, and matched doctorates in Economics having a level lower than the residual average in the field (Table D-6).

[11] See footnote 3.

TABLE D–6. *Mean Intelligence Scores[a] of U.S. Ph.D.'s with U.S. B.A.'s, by Field*

Field	Total, Doctoral Files (N = 11,834)	Matched Cases (N = 8,519)	Residual "Unmatched" Cases (N = 3,315)
Mathematics/ Statistics	69.5	69.4	69.7
Physics	69.1	69.3	68.5
Chemistry	65.5	65.6	65.2
Earth Sciences	65.1	64.6	66.2
Biosciences	62.6	62.5	62.9
Biochemistry	64.7	64.8	64.5
Psychology	65.5	65.2	66.4
Sociology	64.2	64.9	57.4
Economics	65.4	64.6	68.1
Total	65.5	65.5	65.4

[a] Intelligence scores have a population mean of 50 and a standard deviation of 10. A doubling of the reported figures yields rough approximations of Army General Classification Test Scores. See text for a further discussion of these data.

The second measure is related to institutional rather than individual quality and is based on the departmental judges' ratings of graduate programs reported by Allan M. Cartter.[12] These Cartter scores yield a theoretical range in department quality from 0.00 (low quality) to 5.00 (high quality). These scores were averaged for several Bioscience fields and were rescored for all fields, with the range of 1 (high quality; Cartter scores 4.00 and above) to 6 (low quality; Cartter scores under 1.50). Across all fields, no difference in institutional quality of the matched and residual groups is evident. Within fields, only Sociology emerges as having a large difference in departmental quality, with the matched doctorates originating from more superior institutions than the unmatched doctorates in NAS files (Table D-7).

Summary and Conclusions

The problem of coverage in many scientific fields by the National Register of Scientific and Technical Personnel is a serious one. Of the U.S. science doctorates in recent years, only about three-fourths are included. Within fields, there appears to be a good deal of variation in coverage, with the biosciences, having only about two-thirds included, being low. These coverage estimates are probably high if we are to generalize to the coverage of the National Register *in toto.* Some earlier unpublished analyses of three scientific fields by Lindsey Harmon suggest that the recent doctorate recipients are more likely to be in the Register than those from earlier periods.[13] Coverage of those within a field who

[12] See footnote 4.

[13] Harmon, Lindsey R., "A Study of the Collation of the Register of Scientific and Technical Personnel with the Doctorate Records of the Office of Scientific Personnel." Unpublished report on the coverage of Genetics, Mathematics, and Psychology of December, 1961, National Academy of Sciences–National Research Council.

TABLE D–7. *Mean Cartter Quality of Graduate Department of U.S. Ph.D.'s with U.S. B.A.'s, by Field*

Field	Total, Doctoral Files (N = 25,641)	Matched Cases (N = 18,587)	Residual "Unmatched" Cases (N = 7,054)
Mathematics/Statistics	2.78	2.80	2.70
Physics	2.45	2.44	2.49
Chemistry	2.76	2.74	2.81
Earth Sciences	2.65	2.69	2.56
Biosciences	3.00	2.93	3.12
Biochemistry	3.10	3.06	3.17
Psychology	3.02	3.07	2.86
Sociology	2.87	2.63	4.51
Economics	2.99	2.98	3.02
Total	2.85	2.83	2.90

do not hold a doctorate, if included in the field definition, might also be expected to be lower than that of doctorate recipients.

This comparison has been made by the residual method. Its adequacy as an estimate of coverage in the National Register is a function of the comparability of definition of the two files, of the completeness of the matching operation, and of the completeness of the coverage of the universe by the NAS Doctoral Files. On all these points we believe that residual errors, if any, are small, and that the estimate of undercount is close to a "true" figure. The NAS files include over 99 per cent of all doctorates granted in U.S. universities. As indicated above, each National Register case was matched against the total NAS file in all fields, so that errors in identifying field of Ph.D. should not affect the overall estimate of coverage. All but about 3 per cent of the National Register cases were matched, and even if *all* the unmatched cases are included in the numerator, the overall estimate of coverage is only increased by a little more than 2 per cent. Since the comparison is limited to U.S. B.A.-U.S. doctorate recipients, the loss to other countries, or out of the profession, is likely to be minimal. To the extent that persons with a U.S. B.A.-U.S. doctorate are noncitizens *and* have left the country, we have made an overestimate of nonresponse. Within the fields under consideration, about 285 U.S. doctorate recipients in the 1957 to 1962 period were foreign citizens, with a U.S. B.A., and said they were either not going to remain in the United States, or were undecided about remaining after receiving the Ph.D. This is about 1.5 per cent of the matched cases, and would reduce the estimated undercoverage in the Register by about 1.1 per cent.

To the extent that persons trained as Ph.D.'s in science have dropped their professional identification and entered a nonscience field, within eight years after completion of the doctorate, we have made an overestimate of nonresponse. It is hard to see how this figure could exceed 2 or 3 per cent, although we have no precise estimate of the number of persons who vanish from the profession. We conclude that the smallest reasonable estimate of undercoverage of recent doctorates in the Register is 20 per cent.

Sex distributions are not representative for all fields. In some respects, however, representativeness is generally good. Ability measures and departmental quality distributions of matched and residual cases suggest little bias in the National Register as a whole, although the bias in a few fields is significant.

In summary, we cite Robert McGinnis:

> The picture of a scientific discipline that emerges from the National Register is no more clear or accurate than are the methods used to develop it. The professional societies bear a heavy responsibility because of their coordinate role on matters of inclusion in or exclusion of individuals from the Register and on the contents of its biennial questionnaires. The scientific population that the National Register actually represents is problematic. . . . The several professional societies could profit from the National Register data in reaching more adequate definitions, and perhaps greater compatibility across fields, of functional qualifications for field membership. In this same vein, nonrespondents yield poor pictures for these purposes. The two classes of nonrespondents, those within the list of eligibles who do not reply to inquiries and those who are functionally eligible, but who are not included on the list, must be considered. For this reason, it is to the interest of the societies that systematic study of non-response be undertaken.[14]

The estimate in the Introduction to the most recent report of the Register that ". . . the 1964 registration included over 90 per cent of the Nation's science doctorates"[15] is much higher than the estimates derived above. Incomplete coverage is a serious problem if the Register is to be used to estimate population totals (for example, the total number of Chemistry faculty members). For purposes of examining relationships among variables within a field (such as the relationship between age and earnings), the undercoverage may not be a serious problem; but to the extent that coverage varies between fields, by age, or by degree level, it introduces additional problems into the analysis.

The National Science Foundation is now planning a study of nonrespondents to the Register. Our coverage estimates indicate that such a study is badly needed, and should provide information that will greatly improve the value of the Register data for analytic purposes.

[14] McGinnis, Robert, "Planning Science Manpower Mobility Analyses for the National Register of Scientific and Technical Personnel." Unpublished report to the National Science Foundation, May, 1966.
[15] National Science Foundation, *American Science Manpower: 1964,* p. 1.

Appendix E: Sample and Procedures of Analysis in the Survey of Women Doctorate Recipients

The Doctoral files of the National Academy of Sciences, Office of Scientific Personnel list a total of 1,979 women as doctorate recipients in 1957–1958. Their current addresses were obtained through university alumni files and professional directories. These subjects were mailed a 41-item structured questionnaire dealing with work experience, marital status, awards and achievements, publications, domestic and community activities, problems encountered in career development, and other personal data.

Excluding the ineligible cases (that is, 21 deaths, records of six males and nondoctoral graduate students that were misplaced in the Doctoral Files of the Academy, and 21 cases that never received questionnaires owing to a clerical error), the 1,547 completed questionnaires constitute 80.1 per cent of the sample. However, further excluding 69 undelivered questionnaires, we obtained an 83.1 per cent rate of return of completed questionnaires. A short version of the questionnaire was mailed on a postcard to those who had not responded and was completed by an additional 106 (5.7 per cent) women.

Two hundred and nine subjects (10.7 per cent) did not respond to either questionnaire or postcard inquiries. From these cases, a random subsample of 69 subjects who had United States addresses was selected for a telephone follow-up. Thirty-six per cent of this subsample was reached and information secured on their employment and marital status. The rate of unemployment

449

among nonrespondents was higher than it was among respondents (18.2 and 8.6 per cent, respectively). Marital status was identical in both groups. Further, the nonrespondent group contained a greater proportion of foreign-born women and residents of foreign countries than the sample of respondents. Lost or undelivered mail sent overseas may have accounted for part of the nonresponse rate in this group.

Twenty-eight measures of the subject's personal and family background characteristics were selected as predoctoral or "control" variables (see below). These include: year of birth, citizenship status at the time of the doctorate, and grades and scores on measured intelligence obtained when the subject was a high school student; parents' level of education, occupation, and birthplace; the major field of doctorate study (scored as six separate dichotomies), whether or not she received stipend support during graduate training, and the quality of the doctorate institution;[1] and four additional dichotomies: whether or not she was a nun, whether or not she was married at the time of the doctorate, whether or not she is currently married, and whether or not she is currently retired. Although the latter two variables are not, of course, "predoctoral," it was considered necessary to control for their contribution to the criteria before assessing the effects of some of the environmental variables. (See below.)

Nineteen variables describing the subject's environmental experiences since obtaining the doctorate were selected as additional predictors of full-time employment. They were: residence in the United States (vs. foreign residence); size of current home town; number of children (including four dichotomous variables indicating whether the subject has any preschool, elementary school, high school, or college (and older) age children); husband's educational attainment (college graduate, Ph.D., professional degree); husband's occupation (natural science, social science, medicine, business and law, college or university professor); and husband's annual gross income. Also included were three variables describing the subject's postdoctoral career experiences: whether she has been a postdoctoral Fellow; whether her first job was in an academic setting; and whether or not her first job after receiving the doctorate was full time. The criterion or dependent variable for the analysis was whether or not the subject was employed full-time as of December, 1965.

Variables Used in the Stepwise Multiple Regression Analysis

Personal Variables

1. Year of birth (1851 = 01; 1930-80)

---

[1] The subject's score on the quality of doctoral institution was based on a six-point scale that was developed utilizing Allan M. Cartter's data reported in *An Assessment of Quality in Graduate Education,* 1966. A score of one represents the highest overall institutional quality that resulted from averaging the scores that the different departments received. A score of six indicates that the school was not rated.

2. Subject's citizenship at time of doctorate (noncitizen = 2)
3. Measured intelligence
4. High school rank
5. Mathematics GPA
6. Science GPA
7. Father's education
8. Mother's education
9. Father's occupational level
10. Mother worked (yes = 2, no = 1)
11. Mother's occupational level
12. Father's birth origin (Foreign = 2, USA = 1)
13. Mother's birth origin (Foreign = 2, USA = 1)
14. Date of marriage (early marriage = 2)
15. Now married = 2; All others = 1)
16. Has been married = 2; All others = 1
17. Nun = 2; All others = 1
18. Retired = 2

Predoctoral Experiences
1. Fellowship or scholarship = 2 ⎫
2. Assistantship = 2　　　　　　⎬ Stipend Source
3. Own money = 2　　　　　　　 ⎭
4. Physical sciences = 2; All others = 1 ⎫
5. Biosciences = 2; All others = 1　　　 ⎪
6. Social sciences = 2; All others = 1　 ⎬ Subject's Major Field of
7. Psychology = 2; All others = 1　　　 ⎪ Specialization
8. Arts and humanities = 2; All others = 1 ⎪
9. Education = 2; All others = 1　　　　 ⎭
10. Quality of doctorate institution

Postdoctoral Experiences
1. First job after the doctorate (Academic = 2; All others = 1)
2. Employed full-time at first job after the doctorate = 2
3. Postdoctoral fellowship = 2

Present Environment and Family Status Variables
1. Present residence (USA = 2; Foreign = 1)
2. Size of town currently lived in
3. Number of children
4. Preschool children (Some vs. None)
5. Elementary school children (Some vs. None)
6. High school children (Some vs. None)
7. College or older-age children (Some vs. None)

8. College graduate = 2 ⎫
9. Ph.D. degree = 2   ⎬ Husband's Education
10. Professional degree = 2 ⎭
11. Natural sciences = 2; All others = 1 ⎫
12. Social sciences = 2; All others = 1   ⎪
13. College teaching = 2; All others = 1   ⎬ Husband's Occupation
14. Medicine = 2; All others = 1   ⎪
15. Law and business administration = 2; All others = 1 ⎭
16. Husband's gross annual income

METHOD OF ANALYSIS

The statistical method used to analyze the effects of the different variables on employment status was stepwise multiple regression. The stepwise multiple regression analysis computer program was a BIMD computer program with further elaborations and refinements added by Robert Panos of the American Council on Education's Office of Research. By performing the regression analysis in stepwise fashion, control of the effects of each independent variable in a predetermined sequence is possible. Thus, the investigator seeks first to enter into the regression those variables that could bias the relationship between the dependent variable and subsequent independent variables. For instance, in this study we were interested in examining the effects of certain environmental experiences, such as having children, upon the criterion of full-time employment. However, since having children is obviously dependent on certain antecedent conditions (e.g., being married), it is important first to control the effects of these antecedent variables. Otherwise, the apparent "effect" of the environmental variable (having children) on employment status may simply be an artifact of our failure to control the relevant antecedent variables (e.g., being married). It can never be ascertained that all relevant biasing variables have been adequately controlled, but it is important to control as many as possible.

Variables were entered into the regression generally in the chronological order in which they probably would have occurred in the individual's career development. Thus, the last "control" variables entered into the equation were the dichotomies, "retired" and "currently married." Following the regression of the criterion on all control variables, the environmental variables were entered into the equation in a "free" stepwise fashion until no additional variables could significantly reduce the residual sum of squares in the criterion.

The results of these analyses are discussed in Chapter 9.

Publications That Resulted from the Commission Staff Efforts

The following articles and books resulted from the work of the staff of the Commission on Human Resources. Some of them were revised and included as part of this volume, while others represent extensions of the work that is reported in this volume.

The articles that were included in this volume in revised form are:

Astin, Helen S., "Patterns of Career Choices Over Time," *Personnel and Guidance Journal,* vol. 45, 1967, pp. 541–546. (Appears in revised form in Chapter 6.)

Astin, Helen S., "Personal and Environmental Factors Associated with the Participation of Women Doctorates in the Labor Force," *Personnel and Guidance Journal,* vol. 46, 1967, pp. 240–246. (Appears in revised form in Chapter 6.)

Bayer, Alan E., "Nurse Supply: It's Better Than We Thought," *The Modern Hospital,* vol. 109, 1967, pp. 75–79. (Appears in revised form in Chapter 4.)

Bayer, Alan E., "Interregional Migration and the Education of American Scientists," *Sociology of Education,* vol. 41, 1968, pp. 88–102. (Appears in revised form in Chapter 7.)

Bayer, Alan E., "The Effect of International Interchange of High-Level Manpower in the United States," *Social Forces,* vol. 46, 1968, pp. 465–477. (Appears in revised form in Chapter 11.)

The other publications of the Commission staff are:

Astin, Helen S., "Career Development During the High School Years," *Journal of Counseling Psychology,* vol. 14, 1967, pp. 94–98.

Astin, Helen S., "Stability and Change in the Career Plans of Ninth Grade Girls," *Personnel and Guidance Journal,* vol. 46, 1968, pp. 961–966.

Astin, Helen S., "The Woman Doctorate in America: Family and Career Characteristics of Professional Women," *Women's Education,* March, 1968.

Astin, Helen S., "Career Development of Girls During the High School Years," *Journal of Counseling Psychology,* vol. 15, 1968, pp. 536–540.

Astin, Helen S., *The Woman Doctorate in America: Origins, Career, and Family.* Russell Sage Foundation, New York, 1969.

Bayer, Alan E., and Helen S. Astin, "Sex Differences in Academic Rank and Salary Among Science Doctorates in Teaching," *Journal of Human Resources,* vol. 3, 1968, pp. 191–200.

Bayer, Alan E., and John K. Folger, "Some Correlates of a Citation Measure of Productivity in Science," *Sociology of Education,* vol. 39, 1966, pp. 381–390.

Bayer, Alan E., "Birth Order and Attainment of the Doctorate: A Test of Economic Hypotheses," *American Journal of Sociology,* vol. 72, 1967, pp. 540–550.

Bayer, Alan E., "Birth Order and College Attendance," *Journal of Marriage and the Family,* vol. 28, 1966, pp. 480–484.

Bayer, Alan E., and John K. Folger, "The Current State of Birth Order Research," *International Journal of Psychiatry,* vol. 3, 1967, pp. 37–39.

Bayer, Alan E., "The College Dropout: Factors Affecting Senior College Completion," *Sociology of Education,* vol. 41, 1968, pp. 305–316.

Bayer, Alan E., and Lyle F. Schoenfeldt, "Student Interchangeability in Three Year and Four Year Nursing Programs," *Journal of Human Resources* (in press).

Bayer, Alan E., "Marriage Plans and Educational Aspirations," *American Journal of Sociology* (in press).

Bayer, Alan E., Lyle F. Schoenfeldt, and Marsha D. Brown, "Delayed and Normal Progress College Students: A Comparison of Psycho-Social Characteristics and Career Plans," *Proceedings,* American Educational Research Association, Los Angeles, 1969 (in press).

Bayer, Alan E., "The American Brain Gain: The Inflow of Talent for Education and Work," in McGinnis, Robert, editor, *Human Mobility.* Cornell University Press, Ithaca, New York, 1969 (in press).

Bayer, Alan E., and Lyle F. Schoenfeldt, "Talent Flow Through Higher Education," Palo Alto, California: Research monograph of the American Institutes for Research.

Burton, Dee, "Birth Order and Intelligence," *Journal of Social Psychology,* vol. 76, 1968, pp. 199–206.

Folger, John K., "Scientific Manpower Planning in the United States," Chapter 12 in the 1967 *World Yearbook on Education,* Harcourt, Brace & World, Inc., New York.

Folger, John K., "The Balance Between Supply and Demand for College Graduates," *Journal of Human Resources,* vol. 2, 1967, pp. 143–169.

Folger, John K., "Some Relationships Between Ability and Self-Reported Grades," *Sociology of Education,* vol. 40, 1967, pp. 270–274.

Hansen, W. Lee, "The Economics of Scientific and Engineering Manpower," *Journal of Human Resources,* vol. 2, 1967, pp. 191–215.

Hansen, W. Lee, and Glen G. Cain and Burton A. Weisbrod, "Classification of Occupations: Some Problems of Economic Interpretation," in Social Statistics Section: *Proceedings,* American Statistical Association, Washington, 1968, pp. 199–203.

Hansen, W. Lee, Glenn G. Cain, and Burton A. Weisbrod, "Occupational Classification: An Economic Approach," *Monthly Labor Review,* February, 1967, pp. 48–52.

Hansen, W. Lee, *The Supply and Demand for Professional Manpower* (in preparation).

Holtmann, A. G., "Linear Programming and the Value of an Input to a Local Public School System," *Public Finance* (in press).

Holtmann, A. G., "The 'Shortage' of Teachers and the Principle of Equal Net Advantage," *The Journal of Economic Issues* (in press).

Tables and Figures

TABLE

2.1 Total Number of Degrees Granted, by Level: 1956–1965, with Projections for 1966–1975   28

2.2 Distribution of All College Graduates in Occupations for Which College Graduation Is Required, Expected, or Not Expected, by Sex: 1950 and 1960   30

2.3 Average Annual Supply of Male College Graduates, Compared with Demands for Occupational Growth and Replacement, Indicating the Estimated Number Available to Raise the Educational Level of Occupations: 1950–1980   32

2.4 Average Annual Supply of Female College Graduates, Compared with Demands for Occupational Growth and Replacement, Indicating the Estimated Number Available to Raise the Educational Level of Occupations When Only 80 Per Cent of the Women Enter the Labor Force: 1950–1980   32

2.5 Projected Demand and Supply of College Graduates: 1966–1975   35

2.6 Projected Needs for Additional College Graduates to Meet National Goals, and Projected Supply of College Graduates: 1965–1975   38

3.1 Estimated Total Employed Ph.D.'s in Arts and Sciences Fields: 1965   46

3.2 Projections of Bachelor's, Master's, and Doctor's Degrees, by Sex: 1956–1975   47

3.3 Past and Projected Growth in Degree Output in Arts and Sciences Fields and All Fields Combined, by Level: 1956–1975   47

3.4 Number of Fellowships Supported by Federal Predoctoral Fellowship Programs: 1960–1966   56

3.5 Current and Projected Patterns of Student Support for Full-Time Graduate Students   57

3.6 Estimated Advanced Degree Graduates Available to Enter United States Employment in Arts and Sciences Fields, by Period and Degree   61

3.7 Faculty Required for Enrollment Growth and Replacement   63

3.8 Estimates of Proportions of Ph.D.'s Among Teaching Faculty and Ratio of Ph.D.'s Available to New Entrants Required: 1955–1975   66

3.9 Research and Development Expenditures: 1954–1965, with Projections for 1970 and 1975   71

3.10 The Number of Additional Arts and Sciences Ph.D. Research Personnel Who Could Be Supported from Projected Growth in Basic Research Funds   72

3.11 Research and Development Ph.D. Employment Demand Compared with Supply   73

4.1 Percentage of Lawyers in Different Employment Settings: 1948–1963   76

4.2 Ratio of Lawyers to Total U.S. Population: 1900–1980   77

455

4.3 Ratio of Lawyers to Gross National Product: 1950–1980   78

4.4 High and Low Projections of Law School Graduates Based on Student Demand   80

4.5 Applications and Acceptances to Medical Schools: 1952–1953 to 1964–1965   88

4.6 Average Undergraduate Performance Index Scores of Medical vs. All Other Graduate Students, by Overall Quality Rating of Graduate Institutions   90

4.7 Total Physicians, Physicians in Private Practice, and Physicians in Direct Family Service: 1955, 1965, and 1975   91

4.8 Projections of Demand and Supply for Engineers   99

4.9 Projected Demand for New Elementary and Secondary Teachers: 1959–1980   105

4.10 Academic Performance Index of Elementary and Secondary Teachers as a Function of Sex, Undergraduate Major Field, and Entry or Departure from the Teaching Profession: 1962–1964   110

4.11 Academic Performance Index of Persons Who Planned to Enter Teaching, by Sex and Career Destination   112

4.12 Percentage of Persons Who Left Teaching Within Three Years, and Type of Post-Teaching Activity, by Sex, Family Status, and Level of Teaching   113

4.13 Academic Performance Index of Persons Who Stayed in Teaching or Left Within Three Years, by Sex, Family Status, and Level of Teaching   113

4.14 Estimated and Projected Numbers of Social Work Students Enrolled in Professional Programs, and Master's Degree Output: 1955–1975   117

4.15 Average Academic Performance of College Seniors, by Sex and Career Preference   119

4.16 Students Admitted to Schools Offering Initial Programs in Professional Nursing Who Were Graduated, by Type of Program: 1964–1966, with Projections to 1968   124

4.17 Number of Degrees Awarded to Nurses Who Previously Received Professional Qualification: 1956–1965   125

4.18 Number of Graduating Nurses Attaining First Professional Qualifications: 1958–1966, with Projections to 1980   127

4.19 Median Years of School Completed by Arts Professionals, by Sex: 1950 and 1960   133

4.20 The Employment Status of Male Arts Professionals: 1950–1960   134

4.21 Arts Professionals Employed, by Specific Occupation: 1940, 1950, and 1960   135

4.22 Median Earnings of Arts Professionals: 1949 and 1959   136

4.23 Growth of Number of Arts Professionals in Relation to Growth of Population and Recreation Expenditures   137

5.1 Estimates of the Percentage of High School Graduates Attending College the Year After High School: 1956–1965   150

5.2 Proportion of High School Graduates Who Are College Entrants, and Proportion of Eligible Age Group Who Are College Entrants: 1955–1966   151

5.3 Projections of Fall College Enrollment, Full-Time and Part-Time   152

5.4 Relationship of Selected Personal and Background Factors to College Attendance or Nonattendance, by Sex   156

5.5 Average Increase in Selectivity as Reflected in Standard Deviation Scores, by School Size and Rate of Growth: 1961–1964   160

5.6 Percentage Increases in Selectivity as Related to Initial Selectivity: 1961–1964   161

5.7 Estimated Distribution of Entering College Freshmen, by College Selectivity and Degree Level: 1965   163

5.8 Enrollment of Students Ranking in the Top Fifth in Academic Aptitude, by College Selectivity and Degree Level 164

5.9 Relationship of Selected Personal and Background Factors to Junior College or Senior College Attendance, by Sex 166

5.10 Relationship of Selected Personal and Background Factors to Completion of Nonselective or Selective Senior College, by Sex 168

5.11 College Progress, by College Type and Selectivity and by Sex 173

5.12 College Progress, by Academic Aptitude and Sex 174

5.13 Academic Progress of Junior College Transfers to Senior Institutions, by Academic Aptitude and Sex 175

5.14 Proportion of Students Receiving Bachelor's Degrees Among Senior and Junior College Entrants with Similar Academic Aptitude, by Sex 176

5.15 Socioeconomic Background of High Ability Students in the Top Fifth, by Type of College Entered and Sex, with Percentage Completion of Senior College 176

5.16 Relationship of Selected Personal and Background Factors to Dropping Out or Completing College, by Sex 178

5.17 Relationship of Selected Personal and Background Factors to Delayed Completion of Senior College or Completion in Five Years, by Sex 180

5.18 Proportion of Bachelor's Graduates Going On for Graduate Study: 1951–1965 183

5.19 Relationship of Selected Personal and Background Factors to Termination of College with Baccalaureate or Continuation with Graduate School, by Sex 186

5.20 Average Academic Aptitude of Bachelor's Graduates Who Did and Did Not Enter Graduate School, by Undergraduate Selectivity and Sex 189

5.21 Average Undergraduate Academic Performance Index Scores for Students Enrolled in Different Graduate School Strata, by Field and Sex 190

5.22 Average Number of Years from Graduate School Entry to Award of the Doctorate by Field: 1957–1964 192

6.1 Career Choice Distribution in the Ninth Grade and One Year After High School—Males 200

6.2 Proportion of High School Boys Shifting from Each Field Between the Ninth Grade and One Year After High School 201

6.3 Career Choice Distribution in the Freshman and Senior Years of College—Males 203

6.4 Proportion of College Males Shifting from Each Field Between the Freshman and Senior Years of College 204

6.5 Net Percentage Change in the Career Plans of Students Over Time in Four National Samples 205

6.6 Means and Standard Deviations on Selected Aptitude Measures of the Initial Group Choosing Each Career Field and Final Group Choosing Each Career Field 212

7.1 Proportion Changing Region for Doctorate Education and Employment, by Quality of Doctorate Education and Field: 1957–1960 Doctorate Recipients 224

7.2 Mean Quality of Doctorate Education, by Regional Migration Status and Major Field Area: 1957–1960 Doctorate Recipients 225

7.3 Mean Quality of Doctorate Education, by Migration Pattern and Major Field Area: 1957–1960 Doctorate Recipients 225

7.4 Regional Gains and Losses in 1957–1960 Doctorate Recipients from Ph.D. to Employment 227

7.5 Regional Gains and Losses in 1957–1960 Doctorate Recipients from High School to Employment 230

7.6 Proportion of College Graduates in Selected Major Fields Who Were Employed Full-Time in the Same Field Five Years After Graduation, by Sex: 1958 B.A. and M.A. Recipients 232

7.7 Major Field of Baccalaureate and of Doctoral Degrees: 1957–1961 Doctorate Recipients 234

7.8 Reported Major Field of Study at Time of Receipt of the Doctoral Degree and in 1964: 1957–1962 U.S.-Born Doctorate Recipients in Selected Sciences 236

7.9 Percentage Remaining in the Same Field from Doctoral Degree to Employment Position in 1962: Selected 1935–1960 Doctorate Recipients 237

7.10 Proportion of Full-Time Employed 1958 B.A. Recipients Who Changed Occupation, Employer, or Both, Between 1960 and 1963, by Field of B.A. and Sex 238

7.11 Proportion of 1958 Recipients Intending to Change or Not to Change Current Occupation During Major Part of Working Life, by Current Occupation and Sex 239

7.12 Job Setting in 1960 and in 1963, by Sex: 1958 M.A. Recipients Employed Full-Time 240

7.13 Proportion of 1958 M.A. Recipients Intending to Change or Not to Change Current Full-Time Occupation During Major Part of Working Life, by Current Occupation and Sex 241

7.14 Percentage of Doctorate Recipients with No Job Changes During Successive Five-Year Work Periods, by Year of Receipt of the Doctoral Degree 241

7.15 Type of Major Work Activity in 1960, by Number of Years Since Receipt of the Doctoral Degree 242

7.16 Doctoral Degree Recipients in 1957–1962 Changing Employment Setting Between Receipt of the Doctoral Degree and 1964, by Field 243

7.17 Job Setting of First Position After Doctorate, by Major Field and Year of Doctorate: Men Employed in Colleges and Universities in 1964 244

7.18 Job Setting of First Position After Doctorate, by Major Field and Year of Doctorate: Men Employed in Business and Industry in 1964 246

7.19 Job Setting of First Position After Doctorate, by Major Field and Year of Doctorate: Men Employed by U.S. Government in 1964 247

7.20 Net Change in Number of 1957–1962 Doctorate Recipients in Selected Job-Setting Categories Between First Position and 1964, by Field 248

7.21 Proportion of 1957–1962 Doctorate Recipients Engaged Primarily in Research and in Academic Settings in 1964, by Postdoctoral Fellowship Status and Field 249

7.22 Proportion of 1957–1962 Doctorate Recipients Engaged Primarily in Research in 1964, by Postdoctoral Fellowship Status, Work Setting, and Field 251

8.1 Citation Frequency of Those Nominated and Those Not Nominated for a National Research Council Technical Panel: 1957–1959 Doctorate Recipients in Selected Fields 259

8.2 Relationship Between Citation Count and Educational Quality, by Field 259

8.3 Relationship Between Citation Count and B.A.-Ph.D. Time Lapse, by Field 260

8.4 Relationship Between Citation Count and Measured Ability, by Field 260

8.5 Intercorrelations and Multiple Correlations of Predictor Variable and Citation Count, by Field   261

8.6 Mean Citation Count, by Field and Type of Employer   261

8.7 Citation Count of Those Employed in Universities, by Field and Quality of University Employer   262

8.8 Quality of Doctorate-Granting Institution, by Field and Type of Employer in 1964   263

8.9 Relationship Between Citation Count, Quality of Degree-Granting Department, and B.A.-Ph.D. Time Lapse, by Field and Type of Employer   263

8.10 Proportion of Sample with No Citations, by Field and Work Activity   264

8.11 Proporton of Sample with Research as Primary Work Activities, by Field and Type of Employer   264

8.12 Mean Citation Count, by Postdoctoral Fellowship Status, Major Work Activity in 1964, and Field: 1957–1959 Male Doctorate Recipients   266

8.13 Mean Citation Count, by Postdoctoral Fellowship Status, Type of Work Setting in 1964, and Field: 1957–1959 Male Doctorate Recipients   266

8.14 Mean 1964 Gross Annual Professional Income, by Job Setting in 1964, Year of Ph.D., and Field of Ph.D.   269

8.15 Mean Gross Annual Professional Income, by Postdoctoral Fellowship Status, Type of Work Setting, Year of Ph.D., and Major Field of Degree   271

8.16 Mean 1964 Gross Annual Professional Income, by Postdoctoral Fellowship Status, Major Work Activity, Year of Ph.D., and Major Field of Degree   272

8.17 Factors Associated with the 1964 Annual Income of 3,506 Scientists Who Received the Doctoral Degree Between 1957 and 1959   273

8.18 Factors Associated with the 1964 Annual Income of 1,464 Scientists in Colleges and Universities Who Received the Doctoral Degree Between 1957 and 1959   275

9.1 Degree Attainment, by Sex: 1955–1965   284

9.2 Full-Time Employment of Women Doctorate Recipients as a Function of Personal and Environmental Variables   293

9.3 Average Percentage of Time Spent in Each Type of Activity Within Colleges and Universities and in All Work Settings Combined   295

9.4 Differences in Salary, by Field of Doctorate and by Work Setting for Women Doctorate Recipients   298

9.5 Productivity of Women Doctorate Recipients as Measured by Articles Published in the Field of Specialization   299

9.6 Scientific and Scholarly Productivity as a Function of Selected Personal and Environmental Variables   300

10.1 Ability Level and Socioeconomic Status of Twelfth-Grade Students, by Sex: 1960   308

10.2 Percentage of High School Graduates Who Went On to College the Following Year, by Academic Aptitude, Socioeconomic Background, and Sex: 1960   310

10.3 Percentage of Students Attending the First Year of College Who Received Some Form of Scholarship Aid, by Sex, Academic Aptitude, and Socioeconomic Status: 1961   311

10.4 Percentage of Entering College Freshmen Who Attended *Selective* Colleges, by Socioeconomic Status, Sex, and Academic Aptitude: 1961   314

10.5 Percentage of College Completion by 1965 of 1960 High School Seniors, by Aptitude, Socioeconomic Status, and Sex   315

10.6 Percentage of College Entrants Graduating, by Sex, Ability, and Socio-economic Status: Project TALENT National Sample and Wisconsin Sample 318

10.7 The Effect of Socioeconomic Status on College Completion and Graduate School Attendance Among High-Ability Students, by Sex 320

11.1 Average Number of Immigrants per Year, by Decade: 1911–1964 328

11.2 Proportion of Immigrants in Professional, Technical, and Kindred Occupations, by Decennial Year: 1910–1965 328

11.3 Contributions of Immigrants to the Pool of New Natural Scientists and Engineers in the United States: 1949–1964 329

11.4 Proportion of Non-U.S. Citizens Receiving U.S. Doctoral Degrees, by Major Field and Year of Degree: 1959–1966 330

11.5 Baccalaureate Origins of U.S. Doctorate Recipients, by Area of Study and Quality of Doctoral Institution: 1960–1966 332

11.6 Place of First Postdoctoral Position, by Citizenship: All U.S. Doctorate Recipients, 1959–1964 333

11.7 U.S. Citizens Age 18 and Over Enrolled in Schools Outside the United States, by Sex: 1960 335

11.8 Number of 1957–1962 Doctorate Recipients in the 1964 National Register, by Place of Baccalaureate and Doctoral Degree: Selected Sciences 338

11.9 Percentage of Employed Men in Professional, Technical, and Kindred Occupations, by Birthplace of Parents and Age: 1960 340

11.10 Percentage of Men with Four or More Years of College, by Birthplace of Parents and Age: 1960 340

APPENDIX TABLES

A.1 Opening Fall Degree-Credit Enrollments, Institutions of Higher Education 380

A.2 College Enrollments as Reported by the Census Compared with Reports by the Office of Education 381

A.3 Projections of Full-Time Male Enrollments 382

A.4 Projections of Full-Time Female Enrollments 383

A.5 Projections of Part-Time Male Enrollments 384

A.6 Projections of Part-Time Female Enrollments 385

A.7 Projected Total Fall Enrollments in Institutions of Higher Education Compared with U.S. Office of Education Projections: 1966–1975 386

A.8 Enrollments for First Professional Degrees Requiring Preprofessional Training 387

A.9 Projected Full-Time and Part-Time Degree-Credit Enrollments, by Level of Study 388

A.10 Summary: Projected Degree-Credit Enrollments in Institutions of Higher Education 389

A.11 First-Time Enrollments—Male, Compared with High School Graduates and Age Groups 390

A.12 First-Time Enrollments—Female, Compared with High School Graduates and Age Groups 391

A.13 Estimated Distributions of Male College Entrants, by Intelligence Test Score Ranges in 1953 and 1973 for Two Different Assumptions About Enrollment Rates 392

A.14 Estimated Distribution of College Graduates, by Intelligence Test Score Ranges in 1955, 1975, and 1985, by Sex 393

A.15	First-Level Degrees—Males	394
A.16	First-Level Degrees—Females	395
A.17	First-Level Degrees—Total	396
A.18	Percentage That Master's Degrees Are of First-Level Base of Degrees in the Field—Males	397
A.19	Percentage That Master's Degrees Are of First-Level Base of Degrees in the Field—Females	398
A.20	Master's Degrees—Males	399
A.21	Master's Degrees—Females	400
A.22	Master's Degrees, by Field—Total	401
A.23	Percentage That Doctoral Degrees Are of First-Level Base of Degrees in the Field—Males	402
A.24	Percentage of Female to Male Doctorates, by Field	403
A.25	Number of Doctorates, by Field—Males	404
A.26	Number of Doctorates, by Field—Females	405
A.27	Number of Doctorates, by Field—Total	406
B.1	Correlations Among Selected Personal and Environmental Variables: 1960 High School Students	414
B.2	Male High School Seniors Exhibiting Selected Personal and Environmental Factors, by Educational Attainment 5 Years After High School	418
B.3	Female High School Seniors Exhibiting Selected Personal and Environmental Factors, by Educational Attainment 5 Years After High School	420
C.1	Mean Differences Among the Natural Sciences Career Choice Subgroups on Measures of Ability, Personality, and Interest	424
C.2	Mean Differences Among Engineering Career Choice Subgroups on Measures of Ability, Personality, and Interest	425
C.3	Mean Differences Among Business Career Choice Subgroups on Measures of Ability, Personality, and Interest	426
C.4	Mean Differences Among the Health Professions (M.D., D.D.S.) Career Choice Subgroups on Measures of Ability, Personality, and Interest	427
C.5	Mean Differences Among the Law Career Choice Subgroups on Measures of Ability, Personality, and Interest	428
C.6	Mean Differences Among the Clergy Career Choice Subgroups on Measures of Ability, Personality, and Interest	429
C.7	Mean Differences Among the Arts Career Choice Subgroups on Measures of Ability, Personality, and Interest	430
C.8	Mean Differences Among the Teaching Career Choice Subgroups on Measures of Ability, Personality, and Interest	431
C.9	Mean Differences Among the Skilled/Technical Fields Career Choice Subgroups on Measures of Ability, Personality, and Interest	432
D.1	Number of 1957–1962 Doctorates in NAS Doctoral Files and National Register, by Selected Field and Place of Baccalaureate	439
D.2	Number and Percentage of National Register of U.S. Doctorates Located in NAS Doctoral Files, by Field and Place of Baccalaureate	440
D.3	Proportion of NAS Doctorates in National Register, by Field, Place of Baccalaureate, and Year of Ph.D.	442
D.4	Major Field of Doctorate in National Register and NAS Doctoral Files, All Matched Cases with U.S. B.A.'s	443
D.5	Percentage of Female U.S. Ph.D.'s with U.S. B.A.'s in NAS Doctoral Files and National Register, by Field	445
D.6	Mean Intelligence Scores of U.S. Ph.D.'s with U.S. B.A.'s, by Field	446

D.7 Mean Cartter Quality of Graduate Department of U.S. Ph.D.'s with U.S. B.A.'s, by Field   447

FIGURES

3.1 Actual and Projected Number of First-Level Degrees in Arts and Sciences Fields: 1956–1976   48

3.2 Actual and Projected Number of Master's Degrees in Arts and Sciences Fields: 1956–1976   49

3.3 Actual and Projected Number of Doctoral Degrees in Arts and Sciences Fields: 1956–1975   50

3.4 Proportion of All Bachelor's, Master's, and Doctoral Degrees in Arts and Sciences Fields: 1956–1975   51

3.5 Actual and Projected Full-Time Equivalent Teaching Faculty in the Arts and Sciences Fields: 1955–1985   62

4.1 Number of Graduates from Medical and Osteopathic Schools: 1950–1965, with Projections to 1975   87

4.2 Mean Medical College Admissions Test Scores (MCAT) of Accepted, Rejected, and Total Medical School Applicants, for Selected Years: 1952–1965   89

4.3 Actual and Projected Number of Bachelor's, Master's, and Doctoral Degrees in Engineering: 1955–1976   96

4.4 Actual and Projected Number of Engineers: 1960–1975   100

4.5 Ratio of Recent College Graduates Entering Teaching to Total Number of First-Level Degrees and Education Degrees: 1959–1980   107

4.6 Actual and Projected Number of Bachelor's and Master's Degrees in Education, by Sex: 1957–1980   109

4.7 Proportion of Total Nursing Graduates with Baccalaureate, Diploma, and Associate Degrees: 1957–1966   123

4.8 Number of Basic Professional Nursing Programs: 1957–1965   126

4.9 Actual and Projected Number of Professional Nurses in Practice: 1954–1980   129

4.10 Distribution of Arts Professionals, by Industry of Employment: 1950 and 1960   138

4.11 Undergraduate Degree Field of Arts Professionals   141

5.1 Actual and Projected Proportions of Eligible Age Group Who Graduate from High School, by Sex: 1955–1975   148

5.2 College Graduation and Graduate School Attendance in 1965, by College Selectivity (High-Low) and Sex: 1960 High School Seniors Who Attended College   172

6.1 Career Plans of Entering Male Freshmen: 1961 and 1965   208

7.1 A Typology of Interregional Migration Patterns   222

7.2 Type of Employment in 1963 of New College Science Faculty in 1964–1965, by Subject Matter Specialty   242

7.3 Proportion of 1957–1962 Science Doctorate Recipients Receiving Postdoctoral Fellowships   250

9.1 Labor Force Participation of Women, by Age and Educational Attainment: 1950 and 1960   282

9.2 Career Expectations of Women High School Graduates of 1960 and Women College Graduates of 1965   286

9.3 Employment Status of 1957–1958 Women Doctorate Recipients, by Field: 1965   290

9.4 Employment Status of Single and Married Women Doctorate Recipients, by Field: 1965   291

9.5 Academic Rank of Women Doctorate Recipients Employed Full-Time in Colleges and Universities, by Field   297

10.1 Type of College Attended by Entering College Freshmen, by Sex and Socioeconomic Background   313

11.1 Proportion of U.S. Doctoral Degrees Awarded to Those of Foreign Origin, by Field and Decade of Degree   331

11.2 Foreign Region of First Postdoctoral Position for Those Going Abroad, by Citizenship and Field: U.S. Doctorate Recipients of 1959–1964   334

Index

Ability, xxiii–xxiv, xxvi–xxvii, 12, 15, 153–181, 185–191, 209–214, 307–309, 315, 317
  as related to career shifts, 209–314
  as related to college completion, 172–181
  as related to college entrance, xxiii–xxiv, xxvi–xxvii, 153–161
  as related to college preference, 164–166, 168
  as related to graduate school attendance, 155, 177, 185–191
  as related to socioeconomic status, xxiii, 307–309, 315, 317
  levels at college entrance, 158–159
  See also Intelligence
Academic grades. *See* College grades, High school grades
Academic Performance Index. *See* College grades
Academic rank, 296–297
Academic research. *See* Research, academic
Achievement. *See* Professional achievement
Adams, Walter, 150n.
Adjustment mechanisms. *See* Manpower
Admissions. *See* College entrance
Age, 128, 301
  nurses, 128
  women Ph.D. recipients, 301
Agriculture and forestry degrees, 394–406
Alexander, C. Norman, Jr., 153n.
American College Testing Program, 158
American Council on Education, xi, xiii, 203, 204, 207, 208, 213, 286, 287, 361
American Institutes for Research, 407
American Nurses Association, 124, 125, 130n.
American Society for Engineering Education, 54n., 95, 103

Anderson, C. Arnold, 42n., 270n., 315n., 358n.
Applications, 44–74
  bachelor's degrees, 46–48, 51–53
  college teaching, 61–69
  employment, 46, 61–69
  enrollment, 59
  master's degrees, 46–47, 49, 51–52, 60–61
  Ph.D. degrees, 46–47, 50–52, 60–61
  research, 69–74
  stipends, 54–59
  supply and demand, 46, 60–61
  See also Biological sciences, College entrance, Humanities, Physical sciences, Social sciences
Assistantships. *See* Stipends
Association of American Medical Colleges, 89, 202, 285n., 326n., 409n.
Astin, Alexander W., xiii, 52n., 153n., 170n., 199n., 202n., 207n., 316n., 408n.
Astin, Helen S., xii., xiv, 197n., 203n., 205, 214n., 281n., 287n., 296n., 298n., 453, 454
Atomic Energy Commission, 56
Attrition, 13–14, 53–54, 79, 94–97, 102–103, 120, 128, 165, 170–182, 185, 188, 285–286, 349
  as related to ability, 53, 174
  as related to college selectivity, 171–173
  as related to faculty-student relationships, 53–54
  as related to institutional type, 171–182
  as related to sex, 174–176
  engineering, 13, 94–97, 102–103
  graduate school, 185, 188
  junior colleges, 14, 170–174
  law, 79, 188
  nursing, 128
  social work, 120
  women, 285–286
Axelrod, S., 202n.

Babco, Eleanor L., 268*n.*
Bachelor's degrees, xx, 28, 48, 284, 394–396
  production, 28, 48, 284, 394–396
  projections, xx,. 28, 48, 394–396
Bachrach, P. E., 202*n.*
Bain, Robert, 106*n.*
Barber, Bernard, 270*n.*
Barger, Ben, 153*n.*
Barron, Frank, 5*n.*, 256*n.*, 265*n.*
Baumol, William, 132*n.*, 139*n.*
Bayer, Alan E., xii, xiv, 75*n.*, 153*n.*, 217*n.*, 221*n.*, 256*n.*, 296*n.*, 298*n.*, 299*n.*, 325*n.*, 410*n.*, 453, 454
Becker, Gary, 34*n.*
Becker, Susan J., 154*n.*
Beezer, Robert H., 153*n.*
Bennett, William S., Jr., 153*n.*
Berdie, Ralph F., 153*n.*, 154*n.*, 309*n.*
Berelson, Bernard, 190*n.*, 191, 192, 261*n.*, 358*n.*
Bernard, Jessie, 285*n.*, 298, 299*n.*
Biological sciences, 47–55, 60–63, 66, 68, 71–73, 190, 224–228, 268, 330–331, 394–396
  college grades, 190
  college major shifts, 224–226
  college teachers, 61–63, 66, 68
  degrees, 47–53, 60–61, 330–331, 394–396
  employment shifts, 227–228
  fellowships, 54–55
  foreign students, 330–331
  research, 71–73
  salaries, 268
  supply and demand, 60–61
Birth rates, xix–xx, 105
Bombach, Gottfried, 348*n.*
Bowen, William, 132*n.*, 139*n.*
Bowman, Mary Jean, 42*n.*, 369*n.*
Brazer, Harvey E., 409*n.*
Bridgman, Donald S., xii, 28, 284, 375
Brimhall, Dean R., 341*n.*
Brown, David G., 220*n.*, 242, 354*n.*, 357
Brown, Marsha D., 372
Bureau of Census, 10, 28, 30, 120–121, 128*n.*, 131*n.*, 133–136, 138, 152, 217–218, 222*n.*, 282, 289*n.*, 325*n.*, 326*n.*, 328, 335, 336*n.*, 339–340, 361, 375, 377, 378, 381, 383–385, 390, 392
Bureau of Labor Statistics, xi, 34–36, 98*n.*, 115, 116, 120, 128, 150, 222, 361
Bureau of Labor Statistics, Input-Output Model, 25, 35, 36

Bureau of Social Science Research, 12, 106*n.*, 112, 141, 183*n.*, 184, 381
Burton, Dee, 372
Business, 31–33, 38, 199–216, 233–234, 394–406
  career choices, 200–216
  college major shifts, 233–234
  degrees, 394–406
Buswell, Guy T., 299*n.*

Cain, Glen G., 372
Campbell, Ernest Q., 153*n.*
Career choices, xxi, xxiii, 12–14, 197–218, 321, 424–432
  as related to ability, 424–432
  as related to personal and environmental factors, 207–218, 424–432
  as related to socioeconomic status, xxiii, 321
  as related to type of college attended, 199
  distribution, ninth grade, 200
  distribution, one year after high school, 200
  effects of colleges and universities, xxi, 12–14
Career shifts, xxi, 10, 12–13, 198–215, 234–237
  as related to ability, 209–214
  as related to career expectations, 213–215
  as related to college student-faculty interactions, 214
  as related to environmental characteristics, 198
  as related to father's occupation and income, 213–214
  as related to high school variables, 206, 214, 215
  as related to institutional type, 199, 214
  as related to intended major, 213
  as related to interests, 213, 215
  as related to maturity, 203, 206
  as related to personal characteristics, 198
  as related to sex role, 198, 209
  as related to socioeconomic status, 198, 206, 208
  college freshmen, 202–208
  college graduates, 234–237
  college seniors, 203–205
  high school freshmen, 200–201, 205, 209–215

Career shifts— *continued*
  high school graduates, 200–201, 205,
    209–213
  high school seniors, 200–201, 205,
    214–215
  teaching, 10, 12–13
Cartter, Allan M., 9*n*., 45*n*., 69*n*., 74,
    90, 189, 190, 222*n*., 224, 229*n*.,
    255*n*., 256*n*., 259, 261, 262, 263,
    285*n*., 330*n*., 332, 354*n*., 434*n*.,
    450*n*.
Catholic College Selectivity, 159
Cattell, J. McKeen, 341*n*.
Citations. *See Science Citation Index,*
    Productivity
Clark, Kenneth E., 256*n*., 257*n*., 259*n*.
Clarke, Betty, 165*n*.
Clergy, 200–201, 203–204, 207–208,
    210, 213, 216
Cohen, Wilbur J., 409*n*.
Cole, Jonathan R., 257*n*.
Cole, Stephen, 257*n*.
Coleman, James S., 153*n*., 409*n*.
College choice, 14–15, 154, 164–182,
    312–322
  as related to ability, 164–168
  as related to college commitment,
    154, 167, 169
  as related to ethnic-religious variables,
    167, 169
  as related to family of orientation
    variables, 167, 169
  as related to family of procreation
    variables, 167–169
  as related to high school variables,
    167, 169
  as related to interests, 166, 168
  as related to residence, 167, 169
  as related to socioeconomic status,
    14–15, 164, 166, 168, 312–315,
    322
  as related to temperament, 166, 168,
    312–315
College completion, 14, 19–20, 170–182,
    315–322
  as related to ability, 172–181
  as related to college commitment,
    179–181
  as related to ethnic-religious variables,
    179–181
  as related to family of orientation
    variables, 179, 181
  as related to family of procreation
    variables, 172, 179, 181
  as related to high school variables,
    179–181

College completion—*continued*
  as related to institutional selectivity,
    171–173
  as related to institutional type, 14,
    171–182
  as related to interests, 177, 178, 180
  as related to residence, 179, 181
  as related to socioeconomic status,
    19–20, 176–180, 315–322
  as related to temperament variables,
    177–178, 180
  cumulative rates, 170–171
College degrees. *See* Bachelor's degrees,
    Master's degrees, Ph.D. degrees,
    Professional degrees
College enrollment, xxvi–xxvii, 26–29,
    152, 159–182, 217–226, 329–339,
    375–397
  abroad, 335–336, 338–339
  as related to ability, xxvi–xxvii
  as related to high school grades,
    166–169
  as related to institutional growth rate,
    161–165
  as related to institutional selectivity,
    160–165, 167–169, 171, 173
  as related to socioeconomic status,
    159–161, 164–169
  as related to type of institution,
    171–182
  foreign, 329–335
  migration patterns, 218–219
  mobility, 217–226
  projections, xx, 26–29, 152, 375–397
  trends, 375–392
College entrance, xxiii–xxvii, 14–15,
    19–20, 149–173, 309–322
  as related to academic ability,
    xxiii–xxiv, xxvi–xxvii, 15, 19–20,
    149–173
  as related to college commitment,
    154, 157
  as related to ethnic-religious
    variables, 157
  as related to family of orientation,
    variables, 157
  as related to family of procreation
    variables, 157
  as related to high school variables,
    157
  as related to institutional selectivity,
    160–165, 167–169, 171–173
  as related to interests, 155–156
  as related to residence, 157
  as related to sex, 154

College entrance—*continued*
  as related to socioeconomic status,
    xxiii–xxiv, 14–15, 19–20
    153–158, 161, 309–317, 322
  as related to temperament variables,
    155–156
  proportion of age group, 149–152
College Entrance Examination Board,
    158*n*.
College grades, 108, 110–113, 119–120,
    189–190
  as related to graduate and professional
    school enrollment, 120, 189–190
  See also College selectivity
College major, shifts in,
    224–226, 233–234
College selectivity, 27, 159–164,
    171–173, 182, 188–191, 312–315
  as related to college completion,
    171–173, 182
  as related to graduate school
    attendance, 188–191
  as related to institutional growth,
    162–163
  as related to student ability, 159–164
  as related to socioeconomic status,
    312–315
College student geographic mobility,
    217–226
College teachers, xix–xxi, 9–10, 46,
    61–69
  arts and sciences, 61–69
  Ph.D. ratios, xxi, 66
  supply and demand, xix–xxi, 9–10,
    46, 61–69
Commission on Human Resources and
    Advanced Education, xi, xvi, xxiv,
    xxxii, 2, 3, 28, 32, 47, 57, 67, 77,
    90, 95–97, 107, 127, 148, 149,
    151–152, 198, 214, 221, 254, 259,
    284, 290, 316, 324, 390, 408, 433
Committee for the Analysis of
    Engineering Enrollment, 95*n*., 98*n*.
Community colleges. *See* Junior colleges
Cooley, William W., xiii, 154*n*., 199*n*.,
    200, 201, 205, 213*n*., 215*n*., 286,
    308, 311*n*., 361, 408*n*.
Council on Social Work Education,
    117, 121
Crane, Diana, 256*n*., 258*n*.
Creager, John A., 221*n*., 257*n*., 408*n*.
Creativity. *See* Productivity

Darley, John G., 158*n*.
David, Henry, xiii
David, Martin, H., 409*n*.

Davis, James A., xiii, 53*n*., 90, 198*n*.,
    205, 209*n*., 321*n*.
Degrees, xx–xxi, 28, 48–51, 284, 375,
    379, 381, 394–406
  See also Bachelor's degrees, Master's
    degrees, Ph.D. degrees,
    Professional degrees
Dentists, 7, 11, 13
  See also Medicine
Department of Health, Education,
    and Welfare, 115*n*., 121*n*.
Disadvantaged youth. *See* Socioeconomic
    status
Doctor's degrees. *See* Ph.D. degrees
Dropouts. *See* Attrition
DuBois, Cora, 329*n*.
DuBois, Philip H., 293
Duncan, Beverly, 154*n*.
Duncan, Otis Dudley, 270*n*.

Earnings. *See* Salaries
Eckland, Bruce K., 170*n*., 308, 309*n*.,
    317*n*., 319
Economic growth. *See* Gross national
    product
Educational levels, 340
  foreign, 340
Educational objectives, national,
    xxxi–xxxii, 8
Educational system expansion, 1–2, 6–8,
    13–15, 26–29, 151–152, 159–164,
    182–184
  as related to economy, 1–2, 6–8
  graduate and professional schools,
    1–2, 182–184
  junior colleges, 159, 162–164
  senior colleges, 162–164
Educational Testing Service, xi, xiii, 159
Eells, Walter C., 253*n*.
Elder, Glen H., Jr., 153*n*.
Elementary school enrollment, xx, 9
Elementary and secondary school
    teachers, 9–10, 29, 31, 75, 103–114,
    119, 131, 142–143, 190, 200–216,
    233–234, 330–332, 394–406
  ability, 212
  career shifts, 200–216
  characteristics, 111–114
  college grades, 108, 110–113, 119, 190
  college major shifts, 233–234
  degrees, 109, 330–332, 394–406
  departure from teaching profession,
    112–113
  educational level, 31
  foreign students, 330–332
  re-entry into labor force, 104–108

Elementary and secondary school
  teachers—*continued*
  salaries, 131
  supply and demand, xviii–xx, 9–10,
    29, 103–114
Employment fields. *See* Manpower, Occupational distribution
Employment setting shifts, 238–245
Engineering, xvi–xix, 3, 7, 13, 30–31, 75,
  94–103, 142–143, 190, 200–216,
  394–406
  ability, 212
  attrition, 13, 94–97, 102–103
  career choices, 200–216
  census count, 94, 99
  college grades, 190
  degrees, 95–97, 99, 102–103, 394–406
  educational level, 31, 101–103
  graduates, 95–97, 99
  productivity, 101–103
  supply and demand, xvi–xix, 3, 7, 30–
    31, 94–103
Engineering Manpower Commission,
  95–96, 98

Federal government, xviii–xx, xxviii–xxx,
  54–60, 69–74, 347
  fellowships, xxix, 54–60
  funds, xix, xxviii–xxx
  research, xx, 69–74
  role in supply and demand, xxviii–xxx,
    347
  selective service regulations, xxix, 60
  tax policies, xxix
Fellowships, 54–60, 245, 249–250
  pre-doctoral, 54–60
  post-doctoral, 245, 249–250
Fein, Rashi, 29*n*., 34, 85*n*., 90*n*., 91–92,
  93*n*., 355*n*.
Ferriss, Abbott L., 221*n*., 223*n*., 252*n*.,
  267*n*.
Flanagan, John C., 154*n*., 199*n*., 200,
  201, 205, 215, 267, 286, 307*n*., 308,
  311*n*., 407*n*., 408*n*., 411*n*.
Folger, John K., xii, xix, 16*n*., 154*n*.,
  176*n*., 215, 218*n*., 256*n*., 283*n*.,
  299*n*., 454
Foreign students, 86, 92, 329–336,
  337–339
  enrollment in U.S. colleges, 329
  graduate school enrollment, 329
  in medicine, 86, 92, 326
  Ph.D. recipients, 329–334, 337–339
  region of origin, 333–334
  See also Immigrants
Friedwald, E. M., 341*n*.

Garfield, Eugene, 257*n*.
Geographic mobility, xxi–xxii, 15–16,
  217–232
  college, 217–226
  graduate students, 221–226
  job, 226–232
Ghiselin, Brewster, 265*n*.
Ginsberg, S. W., 202*n*., 280, 281
Ginzberg, Eli, 200, 202*n*., 280*n*., 281*n*.
Gist, Noel P., 153*n*.
Glick, Paul C., 268*n*.
Glockel, Galen, 118*n*., 119*n*., 120*n*.
Goals, National. *See* National goals
Gottlieb, David, 185*n*.
Grades. *See* College grades, High school
  grades
Graduate school attendance, 14–15, 54,
  154–155, 171–177, 182–194
  as related to ability, 155, 177, 185–186,
    188–191
  as related to college commitment, 154,
    187
  as related to ethnic-religious variables,
    187
  as related to family of orientation var-
    iables, 187
  as related to family of procreation var-
    iables, 185, 187
  as related to high school variables, 187
  as related to institutional selectivity,
    171–173
  as related to interests, 185–186
  as related to residence, 187
  as related to sex, 184
  as related to socioeconomic status,
    14–15, 185–186
  as related to temperament, 186
  as related to undergraduate institutional
    characteristics, 14–15, 188–191
  percent of bachelor's graduates attend-
    ing, 183
Graduate students, 54–60, 174, 182–194,
  221–226, 329
  ability, 174, 188–189
  Academic Performance Index scores,
    189–190
  attrition, 184–185, 188–189
  completion rates, 184, 191–194
  foreign students, 329
  migration trends, 221–226
  part-time, 183–184
  stipends, 54–60
  undergraduate college grades, 189–190
Greeley, Andrew M., 153*n*., 154*n*.
Greenberger, Martin, 409*n*.
Groat, H. Theodore, 217*n*.

Gross national product, 36, 71, 77–79, 83
  as related to research expenditures, 71
  lawyer-GNP ratio, 77–78, 83
Grubel, Herbert G., 338

Hall, Everette, 153*n.*
Haller, Archie O., 153*n.*, 309*n.*
Hansen, W. Lee, xii, 94*n.*, 97*n.*, 267*n.*,
  270*n.*, 309, 355*n.*, 454
Harmon, Lindsey R., xiii, 46, 54*n.*, 70*n.*,
  191*n.*, 219*n.*, 220*n.*–221*n.*, 233*n.*,
  234, 237, 240*n.*, 241, 242, 255*n.*,
  257*n.*, 281*n.*, 285*n.*, 294, 295*n.*,
  296*n.*, 298*n.*, 330*n.*, 331, 332*n.*,
  337*n.*, 434*n.*, 445, 446*n.*
Harris, Seymour, 26*n.*
Havighurst, Robert, 26*n.*
Health Professions. *See* Medicine, Nurs-
  ing
Henderson, Bonnie C., 437*n.*
Herma, J. L., 202*n.*
Herriott, Robert E., 153*n.*
Hewer, Vivian H., 153*n.*, 283*n.*
High school completion rates, 148–149
High school enrollment projections, xx, 9
High school grades, 149, 153–154
  predictive valve, 149, 153–154
High school graduates, 148–151, 200
  career shifts, 200
  college attendance, 150–151
Hills, John, 27*n.*
Hjelm, Howard F., 153*n.*
Hodge, Robert W., 270*n.*, 357*n.*
Holland, John L., 198*n.*, 200*n.*
Hollis, Ernest V., 220*n.*, 232*n.*, 354*n.*
Holtmann, A. G., xii, 454
Hood, Albert B., 153*n.*, 154*n.*, 309*n.*
Hopper, Janice A., 437*n.*
Hoyt, Donald P., 254, 265*n.*
Humanities, 46–53, 60–66, 68, 73, 190,
  289–290, 394–406
  college grades, 190
  college teachers, 61–66, 68
  degrees, 47–53, 60–61, 394–406
  employment, 46, 289–290
  research, 73
  supply and demand, 60–61, 64–65
Hunt, Shane, 274*n.*
Hutchins, Edwin B., 53*n.*

Iffert, R. E., 165*n.*
Immigrants, xxii–xxvii, 20, 29, 325–343
  average number per year, 327–328
  college enrollment, 329, 335
  educational level, 340
  engineering, 328, 329

Immigrants—*continued*
  Labor Force contribution, 325
  medicine, 326
  natural sciences, 328–329, 341
  occupational distribution, 327–329
  source of high-level manpower, xxvii,
    20, 29, 325–341
  source of second-generation manpower,
    339–340
  See also Foreign students
Immigration and Naturalization Service,
  328
Income. *See* Salaries
Institute of International Education,
  329*n.*, 332*n.*, 333*n.*, 335*n.*
Institute for Scientific Information, 256*n.*,
  257
Intelligence, xxiii, xxvi–xxvii, 392–393
  as related to college attendance, xxiii,
    xxvi–xxvii, 392–393
  as related to college graduation, xxiii,
    393

Jaffee, A. J., 150*n.*
Johnson, Davis, F., 53*n.*
Jobs, 30, 35, 44–45, 61–74
  arts and sciences, 44–45, 61–74
  types of activities, 30, 35, 44–45
  See also Elementary and secondary
    teaching, Engineering, Law, Medi-
    cine, Nursing, Performing arts,
    Social work
Junior colleges, 14, 27, 159, 162–182,
  218, 267, 312–315, 319–323
  ability of students, 164
  attrition, 14, 170–174
  completion rates, 171
  enrollment, 27
  migration trends, 218
  progress of transfers from, 14, 170–177
  selectivity, 159, 162–164
  socioeconomic status of students, 164,
    312–315, 319–320, 322–323
  student characteristics, 162–164, 175

Kershaw, Joseph A., 357*n.*
Klock, Joseph, 27*n.*
Knoell, Dorothy M., 165, 170*n.*, 174*n.*
Korbel, John, 409*n.*
Krasnegor, Rebecca B., 232, 233*n.*, 237*n.*,
  238–241
Kriesberg, Louis, 154*n.*

Labor force. *See* Manpower
Labor reserve, 7, 38–41, 118, 131,
  352–356

Labor reserve—*continued*
retirement, 7, 38–41, 353–354
women, 118, 131, 352–353
Larmon, Elizabeth A., 223*n.*
Law, xix, 75–84, 142–143, 188, 190,
200–216
ability, 212
attrition, 79, 188
career choice, 200–216
census count, 77
college grades, 82, 190
degrees, 79–84
employment settings, 76
enrollment, 79–80, 82–83
income, 83–84
institutional capacity, 77–83
ratio to GNP, 77–78, 83
ratio to population, 77, 83
state ratios, 77
student demand, 77–84
supply and demand, xix, 78–84
Lecht, Leonard A., xiii, 37*n.*, 38, 71,
101*n.*, 111*n.*, 116, 129*n.*
Lee, Calvin B. T., 69*n.*
Lee, Everett S., 223*n.*
Levine, Milton, xiii
Lindenfeld, Frank, 106*n.*
Lohnes, P. R., 423

McConnell, T. R., 299*n.*
McDill, Edward L., 153*n.*
McGinnis, Robert, 448*n.*
McKeachie, W. J., 253*n.*
McKean, Roland N., 357*n.*
McKinnon, Donald, 5*n.*

Manpower, xiv, xvi–xviii, xxi–xxii, xxvi,
xxix–xxxii, 1–13, 15–21, 25–27,
29–33, 37–41, 217–252, 325–341,
347–359, 360–371
adjustment mechanisms, xxx, 348–359
data system, 2, 4, 5, 361
employer mobility, 238, 240–252
employment setting, 242–247
foreign, 20, 325–341
geographic mobility, xxi–xxii, 15–16,
218–232, 356–359
high-level mobility, xxii, 218, 221–242
national goals, xxxi–xxxii, 8, 37–38
occupational mobility, xxvi, 15–16, 30,
223–242, 356–359
occupational upgrading, 29–33, 38–41
planning, xxix, 25–26, 347–359
post-doctoral fellowship recipients,
245, 251
problems, xxxi–xxxii, 2, 3, 26

Manpower—*continued*
production, xxiv
projections, xviii, 26–27
quality substitution, 354–355
regional gain or loss, 220–232
research, 4–6, 249, 360–371
sub-professionals, 355–356
supply and demand, xvii, xviii, 4–12,
29
U.S. Manpower abroad, 336–337
Manpower Development and Training
Act, 3, 347
Manpower Report of the President,
3, 35, 40*n.*
Marcson, Simon, xiii, 261*n.*
Margolis, J., 257*n.*
Maris, Jerome G., 256*n.*
Mason, Ward, 106*n.*
Master's degrees, xix–xxi, 28, 49, 51, 284,
397–401
production, 28, 49, 51, 284, 397–401
projections, xix–xxi, 28, 49, 51,
397–401
Mathematics. *See* Physical sciences
and mathematics
Medicine, xvi, xix, 7, 10–11, 13, 34,
53–54, 75, 84–94, 142–143, 188,
190, 200–216, 326
applications and acceptances, 34, 86–88
attrition, 53–54, 88, 188
career choice, 200–216
college grades, 88, 90, 190
employment settings, 90–91
foreign entrants, 86, 92, 326
graduates, 86–87
health goals, 85
physician-population ratios, 85–86,
90–91
physician productivity, 92–93
physician projections, 92–93
supply and demand, xvi, xix, 10, 84,
91–92
undergraduate grades, 88
Medsker, Leland L., 153*n.*, 174*n.*, 309*n.*
Melichar, Emanuel, 409*n.*
Meltzer, Bernard, 256*n.*
Merrill, Maud A., 283*n.*
Migration. *See* Geographic mobility
Miller, Herman P., 267*n.*
Miller, Norman, 106*n.*, 111*n.*, 183, 184*n.*
Milton, Helen, 71*n.*
Mobility, geographic. *See* Geographic
mobility
Montgomery, James, 165*n.*, 170*n.*
Mooney, Joseph, 185*n.*, 286*n.*
Morgan, James N., 409*n.*

Motivation, 153–158, 254–255, 258–276
  college attendance, 153–158, 254–255
  occupational, 258–276
Mushkin, Selma, 26n.

Nam, Charles B., 16n., 154n., 176n.,
    217, 218n., 219n.
National Academy of Sciences, xi, xii,
    xiii, 2, 70n., 73n., 191n., 192, 243,
    254, 259, 284, 332, 333n., 334
    361, 381, 449
National Defense Education Act, 56, 347
National Education Association, 111,
    295, 296n., 353
National Goals, 8, 37–38
National Goals Commission, 9, 37, 101,
    104, 111, 129
National Goals Project, xxxi, 37, 38, 129
National Institutes of Health, 56, 256
National Merit Scholarship, 53, 207,
    361, 362
National Opinion Research Center, 53,
    57, 82, 106, 108, 110–112, 120,
    189, 190, 349, 381
National Planning Association, xiii, xxxi,
    38
National Register of Scientific and
    Technical Personnel, 73n., 221, 233,
    243, 268, 296, 337, 433–448
National Research Council, xi, 73, 258,
    259, 332–334
National Science Foundation, xi, 28n.,
    40n., 45, 56, 65n., 67n, 97n., 98,
    183, 256, 284, 326, 329, 361,
    433n., 437
Natural sciences, 199–216, 233–234,
    288–290
  career choice, 199–216
  college major shifts, 233–234
  supply and demand, 288–290
Negroes, xxiv–xxvi, 18–19, 119
Neubeck, Gerhard, 153n., 283n.
Nichols, Robert C., 53n., 198n., 205,
    207n.
Nursing, 75, 122–132, 142–143
  age, 128
  attrition, 128
  completion rates, 124
  degrees, 123–128
  educational level, 131
  employment conditions, 131–132
  enrollment, 124
  productivity, 131–132
  salaries, 131
  supply and demand, 125–132

Occupational achievements. See
    Professional achievements
Occupational distribution of college
    graduates, 41–43
Occupational flexibility, 232–245
Occupational mobility, xxii, xxvi, 15–16,
    30, 232–252, 356–359
  business, 232–233, 236–241
  engineering, 232–233, 236–241
  natural sciences, 232–233, 236–241
  social sciences, 232–233, 236–241
  teaching, 232–233, 241
Occupational structure, 31–43
Office of Education, xi, 10, 32, 56n.,
    57, 60, 95, 96, 108n., 127, 151, 152,
    163, 284, 375–380, 382, 387–389,
    392, 394, 407
Oppenheimer, Valerie K., 281n.
Orcutt, Guy H., 27n., 409n.
Osteopathy, 86–87

Pake Report, 73
Palmer, Gladys, 218n.
Panos, Robert J., 170n., 316n., 408n.,
    452
Parmelee, Rexford C., 302n.
Pease, John, 185n.
Performing arts, xix, 75, 132–143,
    200–216, 330–332
  ability, 212
  art professionals–population ratios,
    137, 139
  art professionals–recreational
    expenditures ratios, 137, 139
  career choices, 200–216
  census count, 133, 135
  degrees, 330–332
  educational level, 133, 140–141
  employment status, 133–135, 138
  foreign students, 330–332
  salaries, 136
  supply and demand, xix, 137–143
Ph.D. degrees, xx–xxi, 28, 50–51,
    191–194, 284, 402–406, 433–448
  National Academy of Science Doctoral
    Files and National Register,
    433–448
  production, 28, 50–51, 284, 402–406
  projections, xx–xxi, 28, 50–51,
    402–406
  supply and demand, xx–xxi
Ph.D. degree completion rates, 191–194
  as related to bypassing master's
    degree, 193
  as related to employment, 191
  as related to field, 191–193

Ph.D. degree completion rates—
continued
  as related to interruption, 191–192
  as related to major change, 193
Physical sciences and mathematics,
  46–55, 60–63, 66–68, 71–73, 190,
  224–228, 269, 330–332, 394–406
  college grades, 190
  college major shifts, 224–226
  college teachers, 61–63, 66–68
  degrees, 47–53, 60–61, 330–332,
    394–406
  employment shifts, 226–228
  foreign students, 330–332
  research, 71–73
  salaries, 269
  stipends, 55
  supply and demand, 46, 60–61
Physicians. *See* Medicine
Physics, 53, 185, 245
  See also Physical sciences
Pins, Arnold, 119*n*.
Post-doctoral fellowships, 245–250, 268,
  270–272
  productivity, 268, 270–272
  type of work activity, 246–250
  See also Fellowships
Powers, Lee, 302*n*.
President's Committee on the Status of
  Women, 281*n*.
President's Council of Economic
  Advisers, xxix
Prestige. *See* College selectivity
Productivity, 17, 33–34, 253–258, 268,
  270–272, 298–300
  as related to quality of graduate
    school attended, 17, 258
Professional achievement, xxvii–xxviii,
  16–18, 253–276
  as related to ability, 255, 258–261,
    265
  as related to educational attainment,
    254
  as related to income, 253–254, 268–276
  as related to *Science Citation Index*,
    256–268
Professional degrees, 28
  See also Law, Medicine, Social work
Project TALENT, xi, xiii, 147, 150,
  153–154, 159, 162–164, 170–177,
  183, 189, 190, 199–200, 202, 205,
  209, 212, 214–215, 286, 287*n*.,
  307–309, 315–320, 361, 407–421
Psychiatry, 29, 289–290
Psychology. *See* Social Sciences

Public Health Service, 56, 123, 126,
  128*n*.–130*n*., 131

Quality ratings, college, 162
  See also College selectivity

Race, xxv
Regional mobility. *See* Geographic
  mobility
Rehberg, Richard A., 154*n*.
Research, 46, 69–74, 249, 251, 360–371
  academic, 46, 69–74, 249, 251
  employment, 73–74, 249, 251
  expenditures, 71–72
  future manpower research needs,
    360–371
  non-academic, 46, 69–74, 249, 251
  relation to GNP, 71
  status of manpower research, 360–371
Retirement, 7, 38–41
  See also Labor reserve
Riecken, Henry W., xiii
Rivlin, Alice, 26*n*., 27*n*., 409*n*.
Robson, R. Thayne, xiii
Roe, Anne, 256*n*.
Rossi, Alice S., 281*n*., 283*n*., 292*n*.
Rossi, Peter H., 349*n*., 357*n*.
Ruhe, C. H., William, 86*n*., 87, 88*n*.
Russell, J. D., 351*n*.

Salaries, 268, 271–273
Sanford, Nevitt, 165*n*., 253*n*.
Schloss, Sam, 104*n*.
Schoenfeldt, Lyle F., xiii, 372, 410*n*.
Scholarships. *See* Stipends
Scholastic Aptitude Test, 159–161
Schwartz, Mildred A., 44*n*., 64, 65
Science Citation Index, 256–268, 434–437
Scott, Anthony D., 338*n*.
Searle, Allan D., 72*n*.
Secondary teachers. *See* Elementary and
  secondary teachers
Selectivity. *See* College choice, College
  selectivity
Sewell, William H., 153*n*., 170*n*., 307*n*.,
  309, 316–318, 361
Sex, 154, 156–157, 166–182, 280, 283–286
  as related to college entrance, 154,
    156–157, 166–167
  as related to college completion,
    168–182, 283–286
  discrimination, 280, 285–286
Shah, Vimal P., 153*n*., 170*n*., 307*n*.,
  309*n*., 316*n*., 317*n*., 318
Sharp, Laure, M., xiii, 183*n*., 232, 233*n*.,
  237*n*., 238–241

Shaycoft, Marion F., 307*n*., 312*n*.
Sher, Irving H., 257*n*.
Shryock, Henry S., Jr., 219*n*., 222*n*.
Siegel, Paul M., 357*n*.
Skilled and technical occupations, career choice, 200–216
Smith, William A., 265*n*.
Social Science Research Council, xi
Social sciences and psychology, 47–55, 60–63, 65–66, 68, 71–73, 119, 190, 200–216, 224–228, 233–234, 330–332, 394–406
  ability, 119, 212
  career shifts, 200–216
  college grades, 190
  college major shifts, 224–226, 233–234
  college teachers, 61–63, 65–66, 68
  degrees, 47–52, 60–61, 330–332, 394–406
  employment shifts, 226–228
  foreign students, 330–332
  research, 71–73
  stipends, 54–55
  supply and demand, 60–61
Social work, xix, 29, 75, 114–122, 131
  attrition, 120
  college grades, 119
  degrees, 115–117, 121
  educational level, 115–116, 120–121
  enrollment, 117
  grades, 120
  graduate school, 117, 120–121
  re-entry into labor force, 117–119
  salaries, 117–119, 131
  supply and demand, xix, 29, 115–122
Socioeconomic status, xvi, xxiii–xxvi, xxxv–xxxvi, 14–15, 18–20, 153–158, 305–324
  as related to ability, xxiii, 307–309, 315, 317
  as related to career choice, xxiii, 321
  as related to college choice, 312–315, 322
  as related to college completion, xxiii, 19–20, 315–322
  as related to college entrance, xxiii–xxiv, xxv–xxxvi, 14–15, 19–20, 153–158, 309–317, 322
  as related to college financial aid, 311–312, 321–323
  as related to graduate and professional school enrollment, 320–322
  as related to high school completion, xxv
Soldz, Herbert, xiii, 191*n*., 219*n*., 233*n*., 234, 281*n*., 330*n*., 331, 337*n*.

Spaeth, Joseph L., xiii, 53, 106*n*., 111*n*., 183, 184*n*.
Stipends, 54–60, 245, 249–250
Storer, Norman W., 267, 268*n*.
Stratification, 30–31, 35–37, 161–164
  educational, 161–164
  occupational, 30–31, 35–37
Straus, Murray A., 153*n*., 309*n*.
Suits, Daniel B., 409*n*.
Summerskill, John, 165*n*.
Super, D. E., 202*n*.
Supply and demand, xvii–xix
  See also Manpower
Surgeon General's Consultant Group on Nursing, 128, 132
Szaloczi, Jean, 115*n*.

Talent loss, 14, 277–279, 281, 283–288, 305–307, 310–312, 321–324
  disadvantaged, 14, 305–307, 310–312, 321–324
  women, 281, 283–288
Taylor, Calvin W., 5*n*., 256*n*., 265*n*.
Teachers. *See* College teachers, Elementary and secondary teachers
Terman, L. J., 283*n*.
Tests, xxvii
  as selective device in admissions, xxvii
Tontz, Jay L., 200*n*., 242
Transfers, 14, 170–177
  two-year to four-year colleges, 14
Trent, James W., 153*n*., 309*n*.
Tucker, Allan, 185*n*.
Turner, Ralph H., 153*n*.

Vetter, Betty M., 268*n*.

War, effect on manpower, xxix, 2, 150
Warkov, Seymour, 57*n*., 82*n*., 120*n*., 153*n*.
Wechsler, David, 283*n*.
Weisbrod, Burton A., 372
Weiss, Jeffrey, 92, 93*n*.
Werts, Charles E., 209*n*., 283*n*., 321*n*.
Westby, David L., 154*n*.
White, James J., 302*n*.
Wiesenfelder, Harry, 302*n*.
Wilson, Kenneth M., 191*n*.
Wilson, Logan, 256*n*.
Wolfle, Dael, xiv, xxiv*n*., 2*n*., 3, 4*n*., 46, 65*n*., 77, 79*n*., 149*n*.
Women, xxii, 9–11, 18–19, 29, 40–41, 47, 49, 104–110, 117–119, 280–304, 309–310, 352–353, 450–452
  age, 301
  arts and sciences, 49

Women—*continued*
  attrition, 285–286
  career choice, 286–288
  degrees, xxii, 18, 47, 283–284
  educational attainment, 281–286
  employment, 282–292
  graduate school acceptance rates, 285
  graduate school financial aid, 285
  labor force, 280–282, 288
  marital status, 301
  Ph.D. recipients, xxii, 285, 288–303, 450–452
  productivity, 298–300

Women—*continued*
  re-entry into labor force, 10–11, 19, 29, 40–41, 280–281, 352–353
  salaries, 296–298, 301
  sex role, 283–285, 287–288
  social work occupations, 117–119
  socioeconomic status, 283, 309–310
  teaching, 9, 11, 104–106, 108, 110, 295–296, 302
Woodrow Wilson Fellowships, 58, 185, 188, 285–286
  attrition, 185, 188, 285–286
Work activities. *See* Jobs, Types of activities.